What to study on your way to the _____

Administration Tests

DOS Text Utilities

F1 = opens the HLP file

F3 = allows you to choose an option and modify it

F5 = mark multiple items

Alt+F10 = quick exit

MONITOR Utilities

<Alt><Esc> = toggle between open screens

<Ctrl><Esc> = menu of open screens

NET.CFG example:

Link Driver NE2000

    INT 5

    PORT 340

    MEM D0000

    FRAME ETHERNET 802.2

NETWARE DOS REQUESTER

    FIRST NETWORK DRIVE=F

NetWare has 4 security levels:

Login; Rights; Attributes; File Server

LOGIN validation:

check for password requirement; match ID and password; check user account restrictions

RIGHTS:

Supervisor; Supervisor equivalent; Workgroup Manager; Account Manager; PCONSOLE operator; FCONSOLE operator; User

File System security:

Trustees; Directory and Files rights; Inheritance; Inherited Rights Mask (IRM); Effective rights

Rights:

Access Control; Create; Erase; File Scan; Modify; Read; Supervisory; Write

ATTRIBUTES:

read-only; read-write; sharable; hidden; system; transactional; purge; archive needed; read audit; write audit; copy inhibit; execute only; delete inhibit; rename inhibit

Supported frame types:

ETHERNET_802.3—default for 2.2 and 3.11

ETHERNET_802.2—default for 3.12 and 4.x

ETHERNET_II—for TCP/IP

ETHERNET_SNAP for AppleTalk

TOKEN RING

NetWare file allocation tables support 536,870,912 FAT entries and 2,097,152 DET entries

Three types of caching supported:

Directory caching—copying DET and FAT into file server RAM

Directory hashing—indexes the memory stored DET = 30% fast

File caching—frequently used files in RAM—100 times faster

Installation and Configuration Tests

The 7 steps to installation:

1. Prepare the disk

   FDISK and FORMAT

   CREATE and FORMAT

   CREATE SERVER.311 dir and use SYSTEM-1 disk (has SERVER.EXE on it)

   Create AUTOEXEC.BAT to load SERVER.EXE

   Type **Copy A:*.*** and repeat for SYSTEM-2 and SYSTEM-3

   On 3.12, INSTALL.BAT here asks for File Server Name, Internal IPX Network Number, then

   Copies server boot files from SYSTEM-x into place

   Next: Locale settings, then File Formats, Special Startup Commands (SET), create

   AUTOEXEC.BAT

2. Run SERVER.EXE. It reboots the machine to clear TSRs—gives speed rating

3. Load disk and then communication drivers

   :LOAD C:\SERVER.312 ISADISK

   prompts for parameters—1F0, E

   :LOAD C:\SERVER.312\NE2000

   prompts for parameters—300, 3

   :BIND IPX TO NE2000

   prompt for network number

4. Run Install.NLM

   :LOAD C:\SERVER.312\INSTALL

   Go to Disk Options and choose partition tables

   can change hot fix here

   Go to Volume Options

   make SYS volume

   mount SYS volume

   Go to System Options

   copy SYSTEM and PUBLIC in with 3.11, prompted for each disk one at a time

   Must install from drive A and cannot specify another. To solve this, exit and type :LOAD C:\SERVER.311\INSTALL /J and then specify any other drive using F6

5. Make configuration files—STARTUP.NCF and AUTOEXEC.NCF

6. Install additional NLMS

7. Do clients

   Files copied to WINDOWS\SYSTEM

   NETWARE.DRV; NETWARE.HLP; NWPOPUP.EXE; VIP.386—run DOS apps in enhanced mode;

   VIPX.386 - DOS session task switching; VNETWARE.386—conjunction with POPUP

   Files copied to WINDOWS

   NWADMIN1.INI; NETWARE.INI; ET.INI; NWUSER.EXE; NWUTILS.GRP

CNE 3 Short Course

Dorothy Cady

Drew Heywood

Blaine Homer

Debra Niedermiller-Chaffins

New Riders

New Riders Publishing, Indianapolis, Indiana

CNE 3 Short Course

By Dorothy Cady, Drew Heywood, Blaine Homer, and Debra Niedermiller-Chaffins

Published by:
New Riders Publishing
201 West 103rd Street
Indianapolis, IN 46290 USA

CIP data available upon request

Warning and Disclaimer

This book is designed to provide information about the NetWare network operating system. Every effort has been made to make this book as complete and as accurate as possible, but no warranty or fitness is implied.

The information is provided on an "as is" basis. The author(s) and New Riders Publishing shall have neither liability nor responsibility to any person or entity with respect to any loss or damages arising from the information contained in this book or from the use of the disks or programs that may accompany it.

Publisher	Don Fowley
Publishing Manager	Emmett Dulaney
Marketing Manager	Ray Robinson
Managing Editor	Tad Ringo

Acquisitions Editor
Alicia Buckley

Production Editor
John Sleeva

Copy Editors
Amy Bezek, Fran Blauw,
John Kane, Sarah Kearns,
Stacia Mellinger, Suzanne Snyder,
Phil Worthington, Lillian Yates

Technical Editor
Kurt Schernekau

Associate Marketing Manager
Tamara Apple

Acquisitions Coordinator
Tracy Turgeson

Publisher's Assistant
Karen Opal

Cover Designer
Jay Corpus

Book Designer
Sandra Schroeder

Manufacturing Coordinator
Paul Gilchrist

Production Manager
Kelly Dobbs

Production Team Supervisor
Laurie Casey

Graphics Image Specialists
Jason Hand, Clint Lahnen,
Laura Robbins, Craig Small,
Todd Wente

Production Analysts
Angela Bannan
Bobbi Satterfield

Production Team
Heather Butler. Angela Calvert,
Kim Cofer, Jennifer Eberhardt,
Kevin Foltz, David Garratt,
Erika Millen, Erich J. Richter

Indexer
Chris Cleveland

About the Authors

Dorothy L. Cady is a former senior technical writer for Novell, Inc. in Provo, Utah. Ms. Cady started with Novell in 1990 as a team leader for the Software Testing Department's Documentation Testing Team, helping to ensure the quality of the documentation that ships with NetWare 2, 3, and 4, NetWare Lite, and Personal NetWare products.

Ms. Cady is a Certified Novell Instructor (CNI), a Certified Novell Engineer (CNE), a Certified Novell Administrator (CNA), and an Enterprise CNE (ECNE).

Dorothy is now a freelance writer and instructor with over twenty years experience in the computer industry, both in private and public service. She also is the author of *CNA Study Guide* and *New Riders' Guide to NetWare Certification*, as well as co-authoring many other New Riders books. She is also the author of *Bulletproof Documentation: Creating Quality Through Testing.*

Drew Heywood has been involved in the micro-computer industry since he purchased an Apple IIe in 1979. For the past nine years, he has focused on networking. From 1991 through February 1995, Drew was a product line manager at NRP, where he launched NRP's network book line and expanded the line to include some of the most successful book titles in the industry. Drew and his wife, Blythe, have most recently founded InfoWorks, Inc. to support his dual interests as a computer book author and a consultant. Drew was the author of NRP's *Inside Windows NT Server* and *Inside NetWare, Fourth Edition*, and has contributed to several NRP books, including *Networking Technologies* and *CNE Short Course*, both of which are members of NRP's CNE Training Guide series.

Blaine Homer is a technical editor for *LAN Times*. He writes previews, reviews, and product comparisons. His technical beats includes network hardware, Novell products, network management applications and tools, and network security. Before joining the LAN Times Testing Center, Mr. Homer worked for Novell's internal network management team. He also worked for Novell's IS department repairing hardware and supporting the end user. Mr. Homer does private network installation and consulting. He has a B.S. degree from Brigham Young University's Marriott School of Management, with an emphasis in Information Systems.

Debra Niedermiller-Chaffins is Training Manager for MicroAge of Southeast Michigan in Novi, Michigan. Ms. Niedermiller-Chaffins has been working since 1988 to help organizations develop autonomy and self-sufficiency in training future Certified NetWare Engineers operations. She is a Certified NetWare Instructor and a CNE, specializing in training future CNEs. In addition to teaching, Ms. Niedermiller-Chaffins also supports a small client base, which provides her with a background of real-world networking scenarios. She is the author of *Inside Novell NetWare, Special Edition, NetWare Training Guide: Managing NetWare Systems, NetWare Training Guide: Networking Technologies*, and *Inside NetWare Lite*, also published by New Riders Publishing.

Trademark Acknowledgments

Contents at a Glance

Part V: Service and Support

Part VI: NetWare 3.1x Installation and Configuration

Part VII: NetWare Printing

Table of Contents

Part II: NetWare 3.1x Advanced Administration

16   Setting Up Network Printing and Mail Services   231

17   Setting Up Secure User Access   247

Part IV: Networking Technologies

Part V: Service and Support

Part VII: NetWare Printing

INTRODUCTION

The staff of New Riders Publishing is committed to bringing you the very best in computer reference material. Each New Riders book is the result of months of work by authors and staff who research and refine the information contained within its covers.

As part of this commitment to you, the NRP reader, New Riders invites your input. Please let us know if you enjoy this book, if you have trouble with the information and examples presented, or if you have a suggestion for the next edition.

Please note, though: New Riders staff cannot serve as a technical resource for NetWare or for related questions about software- or hardware-related problems. Please refer to the documentation that accompanies NetWare or to the applications' Help systems.

If you have a question or comment about any New Riders book, there are several ways to contact New Riders Publishing. We will respond to as many readers as we can. Your name, address, or phone number will never become part of a mailing list or be used for any purpose other than to help us continue to bring you the best books possible. You can write us at the following address:

> New Riders Publishing
> Attn: Publisher
> 201 W. 103rd Street
> Indianapolis, IN 46290

If you prefer, you can fax New Riders Publishing at (317) 581-4670.

You can send electronic mail to New Riders at the following Internet address:

`edulaney@newriders.mcp.com`

NRP is an imprint of Macmillan Computer Publishing. To obtain a catalog or information, or to purchase any Macmillan Computer Publishing book, call (800) 428-5331.

NetWare 3.1x
Administration

Understanding NetWare 3.1x Functions and Services

Access to resources is provided by NetWare through three types of utilities—DOS text, command-line, and graphical—which interact with the file server through functions and services. The purpose of this chapter is to cover those functions and services, so you can do the following effectively:

- *Describe network functions and services*

- *Use the network communication system*

- *Use the NetWare file system*

- *Use NetWare utilities*

- *Use the ElectroText Electronic Documentation*

Network Functions and Services

The basic function of a network is to enable you to access shared network resources and provide services to clients. Those services can and often do include:

- File storage and retrieval
- Distributed and centralized processing
- Security
- Printing
- Back up and protection of network data
- Inter-office/department communication
- Network connectivity

File storage and retrieval is provided through physical means—hard disk drives on network file servers—and through logical means—networking software that provides access to the physical hard disks.

Distributed processing is provided through microprocessors found on the system boards of each network workstation. NetWare offers centralized processing by providing network clients with access to mainframes and minicomputer systems that also can be part of the network.

Security features can be implemented at the level of your choice.

Printing services are provided through printers attached to the network at different locations.

NetWare enables you to make backup copies of your network data and NetWare's bindery (user-related information) as well as to choose the type of backup device and software to be used. The SBACKUP utility is provided by default, but you also have the option of using more sophisticated or user-friendly backup programs provided by third-party vendors.

NetWare provides communication across network lines from office to office, workgroup to workgroup, company to company, even country to country. Communication is the key to networking, and communication is provided by NetWare's operating system software. The physical connection enabling communication is accomplished with *network interface cards* (NICs), also known as network boards.

The function of a NetWare file server is to provide network users with the services and functions they need. Those services, described previously, include but are not limited to the following:

- File storage and retrieval services
- Security services
- Printing services

For NetWare file servers to provide these services, special software must be loaded into file server memory (RAM). This software consists of two main pieces: the core *operating system* (OS) and *NetWare Loadable Modules* (NLM).

The core operating system provides three basic services, as follows:

- File storage
- Security (including Packet Signature)
- Routing

NetWare Loadable Modules provide other networking services including:

- Printing services
- File storage management
- Server management and monitoring
- Remote console access
- Network protection services through *uninterruptible power supply* (UPS) management
- Network communication services

To access services and functions, network users connect various types of computers and other devices to the network. Any device connected to the network and capable consequently of requesting services from the network is called a *network client.* Computers connected to the network are included in this group, but most often are referred to as *workstations* rather than network clients.

NetWare supports not only *Disk Operating System* (DOS)-based computers (clients), but the following types of clients as well:

- Microsoft Windows
- Macintosh
- Unix
- OS/2

The Network Communication Process

Hardware requirements for communication include the addition of a network board into an available slot in your computer. Furthermore, the board is then physically connected to the network cabling system, using a specific type of cable and connectors (see fig. 1.1).

Figure 1.1
Basic network communication.

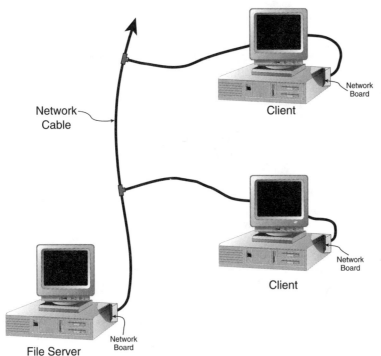

Network Board

Client

Network Cable

Network Board

Client

Network Board

File Server

Your workstation can connect to another network using a different type of cabling and network board scheme. This other connection is accomplished through a network router—a device capable of routing network communications between unlike networks.

After a physical (hardware) connection is made, a software connection must be established. To make a software connection to the network, several files must be loaded into the workstation's memory (see fig. 1.2).

The software your workstation needs to accomplish network communication includes the following:

- LSL.COM (referred to as the Link Support Layer)

- LAN driver (such as NE2000.COM or NE2.COM)

- IPXODI.COM (the communications protocol)

- VLM.EXE (the NetWare DOS Requester)

For the software to function properly, it must be loaded into the workstation's memory in the same order listed. These software elements perform a variety of tasks.

Link Support Layer

The *Link Support Layer* (LSL) implements the ODI specification (see communications protocol). Its primary function is to route network information between the LAN driver and the appropriate communication software. In this capacity, it functions much like a switchboard—it ensures that all communication is sent to its proper destination. The LSL is implemented at each workstation when you load the LSL.COM file.

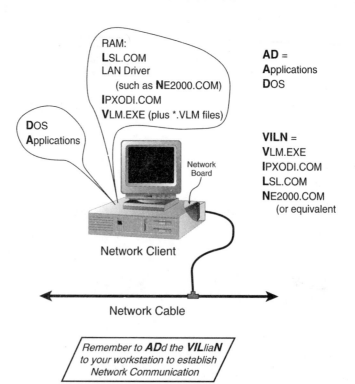

Figure 1.2

Files used for network communication.

RAM:
LSL.COM
LAN Driver
   (such as **NE**2000.COM)
IPXODI.COM
VLM.EXE (plus *.VLM files)

DOS
Applications

Network Board

Network Client

AD =
Applications
DOS

VILN =
VLM.EXE
IPXODI.COM
LSL.COM
NE2000.COM
   (or equivalent

Network Cable

Remember to **AD**d the **VIL**lia**N**
to your workstation to establish
Network Communication

Communications Protocol

The Communications Protocol is a set of rules loaded into workstation memory that determine how communication takes place. NetWare 3.12 follows the *Open Data-Link Interface* (ODI) communications protocol when you load the IPXODI.COM file.

NetWare DOS Requester

The purpose of the NetWare DOS Requester is to allow connection of DOS-based workstations to the network. It functions as a connection point between the workstation's local operating system and the network. A series of files called *Virtual Loadable Modules* (VLM), along with the VLM Manager (VLM.EXE), make up the NetWare DOS Requester. When you load the VLM.EXE file at your workstation, it loads the other required VLMs.

LAN Driver

The LAN driver activates and controls the network board in your workstation. You must load a LAN driver that matches the network board installed in your workstation. NetWare provides LAN drivers for many common network boards. If you are using a network board for which NetWare does not supply a matching LAN driver, simply load the appropriate LAN driver supplied with the network board when you purchased it.

 Not all LAN drivers support the ODI specification. You must use a LAN driver that does support ODI when running on a NetWare 3.12 network. These drivers are referred to as *Multiple Link Interface Drivers* (MLID).

All the network communication files are loaded at the workstation by typing these file names at the DOS prompt or by putting them into your workstation's startup file. After this software is loaded into your workstation's memory, the workstation can send requests for services and data, as well as receive responses and information across the network.

 To help you remember all the software associated with network communications, remember the following sentence, which is also noted in figure 1.2:

To ensure successful communication, remember to **AD**d the **VIL**lai**N** to your workstation:

1. **A.** Applications software

2. **D.** DOS (or other supported workstation operating system)

3. **V.** VLM.EXE

4. **I.** IPXODI.COM

5. **L.** LSL.COM

6. **N.** NE2000 (LAN card for your network board)

Now that your workstation is connected to the file server, you can access network information. To optimize that access, you must understand how the information is arranged on the file server.

The Network File System

NetWare 3.12 file servers provide storage and retrieval of files by giving network clients access to its hard disk(s). Each hard disk is organized into logical structures containing volumes and directories.

Volumes are logical divisions of the hard disk. They are the highest logical level on a NetWare file server (see fig. 1.3). Volumes contain directories, which are the second logical level. Subdirectories and files comprise the third logical level. They cannot be stored directly at the volume level; they are stored in directories, which are stored on volumes.

The NetWare operating system has requirements of its own in order for it to function and provide network services. The logical division into volumes is one of those requirements. Another is that of specific NetWare directories into which NetWare can store and retrieve various files it needs to perform requested functions and to provide required services.

In the DOS environment, NetWare volumes are the logical equivalent to the DOS root. As with the DOS directory structure, the highest level you can access on a NetWare file server hard disk is the root (volume). Also, as with the DOS root, there are specific technical requirements associated with volumes. These specifications include the following:

- A volume name must be two to fifteen characters long and follow the same basic naming conventions as DOS (0-9 and A-Z). However, NetWare volume names can include symbols such as the underscore (_). Volume names are identified by the colon (:) that immediately follows them, so a colon cannot be used in the volume name.

- Each volume name on a file server must be unique to that file server, although the same volume name can be used on other file servers.

Figure 1.3

NetWare file system structure.

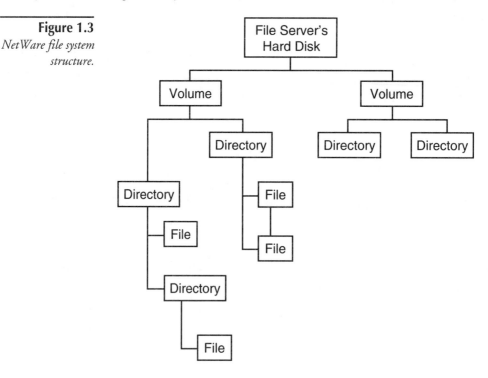

For example, every NetWare file server has a SYS: volume, but no NetWare file server can have two volumes called SYS.

■ A volume can be as large as 32 TB and can span as many as 32 hard disks.

■ A file server can have a maximum of 64 volumes on it, but the total size for all volumes is limited to 32 TB.

Directories are the next-highest level in the NetWare file system structure. Directories can have files and other directories (subdirectories) beneath them. NetWare, like DOS, uses a hierarchical file storage system (see fig. 1.4).

The main function of a NetWare directory structure is to provide organization for files and subdirectories. Each directory, subdirectory, and file has its own name, a name unique within a particular area of the directory structure. You can have more than one subdirectory with the same name if each of these subdirectories are stored beneath a different directory. Because directories, subdirectories, and files are accessed by name, no directory, subdirectory, or file can have the same name as another directory, subdirectory, or file at the same level within the file system structure.

NetWare's directory structure uses drive letters and specific paths. A path begins with the name of the file server and is followed by a volume name, a directory name, and, if appropriate, the names of any subdirectories below that point in the directory structure. A typical NetWare directory path might look similar to the following:

`F:Acct_Server/SYS:Public/Users/Sam`

The letter F is the drive letter assigned to this specific path, as noted by the colon which follows it. In DOS, only drive letters representing actual

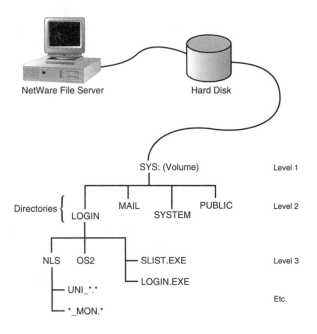

Figure 1.4
NetWare's hierarchical file storage system.

physical drives or logical drives formed by creating DOS partitions are used. In NetWare, every letter of the alphabet can be used as a NetWare drive, assuming your workstation does not need the drive letter to represent a physical or logical DOS drive.

Acct_Server is the name of the file server on which the remainder of this path can be found. When specifying a NetWare path, the name of the file server must be followed by either a forward (/) or a backward (\) slash.

SYS represents the name of the NetWare volume and must be followed by a colon, which indicates that the name that precedes it is a NetWare volume.

USERS is the name of a directory which can be found on the SYS: volume. It is followed by a slash, which is used from here on out in the NetWare path to indicate subdirectories.

SAM is the name of a subdirectory found below the USERS directory. In many network environments, this path would represent the home directory for a network user called SAM, who would use this home directory to file all his personal files. In it he can create other subdirectories and extend the NetWare directory structure to as many levels as the operating system allows.

NetWare requires specific directories to set up and access the files it needs to operate. When you install NetWare, it creates seven directories and installs the files it requires into these directories. The directories NetWare installation creates include the following:

- LOGIN
- MAIL
- PUBLIC
- SYSTEM
- ETC

These directories are all created below the SYS: volume in the file system structure.

LOGIN

The first directory you access on a NetWare file server is the LOGIN directory. It contains several files important to your initial file server access, including SLIST.EXE and LOGIN.EXE.

SLIST

SLIST.EXE is a NetWare utility used to see the names of all file servers that the file server to which you are logging in can see. To make it easier for you to find a particular file server's name, SLIST.EXE provides the list of known file servers in alphabetical order. In addition, SLIST.EXE provides some basic information about each file server. This information includes the following:

- Network
- Node address
- Status

The network address is the assignment of the ipx internal net for the server. The node address in 3.x is always 1.

The status information for a workstation is a little more complex. There are three types of status that can be displayed: blank, Default, and Attached. The status displayed indicates the relationship of this workstation to the file server, not the actual or physical status of the file server.

A blank or no status indicates that there is no current relationship between this workstation and this file server. The fact that the file server is included in the list indicates that the workstation can see this server, but otherwise the workstation and file server have no established relationship.

A Default status indicates the workstation is currently connected to this file server and this is the file server from which you are running any NetWare-related commands.

An Attached status indicates that the workstation has loaded the appropriate files and has established communication with this file server. It often indicates that this was the first server to which the workstation was able to establish a network connection (attachment), so that it could see the LOGIN directory and gain access to the appropriate file server by running the LOGIN.EXE file.

LOGIN

The LOGIN.EXE file enables you to identify yourself to the network using your assigned network USERID (assigned login name), and if applicable, related password. After you successfully identify yourself to the network, you are able to access network files and resources to which you have been given rights.

MAIL

The MAIL directory contains a mail subdirectory that is named with a unique one to eight digit hexidecimal number for each NetWare user. These directories are created for each user when given a USERID and account on the network. These subdirectories contain a user's personal login script, as well as any printer definition files created for the user's personal use. These files are identified as

PRINTCON.DAT files. The Supervisor's mail sub-directory is always identified with just the numeral 1.

PUBLIC

The PUBLIC directory contains all the utilities and commands that most network users are allowed to and might need to access. It also contains files used for defining printers (printer definition files—PDF files), and files the NetWare OS uses when it has to perform various system subroutines (overlay—OVL files). In addition, the PUBLIC directory contains all the help files (*.HLP) for the utilities and commands located in this directory. These help files give you online information related to these utilities and commands to help you properly execute and use them.

SYSTEM

The SYSTEM directory contains those NetWare utilities and command-line commands that only network supervisors and users of equivalent status can use. It also contains the NetWare Loadable Modules (NLM) and files intended for use by the NetWare operating system. Three other directories are sometimes created, as well:

■ ETC

■ DELETED.SAV

■ DOC

ETC

Because correct connectivity is important in the NetWare environment, this directory contains files to be used with TCP/IP connectivity. These files are text files that provide connectivity information about other network devices.

DELETED.SAV

The DELETED.SAV directory contains files that have been deleted and files that at one time were stored in a directory that no longer exists. NetWare enables you to undelete files you have deleted. Furthermore, when configured to do so, it saves the files you have deleted in the directories in which they were originally stored. If you also delete those directories, the deleted files, of course, cannot be stored there and are instead stored in the DELETED.SAV directory.

Deleted files do not appear on the file list when you request a directory listing. To see which files have been deleted and might be recoverable, you must use NetWare's salvage feature.

DOC

NetWare 3.12 ships with a full set of documentation on CD-ROM. It also includes various files required to access this online documentation set. This directory stores the electronic versions of the NetWare manuals, if you choose to install them.

NetWare Utilities

As discussed previously, several of the system-created directories contain utilities that both regular users and network administrators can use. There are three types of *interfaces* (methods of access and control) used by these utilities. The type of interface that a utility uses also is used to identify the type of utility. The three types of network utilities available on a NetWare network include the following:

- DOS text utilities
- Command-line utilities
- Graphical utilities

Though the interface used by a given NetWare utility might differ from that of another utility, together, all these NetWare utilities provide the basic functionality needed to administer and use network resources.

DOS Text Utilities

All DOS text utilities use a menu-based interface. Information shown includes the name of the utility, the version number, the current date and time, the name of the user accessing this utility, and the name of the file server the user is currently accessing. All this information is displayed on the command line.

Figure 1.5 shows the SYSCON main screen.

Within all DOS text utilities you can use function keys to perform basic tasks or functions. The available function keys include the following:

- **F1**   Opens the help (HLP) file for this utility
- **F3**   Enables you to choose an option to modify it
- **F5**   Lets you mark multiple items upon which to simultaneously perform the same action
- **ALT+F10**   Enables you to exit the utility at any given point

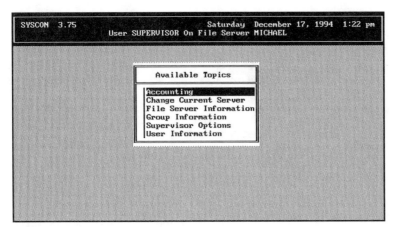

Figure 1.5
*SYSCON DOS text
utility main screen.*

Command-Line Utilities

Command-line utilities have no menu interface and are often provided as an alternative to using either the DOS text utilities or the graphical utilities.

Graphical Utilities

Graphical utilities have a *graphical-user interface* (GUI). Figure 1.6 shows a graphical utility.

As with the command-line utilities, it might not always be easy or instinctive for you to understand how to use a particular utility or how to perform a given task using that utility. To help you, NetWare utilities provide online (on-screen) help that you can access from within the utility. How you access this online help depends on the type of utility you are using—text, command-line, or graphical.

To access help from within a DOS text utility, press F1. DOS text utility help is contact sensitive; meaning, wherever you are within the utility, pressing F1 displays a help screen related to the area of the utility. In the SYSCON utility, for example (refer to fig. 1.5), if you chose the first menu item from the Available Topics menu, you could press F1 to see a help screen related to that specific menu item.

To access help from a command-line utility, type the utility name followed by a blank space, a slash, and a question mark.

To access help from within a graphical utility, choose the Help button from the button bar. The Help button shown previously in figure 1.6 is the question mark displayed as the last button in the button bar.

The ElectroText Electronic Documentation

NetWare provides another online help resource called *Novell ElectroText*, an electronic copy of the entire NetWare 3.12 manual set. If you install it, the ElectroText software can be stored on the file server, a workstation, or accessed from CD-ROM disk.

Novell's ElectroText software is provided through three major components, as follows:

- **Search engine.** Locates information in NetWare's electronic manual set

Figure 1.6

A NetWare graphical utility.

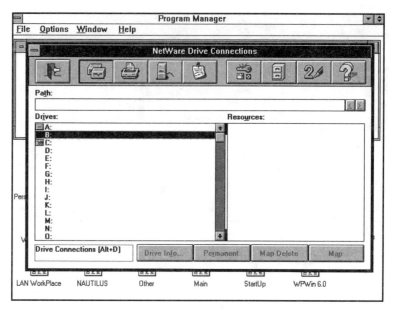

- **Bookshelf.** Contains the NetWare 3.12 set of electronic manuals

- **Viewer.** Enables you to move through, read, and print Novell's electronic documentation

You can only run ElectroText through Windows. From within Windows, select the ElectroText icon. After ElectroText opens, choose the NetWare 3.12 manuals; then open one of the books, such as Concepts or System Administration. Furthermore, before users can access Novell's ElectroText software, you must set up each user's MS Windows workstation to display the icon for starting the feature.

After you have opened a book, you can activate the search engine by using the Search field found at the bottom of either a library or *bookshelf window* (a window containing the collection of available documents) to search for a specific topic. You also can use the outline to choose specific information that you want to read.

Novell's ElectroText software also provides a viewer that is used to open books, navigate through books, and print portions of books; that is, the viewer is used to activate and navigate Novell ElectroText.

Before anyone can use Novell's ElectroText, certain related software must be installed on the network. To install ElectroText, your system must meet the minimum requirements, which include the following:

- At least 30 MB of available disk storage space

- A copy of the program software, ET.EXE

- A copy of the NetWare 3.12 electronic book set

Once you meet these minimum requirements, you can set up the ElectroText software so users can access it from any of the following:

- A Microsoft Windows client

- A NetWare 3.12 file server

- A CD-ROM drive

Questions

1. Which of the following is NOT a service provided by NetWare 3.12?

    ○ A. File storage and retrieval

    ○ B. Distributed and centralized processing

    ○ C. Security

    ○ D. Interoffice telephone communication

2. Of the following, which THREE are provided by the NetWare core operating system?

    ☐ A. File storage

    ☐ B. Packet Signature

    ☐ C. Network management

    ☐ D. Routing

3. The file whose primary function is to route network information between the LAN driver and the appropriate communication software is called _____.

    ○ A. LSL.COM

    ○ B. LAN driver

    ○ C. IPXODI.COM

    ○ D. NetWare DOS Requester

4. The set of rules that determine how the network and workstation communicate is implemented at each workstation when you load the _____ file.

    ○ A. LSL.COM

    ○ B. LAN driver

    ○ C. IPXODI.COM

    ○ D. NetWare DOS Requester

5. The main function of a NetWare directory structure is to do which of the following?

    ○ A. Provide file and directory organization

    ○ B. Emulate the DOS environment

    ○ C. Allow storage of Macintosh files on disk

    ○ D. Provide advanced file system security

6. The directory containing all the utilities and commands that most network users are able to and might need to access is the _____ directory.

    ○ A. SYSTEM

    ○ B. PUBLIC

    ○ C. MAIL

    ○ D. ETC

7. In which directory are the NLMs stored?

   ○ A. SYSTEM

   ○ B. PUBLIC

   ○ C. MAIL

   ○ D. ETC

8. Of the three types of NetWare 3.12 utilities, which type does NOT provide online help?

   ○ A. DOS GUI

   ○ B. Command-line

   ○ C. DOS text

   ○ D. Graphical

9. To activate and navigate DOS text utility help, press the _____ key while the utility is running.

   ○ A. F1

   ○ B. F3

   ○ C. F5

   ○ D. Alt+F10

10. If you choose the help button (?), for which type of utility will you be activating online help?

    ○ A. DOS text

    ○ B. Command-line

    ○ C. NetWare User Tools

    ○ D. GUI

11. The _____ utility requires you to type /? to activate help.

    ○ A. DOS text

    ○ B. command-line

    ○ C. GUI

    ○ D. ElectroText

12. The help system that must be started from inside MS Windows is called _____.

    ○ A. DOS text

    ○ B. command-line

    ○ C. GUI

    ○ D. ElectroText

13. The primary file used to install ElectroText is called _____.

    ○ A. INSTALL.NLM

    ○ B. DYNATEXT.INI

    ○ C. SYSDOCS.CFG

    ○ D. ET.EXE

14. Basic information NOT shown on the main screen of DOS text utilities is _____.

    ○ A. the name of the utility

    ○ B. the utility's version number

    ○ C. the current date and time

    ○ D. None of the Above

15. Login security is provided by _____.

   ○ A. requiring each user to have a unique
         network identification

   ○ B. making passwords mandatory

   ○ C. providing Packet Signature at the
         file server, client, and file server and
         client levels

   ○ D. creating SYS volume at installation

Answers

1. D	9. A
2. A, B, D	10. D
3. A	11. B
4. C	12. D
5. A	13. D
6. B	14. D
7. A	15. A
8. A	

Understanding and Implementing NetWare 3.1x Network Security

There are several aspects of NetWare security that you need to understand, such as the overall design and availability of security, as well as how to implement it. The chapter is broken into the following four sections:

- *Manipulating NetWare network and file system security*

- *Setting up and securing user and group accounts*

- *Implementing network and file system security*

- *Implementing file server console security*

Manipulating NetWare Network and File System Security

The levels of network security and how they work are illustrated in figure 2.1. They consist of the following:

- Login
- Rights
- Attributes
- File server

NetWare's four security levels control access to information on the network. Login security controls user access to the network. Rights security controls user access to network resources. Attributes security controls what users can do with or to network resources. File server security controls user access to the file server through the file server console.

Login Security

This is the first and most rudimentary level of network security. Components consist of a valid network *user ID* (also called the username) and an associated password.

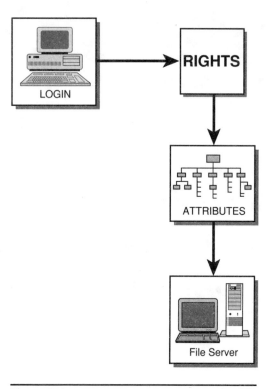

Figure 2.1
The NetWare security levels.

The first step in the login security process is *validating* the user, which involves the following:

- Checking for password requirements
- Matching the user's ID and password
- Checking user account restrictions

NetWare's security system validates network users by checking the login information that the user provides (user ID and password) against the information stored in the NetWare bindery about that user.

Note The NetWare bindery is a database containing three types of information, including the following:

- **Objects.** Physical or logical entities, such as users and groups

- **Properties.** Characteristics of each object in the NetWare bindery, such as password requirements and group members

- **Data sets.** Values assigned to each bindery property, such as the actual password used by a given user

After a network user's ID and password have been checked, the user's request for access is then checked against any restrictions placed on their user account.

User account restrictions control several aspects of network access and use. Restrictions can be set, for example, that specify the days of the week and times of day that a user can log into the network. Other restrictions can limit the number of clients (workstations) from which a user can log in. Intruder detection is a user account restriction feature

that locks a user's account after a predetermined number of incorrect user login attempts have been made.

Most of the account restrictions are related to a user's rights to log into the network. There are different types of restrictions that can be set. Figure 2.2 shows the SYSCON utility's User Information menu.

Some of the different types of user account restrictions you can set—which are included on the SYSCON User Information menu shown in figure 2.2—include the following:

- **Account restrictions.** You can specify account-related restrictions, such as whether a user must have a password, what the minimum length of that password must be, whether the user can change the password, whether the user must periodically change the password, whether the account has an expiration date, and whether the user's connections should be limited.

- **Station restrictions.** You can restrict which network clients a user can log in from.

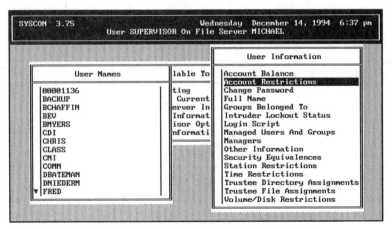

Figure 2.2
SYSCON's User Information menu.

- **Time restrictions.** You can restrict the times of day during which a user can access the network (see fig. 2.3).

- **Volume disk restrictions.** You can limit the amount of space the user can have for file storage on any particular network volume.

You can also set another particularly useful security feature of NetWare known as intruder account detection. *Intruder account detection* enables you to choose whether the network detects and tracks unsuccessful attempts to log in using an invalid network user ID or password, or an incorrect combination of user ID and password.

The SYSCON utility enables you to see the status of a user's intruder account detection. Figure 2.4 shows the status of FRED's intruder account detection—this user's detection feature has not been triggered.

Rights Security

For a validated user to access network resources, the user must have the necessary *rights*, which are the access privileges you give network users. They are an integral part of network security, even though they are oriented toward file system security.

These rights, granted by the network administrator, can be assigned to individual network users (regular users) as well as to other pre-defined types of network users.

 Note   NetWare defines several different types of users. They include the following:

- **Supervisor.** Has all rights to everything on the network

- **Supervisor equivalent.** Has the same rights as the Supervisor

- **Workgroup manager.** Has limited control over a select group of other users, including the right to create or delete users (within that group)

- **Account manager.** Has limited control over a select group of users specifically assigned to him or her (the account manager)

- **PCONSOLE operator.** Can manage existing print queues or print servers but cannot add new ones

- **FCONSOLE operator.** Can manage the network file server using FCONSOLE, if that user has supervisor equivalent rights

- **User.** (Includes regular users and a special user known as Guest.) Can log in to the network and access the network resources granted to them

You protect NetWare's file system using various security features, described as the following:

- Trustees

- Directory and file rights

- Inheritance

- Inherited Rights Mask (IRM)

- Effective rights

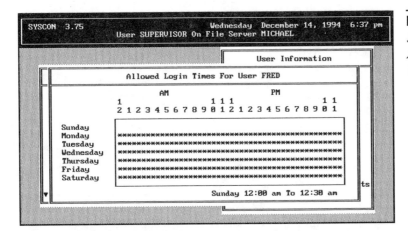

Figure 2.3
SYSCON utility display of Allowed Login Times For User FRED.

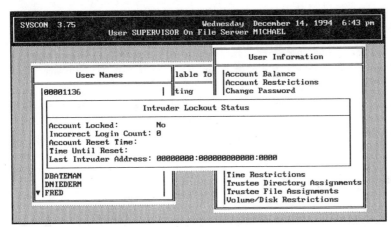

Figure 2.4
The Intruder Lockout Status for user FRED.

You grant rights to users for access to network files and directories by making them trustees of various network files and directories. Use the SYSCON utility to make users trustees, then to grant specific rights to those users. You also can use the SYSCON utility to see which directories a user is a trustee of.

Figure 2.5, for example, shows both the list of Trustee Rights Granted to user FRED and the Trustee Rights Not Granted user FRED to his mail directory.

Rights you can give to network users include the following:

■ **Access Control.** Enables you to modify trustee assignments and the IRM for a directory or file

■ **Create.** Enables you to create files and subdirectories

■ **Erase.** Enables you to delete files and directories

■ **File Scan.** Enables you to see files and directories when you request a directory listing

■ **Modify.** Enables you to change file and directory attributes

■ **Read.** Enables you to open files and read or run them

■ **Supervisory.** Gives you all rights to files and directories

■ **Write.** Enables you to open a file and write to it

One other method in which rights security is implemented is through the use of *Inherited Rights Masks* (IRMs). An IRM is provided for each file and directory at the time it is created. By default, the IRM grants all rights to the file or directory. You can modify the IRM to filter out any rights you do not want users to have for a particular file or directory.

By changing the IRM for a given directory to remove a right, any user who would have inherited that right will no longer have it. The IRM takes effect from the point in the directory at which the

IRM is modified, on down through the balance of that portion of the directory structure.

 Note   An *inherited right* is a right you receive to all subdirectories or files below the level at which the right was granted. Once granted, rights flow through the directory structure until either another set of rights are granted to you or the IRM prevents you from inheriting those rights.

IRMs cannot filter out the Supervisory right. If you give the Supervisory right to an individual, you cannot prevent them from having full access to all files and directories from there on, until you go back and remove the Supervisory right.

Because rights can be granted, can be blocked out, and can flow down through the directory structure, a user's rights at one point in the directory structure can be different than his or her rights at another point in the directory structure. The rights the user ends up with at any point in the directory structure are the user's effective rights.

Figure 2.5
User FRED's Granted and Not Granted Trustee Rights.

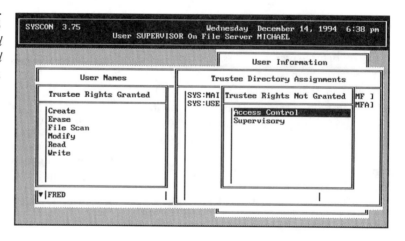

A user's effective rights are determined by looking at the user's inherited rights, the IRM, and any group affiliations or equivalencies the user might have.

In most cases, the explicit rights granted to a user are the same as the user's effective rights. If a user has rights granted because that user is a member of a group, those explicit rights are added to the explicit rights granted to the user at that level in the directory structure, to equal the user's effective rights.

When no rights are explicitly granted to the user, and no rights are granted based on the user's association with a group, the user's effective rights are those that have been granted elsewhere at a higher level in the directory structure, with one exception, the IRM. If an IRM is applied, the rights the IRM filters out are taken away from that user. The only exception is the Supervisory right, which cannot be removed with an IRM.

In addition to enhancing or restricting a user's access to network directories and files using rights, you also can restrict what users can do with directories and files by assigning directory and file attributes.

Attributes Security

Rights are given to users. *Attributes* are attached to files and directories and are given to files by using FLAG and to directories by using the FLAGDIR command. Figure 2.6 shows the FLAG command help screen, which lists the available attributes.

The available attributes include the following:

- **Read Only.** File can be opened and read but cannot be modified

- **Read Write.** File can be opened, read, and modified

- **Sharable.** File can be accessed by multiple users at the same time

- **Hidden.** File is not displayed when a directory listing is requested

- **System.** File is a system file

- **Transactional.** File is one to which the *Transactional Tracking System* (TTS) security feature can be applied

- **Purge.** File is to be completely eliminated so as not to be recoverable when deleted

- **Archive needed.** File is to be archived

- **Read Audit.** Not implemented in NetWare 3.1*x*

- **Write Audit.** Not implemented in NetWare 3.1*x*

- **Copy Inhibit.** File cannot be copied (for use with MAC files only)

- **Execute only.** File can only be run (executed)

- **Delete Inhibit.** File cannot be deleted

- **Rename Inhibit.** File cannot be renamed

File Server Security

File server security refers to the physical security of the network file servers. To make a network file server secure from physical access by others, place the server in an area where physical access can be restricted, such as a locked file server room.

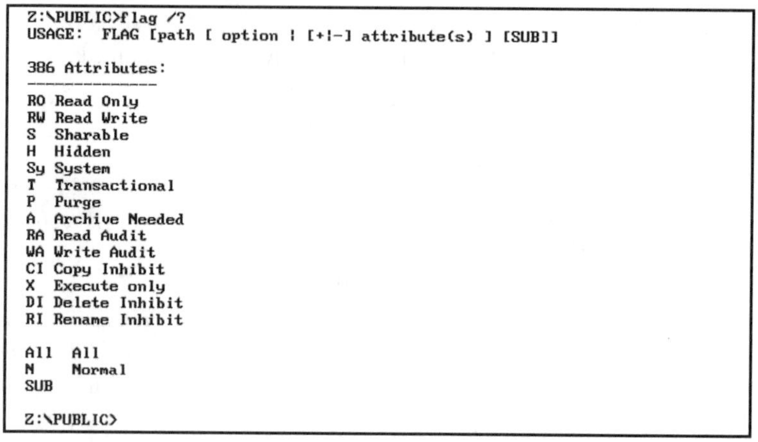

Figure 2.6

FLAG Help screen displaying attributes.

```
Z:\PUBLIC>flag /?
USAGE:  FLAG [path [ option | [+!-] attribute(s) ] [SUB]]

386 Attributes:
-----------------
RO  Read Only
RW  Read Write
S   Sharable
H   Hidden
Sy  System
T   Transactional
P   Purge
A   Archive Needed
RA  Read Audit
WA  Write Audit
CI  Copy Inhibit
X   Execute only
DI  Delete Inhibit
RI  Rename Inhibit

All  All
N    Normal
SUB

Z:\PUBLIC>
```

Two other methods of restricting physical file server console access include setting a console password and setting a password on the remote console utility.

You set a file server console password using the Lock File Server Console option from the MONITOR NLM's Available Topics main menu. When prompted to enter a password, enter a password for the file server console. Then, no user can access the console to load modules or make changes without first knowing the console password.

Whenever you run RCONSOLE, you are prompted for a password. When you load the RCONSOLE-related *NetWare Loadable Modules* (NLM) on the file server, you set that password. RCONSOLE-related NLMs include:

■ REMOTE.NLM

■ RSPX.NLM

Another important security feature of NetWare 3.1x is known as Packet Signature.

Packet Signature is defined at both the NetWare file servers and clients. Once defined, the level of

Packet Signature you set is added to network packets to provide a user/client identification for packets being sent between a particular client and the file server. Packet Signature prevents users from forging network packets to gain greater access to the network than that user was originally granted.

Higher levels of Packet Signature cause greater burden on network traffic. NetWare's Packet Signature security feature, therefore, is designed to let you set the level for the NCP Packet Signature. At the maximum level, when a client logs into a NetWare 3.12 server, the server and client agree upon a single, shared identification key called the *session key*, which is included in every packet sent between the file server and this client until the connection is broken. Each client receives a unique session key each time it connects to the network.

After a client is logged in and a session key is established, the file server checks each packet to make sure it has the client's unique signature, ensuring that each packet it receives is a valid packet. Packets with correct signatures are processed, and all others are discarded. Figure 2.7 shows the NCP Packet Signature process.

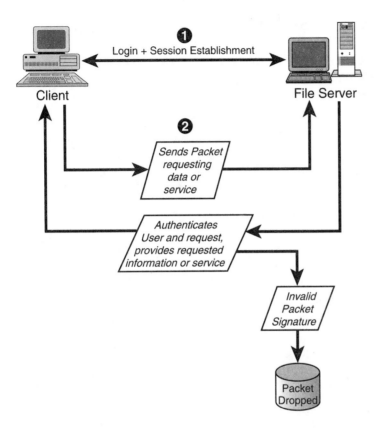

Figure 2.7
The Packet Signature process.

There are various Packet Signature levels you can set. The level is set as a number ranging from 1 to 4 inclusive. Level 1 provides the least amount of security. Level 4 provides the greatest amount of security.

You set signature levels for each server and client by adding **SET NCP PACKET SIGNATURE OPTION** = *number* at the server console *or* in the server's AUTOEXEC.NCF file. To set the Packet Signature level at the client, put **SIGNATURE LEVEL** = *number* in the client's NET.CFG file, indented under the NetWare DOS Requester heading.

Performance issues associated with Packet Signature are discussed in Chapter 12, "Maintaining and Monitoring NetWare 3.1x Servers."

Setting Up and Securing User and Group Accounts

Network security entails much more than just understanding what it is. You must also understand how to implement it. There are different tasks associated with the different types of security features.

Before users can access the network, for example, they need to have a user account on the network. To ensure that users access only those network services to which they are entitled, user network accounts need to have appropriate account restrictions applied to them. In addition, you need to work with and manage both group and user accounts.

Setting up user accounts requires three steps. First, you must establish the account for the user. Second, you must determine whether each user account should have a password associated with it. Third, you must decide whether user accounts will have restrictions applied to them, then implement any restrictions you have chosen to apply.

To simplify the setup of user accounts, you can also establish group accounts. Using group accounts enables you to simultaneously apply rights and restrictions to a group of network users.

Use the SYSCON utility to create user and group accounts. Create user accounts by choosing the User Information option from SYSCON's main menu. Pressing Insert and following the prompts then enables you to create users.

SYSCON also enables you to create group accounts. The process for creating group accounts is very similar to that of creating user accounts. The main difference is that you choose the Group Information option from SYSCON's main menu, instead of the User Information option.

 Note   You can automate the creation of user accounts using the USERDEF and MAKEUSER utilities. These two utilities enable you to define various aspects of user accounts, which will be applied to all user accounts when created.

Implementing Network and File System Security

You implement Network and file system security using the SYSCON and FILER utilities. SYSCON enables you to create users and groups and also enables you to establish user- and group-related security. You can create Workgroup Managers and User or Group Account Managers, as well as Console Operators using SYSCON.

You can also make trustee assignments and apply rights using the SYSCON and FILER utilities.

You make trustee assignments by adding users or groups as trustees of the current directory. To accomplish this task, start the FILER utility and choose Current Directory Information from the Available Topics menu (see fig. 2.8).

When the Directory Information For screen opens, choose Trustees. To add trustees, press Insert, then choose users and groups to be added. If you want to add more than one user or group, first mark each user or group using the F5 key, then press Enter to accept your choices.

You then can give those users and trustees specific rights to that directory or file by returning to the Available Topics FILER menu, choosing Current Directory Information, choosing the trustees to receive rights, pressing Insert to see a list of available rights, marking (F5) those rights that you want to grant, and then pressing Enter.

In addition to granting or revoking rights and trustee assignments using the SYSCON and FILER utilities, you can also use various command-line utilities, including the following:

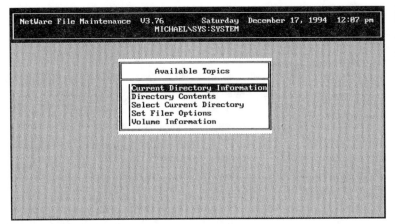

Figure 2.8
FILER's Available Topics menu.

■ RIGHTS

■ TLIST

■ GRANT

■ ALLOW

■ REVOKE

■ REMOVE

Use these utilities to implement security on your network. You can accomplish the same basic tasks with these command-line utilities as you accomplish using the SYSCON and FILER utilities.

Note You can use the SYSCON utility, for example, to set account restrictions. Account restrictions are used to determine whether or not a user can log in to the network, at what times they can log in, and from which workstations they can log in.

You set account restrictions for individual users. You choose the user for whom you want to set account restrictions, therefore, from the User Information screen in SYSCON, then choose

Account Restrictions. From there you choose which account restrictions you want to implement.

You perform the following in SYSCON to set account restrictions:

■ Disable the user's account so that the user cannot log into the network at all

■ Enable the user's account if it has been disabled

■ Set user's account to expire and provide an expiration date on that user's account

■ Remove an expiration date restriction

Command-line utilities are used to accomplish various security-related tasks.

RIGHTS is used to view your effective rights in a given directory, subdirectory, or file. To use RIGHTS, type **RIGHTS [*path*]** and press Enter. Replace *path* with the directory path in which you want to view your rights.

TLIST is used to see the list of trustees assigned to a given directory, subdirectory, or file. To use TLIST, type **TLIST [*path* [USERS | GROUPS]]** and press Enter. Replace *path* with the directory path, and type either **USERS** or **GROUPS** to view either the users or the groups with rights to this directory, subdirectory, or file.

GRANT is used to give trustee rights to a given directory, subdirectory, or file for a specific user or group. To use GRANT, type **GRANT** *rights* **[FOR** *path*] **TO [USER | GROUP]** *name* and press Enter. Replace *rights* with the list of rights you want to grant, inserting a space between each right. To grant Read and File Scan, for example, type **R F** in place of *rights*. Replace *path* with the path to the directory or file, and replace *name* with the name of the user or group to whom you are granting the rights.

ALLOW is used to change the IRM for a directory, subdirectory, or file. To use ALLOW, type **AL-LOW [*path* [TO INHERIT]** *rights*] and press Enter. Replace *path* with the path to the directory, subdirectory, or file, and replace *rights* with the list of rights you want to prevent from flowing down. As with the GRANT command, rights must be separated with a space.

REVOKE is used to take trustee rights to a directory, subdirectory, or file away from a specific user or group. To use REVOKE, type **REVOKE** *rights* **[FOR** *path*] **FROM [USER | GROUP]** *name* **[/***option*] and press Enter. Replace *rights* with the list of rights to be revoked, separating each with a space. Replace *path* with the path to the directory, subdirectory, or file from which the rights are to be revoked. Replace *name* with the user or group name which the REVOKE command is intended to affect. If you want, you can replace *option* with **-SUB** to revoke the rights to all subdirectories within the specified path, or **-F** to revoke the rights

to all files within the path, and within any subdirectories if you also used the -SUB option.

REMOVE is used to remove a user or a group from the list of trustees associated with a directory, subdirectory, or file. To use REMOVE, type **RE-MOVE [USER | GROUP]** *name* **[[FROM]** *path* [*option*] and press Enter. Replace *name* with the name of the user or group. Replace *path* with the path that points to the directory, subdirectory, or file. Replace *option* with one or both of the available options. You can type **-SUB** to remove the users or groups from the trustee list associated with all subdirectories within the specified path, or **-F** to apply the REMOVE command to all files within the path, and within any subdirectories (if you also used the -SUB option).

Implementing File Server Console Security

Securing user access to the network and its resources is an important security system implementation. It is not, however, the only security measure you should take. You should also physically protect your file servers from unauthorized access.

There are two ways to physically protect your file servers from unauthorized access. The first is to lock the file server in a secure area; the second is to provide the console with a password.

You implement console password security from either the file server console or by running one of the remote console utilities—RCONSOLE or ACONSOLE. RCONSOLE is run from a network workstation, ACONSOLE from a workstation that gains access to the network through a modem. The use of a modem and an additional file, which you load at the file server, make up the main difference between using RCONSOLE and ACONSOLE.

Whether you use RCONSOLE, ACONSOLE, or directly access the file server's console, you set the file server password by first loading the MONITOR NLM, then choosing Lock File Server Console from the Available Topics menu. Next, you type a password used to lock the keyboard. You can use any password, including the Supervisor's.

Questions

1. Of the following, which is NOT a level of network security?

   ○ A. Login

   ○ B. Rights

   ○ C. Group accounts

   ○ D. File and directory attributes

2. Which network security level is affected by the user's password?

   ○ A. Login

   ○ B. Rights

   ○ C. User accounts

   ○ D. Attributes

3. To access a NetWare network, a user must first pass through the _____ security level.

   ○ A. login

   ○ B. rights

   ○ C. user accounts

   ○ D. attributes

4. Which utility can be used to set user account password requirements?

   ○ A. GRANT

   ○ B. SYSCON

   ○ C. FILER

   ○ D. TLIST

5. Which of the following restrictions CAN-NOT be turned on or off for individual network user accounts?

   ○ A. Intruder detection

   ○ B. Account restrictions

   ○ C. Time restrictions

   ○ D. Station restrictions

6. Which key is used to choose more than one user or group for simultaneously applying account restrictions?

   ○ A. F1

   ○ B. F3

   ○ C. F5

   ○ D. Alt+F10

7. Effective rights are equal to which of the following?

   ○ A. User's granted rights at the level granted

   ○ B. Supervisor's rights

   ○ C. User's inherited rights less applied IRM

   ○ D. User's granted rights plus granted group rights

8. The file server console can be secured with a password using _____.

   ○ A. AUTOEXEC.NCF

   ○ B. MONITOR.NLM

   ○ C. SYSCON.EXE

   ○ D. FILER.EXE

9. You delete a user or group from the trustee list of a file using the _____ utility.

   ○ A. REMOVE

   ○ B. REVOKE

   ○ C. TLIST

   ○ D. GRANT

10. You CANNOT use the SYSCON utility to complete which of the following tasks?

    ○ A. Change a user's group

    ○ B. Modify a user's security equivalence

    ○ C. Change a user's directory assignment

    ○ D. Calculate a user's effective rights

11. Of the following, which THREE are NetWare rights?

    ☐ A. F

    ☐ B. W

    ☐ C. S

    ☐ D. B

12. To see a list of files in a directory, you must have the _____ right.

    ○ A. F

    ○ B. A

    ○ C. M

    ○ D. E

13. Another way of describing rights that flow down throughout the NetWare directory structure is _____.

○ A. Trustee

○ B. Inheritance

○ C. Effective

○ D. Granted

14. To prevent an executable file from being deleted accidentally, set the _____ attribute on the file.

   ○ A. R

   ○ B. C

   ○ C. X

   ○ D. A

15. Which TWO tasks should be used to implement console security features on the server?

   ☐ A. Lock the file server in a secure place

   ☐ B. Load FDISK at the file server console

   ☐ C. Add a console password

   ☐ D. None of the above

Answers

1. C	9. A
2. A	10. D
3. A	11. A, B, C
4. B	12. A
5. A	13. B
6. C	14. C
7. D	15. A, C
8. B	

3

Accessing NetWare 3.1x Network Services

*W*hen a user's client is prepared to access the network, the user needs to understand how to access and use the network file system. This chapter provides instructions related to preparing a client for network access and to finding and using the network resources the client's user needs, including the following:

- *Installing and configuring a network client*

- *Connecting a workstation to the network*

- *Accessing the network file system*

- *Viewing and managing file system information*

Installing and Configuring a Network Client

Providing networking services requires special hardware and software; so, too, does accessing those services. On a NetWare 3.12 file server, the operating system software provides the services. On a NetWare network client, the client software provides the access to those services. Just as the 3.12 operating system and related files must be installed on the file server, the network client software must be installed on the client.

After backing up your PC's configuration files, change to the drive containing the WSDOS_1 disk. Type **INSTALL** and press Enter to start the client installation. The NetWare Client Install screen opens (see fig. 3.1).

Five steps must be completed to install the NetWare client software. Each is represented on the NetWare Client Install screen.

- Step 1 requires you to provide a path and directory into which the client files will be installed. The C:\NWCLIENT directory is the default. The client installation creates this directory, if it does not already exist. Change the default path if you want the client files installed into a directory other than C:\NWCLIENT.

- Step 2 enables you to choose whether the installation program automatically updates your configuration files as needed. If you answer Yes, the LASTDRIVE=Z statement is added to the client's CONFIG.SYS file, and the CALL STARTNET.BAT statement is added to the client's AUTOEXEC.BAT file.

- Step 3 automatically installs support for Microsoft Windows clients. If your workstation runs Microsoft Windows, type **Yes** at the prompt.

  Step 3 also requires you to provide the path and directory name into which you installed Microsoft Windows. If you installed Microsoft

Figure 3.1

The NetWare Client Install screen.

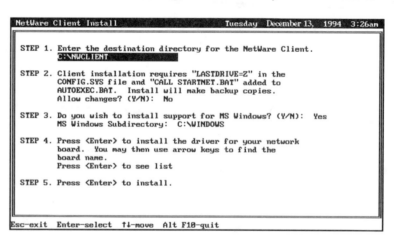

Windows into a directory other than the MS Windows default of C:\WINDOWS, change this field to reflect the actual location of these files.

■ Step 4 requires you to specify your device driver. By highlighting this field and pressing Enter, you are presented with a list of device drivers from which to choose. Your choice depends on the network board installed in your workstation. When possible, the installation software determines which board is installed and fills in the appropriate device driver. You then need to choose the device driver and indicate the settings on your network board.

■ Step 5 starts the installation. Highlight its field and press Enter. The balance of the installation is completed automatically. You only have to make changes to your configuration files if you typed No instead of Yes in step 2. If you typed Yes, your original configuration files are saved in their original location with a BNW extension. You can now reboot your PC, and it will load the appropriate files to boot your workstation as a network client.

Now that you have installed the DOS and Microsoft Windows client software, you can log in to the network. In the event that you cannot access the network, or you have to modify your configuration files at some later date, however, you should know what these files must contain for your workstation to access the network.

CONFIG.SYS provides configuration information for the computer to use when it boots.

The AUTOEXEC.BAT file contains DOS commands to help set up your working environment.

When you install the NetWare client, a command to run the STARTNET.BAT file is added to the AUTOEXEC.BAT file.

The NET.CFG file is not a standard computer configuration file. It is used on NetWare clients to provide commands to help your computer establish and maintain a network connection.

The CONFIG.SYS file must include the LASTDRIVE=Z command, which is added to it by the INSTALL program for the DOS Requester. The NetWare 3.12 client files work with DOS. Unless you include the LASTDRIVE=Z command in the CONFIG.SYS file, DOS assumes that the last available drive is the last drive it can recognize, which is usually represented as drive E. By including this command in the CONFIG.SYS file, you have all other drive letters available for network access.

The AUTOEXEC.BAT file uses a series of commands to load the appropriate network client files. These commands can also be placed in a file called STARTNET.BAT, in which case STARTNET.BAT is called from the AUTOEXEC.BAT file to run the following commands:

```
C:
CD \NWCLIENT
LSL.COM
NE2000 (replace with your LAN driver)
IPXODI
VLM
F:
LOGIN fileserver_name/username
```

These AUTOEXEC.BAT or STARTNET.BAT commands work with the NET.CFG file. The BAT file runs the commands, and the NET.CFG file provides the parameters needed to properly configure the commands when they are run.

The NET.CFG file must include the following lines of information with parameters set to match your LAN board and first network drive.

```
Link Driver NE2000
    INT 5
    PORT 340
    MEM D0000
    FRAME ETHERNET_802.2
NetWare DOS Requester
    FIRST NETWORK DRIVE=F
```

Information needed in the NET.CFG file includes the following:

- **INT number.** The interrupt setting on the network board.

- **PORT number.** The port setting for the network board.

- **MEM address.** The memory address used by the network board.

- **FRAME type.** The frame number used by the network to which you are connecting; NetWare 3.12 uses a default frame type of ETHERNET_802.2.

The NET.CFG file also contains a FIRST NETWORK DRIVE= command. The client installation automatically updates the NET.CFG file with the FIRST NETWORK DRIVE=F line, if you chose Yes in Step 2.

Connecting a Workstation to the Network

Four specific files must be run to access the network. These four files, which must be run in the order listed, include the following:

1. LSL.COM

2. LAN Driver

3. IPXODI.COM

4. VLM.EXE

LSL.COM enables the routing of Network information of different protocols between the LAN driver and the software. LSL.COM is also called the *Link Support Layer.*

Once LSL.COM is run, load the LAN driver for your workstation to your workstation's network board, thus allowing it to establish a connection between the client software and the physical components of the network.

The third file that must be loaded into the workstation's memory is the IPXODI.COM file. When run, this file loads the NetWare IPX protocol, which processes network requests, passing the required information between the NetWare DOS Requester and the Link Support Layer.

Running the VLM.EXE file and its associated files (also referred to as the NetWare DOS Requester) provides a connection point between DOS and applications being run on the client, and the services provided by the network.

Once all these files have been run, your workstation is a network client. You can use it to log in to the network and access available resources.

Accessing the Network File System

Understanding the MAP command is critical to undertanding how to efficently access the NetWare server.

To run the NetWare MAP command, type the following and press Enter:

```
MAP [option] drive_letter:=directory_path
```

With the MAP command, you specify a drive letter (from those specified in the FIRST NETWORK DRIVE and LAST NETWORK DRIVE parameters set in your configuration files), followed by a colon (:), to indicate that it is a drive letter, then you provide the exact path.

Options available with the command include the following:

- **ROOT.** Specifies that the drive is to appear as though it is a root directory, even though the drive can point to a subdirectory several levels deep within the NetWare directory structure.

- **N.** Tells the MAP command to use the next available drive letter instead of waiting for you to specify a letter.

- **DEL.** Lets the MAP command know that you want to remove an existing drive mapping. When you use this option, you must tell the MAP command which drive letter you want it to delete.

You can also use the MAP command without any options, which displays a list of your current drive mappings.

In NetWare, the exact path includes the file server name (if it is not your current default server), followed by a slash, then the volume name, followed by a colon, and finally, the directories and subdirectories that point to the final destination. Each directory and subdirectory is separated by a slash.

To map drive letter P to the PAYROLL directory on the HR volume of the ACCOUNTING file server, for example, type the following line and press Enter:

```
MAP P:=ACCOUNTING/HR:PAYROLL
```

You can map two types of network drives: regular and search. A *search drive* functions like a DOS path drive. NetWare uses mapped search drives to find executable files. Network drives are used to find data files.

To access network applications, you must specify the network drive letter when searching for a data file. When searching for an executable program with a NetWare search drive mapped, however, you can just type the name of the program. NetWare then searches all its mapped search drives until it finds and runs the program.

To map a search drive, you must tell NetWare that you want the mapping to be a search drive. To do so, replace the drive letter in the previous example with **S16**. Using S16 tells NetWare to assign the next available search drive. You can also specify a particular search drive by specifying the numeric order associated with the search pattern.

You can, for example, make the search drive you are mapping the first drive to be used when looking for a program file by replacing the drive letter with **INS S1**. INS indicates that the search drive should be placed in the order indicated, and that existing search drives should be renumbered. The S1 indicates that it is a search drive and that it should be placed in the first position. To map a search drive to the DOS directory so it will search it first whenever it is looking for an executable program, the MAP command would look similar to the following:

```
MAP INS S1:=SYS:PUBLIC/DOS
```

If you fail to include INS, a new directory mapping will be assigned for the specified drive. Omit INS, therefore, when you are reassigning a drive. Include INS when you are adding a new search drive to a particular position in the search drive order.

You can use the MAP command to map to NetWare volumes or to specific directories on NetWare volumes. Once a drive is mapped to at least the volume level on a NetWare file server, you can then use the DOS CD command to move through the NetWare directory structure, if necessary.

After you have mapped search and network drives, you can navigate through the NetWare file server's volume and directory structure to find the network resources you need, using these mappings.

After a drive map has been created, you can access the mapped volume and directories by simply changing your default drive letter to the letter that represents the drive you mapped. You can then access data files stored at that path.

If you mapped search drives to the location of an executable file, you do not have to change first to that search drive to run the program. You can run it from anywhere on the network by typing the program name and letting NetWare's search drive capabilities find and start the program. You should, however, add to your DOS path statement the drive letters that represent your network search drives.

In the following DOS PATH statement of a network client, for example, you can see that two search drives—Z and Y—have been added:

```
PATH C:\;C:\WP51;C:\DOS;C:\
WINDOWS;C:\MOUSE;Z:.;Y:.
```

Because directories are searched for executable files in the same order they're displayed in the DOS path, these two NetWare search drives are the last drives searched when an executable file needs to be found. Keeping your DOS path statement relatively short is an important factor for timely access of files. Include, therefore, only those drive letters that contain executable files and which you use most frequently. Because Z is most often used to represent the search path to the NetWare utilities found in the SYS:PUBLIC directory, you should always include it in the DOS PATH statement.

Viewing and Managing File System Information

Using network and search drives, you can display, modify, and otherwise access available network resources.

NetWare provides several commands and utilities to help you access, view, and manage the NetWare file system. These utilities and commands include the following:

- FILER
- VOLINFO
- CHKVOL
- SLIST

VOLINFO

The VOLINFO utility provides information about each volume on the current NetWare file server, including the volume's name, the amount of storage space available on it, how much of that storage space is still available (unused), the total number of directory entries allowed on this volume, and the number of currently available directory entries (see fig. 3.2).

This screen also shows a menu from which you can choose to view volume information about other file servers.

In addition, the VOLINFO utility enables you to determine how frequently the volume information display is updated (use the Update Interval option from the Available Options menu).

CHKVOL

Use the CHKVOL utility to see information about the current volume. Type **CHKVOL [*path*] [/Continuous]** and press Enter. Replace *path* with the path pointing to the specific volume. Add the /Continuous option to see all the information displayed without stopping.

SLIST

The SLIST utility provides information about NetWare network file servers. To use SLIST, type **SLIST [*Server*] [\Continue]**, and press Enter. Replace *Server* with the file server name, and add \Continue if you want to see a continuous display.

Using SLIST, you can view several items of information, including the following:

- Network file server names
- Network numbers
- Each file server's node address
- The client's current relationship to each server

The network file server name represents the unique name given to that file server when it was installed. No two file servers on the same network can have the same name.

When more than one network exists, the network number identifies one NetWare network from another. It is the number (in hexadecimal format) assigned to the network cable segment for that network.

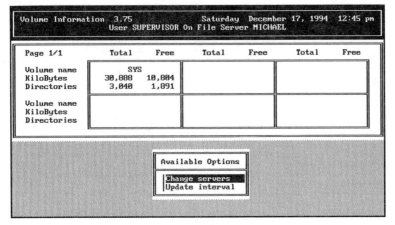

Figure 3.2
The VOLINFO screen.

Each client, file server, directly attached printer or other peripheral device must have something to identify it as unique to the network. This identifier is called the *node address* and is displayed using the SLIST utility.

The status fields show the current relationship of this network client to the listed file server. It does not show the operational status of the file server itself. A status of Default indicates that this is your client's current default directory. The Attached status indicates that this client is currently attached to or logged into this file server. You cannot have any drives mapped to the file server, but if you have a connection, the status is indicated as Attached.

A status of No indicates that you are neither attached nor logged in to this file server.

You can manipulate and otherwise manage directories on NetWare file servers using three basic DOS commands, including the following:

- MD
- RD
- RENDIR

The following two NetWare utilities can be used to obtain information about network directories:

- LISTDIR
- NDIR

LISTDIR

The LISTDIR command enables you to see a listing of network directories.

Type **LISTDIR** *[drive | path]* and press Enter. Replace *drive* with a mapped NetWare drive letter

or replace *path* with a full NetWare directory path, including the name of the file server.

LISTDIR shows all subdirectories found in the specified path, as well as the total number of directories found.

NDIR

The NDIR utility enables you to view information about directories that meet a specific search criteria that you specify.

You can also use NetWare and DOS utilities to manage files on the network. File management includes copying, moving, deleting, salvaging, and purging files.

DOS commands used to copy, move, or delete files include the following:

- **COPY.** Makes a duplicate of a file in another directory
- **REN.** Changes a file name, or moves that file from one directory to another
- **DEL.** Eliminates a file

NetWare utilities used for file management include the following:

- NCOPY
- FILER
- SALVAGE
- PURGE

NCOPY

The NetWare NCOPY command is used to accomplish the same types of tasks that the DOS

COPY or XCOPY commands accomplish. NCOPY, however, is designed to let you manage network files. It can handle extended file information, such as file attributes, which DOS COPY and XCOPY commands cannot.

NCOPY can also verify a successful and accurate copy. The most impressive feature of NCOPY, however, is its capability to use full NetWare paths, including the file server and volume names.

To use NCOPY, type **NCOPY [*path*] [[TO] *path*] option** at the prompt and press Enter. Replace the first *path* with the NetWare path pointing to the file to be copied and the name of the file. Replace the second *path* with the ending location for the copied file. Replace *option* with any of NCOPY's available option parameters.

NCOPY's available option parameters include the following:

- **/S.** Copies all subdirectories

- **/S/E.** Copies all subdirectories, even if they contain no files

- **/F.** Copies sparse files

- **/I.** Informs the user when non-DOS file information will be lost

- **/C.** Copies only DOS information

- **/A.** Copies all files that have the archive bit set

- **/M.** Copies all files that have the archive bit set, then clears that archive bit

- **/V.** Verifies that each write can subsequently be read

- **/H** or **/?.** Views the help screen associated with the NCOPY utility

You can manage directories and files using either DOS or NetWare command-line commands. You can also manage directories and files using three NetWare utilities: FILER, SALVAGE, and PURGE.

FILER

The FILER utility enables you to perform such directory and file management tasks as accessing, viewing, and managing information about network file servers, volumes, directories, and files. From the FILER Available Topics menu you can choose any of the following options:

- **View information about the current directory.** Self explanatory

- **Current Directory Information.** Displays directory information, such as the directory's owner, creation date and time, directory attributes, inherited rights that have been masked out, directory trustees, and your current effective rights in this directory

- **Directory Contents.** Displays a list of all files and subdirectories in the current directory

- **Select Current Directory.** Modifies your current default directory

- **Set Filer Options.** Modifies the defaults used for directory and file information display when using FILER

- **Volume Information.** Displays details about the current volume, including file server and volume names, the disk type and size, and the number of directory entries

If you choose the Current Directory Information option, a screen similar to that shown in figure 3.3 appears.

Figure 3.3

The current Directory Information for SYSTEM screen.

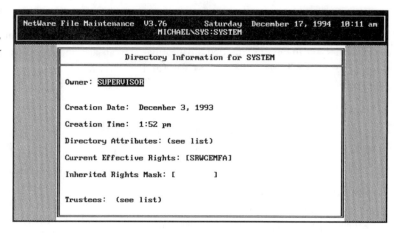

If you choose the Directory Contents option, a screen similar to that shown in figure 3.4 appears.

If you choose the Select Current Directory option, a screen showing the current directory path appears, and you can modify the path if you want.

If you choose Set Filer Options, a screen similar to that shown in figure 3.5 appears.

If you choose Volume Information, a screen similar to that shown in figure 3.6 appears.

SALVAGE

NetWare's SALVAGE utility enables you to retrieve files that were previously deleted. Although the deleted files are no longer included on the list when you issue a directory command, they are still available on the hard disk until purged or written over. Even if you delete the directory in which the file was stored, NetWare saves the directory's deleted files in a directory, DELETED.SAV, found at the root level of the volume containing the deleted files.

To recover deleted files, type **SALVAGE** and press Enter. The main menu for the SALVAGE utility opens, and you can choose from among four available options (see fig. 3.7).

The available four options perform the following:

- **Salvage From Deleted Directories.** Specifies a file pattern to be used by the SALVAGE utility to search for and display deleted directories from which you can choose to recover files

- **Select Current Directory.** Changes from the current directory to another directory, if necessary

- **Set Salvage Options.** Determines sort order when SALVAGE presents the list of deleted files or directories from which you can recover files (see fig. 3.8)

- **View/Recover Deleted Files.** Specifies the Erased File Name Pattern To Match that Salvage is to use when searching for recoverable files and directories

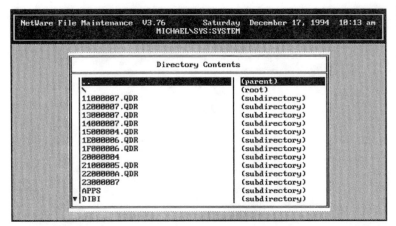

Figure 3.4

The Directory Contents screen.

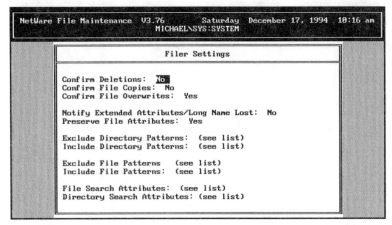

Figure 3.5

The Filer Settings screen.

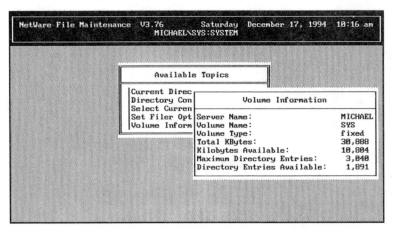

Figure 3.6

The Volume Information screen.

Figure 3.7
The SALVAGE Main Menu Options screen.

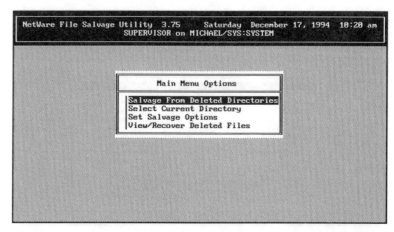

Figure 3.8
The Salvage Options screen.

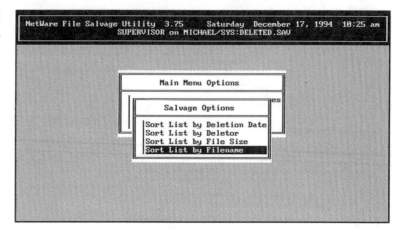

PURGE

Deleted files can be salvaged unless one of two things have happened. At some point, new files overwrite deleted files, starting with the files that have been deleted the longest time. In that case, files remain salvageable for a period of time determined by the free space available on the volume.

It might be desirable to remove files from the volume completely. The process of purging deleted files to make room for new files retards the server. Additionally, you might not want sensitive files to

be salvageable. You remove deleted files using the NetWare PURGE command-line utility. Once purged, files and directories cannot be recovered.

To use the PURGE command, type the following at the system prompt and press Enter:

`PURGE [file_name ¦ wildcard] [/ALL ¦ /A]`

Replace *file_name | wildcard* with either a specific file name or a wild card (that is, ? or *) to request all files with a given filename character(s). You can also use PURGE with the /ALL or the /A option to remove all files from the current directory path.

Questions

1. Of the following, which THREE are steps in the DOS and Microsoft Windows client installation process?

   ☐ A. Install DOS

   ☐ B. Copy files to C:\WINDOWS directory

   ☐ C. Copy client files to the C:\NWCLIENT directory

   ☐ D. Select your network board driver

2. The disk used to install the client is called _____.

   ○ A. INST_1

   ○ B. DOS_INS1

   ○ C. SYSTEM_1

   ○ D. WSDOS_1

3. The directory in which the client files are installed (unless you specify otherwise) is the _____ directory:

   ○ A. C:\WINDOWS

   ○ B. C:\NWCLIENT

   ○ C. C:\WINDOWS\SYSTEM

   ○ D. C:\

4. If you need to recover your modified configuration files after the client installation is complete, you can find them by looking for files with the _____ extension.

   ○ A. BNW

   ○ B. BFR

   ○ C. BKU

   ○ D. OLD

5. Which NetWare client installation step requires that you choose and configure the driver for the network board installed in your computer?

   ○ A. 1

   ○ B. 2

   ○ C. 3

   ○ D. 4

   ○ E. 5

6. Which TWO configuration files do computers generally have before they are set up as network clients?

   ☐ A. CONFIG.SYS

   ☐ B. STARTNET.BAT

   ☐ C. NET.EXE

   ☐ D. AUTOEXEC.BAT

7. Which file contains the NetWare DOS Requester configuration parameters?

   ○ A. CONFIG.SYS

   ○ B. STARTNET.BAT

   ○ C. NET.CFG

   ○ D. AUTOEXEC.BAT

8. Which file contains the LASTDRIVE=Z statement?

   ○ A. CONFIG.SYS

   ○ B. STARTNET.EXE

   ○ C. NET.CFG

   ○ D. AUTOEXEC.BAT

9. The drive letter used most commonly as the drive letter for accessing the LOGIN.EXE file is drive _____.

   ○ A. D

   ○ B. F

   ○ C. G

   ○ D. Z

10. In which order must you load client files to connect to the network?

    ○ A. VLM.EXE, IPXODI.COM, LAN driver, and LSL.COM

    ○ B. LSL.COM, IPXODI.COM, VLM.EXE, and LAN Driver

    ○ C. LSL.COM, LAN driver, IPXODI.COM, and VLM.EXE

    ○ D. IPXODI.COM, LAN driver, LSL.COM, and VLM.EXE

11. Use the _____ utility to see a list of directories in the current path.

    ○ A. RENDIR

    ○ B. MKDIR

    ○ C. NDIR

    ○ D. NEWDIR

12. Use the _____ NetWare command-line utility to make a duplicate of a file with extended file information such as attributes.

    ○ A. NCOPY

    ○ B. COPY

    ○ C. SALVAGE

    ○ D. DUPE

13. You can see the owner of a directory by choosing the _____ option from the FILER Available Options screen.

    ○ A. Current Directory Information

    ○ B. Volume Information

    ○ C. Select Current Directory

    ○ D. Set Filer Options

14. The SALVAGE utility uses the _____ directory to store deleted files when the files' original directory has also been deleted.

    ○ A. DIRECT.DEL

    ○ B. DELETED.SAV

    ○ C. SAVED.FIL

    ○ D. SALVAGE.DIR

15. To permanently remove files that have been deleted, use the _____ utility.

    ○ A. NCOPY

    ○ B. SALVAGE

    ○ C. PURGE

    ○ D. DELETE

Answers

1. B, C, D	9. B
2. D	10. C
3. B	11. C
4. A	12. A
5. D	13. A
6. A, D	14. B
7. C	15. C
8. A	

Managing NetWare Services from the File Server Console

This chapter explains the available NetWare console commands and the steps needed to access the file server console from a workstation. These steps enable you to manage your network file servers from any workstation, rather than having to be in the same physical proximity as the file server console.

The three sections of this chapter address the following:

- Using Console Commands
- Using NetWare Loadable Modules (NLMs)
- Accessing a Server Console From a Workstation

Using Console Commands

NetWare's operating system loads into memory on each file server when you boot that file server. The *core* operating system files provide basic network services, including file storage and retrieval, network security, and routing.

For users to have access to additional network services, such as printing, storage management, and communications, additional server software must be loaded. You provide these additional services by running console utilities, and loading NetWare Loadable Modules (NLMs) on each file server.

When you load the NetWare operating system, you also load software that enables you to manage the network. This software is accessed from the file server console and is therefore referred to as *console commands.*

NetWare provides four types of console commands, which follow:

- Configuration commands
- Installation commands
- Maintenance commands
- Screen display commands

NetWare commands are similar to DOS commands. Just as DOS commands provide DOS operating system access and instructions, NetWare commands provide NetWare operating system access and instructions. DOS commands can be run from any workstation with DOS loaded into its memory. NetWare console commands can be run from any PC with the NetWare operating system loaded into its memory (a NetWare file server).

NetWare console commands—unlike regular NetWare commands, which can be issued from any NetWare client—can only be issued from the NetWare file server console. NetWare console commands can be issued from a NetWare client, however, if they are issued while running a remote session using NetWare's remote console utility, which is discussed later in this chapter.

Understanding the function, purpose, and use of NetWare console commands makes it easier for you to monitor and maintain your network file servers. Each of the four types of NetWare 3.12 console commands are discussed in this chapter.

Configuration Console Commands

Configuration console commands relate to tasks performed to configure various aspects of the NetWare file server. Some of the more important NetWare configuration console commands include the following:

- CONFIG
- NAME
- TIME
- UPS STATUS
- VOLUMES

Installation Console Commands

Installation console commands relate to tasks associated with installing NetWare on the file server. Some of the important NetWare installation console commands include the following.

BIND

Links the local area network (LAN) driver to a communication protocol and to a specific file server LAN board. Type **BIND** *protocol* [**TO**] *LANdriver\boardname* [*driver_parameter*] [*protocol_parameter*] and press Enter. *Protocol* is IP, IPX, and so on. *LANdriver\boardname* is the driver name for the file server's network board. *Driver_parameter* is comprised of the following: DMA number, FRAME name, INT number, MEM number, PORT number, and SLOT number. *Protocol_parameter* is comprised of any parameters unique to the protocol you are binding to the LAN driver.

LOAD

Places an NLM in file server memory. Type **LOAD** [*path*] *NLM_name* [*parameter*] and press Enter. Replace *path* with the full directory path pointing to where the NLMs are stored, if they are not stored in SYS:SYSTEM. Replace *parameter* with any of the valid parameters, as needed. For example, if loading a LAN drive, use the following parameters as needed: DMA number, FRAME name, INT number, MEM number, PORT number, and SLOT number.

MOUNT

Readies a volume for access by NetWare users. Type **MOUNT** *volume_name* and press Enter. Replace *volume_name* with the name of the volume to be mounted or type **ALL** to mount all file server volumes. Mount a CD-ROM disk to use as a read-only volume by typing **CD MOUNT** [*device number*] [*volume_name*] and pressing Enter. Replace *device number* with the CD-ROM device number. Replace *volume_name* with the volume name assigned to the CD-ROM disk.

Maintenance Console Commands

Maintenance console commands relate to tasks associated with maintaining your NetWare file server. Some of the more important NetWare installation console commands include the following.

CLEAR STATION

Disconnects a client from the file server, thus closing any files or tables the client had open. Use this command to clear a client whose workstation has become *hung* (locked up and nonresponsive). Type **CLEAR STATION** *n* (replace *n* with the client's station number) and press Enter.

DISABLE LOGIN

Prevents network users from logging in to the file server. Type **DISABLE LOGIN** and press Enter. Currently logged-in users are not disconnected, but no other users will be able to log in.

DOWN

Closes all open files, writes all dirty cache buffers to disk, and updates the DET and FAT tables before rebooting the file server. Type **DOWN** and press Enter.

ENABLE LOGIN

Enables users to log in to the network if the DISABLE LOGIN command was previously issued. If you downed the file server after using the DISABLE LOGIN command, then rebooted the file server, login is automatically reenabled. Type **ENABLE LOGIN** and press Enter.

REMOVE DOS

Unloads the DOS operating system from the file server's memory. Reboots the server when EXIT is typed after downing the server. Type **REMOVE DOS** and press Enter.

UNBIND

Unlinks a LAN driver from a communication protocol or from the file server's LAN board. Type **UNBIND** *protocol* [**FROM**] *LANdriver* [*driver_parameter*] and press Enter. Replace *protocol* with the communication protocol bound to the LAN driver, and *LANdriver* with the name of the driver previously bound to the LAN board, installed in the file server. *Driver_parameters* may include DMA number, INT number, MEM number, PORT number, or SLOT number.

UNLOAD

Removes NLMs from file server memory. Type **UNLOAD** *loadable_module* and press Enter, replacing *loadable_module* with the name of the NLM to be removed from memory. Use this command to unload LAN drivers, Name Space Modules, Disk drivers, and NLM utilities.

Screen Display Console Commands

Screen display console commands relate to the display of information on the NetWare file server's monitor. The more important NetWare screen display console commands include the following.

BROADCAST

Sends messages to users who are currently logged in or attached to the file server. Type **BROADCAST** "*message*" [**TO**] and press enter, replacing *message* with the 55-character maximum message you want to send.

CLS

Clears the file server's display. Type **CLS** at the console and press Enter. (You can use the OFF command to accomplish the same task.)

EXIT

Restores control of the computer to DOS. Type **EXIT** and press Enter, after first issuing the DOWN command. You can then issue DOS commands at the DOS prompt, update NetWare file server configuration files using DOS commands, or boot the file server.

SEND

Causes a message to be displayed on the client monitors of all users (or specified users) currently logged in or attached to the file server. Type **SEND** "*message*" [**TO**] *username|connection number*] [[**AND,**] *username|connection number*] and press Enter, replacing *message* with the text to be sent, and *username|connection number* with either the name or NetWare file server connection number of the user(s) to receive the message.

Using NetWare Loadable Modules

NetWare Loadable Modules (NLMs) are files loaded into file server memory to provide additional functionality. The NetWare operating system provides basic functionality, such as file management. NLMs provide additional functionality, such as file server monitoring capabilities. NetWare provides a variety of NLMs. Figure 4.1 shows a listing of those NLMs stored in the SYS:SYSTEM directory of a NetWare 3.12 file server.

There are four types of NLMs. The functions they provide are name-space support, disk drivers, NLM utilities, and LAN drivers.

 Note   To help you remember these four types of NLMs, remember that working with NLMs is *Never DUL*.

N = Name space

D = Disk driver

U = Utilities (Management and Enhancement)

L = LAN Drivers

Disk Driver NLMs

Disk driver NLMs are loaded on the file server to enable communication between the NetWare

operating system and the file server's hard disk controller. There are different types of hard disk controllers and, consequently, different types of disk driver NLMs. You need to load the disk driver NLM that is compatible with the disk controller installed in the file server.

To load a disk driver, type **LOAD** ***driver_name parameters*** and press Enter. Replace *driver_name* with the disk driver to be loaded and *parameters* with any parameters that you need and that relate to this disk driver.

You can load the disk driver from the file server console and must do so when you first install NetWare 3.12. If, however, in the process of installing 3.12 and creating the file server configuration files (AUTOEXEC.NCF and STARTUP.NCF), you load the disk driver before creating the configuration files, the command to load the disk driver is included in the configuration file. Then, each time you boot the file server, the disk driver NLM is run and automatically loaded into file server memory.

```
F:\SYSTEM>dir *.nlm /w

 Volume in drive F is SYS
 Directory of  F:\SYSTEM

F: CDROM    NLM : INSTALL  NLM : KEYB     NLM : NUT      NLM : RS232    NLM
F: UREPAIR  NLM : V_MAC    NLM : V_OS2    NLM : 3CBOOT   NLM : ADAPTEC  NLM
F: AFTER311 NLM : AIO      NLM : AIOACI   NLM : AIOCOMX  NLM : AIOCXCFG NLM
F: AIODGCX  NLM : AIODGMEM NLM : AIODGXI  NLM : AIOESP   NLM : AIOWNIM  NLM
F: BREBUILD NLM : BROUTER  NLM : BSETUP   NLM : BSPXCOM  NLM : BSPXSTUB NLM
F: BTRIEVE  NLM : BTRMON   NLM : BUTIL    NLM : CONLOG   NLM : DIBIDAI  NLM
F: DIRECTFS NLM : DPTSIM   NLM : EDIT     NLM : ETHERTSM NLM : FDDITSM  NLM
F: IPCONFIG NLM : IPXS     NLM : LLC8022  NLM : MATHLIB  NLM : MATHLIBC NLM
F: MONITOR  NLM : MSM31X   NLM : NFSFIX   NLM : NFSSHIM  NLM : NLICLEAR NLM
F: NMAGENT  NLM : NOVADIBI NLM : NWSNUT   NLM : PCN2LTSM NLM : PFIXUP   NLM
F: PING     NLM : PROTO    NLM : PSERVER  NLM : REMFILFX NLM : ROUTE    NLM
F: RPL      NLM : RXNETTSM NLM : SBACKUP  NLM : SMDR31X  NLM : SNMP     NLM
F: SNMPLOG  NLM : SPXCONFG NLM : SPXS     NLM : STREAMS  NLM : TAPEDC00 NLM
F: TCPCON   NLM : TCPIP    NLM : TLI      NLM : TOKENTSM NLM : TPING    NLM
F: TSA311   NLM : TSA312   NLM : TSA_DOS  NLM : UINSTALL NLM : UPS      NLM
F: WANGTEK  NLM : WS_MAN   NLM : RSPXSTUB NLM : RSPX     NLM : CLIB     NLM
F: REMOTE   NLM
        81 File(s)  11059200 bytes free

F:\SYSTEM>
```

Figure 4.1
Directory Listing of NetWare 3.12 NLMs.

Management and Enhancement Utility NLMs

Various utility NLMs are used to provide network management and operating system enhancement capabilities. The three major management and enhancement utility NLMs include the following:

- INSTALL
- MONITOR
- UPS

The purpose of the *INSTALL* NLM is to enable you to install and then maintain your NetWare 3.12 file server. The purpose of the *MONITOR* NLM is to provide you with a way to monitor your file server's efficiency and to provide file server console security using the Lock File Server Console option. The purpose of the *UPS* NLM is to provide a software connection between the *Uninterruptible Power Supply* (UPS) and the UPS NLM.

To load any of these three NLMs, **LOAD** *NLM_name parameter* at the file server prompt and press Enter. You can also load these NLMs

from the file server's configuration file. If the NLM you want to load is not stored in the SYS:SYSTEM directory, include the path to the directory containing the NLM before you type the name of the NLM.

When you load a 3.12 NLM, replace *NLM_name* with the actual name of the NLM, such as MONITOR. If the NLM you are loading requires any specific parameters—such as NS used with MONITOR to turn off the "Snake" screen saver, or -P to display the MONITOR main menu with the Processor Utilization option included (see fig. 4.2)—then replace *parameter* with any needed parameters.

INSTALL.NLM

NetWare 3.12 provides the INSTALL NLM so you can install and maintain your 3.12 file server. From the Installation Options menu, you can perform tasks related to the hard disk installed in the file server, volumes on the file server, configuration files, files in the SYSTEM and PUBLIC directories, or additional Novell products.

Figure 4.2
The MONITOR NLM screen.

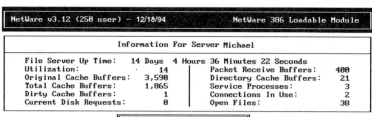

Figure 4.3 shows the Available Disk Options menu that opens when you choose Disk Options from the Installation Options menu. From the Available Disk Options menu, you can perform tasks such as formatting the hard disk, viewing and managing partitions, mirroring the file server's hard disks, or performing a surface test on the hard disks.

MONITOR.NLM

The MONITOR NLM provides a variety of information related to the status and configuration of your NetWare file server. It provides the following information:

- **Connection Information.** Users currently connected to the file server

- **Disk Information.** Number and type of disk drives

- **LAN Information.** LAN drivers installed and related configuration information

- **System Module Information.** List of modules currently loaded on the file server

- **Lock File Server Console.** Capability to provide a password for the console to prevent unauthorized access

- **File Open / Lock Activity.** Option to see which files have been locked

- **Resource Utilization.** Information about file server memory, including statistics such as the current size of each memory pool

- **Processor Utilization.** Option to see active processes from which you can choose to view related statistics

Figure 4.4 shows the information screen for the AES No Sleep Process. This screen opens when you choose AES No Sleep Process from the Available Processes & Interrupts menu. (The Available Processes & Interrupts menu opens when you choose Processor Utilization from the Available Options menu.)

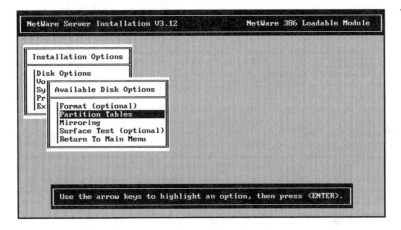

Figure 4.3

The NetWare Server Installation screen.

UPS.NLM

The UPS NLM is not a menu-based NLM. Loading it activates UPS monitoring (once you have connected the UPS hardware to the file server on which you are loading the UPS NLM). After the UPS is attached and you have loaded the UPS NLM, you can verify the current status of UPS by typing **UPS Status** and pressing Enter.

You can also use the UPS NLM to customize the UPS software to fulfill your network's UPS-related needs. When you load UPS, supply the NLM with information about UPS configuration. You can accept the default configuration information supplied by the NLM (see fig. 4.5), but you must use the UPS type and port value specific to the UPS you have attached to the file server.

If your UPS is not correctly configured, is powered off, or is not connected to the file server, a message similar to the one shown in figure 4.6 appears.

Figure 4.4

The AES No Sleep Process screen.

Name	Time	Count	Load
AES No Sleep Process	3,277	18	0.28%
Total Sample Time:	1,179,557		
Histogram Overhead Time:	14,601	(1.23 %)	
Adjusted Sample Time:	1,165,100		

Figure 4.5

UPS NLM configuration defaults.

```
MICHAEL:load ups
Loading module UPS.NLM
   NetWare 386 UPS Monitor
   Version 1.11     December 18, 1990
Available UPS Types: 1-DCB 2-EDCB 3-STANDALONE 4-KEYCARD 5-MOUSE 6-OTHER
UPS TYPE: 1
Support I/O port values are 346, 34E, 326, 32E, 386, 38E
I/O port: 346
Discharge time range:   1 - 3976821 minutes
Discharge time: 20
Recharge time range:   1 - 3976821 minutes
Recharge time: 60
```

Figure 4.6

UPS NLM warning message.

```
WARNING:   Commercial power detected off during UPS installation.
           Check commercial power lines or the UPS.
WARNING:   UPS battery is low.  Repair or replace battery.
WARNING:   UPS hardware configuration error was detected.
           Check for errors in your UPS hardware configuration settings.
   Module initialization failed.
   Module UPS.NLM NOT loaded
```

LAN Driver NLM

LAN driver NLMs establish a communication link between the network board and the driver. Once installed into file server memory, the LAN driver NLM facilitates communication between the file server and the network. To load, type **LOAD** [*path*] *driver* [*parameters*] and press Enter.

Replace *path* with the full path to the directory containing the LAN driver NLM, if it is other than SYS:SYSTEM. Otherwise, the path entry is optional. Replace *driver* with the name of the driver NLM for the file server's network board. Replace *parameters* with any of the appropriate LAN driver parameters and place them inside a pair of square brackets. Parameters that might be needed include: DMA number, FRAME name, INT number, MEM number, NAME board name (if assigned during installation), NODE number, PORT number, and SLOT number.

Accessing a Server Console from a Workstation

You can access the file server's console from the actual file server, or remotely from a workstation (called an *SPX connection* or a *snychronous connection*), using a utility called RCONSOLE, which enables you to emulate the file server's console on the monitor of a workstation connected to the file server. You can also use a utility called ACONSOLE to emulate the file server's console, if you access it from an asynchronous device such as a modem rather than from a workstation connected to the network.

To access a NetWare file server using either a synchronous or an asynchronous connection, you must run the appropriate files at both the file server and the client.

Two NLMs must be loaded at the file server, regardless of whether you are going to access it through an SPX or asynchronous connection. The two NLMs are as follows:

- REMOTE.NLM
- RSPX.NLM

 Note   For an asynchronous connection to this file server, the RS232 NLM must be loaded as well.

REMOTE.NLM

The REMOTE NLM is responsible for the exchange of information between the file server and the client. To load the REMOTE NLM, include the LOAD REMOTE command in the file server's AUTOEXEC.NCF configuration file or type it at the file server console. The correct format for using the REMOTE NLM is as follows:

```
LOAD [path]REMOTE [password]
```

When loading the REMOTE NLM, replace *path* with the drive letter mapped to the directory containing the REMOTE NLM, if it is not stored in the SYS:SYSTEM directory.

Replace *password* with a password you assign to the REMOTE NLM. This password, or the Supervisor's password, can then be used when you later run the RCONSOLE or ACONSOLE utility.

RSPX.NLM

The RSPX NLM loads the SPX driver used by the REMOTE NLM. In addition, it tells the active network clients that it is available. The RSPX NLM *advertises* its presence by sending a specific packet across the network, telling network clients and file servers that it is available for remote access.

Load the RSPX NLM after loading the REMOTE NLM. It, too, can be loaded using the file server's AUTOEXEC.NCF configuration file, or by typing it directly at the console.

To load the RSPX NLM, use the following format, replacing *path* with the drive letter mapped to the directory containing the RSPX NLM, if it is not located in the SYS:SYSTEM directory:

```
LOAD [path]RSPX
```

 Because NetWare requires you to load REMOTE.NLM before loading RSPX.NLM, NetWare will autoload the REMOTE NLM if you issue the LOAD RSPX command before issuing the LOAD REMOTE command.

RS232.NLM

The RS232 NLM is loaded on the file server when the connection to that server is going to be asynchronous. One of the main functions of this NLM is to initialize the modem software. Load the RS232 NLM after loading REMOTE.NLM. To load this NLM, type the following line or place this command into the file server's AUTOEXEC.NCF configuration file:

```
LOAD [path]RS232
```

As with the other NLMs, replace *path* with the path pointing to the location of the RS232 NLM, if it is not stored in the SYS:SYSTEM directory.

After you have loaded the REMOTE NLM and RSPX NLM at a file server (as well as the RS232 NLM if making an asynchronous connection), you can access that server using either the RCONSOLE or ACONSOLE utility. Use the RCONSOLE utility for SPX network connections (through a workstation cabled to the network). Use the ACONSOLE utility for asynchronous network connections (through a modem).

To use RCONSOLE, log in to the network, type **RCONSOLE** at a network client, and press Enter. The Connection Type menu opens. Choose the SPX option and choose the file server to which you want to establish a SPX remote connection. If prompted, provide the password.

After you have connected to the file server, the RCONSOLE utility opens an Available Options menu. Depending on the option you choose, you can perform a variety of tasks. The options available are as follows:

- Select a Screen to View
- Directory Scan
- Transfer Files to Server
- Copy System and Public Files
- End Remote Session with Server (Shift+Esc)
- Resume Remote Session with Server (Esc)

In addition to choosing from the Available Options menu, you can use different keys and key combinations to perform various tasks. Those keys include the following:

*	Displays the RCONSOLE menu
+	Moves forward through server console screens
-	Moves backward through server console screens
Shift+Esc	Exits the RCONSOLE utility
Esc	Resumes your remote console session

 For the first three keys, you must use the numeric keypad. The number and special character keys on the regular keypad will not function.

For all asynchronous connections to a network file server, use the ACONSOLE utility rather than the RCONSOLE utility.

To use the ACONSOLE utility, type **ACONSOLE** at a network client and press Enter. Then choose the Connect to Remote Location option from the ACONSOLE main menu. Provide the phone number to be dialed to access the modem connected to the file server. After the phone connection is made and the Available Servers list opens, choose the file server you want. If prompted, provide the remote console password. From the file server console screen, you can now perform a variety of management tasks. You can perform the same tasks using the ACONSOLE utility as you can using the RCONSOLE utility.

)

Questions

1. Of the following, which THREE are NetWare console command types?

   ☐ A. Screen

   ☐ B. Setup

   ☐ C. Installation

   ☐ D. Maintenance

2. Which TWO console commands CANNOT be used to send messages?

   ☐ A. SEND

   ☐ B. BROADCAST

   ☐ C. RCONSOLE

   ☐ D. ACONSOLE

3. You can use the CLS command at workstations and file server consoles. Which other command can you use at the file server console to accomplish the same task as using CLS?

   ○ A. BROADCAST

   ○ B. EXIT

   ○ C. CLEAR

   ○ D. OFF

4. Which TWO of the following are installation console commands?

   ☐ A. BIND

   ☐ B. EXIT

   ☐ C. MOUNT

   ☐ D. REMOVE DOS

5. You know you are looking at a console command if the file has any one of the following THREE extensions:

   ☐ A. NLM

   ☐ B. DRV

   ☐ C. NAM

   ☐ D. NDS

6. Which of the following console commands is used to link the LAN driver to a communication protocol?

   ○ A. MOUNT

   ○ B. BIND

   ○ C. LINK

   ○ D. EXIT

7. To access a NetWare volume, you must first _____ the volume.

   ○ A. bind

   ○ B. load

   ○ C. mount

   ○ D. format

8. Type _____ to mount a read-only CD-ROM device as a volume.

   ○ A. CD MOUNT 1

   ○ B. MOUNT READONLY CD

   ○ C. CD MOUNT ALL

   ○ D. MOUNT ALL/CD

9. If a user's workstation has hung, use the _____ maintenance console command to remove the connection.

    ○ A. CLEAR ALL

    ○ B. DISABLE LOGIN

    ○ C. EXIT

    ○ D. CLEAR CONNECTION

10. Which THREE commands are configuration commands?

    ☐ A. NAME

    ☐ B. VOLUMES

    ☐ C. MODULES

    ☐ D. CONFIG

11. The THREE most common NetWare NLMs used by a network administrator include _____, _____, and _____.

    ☐ A. MONITOR

    ☐ B. UPS

    ☐ C. RCONSOLE

    ☐ D. INSTALL

12. To see drive status information for one of the file server's hard disks, use the _____ NLM.

    ○ A. MONITOR

    ○ B. CONSOLE

    ○ C. CONFIG

    ○ D. INSTALLATION

13. You cannot choose the _____ option from MONITOR's Available Options menu.

    ○ A. LAN Information

    ○ B. Lock File Server Console

    ○ C. Disk Options

    ○ D. Resource Utilization

14. Which NLM is NOT used for remote console access?

    ○ A. RSPX.NLM

    ○ B. REMOTE.NLM

    ○ C. ASYNC.NLM

    ○ D. RS232.NLM

15. The remote network connection made through a modem is referred to as a/an _____ connection.

    ○ A. REMOTE

    ○ B. INDIRECT

    ○ C. ASYNCHRONOUS

    ○ D. SPX

Answers

1. A, C, D	9. D
2. C, D	10. A, B, D
3. D	11. A, B, D
4. A, C	12. A
5. A, B, C	13. C
6. B	14. C
7. C	15. C
8. A	

Preparing NetWare 3.1x Printing Services for Users

This chapter discusses how NetWare provides shared printing services and how to set up the network so users can access those services. It shows how to redirect print jobs to network printers and how to manage those print jobs after they have been sent to NetWare's printing system. The topics are broken as following:

- *Understanding network printing services*

- *Setting up network printing services*

- *Redirecting print jobs to network printers*

- *Managing network print jobs*

Network Printing Services

The five basic components associated with network printing are as follows:

- Clients
- Printers
- Print queues
- Print servers
- File servers

The four basic steps required to set up network printing include the following:

- Configuring network printing
- Initializing network print servers
- Connecting printers to the network
- Customizing printing services

Basic Network Printing Components

Of the five network printing components, three—printers, file servers, and clients—are very common and should, therefore, be easy to remember. The other two are print queues and print servers.

By now, you should know what file servers and clients are and how they fit into the overall network design. You no doubt know what a printer is, but you need to familiarize yourself with some aspects of using printers on a NetWare network. Consider the following information concerning network printers:

- Printers can be connected to the network in any of three ways. They can be connected to a print server, a workstation, or directly to the network cabling system.

- A printer that is connected to a print server is called a *local* printer, and one connected to a workstation or to the network cable is called a *remote* printer.

- A maximum of 16 printers can be connected to one print server. Because *print servers* (computers running the related print server software) do not have 16 physical ports available—they have only five—printers can be either physically attached to the print server, or logically attached to it. A *physical* connection means the printer is attached by cable to a printer port on the computer. A *logical* connection means the printer is physically attached to either a network work-station or the network cabling and makes a software connection to the print server using the related NetWare printing software. You can physically connect a maximum of five of the 16 printers to ports on the print server.

As just noted, a print server is a computer running special NetWare software. Print servers control network printers. They are responsible for taking print jobs stored in print queues and sending them to the appropriate network printer (see fig. 5.1).

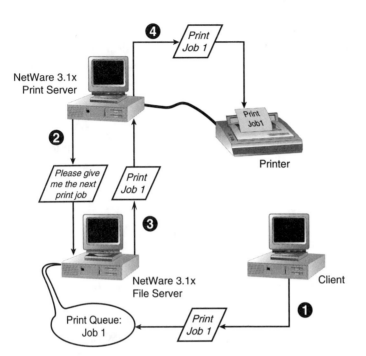

Figure 5.1
*The function of a
print server.*

A *print queue* is simply a directory on a NetWare 3.12 file server that temporarily holds *print jobs* (files waiting to be printed) until the assigned print server can collect the job and send it to a printer.

Network Print Services Setup

To set up network print services, you must complete the following four basic processes:

1. Configure network printing

2. Initialize network print servers

3. Connect printers to the network

4. Customize printing as needed

You configure network printing by defining each network print server, print queue, and printer used on the network. You define these network printing components using the PCONSOLE utility.

Note This installation step easily qualifies as the most tedious of all installation steps. It involves several tasks that must be performed once the PCONSOLE utility is issued. These steps include the following:

■ Creating and configuring print servers

■ Defining the types of printers being used on your network

■ Establishing a logical connection between these different components

The following section discusses the last step in detail.

After defining each print server, print queue, and printer used on the network, you then initialize each of your network print servers.

To initialize a network print server, you load the print server software. Because print servers can be attached to either a NetWare server or to a *dedicated workstation* (one being used for a single function, such as providing access to a network printer), you type **LOAD PSERVER** *print_server_name* at the NetWare server console or **PSERVER** *print_server_name* at the workstation and press Enter. Replace *print_server_name* with the name you assigned to the print server when you first created it.

After the network print servers have been initialized, you must make certain that all network printers are correctly connected to the network. If you intended for printers to be connected directly to the network cable, then connect those printers to the cable. If you intended for some of the printers to be connected to various NetWare file servers or workstations, connect those printers to the appropriate file servers and workstations.

 When you define print servers using the PCONSOLE utility, you specify the type of print server you are defining (local or remote). When you make the physical connection, therefore, be sure to connect them in the same way they were defined.

After you have connected the printer to the network, you can make any modifications needed to customize printing services.

You can, for example, establish default print job configurations for users or define printer forms to be used if not all of your network printing will be done on standard letter-size plain bond paper.

 The last section of this chapter explains how to use the PRINTDEF and PRINTCON utilities to customize network print jobs.

Setting Up Network Printing Services

Network printing is configured by defining each network print server, print queue, and printer used on the network. The PCONSOLE utility is used for this task. You run PCONSOLE from a workstation attached to the network. Log in to the network as a user with Supervisor or equivalent rights, then start the PCONSOLE utility.

Creating a Print Queue

To create a print queue, choose Print Queue Information from the PCONSOLE Available Options menu. The Print Queues screen opens. Press Insert to open the New Print Queue Name box. Type the name of the print queue you want to create and press Enter. The print queue is created, and its name is added to the Print Queues list.

Figure 5.2 shows the Print Queues screen. In this figure, the print queue called PANASONIC_Q is being created. A print queue called LASER_Q already exists.

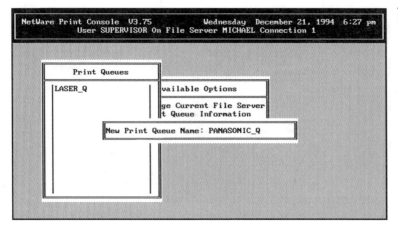

Figure 5.2
Screen associated with creating a print queue.

Creating a Print Server

To create a print server, choose Print Server Information from the PCONSOLE Available Options menu. The Print Server screen opens. If you have not previously created any print servers, it will be empty. Press Insert to open the New Print Server Name box. Type the name of the print server you want to create and press Enter. The print server is created, and its name is added to the list of Print Servers.

Figure 5.3 shows the Print Server screen. In this figure, the print server called LEE_PS is being created. A print server called MICHAEL_PS already exists.

Configuring a Print Server

After creating your print servers, you need to configure each one. To configure a print server, choose it from the Print Servers list. Choose Print Server Configuration from the Print Server Information screen, then choose Printer Configuration to open the Configured Printers list (see fig. 5.4).

If you have not yet configured any printers, the list displays every printer number as Not Installed. Choose a printer number, fill out the form that opens, press Esc, and answer Yes when prompted to save the changes.

The Printer Configuration form requires information about the printer, such as its name, type, and the interrupts and IRQ it uses.

With the printer configured, choose Queues Serviced by Printer from the Print Server Configuration Menu, then choose the printer you defined. When the screen opens displaying the File Server, Queue, and Priority for this print server (blank if no print queues have been added yet), press Insert to display a list of print queues from which to choose (see fig. 5.5). Choose a print queue by highlighting it and pressing Enter. Assign a priority to this print queue (priority 1 has the highest priority). It is now added to the list of print queues to be serviced by this printer.

Figure 5.3

Screen associated with creating a print server.

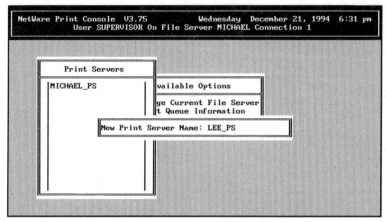

Figure 5.4

The Configured Printers screen.

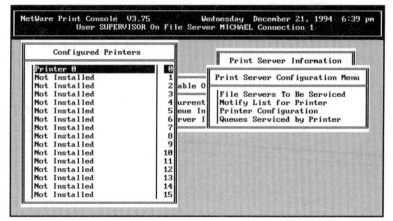

Bringing Up a Print Server

After completing these basic tasks, you must bring up the print server by loading the PSERVER software. Choose Print Queue Information from the PCONSOLE Available Options menu. Then choose the print queue from the Print Queues list. Finally, choose Currently Attached Servers from the Print Queue Information menu and view the name of the print server displayed in the Currently Attached Servers window, as shown in figure 5.6.

To see the name of the print server displayed in the Currently Attached Servers window, you must connect the printer to the file server, workstation, or cable and provide configuration information.

The steps in the previous section explained how to set up the printing-related configuration (print servers, print queues, and printers) using PCONSOLE. The most common mistake people make when setting up printing services is choosing the wrong printer type when filling in the Printer Configuration information (see fig. 5.7).

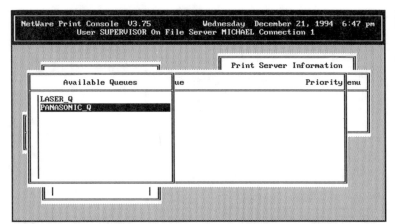

Figure 5.5

Choosing print queues to be serviced by a printer.

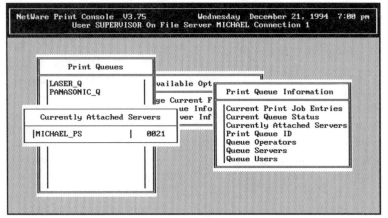

Figure 5.6

The Currently Attached Servers window confirms successful printing installation and configuration.

Local printers are printers that are directly attached to the print server, which may be running as an NLM on a file server or as an EXE on a dedicated print server. For local printers choose either Parallel, LPT1 (or LPT2 or LPT3), or Serial, COM1 (or COM2, COM3, or COM4).

If you did not attach the printer to either a file server with PSERVER.NLM loaded on it or to a PC with PSERVER.EXE running, then choose one of the Remote Parallel, Remote Serial, or Remote Other/Unknown printer types.

Using printers attached to workstations can pose a problem. If the workstation to which the printer is attached is not being used as a dedicated print server, but is being used as a regular workstation with a printer attached, you must run the RPRINTER.EXE utility on the workstation. That way, network users can access the printer attached to a non-dedicated workstation.

Figure 5.7

The Printer Types list.

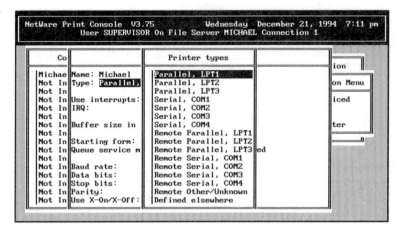

```
NetWare Print Console  V3.75              Wednesday December 21, 1994  7:11 pm
                      User SUPERVISOR On File Server MICHAEL Connection 1

      Co │                  │        Printer types         │              │
         │                  │                              │              │ ion
  Michae │Name: Michael     │ Parallel, LPT1               │              │
  Not In │Type: Parallel,   │ Parallel, LPT2               │              │ on Menu
  Not In │                  │ Parallel, LPT3               │              │
  Not In │Use interrupts:   │ Serial, COM1                 │              │ iced
  Not In │IRQ:              │ Serial, COM2                 │              │
  Not In │                  │ Serial, COM3                 │              │
  Not In │Buffer size in    │ Serial, COM4                 │              │ ter
  Not In │                  │ Remote Parallel, LPT1        │              │
  Not In │Starting form:    │ Remote Parallel, LPT2        │              │
  Not In │Queue service m   │ Remote Parallel, LPT3 ed     │              │
  Not In │                  │ Remote Serial, COM1          │              │
  Not In │Baud rate:        │ Remote Serial, COM2          │              │
  Not In │Data bits:        │ Remote Serial, COM3          │              │
  Not In │Stop bits:        │ Remote Serial, COM4          │              │
  Not In │Parity:           │ Remote Other/Unknown         │              │
  Not In │Use X-On/X-Off:   │ Defined elsewhere            │              │
```

Redirecting Print Jobs to Network Printers

After the printing environment is properly set up, users can send print jobs to network printers. Users can send print jobs from inside application programs, or from the DOS prompt. If the application program understands and uses network printing (if it is *network-aware*), and if the application's print services have been set up to redirect print jobs away from the computer's LPT1 or serial port and toward a network printer, send print jobs using the application directly. There is no need for NetWare's CAPTURE or NPRINT utilities.

If you print directly from applications which are *not* network-aware, or you want to print jobs from a DOS prompt (such as capturing the contents of your monitor's screen to a printer), then NetWare provides two utilities you can use, CAPTURE and NPRINT.

Use the CAPTURE utility (at the DOS prompt) to redirect print jobs from your workstation's LPT or serial ports to network printers. Type **CAPTURE /[*option*]** and press Enter. In place of *option*, you can use any of the available CAPTURE command options.

You can, for example, use /SH to display the current status of the CAPTURE command. Use /Server=*servername* to specify which file server to use. Use /Queue=*queuename* to specify which print queue to use. Figure 5.8 shows the help screen for the CAPTURE command. It displays all the available CAPTURE options.

 Note NetWare also provides a graphical approach to using the CAPTURE command. You can set CAPTURE options using the User Tools for Windows application.

Use the NPRINT utility (also used from the DOS prompt) to print files outside an application. NPRINT uses most of the same options that CAPTURE uses. You can also use PRINTCON to set NPRINT options.

```
F:\SYSTEM>capture /?
USAGE: CAPTURE /SHow /Job=jobname /Server=fileserver /Queue=queuename /Local=n
/Form=form or n /CReate=path /Copies=n (1-255) /TImeout=n /Keep /Tabs=n (1-18)
/No Tabs /Banner=bannername /NAMe=name /No Banner /FormFeed /No FormFeed
/AUtoendcap /No Autoend /NOTIfy /No NOTIfy /DOmain=domain
 /EndCapture /CAncel /ALL

F:\SYSTEM>
```

Figure 5.8

The CAPTURE command help screen displaying available options.

Managing Network Print Jobs

Once you send print jobs to a network print queue, occasions arise when you need to make modifications to, or otherwise manage, those print jobs.

Using the PCONSOLE utility, you can choose Current Print Job Entries from the Print Queue Information menu to then choose a print job to manage.

The Print Queue Entry Information screen opens (see fig. 5.9).

It displays information about the current print job. From this screen, you can choose any of the options shown in table 5.1 and perform the associated actions.

If you submitted the print job, you can modify most of these fields. Some of these fields can only be modified by a user with Supervisor rights or who has been assigned as a print queue operator.

When you submit a print job, many of the fields displayed on the Print Queue Entry Information screen for this job are already filled because they have default entries. You can set some of these defaults by customizing your print job defaults using the PRINTDEF and PRINTCON utilities.

The PRINTCON utility lets you customize print job configurations. Using PRINTCON, you can create special printer setup configurations, edit existing print job configurations, or copy print job configurations from one network user to another.

 Users can have their own print job configurations. To make a copy of one user's print job configuration so it can be used by another user, choose the Copy Print Job Configurations option from the Configure Print Jobs Available Options menu. You are prompted for the *Source* User (whose print job configuration file you want to make a copy of), as well as the *Target* user (the user to whom you want to give the copy of the print job configuration file).

To create a print job configuration, use the Edit Print Job configurations option in the Configure Print Jobs Available Options menu. A list of available print jobs is displayed. To create a print job, press Insert, provide a name for the print job, and set configuration information in the Edit Print Job Configuration screen. As figure 5.10 shows, many of the same fields that are included in the Print Queue Entry Information screen are included in the Edit Print Job Configuration screen (refer to fig. 5.9).

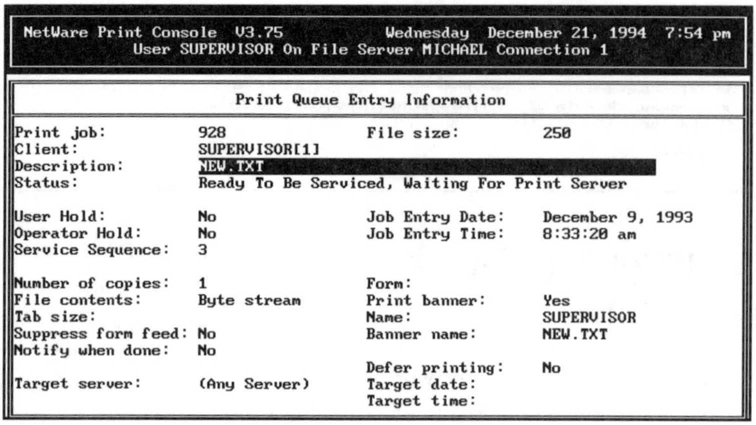

Figure 5.9

The Print Queue Entry
Information screen.

```
┌─────────────────────────────────────────────────────────────────────┐
│ NetWare Print Console  V3.75          Wednesday  December 21, 1994  7:54 pm │
│           User SUPERVISOR On File Server MICHAEL Connection 1        │
├─────────────────────────────────────────────────────────────────────┤
│                    Print Queue Entry Information                    │
│  Print job:        928            File size:       250             │
│  Client:           SUPERVISOR[1]                                   │
│  Description:      NEW.TXT                                         │
│  Status:           Ready To Be Serviced, Waiting For Print Server  │
│                                                                     │
│  User Hold:        No             Job Entry Date:  December 9, 1993 │
│  Operator Hold:    No             Job Entry Time:  8:33:20 am      │
│  Service Sequence: 3                                               │
│                                                                     │
│  Number of copies: 1              Form:                            │
│  File contents:    Byte stream    Print banner:    Yes            │
│  Tab size:                        Name:            SUPERVISOR     │
│  Suppress form feed: No           Banner name:     NEW.TXT        │
│  Notify when done:  No                                            │
│                                   Defer printing:  No            │
│  Target server:    (Any Server)   Target date:                   │
│                                   Target time:                   │
└─────────────────────────────────────────────────────────────────────┘
```

Table 5.1
Print Queue Entry Information Options

Option	Action
Description	Delete or modify the contents to describe this file more accurately.
User Hold	Prevent this file from printing now by placing a user hold. You can later use this field to remove the hold.
Operator Hold	Prevent another user's file from printing immediately— if you have the rights (must be Supervisor or Print Queue Operator)—or remove the hold.
Service Sequence	Change the position of the job in the queue, if you are the Print Queue Operator.
Number of Copies	Specify how many copies will be printed.
File Contents	Specify whether the formatting of this file is to be designated by the application that submitted it (Byte stream), or by the printer (Text), which converts tabs in the document into spaces.
Suppress Form Feed	Advance the printer's paper to the top of the next page after your job is printed (No), or do not advance it (Yes).
Notify When Done	Specify that you want a broadcast message to tell you when your print job is printed (Yes), or not (No).

Option	Action
Target Server	Choose the file server you want to have service your print job if you want to indicate a specific server or let any server take care of it for you (Any Server).
Form	Choose a predefined form from the list of defined forms.
Banner	To identify print jobs being submitted by other users, choose Yes if you want a header page to print before your print job.
Name	If you chose Yes to Banner, enter the text you want to have displayed on the banner. The default is your network UserID, but you can type something else if you want.
Banner Name	Type in the file name being printed—or any other information you want printed on another area of the banner page.
Defer Printing	Choose Yes to print it at a specified date and time, then fill the Target date and Target time fields. Choose No and the print job will print as soon as it becomes priority one at the print queue.
Target Date	Insert the date you want the print job to be printed if you chose to defer the print job.
Target Time	Insert the time of the day you want the job to be printed if you chose to defer its printing to a later time.

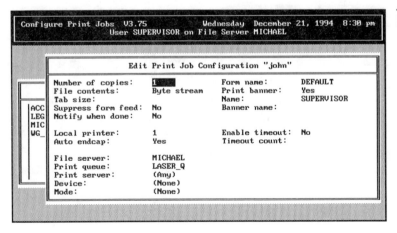

Figure 5.10

The Edit Print Job Configuration screen.

Use the PRINTDEF utility to add printer defini-
tions and names, or form definitions for printing.
To start this utility, type **PRINTDEF** and press
Enter.

From the Printer Definition Utility PrintDef Options menu, you can choose either Printer Devices
or Forms. If you choose Printer Devices, you can do
the following:

- Create printer names and definitions
- Edit printer names and definitions
- Delete printer names and definitions
- Import a printer name and definition
- Export a printer name and definition

You can customize how your printer prints. For
example, if you want your printer to condense the
type when it prints a specific document, you can set
up a series of printer escape sequences (series of
ASCII codes) that tells the printer precisely how
to print in condensed mode. You then save these

escape sequences as a function. To each function,
you assign a function name, so you can use the
function whenever you want to print a file using the
printer sequences defined by it.

You can also use the Printer Definition utility to
define forms to be used on your network printers.
If, for example, you want to print on paper that is
5×7 inches instead of 8 1/2×11, you can define
such a form using this utility.

To create a form, choose Forms from the Printer
Definition Utility PrintDef Options menu. When
the Forms screen opens, press Insert to open the
Form Definition screen (see fig. 5.11). Name the
form, assign a form number, and provide the length
(number of lines on the form) and width (number
of characters per line) of the form.

In the preceding example of a 5×7-inch form, and
if your printer prints 6 lines per inch of length and
10 characters per inch of width, you would type **42**
(seven times six) in the Length field and **50** (five
times ten) in the Width field.

Figure 5.11

*The Form Definition
screen.*

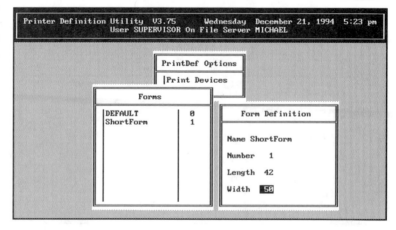

Questions

1. The network printing component to which you can logically connect a printer is the _____.

   ○ A. file server

   ○ B. client

   ○ C. print queue

   ○ D. print server

2. When you send a job to be printed, it goes first to the _____.

   ○ A. file server

   ○ B. client

   ○ C. print queue

   ○ D. print server

3. The second step in the basic printing setup is to _____.

   ○ A. configure network printing

   ○ B. connect the printers to the network

   ○ C. initialize network print servers

   ○ D. customize printing

4. To initialize a network print server, load _____ at the _____.

   ○ A. PSERVER.EXE, file server

   ○ B. PSERVER.NLM, file server

   ○ C. PRINTCON, file server

   ○ D. PRINTCON, workstation

5. Which utility do you use to create print queues?

   ○ A. PSERVER

   ○ B. PRINTCON

   ○ C. PRINTDEF

   ○ D. PRINTER

6. Of the following, which is NOT an item of information provided on the Printer Configuration form?

   ○ A. Printer Name

   ○ B. Interrupt

   ○ C. Print Queue

   ○ D. IRQ

7. How can you tell that you were successful at completing all the printing services setup tasks?

   ○ A. You can send jobs to print queues.

   ○ B. The Current Attached Servers window displays the name of the print server.

   ○ C. You can load the print server on a file server.

   ○ D. You can change printer types without effecting the quality of print services.

8. The THREE utilities used to send print jobs to network printers by redirecting them include:

   ☐ A. User Tools

   ☐ B. PRINTCON

   ☐ C. CAPTURE

   ☐ D. NPRINT

9. Change the _____ field to prevent your print job from being printed until a later date.

   ○ A. Operator Hold

   ○ B. Service Sequence

   ○ C. Suppress Form Feed

   ○ D. User Hold

10. If you have rights, you can modify the _____ job field to specify when a job is to print.

    ○ A. Operator Hold

    ○ B. Service Sequence

    ○ C. Suppress Form Feed

    ○ D. User Hold

11. To customize print jobs, use the _____ utility.

    ○ A. PRINTDEF

    ○ B. PCONSOLE

    ○ C. PRINTCON

    ○ D. PSERVER

12. You CANNOT _____ with the PRINTDEF utility.

    ○ A. edit printer names and definitions

    ○ B. create special printer setup configurations

    ○ C. create printer names and definitions

    ○ D. import a printer name and definition

13. Which utility lets you copy one user's print job information to another user?

    ○ A. PRINTCON

    ○ B. PCONSOLE

    ○ C. PRINTDEF

    ○ D. PSERVER

14. Which THREE are valid ways to connect a printer to the network physically?

    ☐ A. Attach it directly to the cable

    ☐ B. To a NetWare file server running PSERVER

    ☐ C. To a workstation

    ☐ D. To a workstation running PCONSOLE

15. You can connect a maximum of _____ printers to a NetWare 3.12 print server.

    ○ A. 5

    ○ B. 8

    ○ C. 11

    ○ D. 16

Answers

1. D

2. D

3. C

4. B

5. B

6. C

7. B

8. A, C, D

9. D

10. A

11. C

12. B

13. A

14. A, B, C

15. D

Preparing Other NetWare 3.1x Services for Users

As a network administrator, it is your job to help make it easier for your users to access the network, including the services, programs, and data files that they need. This chapter discusses the guidance and suggestions that Novell provides, as well as those features of NetWare that help you to make the user's access to the network and its services as easy as possible. Topics include:

- *Adding network application software*

- *Understanding login scripts and their function*

- *Building system and user login scripts*

- *Understanding the NetWare menu system*

■ Creating and running a NetWare 3.12 menu

■ Converting older NetWare menus

■ Understanding NetWare basic MHS

■ Setting up and administering basic MHS

■ Using First Mail

Adding Network Application Software

When choosing application software to put on your network, consider these seven suggested guidelines to make your choices easier and more successful:

■ Choose application software that is compatible with your network operating system.

■ Choose and verify that the software is designed for multiple users.

■ Establish a directory structure into which you can place the application software before you install it and place different application software files in subdirectories within that directory. Load it all in one area of the network directory structure.

■ After the directory structure is in place, install the application software, following the installation instructions provided by the application software's manufacturer.

■ After the application software files are installed, flag them as Shareable/Read Only (S, RO) to secure against viruses and to enable

multiple users to access the files without changing, copying, or deleting the files.

■ Ensure that users have a search drive mapped to the directory containing the application software's executable files. In addition, grant the Read (R) and File (F) scan rights to each group or individual network user so they have the right to run these programs.

■ If necessary, increase the number of memory buffers and the number of files that can be opened simultaneously in the CONFIG.SYS file on the file server, as well as on user's workstations. Do not make this modification to CONFIG.SYS unless you have determined that the current settings for these two parameters are insufficient.

To load applications software, complete the following steps:

1. Create a directory structure for the application software (if it does not already exist).

2. Copy the application software to its specific directory.

3. Create or update the CONFIG.SYS file (as previously discussed).

4. INSTALL the application software by following the instructions that came with the application program.

5. Flag the application program files so no one can delete, copy, or modify them, as well as to provide some virus protection.

6. Verify that the application runs correctly.

7. Grant users and groups the necessary rights (R and F) to the application software.

8. Create a search drive to the directory. If you put the search drive into the system login script (see the following section for information on login scripts), all the users can access it without having to create search drives for themselves.

The Function of Login Scripts

There are three types of NetWare login scripts:

- System
- User
- Default

System login scripts set up the network environment with general-use information. The system login script, for example, is the most common place to put a search drive mapping to network applications. By placing this search drive mapping in the system login script, which is run first whenever a user logs in to the network, necessary search drive mappings are created for each user.

The user login script enables you or the user to establish a user-specific environment. User login scripts, for example, can contain network drive mappings to the user's home directory and related subdirectories.

The default login script is part of the LOGIN.EXE file. If no user login script exists, the default login script runs, setting up essential environment variables, such as a drive mapping to the SYS:PUBLIC directory. After a user login script is created, the default login script is not run for that user. (This is true even if the user's login script contains only blank lines.) If you want to prevent the default login script from running even when no user login script exists, enter the **NO_DEFAULT** command in the system login script.

Build System and User Login Scripts

Although the default login script is part of the LOGIN.EXE file, and, as such, does not need to be created by the network administrator or by a user, the same is not true of the system and user login scripts.

Table 6.1 shows the available login script commands. These commands can be used in both system and user login scripts, with one exception: You *must* place the NO_DEFAULT command into the system login script if you do not want the default login script to be run when a user does not have a user login script.

 Note Login script commands that have a percent sign (%) in front of them are called identifier variables. An *identifier variable* is a special command that, when run, is replaced by the actual item of information that the identifier variable represents. The LOGIN_NAME identifier variable, when included as %LOGIN_NAME in a login script command, for example, is replaced by the actual UserID of the user running this login script.

Table 6.1
Login Script Commands

Command	Purpose	Example
#	Is followed by a program name, runs an external DOS program, then returns to the login script.	#PS.EXE
*	Indicates the following is a remark—for information purposes only—and is not run as a command.	* This section is only run on Mondays
BREAK	Used with ON or OFF to let the user stop or not stop the login script from running.	BREAK OFF
COMSPEC	Tells where to find the DOS COMMAND.COM file.	COMSPEC=C: \COMMAND.COM
DISPLAY	Types a text file to the screen.	DISPLAY Z:USER.TXT
DRIVE	Specify first (default) drive for user after login script is run.	DRIVE F:
END	Used with IF...THEN...ELSE to specify the end of this conditional statement.	IF MEMBER OF "HR" THEN ATTACH HR1\PR: END
FDISPLAY	Types a text file to the screen, but removes printer and other codes.	FDISPLAY Z:USER.TXT
FIRE PHASERS	Sets the user's computer to repeat a sound for a given number of times.	FIRE PHASERS 3
GREETING_TIME	Specifies time of day such as morning or evening.	WRITE "GOOD % GREETING_TIME"

Command	Purpose	Example
HOUR24	Determines the hour based on a 24-hour day.	IF HOUR24 "18" THEN WRITE "Go home!" END
IF...THEN...ELSE	Lets you run nested (up to 10 levels) condition statements.	IF TUESDAY THEN WRITE "Meet at 3" ELSE...WRITE "Hello" END
INCLUDE	Runs a DOS text file as part of the login script.	INCLUDE Z:TUES.TXT
LOGIN_NAME	Use's the user's login name.	WRITE "Hello %LOGIN_NAME"
MACHINE	Determines computer type if not an OS/2 computer.	S3:=S2\SYS:PUBLIC\ %MACHINE\%OS\ %OS_VERSION
MAP	Creates or modifies a drive mapping or displays current drive mappings.	MAP F:=SYS:USERS\ %LOGIN_NAME
NDAY_OF_WEEK	Determines day of week, using 1 through 7 (Sunday through Saturday).	IF NDAY_OF_WEEK = "02" THEN WRITE "Oh No!" ELSE WRITE "We made it!" END
OS	Determines the type of DOS running on the user's PC.	S3:=S2\SYS:PUBLIC\ %MACHINE\%OS\ %OS_VERSION
OS_VERSION	Determines the DOS version running on the user's PC.	S3:=S2\SYS:PUBLIC\ %MACHINE\%OS\ %OS_VERSION
PAUSE	Stops program execution until user presses a key.	PAUSE

continues

Table 6.1, Continued
Login Script Commands

Command	Purpose	Example
REMARK	Indicates that what follows is a remark—for information purposes only—and is not run as a command.	REMARK This section is only run on Tuesdays.
SET	Sets DOS variables.	SET PROMPT = "PG"
STATION	Displays the client's connection number.	WRITE "Your connection number is %STATION
WRITE	Prints information inside quotations to the monitor.	WRITE "Hello"

You can create login scripts by completing the following steps:

1. Log in to the network with Supervisor rights if you want to create a system login script or a user login script for someone other than yourself.

2. Start the SYSCON utility.

3A. If you want to create a system login script, choose Supervisor Options from the SYSCON Available Topics menu, then choose System Login Script system login.

3B. Choose User Information from the SYSCON Available Topics menu, then choose a user's name to create your own user login script, or, if you have Supervisor rights, another user's login script.

4. If you are creating a user login script, you can choose to copy another user's login script. Type the name of the user whose user login script you want to copy when you are prompted with Read Login Script From User, as shown in figure 6.1.

5. Modify a user script copied from another user or create a login script by using the commands shown in table 6.1.

6. Press Esc to exit the login script file and click on Yes to save the file.

Figure 6.2 shows the system login script for the file server called MICHAEL.

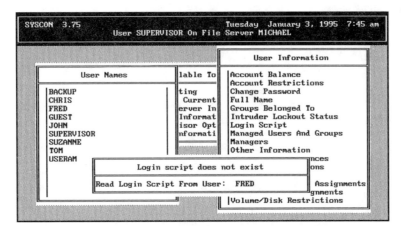

Figure 6.1
The Read Login Script From User prompt.

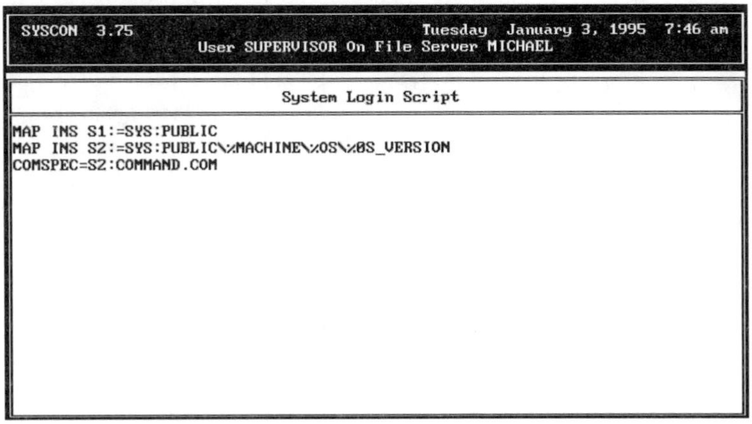

Figure 6.2
Sample System Login Script.

The NetWare Menu System

A *menu* is a screen from which you can choose various options to accomplish various tasks. Some NetWare utilities, such as SYSCON and FILER, provide a menu from which you can make your selections.

NetWare lets you create custom menus using any DOS text editor, and its menuing software program—MENUMAKE.

NetWare menus consist of the following four basic components:

- The main menu

- Submenus

■ Commands

■ Prompts for user input

The main menu must have a title and contain a list of options from which the user can choose. Each option must include commands to be executed when the option is chosen. Submenus must also have a title, as well as options and commands.

There are two types of commands used in a NetWare menu: Organizational and Control. *Organizational commands* determine the layout or arrangement of the menu. *Item commands* define the options available in each menu.

The following are Organizational commands:

■ MENU

■ ITEM

The MENU command identifies the start of each menu. Use the MENU command by including it in the text file, followed by a two- to three-character menu number (01 through 255), a comma, and a menu name. This MENU command must be left-justified whenever it is used.

Use the MENU command as shown in the following example:

```
MENU 01, User Utilities
```

The ITEM command specifies the options to be included on the menu. ITEM lines are indented beneath MENU lines. Include one ITEM line for each option on the menu.

For example, use the ITEM command as shown in the following line:

```
MENU 01, User Utilities
    ITEM Word Processing
```

The ITEM command also has options that can be used with it:

■ **BATCH.** Removes the menu program from RAM and runs the CHDIR option

■ **CHDIR.** Returns the user to the default directory after the chosen menu option has completed its last associated command

■ **PAUSE.** Suspends action until the user presses a key

■ **SHOW.** Displays in the upper left corner of the screen the name of a DOS command being run, if it is being run because of a user's choice of a specific menu option

These ITEM options are used below the ITEM command. They must be indented farther than the ITEM command.

For example, use the EXEC ITEM option as shown below:

```
MENU 01, User Utilities
    ITEM Word Processing
        EXEC WP
```

In addition to the two Organizational commands, there are six Control commands:

■ **EXEC.** Runs the command whose executable file name follows the EXEC command

■ **GETO.** Accepts but does not require the user to provide input to a prompt that is displayed as the result of the user choosing a menu option

■ **GETP.** Stores the user's input for later use, as specified based on numbered identifier variables preceded by a percent sign

■ **GETR.** Requires that the user input valid information (such as a numeric when a numeric is required) before the menu will continue

Note GET commands prompt the user to provide input. You can use up to 100 GET commands per ITEM.

You must place any GET commands between the ITEM and EXEC lines associated with them.

When you use GET commands, the command must be entered as follows, using {curly braces} when indicated, and replacing unused parameters with commas:

```
GETxinstruction{prepend}length,prefill,
  ➥SECURE{append}
```

Replace *instruction* with what you want to appear on the screen.

Replace *prepend* with any information that you want placed in front of the user's response. Place the prepended information in curly braces.

Replace *length* with the number of characters allowed for the user's response.

Replace *prefill* with any information you want to put into the user's answer field as a default answer.

Use SECURE to cause only asterisks to be shown when the user types a response.

Replace *append* with information to be placed at the end of the user's typed input.

■ **LOAD.** Suspends the current menu to load and run another menu that is stored in a separate file.

■ **SHOW.** Retrieves the submenu as specified by the submenu number. The difference between the SHOW and the LOAD commands is that the SHOW command is used when the submenu is contained within the same file as the original menu. The LOAD command calls a menu contained within a separate file.

Create and Run a NetWare 3.12 Menu

After you have created a menu, such as the one shown in figure 6.3, you must prepare the menu to be used.

Figure 6.3
Sample NetWare menu.

To prepare a menu for use, complete the following steps:

1. Create or edit the menu as needed, using any DOS text editor.
2. Compile the menu by running the MENUMAKE utility, as shown in figure 6.4. To run this utility, type **MENUMAKE *[path]textfile***, replacing *path* and *textfile* with the path and the name of the DOS text file containing the menu commands. Press Enter.
3. Run the menu by using the NMENU command, followed by the path to and the name of the DAT file created by the MEMUMAKE utility.

   Create, for example, a text file with menu commands called USERMENU. Next, run the MENUMAKE utility to compile this file, creating a file called USERMENU.DAT. Then run the file by typing **NMENU USERMENU** and pressing Enter. The menu is displayed (see fig. 6.5).

F:\SYSTEM>MENUMAKE USERMENU.SRC
Novell Menu Script Compiler v3.12 (930420)
(c) Copyright 1993, Novell, Inc. All rights reserved.
F:\SYSTEM\USERMENU.SRC:
F:\SYSTEM\USERMENU.DAT written.
F:\SYSTEM>

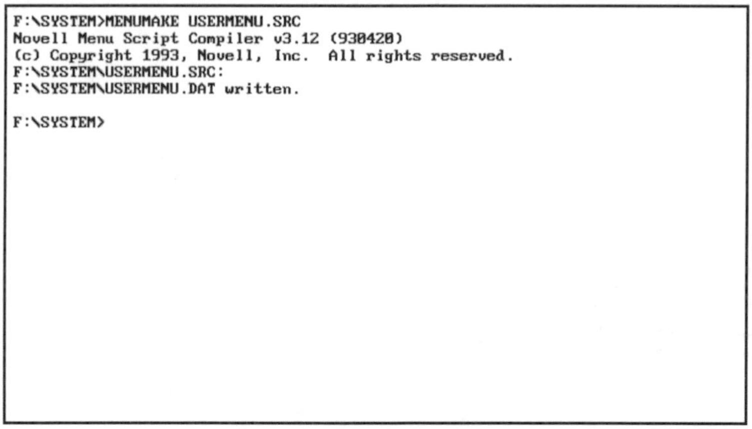

Figure 6.4
Using MENUMAKE to create a menu file.

Novell Menu System V3.12
Tuesday January 3, 1995 8:00am
User Utilities
A. Word Processing
B. File Management
C. Run DOS Command
F2=Session Information
F1=Help

Figure 6.5
User Utilities menu.

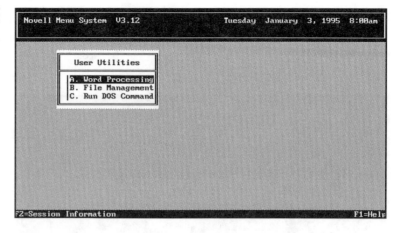

Convert Older NetWare Menus

Pre-NetWare 3.12 menu files had an MNU extension. To convert an older menu, run the MENUCNVT program. To run this program, type **MENUCNVT** *filename.mnu* and press Enter.

After you have converted the menu file, compile it using the MENUMAKE utility, as previously described.

Understand NetWare Basic MHS

Novell's NetWare Basic *Message Handling Service* (MHS) is the software that delivers electronic mail messages. NetWare Basic MHS lets users on a single-server network send electronic mail messages to each other. After Basic MHS receives a mail message from a mail application, it delivers it to the appropriate electronic mailbox.

Set Up and Administer Basic MHS

Basic MHS is installed at the file server console. Basic MHS can only be used on NetWare networks with a single file server. You install Basic MHS on the file server by accessing the server directly from the file server console.

Install Basic MHS

Basic MHS ships with NetWare 3.12 and is installed as if it were an optional Novell product, using the Prodcut Options selection from the INSTALL.NLM.

To start the installation of Basic MHS, type **LOAD INSTALL** at the file server console.

Add a User

Basic MHS installs an administration utility during installation. Before you can run and use this utility, you must run BREQUEST.EXE at the client. Then activate the administrative utility by typing **ADMIN** and pressing Enter.

To add a mail user, choose Users from the Admin Functions menu, press Insert, then type a name for the new user's account and fill in other information as needed. Add users by repeating this process.

Create a Distribution List

You also use the ADMIN utility to create a list of users to whom you can send mail messages. To create a distribution list, choose Distribution Lists from the Admin Functions menu and press Insert. Next, fill in the requested information and press Esc. Choose Yes to save the distribution list.

Use First Mail

As a network administrator, you use the ADMIN utility to prepare Basic MHS for users. Basic MHS provides the background processing and managing features for e-mail. Network users can run First Mail—the NetWare utility that provides the user interface for electronic messaging—or any other e-mail program that uses the *Standard Message Format* (SMF) to send, read, and manage their e-mail messages.

Send Mail Using First Mail

To create and send a mail message, type **MAIL** and press Enter. Choose Send a mail message from the Mail Options menu and type the recipient's user name in the To field. Then type a brief topic description in the Subj field and the message in the blank area, and press Ctrl+Enter to send the mail message.

Read Mail Using First Mail

To read a mail message, type **MAIL** and press Enter. Choose Browse mail messages from the Mail Options Menu, then choose the message you want to read. Press Esc to return to the list of messages and you can choose another message.

 To help you decide which messages are most important—which should be read promptly and which can wait— First Mail provides three useful items of information for each message displayed in the list of available messages. If the sender filled out all fields, you will see information that tells you the date and time the message was created, who sent the message, and to what the subject of the message relates.

Questions

1. Which TWO of the following are guide-lines to consider when choosing application software?

   ☐ A. Usable by only one person at a time

   ☐ B. Flag files SRO

   ☐ C. Load before DOS

   ☐ D. Network OS compatibility

2. The correct order for loading application software is which of the following?

   ○ A. Create directory structure, copy software, update CONFIG.SYS file, INSTALL software, and flag files

   ○ B. Update CONFIG.SYS file, create directory structure, flag files, and INSTALL software

   ○ C. INSTALL software, update CONFIG.SYS file, create directory structure, and copy software

   ○ D. Create directory structure, copy software, flag files, and update CONFIG.SYS file

3. Which of the following is NOT a type of login script?

   ○ A. System

   ○ B. User

   ○ C. Network

   ○ D. Default

4. The login script that runs when no individual login script exists for a user is called the _____ login script.

   ○ A. System

   ○ B. User

   ○ C. Network

   ○ D. Default

5. The _____ login script sets up the network environment with general-use information.

   ○ A. System

   ○ B. User

   ○ C. Network

   ○ D. Default

6. To establish a specific environment for an individual, create a _____ login script.

   ○ A. System

   ○ B. User

   ○ C. Network

   ○ D. Default

7. Which of the following statements about the default login script is true?

   ○ A. It is part of the LOGIN.EXE file.

   ○ B. It executes after the user's login script.

   ○ C. It does not run if a system login script exists.

   ○ D. It runs before the network login script.

8. To run an external DOS command from inside a login script, preceed the command with _____.

   ○ A. #

   ○ B. *

   ○ C. %

   ○ D. INCLUDE

9. To run a DOS text file as part of the login script, use the _____ command.

   ○ A. #

   ○ B. *

   ○ C. %

   ○ D. INCLUDE

10. Which TWO statements about login scripts are true?

    ☐ A. To create a user menu, choose User Information in SYSCON.

    ☐ B. You can copy one user's login script to create a script for another user.

    ☐ C. You can create login scripts for any user regardless of your network rights.

    ☐ D. You create user login scripts to customize their environment and make access to network resources easier for the user.

11. The NetWare software used to create a menu is called _____.

    ○ A. SYSCON

    ○ B. FILER

    ○ C. MENUMAKE

    ○ D. MENUCNVT

12. Which command identifies the start of a NetWare menu?

    ○ A. MENU

    ○ B. START

    ○ C. ITEM

    ○ D. BATCH

13. Of the following, which is NOT an option of the ITEM command?

    ○ A. BATCH

    ○ B. CHDIR

    ○ C. SHOW

    ○ D. MENU

14. Use the _____ command to run a Net-Ware menu.

    ○ A. MENUMAKE

    ○ B. NMENU

    ○ C. USERMENU

    ○ D. DAT

15. NetWare menus created before NetWare 3.12 can be changed to run in a 3.12 environment using which TWO menu commands?

    ☐ A. NEWMENU

    ☐ B. MENUDAT

    ☐ C. MENUCNVT

    ☐ D. MENUMAKE

Answers

1. B, D
2. A
3. C
4. D
5. A
6. B
7. A
8. A
9. D
10. A, D
11. C
12. A
13. D
14. B
15. C, D

Protecting the NetWare 3.1x Network

Features such as passwords, login user IDs, NCP Packet Signature, and others help protect your network from unauthorized access. Unauthorized access is not the only problem that you can experience with your NetWare file server, however. Power outages and hard disk crashes are two other problems from which your file server might suffer. NetWare helps you deal with these types of problems by providing three data integrity features. This chapter discusses those three features with topics including the following:.

- *Understanding system fault tolerance*

- *Understanding storage management services*

- *Backing up and restoring NetWare file servers*

Understanding System Fault Tolerance

System Fault Tolerance (SFT) is one of NetWare's network data protection systems. It includes a variety of approaches to maintaining the integrity of data on your NetWare file server.

SFT helps to ensure your network's data integrity through several key features (see fig. 7.1). These features include the following:

- Disk mirroring
- Disk duplexing
- Duplicate FATs and DETs
- Hot fix
- Read-after-write verification
- TTS
- UPS Monitoring

Table 7.1 shows these SFT features and briefly describes each of them.

Figure 7.1
Features of SFT.

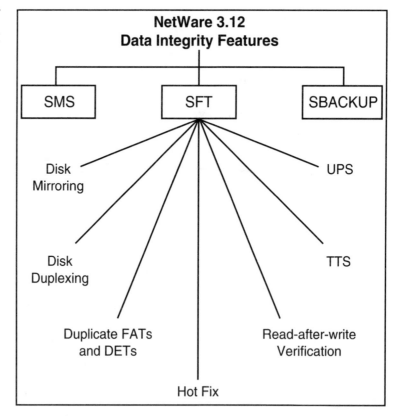

Table 7.1
NetWare's SFT Features

Feature	Description	Purpose
Disk Duplexing	NetWare duplicates data from the NetWare partition of one hard disk to that of another hard disk, using a different adapter, cable, and controller.	To protect data from hard disk failure.
Disk Mirroring	NetWare duplicates data from the NetWare partition of one hard disk to that of another hard disk, using the same adapter, cable, and controller.	To provide a second copy in case of hard disk failure.
Duplicate FATS and DETS	NetWare duplicates the *File Allocation Table* (FAT) and *Directory Entry Table* (DET) to different parts of the hard disk.	To ensure the OS always has access to these tables.
Hot fix	When a bad block is identified, hot fix redirects the data to another area on the hard disk.	To store data in a valid area of the hard disk.
Read-after-Write Verification	When data is stored in a block on the computer's hard disk, read-after-write verification checks that block of data to make certain it can be read. After several unsuccessful tries, it marks the hard disk block as bad and saves the data to another location.	To verify the readability of the data that it just wrote to disk.
TTS	Tracks database transactions to ensure either that all related database changes are saved to the database or that no changes are saved.	To protect the integrity of database files.
UPS	This software lets you control an *Uninterruptible Power Supply* (UPS) connected to your network server.	To protect your server from power outages/fluctuations.

Understanding Storage Management Services

Centralized data storage and access brings with it the increased possibility of the loss of a major amount of your network data due to a hard drive crash. NetWare provides a feature called *Storage Management Services* (SMS) to allow data to be stored and retrieved on your network.

NetWare provides SMS as a group of NetWare Loadable Modules (NLMs). One of the most important aspects of SMS is its design. SMS enables you to back up and restore your network's file system using the SMS-compatible backup software and hardware of your choice. SMS also lets you back up and restore files regardless of the local operating system that you are using. SMS supports DOS, OS/2, Macintosh, Windows, and Unix file systems.

One of the main ways to use a file storage management system is to make regular backups of your network's file system. The next section of this chapter shows you how to use the backup software NetWare provides. This software is called SBACKUP. To ensure data integrity, you must establish a regular schedule of backing your network's data, whether you use SBACKUP or another backup-and-restore software.

The regularity of network backup is important. If you have to restore a network backup, the more current and complete that backup is, the less work you will have to do to reconstruct your network data. Because regular and consistent backups are important, Novell describes some backup techniques that you should consider implementing in your network environment. These techniques include the following:

- Full backup

- Incremental backup

- Differential backup

A *full backup* involves backing up all files on a NetWare file server. You can back up the files on the file server that is running the backup software, or on any other NetWare file server. When you do a full backup, you back up all files on a file server, including bindery and system files. A full backup also causes the *modify bit* (a flag set on a file that indicates whether its contents have changed since the last time this file was backed up) to be reset for each file that is backed up. You should do the first full backup on your NetWare network shortly after you have installed it.

In addition to doing a full backup, you can also choose to back up any of the following:

- Certain directories

- All files that changed after you ran the last backup

- Files ending with a specific file name extension

If you choose to do a backup following one or more of these options, then you are not doing a full backup. Instead, you are doing either an incremental backup or a differential backup.

When you do an *incremental backup*, you back up all files that have been created in or copied to a specific directory since you ran the last backup. You also back up any files in the specified directory that have been modified since the last time you ran a backup. When you do an incremental backup, all file modify bits are cleared.

When you do a *differential back up*, you are backing up all data that has changed since you ran the last full backup. With a differential backup, it does not matter whether the changed files were backed up by an incremental backup because the modify bit is not cleared. This enables you to do an incremental backup later, and back up these files as well.

Knowing when to do network backups is only part of the process. You also need to know how to do those backups. If you are using a backup software package provided by anyone other than Novell, you must follow the instructions provided by that software package. If you choose to use the backup software provided with NetWare 3.12, then follow the instructions for using SBACKUP.

Back Up and Restore NetWare File Servers

Before using SBACKUP, it might help you to be familiar with two of Novell's related terms, as follows:

- **Host.** The file server that has the backup device attached to it.

- **Target.** The file server (or workstation) that contains the files being backed up.

To back up files on a NetWare 3.12 file server or client, complete the following steps:

1. LOAD the TSA312.NLM on the target file server.

2. Load the backup device drivers on the host server if they have not already been loaded.

 If you automated the process of loading the backup device drivers using the file server's AUTOEXEC.NCF file, you do not need to complete step 2.

3. Load SBACKUP at the host server.

4. Provide your supervisor user name if prompted, along with the password.

5. If the Select the Device Driver menu is displayed, choose the device driver for the backup hardware you have attached to your file server.

6. Choose Select Target to Backup/Restore option from the SBACKUP Main Menu to choose the file server or workstation whose files you will back up.

7. If prompted, provide a user name and password for the target server.

8. Choose Backup Menu from the Main Menu

9. When the Backup Menu window appears, as shown in figure 7.2, choose Select Working Directory and provide a path to where the backup session files, such as the error log, should be saved.

Figure 7.2
The Backup Menu.

10. When prompted, fill in the Backup Options fields, then press Esc.

11. When prompted to Proceed with Backup, choose Yes.

12. Choose Start Backup Now to begin the backup session.

13. When the backup is complete, press Enter to redisplay the Backup Menu, then press Esc to return to the Main menu.

 If you are backing up a network DOS client instead of a file server, you first must load the TSA_DOS.NLM at the host. Loading TSA_DOS.NLM, automatically loads the following additional NLMs:

- STREAMS.NLM

- SMDR31X.NLM

- TLI.NLM

- SPXS.NLM or IPXS.NLM

In addition, you must load the TSA_SMS.COM file at the workstation whose files you want to back up. The best way to do this is to modify the client's AUTOEXEC.BAT file to load the TSA_SMS.COM file, then reboot the client to load the TSA_SMS.COM file automatically.

After you have done this, continue with the step that has you loading the SBACKUP NLM at the file server.

You can also back up an OS/2 client by loading the TSA_OS2.NLM at the file server, just as you would load the TSA_DOS.NLM if you were backing up a DOS client.

Questions

1. To back up only files changed since the last backup, perform a/an _____ backup.

   ○ A. full

   ○ B. incremental

   ○ C. differential

   ○ D. custom

2. To back up a DOS client, run the _____ file at the DOS client.

   ○ A. SMDR.NLM

   ○ B. TSA_OS2.COM

   ○ C. TSA_DOS.COM

   ○ D. TSA_SMS.COM

3. Which of the following is NOT a feature of SFT?

   ○ A. Disk mirroring

   ○ B. Disk duplexing

   ○ C. Duplicate FATs and DETs

   ○ D. Hot Repair

4. The SFT feature that verifies the readability of data after it has been written to the hard disk is _____.

   ○ A. hot fix

   ○ B. UPS

   ○ C. read-after-write

   ○ D. duplicate FAT

5. Which THREE files are automatically loaded when you load TSA_DOS.NLM.

   ☐ A. STREAMS.NLM

   ☐ B. SMDR31X.NLM

   ☐ C. DOS_SMS.NLM

   ☐ D. TLI.NLM

6. The feature of SFT that lets you back up and restore your network's file system using compatible backup software and hardware is called _____.

   ○ A. SMS

   ○ B. UPS

   ○ C. SOS

   ○ D. FATS

7. If you are backing up a network DOS client instead of a file server, you must first load the _____ at the _____.

   ○ A. TSA_DOS.NLM, target

   ○ B. TSA_DOS.NLM, host

   ○ C. TSA_SMS.COM, target

   ○ D. TSA_SMS.COM, host

8. Tracking database transactions is a feature of _____.

   ○ A. TTS

   ○ B. SMS

   ○ C. UPS

   ○ D. NLM

9. To protect your network from failure of the hard disk channel, which SFT feature should you implement?

   ○ A. UPS

   ○ B. Duplicate FAT

   ○ C. Disk mirroring

   ○ D. Duplicate DET

10. The SFT feature that you should implement to protect against a bad disk drive adapter card is _____.

   ○ A. duplicate FAT

   ○ B. disk duplexing

   ○ C. disk mirroring

   ○ D. duplicate DET

Answers

1. B

2. D

3. D

4. C

5. A, B, D

6. A

7. B

8. A

9. C

10. B

PART

II

NetWare 3.1x Advanced Administration

Understanding NetWare 3.1x Server Basics

As a network administrator, server startup, monitoring, and maintenance are among your primary duties. To successfully maintain and monitor your network's NetWare 3.1x file servers, you must understand various aspects of the 3.1x operating system and its primary component—the NetWare file server. This chapter is designed to provide you with advanced information about the NetWare 3.1x file server.

After reading this chapter, you will be able to:

■ *Understand server components*

■ *Work with server configuration files*

■ *Describe network communication*

■ Understand name-space support

■ Start a NetWare 3.12 server

Understanding Server Components

Personal computers consist of two primary components: hardware and software. The hardware of a PC includes such physical components as a monitor, keyboard, central processing unit (CPU), and so on. Software includes the operating systems, communication programs, and so on.

A NetWare 3.1x file server, which runs on an Intel-based PC, also consists of two primary components: hardware and software. By understanding the components of a 3.1x file server, you can better understand how a file server provides network services to multiple users. Consequently, you also can better understand how to successfully maintain and monitor your network's 3.1x file servers.

NetWare 3.1x Server Hardware Components

Because a NetWare 3.1x file server runs on an Intel-based PC, the hardware components of the file server are the same as those of a PC. Three of these common components, however, are especially important to a NetWare file server:

■ Microprocessor

■ Memory

■ Hard disk

There is one other hardware component that is not originally part of a PC. It is, however, an important part of a file server (see fig. 8.1). That component is the network board and its associated cabling.

Microprocessor

To install NetWare 3.1x file server software on your PC, you must have at least an Intel 80386 microprocessor. Intel 80486 microprocessors generally are capable of processing service requests at a greater speed than are 80386 microprocessors. A PC with an 80486 microprocessor, therefore, often is more suitable as a NetWare file server than a PC with an Intel 80386 microprocessor, although both can be used.

Table 8.1 provides a quick comparison of some of the features of Intel 80386 and 80486 microprocessors.

Table 8.1
Intel 80386 Versus 80486 Microprocessors

Feature	80386	80486
Register	32-bit	32-bit
Data Bus	32-bit	32-bit
Clock Speeds	16, 20, 25, and 33	25, 33, 50, and 66

PCs using the Intel Pentium microprocessor also can be used as NetWare 3.1x file servers. The Pentium microprocessor still uses the 32-bit address bus, but has a data bus with a 64-bit width. In addition, Pentiums currently run at 60 MHz and 66 MHz, although faster versions are planned.

The Pentium microprocessor also can execute two commands at once, instead of just one command at a time, which is what the 80386 and 80486 micro-processors currently are capable of doing. The Pentium has two data pipelines, not one. NetWare 3.1x is not designed, however, to take advantage of this Pentium microprocessor feature.

Memory

The NetWare 3.1x file server requires a minimum of 4 MB of random access memory (RAM) with which to temporarily store and retrieve needed data. The file server can access and use as much as 4 GB of RAM.

Hard Disk

One of the main benefits of networking is the capability to store data and program files on the network's file servers. Data and program files are

stored on one or more file server hard disks. Those hard disks can be internal or external to the file server, but there must be at least one hard disk.

The first hard disk usually contains both a DOS partition and a NetWare partition. The DOS partition is used to boot the PC and to start the file server. (SERVER.EXE is stored on the DOS partition.) A DOS partition is not mandatory, however, because the PC can be booted and the SERVER.EXE file can be loaded from a floppy disk (not recommended).

The NetWare partition stores the other file server files. It is divided into one or more NetWare volumes. Each 3.1x file server must have at least one volume. That volume is always named SYS.

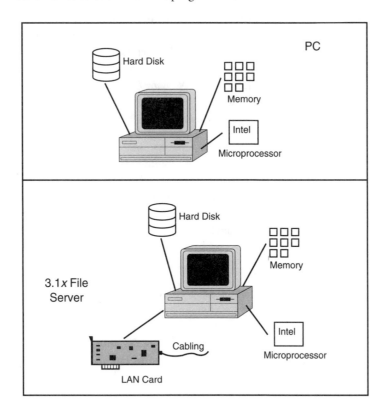

Figure 8.1
PC and file server components.

Each file server can have only one volume called SYS, but it can have more than one volume. Other volumes can be located on the same hard disk, or on additional hard disks, as long as no two volumes on any single NetWare 3.1x file server have the same name.

All NetWare volumes must be placed on NetWare partitions. These volumes cannot be placed on DOS partitions. You can, however, put more than one volume on a NetWare partition.

You can have more than one hard disk on your NetWare file server as well, as long as the total disk space does not exceed 32 TB (*terabytes*). Each additional hard disk must have its own NetWare partition, however, which you create by using the INSTALL utility.

Network Board and Cabling

Each NetWare file server must have at least one network board installed, although file servers can have several boards installed to enable communication among different networks. The network board is responsible for the physical communication between network file servers and clients. When multiple boards (up to a maximum of 16) are installed in a file server, that file server performs another duty—that of a network router.

The cabling system connects the network boards to each other. When different types of network boards are installed in a NetWare file server, different types of cabling systems might also be required.

NetWare 3.1x Server Software Components

In addition to the physical or hardware components required to create a network, software components are needed. The file server must contain three types of software:

- SERVER.EXE
- Disk driver
- LAN driver

This software is described in the following sections.

SERVER.EXE

The main operating system file, which is responsible for performing various NetWare operating system functions, is the SERVER.EXE file. It is loaded into file server memory as a DOS executable file. Once loaded, DOS no longer controls the PC, although it remains resident in memory and provides services if requested.

SERVER.EXE provides limited services. Its primary function is to provide a platform (software bus) to which other network services can attach. These other network services, provided through files known as *NetWare Loadable Modules* (NLMs), ensure that NetWare provides basic networking and advanced services.

Two of the most common and most important services include communication between the file server and the PC's hard disk, and communication between the file server and the PC's network board (see fig. 8.2). These services are provided through software files called disk drivers and LAN drivers.

Disk Driver

Most NLMs are files with an NLM extension. Disk driver NLMs have a DSK extension, however, because they are specialized NLMs. They are responsible for enabling communication between the LAN board installed in the PC with

SERVER.EXE loaded, and the *disk controller*—the PC's hard disk system interface.

As with SERVER.EXE, disk driver NLMs are stored in the server boot directory—SERVER.312. The disk driver NLM appropriate to the architecture of the disk controller in the PC is loaded into the file server's memory after SERVER.EXE has been loaded.

 Note Common disk controller architectures supported by and shipped with NetWare 3.12 include the following:

■ SCSI

■ IDE

■ ISA

■ EISA

■ Microchannel

Unlike SERVER.EXE, which is loaded into RAM by running the DOS-based SERVER executable file, NLMs are loaded into memory by executing a NetWare command called LOAD. You can load any NLM into file server RAM by using the LOAD command. The proper format for the LOAD command follows:

LOAD *NLM_name*

The purpose of the disk driver NLM is to enable communication between the NetWare server and the disk driver. Therefore, the NetWare server (SERVER.EXE) is loaded first, followed by the disk driver. Loading the disk driver then enables the file server to *mount* (prepare for network users to access and use the stored information) NetWare volumes. By default, loading the file server disk driver automatically mounts the required NetWare SYS volume.

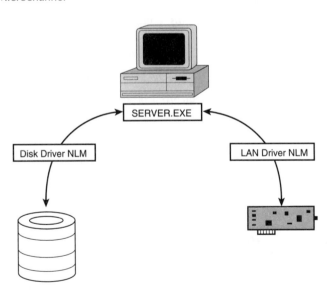

Figure 8.2
Important services provided by NLMs.

Note You must tell the file server to mount any other volumes created when you installed NetWare. To mount other NetWare volumes, use the MOUNT command.

You can MOUNT any single volume by typing **MOUNT *volume_name*** at the file server console and pressing Enter, or by including this command in the file server's AUTOEXEC.NCF file (discussed in the following section).

You can MOUNT all other NetWare volumes by issuing the MOUNT ALL command, replacing *volume_name* with the word ALL. This command also can be issued at the file server console, or placed into the file server's AUTOEXEC.NCF file to automate its execution.

LAN Driver

After the server file (SERVER.EXE) and the disk driver file are loaded into RAM, and the file server volumes (SYS volume as a minimum) have been mounted, you must load the LAN driver into RAM. The LAN driver is responsible for providing a communication interface between the LAN board and the NetWare file server. LAN drivers also are specialized NLMs. These drivers have a LAN file extension.

One of the more common network boards is the NE2000 board. Its associated LAN driver file is NE2000.LAN. To load the NE2000 LAN driver file, type **LOAD NE2000** at the file server console and press Enter. As with loading disk drivers, this process can be automated by placing this command in the AUTOEXEC.NCF file.

Unlike the disk driver NLMs stored in the DOS SERVER.312 directory with SERVER.EXE, LAN NLMs are stored on the NetWare SYS volume in the SYSTEM directory (see fig. 8.3). Because LAN drivers are stored on the SYS volume, they cannot be loaded until the disk driver has been loaded. Loading the disk driver automatically mounts the SYS volume.

Loading the LAN driver into file server RAM is not, by itself, sufficient to enable communication between the NetWare server and the LAN board. To enable communication, the LAN driver also must have a software link established between the LAN driver and its related *communication protocol* (a set of rules that enables information to be prepared, sent, and received between two or more points on the network). To establish this communication, the NetWare BIND command must be issued.

To BIND the *Internetwork Packet Exchange* (IPX) protocol to the NE2000 LAN board, for example, after issuing the LOAD NE2000 command, type the command **BIND IPX TO NE2000** at the file server console and press Enter. You also can automate this command by placing it into the AUTOEXEC.NCF file following the LOAD *LAN_driver* command.

The file server, the network board, and the communication protocol are treated as separate entities. As such, each of these server components must have a network number assigned to it. This network number, also referred to as a *network address*, uniquely identifies each of the network components. These identifiers follow:

- Server = IPX internal network number

- Communication protocol = network address

- Network board = node address

You tell the server what the server's IPX internal network number is after you load SERVER.EXE. The file server's IPX internal network number must be unique for each file server on the network.

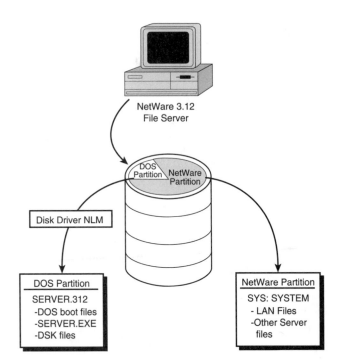

Figure 8.3
*Location of file server
software components.*

You tell the server what the communication protocol network address is when you BIND the communication protocol to the LAN driver. The network address is common to all file servers on the network.

The server determines the node address for itself from information from the network board. Many boards, including Ethernet and Token-Ring, encode a unique number in the card's ROM. Some boards, such as ARCnet, require you to set address information on the board directly using dip switches. Some boards permit you to set the board number with the network board's configuration files prior to installing the board in the file server. The node address must be unique for each network board on the network.

Working with Server Configuration Files

You can load the NetWare server and associated startup files manually from the NetWare file server console. Loading the required files from commands contained in text files called server configuration files is a much easier process, however, and is less prone to error.

Like your PC, which has its own startup configuration files (CONFIG.SYS and AUTOEXEC.BAT), the NetWare file server also can have startup configuration files. These files are called STARTUP.NCF and AUTOEXEC.NCF.

Because the NetWare file server is loaded on a PC, the PC runs its own CONFIG.SYS and

AUTOEXEC.BAT files when you boot the PC. To then load the NetWare file server, you must run the DOS-based SERVER.EXE file. After SERVER.EXE is run, STARTUP.NCF and AUTOEXEC.NCF are executed, if available.

To automate the entire startup process so that SERVER.EXE is loaded each time you boot the PC containing the NetWare file server files, add the SERVER.EXE command to the PC's AUTOEXEC.BAT file. Then when you boot the PC, the required file server files are loaded and run, as shown in figure 8.4.

STARTUP.NCF

The STARTUP.NCF file is used to hold commands that configure the NetWare server. It is stored in the same directory as SERVER.EXE, which is the C:\NETWARE.312 directory created as the default during installation.

Two types of commands are found most frequently in the STARTUP.NCF file: the LOAD and SET commands.

The LOAD Command

The LOAD command, when used in the STARTUP.NCF file, is used primarily for loading disk drivers. It also is used outside of the STARTUP.NCF file, however, to load LAN drivers, name-space modules, and NLMs.

Follow this format when using the LOAD command to load a disk driver:

```
LOAD [path]disk_driver [driver parameter...]
```

A typical LOAD statement in a STARTUP.NCF file might look similar to this example:

```
LOAD ISADISK port=1F0 int=D
```

Note Hexadecimal numbers, such as the D in int=D, are commonly used when specifying configuration parameters.

The SET Command

The SET command is used in the STARTUP.NCF file to configure operating system parameters. These parameters customize server features to better meet your networking needs.

Five categories of SET commands are commonly used in the STARTUP.NCF file:

- Communications
- Memory

Figure 8.4
Automating the loading of the NetWare server.

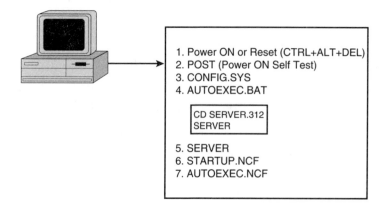

1. Power ON or Reset (CTRL+ALT+DEL)
2. POST (Power ON Self Test)
3. CONFIG.SYS
4. AUTOEXEC.BAT

   ```
   CD SERVER.312
   SERVER
   ```

5. SERVER
6. STARTUP.NCF
7. AUTOEXEC.NCF

- File caching

- Disk caching

- Miscellaneous

Use the following line when placing SET commands into the STARTUP.NCF file:

```
SET [parameter]
```

A typical SET command used in the STARTUP.NCF file might look similar to the following:

```
SET Minimum File Cache Buffers=20
```

 Creating a STARTUP.NCF file to automate server startup procedures makes your life as a network administrator much simpler. If you occasionally need to load the server without running the STARTUP.NCF file, however, you can do so by typing the **SERVER** command followed by **-S\path\filename** and pressing Enter to load an alternate STARTUP.NCF file; or you can type **SERVER -NS** and press Enter to load SERVER.EXE.

AUTOEXEC.NCF

The AUTOEXEC.NCF file is used to hold information that the NetWare server needs when it is booting. This file is stored in the same directory as the LAN and other network files—SYS:SYSTEM. Four items of information that the server needs when booting are stored in this file:

- Name of the file server

- Internal network number

- Command to LOAD the LAN driver

- Command to BIND the protocol to the LAN driver

 As with the STARTUP.NCF file, you can load SERVER without running the AUTOEXEC.NCF file by typing **SERVER -NA** at the file server console and pressing Enter.

As mentioned previously, the LOAD command is used primarily for loading disk and LAN drivers. It also can be used in the AUTOEXEC.NCF file, however, to load name-space modules and other needed NLMs. For example, you can automatically load the MONITOR utility each time you boot your NetWare file server by placing the following command in the AUTOEXEC.NCF file:

```
LOAD MONITOR
```

The AUTOEXEC.NCF file also can contain *console commands* (commands that can be entered at the file server console), such as the following:

- **ABORT REMIRROR.** Stops the automatic remirroring of disks

- **BROADCAST.** Sends messages to network users

- **CD MOUNT.** Mounts a CD-ROM volume

- **DISPLAY SERVERS.** Displays a list of all NetWare servers that the router recognizes

These server configuration files can be created or edited from the file server console in either of two ways. You can create or edit the STARTUP.NCF and AUTOEXEC.NCF files by using the IN-STALL or EDIT NLM commands.

To create or edit these files using the INSTALL NLM, type **LOAD INSTALL** at the NetWare file server console. Choose System Options from the Installation Options menu, then choose one of the following from the Available System Options menu:

- Create AUTOEXEC.NCF file

- Create STARTUP.NCF file

- Edit AUTOEXEC.NCF file

- Edit STARTUP.NCF file

Fill in the blank file window or edit the existing information contained in the file window. Save your changes when you exit.

To create or edit these files using the EDIT NLM, type **LOAD EDIT** at the file server console and press Enter. Type the name of the file to be created or edited, preceded by the path for that file and press Enter. To edit the AUTOEXEC.NCF file, for example, type **SYS:SYSTEM\AUTOEXEC.NCF** and press Enter. Create or modify the file as needed, and save your changes before exiting.

You can also edit the AUTOEXEC.NCF file by using the SYSCON utility. To edit this file using SYSCON, log in to the file server from a network client. Log in as a user with Supervisor rights. Type **SYSCON** and press Enter. Next, choose Supervisor Options from the Available Topics menu. Then choose Edit System AUTOEXEC file from the Supervisor Options menu (see fig. 8.5). Be sure to save your changes when you have finished editing this file.

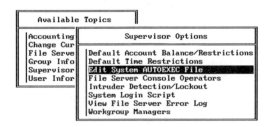

Figure 8.5
Using SYSCON to edit AUTOEXEC.NCF.

Describing Network Communication

Communication is key to any network. Without successful communication, you cannot access network application programs, store and retrieve data files, or print to any printer that is not directly attached to your computer. For network communication to be successful, however, the network operating system must be capable of dealing with differences between types of computers, the communication protocols they support, and the architecture of various files. NetWare 3.1*x* is capable of handling these differences.

One useful feature of 3.1*x* is that it enables you to store data files on network file servers that are not named using DOS naming conventions. NetWare also enables you to store non-DOS file names in their original file-name formats. In addition to retaining the file's non-DOS file name, 3.1*x* stores associated information about these files, such as the following:

- File attributes

- Special non-DOS legal characters

- Case-sensitivity

NetWare provides NLMs that support non-DOS file names. If you use OS/2, Macintosh, NFS, or FTAM file names, you can load the related NLMs onto your NetWare file servers to support these non-DOS file names.

Supported Name Spaces

NetWare 3.1*x* offers two name-space NLMs:

- OS2.NAM to support OS/2 file-naming conventions

■ MAC.NAM to support Macintosh file-naming conventions

If you also need to support NFS (Unix) and FTAM (GOSIP) file-naming conventions on your NetWare 3.1x network, you can purchase the NFS.NAM and FTAM.NAM NLMs for your network.

NetWare supports different operating environments, including those used by minicomputers, mainframe computers, network operating systems, and workstations. Supported name-space protocols are as follows:

■ OS2

■ MAC

■ NFS

■ FTAM

Supported Frame Types

In order for NetWare to support all these environments, it must support *multiple protocols* (conventions or rules used to define how different endpoints on the network will communicate), and a variety of *frame types* (specifications that indicate the format of the data being transmitted in a packet).

 Note Protocols are responsible for providing various operating systems with the following capabilities:

■ Accessing the network media

■ Transporting information across the network

■ Sharing resources on the network

Access to the network media enables clients to send *packets* (addressed and defined groups of data) across the network. Each packet uses a specific frame type. Before another device on the network can accept a transmitted packet, that other device must be using the same frame type as the device that sent the packet.

NetWare 3.12 supports Ethernet 802.2 as its default frame type. It also, however, supports various Ethernet and Token-Ring frame types.

NetWare 3.12 supports the following Ethernet frame types:

■ Ethernet II

■ 802.2

■ 802.3 (Raw)

■ SNAP

The Ethernet II frame type supports both IPX and TCP/IP communication protocols. If you use one of these protocols in your NetWare server to bind that protocol to the network board, you include the following command in your startup file:

```
BIND protocol TO lan driver¦boardname [driver
parameters][protocol parameters]
```

For example, include entries similar to the following in your AUTOEXEC.NCF file if you use IPX, Ethernet II, and a NE2000 network board in your file server.

```
LOAD NE2000 PORT=300 PORT=300
FRAME=Ethernet_II
BIND IPX TO NE2000 NET=01DC01
```

The 802.2 frame type is also an Ethernet frame type. It also supports both IPX and TCP/IP communication protocols. If you use one of these protocols in your NetWare server, bind that protocol to the network board by including the BIND command in your AUTOEXEC.NCF file, as shown in the following example:

```
LOAD NE2000 INT=3 PORT=300 FRAME=802.3
BIND IPX TO NE2000 NET=01DC02
```

The 802.3 (Raw) frame type is another Ethernet frame type. It supports IPX, but does not support TCP/IP. If you use the IPX protocol with the 802.3 frame type in your NetWare server, bind this protocol to the network board using the BIND command in the AUTOEXEC.NCF startup file, as shown in the following example:

```
LOAD NE2000 INT=3 PORT=300 FRAME=802.3
Bind IPX TO NE2000 NET=01DD
```

The SNAP frame type is also an Ethernet frame type. It supports the AppleTalk communication protocol. If you use AppleTalk in your NetWare server, BIND this protocol to the network board using the BIND command in your AUTOEXEC.NCF startup file, as shown in the following example:

```
LOAD NE2000 INT=3 PORT=300
FRAME=Ethernet_SNAP
BIND AppleTalk TO NE2000
```

NetWare 3.12 supports the following Token-Ring frame types:

- Token-Ring
- Token-Ring_SNAP

The Token-Ring frame type supports the IPX communication protocol. If you use the IPX protocol with a Token-Ring frame type in your NetWare server, BIND this protocol to the network board by including the BIND command in your startup file, as shown in the following example:

```
LOAD Token INT=5 PORT=20a FRAME=Token_Ring
BIND IPX TO Token NET=2201AD
```

The Token-Ring_SNAP frame type is also a Token-Ring frame type. It supports the AppleTalk communication protocol, as well as the TCP/IP communication protocol. If you use either of these protocols with Token Ring in your NetWare server, BIND the chosen protocol to the network board by including the BIND command in your AUTOEXEC.NCF startup file, as shown in the following example:

```
LOAD Token INT=5 PORT=20a FRAME=Token-
Ring_SNAP
BIND IP TO Token ADDR=110.111.1.1
```

Supported Protocols

NetWare supports several communication protocols, which Novell refers to as the *NetWare Protocol Suite* (see fig. 8.6).

The communication protocols included in the NetWare protocol suite follow:

- Internetwork Packet Exchange (IPX)
- Sequenced Packet Exchange (SPX)
- Routing Information Protocol (RIP)
- Service Advertising Protocol (SAP)
- NetWare Core Protocol (NCP)
- Packet Burst

The IPX communication protocol is used by both NetWare file servers and *routers* (devices that transfer network packets between different networks).

The advantage of the IPX communication protocol is that it does not require the receiving client to acknowledge the packet's delivery, a process referred to as a *connectionless delivery*. IPX addresses the data packet, sends it out to the proper network, and then delivers the packet based on the node address of the computer.

The SPX communication protocol layers on top of IPX to add reliable delivery service. SPX is a connection-oriented communication protocol that ensures that all data packets are received properly. If SPX does not receive a response to its request for verification of receipt, the data packet is retransmitted.

The RIP communication protocol is used by network routers to exchange information about network routes. It enables network clients to determine which path through the network is the best one to take in order to deliver a packet.

The SAP communication protocol is used by each device on the network to announce (advertise) its service, its name, and its network address. This protocol tells all other devices on the network what network service these devices can expect to find, and where they can expect to find it. A NetWare print server, for example, would advertise its provision of printing services, its print server name, and its network address.

 You can use the TRACK ON console command to see continuous information about RIP and SAP network packets that are being sent from and received by the file server. TRACK ON causes file-server, network-routing, and network-connection request information to be displayed continuously on the file server's monitor. To discontinue the display of RIP and SAP traffic, issue the TRACK OFF command at the file server console.

Each file server keeps a record of all RIP and SAP information that has been broadcast on the network. This information then can be used for routing packets across the network over the best route. Sometimes the routing information becomes corrupted. You can clear the router tables by issuing the RESET ROUTER console command. The previous router tables then are cleared, and a new router table is created.

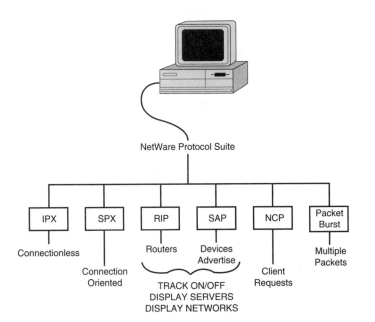

Figure 8.6
The NetWare protocol suite.

Because file servers keep information about other servers on the network, you can see a list of known services that have advertised with SAP by issuing the DISPLAY SERVERS console command, which also shows you how many network routers (known as the number of *hops*) a packet traveling from this file server to another file server must make to reach its destination.

The DISPLAY NETWORKS console command reveals the network numbers of all networks this file server can recognize and tells you how many hops are needed to reach each network.

The NCP communication protocol is used by the NetWare operating system to accept, interpret, and respond to requests from network clients for network services. When a user loads the connection files at his client and requests a network connection, for example, the related NCP responds to the client's connection request.

The Packet Burst communication protocol enables network clients to combine multiple packets and send them across the network in a series. Only after several packets have been sent is an acknowledgment of packet receipt required. The Packet Burst protocol reduces network traffic by reducing the number of acknowledgment packets that must be sent.

Packet Burst might be supported on some servers but not on others. Each network client, therefore, must negotiate with other network devices to determine whether they support Packet Burst. Network clients that support it also must negotiate with each other to determine the largest Packet Burst size that both clients can manage successfully.

Although not part of the NetWare protocol suite, support for the primarily Unix-based TCP/IP protocol is shipped with NetWare 3.1x in the form of

NLMs. These NLMs enable Unix clients or hosts to send packets through NetWare network file servers, and provide support for some Unix-based applications, such as NFS.

Before support for the Unix-based TCP/IP protocol is available on a NetWare 3.1x server, the TCP/IP-related NLMs must be installed on the NetWare server. As with all NLMs, the TCP/IP-related NLMs are installed on a NetWare file server using the LOAD console command.

To load the TCP/IP-related NLMs, type the following command at the NetWare file server console and press Enter:

LOAD TCPIP

NetWare then automatically loads six other related NLMs:

- **STREAMS.NLM**. Provides an interface between the NetWare operating system and various communication protocols, making the communication protocol transparent to the operating system.

- **SNMP.NLM**. (Simple Network Management Protocol.) Makes it possible for TCP/IP-based network management clients to share network node information.

- **CLIB.NLM**. Provides a library of C programs required by NLMs.

- **AFTER311.NLM**. Loads a post NetWare 3.11 NLM.

- **IPXS.NLM**. Provides a protocol stack for service NLMs that need STREAMS-based IPX protocol services.

- **TLI.NLM**. Provides a communication interface between STREAMS and user applications.

Understanding Name-Space Support

NetWare supports different operating system's file naming conventions. It does so by providing NLMs that you can load. If you want to store files on the NetWare server that follow the Macintosh file naming conventions, for example, you can load the MAC.NAM NLM.

NetWare provides name-space support for DOS file names as part of the operating system files. You do not have to load an additional NLM to provide DOS name-space support.

In contrast, to use non-DOS file names, you do have to load separate NLMs to support OS/2 (OS2.NAM), Macintosh (MAC.NAM), Unix (NFS.NAM), and GOSIP (FTAM.NAM) name spaces.

Before you can use non-DOS file names, you must prepare the NetWare volume. Issue the following two commands:

```
LOAD name_space.NLM
ADD NAME SPACE TO volume_name
```

To use OS/2 file names on the SYS volume, type **LOAD OS2** and press Enter. Then type **ADD NAME SPACE TO SYS** and press Enter. To add Macintosh name-space support to the SYS volume, type **LOAD MAC** and press Enter.

You must issue the LOAD command for each name-space NLM you want to load. After all name-space NLMs are loaded, you issue the ADD NAME SPACE TO *volume_name* command. Even though you issue separate LOAD commands for each type of name space you want to use, you only issue the

ADD NAME SPACE TO *volume_name* command once for each volume to which you are adding name-space NLMs.

Starting a NetWare 3.12 Server

Before you can issue any console commands, including the LOAD command, you must start the NetWare file server. After the server's startup files are created, you can start the server automatically each time you boot the file server.

To start a NetWare file server, complete the following steps:

1. Boot DOS on the computer.

2. Change to the directory containing the SERVER.EXE file so it can be loaded into RAM.

3. Type **SERVER** and press Enter to load the NetWare operating system.

4. Load the disk driver from the DOS partition so the server can access the disk and see the NetWare partition and volumes.

5. Mount volume SYS and any other NetWare volumes so that file and bindery information can be cached into RAM for quicker access.

6. Load the LAN driver to activate the network board.

These steps start the NetWare file server. Each step, except for physically powering up the PC, can be automated using the computer's startup files and the file server's startup files.

Questions

1. THREE hardware components that are particularly important to a NetWare file server are the _____, the _____, and the _____.

   ☐ A. Microprocessor

   ☐ B. Printer

   ☐ C. Memory

   ☐ D. Hard disk

2. Which TWO of the following hardware components are exclusive to file servers and workstations and are not part of a standard PC?

   ☐ A. Network board

   ☐ B. Network cabling

   ☐ C. Microprocessor

   ☐ D. Hard disk

3. The minimum microprocessor required to run a NetWare 3.1x file server is_____.

   ○ A. Intel 80286

   ○ B. Intel 80386

   ○ C. Pentium

   ○ D. Motorola MC68000

4. Which of the following is NOT mandatory on a NetWare 3.1x file server?

   ○ A. A minimum of 4 MB of RAM

   ○ B. An Intel 80386 or higher microprocessor

   ○ C. A DOS partition on the file server's hard disk

   ○ D. A NetWare partition on each file server volume

5. You can use more than one hard disk on your NetWare file server as long as _____.

   ○ A. you install a DOS partition on each hard disk

   ○ B. all hard disks have a SYS volume

   ○ C. you do not install more than three hard disks on any one file server

   ○ D. the total hard disk space does not exceed 32 TB

6. The hardware responsible for the physical communication between the file server and network clients is the _____.

   ○ A. network board

   ○ B. LAN driver

   ○ C. hard disk

   ○ D. SYS volume

7. Installing more than one network board in a file server also makes it a network _____.

   ○ A. client

   ○ B. driver

   ○ C. router

   ○ D. workstation

8. The maximum number of Network boards that can be installed in a NetWare 3.1x file server is _____.

   ○ A. 8

   ○ B. 12

   ○ C. 16

   ○ D. 18

9. Which of the following is NOT considered a NetWare file server software component?

   ○ A. IPXODI.COM

   ○ B. SERVER.EXE

   ○ C. LAN driver

   ○ D. Disk driver

10. Which term best describes the primary function of the main NetWare operating system file?

    ○ A. Communication tool

    ○ B. Software bus

    ○ C. Connection driver

    ○ D. LAN driver

11. Of the following file-name extensions, which one is NOT a NetWare Loadable Module (NLM)?

    ○ A. NLM

    ○ B. NCF

    ○ C. NAM

    ○ D. LAN

12. Which TWO of the following are NOT NetWare file server startup files?

    ☐ A. AUTOEXEC.EXE

    ☐ B. AUTOEXEC.NCF

    ☐ C. CONFIG.NCF

    ☐ D. STARTUP.NCF

13. Which of the following statements is true?

    ○ A. SERVER.EXE is run after file server configuration files are run.

    ○ B. SERVER.EXE is run before STARTUP.NCF is run.

    ○ C. You can add SERVER.EXE as a line to the PC's CONFIG.SYS file to automate server startup.

    ○ D. STARTUP.NCF is stored in the SYS:SYSTEM directory.

14. Which TWO commands are used to customize server configuration files?

    ☐ A. LOAD

    ☐ B. SET

    ☐ C. INSTALL

    ☐ D. RUN

15. The SET command is NOT used to configure _____.

    ○ A. communications

    ○ B. memory

    ○ C. disk caching

    ○ D. installation

16. Which THREE NetWare utilities can you use to modify file server configuration files?

    ☐ A. SYSCON

    ☐ B. NAMESPACE

    ☐ C. INSTALL

    ☐ D. EDIT

17. Which TWO name-space NLMs must be purchased separately from NetWare 3.12 if you need to use them?

    ☐ A. NFS

    ☐ B. OS2

    ☐ C. MAC

    ☐ D. FTAM

18. Which of the following is NOT a name space the NetWare supports by loading a specific name-space module?

    ○ A. DOS

    ○ B. NFS

    ○ C. OS2

    ○ D. FTAM

19. The default frame type supported by NetWare 3.12 is _____.

    ○ A. Ethernet II

    ○ B. 802.2

    ○ C. 802.3

    ○ D. SNAP

20. The frame type that supports IPX but does not support TCP/IP is _____.

    ○ A. Ethernet II

    ○ B. 802.2

    ○ C. 802.3

    ○ D. SNAP

21. The Token-Ring frame type that supports AppleTalk is _____.

    ○ A. 802.2

    ○ B. 802.3

    ○ C. Token-Ring

    ○ D. SNAP

22. Which of the following protocols is NOT part of the NetWare protocol suite?

    ○ A. SAP

    ○ B. IPX

    ○ C. TCP/IP

    ○ D. Packet Burst

23. To install support for TCP/IP, you must load the _____ NLM at the NetWare file server console. Other related NLMs are loaded for you.

    ○ A. STREAMS

    ○ B. TCPIP

    ○ C. CLIB

    ○ D. TLI

24. Which TWO console commands must be used to provide name-space support on a NetWare 3.1x file server?

    ☐ A. ADD NAME SPACE TO

    ☐ B. LOAD

    ☐ C. INSTALL

    ☐ D. TRACK ON

25. Which of the following shows the correct order for starting a NetWare file server?

    ○ A. Boot DOS, load disk driver, load SERVER, mount SYS

    ○ B. Boot DOS, load SERVER, load LAN driver, mount SYS

    ○ C. Boot DOS, load SERVER, load disk driver, mount SYS, load LAN driver

    ○ D. Boot DOS, load LAN driver, load disk driver, load SERVER, mount SYS

Answers

1. A, C, D	14. A, B
2. A, B	15. D
3. B	16. A, C, D
4. C	17. A, D
5. D	18. A
6. A	19. B
7. C	20. C
8. C	21. D
9. A	22. C
10. B	23. B
11. B	24. A, B
12. A, C	25. C
13. B	

Understanding Memory and Performance in NetWare 3.1x Servers

The amount of system memory available to the NetWare 3.1x file server greatly affects its performance. To help ensure that the NetWare operating system has enough available memory, NetWare divides the available system memory into groups called memory pools. Each memory pool is set aside to be used in processing specific types of service requests, or for storing information about the status of a file server's resources.

NetWare file servers require a minimum of 4 MB of system memory, but can address as much as 4 GB of memory. This chapter discusses how NetWare 3.1x allocates and uses system memory, and the ways in which server performance is affected by NetWare's handling of system memory.

After reading this chapter, you will be able to do the following:

■ Understand how server memory works

■ Determine server memory requirements

■ Use memory-related console commands

■ Optimize performance using SET parameters

■ Understand how protocols affect performance

■ Semi-permanent

■ Alloc short term

■ Cache movable

■ Cache non-movable

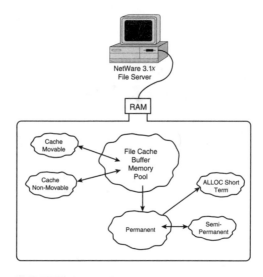

How Server Memory Works

If your file server's hard disk drive is no larger than 80 MB, the NetWare 3.1x operating system can function with as little as 4 MB of system memory. Larger hard disks require greater amounts of memory. To address and use this wide range of available system memory, the NetWare operating system divides that memory into groups that it refers to as memory pools.

Memory Pools

NetWare uses six pools, as shown in figure 9.1.

The six NetWare 3.1x memory pools include the following:

■ File cache buffer

■ Permanent

Figure 9.1

NetWare 3.1x memory pools.

Each memory pool has its own features, content, and method of using resources. Table 9.1 provides a comparison of some of the information related to these six memory pools.

Table 9.1
Comparison of NetWare 3.1x Memory Pools

Memory Pool	Features	Resource Use
File cache buffer	Takes all free memory when the server boots	Lends buffers to NLMs
		Allocates enough memory to cache volume's entire FAT
	It is the memory pool from which other pools draw	
		Caches portions of volume's DET
	Cache files that users are accessing	
		Uses buffers to build a directory name Hashing table
		Uses buffers to build Turbo FAT indexes for all open, randomly-accessed files
Permanent	Used as memory source for semi-permanent and alloc pools	Used by the NetWare operating system to store long-term information such as permanent tables, directory cache buffers, and packet receive buffers
Semi-permanent	Subdivision of the permanent memory pool	Used by LAN drivers and disk drivers
	Used for limited memory needs	
Alloc short term	Supplies short term memory needs	Used by utilities with pop-up window
	Also called *alloc memory*	Stores information related to: Mappings & connections Service requests
		Open/locked files
	Released memory is returned to this memory pool	Service advertising Broadcast messages NLM and Queue manager tables

continues

Table 9.1, Continued
Comparison of NetWare 3.1*x* Memory Pools

Memory Pool	Features	Resource Use
Cache movable	Gets its memory from file cache buffer pool	Used by FAT, Hash, and other system tables
	Also called *movable memory*	
	Its memory space is moved around to optimize memory	
	Returns unused memory to file cache buffer pool	
Cache non-movable	Used for loading modules into memory	Lists memory buffers temporarily assigned
	Handles large memory buffers	
	Does not move memory	
	Returns released memory to file cache buffer pool	

NetWare File Server Memory Components

Memory pools are NetWare's way of dividing and allocating available memory, which is used to manage NetWare's three major file server memory components, which follow:

- Cache buffers
- Tables
- Disk blocks

Cache Buffers

Cache buffers are areas of RAM where the most frequently accessed files are stored. NetWare's file cache buffer memory pool is used to accommodate the RAM requirements of cache buffers, of which there are three types:

- File cache buffers
- Directory cache buffers
- Packet receive buffers

File cache buffers are the primary type of cache buffer and the main portion of the file cache buffer pool. They are temporary storage areas for files—or portions of files—users need.

File cache buffers temporarily store files that have been read from the hard disk. When a user requests a file, the file is read from the hard disk and stored in a file cache buffer. Future requests by the user to read this file then can be fulfilled from the file cache buffer rather than the hard disk.

 • Note   File cache buffers make it possible for files to be read as much as 100 times faster than when read from disk.

File cache buffers also temporarily store files that have been modified by the user, but have not yet been written back to the hard disk. When the file cache buffers contain such modified files, the file cache buffers are called *dirty cache buffers.*

All user requests for files are serviced from the file cache buffers, which means that anytime a user requests a file, the server first checks the cache to determine whether the file is already there. If it is, the server provides the requested file. If the file is not already stored in a file cache buffer, the server checks the disk for the file. When the file is found, the server stores a copy in the file cache buffer, and then it provides a copy to the user's client (workstation).

Directory cache buffers are also a portion of server memory. Rather than hold files, however, directory cache buffers store directory table information.

Packet receive buffers temporarily hold packets as they are received from network clients. Once the file server is free to process and route the received packet, it retrieves the packet from the packet receive buffer and processes it as needed. Packet receive buffers are particularly useful when

network traffic and file server processing is heavy. Packets received when the server is too busy to immediately process them would be lost without a packet receive buffer temporary storage area.

Tables

Tables are used to find files stored on the hard disk and to track properties of those files. There are two types of tables:

■ Directory tables

■ File allocation tables

Directory tables are located on each volume, and they contain information related to the files, directories, and trustees (if appropriate) used by NetWare file server clients.

Directory tables contain various items of information (see fig. 9.2). The following are the two main categories of information:

■ Name-space information

■ Directory-related information

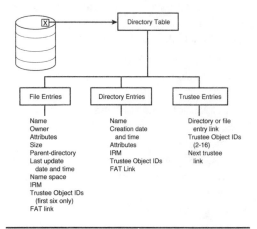

Figure 9.2
Directory table entry information.

Because of the increase in table entry size required for non-DOS name spaces, adding a name space to a NetWare volume requires that there be at least 10 MB of available disk space.

Disk Blocks

To store information on a disk, the disk first must be divided logically into storage areas called *disk blocks*. Disk blocks can be allocated in different sizes—4, 8, 16, 32, and 64 KB blocks are common sizes. Two types of blocks are created when a disk is divided:

- Disk allocation blocks
- Directory table blocks

Disk allocation blocks are used to store files. NetWare's default disk allocation block is 4 KB. If a file to be stored on a NetWare volume is larger than 4 KB, several disk allocation blocks can be used to store it.

 When multiple blocks are used to store a file, each block contains a link to the preceding and the following block. The FAT tracks the links, subsequently keeping track of which blocks contain all the pieces of any given file.

Directory table blocks are always set at the smallest block size—4 KB. Each 4 KB directory table block can contain up to 32 entries. Each entry can be as large as 128 bytes. Each NetWare volume can contain up to 65,536 directory entry blocks. Therefore, the maximum number of directory table entries per volume can be 2,097,152:

$$65,536 \times 32 = 2,097,152$$

To allow as much room on the disk as possible for use by files, NetWare initially allocates only six directory table blocks. If more directory table blocks are needed, NetWare allocates them one at a time.

NetWare Server Memory

Various aspects of the NetWare file server must have some server memory allocated to them. How well memory is allocated can affect how efficiently your NetWare file server performs.

 NetWare helps ensure that memory is allocated adequately because it can dynamically allocate needed memory. You must, however, make some decisions regarding memory as a NetWare administrator.

Your first decision relates to the loading of two specific NetWare resources, which follow:

- NLMs
- Name spaces

Your second decision, discussed in the following section, relates to calculating how much memory your file server must have to function.

NetWare Loadable Modules return memory to the pool once they are done using it. But you still need to know approximately how much memory you need to load and run the NLMs you want on your NetWare server.

When determining how much memory your NetWare server will need for NLMs, consider the following:

■ What other NLMs must be loaded when you load the specific NLM you have chosen? When you load the SBACKUP NLM, for example, you also must load the appropriate TSA NLM. You need to take into consideration how much memory all the related NLMs require.

■ Whether a particular NLM will require additional memory to run.

When adding name-space support to a NetWare volume, consider the following:

■ Extra cache memory will be needed to accommodate the increase in directory table information and size.

■ Partially due to its two forks (data and resource), Macintosh name-space support requires more memory than any other name space.

Determining Server Memory Requirements

Because of all the variables that go into the use of NetWare file server memory, it is important that you make sure your file server has sufficient memory to function. NetWare 3.1x's minimum memory requirement of 4 MB is a good place to start. However, 4 MB is only enough to operate a NetWare file server using the minimum configuration. If you want your NetWare file server to function at its peak efficiency, you must determine how much memory is required for it to do so, and then ensure that an adequate amount of memory—or more—is provided.

Before you can determine the memory requirement for your NetWare 3.1x file server, you must have a good idea of the functions and services it must provide your network users. Once you understand what is needed from the network, you can calculate the memory requirements for each of your file servers.

Before attempting to calculate the memory requirements for each NetWare file server, consider the following variables:

■ NetWare 3.1x's minimum memory requirement of 4 MB

■ Which NLMs will be loaded on the file server

■ Size of each file server hard disk

■ Size of each volume on the file server

■ Block size used (4, 8, 16, 32, or 64 KB)

■ Anticipated maximum number of entries in each volume's directory table

■ Number of file and directory cache buffers allocated for caching

To calculate each file server's total memory requirements, use the following information and formulas:

1. Calculate memory requirements for each *DOS volume* (a volume without name space loaded), using the following instructions:

    1a) Calculate the total MB of space on all of the file server's DOS volumes:

    Size (in MB) of 1st DOS volume

    + Size (in MB) of 2nd DOS volume

    + Size (in MB) of all other DOS volumes
    _____

    Total MB of DOS volume space

If the DOS volumes on your NetWare file server have not been set up so that the disk allocation block is the same for each volume (all configured to 4 MB or all configured to 8 MB, and so forth), do not add the space on each volume to get a total DOS volume space. Rather, multiply each DOS volume's space separately against the factor (.023) shown in the following step:

1b) Multiply the total MB DOS volume space by a factor of .023:

Total (MB) DOS volume space
.023 (2.3%)
⎯⎯⎯⎯⎯⎯⎯⎯⎯⎯⎯⎯⎯⎯⎯
Total DOS volume space

1c) Divide the total DOS volume space by the disk allocation block size of the volume(s). The default is 4 KB on NetWare 3.1x file servers and is the size used in the following example:

Total DOS volume space
÷ 4 KB DOS volume block size
⎯⎯⎯⎯⎯⎯⎯⎯⎯⎯⎯⎯⎯⎯⎯
Total memory required for DOS volumes

Novell shows this step (for DOS volumes) as the following formula:

Memory (M) = .023 × volume size (in MB) ÷ block size

2. Calculate memory requirements for each *non-DOS volume* (a volume *with* name space loaded), using the following instructions:

2a) Calculate the total MB of space on all the file server's non-DOS volumes:

Size (in MB) of 1st non-DOS volume
+ Size (in MB) of 2nd non-DOS volume
+ Size (in MB) of all other non-DOS volumes
⎯⎯⎯⎯⎯⎯⎯⎯⎯⎯⎯⎯⎯⎯⎯
Total MB of non-DOS volume space

If the non-DOS volumes on your NetWare file server have not been set up so that the disk allocation block is the same for each volume (all configured to 4 MB or all configured to 8 MB, and so forth), do not add the space on each volume to get a total non-DOS volume space. Rather, multiply each non-DOS volume's space separately against the factor (.032) shown in the following step:

2b) Multiply the total MB non-DOS volume space by a factor of .032:

Total (MB) non-DOS volume space
× .032 (3.2%)
⎯⎯⎯⎯⎯⎯⎯⎯⎯⎯⎯⎯⎯⎯⎯
Total non-DOS volume space

2c) Divide the total non-DOS volume space by the disk allocation block size of the volume(s). The default is 4 KB on NetWare 3.1x file servers, and is the size used in the following example:

Total non-DOS volume space
÷ 4 KB non-DOS volume block size
⎯⎯⎯⎯⎯⎯⎯⎯⎯⎯⎯⎯⎯⎯⎯
Total memory required for non-DOS volumes

Novell shows this step (for non-DOS volumes) as the following formula:

Memory (M) = .032 × volume size (in MB) ÷ block size

3. Calculate the total file server memory requirements according to the following instructions:

   3a) Add the total memory required for DOS volumes to that required for non-DOS volumes:

   Total memory required for DOS volumes

   + Total memory required for non-DOS volumes

   _____

   Total memory required for all volumes

Novell shows this step (for adding DOS and non-DOS volume memory together) as the following formula:

Total Volume Memory (M) = $M_{DOSvol1}$ + $M_{DOSvol2}$ + $M_{notDOSvol}$

   3b) Now add 2 MB of memory to the total memory required for all volumes (total volume memory):

   Total volume memory

   + 2 MB

   _____

   Total file server memory required (rounded to next highest MB)

Novell shows this step (for calculating the total file server memory required) as the following formula:

2 MB + Total Volume Memory = Total MB (rounded to higher)

After NetWare 3.1x is installed, you can view memory usage information by using the MONITOR console utility (see fig. 9.3).

The MONITOR console utility provides information about the file server, including that which affects memory usage, such as the following:

■ **Original cache buffers.** Number of buffers you originally assigned for caching purposes.

■ **Total cache buffers.** Number of buffers available for caching files. Each time you LOAD an NLM, this number decreases.

■ **Dirty cache buffers.** Number of buffers currently in use. If this number is consistently close to the number of total cache buffers, you might need to increase the number of cache buffers for this file server. You might need to add more memory to this file server to add more cache buffers.

■ **Packet receive buffers.** Number of buffers set aside to provide temporary storage to network packets as they arrive at the file server.

```
NetWare v3.12 (250 user) - 11/11/94          NetWare 386 Loadable Module

                        Information For Server Michael

    File Server Up Time:   14 Days  4 Hours 40 Minutes 45 Seconds
    Utilization:              17       Packet Receive Buffers:   400
    Original Cache Buffers: 3,590      Directory Cache Buffers:   21
    Total Cache Buffers:    1,865      Service Processes:          3
    Dirty Cache Buffers:        0      Connections In Use:         2
    Current Disk Requests:      0      Open Files:                38
```

Figure 9.3

The MONITOR console utility showing file server information.

- **Directory cache buffers.** Number of buffers set aside to handle directory caching. Remember when assigning the maximum number of directory cache buffers that the more directory cache buffers you allow the operating system to assign, the fewer buffers there will be available for file caching. Careful balance between the two is important to the efficient operation of your file server.

Using Memory-Related Console Commands

The MONITOR console utility enables you to see a great deal of information about your NetWare file server. It is not, however, the only utility related to NetWare file server memory. In addition to the MONITOR console utility, there are two other console commands you can use to manage your NetWare 3.1x file server's memory.

The two NetWare file server console commands related to memory follow:

- MEMORY

- REGISTER MEMORY

These commands are discussed in the following sections.

The MEMORY Console Command

You use the MEMORY console command to see information about the total amount of addressable memory installed in your NetWare 3.1x file server.

After you type **MEMORY** at the file server console and press Enter, a display similar to the following appears:

```
Total server memory: 8,831 Kilobytes
```

By default, NetWare 3.1x automatically can address up to 16 MB of memory if the file server uses an *Enhanced Industry Standard Architecture* (EISA) bus. If the file server uses an *Industry Standard Architecture* (ISA) or microchannel bus, 3.1x can address memory above 16 MB, if it is configured to do so, by using the REGISTER MEMORY command.

 Note If your NetWare 3.1x file server has an AT bus disk adapter or network board installed, and it uses *Direct Memory Access* (DMA) or bus mastering, the file server cannot address memory above 16 MB. In this case, to prevent problems on your file server, you must enter the following SET parameter into the file server's STARTUP.NCF file:

```
Auto Register Memory Above 16 Megabytes=OFF
```

This SET parameter cannot be entered at the console prompt or in the AUTOEXEC.NCF file. To activate this set parameter from the STARTUP.NCF file, reboot the file server.

The REGISTER MEMORY Console Command

When you know you have more than 16 MB of memory in your file server, but the NetWare operating system is not recognizing that additional memory, you should suspect one of two conditions:

- Your NetWare 3.1*x* file server has an AT bus disk adapter or network board installed that uses DMA or bus mastering.

- You have not yet registered that additional memory with the NetWare operating system.

To register the additional memory with the NetWare 3.1*x* operating system, place the following console command in the file server's AUTOEXEC.NCF:

```
REGISTER MEMORY start length
```

Replace *start* with the hexadecimal number that represents the starting address of the additional memory. The usual address is 0×1,000,000, which equals 16 MB.

Replace *length* with the hexadecimal value that represents the end of the additional memory. If you have 24 MB of total memory installed in your NetWare file server, for example, you would use the following command:

```
REGISTER MEMORY 0×1000000 800000
```

 Note The *length* field must contain a hexadecimal number that is divisible by 10h×10. If you don't know the hexadecimal number for the amount of memory installed in your file server, you can find a chart listing start and length values for standard computers in Novell's NetWare 3.12 *System Administration* manual.

To place the REGISTER MEMORY command into the file server's AUTOEXEC.NCF file, you can use the SYSCON utility. As figure 9.4 shows, this command must be placed after the lines that provide the file server's name and its IPX internal network number.

Obviously, it is important that your NetWare file server be capable of accessing all the memory installed in it. It's also important that you are able to monitor and manage the file server's memory. Part of monitoring and managing your NetWare file server, including its memory, is setting parameters that optimize your NetWare 3.1*x* file server's performance. Various SET parameters can help you optimize your 3.1*x* file server's resources.

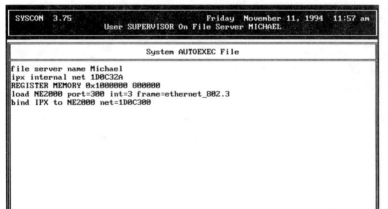

Figure 9.4
The REGISTER MEMORY command in the AUTOEXEC.NCF file.

Optimizing Performance Using SET Parameters

In addition to the MONITOR console utility and the two console commands used to manage the 3.1x file server's memory, there also are several SET parameters you can use. The SET AUTO REGISTER MEMORY ABOVE 16 MEGABYTES=OFF is just one of them.

The categories of other SET parameters include the following:

- Communications
- Memory
- File caching
- Directory caching
- Miscellaneous

The SET parameters engaged, coupled with how they interact with other SET parameters, can result in unexpected file server performance. Therefore, before learning which SET parameters can be used to optimize a NetWare 3.1x file server's performance, it is useful to understand just how SET parameters interact.

The 3.1x operating system is designed to configure dynamically many of its performance factors so that its performance is optimized by default. The key operating system functions NetWare dynamically optimizes include the following:

- The number of service processes it needs to handle disk reads and writes

- The number of packet receive buffers it allocates (up to the configured maximum) to handle all incoming packets

- The number of directory cache buffers (up to the configured maximum) it needs to cache as many of the directory information requests that it receives as possible

Although you can configure many SET parameters, some of the more important ones follow:

- Maximum physical receive packet size
- Maximum packet receive buffers
- Minimum packet receive buffers
- Maximum alloc short term memory
- Cache buffer size
- Minimum file cache buffers
- Maximum concurrent disk cache writes
- Immediate purge of deleted files
- Maximum directory cache buffers
- Minimum directory cache buffers
- Maximum service processes

Table 9.2 lists each of these SET parameters, reveals suggested or default settings for these parameters, and provides a brief summary of how changing each parameter might alter the performance of your NetWare 3.1x file server. Also note in the table that those parameters that must be set in the STARTUP.NCF file are shown in a **bold** typeface.

Table 9.2
SET Parameters That Affect File Server Performance

Parameter	Suggested or Default Setting	Performance Summary/Suggestions
MAXIMUM PHYSICAL RECEIVE PACKET SIZE	Token Ring=4204 Ethernet=1514 Range=618–24682	Set only to actual size of largest packet to prevent wasted buffer space
MAXIMUM PACKET RECEIVE BUFFERS	Default=400 Range=50–2000	Increase to prevent sudden peak usage, but impacts permanent memory pool
MINIMUM PACKET RECEIVE BUFFERS	Default=100 Range=10–1000	Increase to improve server response time
MAXIMUM ALLOC SHORT TERM MEMORY	Default=8 MB (8388608) Range=50000–33554432	Increase if server cannot do assigned tasks because pool is at its limit
CACHE BUFFER SIZE	Default=4096 bytes Options=4096, 8192, and 16384	Increase to improve server performance if block sizes are more than 4 KB, but optimum is buffer=block size
MINIMUM FILE CACHE BUFFERS	Default=20 Range=20–1000	Lower if too high a setting limits NLM loading due to insufficient memory
MAXIMUM CONCURRENT DISK CACHE WRITES	Default=50 Range=10–1000	Increase if a write-intensive network, decrease if a read-intensive network
IMMEDIATE PURGE OF DELETED FILES	Default=ON	Change to OFF to reduce server activity and enable salvage feature
MAXIMUM DIRECTORY CACHE BUFFERS	Default=500 Range=20–4000	Increase to speed up directory searches, or reduce to save memory
MINIMUM DIRECTORY CACHE BUFFERS	Default=20 Range=10–2000	Increase if MONITOR shows 100% or more, or if directory searches are slow
MAXIMUM SERVICE PROCESSES	Default=20 Range=5–40	Increase to fix low memory temporarily, until you can add more file server memory

SET parameters are not alone in affecting the NetWare 3.1x file server's performance. Some protocols are capable as well.

How Protocols Affect Performance

Two protocols NetWare 3.1x includes can have an important impact on your NetWare file server:

- Large Internet Packet (LIP)

- Packet Burst

LIP

The LIP protocol is active, by default, at both the NetWare 3.12 file server and the client. You can disable LIP if you choose to do so. To disable LIP, enter the following command at the file server console:

```
SET ALLOW LIP=OFF
```

Although you can disable LIP, leaving LIP enabled provides enhanced network performance whenever packets must be sent across *network routers* (a file server, dedicated computer, or a workstation that contains multiple network boards of different topologies).

Some routers have difficulty handling packet sizes larger than 576 bytes (512 bytes of data plus 64 bytes of header information). Because some routers can handle larger packet sizes, however, LIP enables larger packet sizes to be sent across routers, as long as both the server and the client agree to the negotiated larger packet size. The maximum size of a packet depends on what the file server can accommodate. This information may be hardcoded into the router, in which case, LIP has no effect.

Figure 9.5 shows the logic of LIP in a NetWare 3.12 network.

Figure 9.5
The logic of LIP.

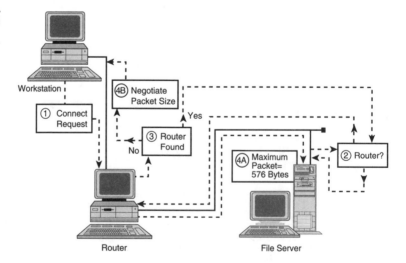

Packet Burst

The Packet Burst protocol also affects the performance of the NetWare file server because it expedites the transfer of read-and-write *NetWare Core Protocol* (NCP) packet requests. By default, Packet Burst is enabled at NetWare 3.12 file servers. If the client requesting NetWare services is not capable of taking advantage of the Packet Burst protocol, the NetWare file server communicates with the client on a one-on-one request/response basis.

Packet Burst improves network performance because it does the following:

- Reduces network traffic by not requiring that each individual packet be sequenced and acknowledged

- Monitors the network for dropped packets and retransmits only those that were dropped

Questions

1. The type of memory pool used by a pop-up window such as the MONITOR utility is called _____.

   ○ A. file cache buffer memory

   ○ B. permanent memory

   ○ C. semi-permanent memory

   ○ D. alloc short term memory

2. LAN drivers and disk drivers are stored in the _____ memory pool.

   ○ A. file cache buffer

   ○ B. permanent

   ○ C. semi-permanent

   ○ D. alloc short term

3. A network packet that CANNOT be processed immediately would be stored temporarily in the file server's _____ memory pool.

   ○ A. file cache buffer

   ○ B. permanent

   ○ C. semi-permanent

   ○ D. alloc short term

4. Which memory pool CANNOT be used by NetWare Loadable Modules?

   ○ A. File cache buffer memory

   ○ B. Permanent memory

   ○ C. Semi-permanent memory

   ○ D. Alloc short term memory

5. All other memory pools obtain additional memory from the _____ pool.

   ○ A. file cache buffer memory

   ○ B. permanent memory

   ○ C. semi-permanent

   ○ D. alloc short term

6. Which of the following is NOT a major NetWare 3.1x file server memory component?

   ○ A. Cache buffers

   ○ B. ROM

   ○ C. Tables

   ○ D. Disk blocks

7. Areas of RAM where the most frequently accessed files are stored are known as _____.

   ○ A. cache buffers

   ○ B. ROM

   ○ C. tables

   ○ D. disk blocks

8. NetWare 3.1x finds files that have been stored on the hard disk by checking its _____.

   ○ A. Cache buffers

   ○ B. ROM

   ○ C. Tables

   ○ D. Disk blocks

9. The logical storage areas on the disk used to store files are called _____.

   ○ A. cache buffers

   ○ B. ROM

   ○ C. tables

   ○ D. disk blocks

11. The primary type of cache buffer is called the _____.

   ○ A. file cache buffer

   ○ B. directory cache buffer

   ○ C. packet receive buffer

   ○ D. dirty cache buffer

12. The cache buffer that temporarily stores files that have been read from, or are being written back to, the hard disk is called the _____.

   ○ A. file cache buffer

   ○ B. directory cache buffer

   ○ C. packet receive buffer

   ○ D. dirty cache buffer

13. Where in memory is directory table information stored?

   ○ A. Directory entry table

   ○ B. File allocation table

   ○ C. Packet receive buffer

   ○ D. Directory cache buffer

14. Buffers that hold service requests yet to be processed are _____.

   ○ A. file cache buffers

   ○ B. directory cache buffers

   ○ C. packet receive buffers

   ○ D. dirty cache buffers

15. Buffers that hold files not yet written back are called _____.

   ○ A. file cache buffers

   ○ B. directory cache buffers

   ○ C. packet receive buffers

   ○ D. dirty cache buffers

Answers

1. D		9. D	
2. C		10. A	
3. B		11. A	
4. B		12. D	
5. A		13. D	
6. B		14. C	
7. A		15. D	
8. C			

Working with NetWare 3.1x Clients

ile servers are a key component in any network. Another key component is the client *(a workstation using appropriate NetWare software in order to access and use resources on the network). NetWare 3.12 networks can include several types of clients, such as DOS, Apple Macintosh, Unix, IBM OS/2, and Microsoft Windows. Regardless of the type of client you use, your ultimate goal is to gain access to the network so you can utilize the resources it provides.*

As a network administrator, you are responsible for ensuring that each network client can connect to and access resources on the network. The better you understand the design and abilities of 3.1x client software, the easier it is for you to install, update, and maintain your network clients.

Although different client types can access a NetWare network, the most common types include DOS and Microsoft Windows clients. This chapter explains what you need to know about DOS and Windows clients in order to successfully install, update, and maintain them.

After reading this chapter, you will be able to:

■ Understand the ODI environment

■ Install and update client workstations

■ Work with the NetWare DOS Requester

■ Support read-only and diskless network devices

The ODI Environment

One area of network management that is often the source of major problems is client administration. Although a NetWare network might only have several NetWare file servers to maintain, it may have several hundred clients, many of which you might be responsible for managing. Even if you do not have total responsibility for client management, you may at least be responsible for setting up the client environment and making sure that it functions correctly.

On a NetWare 3.1x network, DOS and Windows clients follow the *Open Data-Link Interface*. ODI was chosen for 3.1x networks because it supports several protocols as well as multiple LAN drivers on 3.1x file servers.

ODI is one of two major client pieces that you enable at each network client to provide communication between the client and the network. The other major client piece is the NetWare DOS Requester.

 NetWare 3.1x clients use ODI communication and connection files. If the NetWare client also supports Windows, then additional Windows-related files must also be used on the client, and can be updated using WSUPDATE. The 3.1x DOS-based client, moreover, needs to have the NetWare DOS Requester loaded in order to access NetWare network resources.

Understanding both the NetWare DOS Requester and the architecture and related files of ODI makes it easier to set up and upgrade 3.1x network clients. Because ODI provides the model to which other client pieces belong, ODI is discussed here first.

ODI implements the *Open System Interconnection* (OSI) model. The OSI model was designed to provide companies with guidance and direction when developing methods of network communication, by establishing recommendations to be followed during development.

OSI defines seven layers (see fig. 10.1). At each layer, the procedure that should be followed in order for one computer to send information or requests across the network to another computer is defined. These definitions help developers see what particular processes should take place at any given point in the model. How those processes occur is up to the developer.

| Application |
| Presentation |
| Session |
| Transport |
| Network |
| Data Link |
| Physical |

Figure 10.1
The OSI reference model.

As you can see from figure 10.1, the name of each OSI layer is based on the primary function for which the layer provides development guidelines.

- **Application.** Provides the communication interface between network applications and lower-layer protocols.

- **Presentation.** Provides rules for encoding data so it can be successfully communicated between unlike computers.

- **Session.** Provides a type of fault tolerance by ensuring that all activities related to a transaction are complete before the transaction is passed on to the next layer.

- **Transport.** Provides a variety of transport services such as error recovery and reliability.

- **Network.** Provides both connection-oriented and connectionless network services.

- **Data Link.** Provides logical link control defined by various standards including IEEE 802.2, 802.4, and others.

- **Physical.** Provides local area network standards that include the physical layer components of three IEEE standards—802.3, 802.4, and 802.5.

ODI implements the OSI reference model, choosing modules to implement that fill the particular communication need at various places in the communication process.

The ODI method of implementing OSI provides the following benefits:

- Allows for maximum flexibility of the network

- Makes client/server connections primarily transparent to the user

- Requires no additional investment in network equipment

- Supports multiple LAN drivers on each NetWare 3.1x file server and client

- Supports multiple protocols on each NetWare 3.1x file server and client, including—but not limited to—IPX/SPX, TCP/IP, AppleTalk, OSI TP4, and DEC LAT

In some instances, the software that implements the OSI reference model is directly related, layer for layer, to the model itself. For example, the Network Board (also referred to as the *Network Interface Card* or NIC) is an implementation of the Physical layer of the OSI model. In addition, IPX (the communication protocol that Novell uses to send data packets between clients and servers) is an implementation of the network layer.

Other software that NetWare uses to implement the OSI reference model includes the Link Support Layer (LSL) and the Multiple Link Interface Driver (MLID). The LSL and MLID software are an implementation of the OSI model's data link layer (see fig. 10.2).

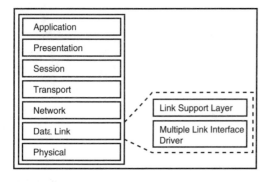

Figure 10.2

Software implementation of OSI layers.

The link support layer, implemented by means of LSL.COM, links the network board to the appropriate MLID. This link ensures that each packet is routed through the appropriate *protocol stack* (a group of communication protocols that establish the rules of communication across the network and which is used above the data link layer of the OSI Reference model). The LSL acts like a switchboard, routing network packets to their correct destination.

The MLID is somewhat less independent in its handling of network packets than the LSL, although its function is no less important. MLIDs are LAN driver files, such as NE3200.COM, that copy specific identification information about an incoming packet, and send that information along with the packet to the LSL. When a packet is being sent out of the file server, the MLID copies the needed packet identification information into the packet and sends it out to the network (see fig. 10.3).

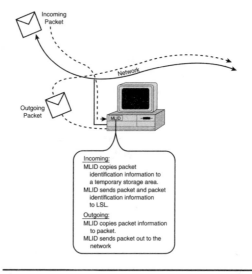

Figure 10.3

Functions of the MLID.

Other software required for connection to the network includes the protocol stack files. The makeup of the protocol stacks depends on the types of protocols used on the network.

A network using IPX, for example, would include the IPX protocol stack, which is implemented on a NetWare 3.1x client by loading the IPXODI.COM file.

Before a client can load the IPXODI.COM and other communication and control files, the client must have those files installed and any related files updated.

Installing and Updating Client Workstations

When you install or update a network client, several files are either copied to the client or modified. What occurs depends at least in part on whether or not the network client requires Windows support.

Installing Client Workstations

When you install client workstation files on a client that uses Windows, two processes occur.

First, two sets of files are copied to the client's hard disk, as shown in table 10.1. One set of files is copied to the \WINDOWS\SYSTEM directory. The second set is copied to the \WINDOWS directory.

Table 10.1
Microsoft Windows Files Affected During Client Installation

Directory Where File's Installed	Name of File	Function/Purpose of File
\WINDOWS	ET.INI	Initializes Novell's ElectroText (Electronic Documentation) file
\WINDOWS\SYSTEM	NETWARE.DRV	Allows access to the NetWare network from an MS Windows application
\WINDOWS\SYSTEM	NETWARE.HLP	Provides help for clients running MS Windows
\WINDOWS	NETWARE.INI	Provides configuration information to customize the MS Windows driver
\WINDOWS	NWADMIN.INI	Sets MS Windows user tools options
\WINDOWS\SYSTEM	NWPOPUP.EXE	Displays network-related messages inside MS Windows applications
\WINDOWS	NWUSER.EXE	Loads the MS Windows NetWare User Tools
\WINDOWS	NWUTILS.GRP	Provides access to the NWUSER group in the MS Windows Program Manager
\WINDOWS\SYSTEM	VIPX.386	Lets users run DOS-based applications from within Enhanced Mode MS Windows
\WINDOWS\SYSTEM	VNETWARE.386	Works with NETWARE.DRV and NWPOPUP.EXE to show broadcast messages

The second process that occurs when you install the NetWare 3.1x networking files on the client involves several changes made to the following three Microsoft Windows configuration files:

- PROGMAN.INI

- SYSTEM.INI

- WIN.INI

The PROGMAN.INI Windows configuration file is changed to include an additional entry under the [Groups] section. This entry specifies the group number and sets the path to the executable NWUSER file. Figure 10.4 shows a PROGMAN.INI file with the related group information in bold.

```
[Settings]
Window=66 29 578 365 3
display.drv=qvision8.drv
Order= 10 6 19 14 3 1 17 9 7 11 4 15 8 13 18 12 2 20 5
SaveSettings=1
AutoArrange=1
MinOnRun=0

[Groups]
Group1=C:\WINDOWS\MAIN.GRP
Group2=C:\WINDOWS\ACCESSOR.GRP
Group3=C:\WINDOWS\NAUTILUS.GRP
Group4=C:\WINDOWS\STARTUP.GRP
Group5=C:\WINDOWS\APPLICAT.GRP
Group6=C:\WINDOWS\NWUSER.EXE
¤
```

Figure 10.4
Sample PROGMAN.INI file.

The SYSTEM.INI Windows configuration file is changed to include entries under three categories. The affected categories and their related changes are shown as bolded entries in figure 10.5.

```
[boot]
network.drv=netware.drv
taskman.exe=C:\WINDOWS\TASKMGR.EXE
mouse.drv=lmouse.drv
language.dll=English
keyboard.drv=keyboard.drv
system.drv=atrnsys.drv

[keyboard]
type=4

[boot.description]
network.drv=NetWare.drv
keyboard.typ=Enhanced 101 or 102 key US and Non US keyboards
mouse.drv=Logitech
language.dll=English (American)
system.drv=MS-DOS System
codepage=437
display.drv=COMPAQ QVision, 640x480x256, sm. res.

[386Enh]
network=*vnetbios,vnetware.386,vipx.386
TimerCriticalSection=10000
OverlappedIO=off
device=fastback.386
32BitDiskAccess=OFF
```

Figure 10.5
Sample SYSTEM.INI file.

The WIN.INI MS Windows configuration file is changed to include an entry that loads the NWPOPUP.EXE file, as shown in bold characters in figure 10.6.

After the initial installation of client files, updates to these files may be periodically released by Novell. Updates should be implemented on your NetWare 3.1x file servers as soon as possible.

```
[windows]
spooler=yes
load=nwpopup.exe
Beep=yes
NullPort=None
BorderWidth=3
CursorBlinkRate=530
DoubleClickSpeed=452
Programs=com exe bat pif
Documents=
DeviceNotSelectedTimeout=15
TransmissionRetryTimeout=45
KeyboardDelay=2
KeyboardSpeed=31
ScreenSaveActive=1
ScreenSaveTimeOut=480
DosPrint=no
NetWarn=0
CoolSwitch=1
DefaultQueueSize=32
PrinterSetup=1
device=HP LaserJet IIIP PostScript,pscript,LPT1:

[Desktop]
Pattern=116 84 84 84 84 84 84 92
Wallpaper=butterly.bmp
```

Figure 10.6
Sample WIN.INI file.

Updating Client Workstations

You can update client files by running WSUPDATE from the DOS command line at the network client. WSUPDATE.EXE is, however, located on the NetWare file server, not the client. Therefore, you must be logged in to the NetWare 3.1x file server to run WSUPDATE.

You can automate client file updating by placing the WSUPDATE command and associated parameters into a file server's system login script. Using this method updates each client's files at the time the user logs in to the network. Because you only have to initiate the update once (at the login stage instead of with each client), the possibility for error is reduced considerably.

Automating client file updating is more efficient than physically moving from client to client, logging in, and running WSUPDATE from the client. You should, however, use great care when placing this command in the system login script, as different types of network clients often use different types of files.

 Note Although WSUPDATE is primarily used for updating client files, you can also use it to update files on other NetWare servers by using the /ALL option with it, as described later.

To use WSUPDATE for updating files, use the following syntax:

`WSUPDATE[source_path][destination_path][/options]`

Replace *source_path* with the full path and filename of the most current version of the file being used for updating other copies of this file. To make it possible for users to access this file, copy it into the SYS:PUBLIC directory, particularly if you are going to automate the update using the system login script.

Replace *destination_path* with only the predefined drive letter (do not specify a directory) followed by a colon and the name of the file being updated. If you want to specify a local drive, use ALL or ALL_LOCAL in place of the *destination_path* just described. Using ALL searches all network drives. Using ALL LOCAL searches all local drives.

Replace */options* with one or more option parameters, preceding each one you use with a slash (/). Available option parameters and additional details about the syntax for the WSUPDATE utility are shown in figure 10.7.

Figure 10.7
WSUPDATE
Help screen.

```
Usage: WSUPDATE [/F=<InFile>|<SourcePath>] <DestDrive:DestFile> [/option...]]
       /F=<InFile> - specify a configuration file or
        SourcePath - file to update
       DestDrive = <drive letter:> | ALL: | ALL_LOCAL:
       DestFile - the name of the file to update (optional)
       [/[C]opy over old | /[R]ename old]
       /[S]ubdirectory - scan all subdirectories
       /read-[O]nly - update read-only files
       /[L]logfile=filename - create a log file called filename
       /[N]ew file - create <DestFile>,<DestFile> must be full destination path
        with file name
       /[V] [=<drive letter>] - update config.sys with LASTDRIVE=Z
        use <drive letter> for boot drive if not C.
```

The options available for WSUPDATE include:

■ Search options:

/ALL or **/ALL_LOCAL.** Searches all network drives, or all local drives

/S. Searches for the files to be updated in all subdirectories of the *destination_path*

■ File update options:

/O. Updates all files, even those flagged as Read-Only

/C or **/R.** Use these options to **C**opy the new file over the old file without saving a backup of the old file, or to first **R**ename the old file

■ Destination options:

/F=[path/file]. Directs the WSUPDATE command to a file containing required WSUPDATE options so that no options used with this command are run

/L=[path/file]. Directs the WSUPDATE command to the appropriate path for recording its operations in a log file

/N. Creates a new file and path if one does not already exist

■ Other options:

/V=[<drive letter>]. Adds the LASTDRIVE= command to the CONFIG.SYS file (replaces <drive letter> with the actual last drive letter, usually the letter Z)

■ Help:

/?. Use this option to get help information online

The support of clients running Windows by installing or updating the client files is important for those clients. Regardless of whether or not the DOS client uses MS Windows, the DOS client requires the NetWare DOS Requester in order to access the 3.1x network.

Working with the NetWare DOS Requester

In addition to the communication and connection files previously discussed, DOS clients need other files in order to establish communication with network devices. These files are collectively referred to as the *NetWare DOS Requester*.

The NetWare DOS Requester consists of a series of files that provide services such as redirecting print jobs, maintaining network connections, and handling network packets. The NetWare DOS Requester also provides expanded and extended memory support, allows unneeded files to be swapped in and out of memory (thus making more efficient use of memory), and eliminates duplication of effort between the NetWare shell and DOS.

The modularity of the NetWare DOS Requester allows third-party and future NetWare services to be easily added to NetWare clients. Modularity is provided through a variety of program files called *Virtual Loadable Modules* (VLMs). Each VLM performs specific services.

 Note Some client VLMs are required, but a few VLMs are optional. You can save memory by not loading the optional VLMs. The load order of VLMs is important, however. If you choose not to load optional VLMs, the best way to prevent them from being loaded is to rename them. VLMs have a VLM extension. Rename unnecessary VLMs by changing their VLM extension to something else.

VLMs are of three types, as follows:

- **DOS redirection VLMs.** REDIR.VLM provides DOS redirection services. It tricks the DOS client into believing it is looking at another DOS drive when it sees the NetWare file server.

- **Service protocol VLMs.** NWP.VLM, FIO.VLM, and PRINT.VLM provide specific services to the network client. NWP.VLM is responsible for establishing and maintaining network connections. It also handles broadcast messages and the implementation of different Novell file server types, such as *NetWare Directory Services* (NDS), Bindery, and NetWare Lite. FIO.VLM handles the file transfer protocol, including cached, noncached, and burst mode read/write requests. PRINT.VLM provides printing services.

- **Transport protocol VLMs.** TRAN.VLM provides services related to server connection maintenance, the transportation of network packets, and other transport-related services.

The NetWare DOS Requester modules available with NetWare 3.1x are shown in table 10.2.

Table 10.2
NetWare DOS Requester Virtual Loadable Modules

Module's File Name	*Purpose of the Module*	*Parent VLM*
AUTO.VLM	Automatically reconnects a client to a server when the server is available	
BIND.VLM	Lets clients on NDS networks access Bindery-based servers (NetWare 3.1x and earlier versions)	NWP.VLM

continues

Table 10.2, Continued
NetWare DOS Requester Virtual Loadable Modules

Module's File Name	Purpose of the Module	Parent VLM
CONN.VLM	Tracks connection information and makes it available to other VLMs as needed	
FIO.VLM	Supports file access	
GENERAL.VLM	Provides general functions needed by other VLMs	
IPXNCP.VLM	Adds NCP header information to packets and passes them off to IPX	TRAN.VLM
NDS.VLM	Lets clients on Bindery-based NetWare servers access NDS-based (NetWare 4.x) servers	NWP.VLM
NETX.VLM	Provides backward compatibility for applications using the old NetWare shell	
NWP.VLM	Coordinates services with the VLMs for which it is responsible (its Child VLMs)	
PRINT.VLM	Redirects printing requests to the network	
RSA.VLM	Provides re-authentication for NDS	NWP.VLM
REDIR.VLM	Working with DOS, redirects non-DOS requests to the network	
SECURITY.VLM	Provides packet security when needed	

Only four of the VLMs listed in table 3.2 are considered optional. All others are required. The four optional VLMs include:

- NDS.VLM

- PRINT.VLM

- AUTO.VLM

- RSA.VLM

All VLMs are loaded and managed using the NetWare DOS Requester's VLM manager—VLM.EXE.

To load the NetWare DOS Requester, run the VLM.EXE file, followed by any parameters needed by your client's particular configuration. For example, you can load a portion of the NetWare DOS Requester into expanded memory (if available on the client) by typing **VLM /Me**, and pressing Enter at the client's system prompt. You can also load the NetWare DOS Requestor into extended memory (VLM IMX) or conventional memory. In addition, you can load the NetWare DOS Requester from either of two client startup files, including:

- AUTOEXEC.BAT

- STARTNET.BAT

Besides the /M parameter, which lets you specify the area of memory into which the NetWare DOS Requester is to be loaded, there are several other parameters available with VLM.EXE. Available parameters include:

- **/C=[path/]filename.ext.** If you use a configuration file other than NET.CFG, this parameter specifies that another configuration file is to be used, and where that file is located.

- **/D.** This parameter displays diagnostic information related to the NetWare DOS Requester.

- **/Mx.** This parameter tells the NetWare DOS Requester which area of memory it is to load into. Replace x with C for conventional memory, X for extended memory, or E for expanded memory.

- **/PS=<server name>.** This parameter specifies which NetWare 3.1x file server the NetWare DOS Requester is to seek out and attach to (called the Preferred Server) when loading. Replace *server name* with the actual name of the file server.

- **/PT=<tree_name>.** This parameter specifies which NetWare 4.x network tree the NetWare DOS Requester is to seek out to establish the network connection when loading.

- **/U.** This parameter unloads the NetWare DOS Requester from the client's memory.

- **/Vx.** This parameter provides details about the NetWare DOS Requester while it is loading. (V stands for verbose.) Four levels of detail are available. Replace x with the level you prefer. Available levels are numbered 0 through 4.

- **/?.** This parameter displays the help screen shown in figure 10.8.

You can use the NET.CFG file to configure the NetWare ODI environment and to specify configuration options for the NetWare DOS Requester.

Figure 10.8

NetWare DOS Requester (VLM) help screen.

```
(C) Copyright 1993 Novell, Inc.  All Rights Reserved.
Patent pending.

Available command line options:
/?      Display this help screen.
/U      Unload the VLM.EXE file from memory
/C=[path\]filename.ext
        Specify a configuration file to use (Default is NET.CFG).
/Mx     The memory type the VLM.EXE file uses where x is one of the following:
        C = Conventional memory.
        X = Extended memory (XMS).
        E = Expanded memory (EMS).
/D      Display the VLM.EXE file diagnostics.
/PS=<server name>
        Preferred server name to attach to during load.
/PT=<tree name>
        Preferred tree name to attach to during load.
/Vx     The detail level of message display where x is one of the following:
        0 = Display copyright and critical errors only.
        1 = Also display warning messages.
        2 = Also display VLM module names.
        3 = Also display configuration file parameters.
        4 = Also display diagnostics messages.

C:\NWCLIENT>
```

To modify the NET.CFG file to include ODI-related configuration information, include the following:

■ A Link Driver section, which includes applicable information for naming your network driver and identifying various related hardware settings.

This section must have a left-justified section head titled **Link Driver *driver_name*.** (Replace *driver_name* with the name of the network board driver used in this client.)

The following lines of information, where applicable, must be included as options (indented at least one space) under this section head:

DMA [#1|#2] *channel number*

INT [#1|#2] *interrupt_request_number*

MEM [#1|#2] *hex_start_address[hex_length]*

PORT [#1|#2] *hex_start_address*

SLOT *number*

FRAME *frame_type*

■ A Link Support section is also needed. It, too, must be left-justified and is entered as **Link Support**.

The following lines of options, where applicable, are included, and must also be indented at least one space under this section head:

BUFFERS *number [size]*

MEMPOOL *number*

MAX BOARDS *number*

MAX STACKS *number*

To modify the NET.CFG file to include NetWare DOS Requester-related configuration information, include applicable options from the following list. Remember to indent each option at least one space under the left-justified heading called NetWare DOS Requester. The available options include:

AUTO RECONNECT=

AUTO RETRY=

BIND RECONNECT=

CACHE BUFFERS=

CACHE BUFFERS SIZE=

CACHE WRITES=

CHECKSUM=

CONNECTIONS=

FIRST NETWORK DRIVE=

LARGE INTERNET PACKETS=

LOAD CONN TABLE LOW=

LOAD LOW IPXNCP=

LOCAL PRINTERS=

MAX TASKS=

MESSAGE LEVEL=

PB BUFFERS=

PREFERRED SERVER=

PRINT BUFFER SIZE=

PRINT HEADER=

PRINT TAIL=

SEARCH MODE=

SIGNATURE LEVEL=

USE DEFAULTS=

VLM=

Figure 10.9 shows a sample NET.CFG file for a NetWare network client. It includes some of the most common parameters used by the NetWare DOS Requester.

```
Link support
    Buffers 8 1586
    MemPool 4096

Link driver NE2000
    INT 5
    PORT 340
    MEM D0000
    FRAME Ethernet_802.2

Netware DOS Requester
    FIRST NETWORK DRIVE = F
    NETWARE PROTOCOL = PNW,BIND,NDS
    PREFERRED SERVER = MICHAEL
    SHOW DOTS = ON
    VLM = NMR.VLM


Protocol IPX
        IPX SOCKETS 45
```

Figure 10.9
Sample NET.CFG File.

Supporting Read-Only and Diskless Network Devices

Currently, read-only devices are compact disc devices being used as CDROM volumes. NetWare 3.1*x* makes available an NLM called CDROM.NLM. As with all NLMs, you load this one by typing **LOAD CDROM** at the file server console, and pressing Enter. You also can include this NLM load command in the file server's startup file.

Once the CDROM.NLM is loaded, you must use the MOUNT command to make this volume available. Type **CD MOUNT** *[device_number]* *[volume_name]* and press Enter at the file server console to mount the CDROM volume. Replace *device_number* with the device or drive number that specifies the CD-ROM drive's system interface. Replace *volume_name* with the name assigned to this volume.

The CD utility, followed by an appropriate command word, allows you to obtain CD-ROM information.

You can see a list of available CD-ROM devices by typing **CD DEVICE LIST** at the file server console and pressing Enter.

You can obtain help information related to the CD-ROM device by typing **CD HELP** and pressing Enter.

You can also see information from the root directory of a CD-ROM volume by typing **CD DIR** [*device_number*] [*volume_name*] and pressing Enter.

Beside providing support for read-only devices, NetWare 3.1x also supports *diskless clients* (workstations with no attached hard disk or floppy disk drives).

As a network administrator, you must prepare the NetWare file server to support diskless clients. To prepare the file server, install the related NLM, called **RPL.NLM**, and bind it to the network board.

Any required bootstrap files must be located in the file server's SYS:LOGIN directory. Run the DOSGEN utility to create remote boot disk image files to be placed into the SYS:LOGIN directory.

Questions

1. ODI stands for _____.

   ○ A. Open Data-Link Interface

   ○ B. Open Data-Connect Interface

   ○ C. Open Data Interconnect

   ○ D. Open Data-Systems Interconnect

2. Which TWO of the following are supported by ODI?

   ☐ A. Multiple file servers

   ☐ B. Multiple protocols

   ☐ C. Multiple LAN drivers

   ☐ D. Multiple clients

3. Of the following, which is NOT an OSI layer?

   ○ A. Application

   ○ B. Transportation

   ○ C. Presentation

   ○ D. Physical

4. The purpose of the OSI model is to _____.

   ○ A. define exactly what procedure must be followed

   ○ B. separate software from hardware processes

   ○ C. show the processes that should take place at any given point

   ○ D. force companies to comply with communication rules

5. The layer of the OSI model that provides the interface between network applications and lower-layer protocols is _____.

   ○ A. application

   ○ B. presentation

   ○ C. session

   ○ D. network

6. The layer of the OSI model which provides rules for encoding data for successful communication is _____.

   ○ A. application

   ○ B. presentation

   ○ C. session

   ○ D. network

7. The _____ OSI model layer provides both connection-oriented and connectionless network services.

   ○ A. application

   ○ B. presentation

   ○ C. session

   ○ D. network

8. Which of the following is NOT a benefit of the modular implementation of the OSI reference module?

   ○ A. Flexibility

   ○ B. Transparent client/server connection

   ○ C. Concentration on a single network protocol

   ○ D. No additional equipment investment required

9. NetWare implements the Link Support Layer of the OSI reference model with the _____ file.

    ○ A. IPXODI.COM

    ○ B. NEx.COM

    ○ C. LSL.COM

    ○ D. NETX.COM

10. Which of the following is an MLID file?

    ○ A. IPXODI.COM

    ○ B. LSL.COM

    ○ C. NETX.COM

    ○ D. NE2000.COM

11. Which THREE are files copied to the \WINDOWS\SYSTEM directory during client installation?

    ☐ A. ET.INI

    ☐ B. NETWARE.DRV

    ☐ C. NETWARE.HLP

    ☐ D. NWPOPUP.EXE

12. During client installation, the _____ file is copied to the \WINDOWS\SYSTEM directory to let users run DOS-based applications from within Enhanced Mode MS Windows.

    ○ A. NETWARE.INI

    ○ B. NWUTILS.GRP

    ○ C. VIPX.386

    ○ D. VNETWARE.386

13. To see which group was added to Windows Program Manager during client installation, look at the _____ file.

    ○ A. NETWARE.INI

    ○ B. SYSTEM.INI

    ○ C. WIN.INI

    ○ D. PROGMAN.INI

14. Which of the following INI files is not modified during client installation?

    ○ A. NETWARE

    ○ B. SYSTEM

    ○ C. WIN

    ○ D. PROGMAN

15. The file used to update existing client files is _____.

    ○ A. CLIENT.UPD

    ○ B. INSTALL.EXE

    ○ C. WSUPDATE.EXE

    ○ D. NETWARE.EXE

Answers

1. A	9. C
2. B, C	10. D
3. B	11. B, C, D
4. C	12. C
5. A	13. D
6. B	14. A
7. D	15. C
8. C	

Setting Up and Maintaining NetWare Print Services

To use NetWare 3.1x print services, you must first set up the printing environment. After that has been accomplished, you can concentrate on improving, customizing, and maintaining network print services using some of NetWare's advanced printing capabilities.

This chapter shows you how to use NetWare's advanced print services so that you can customize and maintain printing on your 3.1x network. After reading this chapter, you will be able to do the following:

- *Understand advanced printing services*

- *Create default print job settings*

- *Print documents using default settings*

- *Maintain network printing services*

Advanced Printing Services

When you set up basic printing services on your NetWare network, you completed the following four main steps:

1. Using PCONSOLE to configure basic printing environment components including print queues, print servers, and printers.

2. Running PSERVER at either a NetWare file server or a dedicated print server to initialize the print server.

3. Connecting all the network printers to the network.

4. Using NetWare 3.1x utilities such as PRINTCON and PRINTDEF to provide some basic customization of NetWare printing services.

Now that the basic printing services are running smoothly, consider ways in which you can customize and maintain those services. Before you jump right in and start making modifications to the network's printing environment, however, you might find it helpful to consider some advanced printing setup and management design.

Designing your network printing environment is relatively easy when your network is small and you have only one or two file servers and only one or two print servers. When your network begins to grow, however, printing setup and design issues become a little more complex. To implement and maintain advanced printing services successfully, you must consider the needs of your network and its users, as well as issues related to advanced printing setup and management design.

In assessing the print service needs of your network, you must consider the following higher-level performance issues:

- **Capacity of your network printers.** By monitoring the print jobs in each print queue, you can determine when peak printing loads occur, then decide whether your current network printers are capable of handling those peak loads. If they are not, you can make modifications to accommodate the peak loads.

- **Necessity for multiple print queues for each printer.** If after monitoring print jobs in print queues you determine that high-priority print jobs are not being serviced as soon as they should be, you can consider adding print queues to each printer.

- **Priority assigned to each print queue.** By adding print queues and assigning them different priorities, you can ensure that high-priority jobs are printed before low-priority jobs.

- **Necessity for multiple printers per print queue.** Again, monitoring print jobs in print queues helps you see whether you have enough network printers to handle all of your network's printing needs. If print job requests are always backlogged in the print queues, you might con-sider adding more printers to one or more of the print queues.

- **Network printers of different types.** You can provide support on your NetWare 3.1x network for non-DOS-compatible printers, such as Unix or AppleTalk printers, by installing additional software, available from Novell authorized resellers, and using PCONSOLE to define these printers.

In addition to having to assess the printing requirements and needs of your network's users, you will be faced with the following two advanced printing setup and management design issues:

■ Working with multiple file servers

■ Designing multiple print queues

You can set up a network print server to accept print jobs from several network file servers. The number of file servers that you assign to a single print server depends on factors such as the following:

■ How close the printer is to those file servers

■ What logical groups of network users can reasonably access the associated printers

■ The type of printing environment in your company (job shop or individual printing assignments)

Other factors can affect your decision as well. Regardless of the reasons, if you choose to service several NetWare file servers from a single print server, you must make the appropriate changes to your printing environment. The changes you need to make include the following:

1. Creating a print queue on each of the NetWare file servers that will be submitting print jobs to the print server.

2. Defining a print server on each file server. These print servers must have the same name as that of the print server. If the print server that will be providing the printing services is called PS_MICHAEL, for example, then you must define a print server on each file server and identify it as PS_MICHAEL.

3. Defining printers for each file server that also have the same printer number and printer name as the printers on the print server.

4. Assigning each printer to one of the print queues that you created.

5. Choosing the file servers for which the print server will service job orders.

 You make the choices in step 5 by selecting servers from the list of available servers. This list is displayed when you press the Insert key from within the Print Server Configuration menu of the File Servers to be Serviced screen in the PCONSOLE utility.

It is relatively easy to set up several print queues to service print jobs on the network. The important issue to consider is the design and use of those print queues.

This book assumes that you have some experience as a NetWare administrator, so an effective place to start is to look at the current print queues on your server. Checking the Current Queue Status option in PCONSOLE for each of your print queues shows you, among other things, print jobs currently in the queue. From this screen you might be able to determine such things as whether the print queue is servicing too many print jobs, if low-priority print jobs are beating out more important print jobs simply because they arrived at the queue first, and other related print job status information.

Gathering and reviewing information about the status of print jobs in print queues helps you decide if your current print queue design and setup is sufficient for your network's current and future needs. If you believe that some changes might benefit the network and its users, then you can consider making changes in some or all of the following areas:

- **Assignments of print queue users.** Consider whether you can change the assignment of print queue users to make better use of workgroups or of the arrangement of print queue users.

- **Print queue priorities.** If you have not as-signed different priorities to different print queues, changing print queue priorities can help ensure that critical jobs are printed before those that can safely wait to be printed.

- **Increasing or reducing the number of print queues.** If there simply are so many jobs in the print queue that there is always a wait for printing services, then perhaps you should add more print queues.

- **Assignment of print queue and print server operators.** Consider delegating some of the responsibility for print queue and print server management to other company employees. Assigning other users to be print queue opera-tors and print server operators can relieve you of some of the daily responsibilities associated with troubleshooting and problem solving related to print queues and print servers.

Careful consideration, effective design, and proper implementation of the use of multiple servers on the network, as well as effective design of print queues will enhance your network printing envi-ronment. In the case of print queue management, modifications such as those previously discussed also can relieve you of some of the daily burden associated with managing your network's printing environment.

Creating Default Print Job Settings

When using network print services, some aspects of printing can be a little more complex than if you simply had a printer attached to your workstation's LPT port. Tasks that often become a little more cumbersome include the following:

- Redirecting screen displays to a network printer

- Redirecting print jobs from within applica-tions to a network instead of a local printer

- Redirecting data to a network file

To simplify these types of printing tasks on a network, NetWare 3.1x provides utilities that enable you to specify and automate your print-ing configurations. NetWare also provides utilities that enable you to automate your printing configu-rations. The NetWare CAPTURE utility, for example, enables you to specify what to do with network print requests when the print jobs are not automatically network compatible. The NetWare PCONSOLE utility enables you to view print queues, print servers, and printers on the network, as well as view and manipulate your own network print jobs.

The NetWare PRINTCON utility enables you to automate your CAPTURE and PCONSOLE settings by specifying defaults to be used when printing jobs that are not automatically network compatible.

Before CAPTURE and PCONSOLE settings are automatic, you must create different print job settings that can be used when needed. These print job settings are called *default print job settings*. You create default print job settings using the PRINTCON utility.

To create a new default print job setting, run the PRINTCON utility and choose the Edit Print Job Configurations option from the Available Options menu to display the Print Job Configuration screen, as shown in figure 11.1.

From the Print Job Configuration screen, you add a new print job configuration by pressing Insert, typing a name for the new configuration, and pressing Enter. This action opens the Edit Print Job Configuration screen for the print job

configuration you are adding. Figure 11.2 shows the Edit Print Job Configuration screen that opened when creating a new print job called LEGAL.

If you do not create print job configurations, users need to specify CAPTURE options before printing jobs from their workstations' screens or from applications that are not network-compatible. Table 11.1 lists the fields included in the Edit Print Job Configuration screen and shows their equivalent CAPTURE option.

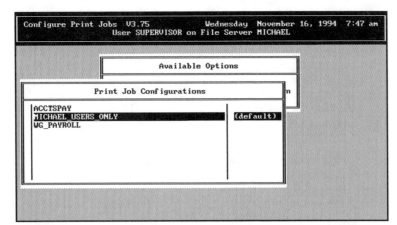

Figure 11.1
The Print Job Configurations screen.

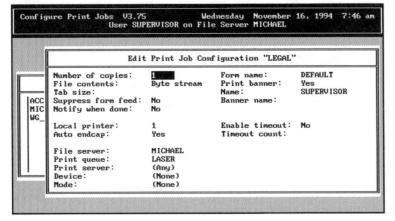

Figure 11.2
The Edit Print Job Configuration screen.

Table 11.1
Print Job Configuration and CAPTURE Options

Edit Print Job Configuration Field Option	*Description of Field*	*Related CAPTURE*
Number of copies	Tells how many copies should be printed	/Copies=*n*
File contents	Indicates if file is a text file or a byte stream file	(none)
Tab size	Specifies number of spaces in a tab, if applications do not predefine the number of spaces	/Tabs=*n*
Suppress form feed	Specifies whether to feed a blank form after job is printed	/FormFeed
Notify when done	Indicates if a message should be sent to tell the user his job has finished printing	/NOTify
Local printer	Specifies that the LPT port is used to capture the job	/Local=*n*
Auto endcap	Sends data waiting to be printed to printer when the application is closed	/AUtoend
File server	Indicates which server should receive the print job	/Server=*name*
Print queue	Indicates which queue should receive the print job	/Queue=*name*
Print server	Indicates which print server is being used for the print job	(none)
Device	Specifies which device to use as defined in the file server's PRINTDEF database	(none)
Mode	Specifies the mode to use as defined in the file server's PRINTDEF database	(none)

Edit Print Job Configuration Field Option	Description of Field	Related CAPTURE
Form name	Indicates the form to use to print the job	/Form=*name* or *n*
Print banner	Tells whether to print a banner page before printing job	/No Banner
Name	Shows the name of the user submitting the print job	/NAMe=*name*
Banner name	Text to appear on lower part of banner page	/Banner=*name*
Enable timeout	Tells the program to print without exiting application after a specified time period has elapsed	(none)
Timeout count	Specifies the time period to use for Enable timeout	/TImeout=*n*

Printing Documents Using Default Settings

After a default print job configuration has been created using PRINTCON, users can issue print job requests using that default print job configuration.

When a print job configuration such as the one shown as LEGAL is created, users can tell print jobs to use this configuration. Specifying that jobs use a default configuration enables users to issue the CAPTURE command with only one option: that which specifies the configuration job to use.

Network users also can skip using the CAPTURE command. If they do not issue any capture command, the default print job configuration information is used.

To specify a job configuration defined in PRINTCON, use the following CAPTURE command:

`CAPTURE J=job name`

In the earlier Edit Print Job Configuration example, to use the previously created LEGAL job configuration, you would type **CAPTURE J=LEGAL** at your workstation and press Enter.

Maintaining Network Printing Services

After you have set up and configured network printing services, you then need to maintain those services. Maintenance issues can include items such as the following:

- Managing printers

- Converting remote printers to private status

- Making permanent and temporary changes to printing features such as print queue settings and notification lists

Some of the printing management/maintenance tasks that you can perform with the PSC and PCONSOLE utilities include checking printer status, stopping and restarting print jobs, and mounting forms.

Checking Printer Status

You can check the status of a printer by using either the PSC utility or the PCONSOLE utility. To check the status of a printer using the PSC utility, type the following and press Enter:

`PSC PS=print_server_name P=printer_number Stat`

To check the status of a printer using the PCONSOLE utility, first run the PCONSOLE utility, then choose Print Server Information from the Available Options menu. Next, choose a print server from the Print Servers list; the Print Server Information menu opens. From that menu, select Printer. Now select the printer whose status you want to see. You now can see the printer status information for this printer.

Stopping and Restarting Print Jobs

You can stop and restart print jobs using either the PSC or PCONSOLE utilities. To stop a print job using PSC, type the following at the prompt and press Enter:

`PSC PS=print_server_name P=printer_number PAU`

To stop the printing of the current print job using PCONSOLE, and otherwise temporarily suspend printing on a printer, complete the following steps from inside the Status of *Printer_name* screen:

1. Choose Printer Control.

2. Choose Stop Printer from the Printer Control menu.

To restart a stopped print job using PSC, type the following command at the prompt, then press Enter:

`PSC PS=print_server_name P=printer_number STAR`

To restart a stopped print job using PCONSOLE, select Start Printer from inside the Printer Control menu.

Mounting Forms

You can mount forms using either the PSC utility or the PCONSOLE utility. To mount a form using the PSC utility, type the following at the prompt and press Enter:

`PSC PS=print_server_name P=printer_number MO F=n`

Replace n with the number of the form you want to mount. Forms must be predefined using the PRINTDEF utility.

To mount a specific form using the PCONSOLE utility, complete the following steps:

1. Start PCONSOLE.

2. Choose Print Server Information from the Available Options menu.

3. Choose a print server form the Print Servers list.

4. Choose Print Server Status/Control from the Print Server Information menu.

5. Choose a printer from the list of Active Printers.

6. Choose Mounted Form.

7. Type the number of the form you want to mount (as previously defined using the PRINTDEF utility), then press Enter.

You can use the PSC utility to accomplish another task: converting a remote network printer to a private workstation printer for local-only printing. To change a remote network printer from shared to private status, type the following command at the workstation's prompt and press Enter:

```
PSC PS=print_server_name P=printer_number PRI
```

To restore the now private printer to a network printer, type the following command at the workstation's prompt and press Enter:

```
PSC PS=print_server_name P=printer_number SH
```

Another management/maintenance task you can perform is that of changing print queue and notification lists settings. Some of these changes are permanent changes, such as creating print queues, whereas others are considered temporary, such as assigning a print queue operator.

You can use the PCONSOLE utility to make permanent changes, such as adding print queues, and temporary changes. Two temporary changes that you can make are adding users to the printer notify list and temporarily assigning a print queue to a printer.

Adding Users to the Printer Notify List

To temporarily add users to the printer notify list, first make sure that the print server is up and running, then run the PCONSOLE utility at your workstation and complete the following steps:

1. Choose Print Server Information.

2. Print Server Status and Control.

3. Choose Notify List for Printer.

4. Add users as needed.

 Some of the menu options for making changes are available only when the print server is running. The Print Server Status and Control option is one of them.

The users you add will continue to be part of the notify list until you down the print server.

Assigning a Print Queue to a Printer

Sometimes a print queue becomes overloaded with print job requests (too many requests or very large print jobs). To relieve the burden on a given printer, you can assign one or more of the print queues to different printers.

To temporarily assign a print queue to another printer, complete the following steps:

1. Start PCONSOLE at your workstation by typing **PCONSOLE** and pressing Enter.

2. Choose Print Server Information.

3. Choose Print Server Status and Control.

4. Choose Queues Serviced by Printer.

5. Reassign the print queue.

Questions

1. Which of the following is NOT a step involved in setting up basic print services?

   ○ A. Create default print job settings

   ○ B. Connect printers to the network

   ○ C. Run PSERVER

   ○ D. Configure print queues, servers, and printers

2. The advanced print setup consideration that takes into account peak printing loads is which of the following?

   ○ A. Priority assigned to the print queue

   ○ B. Multiple print queues for each printer

   ○ C. Multiple printers per queue

   ○ D. Capacity of network printers

3. Which of the following is NOT an advanced network printing environment design consideration?

   ○ A. Types of network printers

   ○ B. Number of printers per print queue

   ○ C. Location of printers on network

   ○ D. Capacity of network printers

4. The utility used to define non-DOS-compatible printers, such as Unix or AppleTalk, is the _____ utility.

   ○ A. PSC

   ○ B. PCONSOLE

   ○ C. PRINTCON

   ○ D. PRINTDEF

5. TWO advanced printing setup and management design issues to be considered include _____ and _____.

   ☐ A. print server location

   ☐ B. multiple file servers

   ☐ C. multiple print queues

   ☐ D. file server location

6. Which of the following is NOT a change that you must make to accommodate multiple print servers on your network?

   ○ A. Attaching a printer to each print server

   ○ B. Creating a print queue on each file server

   ○ C. Defining a print server on each file server

   ○ D. Choosing which file servers the print server will service

7. Which network printing task is NOT a reason to create default print job settings?

   ○ A. Print all documents to your local printer

   ○ B. Redirect screen displays to a network printer

   ○ C. Send print jobs to a file

   ○ D. Print from applications that are not designed for use on a network

8. The TWO utilities that enable you specify details such as number of copies and tab size for print jobs that must be redirected are _____ and _____.

   ☐ A. PRINTCON

   ☐ B. PRINTDEF

   ☐ C. PCONSOLE

   ☐ D. CAPTURE

9. The NetWare utility that enables you to automate print job details such as tab size is _____.

   ○ A. PRINTCON

   ○ B. PRINTDEF

   ○ C. PCONSOLE

   ○ D. CAPTURE

10. The equivalent CAPTURE command for the Suppress form feed field in the Print Job Configuration screen is _____.

    ○ A. /C=n

    ○ B. /F

    ○ C. /NAM=n

    ○ D. /NFF

11. The _____ Print Job Configuration field specifies how many spaces should be used for tabs if the application does not have print formatting instructions.

    ○ A. File Server

    ○ B. Form Name

    ○ C. Enable Timeout

    ○ D. Tab Size

12. If you do NOT want a cover page to be printed before your print job, specify _____ in the CAPTURE command.

    ○ A. /NB

    ○ B. /B=name

    ○ C. /Q=name

    ○ D. /T=n

13. To print a document using a job configuration defined in PRINTCON, use the _____ CAPTURE command.

    ○ A. /N=name

    ○ B. /B=name

    ○ C. /J=name

    ○ D. /T=n

14. To stop a print job using the PSC command, which option should you add to the command?

    ○ A. STAT

    ○ B. STOP

    ○ C. START

    ○ D. MO F=n

15. To convert a remote network printer to private use, use the _____ command.

    ○ A. PCONSOLE

    ○ B. PSC

    ○ C. PRINTCON

    ○ D. PRINTDEF

Answers

1. A

2. D

3. C

4. B

5. B, C

6. A

7. A

8. C, D

9. A

10. D

11. D

12. A

13. C

14. B

15. B

Maintaining and Monitoring NetWare 3.1x Servers

NetWare file servers are the key components in the NetWare network. Without them, clients are only PCs cabled together using network boards and cabling. They can do little more than function as stand-alone computers.

Your network users may actually prefer the functionality of their stand-alone PCs to that of a network plagued with poor performance. It is your responsibility as a network administrator to keep the network functioning at peak performance.

The best way to ensure the performance of your network is to periodically monitor and adjust various performance factors. This maintenance requires a knowledge and understanding of those factors.

This chapter is designed to help you understand your network and some specific performance factors. After reading this chapter, you will be able to perform the following:

- Understand network performance

- Monitor server information

- Perform server maintenance

- Set server time

- Understand routing information

- Create file server batch files

Understanding Network Performance

The amount of storage space your file servers contain and the number and type of application programs they provide are important to your users. Slow or inadequate network performance, however, will bring more complaints from users than almost anything else. To keep the network running at peak performance, it must be maintained.

Maintaining network performance is mostly a balancing act. Four different factors must be kept in order, and they are as follows:

- Communication

- Hardware

- Environment

- Memory

Communication refers to the compatibility of the file server's bus architecture and the network boards used in the file server. If your file server's bus architecture is 32-bit, then using 32-bit network boards helps to ensure the efficient transmission of packets through the file server.

Hardware refers to computer equipment chosen for the network file server and clients. For quicker processing, choose PCs with CPUs that have higher speeds, as well as file servers and workstations with larger bus architectures. Slow workstations can bottleneck the network's processing and reduce network performance.

Environment refers to the needs and uses of your network. A network supporting large quantities of file server disk reads and writes functions less efficiently than one that requires fewer disk reads and writes, given the same hardware. Supporting large quantities of disk reads requires additional file server RAM for caching. Supporting large quantities of disk writes requires faster disk controllers and hard drive systems.

Memory refers primarily to file server memory. In NetWare 3.1x, memory is arranged into logical pools and allocated dynamically (as needed). The more RAM provided in the network file servers, the better response you can expect from your network servers. NetWare 3.1x also automatically balances memory pools after the server has been running for a period of time. You can change memory pool SET parameters to help expedite or customize memory pool balance.

Other aspects of NetWare can affect network performance, one of those being NCP Packet Signature.

NCP Packet Signature is a NetWare security enhancement that ensures that each packet received by a file server from a workstation is the same packet originally sent by that workstation. Its purpose is to prevent individuals from creating counterfeit packets, modified packets that grant the user greater rights to the network than were originally provided. NCP Packet Signature provides significant improvements in network security. Along with those improvements, however, comes additional network overhead. Additional NCP Packet Signature overhead can impact network performance, as can the types of services provided by your network.

For example, any load-intensive task on the network can have a negative impact on the client's performance when NCP Packet Signature is implemented. This is particularly noticeable to clients when they perform tasks such as transferring large databases or other files.

Network clients that commonly request less resource-intensive network services, such as word processing, are not likely to notice any performance degradation.

If you do experience a reduction in performance with the implementation of NCP Packet Signature, consider making the following changes or upgrades:

■ Changing file server hardware to PCs containing Intel 80486 CPUs running at a minimum of 50 MHz

■ Upgrading all clients to at least 80386 CPUs

■ Updating all NetWare utilities to those released with NetWare 3.12, especially the LOGIN and ATTACH utilities

■ Setting NCP Packet Signature levels at the client and file server to only the maximum level of security the network requires

NCP Packet Signature enables you to set the level of security to be provided.

 Note After you start the file server, you can increase the NCP Packet Signature level, but you cannot decrease it. Therefore, set the NCP Packet Signature to the lowest level with which you feel comfortable, and increase it later if it is not sufficient.

You have four NCP Packet Signature levels from which to choose: 0, 1, 2, and 3. Level 1 is the default for NetWare clients. Level 2 is the default for NetWare file servers. Levels 3 and 4 have the greatest impact on network performance. The higher you set the number, the higher the level of packet security. Higher security tends to increase network traffic, thus slowing network performance.

You set the NCP Packet Signature levels at file servers and client workstations. To set the NCP Packet Signature level for the file server, add the following to the file server's STARTUP.NCF file:

```
SET NCP PACKET SIGNATURE OPTION=number
```

To set the NCP Packet Signature level at the client workstation, add the following line to the client's NET.CFG file:

```
SIGNATURE LEVEL=number
```

The level set at any of the file servers can be different from the level set at each of the clients. Table 12.1 lists the available NCP Packet Signature levels.

Table 12.1
Levels of NCP Packet Signature

Level	Default	Description
0		The file server does not sign any packets.
1	Client	The file server will sign packets if the client requests that packets be signed.
2	Server	The file server will sign packets if the client is able to sign packets as well.
3		The file server will sign all packets and require the client to do so as well; if the client does not sign, the file server will not allow the client to log in.

Monitoring Server Information

Before you can improve the performance of your network, you must understand how well the network's individual file servers are currently performing. The MONITOR utility provides a great deal of information concerning your file server's performance. Run MONITOR on each file server and view several items of information, including the server's, which follow:

- Resource and processor utilization
- Memory statistics
- Hard disk drive status

MONITOR is a server console utility. You can access MONITOR from a workstation using NetWare's remote console feature. To start MONITOR, type the following command at the file server console:

LOAD MONITOR

 Note If you include the /P option with the LOAD MONITOR command, the Processor Utilization option also is displayed on the Available Options menu that opens.

When the MONITOR console utility is loaded, a screen appears displaying basic network information, including server memory statistics. The top of that screen is similar to the one shown in figure 12.1. It contains several items of information about your network, including information related to file server and network performance, and resource and processor utilization.

Six of the items on the MONITOR utility's main screen are particularly useful for verifying file server and network performance. These six items include the following:

- Utilization
- Total Cache Buffers
- Dirty Cache Buffers
- Packet Receive Buffers
- Directory Cache Buffers
- Service Processes

The Available Options menu contains the following two options from which to choose to view server memory statistics:

- System Module Information
- Resource Utilization

The six file server and network performance items, as well as each of the two Available Options menu memory statistics items, are discussed in this section to help you monitor and maintain your network's performance.

Resource and Processor Utilization Information

Table 12.2 provides important information related to the six file server and network performance items listed previously.

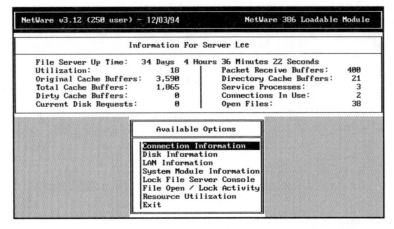

Figure 12.1

MONITOR Utility main screen.

Table 12.2
Relevant Resource and Processor Utilization Information

Item Name	Description	Information to Note
Utilization	The percent of file server processing currently being used.	Varies inversely to the Polling Process ability percentage shown in MONITOR's Process Utilization screen (LOAD MONITOR /P).
		High percentage might mean the following: Network board using CPU cycles
		NLM using processing time
		High percentage does not necessarily mean the CPU needs more processing power.
Total Cache Buffers	Quantity of RAM still available for cache buffers to use.	If server performs too slowly, add more RAM to increase cache buffers.
		If Cache Buffers statistic in Server Memory Statistics screen is below 20%, add more RAM.
		Cache Buffers should range from 40–60%.
Dirty Cache Buffers	Number (not %) of cache buffers that hold information not yet saved back to the hard disk.	Calculate percentage by dividing this number into Total Cache Buffers number.
		If over 70%, change MAXIMUM CONCURRENT

Item Name	Description	Information to Note
		DISK CACHE WRITES Set parameter to a higher number.
Packet Receive Buffers	Number of buffers the server uses to hold client service requests when the processor cannot immediately handle them.	Each buffer is equal to 1 KB of memory. The default value is 100. Can change using the MINIMUM and MAXIMUM PACKET RECEIVE BUFFERS Set commands. If there's an increase in the number of Service Processes, you can lower this number.
Directory Cache Buffers	Number of buffers for directory caching.	Increases in number of searches will increase this number to the maximum you allocated. Allocate with the MINIMUM and MAXIMUM DIRECTORY CACHE BUFFERS Set command.
Service Processes	Number of task handlers allocated for processing client requests.	The only way to remove memory given to service processes is to down and reload the server. Increase the default setting (by 5) if this number is close to 20, and there is enough available cache buffer memory.

Memory Statistics

To view file server memory statistics, use the following two MONITOR Available Options menu choices:

- System Module Information
- Resource Utilization

When you choose System Module Information from the Available Options menu, you will see a screen similar to the one shown in figure 12.2. It contains a list of system modules, such as the network card and the NetWare 386 Console Monitor.

Choosing a module from the System Module screen provides two basic items of information about that module, as follows:

- **Module Size.** The number of bytes of memory taken by this module while it is loaded

- **Load File Name.** The name of the NetWare Loadable Module that you placed into server memory using the LOAD command

A menu from which you can choose to view additional information about that network module is also shown. This menu is called Resource Tags (see fig. 12.3).

You can choose to view several items from the Resource Tags menu. What you choose depends on the type of information for which you are searching and on the system module you have selected.

For example, if you want to view information about the MONITOR utility's use of Alloc Short Term memory, first choose NetWare 386 Console Monitor from the System Modules screen, then choose Alloc Memory from the Resource Tags menu. Figure 12.4 shows the Resource Information window that appears after Alloc Memory has been selected.

Figure 12.2
The System Module screen.

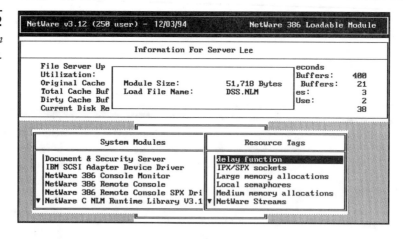

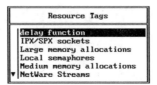

Figure 12.3

The Resource Tags menu.

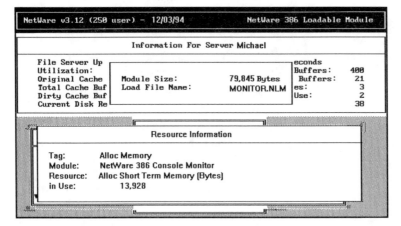

Figure 12.4

The Resource Information screen.

The Resource Information screen provides the following information:

■ **Tag.** The Resource Tag you chose to view

■ **Module.** The module for which you are viewing requested information

■ **Resource.** The type of resource you chose to view, and how it is provided—usually shown as bytes

■ **In Use.** The number of bytes currently being used by this module

Resource tags are NetWare's way of tracking the various memory-related resources your network is using. You can view this information to help deter-

mine whether or not you can unload some modules to temporarily free up memory. You can also use this information when adding new modules to help determine whether or not you want the modules loaded only as needed because of the quantity of resources that they may use.

Hard Disk Drive Status

You can also use the MONITOR utility to view information related to the health of the file server's hard disks.

To view disk-related information, choose Disk Information from MONITOR's Available Options menu. Several items of information about the hard disk will be displayed on the screen. These items include the following:

- Driver name (such as ISADISK.DSK)
- Disk size
- Number of partitions on the disk
- Status of disk mirroring (Mirrored or Not Mirrored)
- Status of Hot Fix
- Partition blocks
- Data blocks
- Redirection blocks
- Redirected blocks
- Reserved blocks

Of these items, three need to be watched in order to monitor the status of your file server's hard disk. They include the following:

- Redirection blocks
- Redirected blocks
- Reserved blocks

Approximately once a week, check these three numbers. Add together the number of Redirection Blocks and the number of Reserved Blocks. If the total number of Redirection plus Reserved Blocks is approximately half the number of Redirected Blocks, then your hard disk may be on the verge of failing. Consider backing up your hard disk, running the INSTALL utility to perform a hard disk surface test, and replacing the hard disk if the surface test fails.

Performing Server Maintenance

Understanding how your server is performing and making modifications to improve its performance is not always enough. Sometimes, problems with your network are the result of other unrelated problems.

For example, the NetWare file server's *bindery* (a database of network information such as users, account restrictions, and so forth) becomes corrupt. Problems with removing user accounts or changing a user's account restrictions cannot be fixed by adding more system memory. Instead, you must correct the bindery.

You can have other types of network problems as well, such as volume errors or corruption of network files. NetWare provides the following four utilities to help correct these types of problems:

- BINDFIX
- BINDREST
- VREPAIR
- SBACKUP

Run BINDFIX for any server you suspect might have corrupted bindery files. Running BINDFIX corrects problems such as user names that you cannot delete, and passwords that you cannot change.

Run BINDREST when you have run BINDFIX but need to restore the bindery to its previous version. That is, run BINDREST when you want to undo the bindery changes you made running BINDFIX.

Use VREPAIR to make volume repairs and to remove name space from a NetWare volume.

Use SBACKUP to make copies of files and programs on the NetWare file server. You also use SBACKUP to restore copies of files and programs that were made using SBACKUP.

BINDFIX and BINDREST

BINDFIX and BINDREST use the following three bindery files stored in the SYS:SYSTEM directory on the file server:

- NET$OBJ.SYS
- NET$PROP.SYS
- NET$VAL.SYS

When you run BINDFIX, it makes a copy of each of these three files, then renames the three bindery files with an OLD extension. BINDREST uses the files with the OLD extension to restore the previous bindery files.

Both BINDFIX and BINDREST are utilities run from the workstation. Log in to the file server as a user with Supervisor rights. After making sure that all users are logged out of the file server, change to the SYS:SYSTEM directory and run BINDFIX by typing **BINDFIX** and pressing Enter.

BINDFIX then runs several checks on the bindery, finding and repairing problems such as the following:

- Errors in the bindery causing bindery error messages to appear on the file server console

- The "unknown server" error message you might receive when printing to your default server

- User names, passwords, or rights you cannot change; or, in the case of user names, you cannot delete

When BINDFIX is complete, there will be corrected copies of the NET$OBJ.SYS, NET$PROP.SYS, and NET$VAL.SYS files. The previous versions exist as NET$OBJ.OLD, NET$PROP.OLD, and NET$VAL.OLD.

If running BINDFIX did not solve your bindery problems, you can restore the previous versions of these files by typing **BINDREST** and pressing Enter. BINDREST then restores the OLD files, effectively undoing all of the changes made when you ran BINDFIX.

VREPAIR

VREPAIR is a NetWare NLM. You use VREPAIR to accomplish two primary tasks.

One task for which you use VREPAIR is to make volume repairs. You also use VREPAIR to remove name space from a NetWare volume.

Other reasons to use VREPAIR include the following:

- A volume will not mount as the result of a hardware failure

- A hardware failure has caused disk read errors

- A volume is corrupted due to a hardware failure

- Mirroring errors occur when the file server boots

- Memory errors occur

- A volume will not mount because name space has been added to it

Unlike most NLMs, VREPAIR is stored on the DOS partition of the NetWare file server. The name space NLMs are also stored on the DOS partition, instead of the NetWare partition.

 To run VREPAIR, you must first dismount the NetWare volumes that are to be repaired. When the volumes are dismounted, you cannot access them. If the SYS volume is dismounted, you cannot access VREPAIR.NLM to repair the SYS volume. Therefore, it is good practice to keep a copy of the VREPAIR.NLM file on the server's boot partition where the file can be accessed after SYS has been dismounted.

To run VREPAIR, notify all network users to log out of the file server. Once all users are logged out, you can dismount the volumes to be repaired and run VREPAIR.

To remove name space support from a volume, complete the following steps:

1. Notify all users to log out of the file server.

2. Make sure that the VREPAIR.NLM and the name space NLM (such as V_MAC.NLM or V_OS2.NLM) are stored on the DOS partition of the file server.

3. Issue the SEARCH ADD command and add the DOS path for these NLMs to the file server's NLM search path.

4. Type **LOAD INSTALL**, choose Volume options, select the volume to be dismounted, then choose status to dismount the volume containing the name space you want to remove. Or type **DISMOUNT volume_name** and press Enter.

5. From the console prompt, type **LOAD VREPAIR** and press Enter.

6. From the VREPAIR menu, choose option 2—Set Vrepair Options.

7. Change the Current Vrepair Configuration field to read Remove Name Space Support from the Volume, by choosing Option 1.

8. Choose the name space to be removed.

9. Choose Option 0 to return to the main menu.

10. Choose Repair a Volume from the main menu, and choose the volume to be repaired.

11. Start VREPAIR.

12. After VREPAIR has completed its process, it prompts you to tell it whether or not to write its repairs to the disk. Choose Yes to Write Repairs to the Disk. This removes name space from the volume.

    If you need to remove other name spaces, repeat the process.

13. Choose Exit (Option 0) to exit from VREPAIR.

14. Remount the dismounted volume.

 You can also verify that name space has been removed by issuing the VOLUMES command at the file server console.

SBACKUP

The SBACKUP utility lets you back up several pieces of your network, including:

- DOS and OS/2 workstations
- Network file system
- BTRIEVE and NDS databases

SBACKUP also lets you restore any of these network pieces you previously backed up using SBACKUP.

SBACKUP consists of eight modules. Together, these modules provide the software you need to back up and restore your network's important files.

Of these eight modules, three are particularly important. They include:

- Storage Device Interface (SDI)
- NetWare Server TSAs
- Workstation TSAs

You load the SDI software on the file server to which your backup tape device is attached. Using device drivers, the SDI passes commands and information between the tape device and the backup utility. A file server with an attached backup device and the SDI software is called the host server.

You load NetWare Server TSAs on the file servers whose files you want to back up. These file servers are called target servers. The TSAs communicate with the file server backup software. A host server can also be a target server.

You load workstation TSAs on DOS or OS/2 workstations so you can back up the local hard disks on these workstations.

Software you back up is referred to either as parent or child software. A *parent* is any data set that is capable of having subordinate data sets. A *child* is any data set that cannot have subordinate data sets.

A directory, for example, can have subdirectories or files stored below them. Subdirectories can have other subdirectories or files stored below them. Therefore, directories and subdirectories are parents. A file cannot have directories or other files stored below it; therefore, a file is a child.

While NetWare provides SBACKUP, many companies choose alternative backup and restore utilities. SBACKUP is functional, but it is not the easiest to use of available backup software. Understanding the basics of SBACKUP, however, particularly the terms and features just described, is helpful to you as a network administrator.

There are other utilities NetWare provides to help you monitor and maintain your network. Two of those are the SET TIME and SET TIMEZONE commands.

Setting Server Time

Use the SET TIME command to set the clock time and date on the file server. Use the SET TIMEZONE command to set the time zone (such as Pacific Standard Time) for your file server.

To set the current date and time on your file server, type the following command at the file server console:

`SET TIME mm/dd/yy h:m:s`

Replace *mm/dd/yy* with the month, day, and year to which you want to set the server. For example, to set the server date to January 1, 1995, type **SET TIME 01/01/95** and press Enter.

You also use the SET TIME command to change the time on the file server. For example, to set the file server time to 1:32 a.m., type **SET TIME 1:32:00** and press Enter.

To set the time zone, use the SET TIMEZONE command. For example, to set the time zone on your file server to daylight savings time in the Pacific zone, type **SET TIMEZONE PST8PDT**.

Understanding Routing Information

Another important responsibility of a network administrator is understanding routing information.

The TRACK ON console utility enables you to view the traffic on your network. To use this utility, type **TRACK ON** at the file server console. Figure 12.5 shows the type of information displayed when the TRACK ON utility is used.

A *Routing Information Protocol* (RIP) packet exchanges information between network routers. This information is then used by each router to determine the best route to take between two points to send a packet to its final destination as quickly as possible.

A *Service Advertising Protocol* (SAP) packet advertises the service provided and the name and address of network devices that provide network services. For example, file servers and print servers are network devices that provide network services to network clients.

The TRACK ON utility provides information for each RIP and SAP packet sent in or out of the network file server. Packet information common to both RIPs and SAPs includes the following:

■ **Direction of the packet.** Indicates whether the packet was received (IN) by the file server or sent (OUT) by the file server. For example, a SAP packet can display on the screen as IN.

■ **Network address.** Shows the LAN address of the network card that sent or received the packet. For example, a network address looks something like 000004AD, followed by a colon, which separates it from the node address.

■ **Node address.** Shows the address of the device (server or router) on the network node. For example, in a RIP packet that is a broadcast message, the node address is displayed as a series of Fs (FFFFFFFFFFFF).

Figure 12.5

The TRACK ON utility displays information about RIP and SAP network packets.

```
IN  [ABCD0012:00001B01112B]       10:03:19AM       SERVER3      3
OUT [ABCD003C:FFFFFFFFFFFF]       10:03:19AM       SERVER3      4
IN  [ABCD0012:00001B01112B]       10:10:03AM       SERVER1      5    SERVER3  3
    DOCSERVER      3             ISSERVER    2   ENGINEER     4    PROVO    6
    DOCMASTER      4
IN  [ABCD0012:00001B01112B]       10:10:04AM       SERVER1      5
    DOCSERV1       3             ISSERVER    4   ENGINEER     2
    DOCMASTER
<Use ALT ESC or CRTL ESC to switch screens, or any other key to pause>
```

- **Packet time.** Indicates the time the packet was sent in or out. For example, time is displayed as hh:mm:ss, followed by either am or pm (11:05:33am).

- **Net number.** Represents the number of the specific network (cabling system). For example, 000BAD1234 would be a valid net number.

- **Hops and/or ticks.** The number of routers between the sending and receiving devices are *hops*. One hop equals one router. A *tick* is the number of $1/18$th-of-a-second increments it takes for the packet to reach its specified destination, when sent from this server. For example, in the case of SAPs, only the number of hops is shown (2). In the case of RIPs, both the number of hops and ticks are shown, separated by a slash ($2/3$).

Viewing route information using the TRACK ON utility can help you find problems with your network.

Creating File Server Batch Files

You can create batch files on the network file servers to help automate some of the processes that need to be performed. One of the most common uses for a server batch file is downing a file server from a remote console.

To create a server batch file, you can use the EDIT.NLM. You can also create a server batch file using any ASCII text editor. Your server batch file must be named with an NCF extension and must be stored in the SYS:SYSTEM directory of your NetWare file server.

To create a batch file that you can use to down a file server from a remote location, include the following three lines in the NCF file:

```
REMOVE DOS
DOWN
EXIT
```

To fully reboot a file server from a remote console using this server batch file, you must make sure that the AUTOEXEC.BAT file on the file server will automatically load the file server. To accomplish this, include the following two commands in the file server's AUTOEXEC.BAT file:

```
CD \SERVER.312
SERVER
```

After creating a batch file and updating the file server's AUTOEXEC.BAT file, when you log into this file server from a remote console and type the name of the NCF file you created, you will reboot the file server.

Questions

1. Which of the following is NOT a factor that affects network performance?

   ○ A. communications

   ○ B. hardware

   ○ C. software

   ○ D. memory

2. The compatibility of the file server's bus architecture and the network boards that you use in your file server is an example of the _____ factor that affects network performance.

   ○ A. communication

   ○ B. Hardware

   ○ C. Software

   ○ D. Memory

3. The network performance feature that is also a security feature is known as _____.

   ○ A. Communication

   ○ B. NCP Packet Signature

   ○ C. RAM

   ○ D. RIP

4. Implementing which TWO of the following changes will improve network performance if performance is reduced when implementing NCP Packet Signature?

   □ A. Upgrading file servers to 80486 processors

   □ B. Using only NetWare 3.12 utilities

   □ C. Setting NCP Packet Signature to level 4

   □ D. Upgrading clients to at least 80286 processors

5. Which of the following statements about NCP Packet Signature is true?

   ○ A. Level 2 is the default for clients.

   ○ B. Level 4 is the default for servers.

   ○ C. You must implement the same level at servers and clients.

   ○ D. It lets you set the level of security.

6. The level of NCP Packet Signature at which the file server will sign packets if the client is able is_____.

   ○ A. 1

   ○ B. 2

   ○ C. 3

   ○ D. 4

7. Which of the following is NOT an NCP Packet Signature level option?

   ○ A. 1

   ○ B. 2

   ○ C. 3

   ○ D. 4

8. What step must you take to see the Processor Utilization option in the MONITOR utility?

   ○ A. Choose Resource Utilization, then choose Processor from the MONITOR main menu

   ○ B. Add the /P option when running MONITOR

○ C. Load MONITOR before AUTOEXEC.NCF is loaded

○ D. Both A and B are options

9. Which item of information displayed on MONITOR's main menu is not used to verify file server and network performance?

○ A. Utilization

○ B. Total Cache Buffers

○ C. File Server Name

○ D. Service Processes

10. Which TWO Available Options menu choices let you view server memory statistics?

☐ A. System Module Information

☐ B. Resource Utilization

☐ C. Permanent Memory Pool

☐ D. Disk Options

11. To see the percent of file server processing capability currently being used, view the _____ information in MONITOR.

○ A. Utilization

○ B. Total Cache Buffers

○ C. System Module Information

○ D. Disk Options

12. If file server performance is too slow, add more _____ to the file server.

○ A. file server processes

○ B. total cache buffers

○ C. RAM

○ D. disk sspace

13. If Cache Buffers falls below _____ percent, add more RAM.

○ A. 10

○ B. 20

○ C. 40

○ D. 60

14. Total Cache Buffers should range from _____ to _____ percent.

☐ A. 10

☐ B. 20

☐ C. 40

☐ D. 60

15. Increases in the number of searches increases the number of _____ to the maximum that you allocated.

○ A. total cache buffers

○ B. directory cache buffers

○ C. packet receive buffers

○ D. service processes

Answers

1. C		9. C	
2. B		10. A, B	
3. B		11. A	
4. A, B		12. C	
5. D		13. B	
6. A		14. C, D	
7. D		15. B	
8. B			

Supporting and Protecting NetWare 3.1x Servers

It doesn't matter how efficient your network file server is if it encounters a virus or if its hard disk crashes. Therefore, in addition to monitoring and improving your network's performance, you must also protect it.

You protect your servers from viruses by implementing several steps or approaches to network protection. You ensure that you can restore older versions of your network files by following a regular backup program. This chapter discusses these two topics.

After reading this chapter, you will be able to do the following:

- Implement virus protection

- Conduct backups and restores

Implementing Virus Protection

A computer *virus* is a software program that spreads throughout a computer (or network) in much the same way a virus spreads throughout your body. Protecting a computer or network from a virus is mostly a matter of prevention. It is much easier to prevent a virus from gaining access to any of your computers than it is to try to cure that virus later.

The best way to keep your body free of a virus is to prepare for it, to prevent it with good personal habits. Good security habits go a long way toward preventing your network from being infected as well.

Viruses come from many sources, including pre-packaged, shrink-wrapped, licensed software (though this occurrence is rare). Other sources might include:

- Bulletin board services (BBS)

- Data disks used on network clients

- Illegal copies of software programs

You can take several approaches to prevent your network from being invaded by a virus (see fig. 13.1).

Figure 13.1

Protecting your network from viruses.

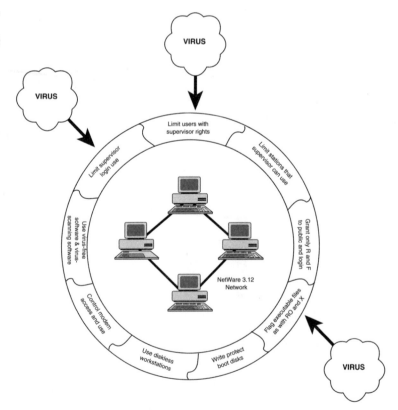

The greater your rights on the network, the more widespread the damage a virus can do. Because most viruses function by attacking the executable program files, a user with the right to change the read-only flag on executable files can make those files more susceptible to attack. To limit the amount of damage a virus can do when it enters the network because of something you did, only use your Supervisor login when necessary. In addition, limit the number of users with Supervisor or equivalent rights.

You should also limit the number of users on your network who have Supervisor rights. In addition, you can limit which network workstations from which the Supervisor user can log in.

For example, limit the Supervisor's login to your regular workstation and one other backup workstation. Then, no one can log in to the file server as user Supervisor, unless he or she is attempting to do so from your workstation, or from the alternate workstation.

Control access to the network and its files by implementing all or most of the following:

- Grant all users only the Read and File Scan rights to common directories such as PUBLIC and LOGIN

- Flag all executable NetWare system and software application files with the Read Only, and, if appropriate, Execute Only NetWare flags

- Make sure all boot disks are designed as write-protected disks

- Convert workstations to diskless workstations where possible

- Control access to and use of modems on your network

Make every effort to ensure that disks used on your network are free of any viruses by implementing the following:

- Purchase new software from reliable manufacturers and vendors

- Only install software you have verified to be virus-free by running virus-scanning software on it before it is installed

- Provide network users with access to virus-scanning software and insist they scan all disks prior to using them when attached to the network

- Have users check-in any disks they are bringing into the office so they can be scanned

- Only use working copies of disks that have been write-protected, using original disks only when you must

Two other important guidelines for protecting your network from viruses include:

- Training and educating your network users as to the problems, symptoms, and procedures associated with network viruses

- Maintaining adequate backups for restoring network files from tapes that have not been infected

Should your network become infected with a virus, you need to be prepared. Make certain you are familiar with the different types of viruses so you can recognize their symptoms. Also, train yourself in the procedures that must be followed to eradicate these viruses.

If you get a virus on your network that you cannot eliminate with virus-protection software, your next best option is to restore a backup that pre-dates the introduction of the virus into your network. It might not be possible for you to determine exactly when the virus was introduced. If you have maintained adequate protection measures, however, you might be able to determine approximately when the virus entered your network.

If you run antivirus software and make every effort to remove the virus from the network, but it does not eliminate the virus, you can choose and restore a backup. NetWare provides SBACKUP to ensure that you have at least a minimal backup and restore function for your network. Of course, you cannot restore network files using SBACKUP unless you originally made the backups using SBACKUP. In the event that you do not use an alternative backup

method, the next section of this chapter explains how to use SBACKUP to conduct network backups and restores.

Backups and Restores

As indicated in Chapter 12 of this course section, you can use the SBACKUP utility to back up and restore several pieces of your network (see fig. 13.2), including the following:

- DOS and OS/2 workstations

- Network file system

- BTRIEVE and NDS databases

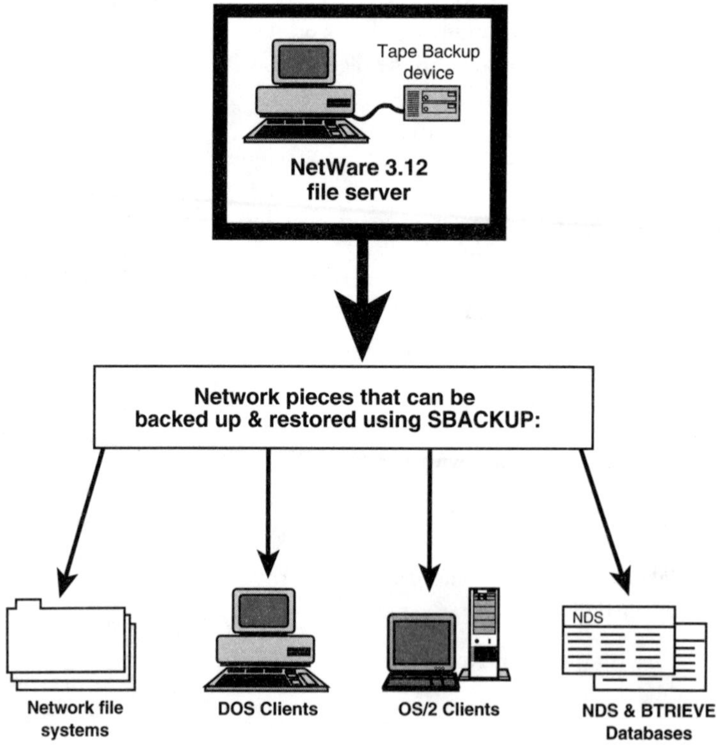

Figure 13.2

Types of network information you can back up.

SBACKUP provides eight modules with which to back up and restore your network's important files. Some of these modules you load on the host server, which is the file server to which your backup tape device is attached. For example, SBACKUP includes the Software Device Interface (SDI) module to pass commands and information between the tape device and the backup utility.

Some of these modules you load on *target servers*, which are the file servers whose files you want to back up, and some modules you load on the *target clients*, which are workstations whose local hard disks you want to back up.

Backing Up a File Server Bindery

Although you can back up and restore all data and files on your network, sometimes it is most important to back up and restore the file server's bindery files, particularly after NetWare is first installed, you have made many corrections to the bindery, or you have run BINDFIX to repair a corrupted bindery. You do not need to back up the file server's bindery each time you backup your network, as long as you have not made any bindery-related changes. If you add or delete users, change a user's rights, or perform other administrative tasks that affect the file server's bindery, then you should make a new backup of the file server's bindery.

To back up a file server's bindery and trustee assignments using NetWare's SBACKUP utility, complete the following steps:

1. Make a preliminary review of your file server and SBACKUP. This review includes the following:

   ■ Make sure there is sufficient memory on the host server. Load the MONITOR.NLM and verify that

the file server has at least 1 MB of available memory.

   ■ Know passwords for the user who will conduct the backup (Supervisor or other user with Supervisor rights) and, if you are conducting a client backup, for that workstation as well.

   ■ Remember any special path you are using for storing or retrieving session files.

2. Prepare the backup device (power it on, load the appropriate backup tape, and so forth).

3. Type **LOAD TSA312** at the target server console and press Enter. This command loads the NetWare 3.12 file server's Target Service Agent (TSA), so the file server's bindery can be backed up.

If backing up a NetWare 3.11 file server, use TSA311.NLM rather than TSA312.NLM.

4. Depending on the backup device you are using, load the related drivers at the console of the host server.

If you have not already done so, edit the DIBI2$DV.DAT file stored in SYS:SYSTEM of the host server before completing the next step.

Remove any lines for device drivers your backup device does not use. You may also have to add the driver name and controller board settings for your particular backup device.

Flag the DIBI2$DV.DAT file to Normal, then edit the DIBI2$DV.DAT file by typing the following command at the file server console and pressing Enter:

```
LOAD EDIT SYS:SYSTEM\DIBI\DIBI2$DV.DAT
```

If using a WANGTEK DIBI-II driver, you only have to load the SBACKUP NLM.

If using a DIBIDAI DIBI-II driver, type the following commands, where *nnnn* is the number of the host adapter, and press Enter after each:

LOAD AHA*nnnn*

LOAD TAPEDAI

If using a TAPEDC001 DIBI-II driver, type **LOAD ADAPTEC** and press Enter.

5. Type **LOAD SBACKUP.NLM** at the host server and press Enter.

6. When prompted, provide your user name and password.

7. If prompted, choose the appropriate device driver for the type of backup device you are using.

8. If prompted, choose a target to back-up.

9. From the Main menu, choose Backup Menu.

10. Choose Select Working Directory from the Backup menu and specify where the backup session files are to be stored.

11. In the Backup Options window, choose to back up the bindery in the What to back up: field. The default is NetWare Server.

12. Fill in other fields and make other choices as needed, then press Esc.

13. Choose Yes when prompted to Proceed with Backup.

14. Choose Start Backup Now and follow any additional prompts for inserting media (tapes), and so forth.

When the backup is complete, you can View the Error Log or just press Esc to return to the Main Menu. Then you can either exit SBACKUP, choose a different target to back up, restore previous backups, or choose to back up a network client.

Backing Up a Network Client

You can choose to back up a network client for any of several reasons. One good reason, particularly with DOS clients, arises when those clients are running Novell's Personal NetWare networking product. If they are, other users might also be accessing this client's hard disk. Backing up this client under this situation provides a measure of security for all network users who access the client.

Just as the SBACKUP utility is used to back up the file server's bindery, you employ SBACKUP to back up a client. However, some of the components needed to perform a client backup differ from those used to back up another file server on the network.

Prepare a NetWare DOS client for backup with the SBACKUP.NLM by completing the following steps:

1. Type **LOAD TSA_DOS** at the host server and press Enter. Several other NLMs are automatically loaded, including the following:

    ■ **STREAMS.NLM.** Provides a common interface between NetWare and the different transport protocols

    ■ **SMDR31X.NLM.** Provides an interface to the backup device driver for communication of device commands such as read, write, rewind, and eject

- **TLI.NLM.** Provides an interface between STREAMS and end-user's application programs

- **SPXS.NLM** or **IPXS.NLM.** Provides access between STREAMS and the related protocol: Sequenced Packet Exchange (SPX) or Internetwork Packet Exchange (IPX)

2. Modify the client's AUTOEXEC.BAT file to load TSA_SMS.COM. Then, reboot the client to automatically load the TSA_SMS.COM file.

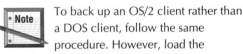 You only have to perform step 2 one time on each client whose hard disk you will be backing up. Thereafter, each time you boot any of these clients, the client's AUTOEXEC.BAT file automatically loads the TSA_SMS.COM file, preparing that client to be backed up.

3. Load SBACKUP at the host server.

4. Choose the client target you want to back up, and follow the prompts.

5. When the backup of the client is finished, exit SBACKUP.

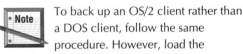 To back up an OS/2 client rather than a DOS client, follow the same procedure. However, load the TSA_OS2.NLM at the file server, rather than the TSA_DOS.NLM, and choose the OS/2 icon at the client instead of loading the TSA_SMS.COM file.

Questions

1. Which of the following statements about protecting your network from viruses is true?

   ○ A. The greater your rights on the network, the more damage the virus can do.

   ○ B. Limiting the Supervisor's number of login workstations has no effect on virus intrusion.

   ○ C. The only way to protect against viruses is to write-protect all disks.

   ○ D. Purchasing software from reputable vendors is a guarantee against virus intrusion.

2. To ensure that disks used on your network are free of any viruses, you can do all of the following EXCEPT:

   ○ A. Give network users access to virus scanning software.

   ○ B. Purchase new software from reliable vendors.

   ○ C. Install only software that has been virus tested.

   ○ D. None of these options help ensure network protection.

3. TWO additional guidelines you can implement to protect your network from viruses include:

   ☐ A. Training and educating network users

   ☐ B. Maintaining adequate backups

   ☐ C. Cleaning up all hard disks

   ☐ D. Installing virus software on each file server

4. Which of the following CANNOT be backed up using SBACKUP?

   ○ A. Network files

   ○ B. DOS workstations

   ○ C. OS/2 workstations

   ○ D. Macintosh workstations

5. In order to use SBACKUP on your network, your file server must have at least _____ of memory.

   ○ A. 1 MB

   ○ B. 2 MB

   ○ C. 4 MB

   ○ D. 8 MB

6. The file server to which the tape backup device is attached is called the _____.

   ○ A. parent

   ○ B. child

   ○ C. host

   ○ D. target

7. If you want to back up the files on the hard disk of a DOS client, which TWO files must be loaded?

   ☐ A. TSA_DOS on the file server

   ☐ B. TSA_DOS on the client

   ☐ C. TSA_SMS on the file server

   ☐ D. TSA_SMS on the client

8. To back up an OS/2 client, load the _____
   file at the file server.

   ○ A. TSA_DOS

   ○ B. TSA_SMS

   ○ C. TSA_OS2

   ○ D. TSA_ICON

9. Which of the following files is NOT loaded
   when TSA_DOS is loaded?

   ○ A. STREAMS

   ○ B. SMDR31X

   ○ C. SPX

   ○ D. TSA

10. Of the following statements, which TWO are
    true?

    ☐ A. TSA_DOS.NLM is loaded at the
       host server.

    ☐ B. STREAMS.NLM is automatically
       loaded when TSA_DOS is loaded.

    ☐ C. You cannot load both TSA_SMS
       and TSA_DOS when backing up a
       DOS client.

    ☐ D. None of the above statements are
       true.

Answers

1. A	6. C
2. D	7. A, D
3. A, B	8. C
4. D	9. D
5. A	10. A, B

NetWare 4.1 Administration

Understanding NetWare 4.x

*T*hose of you already familiar with NetWare 3 networks will find several differences, as well as several similarities, in the way NetWare 3 and NetWare 4 provide basic network services. The purpose of this chapter is to lay the foundation for a more complete understanding of how to administer a NetWare 4 network. To accomplish that goal, this chapter provides information about the following topics:

■ *Basic network components and function*

■ *NetWare Directory Services and the Directory tree*

Basic Network Function and Components

When discussing a network in the context of Novell networks, the type of network being discussed is a *client-server* network (one in which at least one computer functions as a network file server, providing services to other network computers called clients).

Basic Network Function

The basic function of a network is to enable users to share resources, as well as to access resources through other networks or remote hosts. This capability is provided by software (called the *operating system*) that controls the access to network resources. NetWare 4 is a network operating system.

Network Components

A network consists of two or more computers connected in a manner that enables them to share resources, as well as to access resources through other networks or remote hosts. The definition of a network generally includes the physical components associated with a network. At a minimum, those components include the following:

- File server
- Workstation
- Network board (one for each file server and workstation)
- Communications media

NetWare 4 networks include computers running the NetWare 4 operating system. These computers are called *network servers*.

A *client* is any device that requests services or resources from a server. The most common type of client is a computer, commonly called a *workstation*, used to access network resources. NetWare 4 supports computers running the following computer operating systems:

- DOS
- Microsoft Windows
- OS/2
- Macintosh
- Unix

A *network board* is a circuit board that provides communication between computers.

Communications media is the connection (link) between network boards. Two of the most commonly used communications media are coaxial cable and twisted-pair.

Another basic component of a network includes peripheral devices (such as printers or modems). Although not a required minimum component, peripherals usually are considered part of a network's basic hardware components.

NetWare Directory Services and the Directory Tree

You already may be familiar with the term *directory services*. In general, the term refers to the directory and file structure associated with a network file server's storage of programs and user data. In NetWare 4, as in other NetWare and competing network products, directory services remain the same. In NetWare 4; however, the term *NetWare Directory Services* (NDS) refers to something other than the NetWare directory and file structure. NDS refers to the directory or naming service for the database of network resources that NetWare 4 maintains. An understanding of NDS, what it is and how it differs from the network's general directory services, is key to understanding and administering a NetWare 4 network.

Understanding NDS

Unlike the directory services provided by the network, NDS does not provide directory and file services. Instead, NDS provides information about and access to all the network's logical resources.

For example, general directory services would provide you with information about and access to a specific user data file. NDS, however, provides information about and access to such things as the user's network account, rather than a particular file the user has stored on the network. This means that, through NDS, you can find out information about the user's account, such as the user's full name, login identification, telephone number, and other related information.

Networks provide access to a wide variety of network services, including the following:

- Printing
- Security
- Electronic messaging

NetWare Directory Services (NDS) is another type of network service. NDS, like other network services, is provided by file servers on the network. Only NetWare 4 file servers (as opposed to NetWare 3 or NetWare 2) can provide NDS.

The primary responsibility of NDS is to provide information about and access to network services. All network client requests for network services must use NDS. When a network client requests information about network resources, services from the network, or access to network services, NDS locates the necessary information and then provides the requested information, service, or access.

NDS is a replicatable, partitionable, distributed database containing information about network resources. Because it can be *replicated* (copied), *partitioned* (divided), and distributed, all or any specified portion or copy of the database can be stored on any NetWare 4 file server in the network. This means that, although entire copies or copies of portions or divisions (*partitions*) of the database may be stored on different servers in the network, the information contained within NDS can be made accessible from any client on the network. This is what gives NetWare 4 its global design.

Understanding the NDS Database

The NDS database is made up of the following three named items:

- Objects
- Properties
- Values

Objects

Every resource available on the network is represented in the NDS database as an object. An *object* is simply a record of information about that particular network resource. The network resource itself—whether a physical resource, such as a printer, or a logical resource, such as a group of users—is represented in the NDS database as an object.

The following three *object classes,* or types of objects, are allowed in the NDS database (see fig. 14.1):

- [Root]

- Container

- Leaf

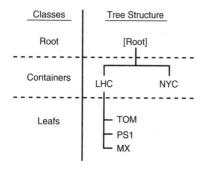

Figure 14.1

NDS object classes.

As with the general directory structure, the NDS directory structure is referred to as a *tree structure.* This description is appropriate because the NDS directory structure is arranged hierarchically, much as directories, subdirectories, and files are arranged in a hierarchical order resembling an upside-down tree in the general directory structure. In addition, as the DOS-based general directory structure has a top, represented by a drive letter and referred to as the *root,* the NDS structure begins with a top level, also called the root. In NDS, the root is referred to as the *Root object,* and is referenced as [Root] or [Treename].

 There can be only one Root per NDS database. That root can contain only Country, Organization, and Alias objects.

In the general Directory tree structure, directories and files exist. In the NDS tree structure, container objects and leaf objects exist.

A *container object* is any NDS object that can contain or hold other objects. Container objects are similar to directories in the general directory structure, because directories can contain other directories or files.

 Although sometimes referred to as a container object, [Root] is not a true container object for the following reasons:

- It is created by NetWare 4 when the first NetWare 4 server is installed on the network.

- You cannot move, delete, or rename it.

Following are the three defined classes of container objects:

- **Country (C).** Used to provide a logical division of the tree into countries, using two-character abbreviations (such as US for United States of America)

 This class of container objects is optional. If used, it must be placed immediately below [Root]. You can only place Organization and Alias objects beneath the Country container.

- **Organization (O).** Used to provide a logical grouping of network resources, such as entire companies or only departments within a company.

Note This class of container objects is required. Organization objects can be placed in Country or in other Organization objects, but cannot be placed in Organizational Unit objects. All objects (except an Alias object that points to [Root], Country, or Organization) can be placed in an Organization container.

- **Organizational Unit (OU).** Used to provide additional logical grouping of network resources into subgroups, such as company departments or teams.

Note This class of container objects is optional. It can contain other OUs, and all objects except [Root], Country, and Organization. In addition, although it can contain Alias objects, it cannot contain any Alias objects that point to [Root], Country, or Organization.

A *leaf object* is any NDS object that cannot contain or hold other objects. Leaf objects are similar to files in the general directory structure, because files cannot contain or hold other files or directories.

Of the variety of leaf objects that exist, the following are some that are frequently referenced:

- **Alias.** A pointer to another object in the database

- **Computer.** Print server or other computer that does not provide file storage and retrieval services (such as a router)

- **Directory Map.** Path pointer, usually directed at a frequently used path such as an application directory

- **Group.** List of users in need of common access rights

- **NetWare Server.** Network file server

- **Organizational Role.** A position or responsibility to which different users can be assigned at different times

- **Print Server.** Network print server

- **Printer.** Printer physically connected to the network

- **Profile.** Login script for multiple users

- **Print Queue.** Queue into which print jobs can be placed to be processed

- **User.** Network user

- **Volume.** Physical volume on a NetWare file server

Properties

For each object on the network, the NDS database can store certain types of information. The types of information about any given object (that can be stored in the NDS database) are called that object's *properties*.

For example, the NDS database can store various types of information about the User object, including the user's name, address, telephone number, and so on. These types of information constitute some of the properties of the User object.

Although some properties are the same for different object classes, some object classes may have properties that are more specific to that object class.

For example, every object class contains the Access Control List (ACL) property. Only leaf objects, such as Directory Map, User, and so on, can have a Common Name (CN) property, however.

Values

The information stored in each of an object's properties is called that property's *value.*

For example, the value of the ACL property for a given object is the list of other objects that can access this object. This is true regardless of the class of object with which the ACL property is associated. In other words, the ACL property of a User object and the ACL property of a Printer object contain the same type of information (a list of users with access to the object), even though the actual content (value) of the list may differ (see fig. 14.2).

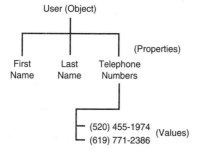

Figure 14.2

Property values.

Questions

1. The software that controls the access to network resources is called the _____ software.

   ○ A. operating system

   ○ B. workstation

   ○ C. client

   ○ D. peripheral

2. The basic function of a network is to _____, as well as to _____.

   ☐ A. print documents

   ☐ B. allow users to share resources

   ☐ C. provide access to remote resources

   ☐ D. save money

3. The _____ operating system is NOT supported by NetWare 4.

   ○ A. Unix

   ○ B. DOS

   ○ C. Macintosh

   ○ D. LSL

4. A _____ is any device that requests services or resources from a server.

   ○ A. media

   ○ B. peripheral

   ○ C. server

   ○ D. client

5. Although not required minimum components, _____ are usually considered part of the basic hardware components of a network.

   ○ A. media

   ○ B. peripherals

   ○ C. servers

   ○ D. clients

6. Country, Organization, and Organizational Unit are all _____ objects?

   ○ A. leaf

   ○ B. container

   ○ C. ACL

   ○ D. [Root]

7. Of the following, which THREE are named items in the NDS database?

   ☐ A. object

   ☐ B. property

   ☐ C. leaf

   ☐ D. value

8. A list of objects with access to another object is called the _____ of this object's ACL.

   ○ A. property

   ○ B. value

   ○ C. object

   ○ D. information

9. To make it easy to assign different users to a specific position or job responsibility, you can create a(n) _____ leaf object.

   ○ A. Alias

   ○ B. Printer

   ○ C. Organizational Role

   ○ D. User

10. If you want to see whether user Mary has access rights to a printer object, you must see the _____ of the printer's ACL.

   ○ A. value

   ○ B. property

   ○ C. object

   ○ D. purpose

Answers

1. A
2. B, C
3. D
4. D
5. B
6. B
7. A, B, D
8. B
9. C
10. A

Setting Up and Securing the Network File System

Chapter 14, "Understanding NetWare 4.x," introduced you to the aspect of NetWare 4 that constitutes the most significant change from earlier versions of NetWare— NetWare Directory Services. This chapter explains how to set up and secure the network and its associated file system, one main aspect of NetWare that has remained relatively consistent throughout various versions.

One major network file-system difference between NetWare versions is related to how you perform the actual setup and security. In NetWare 4, the two main utilities used to set up and secure the NetWare network file system are the Graphical User Interface (GUI) utility called NetWare Administrator, along with NETADMIN, its DOS-based equivalent.

This chapter discusses setting up and securing the network file system under NetWare 4, and provides information about the following topics:

■ Designing, planning, and creating the network file system

■ Understanding and planning basic file system security

■ Implementing basic file system security

Designing, Planning, and Creating the Network File System

NetWare uses volumes and directories to organize files and data. *Volumes,* created during the installation of NetWare file servers, are the basic building blocks of the network's file system structure. The volume called SYS contains the NetWare operating system and associated files.

Other volumes can be created to do the following tasks:

■ Hold applications

■ Store user data

■ Accommodate different operating systems (particularly if they use non-DOS file-naming conventions, such as Macintosh and OS/2)

■ Increase system fault tolerance

■ Any other logical use

Because volumes are the basic building blocks, they should be carefully planned before implementation. Careful planning makes it easier to back up and restore data on the network, implement security, make efficient use of disk space, and administer the network. NetWare 4's installation software starts the planning process by creating the first volume for you, and placing required directories and NetWare operating system files on that volume.

The volume and directories created during installation are shown in figure 15.1.

Figure 15.1

NetWare 4 installed volume and directories.

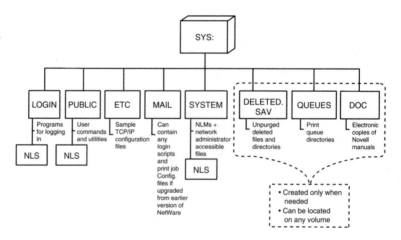

Additional directories, which network administrators may add in order to create an efficient directory structure, can include the following:

- **User data.** To provide an area where users can place their files

- **Applications.** To install various network applications, making it simpler to update and maintain application programs

 With a separate applications directory, you can separate the program files (EXE, BAT, and COM files) from user-created data files. This separation contributes to the logical structure of your network file system design, and makes it easier to add new applications to the network, as well as to update to newer versions.

- **Configuration.** To store configuration files for various network applications

- **DOS.** To make it easy for users to access DOS commands for various versions of DOS

 If you establish a DOS network directory, set the COMSPEC command for each workstation to point to the network DOS directory containing that workstation's version of DOS. This helps to ensure that the workstation can find the correct version of COMMAND.COM when exiting network applications.

- **Shared data.** To let groups of users with common data needs share a common directory

Understanding and Planning Basic File System Security

When planning and implementing network file system security, you should understand the following basic concepts related to file system security:

- Directory and file rights

- Trustee assignments

- Inheritance

- Reassignment of rights

- IRF (Inherited Rights Filter)

- Security equivalence

- Effective rights

To implement file system security, you must first understand each of these basic security concepts. This section describes each of these concepts and relates them to NetWare 4 file system security.

Directory and File Rights

Before you can access any file or directory, you must have the right to access it. Just as there are different ways to manage or manipulate a file or directory, there are different types of rights you can have. For example, if you want to read a file, you need the right to read the file. In NetWare 4, the right you need in order to read a file is called the Read right. NetWare 4 file and directory rights are shown in table 15.1.

Table 15.1
NetWare 4 File and Directory Rights

Right	Abbreviation	What You Can Do with This Right
File Scan	F	See files and directories
Erase	E	Delete files and directories
Write	W	Open and modify a file
Supervisor	S	Everything all other rights enable you to do
Create	C	Make new files or directories
Read	R	Open and read or run files
Access Control	A	Change trustee assignments and IRF
Modify	M	Change attributes or name

Trustee Assignments

In NetWare 4, rights are assigned to objects in the NDS tree. A *trustee* is an object (such as a user, group, or container) that has been assigned rights to another object. Before an object can have rights to a directory or file, that object must be defined as a trustee of the volume on which the directory or file is stored (placed on the Volume object's trustee list). The trustee can then be given rights to the directory or file as previously listed in table 15.1. Giving rights to a trustee is also known as *making a trustee assignment.*

Inheritance

You assign rights to a trustee for a directory or file at a specific level in the directory structure. The rights you assign to that trustee then flow down through the directory structure to other directories and files contained at and below the level at which you made the assignment. When a right is granted in a *parent directory* (a directory immediately above

any subdirectory), that right is granted also to all *children* (subdirectories and files) contained below the parent directory. This flow of rights is called *inheritance.* The rights received by other directories and files as a result of this process are said to have *inherited* those rights.

 Note   Container objects can also be called parent or child objects. *Parent* container objects are those which hold other container or leaf objects. *Child* objects are the container or leaf objects contained within a container object.

Reassignment of Rights

After you have made a rights assignment, you can change an object's rights at a lower level in the directory structure in either of two ways: by granting the object different rights at a lower level in the directory structure, or by using the IRF.

Granting a specific set of rights to a trustee at a level in the tree below the level at which you first granted rights is called a *reassignment of rights.* You can reassign rights whenever you need to change a trustee's access to the file system or to NDS objects. The drawback to reassigning rights is that you then need to keep track of which rights you assigned and where you assigned or reassigned those rights. When assigning or reassigning rights to multiple trustees for multiple objects, you can easily lose track of exactly which rights any given trustee may have been assigned. Using an IRF may be a better option.

IRF

The IRF is a list of all available rights at any given point in the tree. Its function is to control the flow of rights through the tree. Using the IRF, you can prevent one or more rights from being inherited. The IRF applies to all trustees and can permit or prevent any or all available rights from flowing down.

 Note In NetWare 4, unlike NetWare 3, the Supervisor property and Supervisor object rights can be blocked by using an IRF.

The only rights the IRF cannot filter out are those rights granted to a trustee at the same level on which the IRF is implemented. That is, the IRF cannot filter out a trustee assignment made at the same level as the IRF.

Security Equivalence

Objects (such as users, groups, and containers) are made trustees of directories, files, or other objects. The trustee is then given various rights, which determine the access the trustee has to the directory, file, or object. To simplify the assignment of rights, you can make an object *security equivalent* to another object. By doing so, any rights the first trustee has then also become rights of the object assigned security equivalence.

For example, every User object has a Security Equal To property, the value of which is a list of other objects. The objects included in that list have all the same rights to other objects, directories, and files that the original User object has.

Effective Rights

A User, Group, or Organizational Role object can obtain rights to the NetWare file system in several ways. Objects can obtain rights through the following methods:

- Trustee assignments
- Security equivalence
- Inheritance
- Parent containers
- The [Public] trustee
- Default rights assignments

The first two methods only grant rights to objects if a user with sufficient rights plans and implements security to make use of trustee assignments and security equivalence. These two methods have already been discussed.

The next two methods—inheritance and parent containers—grant rights based on other aspects of security, such as the trustee assignments and security equivalence that have been granted. These methods also have already been discussed.

The last two methods in the list—the [Public] trustee, and default rights assignments—are discussed next to help you better understand effective rights.

The [Public] Trustee

The [Public] trustee is a unique trustee, which is part of NDS when the first NetWare 4 file server is created. This trustee can be used to give the Read and File Scan right to anything *connected* (NetWare DOS Requester is loaded but the user has not yet logged in to the network) to the network by simply making [Public] a trustee of an object, directory, or file.

 Granting rights to the [Public] trustee enables you to give all users and objects Read and File Scan rights without requiring that they first be logged in to the network. The Read and File Scan rights are granted to the [Public] trustee by default.

The Read and File Scan rights granted to [Public] by default are not the only default rights in NetWare 4. The other default rights assignments are discussed next.

Default Rights Assignments

If you choose to create a user directory when the User object is created in NDS, the User object is given all file system rights, except Supervisor, to its user directory. In addition, the following objects are given Supervisor rights in the file system:

■ Objects with NDS Supervisor object rights to the Server object

■ Bindery Services Supervisor object

The user who created the NDS file server object is also given all rights to that object, including the file system Supervisor right.

Regardless of the method through which a User, Group, or Organizational Role object obtains rights to the NetWare file system, the rights obtained at any given point in the file system are called *effective rights*. The NetWare operating system calculates the object's effective rights at any point in the file system to determine what access the object will be given. To ensure network security, the network administrator must also be able to ascertain effective rights for specific users.

To determine effective rights, you must first know which rights have been granted through various objects. To find this information, check trustee assignments for the User object itself. Next, see whether the User object has been given any security equivalencies, or whether it is part of a Group. Also, check rights assigned to the User object's parent container, as well as any containers above it from which the User object can inherit rights. This means that you need to know which rights these container objects have, and whether those rights were specifically granted to the container, assigned by default, or assigned to [Public].

When you know which rights the User object has been granted or inherited, follow the flow of those rights through the tree. Remember to take into account any IRFs that may filter out any or all of those rights.

Implementing Basic File System Security

When planning file system security, you must consider the following two main factors:

■ Rights flow down from the top and, therefore, should be planned from the top down.

■ Trustee assignments also should be planned.

When planning and designing for top-down file system security, including trustee assignments, consider the following:

■ Design from limited access to greater access, from the highest level of the tree to the lowest level (top-down).

■ Give each trustee only the rights needed at each level.

■ Use inheritance to simplify rights flow, as necessary, and use the IRF to eliminate rights flow when specific rights are no longer needed.

■ Plan rights, starting at [Root], to flow down to the directories, subdirectories, and files.

■ Grant rights only as high in the file system structure as necessary.

■ Plan and make rights assignments to groups first, individual users next, and security equivalencies last.

One more issue to consider when planning file system security is the attributes that can be assigned to individual files and directories. Table 15.2 shows the available file and directory attributes.

 The Archive Needed, Hidden, Read Only, Read Write, and System attributes are DOS attributes. The Copy Inhibit, Delete Inhibit, and Rename Inhibit attributes are applied to Macintosh files only.

To implement file system security, use the network administration tools provided by NetWare. The two primary tools you use are the NetWare Administrator and NETADMIN utilities.

Using the NetWare Administrator and NETADMIN utilities you can accomplish several tasks, many of which are security-related, including:

■ Grant, revoke, and reassign rights

■ View effective rights

■ Set IRFs

■ Manage directory and file attributes

■ Manage directory and file trustee lists

■ Manage Group, User, and other objects

Table 15.2
File and Directory Attributes

Attribute	Abbreviation	Apply To
Archive Needed	A	Files
Can't Compress	Cc	Files
Compresses	Co	Files

continues

Table 15.2, Continued
File and Directory Attributes

Attribute	*Abbreviation*	*Apply To*
Copy Inhibit	Ci	Files
Delete Inhibit	Di	Files and directories
Don't Compress	Do	Files and directories
Don't Migrate	Dm	Directories
Don't Suballocate	Ds	Files
Execute Only	X	Files
Hidden	H	Files and directories
Immediate Compress	Ic	Files and directories
Migrate	M	Files
Normal	N	Files and directories
Purge	P	Files and directories
Read Only	Ro	Files
Read Write	Rw	Files
Rename Inhibit	R	Files
Rename Inhibit	Ri	Directories
Shareable	Sh	Files
System	S	Files and directories
Transactional	T	Files

Note To use the NetWare Administrator and NETADMIN utilities, as described in the following sections, you must have the utility running and be pointed to the correct location in the directory tree.

Granting, Revoking, and Reassigning Rights

You can use both the NetWare Administrator and the NETADMIN utilities to grant, revoke, and reassign rights.

Using NetWare Administrator to Grant, Revoke, and Reassign Rights

To grant rights by using the NetWare Administrator utility, first choose the object from the main NetWare Administrator window, then choose Rights to Files and Directories. Next, choose the Add button. When the Select Object window opens, select the files and directories to which the object is to be granted rights (see fig. 15.2).

After an object has been granted rights to directories and files in a volume, those rights can be reassigned (modified) or deleted. To reassign or delete rights, choose Rights to Files and Directories from the main NetWare Administration window, and then from the Rights to Files and Directories User window (see fig. 15.3), mark or unmark the rights to be granted or revoked, or remove the user as a trustee by choosing the Delete button.

Using NETADMIN to Grant, Revoke, and Reassign Rights

To grant, revoke, or reassign rights by using the NETADMIN utility, first choose the object from the Object menu's Class list. Then, from the Actions for user: *username* screen, choose the View or edit rights to files and directories option.

Next, provide the Volume Object name and the beginning path, to specify where the object will be granted rights. Also choose whether rights will be granted only for directories at the defined path, only for files, or for both directories and files, and whether subdirectories will be included.

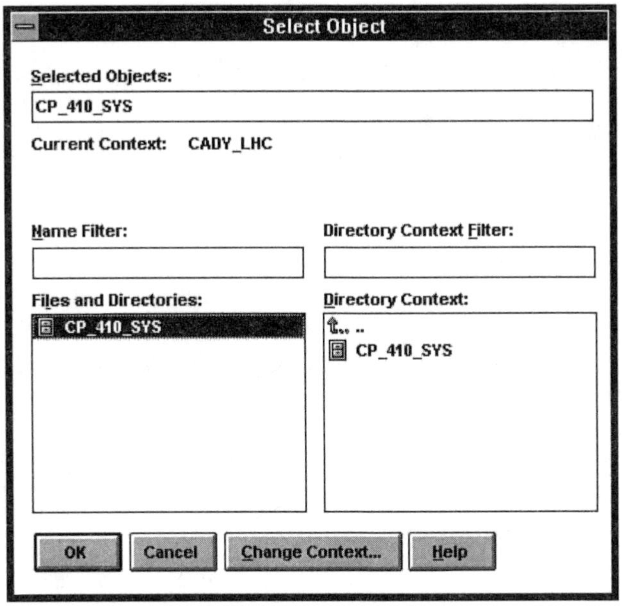

Figure 15.2

The Select Object window.

Figure 15.3

The Rights to Files and Directories window for user Michelle.

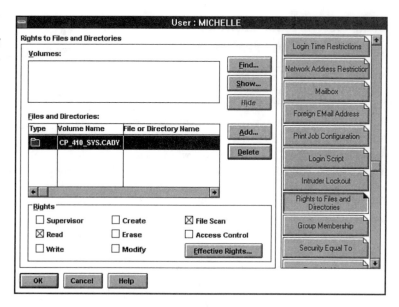

Now press F10 to display the list of trustee rights. If no rights have been assigned to this object, the list is blank. To assign (add) rights, press Insert and specify the Directory in which trustee should be added. Default rights are granted. To modify those rights, press Enter, then add to the list of available rights by pressing Insert and marking or choosing the additional rights to be assigned.

Follow this same process to revoke (or reassign) rights, modifying the list of rights assigned to this object as necessary.

View Effective Rights

Whether you are running the NetWare Administrator or the NETADMIN utility, you can view effective rights by following the same basic procedure used to grant, reassign, or revoke rights. The main difference, of course, is that you view the rights but do not modify them.

 Note   You can also use the RIGHTS command to see effective rights.

Setting IRFs

IRFs can be set anywhere in the file system structure. Before setting an IRF, make sure that you are pointed to the exact location in the file system structure where you want to set or modify the IRF. Then, using either NetWare Administrator or NETADMIN, you can set or modify the IRF.

Using NetWare Administrator to Set IRFs

To set an IRF by using NetWare Administrator, complete the following steps:

1. Select the directory or file from the NetWare Administrator window.

2. Choose Details from the **O**bject pull-down menu.

3. Choose either the Trustees of this File or Trustees of this Directory button, depending on whether you originally selected a file or directory.

4. Mark, unmark, or leave unchanged the box next to each right listed in the Inheritance Filter portion of the Trustees of this File or Directory window (see fig. 15.4).

 Note If a right is grayed out, or shown in gray instead of black ink, that right is unavailable. A mark (X) in the box next to a right indicates that the right can be inherited. To prevent inheritance of a right, unmark the box next to that right.

Using NETADMIN to Set Volume Object IRFs

To set IRFs by using the NETADMIN utility, complete the following steps:

1. Choose the Volume object from the **O**bject, Class list.

2. Choose View or edit the trustees of this object from the Actions for volume: *volume_name* menu.

3. Choose Inherited Rights Filters from the Trustees of this object menu.

4. Press Insert to see a list of properties that can be filtered.

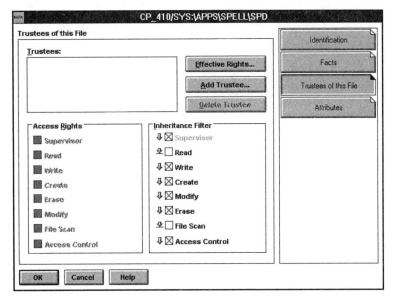

Figure 15.4
The Trustees of this File window.

5. Choose the properties to be filtered.

   For example, to restrict the Object Rights property, choose [Object Rights] from the Properties menu. The [Object Rights] property is then listed on the Inherited Rights Filters screen.

6. Choose an item from those listed on the Inherited Rights Filters screen. A list of the rights that are allowed (not currently screened out by the IRF) is displayed.

   For example, choose [Object Rights]. The Entry rights allowed screen opens, displaying the object rights currently not screened out by the IRF.

7. Modify rights to be allowed by pressing Insert to see a list of rights from which to choose to add. Or delete rights from the list of rights currently not screened out by the IRF.

Managing Directory and File Attributes

Directory and file attributes can be managed by using the NetWare Administrator utility. You cannot use the DOS-based NETADMIN utility to change directory or file attributes. To change directory or file attributes from DOS, use FILER.

To manage directory and file attributes by using NetWare Administrator, first choose the volume and then expand the directory structure until you find the directory or file whose attributes you want to manage.

Next, choose the directory or file itself. When the Identification window for this directory or file opens (see fig. 15.5), choose the Attributes button.

In the Attributes window (see fig. 15.6), mark or unmark attributes as necessary, then choose OK to display the previous window.

Figure 15.5

The Identification window.

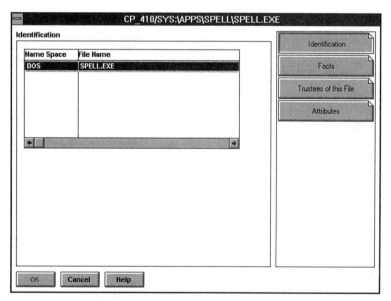

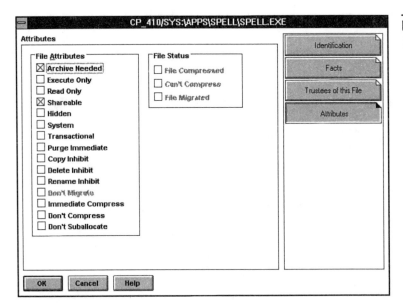

Figure 15.6
The Attributes window.

Managing Directory and File Trustee Lists

To manage directory and file trustee lists, select the object from the list of objects in NetWare Administrator. Then choose Trustees of this object from the **O**bjects pull-down menu. In the Trustees window (see fig. 15.7), you can see which other objects are currently included on this object's list of trustees. By using the buttons in this window you can perform the following tasks:

- Add trustees
- Delete trustees
- Modify a trustee's object and property rights
- View a trustee's effective rights
- Modify the IRF

Managing Group, User, and Other Objects

Before you can manage an object, it must exist. If the object does not already exist, you can create it by using the NetWare Administrator or NETADMIN utilities.

Using NetWare Administrator to Create and Manage Group, User, and Other Objects

To use the NetWare Administrator utility to create an object, first select (from the NetWare Administrator window) the container where the object is to be added, then choose Create from the **O**bject pull-down menu (see fig.15.8).

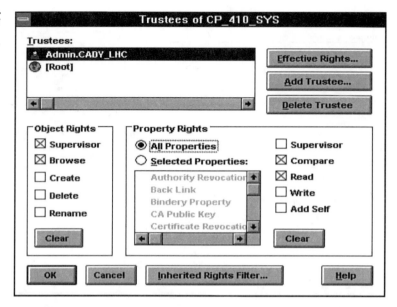

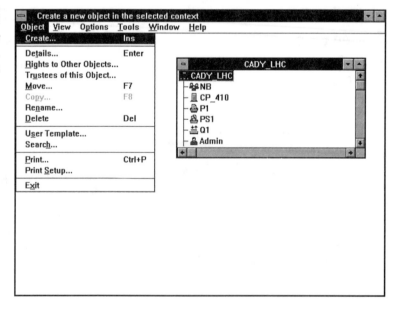

Using NETADMIN to Create and Manage Group, User, and Other Objects

To use the NETADMIN utility to create an object, press Insert at the Class, Object screen, select the type of object to be created from the Select an object class screen, then provide the requested information.

When creating a Group object, for example, you provide a name and mailbox location.

When objects exist in the NDS tree, you can manage those objects. Various management tasks can be performed on an object.

You can use NETADMIN to delete objects, for example, by selecting the object from the list of objects, pressing Delete, and confirming the deletion.

You can use NETADMIN to perform the following management tasks as well:

- Viewing or editing properties of the object

- Renaming the object

- Moving the object

- Viewing or editing rights to files and directories

- Viewing or editing the trustees of the object

Each of these management tasks is performed by choosing the appropriate option from the Actions for *Object: Object_name* menu, and then providing requested information.

In addition to using the NetWare Administrator and NETADMIN utilities, you can also use the RIGHTS command to grant, revoke, and view information about rights from the DOS prompt.

 The RIGHTS command is frequently used for the following reasons:

- To view trustees (RIGHTS /T)

- To see your effective rights (RIGHTS)

In addition, you can use the NDIR command to view information about files and directories.

 Following are two lesser-know but useful NDIR options:

- **/VOL.** Enables you to view volume information

- **/SPA.** Enables you to view space information

In addition to RIGHTS and NDIR, you can use the menu utility FILER to perform various file and directory tasks.

Questions

1. The basic building blocks of the NetWare file system structure are _____.

   ○ A. volumes

   ○ B. directories

   ○ C. files

   ○ D. databases

2. Which TWO are created during installation?

   ☐ A. USER

   ☐ B. SYS

   ☐ C. DELETED.SAV

   ☐ D. ETC

3. The _____ does NOT *t* have to be considered when you plan and implement network file system security.

   ○ A. physical location of user ADMIN

   ○ B. rights inheritance

   ○ C. IRF

   ○ D. directory and file rights

4. Which of the following correctly lists the hot keys for NetWare 4 file and directory rights?

   ○ A. NOMFILES

   ○ B. RUNFASTR

   ○ C. FEWSCRAM

   ○ D. SUPERMAN

5. A/an _____ is a/an _____ assigned rights to a directory or file.

   ○ A. reassignment of rights, object's

   ○ B. IRF, object's

   ○ C. object, inheritance

   ○ D. trustee, object

6. Which of the following is TWO one of the ways a User, Group, or Organizational Role object can obtain file system rights?

   ○ A. Trustee assignment

   ○ B. Security equivalent

   ○ C. Parent container

   ○ D. Child container

7. Of the following, which TWO are default rights assigned to [Public]?

   ☐ A. Read

   ☐ B. Write

   ☐ C. Access control

   ☐ D. File scan

8. Migrate, Normal, and Purge are all known as _____.

   ○ A. Trustee assignments

   ○ B. Object rights

   ○ C. File attributes

   ○ D. Default [Public] rights

9. To view effective rights, you CANNOT use the _____ utility/command.

   ○ A. NETADMIN

   ○ B. NetWare Administrator

   ○ C. RIGHTS

   ○ D. REVOKE

10. When a right is grayed out, what does it mean?

    ○ A. The right has been revoked.

    ○ B. The right is unavailable.

    ○ C. The right can only be granted to
           ADMIN.

    ○ D. The right can only be granted to leaf
           objects.

Answers

1. A

2. B, D

3. A

4. C

5. D

6. D

7. A, D

8. C

9. D

10. B

16

Setting Up Network Printing and Mail Services

*S*hared printing and electronic mail are two particularly useful features of a network. NetWare 4 provides both of these services. This chapter discusses network printing and electronic mail within a NetWare 4 network, and provides information about the following topics:

- Setting up print services

- Customizing and managing print jobs

- Controlling access to and management of printing

- Installing and configuring messaging services

Setting Up Print Services

The process of setting up NetWare 4 print services includes setting up both hardware and software components. Hardware components include the following:

- Printers
- Servers
- DOS workstations
- Cabling

NetWare 4 printing software components include the following:

- PSERVER.NLM
- NPRINTER.NLM
- NPRINTER.EXE

In addition to setting up these hardware and software components, when you set up NetWare 4 printing you must also create the following three NDS objects:

- Print Servers
- Print Queues
- Printers

Setting Up Printing Hardware and Running Related Software

The first step in making shared printing available is to set up the hardware associated with printing on a NetWare 4 network, and to run the related software. You must consider the following hardware-related printing setup issues:

- Connecting a printer to a NetWare server
- Connecting a printer to a DOS workstation
- Bringing up a print server

Connecting a Printer to a NetWare Server

In order to have print services on a NetWare 4 network, at least one of the NetWare 4 file servers must also be functioning as a NetWare 4 print server. In NetWare 4, printers can be attached to any of the file servers, regardless of whether the file server is also functioning as a print server.

 For more information about print servers, see the "Bringing Up a Print Server" section, later in this chapter.

To physically connect a printer to a NetWare server, attach the printer cable to a printer port on the file server.

 If an NDS Printer object has not yet been created for this printer, you must create one before this printer is accessible to the network. (Instructions for creating NDS Printer objects are provided later in this chapter.) In addition, a network print server must be up and running, instructions for which are also discussed later in this chapter.

 When the printer is attached to a NetWare 4 file server that is not also a print server, you must configure the Printer object for this printer to be Manual Load.

Connecting a Printer to a DOS Workstation

As long as the NetWare print server software is loaded on at least one NetWare file server, you can attach printers to DOS workstations as well as to file servers.

Connect printers to workstations the same way you connect them to file servers—by cabling them to the computer's printer port. Then, activate workstation-related printing software by running NPRINTER.EXE on the workstation. To run NPRINTER.EXE, type **NPRINTER** *[printer\print_server printer_number]* at the workstation keyboard, and press Enter. Replace *printer* with the name of the Printer object created for this printer, or replace *print_server* with the print server name assigned to this printer. If you chose to provide a print server name instead of a Printer object, you must also provide a printer number, replacing *printer_number* with the logical printer number assigned to this printer.

 As with printers attached to file servers, a print server must exist somewhere on the network. In addition, an NDS Printer object for this printer must be created before you load NPRINTER.EXE. Furthermore, when the printer is attached to a workstation, you must configure the Printer object to be Manual Load.

Bringing Up a Print Server

A *print server* is a NetWare file server on which PSERVER.NLM and NPRINTER.NLM have been loaded to provide printing services. A print server is responsible for sending print job requests to assigned printers.

In NetWare 4, you bring up a print server by loading PSERVER.NLM on a NetWare 4 file server, which automatically loads NPRINTER.NLM.

 When the printer is attached to a print server, you must configure the Printer object to be Auto Load (also called *Local*).

To load the print server software on a NetWare 4 file server, type the following command at the file server console, and press Enter:

```
LOAD PSERVER .cn=print_server.ou=name.o=name
```

Replace *.cn=print_server.ou=name.o=name* with the specific context and common name assigned to the print server.

 To ensure that the print server is loaded each time the file server is loaded, add the preceding command to the AUTOEXEC.NCF file.

When a print server is up, it can service up to 255 printers and any number of assigned print queues.

Table 16.1 summarizes NetWare 4 printing services. It shows where printers can be connected, and how their printing services are made available on a NetWare 4 network.

Table 16.1
Summary of Printing Options in NetWare 4

Printer Connected to	Software to be Loaded/Run	Printer Object Load Configuration
File Server	NPRINTER.NLM	Manual Load
Print Server	PSERVER.NLM	Auto Load
	NPRINTER.NLM	
Workstation	NPRINTER.EXE	Manual Load

Creating NDS Print Objects

The second major task associated with setting up network printing is to create necessary related NDS printing objects, of which there are the following three types:

■ Print servers

■ Print queues

■ Printers

You can create these objects manually, or you can run the Quick Setup option provided in PCONSOLE to automatically create one of each of these objects. When you use PCONSOLE to set up printing services, only one of each type of object is created. You must create additional objects manually if you need more than one Print server, Print queue, and Printer object on your network.

To run the Quick Setup option in PCONSOLE, complete the following steps:

1. Run PCONSOLE from the DOS prompt by typing **PCONSOLE** and pressing Enter.

2. Choose Quick Setup (see fig. 16.1).

3. Modify any default fields that need to be changed, and provide appropriate printer values as necessary.

4. Press F10.

You can also create Print server objects, Print queue objects, and Printer objects by using the NetWare Administrator utility. To create any of these objects, run the NetWare Administrator utility, and set the current context (location in the tree) to the location in the NDS tree where you want the object to reside. Then choose Create from the Object pull-down menu, and continue creating the object, depending on its type, as described in the following sections.

Creating Print Server Objects

To create a Print Server object, complete the following steps:

1. Choose Print Server from the list of object classes.

2. Provide a name for the Print Server.

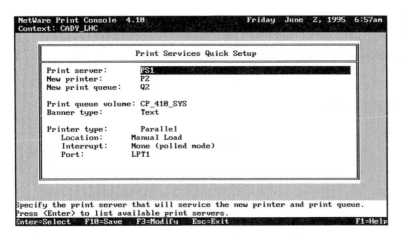

Figure 16.1

The PCONSOLE Quick Setup screen.

3. Mark the Define Additional Properties box (see fig. 16.2).

Figure 16.2

The Create Print Server window.

4. Choose Create.

5. Fill in at least the minimum information necessary (the Print Server object name and Printer objects to be managed by this Print Server object).

6. Choose OK.

Note When a Print Server object is created, default rights and assignments are created for the Print Queue Operator, Print Queue User, and the Print Server Operator List.

Creating Print Queue Objects

To create a Print queue object, complete the following steps:

1. Choose Print Queue from the list of object classes.

2. Choose the type of Print Queue object (Directory Service Queue or Reference a Bindery Queue).

3. Provide at least the minimum information necessary for a Print Queue object (a name for the print queue, and the name of the volume where the print queue is to be placed).

4. Mark the Define Additional Properties box (see fig. 16.3) if additional information (such as a description, location, operator flags, and so on) is to be provided.

Figure 16.3
The Create Print Queue window.

 If you chose to define additional properties, fill in the information you want to provide on the form that opens (Print Queue Identification), then choose OK on this form.

5. Choose OK.

Creating Printer Objects

To create Printer objects, complete the following steps:

1. Choose Printer from the list of object classes.

2. Provide a name for the printer.

3. Mark the Define Additional Properties box (if necessary).

 Fill in additional information, as necessary, if you chose to define additional properties, then choose OK.

4. Choose Create.

Customizing and Managing Print Jobs

Some aspects of a network print job can be customized. With NetWare 4, you can choose what to customize, and then create custom print jobs.

You can, for example, choose whether to have a banner page printed before each print job, or whether a special form should be used with a particular print job. In addition, NetWare 4 enables you to manage various aspects of print jobs (such as which print queue a print job can use).

In addition to customizing print jobs, you can manage print jobs. Print job management includes management of print queues, print servers, and printers.

Customizing Print Jobs

To create customized print jobs, use the NetWare Administrator or PRINTCON utilities. You can then use these customized print jobs when you use the CAPTURE or NPRINT *Job* option.

To create print job configurations by using NetWare Administrator, first choose the level at which you want the print job configuration to be placed.

Note If you create the print job configuration at the container level, all user objects in that container have access to the print job configuration by default. To ensure that only a specific user has access to the print job configuration, create it at the user object level.

After you select the level, choose Details from the Object pull-down menu. Next, choose Print Job Configuration from the list of available objects. Choose the New button, then fill in the necessary fields in the Print Job Configuration window (see fig. 16.4).

When you create a print job configuration, you must include at least a name for the print job configuration (Print Job Name) and choose a printer or print queue object for the print job configuration to use (Printer/Queue). Other fields can be left at their default settings, or can be modified as necessary. Table 16.2 lists the fields in the Print Job Configuration window, and briefly explains their function.

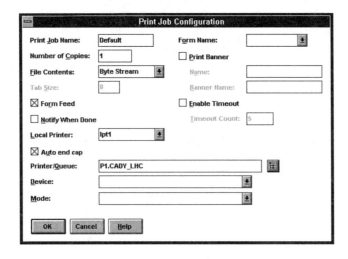

Figure 16.4

The Print Job Configuration window.

Table 16.2
Print Job Configuration Fields

Field Name	Hot Key	Function
Print Job Name	J	Provides name to be used when choosing a print job
Form Name	O	Chooses form used when this print job configuration is chosen
Number of Copies	C	Number of copies (1 to 65,000) to be printed when this print job configuration is used
Print Banner	P	Specifies whether banner page should be printed at beginning of each job that uses this configuration
Name	A	Any name that identifies owner of print job; placed on the banner page (default is user's login name)
Banner Name	B	Name that identifies the print job itself; default is either the file name (NPRINT commands) or the port number (CAPTURE commands)
File Contents	F	Text (tab commands are understood and their size can be set), or Byte stream (no tabs)
Tab Size	S	Number of spaces to be used between tab stops
Form Feed	R	Specifies whether form should be ejected from printer after print job is complete
Enable Timeout	E	Specifies whether print job should be considered complete after specified amount of time has elapsed since last command was sent to printer
Timeout Count	T	Specifies how much time can elapse before job is considered complete when Enable Timeout option is used
Notify When Done	N	Determines whether print job's originator (workstation) should receive notification when job has been printed
Local Printer	L	Indicates which printer port (LPT1 through LPT9) printer is attached to
Auto end cap	U	Automatically closes print queue file when print job has been printed
Printer/Queue	Q	Specifies printer or queue this print job configuration should use
Device	D	Specifies print device to be used for jobs that use this configuration
Mode	M	Enables you to choose a print mode, as determined by print device you chose

Managing Print Jobs

Print servers, print queues, and printers periodically require administrator intervention. Intervention may include such tasks as preventing new print servers from adding jobs to print queues, deleting print jobs from a print queue, or pausing, stopping, and restarting the printer. These tasks, as well as many other print job management tasks, can be accomplished by using either of the following utilities:

- PCONSOLE
- NetWare Administrator

Managing Print Jobs with PCONSOLE

You can accomplish several print job management tasks by running PCONSOLE at a workstation, then choosing one of the following from the PCONSOLE Available Options menu:

- Print Queues
- Printers
- Print Servers

To manage print queues, choose Print Queue from the Available Options menu, choose the print queue to be managed, then choose what you want to manage from the Print Queue Information menu (see fig. 16.5).

You can choose to perform various print queue management tasks by choosing any of the following from the Print Queue Information menu:

- **Print Jobs.** Enables you to add (press Ins) print jobs to the queue, cancel (press Del) print jobs, or change fields on a print job's information screen (choose the print job).

- **Status.** Enables you to view information about the print queue. This information includes the number of jobs currently in the queue, the number of active print servers for this queue, and the status (YES/NO) of operator flags.

- **Attached print servers.** Enables you to see which print servers can service this print queue.

- **Information.** Enables you to see the Object ID assigned to this print queue, the name of the file server associated with this print queue, and the volume in which this queue is located.

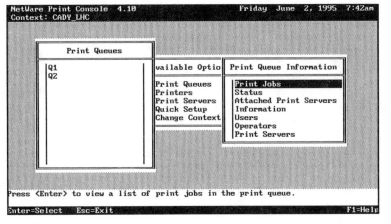

Figure 16.5

The Print Queue Information menu.

Figure 16.6

The Print Server Information menu.

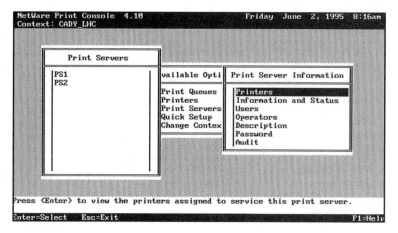

- **Users.** Enables you to add or remove users from the list of authorized users.

- **Operators.** Enables you to add or remove operators from the list of authorized print queue operators.

- **Print Servers.** Enables you to add or remove print servers from the list of authorized print servers.

You can choose to perform various print server management tasks by choosing any of the following from the Print Server Information menu (see fig. 16.6):

- **Printers.** Enables you to add, Delete, rename (press F3), or modify the configuration of a printer (choose the printer)

- **Information and Status.** Enables you to shut down the print server, or change its name

- **Users.** Enables you to add or Delete users authorized to send jobs to this print server

- **Operators.** Enables you to add or Delete objects that can manage this print server

- **Description.** Enables you to edit the description associated with this print server

- **Password.** Enables you to change this print server's password

- **Audit.** Enables you to turn auditing for the print server on or off, set the maximum allowable size for the audit file, and view and delete the audit file

You can modify various items of printer-related information as well, by first choosing Printers from the Available Options menu, then choosing a specific printer. Figure 3.7 shows the Printer Configuration screen for the printer named PS1.

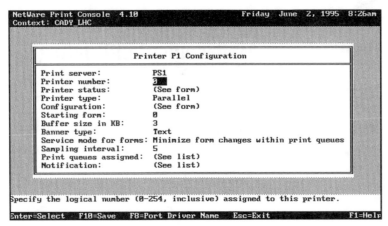

Figure 16.7
The Printer Configuration screen.

You can modify information for the printer by choosing any of the following fields from the Printer Configuration screen:

- Printer number
- Printer status
- Printer type
- Configuration (of the printer itself)
- Starting form
- Buffer size in KB
- Banner type
- Service mode for forms
- Sampling interval
- Print queues assigned
- Notification (list of objects to be notified)

Managing Print Jobs with NetWare Administrator

To manage print jobs by using the NetWare Administrator utility, select the print object (Print Server, Printer, or Print Queue) you want to manage from the NetWare Administrator, then choose

Details from the Object pull-down menu. Then, depending on the type of printing object you chose, either fill in or modify the fields on the forms associated with each type of print object.

The following forms are associated with the Print Queue object:

- Identification
- Assignments
- Operators
- Users
- Job list

Forms associated with the Print Server object include the following:

- Identification
- Assignments
- Users
- Operator
- Auditing log
- Print layout

These forms are associated with the Printer object:

- Identification
- Assignments
- Configuration
- Notification
- Features
- See also
- Printer status

Controlling Access to and Management of Printing

To spread out the responsibility for managing network printing, various types of users can be assigned to perform various tasks. Different types of users have different rights and responsibilities for managing printing. Table 16.3 shows the types of users who can manage printing services, and the management duties they are given by default.

Table 16.3
Default Network Printing Management User Capabilities

User Type	Default Tasks That Can Be Performed
Container Supervisor	Create and delete Printer objects Create and delete Print Server objects Create and delete Print Queue objects Change print queue list of users Change print queue list of operators Change assignment of print queues Change Notify list Monitor print servers
Printer Notify List	Receive error messages from a printer
Print Queue Operator	Manage print jobs in print queue for self and others Change print queue operator flags
Print Server Operator	Change assignment of print queues Change Notify list Change status of printer Bring down a print server (unload print server files)
Print Queue User	Submit, modify, and remove own jobs in print queue
Print Server User	Monitor print servers Receive error messages from a printer

Installing and Configuring Messaging Services

Messaging services are concerned primarily with active communication between network users. Messaging services are responsible for storing, retrieving, and delivering communications in many forms (binary data, text, graphics, and video and audio data).

To accomplish network communication, NetWare's messaging services provide a *messaging engine* (technology that has been integrated with NDS to accommodate the transportation, storage, and retrieval of network communications), *mailboxes* (electronic storage locations for individual network users), and *messaging applications* (utilities to simplify access to and use of network messaging services).

 Although various NetWare-compatible applications can be used to access and use messaging services, NetWare 4 includes a basic NDS-aware electronic mail application called FirstMail, the use of which is discussed in Chapter 8, "Accessing and Using Network Resources."

Before you can use NetWare's Message Handling Services (MHS), it must be installed. You can install MHS when you install the NetWare 4 file server, or you can install it later. To install MHS when you install NetWare 4, you must choose the Customized installation option. Otherwise, you install MHS by using INSTALL.NLM.

Before you can install MHS, your file server must meet the following minimum requirements:

- 500 KB of RAM available

- 2.5 MB of hard disk space to store MHS programs, plus additional disk space for user mailboxes

- A CD-ROM drive

 To handle 10 network users who need no more than 100 messages per day, the file server must meet the following minimum requirements:

- 80386 microprocessor

- 12 MB file server RAM

- 65 MB hard disk space

To install MHS, either load INSTALL.NLM after the NetWare 4 file server has been installed, or choose the customized installation path during the NetWare 4 file server installation. Then complete the following steps:

1. Choose Product options.

2. From the Other Installation Actions menu, choose the Choose an item or product listed above option.

3. From the Other Installation Items/Products menu, choose Install NetWare MHS.

4. Choose the path.

 If the current path does not point to the location of the NETMAIN.ILS file, press F3 and change the path.

5. When the Postmaster General Authentication window opens, enter (in the Name field) the name of the user responsible for administration of MHS, making certain to provide the

user's complete context; then (in the Password field) enter the user's password, and press Enter.

6. Choose the volume on which the MHS database is to be installed (if the NetWare 4 server has multiple volumes), and press Enter.

7. Modify the AUTOEXEC.NCF file to include the LOAD MHS command.

 Choose NCF file options from the Installation Options menu to modify the AUTOEXEC.NCF file. Remember, the server must be taken down and reloaded before any changes made to the AUTOEXEC.NCF file will become effective.

During the basic installation of NetWare 4, the Messaging Services object is created. When the Messaging Services object exists, mailboxes must be assigned to NDS objects. Assign mailboxes to any of the following NDS objects:

■ Users

 To assign a mailbox to a user, use the Messaging Server object and choose the Users property.

■ Groups

■ Organizational Role

■ Organizational Unit

In addition, you can create distribution lists by choosing Create from the NetWare Administrator Objects pull-down menu, then choosing Distribution List. Provide a name for the distribution list, then add users, groups, and other NDS objects as appropriate.

 If your network contains a gateway, you can add the External Entity object so that messages can be sent to users not included in the list of NDS users.

Questions

1. Of the following, which one CANNOT be used to provide printing services to the network?

   ○ A. Print server

   ○ B. File server

   ○ C. Workstation

   ○ D. Stand-alone computer

2. Which TWO commands load the print server software on a NetWare 4 file server?

   ☐ A. LOAD NPRINTER.NLM

   ☐ B. LOAD PSERVER.NLM

   ☐ C. INSTALL PSERVER.NLM

   ☐ D. INSTALL PSERVER.EXE

3. The _____ PCONSOLE option automatically sets up printing services.

   ○ A. Automatic Setup

   ○ B. Print Install

   ○ C. Basic Setup

   ○ D. Quick Setup

4. Of the following, which one allows you to create Print Server objects, Print Queue objects, and Printer objects?

   ○ A. NETADMIN

   ○ B. PSERVER

   ○ C. NetWare Administrator

   ○ D. CAPTURE

5. The minimum information required when creating a Print Queue object is _____.

   ○ A. a print queue name only

   ○ B. a print queue name and volume

   ○ C. a volume only

   ○ D. a print queue name, volume, and print server

6. Which of the following is NOT a true statement?

   ○ A. If you create a print job configuration at the container level, all user objects in that container have access to it by default.

   ○ B. You can create a print job by choosing the Details option from the NetWare Administrator Object pull-down menu.

   ○ C. The minimum information you must provide when creating a print job configuration is the volume on which it is to be stored.

   ○ D. When managing printing on a NetWare 4 server, you must consider management of print queues, print servers, and printers.

7. Of the following, which TWO are fields you can fill in when you create a print job configuration?

   ☐ A. File Server Name

   ☐ B. No End Cap

   ☐ C. File Contents

   ☐ D. Timeout Count

8. The _____ option on the Print Queue Information menu enables you to view information about the print queue, such as the current number of jobs in the queue.

   ○ A. Print jobs

   ○ B. Status

   ○ C. Information

   ○ D. Print Servers

9. To delete the print server's audit log, choose the _____ option from the Print Server Information menu.

   ○ A. Information and Status

   ○ B. Description

   ○ C. Operators

   ○ D. Audit

10. When you want to give another network user the responsibility for downing a print server, you can create a _____ object.

   ○ A. Print Server Operator

   ○ B. Print Server User

   ○ C. Container Supervisor

   ○ D. Print Server Supervisor

Answers

1. D

2. A, B

3. D

4. C

5. B

6. C

7. C, D

8. B

9. D

10. A

Setting Up Secure User Access

*N*etwork security is both a software and a hardware issue. Hardware security may include such issues as controlling physical access to network file servers and providing protection against power surges and losses.

NetWare software security includes both file system and NDS (Network Directory Services) security. Although security issues between the two are often similar—file system security controls access to files and directories, and NDS security controls access to NDS objects—NDS and file system security are separate issues. In this chapter, only issues related to NDS security (and not to file system or hardware security) are discussed.

This chapter, because it focuses on providing secure access to the network for network users, discusses the following security and network access issues:

- Understanding and implementing security

- Ensuring secure network access through user objects

- Automating network access through a DOS workstation

Understanding and Implementing Security

In NetWare 4, all network resources such as users, groups, and so on are recorded as objects in the NDS database. Just as access by users to network directories and the files they contain is regulated by file system security, access to the network and the resources it provides is regulated by NDS security. NDS security controls who can access NDS objects and the properties associated with them.

To gain access to the network, users must first have a User object created by the network administrator. (See the "Ensuring Secure Network Access through User Objects" section of this chapter for information about how to create User objects.)

NDS User objects must be assigned, at a minimum, a Login Name property value, and a Last Name property value. This information, along with other property values (including password requirements and values) is then stored in the NDS database. The user then logs in to the network, using the Login Name and Password property values. Login security compares these two values, checks for any restrictions that may have been set up for this User object, verifies that a valid User object and Password combination were used, and if not, tracks login attempts based on any set Intruder Limits. Then, if everything is correct, login security authenticates the login request and grants the User object access to NDS network resources.

To access NDS resources on the network, the user seeking access must first have been given the necessary NDS rights. Before rights can be granted to a User or other NDS object, however, that object must be made a trustee of the NDS resource. Then various rights such as Browse, Create, and so on can be assigned.

 Note An object is made a trustee of another object by adding the first object to the Object Trustees ACL (Access Control List) of another object. To simplify this process, using the NetWare Administrator utility, you can drag one object on top of another object and drop it there. This process automatically makes the dragged object a trustee of the receiving object.

For example, to give user object SAM the right to see all objects in container PAYROLL, user object SAM must be added to the Object Trustees (ACL) property for the PAYROLL container. Using the NetWare Administrator utility, User object SAM can be dragged on top of the PAYROLL container object and dropped. Then user object SAM must be given the Browse object right.

Note also that every object in the NDS tree has an Object Trustees (ACL) property.

Unlike the file system, which has only one set of rights, NDS has two sets of rights that can be assigned—object rights and property rights. *Object rights* are used to control what access an object has to another object. *Property rights* are used to control what access an object has to the information contained in an object's different properties.

For example, if you give user object SAM the Browse object right to container PAYROLL, user SAM will be able to see all objects within and below that container. If you then also give user object SAM the Read property right to the PAYROLL container, user object SAM will be able to see the values contained in each of this container's properties.

Table 17.1 lists all object and property rights, provides a brief description of each, and lists the type of right (object or property).

When assigning property rights, you can choose between assigning all property rights for the object (choose the All Properties option when assigning property rights for the object), or assigning only specific property rights (choose the Selected Properties option, then choose which rights to assign to which properties).

Another similarity between NDS and the file system is that of inheritance. The file system and NDS both have a structure of rights inheritance. Both object and property rights flow down through the NDS tree structure to containers and subcontainers in much the same way that rights flow down through the file system structure from directories to subdirectories and files.

As with file system rights, the flow of object and property rights can be stopped or blocked at any lower level in the tree. To block rights at lower levels in the NDS tree, either make a new trustee assignment, or implement the IRF (Inherited Rights Filter) at the level in the tree where you want to block the flow of rights.

Rights assigned individually by using the Selected Properties option overwrite any rights assigned by using the All Properties option. This NDS feature makes it possible to make new trustee assignments at lower levels in the tree without having to first make specific or selected assignments at each higher level in the tree. Because rights assigned through the Selected Properties option cannot be inherited, selected assignments at each level in the tree would be necessary if the All Properties option were not first chosen at some higher level in the tree.

Table 17.1
List of Object and Property Rights

Type of Right	Name of Right	Description
Object	Browse	See objects in the tree
Object	Create	Create new objects
Object	Delete	Delete objects in the tree
Object	Rename	Change an object's name
Property	Add Self	Add or remove self as a value
Property	Compare	Compare any value to itself
Property	Read	Read a property's values
Property	Write	Add/change/delete values
Object	Supervisor	Access all properties of the object
Property	Supervisor	See and manipulate all values

In the file system, users can be made security equivalent to another user in order to gain the same access as another user. In NDS, objects can also be made security equivalent to other objects. By default, each User object within a container of the tree is made security equivalent to the container in which it resides.

For example, when the container object HOME is made a trustee of another NDS object, such as the server object LHC_CADY, all user objects residing in the HOME container are also made trustees of the LHC_CADY server object.

There are several methods whereby an object can receive various object and property rights. Some of them have already been mentioned, including being made a trustee of an object and given object and property rights to that object, or being made security equivalent to a container. Because, as with the file system, there are several ways a user object can receive rights or have them modified or revoked, the term *effective rights* applies to both file system security and NDS security.

To determine the effective rights of an NDS object, you must consider all of the following:

- All explicit trustee assignments given to that User object

- Any Group objects to which the User object has been added

- The rights of the container in which the User object resides

- Whether the User object is also an occupant of an Organizational Role object

- All security equivalencies to other User objects granted to this User object

- Rights granted by default, such as those given to the [Public] trustee, which apply universally to all User objects

 Note In addition, you must also consider where in the NDS tree you are located (current context) when determining effective rights, and whether the IRF has prevented any of the User object's rights from flowing down to this level in the tree.

Unlike file system security, the Supervisor right can be blocked with the IRF in NDS security. This must also be taken into consideration when calculating effective rights.

When NDS is installed, a NetWare 4 file server is added to (installed in) the network, or a User object is created, certain default rights are assigned at various locations in the NDS tree. Table 17.2 lists the associated rights assigned by default to various trustees when each of these three actions occur on the network.

Default rights assignments are designed to take care of common rights needs. Sometimes, however, default assignments are not sufficient; additional rights are necessary to enable users to access other network resources, or to manage NDS objects and properties. When additional rights assignments are needed, consider the following:

- Grant the Read right to the Path property or to the All Properties option to enable a user to access a Directory Map object

- Grant the Read right to the Login Script property of the All Properties option to enable a user to access and use a Profile Login Script object

Table 17.2
NDS Default Rights Assignments

Action	*Trustee*	*Right Assigned*
[Root] is created	[Public] User object ADMIN	Browse right to [Root] Supervisor object right to [Root]
Server object added	Server object Object's creator [Public]	Supervisor object right to itself Supervisor object right to the server object Read right to Messaging Server property
User object created	User object	Read to All Property Rights, and Read and Write to Login Script and Print Job Configuration properties
	[Root]	Read to Network Address and Group Membership properties
	[Public]	Read to Default Server property

Also, consider the following as guidelines for assigning additional NDS rights:

■ Verify the current default assignments before making changes

■ Use the Selected Properties option instead of the All Properties option whenever feasible, to help protect network information and assign specific rights rather than general rights

■ Grant the Write property right to the Object Trustees (ACL) property of an object only when truly necessary, to avoid giving the trustee the ability to grant all rights (including Supervisor) to any trustee

■ Exercise caution when granting the Supervisor object right to a Server object, or the Write property right to the Object Trustees (ACL) property of the Server object, because both actions grant Supervisor file system rights to all associated file server volumes

■ Filter out the Supervisor right with an IRF only after making certain that another object with the Supervisor right has been assigned to the container so as to prevent a total lockout of the ADMIN and, subsequently, no management capabilities in that branch of the tree

Ensuring Secure Network Access through User Objects

Before a user can access network resources, the user must have a User object in the NDS database. The NetWare 4.1 installation software creates the ADMIN User object, and gives that User object all rights to the NDS tree. The network Administrator (ADMIN User object) then creates other User objects. How to create and manage User objects is the focus of this section.

Two NDS utilities—NetWare Administrator and NETADMIN—enable you to create and manage NDS User objects. Using either of these two utilities, you can do the following:

■ Create and use a User_Template

■ Create User objects

■ Manage User objects

Creating and Using a User_Template

A User_Template lets you set up a master from which all property values can be copied to a User object each time you create a new User object. This can greatly reduce the amount of setup work you must perform for each new User object. You can create a User_Template in any of three ways, all of which involve the NetWare Administrator utility. You cannot create a User_Template with NETADMIN. You can create a User_Template in the following three ways:

■ By using the User_Template option from the Object pull-down menu

■ By choosing to create a User object, and calling it User_Template

■ By choosing to create a User_Template when you create an Organization object or an Organizational Unit object

To create a User_Template with the NetWare Administrator utility, log in to the network as a user with Supervisor rights, open the NetWare Administrator utility, change your current context to point to the container where you want to create the User_Template, and then, depending on the method you chose to create a User_Template, complete the appropriate set of steps.

If you want to use the User_Template option from the Object pull-down menu, complete the following steps:

1. Choose User_Template from the **O**bject pull-down menu.

2. Provide a **G**iven Name, at a minimum.

3. Fill in other fields on this Identification page as necessary (see fig. 17.1).

4. Choose other pages such as Environment, Login Restrictions, and so on, and fill in fields as necessary.

5. When you have filled in all appropriate fields on all necessary pages, choose OK to save your changes.

If you want to create a User object and call it User_Template, complete the following steps:

1. Choose **C**reate from the **O**bject pull-down menu, then choose User.

2. Type **User_Template** in the Login Name field, then type **Template** in the Last Name field. (Both fields must be filled in to create a User object, with User_Template in the Login Name field indicating to the operating system that this User object is a User_Template.)

3. Expand the tree, if necessary, until you can see the User_Template object, then choose that object (see fig. 17.2).

4. Choose the User_Template object to open the User: User_Template Identification window.

5. Provide a **G**iven Name, at a minimum.

6. Fill in other fields on this Identification page, as necessary.

7. Choose other pages such as Environment, Login Restrictions, and so on, and fill in fields as needed.

8. When you have filled in all appropriate fields on all necessary pages, choose OK to save your changes.

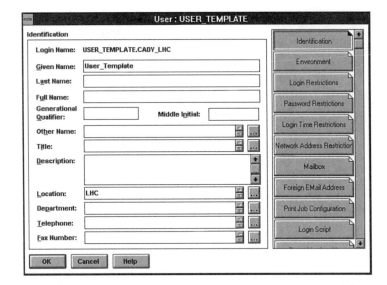

Figure 17.1
The User_Template Identification page.

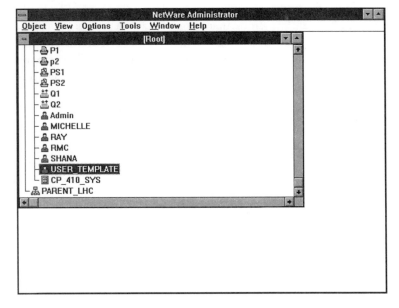

Figure 17.2
The expanded tree, showing User_Template.

If you want to create a User_Template when you create an Organization object or an Organizational Unit object, then complete the following steps:

1. Choose **C**reate from the **O**bject pull-down menu, then choose either Organization (if your context is [Root]) or Organizational Unit (see fig. 17.3).

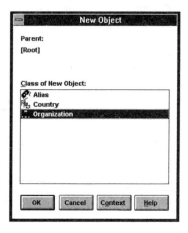

Figure 17.3
The New Object window.

■ **Note** Because you will create Organizational Unit objects far more often than Organization objects, the balance of the numbered steps explain only how to create a User_Template when you create an Organizational Unit object. This note explains the remaining steps for creating a User_Template when you create an Organization object:

■ Choose Organization from the New Object menu.

■ Provide a name for the object.

■ Mark the Define User Defaults box.

■ Choose Create. The User_Template is created.

■ To see and modify this User_Template, expand the tree until you can see the User_Default object, then choose the User_Default object and provide the necessary information.

2. When the Create Organizational Unit window opens, type **User_Template** in the Organizational Unit **N**ame field.

3. Mark the Define **U**ser Defaults box, and choose Create.

4. To see and modify this User_Template, expand the tree until you can see the User_Template object, then choose the User_Template object and provide the necessary information.

After you create the User_Template, you can choose to apply it to each User object you subsequently create. In addition, you can edit the User_Template, changing what is applied to new users when they are created. You change the User_Template by running the NetWare Administrator utility, expanding the tree, choosing the User_Template object, then modifying information on the various screens. When all information is satisfactory, choose OK.

You can also modify a User_Template, using the NETADMIN utility, by following these steps:

1. Choose Manage objects from the NetAdmin Options menu.

2. Choose the User_Template object.

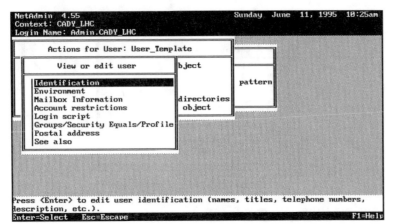

Figure 17.4
The View or edit user screen.

3. Choose View or edit properties of this object from the Actions for *object: object_name* menu.

4. Choose the page (Identification, Environment, Mailbox information, and so on) whose contents you want to edit (see fig. 17.4).

5. Make the necessary changes, then press F10 to save those changes.

After you create a User_Template and modify it to suit your network's particular needs, you can apply that User_Template each time you create a User object.

You can create User objects using either the NetWare Administrator or NETADMIN utilities. When using the NetWare Administrator utility, mark the Use User Template box in the Create User box to apply the User_Template when creating a user (see fig. 17.5).

When using the NETADMIN utility, set the Copy the User Template Object? to Yes (the default) in the Create User Object screen.

The following section explains how to create User objects, using the NetWare Administrator and NETADMIN utilities.

Figure 17.5
The Create User box.

Figure 17.6
*The Select an object
class screen.*

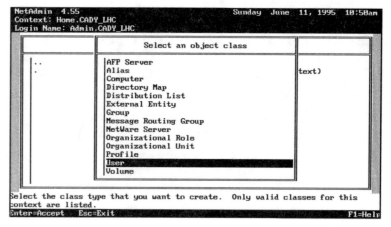

Creating User Objects

To create a User object by using the NetWare Administrator utility, complete the following steps:

1. Choose **C**reate from the **O**bject pull-down menu, then choose User.

2. Type, in the Login **N**ame field, the name the user is to use when logging in to the network.

3. Type the user's last name in the **L**ast Name field, if you choose to provide this information; then mark any of the appropriate boxes (such as **U**se User Template), providing any additional information as requested (such as the path to the user's home directory if creation of a home directory was chosen as an option).

4. Choose **C**reate.

To create a User object by using the NETADMIN utility, complete the following steps:

1. Change your current context to the context where the User object is to be created.

2. Press the Ins key, and choose User from the Select an object class screen (see fig. 17.6).

3. Type, in the Login **N**ame field, the name the user is to use when logging in to the network.

4. Type the user's last name in the **L**ast Name field, then provide any additional related information, as necessary.

5. Press F10 to save this information and create the User object.

Managing User Objects

User objects in particular require regular maintenance. New User objects need to be added, whereas others need to be deleted or modified. Security issues such as login restrictions must also be dealt with. The following common User object management tasks are discussed in this section:

- Adding and changing User object property values

- Setting account restrictions

- Implementing and resetting intruder detection

Note To pass the NetWare 4.1 Administration CNE test, you must be able to perform each task in the preceding list, using the NetWare Administrator utility. Therefore, only the steps to be followed for performing these tasks by using the NetWare Administrator utility are discussed here (even though both the NetWare Administrator and NETADMIN utilities can be used to perform these tasks).

Adding and Changing User Object Property Values

To add or change a User object's property values, log in to the network as a user with Supervisor rights, start the NetWare Administrator utility, and complete the following steps:

1. Expand the directory tree, then choose the User object whose property values you want to add or change.

2. From the User Identification page, choose the property or choose another page containing properties whose values are to be added or changed. (See table 17.3 for a list of pages and some of the more frequently referenced property values you can add or change on each page.)

3. When you have made all necessary additions or changes, choose OK to save all changes.

 Note If you choose Cancel instead of OK, all changes on all pages are lost. You must choose OK to save all changes.

Table 17.3
Some User Object Pages and Their Common Properties

Page Name	Property	Description
Identification	Login Name	Name used by user to identify him/herself to the network and gain access to its resources
	Given Name	User's first name
	Last Name	User's last name
	Title	Job function or responsibility
	Department	Department or division in which user works
	Telephone	User's telephone numbers
	Fax Number	User's FAX number
Environment	Default Server	Complete context for user's default file server, as set in Preferred Server statement of workstation NET.CFG file
	Home Directory	Location (volume and path) of user's home directory

continues

Table 17.3, Continued
Some User Object Pages and Their Common Properties

Page Name	Property	Description
Mailbox	Mailbox Location	Name of messaging server where user's mailbox is stored
	Mailbox ID	Unique name for this user's mailbox, as stored in NDS database
Print Job Configuration	Print Job Configurations	Enables you to add, modify, or delete an existing configuration, or change the default print job configuration for this user
Login Script	Login Script	Holds login script commands specific to this user
	Profile	Enables you to specify a profile login script to be activated when this user logs in to the network
Intruder Lockout	Account Locked	Enables you to unlock a locked user account
Rights to Files and Directories	Volumes	Enables you to find, show, or hide names of any volumes on which the user has File or Directory rights
	Files and Directories	Enables you to see all files or directories to which this user has a trustee assignment
	Rights	Displays user's Trustee rights assignment for specified file or directory
	Effective Rights	Enables you to see the \ effective rights for this object
Group Memberships	Memberships	Displays groups of which this user is a member, and enables you to Add this user to a group, or Delete this user from a group
Security Equal To	Security Equals	Displays list of objects to which this User is security equal, and enables you to Add objects to and Delete objects from the list

Setting Account Restrictions

Set account restrictions by using the following pages from the NetWare Administrator utility:

■ Login Restrictions

■ Password Restrictions

■ Login Time Restrictions

Table 17.4 shows a list of user account-restriction-related pages, and several of their more frequently used user properties.

Table 17.4
List of User Account-Restriction Pages and Common User Properties

Page Name	Property	Description
Login Restrictions	Account Disabled	Enables you to prevent user from logging in to network
	Account has Expiration Date	Sets date and time on which user's account will expire
	Limit Concurrent Connections	Enables you to limit number of workstations from which user can be simultaneously logged in to the network
Password Restrictions	Allow User to Change Password	Enables you to specify whether user can change his or her own password
	Require a Password	Enables you to force user to have a password for his or her user account
	Minimum Password Length	Indicates minimum number of characters required for a password, if one is required
	Force Periodic Password Changes	Enables you to require that users change their passwords at specified regular intervals
Login Time Restrictions	Reset	Use to reset segments of time you blacked out to prevent this user from accessing the network during those time segments

Implementing and Resetting Intruder Detection

To implement intruder detection, complete the following steps:

1. Select the level of the tree where you want to implement intruder detection.

2. Choose **D**etails from the Object pull-down menu.

3. Choose the Intruder Detection page button to open the window shown in figure 17.7.

4. Mark the Detect Intruders and Lock Account After Detection boxes.

5. Accept the default values for the associated properties, or change the values as necessary.

6. Choose OK to save the changes.

To reset intruder detection on a user's account, using the NetWare Administrator utility, expand the tree to display objects, choose the User object, then choose the Intruder Lockout page from the NetWare Administrator utility. From this page you can set or change various Intruder Lockout properties. Table 17.5 shows a list of user Intruder Lockout properties that you can set or change.

Figure 17.7

The Intruder Detection window.

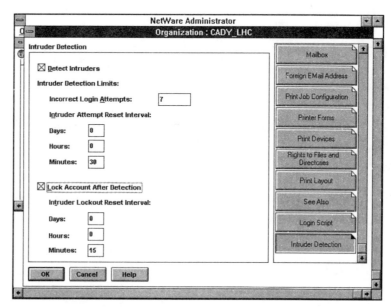

Table 17.5
Intruder Lockout Properties

Property Name	*Description*
Account Locked	When marked, indicates that an attempt to log in to network using this user's login name and an incorrect password occurred, unsuccessfully, several times
Incorrect Login Count	Indicates number of attempts made to log in, using the incorrect password
Account Reset Time	Indicates at what time account will be unlocked, if currently locked, or at what time Incorrect Login Count will be reset
Last Intruder Address	Displays workstation network address from which last incorrect login attempt was made

Automating Network Access through a DOS Workstation

After security and access for users is set up and configured at the NDS database and file server level, the user's workstation must be set up to enable the user to access the network. In addition, after basic workstation installation has been accomplished, workstations should have their configuration files set up so as to automate the process of loading files and preparing for logging in to the network.

Setting up a user's workstation and automating the process of loading files in preparation for network log in involves the following two procedures, both of which are discussed in this section:

■ Installing NetWare Client for DOS and MS Windows

■ Modifying workstation files to automate network connection

Installing NetWare Client for DOS and MS Windows

A workstation that is to be connected to a NetWare 4 network must meet the following minimum requirements:

■ IBM (or compatible) XT, AT, 8088 (or higher) microprocessor

■ 4 MB hard disk space for a DOS or MS Windows Client

 Note If less than 5 MB of disk space is available when you install the NetWare Client for DOS and MS Windows software, you receive an `Insufficient disk space` error message.

The NetWare Client for DOS and MS Windows software can be installed from disk, or across the network from the SYS:PUBLIC\CLIENT \DOSWIN directory. Set up for installation by placing the WSDOS_1 disk in a disk drive, or by logging in to a NetWare 4 file server and mapping a drive to the SYS:PUBLIC\CLIENT\DOSWIN directory. Then install the NetWare Client for DOS and MS Windows software by completing the following steps:

1. Type **Install** and press Enter.

2. Accept C:\NWCLIENT as the default directory where the client files will be stored, or change this field on the NetWare Client Install screen (shown as step 1 in fig. 17.8) to reflect a different location.

3. If you prefer to modify the client's AUTOEXEC.BAT and CONFIG.SYS files manually, change the YES default in step 2 to NO when you are prompted to `Allow changes? (Y/N)`.

4. If the client has MS Windows installed, change the NO default in step 3 to YES when you are prompted to `Install support for MS Windows? (Y/N)`.

Figure 4.8

The NetWare Client Install screen.

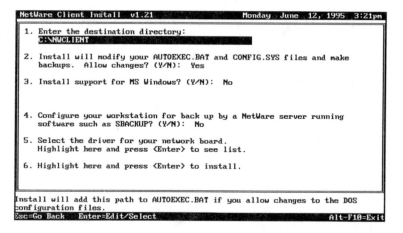

Figure 4.9

The screen for configuring client backup.

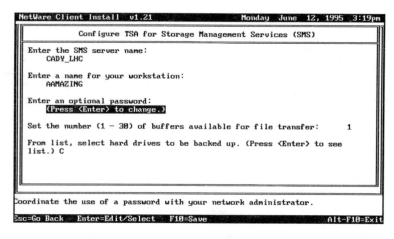

5. If you want this client to have its hard disk backed up from the file server, change the NO default in step 4 to YES when you are prompted to Configure your workstation for back up by a NetWare server running software such as SBACKUP (Y/N).

If you choose to allow this client to be backed up, you are prompted with a screen that enables you to Configure TSA for Storage Management Services (SMS). Figure 17.9 shows this screen with entries for a client on the CADY_LHC file server.

6. Choose a network board driver for the network board installed in this client from step 5 on the NetWare Client Install screen, by choosing Highlight here and press <Enter> to see list (step 5).

If a network board and driver are already installed when you run the NetWare Client for DOS and MS Windows install program, and the install program can recognize the board, a message window indicating that the board has been recognized is displayed (see fig. 17.10). Press Enter to continue.

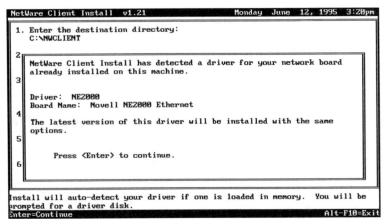

Figure 17.10

The Network Board Driver Detected message screen.

If no board is detected, or you want to change the selected board, you can choose from a list of network boards.

7. Select step 6 (Highlight here and press <Enter> to install), then press Enter to install the NetWare Client for DOS and MS Windows software.

Modifying Workstation Files to Automate Network Connection

If you chose not to let the client installation software modify the AUTOEXEC.BAT and CONFIG.SYS configuration files, you must modify them yourself. In addition to the AUTOEXEC.BAT and CONFIG.SYS files, you will have to work with the NET.CFG file, and possibly with the STARTNET.BAT file.

The CONFIG.SYS file must contain the following line for workstations you want to make NetWare 4 clients (or from which you want to access NetWare 4 resources):

```
LASTDRIVE = Z
```

The AUTOEXEC.BAT file must contain either a call to the STARTNET.BAT file (@CALL C:\NWCLIENT\STARTNET.BAT), or the lines

that are part of the STARTNET.BAT file, as shown in the following paragraph.

If used, the STARTNET.BAT file contains the following lines:

```
C:
CD \NWCLIENT (or replace with the directory
where the NetWare Client for DOS and MS
Windows files are stored)
LSL.COM
NE2000 (replace with the driver file used by
this client)
IPXODI
VLM
F:
LOGIN user_login_id (replace user_login_id
with this user's login name)
```

The NET.CFG file provides configuration information for the workstation's connection software. This file must contain at least a Link Driver driver_name command with parameters, and a NetWare DOS Requester heading with two additional entries, as shown in the following example of a NET.CFG file:

```
Link Drive NE3200
     INT 5
     PORT 300
NetWare DOS Requester
     FIRST NETWORK DRIVE = F
     PREFERRED SERVER = CADY_LHC
```

Questions

1. The first step you must perform before granting the Browse object right to a specific user is to _____ .

   ○ A. move the User object to the other object's container

   ○ B. grant the Browse object right to a group to which the user presently belongs

   ○ C. create a group and add the User object to it

   ○ D. make the User object a trustee (add it to the object's ACL)

2. The _____ and _____ property rights enable you to read a property's values.

   ☐ A. Add Self

   ☐ B. Read

   ☐ C. Supervisor

   ☐ D. Browse

3. Which of the following is NOT a true statement?

   ○ A. Rights assigned individually, using the Selected Properties option, overwrite any rights assigned by using the All Properties option.

   ○ B. Both the file system and NDS have a structure of rights inheritance.

   ○ C. You can block the Supervisor right in both the file system and NDS.

   ○ D. When the [Root] object is created, only [Public] and ADMIN are assigned default rights to [Root].

4. A _____ can be used to simplify creation of User objects.

   ○ A. User_Template

   ○ B. User_Map

   ○ C. User_Object

   ○ D. User_Container

5. The field you must fill in on the User_Template Identification page when creating a User_Template object is _____ .

   ○ A. Last Name

   ○ B. Given Name

   ○ C. Login Name

   ○ D. Other Name

6. To create a User object with the NetWare Administrator utility, what option do you choose from the Object pull-down menu?

   ○ A. User

   ○ B. Details

   ○ C. Add

   ○ D. Create

7. Of the following, which THREE are true statements:

   ☐ A. The Identification page of a User object contains the user's Given name.

   ☐ B. The Environment page of a User object contains the user's Home Directory.

   ☐ C. To specify a Profile login script to be used, open the Login Restrictions page for the user.

   ☐ D. To unlock a user's account, use the Intruder Lockout page for that user.

8. To set a date and time when a user's account will expire, you must open the _____ page for that User object.

   ○ A. Identification

   ○ B. Login Restrictions

   ○ C. Password Restrictions

   ○ D. Intruder Lockout

9. Which of the following is NOT a property of a user's Intruder Lockout page?

   ○ A. Incorrect Login Count

   ○ B. Reset

   ○ C. Account Locked

   ○ D. Last Intruder Address

10. To specify drive Z as the last network drive, place the _____ statement into the _____ client configuration file.

   ○ A. LAST DRIVE = Z, AUTOEXEC.BAT

   ○ B. LASTDRIVE = Z, STARTNET.BAT

   ○ C. LASTDRIVE = Z, CONFIG.SYS

   ○ D. LAST DRIVE = Z, NET.CFG

Answers

1. D

2. B, C

3. C

4. A

5. B

6. D

7. A, B, D

8. B

9. B

10. C

18

Customizing User Access

To some extent, setting up a user's workstation for network access customizes that user's access to the network. In reality, however, the setup process customizes the client's access more than the user's access. Other options for customizing user access exist. This chapter provides information about the following two options:

- *Login scripts*

- *Menus*

Creating Login Scripts

NetWare 4 has four types of login scripts: container, default, profile, and user. The NetWare administrator can create all of them except the default login script.

 The default login script is part of the LOGIN.EXE file, and cannot be created or modified by network users. It runs only if no user login script exists. To prevent it from running when no user login script exists, place the NO_DEFAULT command in a container or profile login script.

Container Login Script

The *container* login script is the first login script run when a user logs in, if such a login script exists in the user's parent container. Used primarily to establish the general environment for the user, the container login script may include commands to perform such tasks as the following:

■ Establish global network assignments

■ Provide actions, associated with the user's login, that are relatively unique to users in the parent container (such as mapping drives and starting menus or applications)

■ Set up access to various network files and printers

Figure 18.1 shows a sample container login script for the Organization: CADY_LHC container.

To create a container login script, complete the following steps:

1. Log in to the network as a user with Supervisor rights, then start the NetWare Administration utility.

2. Expand the NDS tree to display the container where you want to create the login script, then highlight (select) that container.

3. Choose **D**etails from the Object pull-down menu.

4. Choose the Login Script page button.

5. Type the login script commands you want to place in this container login script (refer to fig. 18.1).

6. Choose OK.

Profile Login Script

The *profile* login script executes after the container login script, if a container login script exists. Frequently, a profile login script is used to provide (to users whose User objects are in a different parent container) the same types of conditional operations that the container login script provides for this container's users.

You can, for example, set up the profile login script to do the following:

■ Map network drives

■ Send messages

■ Provide access to printers

The profile login script is a property of the Profile object (see fig. 18.2).

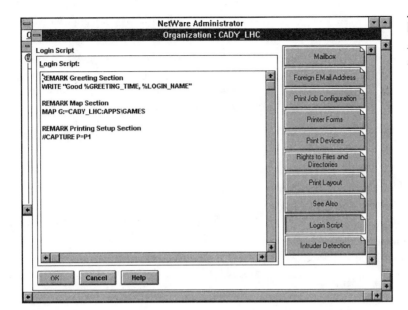

Figure 18.1
A sample container login script.

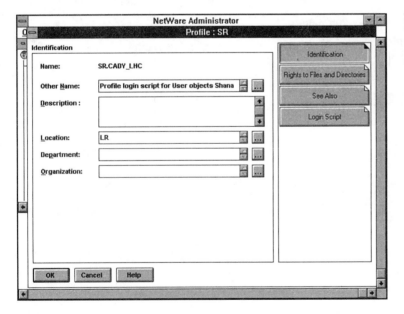

Figure 18.2
The Profile object SR Identification page.

To create a profile login script, complete the following steps:

1. Log in to the network as a user with Supervisor rights, then start the NetWare Administration utility.

2. Expand the NDS tree to display the container where you want to create the profile login script.

3. Choose **C**reate from the Object pull-down menu.

4. Type a name for the profile login script, then mark the **D**efine Additional Properties box, and choose **C**reate (see fig. 18.3).

5. When the Profile: *profile_name* Identification page opens, choose the Login Script page button.

6. Type the login script commands you want to place in this login script.

7. Choose OK.

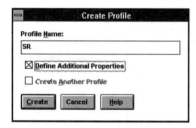

Figure 18.3
The Create Profile dialog box.

User Login Script

The *user* login script runs after the container and profile login scripts (if applicable) have run. If a user login script exists, the default login script will not run. Therefore, the user login script should contain at least basic system mappings (if such mappings have not been provided in one of the other types of login scripts). Following are other common uses for a user login script:

- Running commands that apply only to this user

- Setting up connection to printers commonly accessed by this user

- Sending to the user notices or reminders based on specific days of the week

- Starting, at the time the user logs in to the network, any menus and applications used frequently by this user

The user login script is a property of the User object (see fig. 18.4).

To create a user login script, complete the following steps:

1. Log in to the network as a user with Supervisor rights, then start the NetWare Administration utility.

2. Expand the NDS tree to display the User object for whom you want to create a user login script, then select that User object.

3. Choose **D**etails from the Object pull-down menu.

4. Choose the Login Script page button.

5. Type the login script commands you want to place in this user's login script.

6. Choose OK.

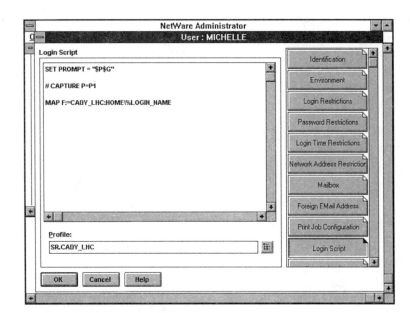

Figure 18.4

The User object MICHELLE login script page.

 Note You can also specify a profile login script to be run for this user when he or she logs in to the network. To specify a profile login script, choose the **P**rofile field and enter the complete name of a profile login script. If you choose to run a profile login script for this user, the profile login script is executed before the user login script.

When you create a login script of any type, you must use specific commands in the proper context. In addition, you must apply the following rules:

■ Only one command can be entered on each line.

■ Blank lines can be inserted with no effect.

■ When using variables in a command, they must be preceded by the percent (%) sign.

 Note A *variable* is a term that tells the computer to replace the term with its equivalent value. For example, the variable %LOGIN_NAME tells the computer to use the user's actual login name, rather than the term %LOGIN_NAME.

■ Variables should be written in uppercase letters.

Table 18.1 lists several of the most commonly used login script commands available for NetWare 4 login scripts.

Table 18.1
NetWare 4.1 Login Script Commands

Command	Description	Example
#	Executes an external command	#CAPTURE P=P1
CLS	Clears the monitor	CLS
COMSPEC	Tells the PC where to find the COMMAND.COM file	COMSPEC=S3:COMMAND.COM
DISPLAY *file*	Prints a text file to the screen	DISPLAY AUTOEXEC.BAT
DRIVE	Specifies the default drive letter	DRIVE G
EXIT *file*	Ends the login script and runs a file	EXIT TODAY1.BAT
FIRE PHASERS	Causes the computer to beep	FIRE PHASERS 2 times
MAP	Sets a drive mapping or displays current settings	MAP G:=CADY_LHC:APPS
REMARK	Indicates that anything that follows is not to be run	REMARK This login script was last changed on 6/95
WRITE	Displays a message on the screen	WRITE "Remember your daily report!"

Creating Menus

When a user logs in to the network, you can simplify the user's access to resources by providing a menu of items from which to choose. Generally, if the user always accesses only one utility and rarely accesses any other network resources, a menu is unnecessary. If the user must access three different application programs, for example, then a menu from which to choose may be very useful. To enable the user to access a menu, you can use the EXIT *file* command in the user's login script, replacing *file* with the name of the menu.

Before a user can access a menu, that menu must be created. To create a menu, type the menu commands in a file, using the correct order and terminology. Use any DOS text editor to create the file. Save the file with an SRC extension.

For example, if you want to create a menu file for a group of users to access various applications in the Accounts Payable department, you might create a DOS text file called AP.SRC.

After you create the basic source file, you compile that source file, the result of which is a usable menu file with a DAT extension. This file can then be run for user access. To compile the source file, you use the MENUMAKE command followed by the name of the source file.

For example, to compile the AP.SRC file, type **MENUMAKE AP** and press Enter. The result, if your efforts are successful, is a usable menu file called MENUMAKE.DAT.

 If you chose to name the source file with an extension other than SRC, specify the complete file name (including the extension) when you compile the file. If, in the preceding example, you had named the menu source file AP.TXT instead of AP.SRC, you would have to type **MENUMAKE AP.TXT** when compiling the source file.

If the source file does not compile successfully, you probably have made some mistakes in specifying the commands in the menu source file. (Commands specify such things as what the menu is to look like when it runs, and how the menu is to process information and execute commands.) To successfully compile the source menu, you must correct the errors. To correct the errors, you need to understand not only the commands themselves, but also the requirements for using commands.

NetWare menu source files can contain only two types of menu script file commands—organizational and control commands.

Organizational commands specify what the menu will look like when it displays on-screen. The following are the two organizational commands:

■ MENU

■ ITEM

Control commands specify which commands to execute and how to process information provided. There are four basic control commands, one of which has three alternative uses. The following are the four control commands:

■ EXEC

■ LOAD

■ SHOW

■ GET*X*

 When you use any of the commands in a menu source file, the commands must be typed in uppercase letters.

In addition to the commands, the menu source file contains options that can be used with each command. For example, when you use the ITEM command, you can also use its associated BATCH option. Doing so enables you to remove the otherwise memory-resident menu from the workstation's memory, thereby freeing up room in which to load application programs and files.

Table 18.2 shows each of the organizational and control commands, as well as the options that can be used with each command. The table also provides the format to be followed when you use the command, a list of options that can be used with each command, and a brief description of those options.

Table 18.2
NetWare 4.1 Menu Commands and Options

Command	Command Description and Format	Options and Descriptions
MENU	Specifies start of each menu screen, along with number and name of menu **Format:** `MENU menu_number, menu_name`	No options available
ITEM	Defines menu options **Format:** `ITEM item_name {options}`	BATCH—removes menu from memory CHDIR—returns to default directory after a menu option is chosen PAUSE—displays "Press any key to continue" message and pauses until a key is pressed SHOW—displays name of a DOS command being run when one has been requested
EXEC	Runs a specified command **Format:** `EXEC {option}`	EXIT—closes menu and exits to the DOS prompt DOS—shells out to DOS requiring the user to type **EXIT** to return to the menu. LOGOUT—closes menu and logs user out of network, returning user to DOS prompt
LOAD	Runs another menu from within this menu, when the other menu was created as a separate menu file **Format:** `LOAD menu_name.DAT`	No options available
SHOW	Runs submenus created as part of this menu; can be used to display up to 255 submenus **Format:** `SHOW menu_number`	No options available
GETX	Prompts for user input. If X is replaced with the letter O, input is *optional*. If X is replaced with the letter R, input is *required* before additional processing can be done. If X is replaced with the letter P, input provided by the user is stored for later use. **Format:** `GETX instruction{prepend}` ➥`length,prefill[append]`	No options available

Note When the GET*X* command is used, the user must press F10 before processing will continue. In addition, the following rules apply to the use of GET*X* in menus:

- GETX must be placed between the ITEM command and any EXEC command associated with it.

- You may use no more than 100 GET*X* commands per ITEM.

- You can prompt the user for a response no more than 10 times per dialog box, or you can use the caret (^) symbol to place each prompt in its own dialog box.

- Each prompt must be on a separate line in the menu file.

The following sample menu source file is named TEST.SRC:

```
MENU 01,Menu Options
  ITEM ^BNetWare Commands
    Show 10
  ITEM ^AApplications
    Show 20
  ITEM ^DLogout
```

```
    EXEC LOGOUT
  ITEM ^CClose Menu
    EXEC EXIT

MENU 10,NetWare Commands
  ITEM NLIST
    GETO Class Name and Option:{}25,,{}
    EXEC NLIST
  ITEM DIR {PAUSE}
    GETO Drive letter:{}25,,{}
    EXEC DIR

MENU 20,Applications
  ITEM Word Processor
    EXEC C:\WP\WP.EXE
  ITEM Screen Shots
    EXEC C:\COLLAGE\SNAP C:\BOOKS
```

After running the MENUMAKE utility to compile this source file, the menu file called TEST.DAT is created. The user can then run this menu by typing **NMENU** followed by the name of the menu. For example, when the user types **NMENU TEST.DAT** at the prompt and presses the Enter key, the result is the menu shown in figure 18.5.

 Note The user must have Read and File Scan rights to the directory containing the menu file, and Read, File Scan, and Write rights to the user's directory.

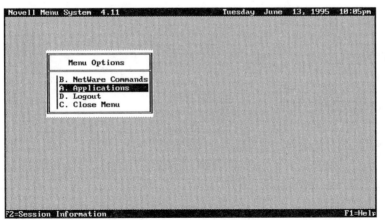

Figure 18.5
Menu displayed from running the TEST.DAT file.

Questions

1. Which of the following is NOT a type of login script?

   - ○ A. Container
   - ○ B. Profile
   - ○ C. Optional
   - ○ D. User

2. The _____ and _____ login scripts can be selected from inside the User object's Login Script page.

   - ☐ A. container
   - ☐ B. profile
   - ☐ C. optional
   - ☐ D. user

3. The _____ login script is NOT run for a user whose parent container is not the same as that of this login script.

   - ○ A. container
   - ○ B. profile
   - ○ C. optional
   - ○ D. user

4. Which of the following is NOT a true statement?

   - ○ A. The user login script is used to run commands that apply only to the user.
   - ○ B. A profile login script must be given a name.
   - ○ C. The user login script is a property of the User object.
   - ○ D. None of the preceding statements is true.

5. Which rule relates to creating login scripts?

   - ○ A. Variables must be preceded by a percent (%) sign.
   - ○ B. Multiple commands can be entered on the same line, if separated with commas.
   - ○ C. Only Organizational and Control commands are used when you create login scripts.
   - ○ D. All of the preceding rules relate to creating login scripts.

6. If both types of login scripts are run, the _____ login script executes before the user login script.

   - ○ A. container
   - ○ B. default
   - ○ C. profile
   - ○ D. optional

7. Of the following, which THREE are valid login script commands?

   - ☐ A. CLS
   - ☐ B. #
   - ☐ C. PLAY SOUND
   - ☐ D. WRITE

8. A file with a _____ extension is a menu source file.

   - ○ A. DAT
   - ○ B. SOU
   - ○ C. SRC
   - ○ D. EXE

9. To start an application from a menu, you must use the _____ control command.

   ○ A. EXEC

   ○ B. LOAD

   ○ C. SHOW

   ○ D. GET*X*

10. The user must have _____ and _____ security rights to access a menu file.

   ○ A. File Scan, Write

   ○ B. Write, Read

   ○ C. File Scan, Write

   ○ D. Read, File Scan

Answers

1. C

2. B, D

3. A

4. D

5. A

6. C

7. A, B, D

8. C

9. A

10. D

Using NetWare Console Commands

NetWare 4 file servers enable you to store, access, and manage files and the NDS database, and to provide services that network users request. The ability to access, manage, and protect NetWare 4 file servers is, therefore, of paramount importance. Access to NetWare servers is provided through console commands. The basic design of the NetWare 4 operating system (the core OS) and its associated NLMs (NetWare Loadable Modules) also provides access.

This chapter discusses the NetWare console commands and NLMs commonly used to protect and access NetWare 4 file servers. Also included here is information about the use of console commands, NLMs, remote console access, and SBACKUP. The chapter addresses the following topics:

■ Understanding and securing the NetWare 4 file server

■ Implementing and using remote console management

■ Enhancing file server security by using SBACKUP

Understanding and Securing the NetWare 4 File Server

The NetWare 4 file server provides access to resources on the network, and provides services requested by users. To provide access to resources and services, the NetWare 4 file server interface provides console commands and NLMs. NLMs are also one portion of the NetWare operating system. The other portion is called the *NetWare core OS*.

NLMs provide added functionality. By loading different NLMs on the file server, you can pick and choose what functionality you implement. NLMs that provide services such as linking disk and LAN drivers are always loaded on every NetWare 4 file server. NLMs that provide services such as management utilities may be loaded only when they are needed.

NetWare 4 provides the following four types of NLMs:

■ **Disk drivers.** These NLMs are responsible for controlling communication between the NetWare 4 operating system and the computer's hard disk drives. Standard NetWare disk driver NLM files use a DSK extension. The newer NPA (NetWare Peripheral Architecture) files have CDM and HAM extensions.

■ **Name space modules.** Thanks to these NLMs, files whose names are not based on DOS file-naming conventions can be stored in the NetWare 4 file system. Name space files have a NAM extension.

■ **Network board (LAN) drivers.** These NLMs are responsible for controlling communication between the NetWare 4 operating system and the network board. LAN driver files have a LAN extension.

■ **NLM utilities.** These NLMs are utilities that are run from the file server console or from a workstation running the remote console software. The NLM utilities provide access to monitor and configure file server software. The NLM utility modules have a NLM extension.

To load an NLM, type the following command at the file server console, and press Enter:

LOAD *NLM_name [parameters]*

Replace *NLM_name* with the name of the NLM to be loaded. If the NLM is not currently found in the SYS:SYSTEM directory, which is the default location for NLMs, you can also specify the path to the NLM before providing the name of the NLM to be loaded.

Replace *[parameters]* with any parameters to be used when loading this specific NLM. For example, to change the keyboard type at the file server, type **LOAD KEYB** *keyboard_type*, replacing *keyboard_type* with the type of keyboard. The type of keyboard you enter in place of the *keyboard_type* command is a parameter of the LOAD KEYB command.

Table 19.1 shows a list of some of the more commonly used NLMs.

The NetWare core OS runs on every NetWare 4 file server. Without it, a NetWare 4 file server is not a file server, but just another computer physically attached to the network. The NetWare core OS provides the following five basic services:

- Authentication of network users
- File system services
- NetWare Directory Services
- Network security
- Routing services

Table 19.1
Commonly Used NLMs

NLM	NLM Type	Function
ISADISK.DSK	Disk driver	Controls ISA hard disks
INSTALL.NLM	NLM utility	Installs and configures NetWare
MAC.NAM	Name space	Allows files using Macintosh naming conventions to be stored on and retrieved from a NetWare file server
MONITOR.NLM	NLM utility	Displays NetWare OS statistics
OS2.NAM	Name space	Allows files using OS/2 naming conventions to be stored on and retrieved from a NetWare file server
RSPX.NLM	NLM utility	Permits remote access to the file server console
NE2000.LAN	LAN driver	Controls NetWare 4 OS communication with the network board
PSERVER.NLM	NLM utility	Loads NetWare print server software on a file server

NLMs provide network services, and a means of controlling and configuring those services. The core OS also provides a means of accessing and controlling the NetWare operating system. It provides utilities, called *console commands*, which can be run from the NetWare OS system prompt. Just as NLMs can be compared to external DOS commands, NetWare console commands are similar to internal DOS commands. Following are several of the more commonly used NetWare console commands:

- **BROADCAST.** Use to send a message to workstations with current network connections

- **CLS.** Use to clear the console screen displaying only the system prompt

- **CONFIG.** Use to view the file server's name and its network (LAN) configuration information

- **DOWN.** Use to unload the operating system software

- **EXIT.** Use to return to the DOS prompt after using the DOWN console command

- **HELP.** Use to view information about NLMs and console commands (see fig. 19.1)

- **LOAD.** Use to run NLMs by placing them into file server memory

- **MODULES.** Use to view a list of currently loaded NLMs

- **UNLOAD.** Use to remove NLMs from file server memory

Figure 19.1

Display of the Help BROADCAST console command.

```
CP_410:help broadcast
BROADCAST "message" [[TO] username|connection_number] [[and!,] username!
           connection_number...]
Send a message to all users logged in or attached to a file server or to a
list of users or connection numbers.
Example:  broadcast "Please delete unneeded files to free disk space"

CP_410:
```

Implementing and Using Remote Console Management

Loading NLMs and entering console commands while sitting at the network file server is not always convenient, or even possible. NetWare provides remote console management NLMs and a utility to enable you to access the file server console from a workstation just as easily as if you were sitting at the file server console.

To use the remote console utility, you need to load the associated NLMs at the file server (REMOTE.NLM and RSPX.NLM or RS232.NLM), then log in to the file server and run the RCONSOLE utility.

 Note Add the command to load the remote console management NLMs to the file server's AUTOEXEC.NCF file to ensure that remote console management is always available.

Connection to a file server can be made from a workstation attached directly to the network, or from a workstation attached to the network through a modem. The first type of connection is referred to as an *SPX connection.* The second type of connection is referred to as an *asynchronous connection.* With both types of connection, the REMOTE.NLM must be loaded when you implement remote management on a file server. If the type of connection you will be using is an SPX connection, you must also have the RSPX.NLM loaded. If the type of connection you will be using

is asynchronous, you must also have the RS232.NLM loaded. Then, when you run the RCONSOLE utility, you choose the type of connection from the first RCONSOLE screen, as shown in figure 19.2.

If you choose the SPX connection type, choose the file server whose console you want to work with, then provide the remote console password when prompted. In addition to loading and unloading NLMs and issuing file server console commands, you can press Alt+F1 to activate the RCONSOLE Available Options menu (see fig. 19.3), and then choose to perform any of the following tasks:

- Change from one screen to another (Select a Screen to View)

- See directories and files on the DOS partition of the file server's hard disk (Directory Scan)

- Copy files from the workstation to the file server (Transfer Files To Server)

- Temporarily change to the workstation's DOS prompt, then return by typing **EXIT** (Invoke Operating System Shell)

- Quit RCONSOLE (End Remote Session With Server)

- Close the Available Options menu and redisplay the console (Resume Remote Session With Server)

- See the network address of this workstation (Workstation Address)

- Manipulate when typing done at the keyboard will be processed (Configure Keystroke Buffering)

Figure 19.2
RCONSOLE's Connection Type screen.

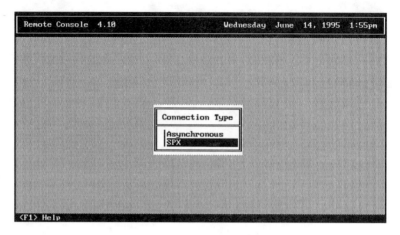

Figure 19.3
RCONSOLE's Available Options menu.

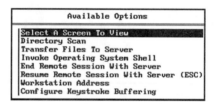

Some keystroke combinations also enable you to perform tasks. By pressing Alt+F3, you can move forward through server console screens; press Alt+F4 to move backward through server console screens. You can exit RCONSOLE by pressing Alt+F2, or close the Available Options menu and resume the remote session with the server by pressing the Esc key.

If you chose the asynchronous connection type, both the workstation and the file server must have an attached modem. After you choose Asynchronous, you can choose to Connect To Remote Location; then choose the location, or configure location information by choosing the Configuration menu option.

One way to secure your network file server is to require a password on the RCONSOLE utility. Other methods include locking up the server itself,

using the console password feature available in MONITOR.NLM, or the SECURE CONSOLE command. Another way to help secure your file server is to back up the files and programs stored on it.

Enhancing File Server Security Using SBACKUP

Many compatible backup utilities are available for backing up and restoring NetWare files and programs. Because not everyone wants to spend the additional money to purchase this software, however, NetWare 4 includes the SBACKUP utility.

Regardless of which backup software you use, it can provide sufficient security only if it is used regularly. To ensure regular use of the backup software, you should assign the responsibility for routine backup to a specific network user. In addition, you should decide which backup strategy is most appropriate for your network.

 Note When you assign the responsibility for network backup, you must also assign the following rights:

- To back up the NetWare server's file systems, the user must have Read and File Scan rights.

- To back up NDS, the user must have the Browse object right and the Read property right.

- The user must also know the password for each workstation to be backed up, as well as for the file servers being backed up (Target) or running the backup software (Host).

You can choose from the following three basic backup strategies:

- **Full.** Backs up all files and clears the Modify bit

- **Incremental.** Backs up all files created or changed since the last full or incremental backup, and clears the Modify bit

- **Differential.** Backs up all files created or changed since the last full backup, and clears the Modify bit

 Note You can combine the full backup with either the incremental or differential backup strategies, but you should not combine incremental and differential backup strategies.

Before you can back up file servers and workstations, certain files must be loaded on the file server or the workstation. To back up a file server, a driver for the backup device must be loaded on the Host file server. The appropriate TSA file must be loaded also. Then SBACKUP must be loaded.

For example, to backup a NetWare 4.1 file server, including the NDS database, load TSA410.NLM and TSANDS. To back up a NetWare 3.12 server, load TSA312.NLM. To back up a NetWare 3.11 server, load TSA311.NLM. To backup a NetWare 2.2 server, load TSA22.NLM. After you have loaded the TSAs for each type of server you will be backing up, then load the SBACKUP.NLM.

 Note If you are going to back up a workstation's hard disk, you must load the TSADOS.NLM at the file server, and the TSASMS.COM file at the workstation.

To back up a network file server, load the previously indicated files (TSA*xxx*.NLM and SBACKUP.NLM), then complete the following steps:

1. From the SBACKUP Main menu, choose Change Target to Backup From or Restore To.

2. Choose a *server_name*. NetWare File System to back up.

3. Provide a user name and password when prompted.

 Note The user name should be either the network administrator's name, or the name of another user who has been granted the necessary rights to run backups and restores.

Figure 19.4

SBACKUP's Main Menu.

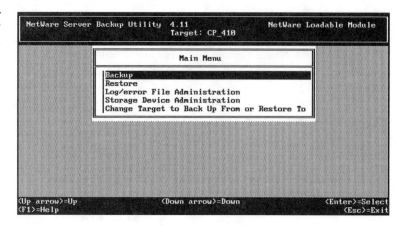

```
NetWare Server Backup Utility  4.11            NetWare Loadable Module
                              Target: CP_410

                              Main Menu

              Backup
              Restore
              Log/error File Administration
              Storage Device Administration
              Change Target to Back Up From or Restore To




<Up arrow>=Up            <Down arrow>=Down              <Enter>=Select
<F1>=Help                                              <Esc>=Exit
```

4. Choose Backup from the Main Menu (see fig. 19.4).

5. Choose a backup device if more than one is available and the option to choose is provided.

6. Provide a location for the session log file and error file.

7. Choose the type of backup to be performed.

8. Provide a description for this backup.

9. Choose to proceed now.

10. Insert the tape or other media being used and provide a label for the media, then continue with the backup, swapping out new tapes as necessary.

Note You can also back up a network workstation by loading the previously indicated files (TSADOS.NLM and SBACKUP.NLM at the server, TSASMS.COM at the workstation), choosing Change Target to

Backup From or Restore To from the Main menu, then choosing a *server_name.DOS Workstation TSA* to back up, and following the basic procedure used to back up a file server.

Restore backups by choosing Restore instead of Backup from the SBACKUP Main menu. As prompted, provide the same restore-related information you provided for the original backup, such as the location of the session files and the device to restore from. In addition, when you restore, you must specify the type of restore—one file or directory, an entire session, or a custom restore. Then proceed with the restore, swapping in tapes as necessary.

Questions

1. Access to the network and other basic resources is provided through _____.

   ○ A. NLMs

   ○ B. the core OS

   ○ C. RCONSOLE

   ○ D. name space modules

2. The NLMs responsible for controlling communication between the OS and the hard disk drives are _____.

   ○ A disk drivers

   ○ B. name space modules

   ○ C. network board (LAN) drivers

   ○ D. NLM utilities

3. The ISADISK.DSK is NOT _____.

   ○ A. an NLM

   ○ B. responsible for controlling ISA hard disks

   ○ C. a disk driver

   ○ D. a console command

4. NLMs are stored in _____ by default.

   ○ A. SYS:PUBLIC

   ○ B. SYS:LOGIN

   ○ C. SYS:ETC

   ○ D. SYS:SYSTEM

5. Which is NOT a basic service provided by the NetWare core OS?

   ○ A. Authentication

   ○ B. NDS

   ○ C. OS Statistics

   ○ D. Routing

6. Of the following, which is NOT a remote-console-related NLM?

   ○ A. REMOTE.NLM

   ○ B. RSPX.NLM

   ○ C. MODULE.NLM

   ○ D. RS232.NLM

7. Of the following, which THREE are NetWare console commands?

   ☐ A. CLS

   ☐ B. BROADCAST

   ☐ C. NLIST

   ☐ D. UNLOAD

8. A _____ backup backs up all files created or changed since the last full backup, and doesn't clear the modify bit.

   ○ A. Custom

   ○ B. Incremental

   ○ C. Differential

   ○ D. Full

Answers

1. B

2. A

3. D

4. D

5. C

6. C

7. A, B, D

8. C

Managing the Directory Tree and File System

As a NetWare 4 network administrator, your responsibilities may include such tasks as planning NDS, setting up resources and making them accessible, automating the user's environment, organizing and managing the directory structure, and managing and keeping the entire network running. The simplicity or difficulty of this last task—managing and keeping the entire network running—depends on the success of each of the other tasks, particularly that of planning, organizing, and setting up the network.

This chapter is designed to provide you with the basic information you need to know in order to successfully manage NetWare Directory Services, as well as the directory structures, files, and volume space used by NetWare 4 file servers. To that end, this chapter provides information on the following topics:

- Managing the file system

- Naming Directory tree objects

- Accessing objects in the Directory tree

- Automating user access to the Directory tree

Managing the File System

To successfully manage the file system, you must be able to manage directories, files, and space on the NetWare volume. Many of the DOS utilities you use for managing DOS directories and files can be used also to manage NetWare directories and files. In addition, NetWare provides the following utilities for file system and volume management:

- FILER

- FLAG

- NDIR

- NCOPY

- NETADMIN

- NetWare Administrator

- RENDIR

As a network administrator, you probably have had experience with most of these utilities, using them to perform file system management tasks. Because the NetWare Administrator is a relatively new utility and is specific to NetWare 4, your experience with this utility may be limited. Detailed

knowledge of this utility is important to passing the NetWare 4 Administration CNE exam. Therefore, the NetWare Administrator utility is used in most of the tasks explained in this section.

The following file, directory, and volume management tasks are discussed:

- Creating directories

- Viewing and modifying directory information

- Renaming directories

- Deleting directories and their contents

- Copying and moving directory structures

- Copying and moving files

- Viewing and modifying file information

- Deleting, purging, and salvaging files

- Managing volume space

 You are assumed to have the necessary rights to perform all the tasks discussed in this section. In addition, the instructions are based on the assumption that you already have the Network Administrator utility running, and that you have expanded the Directory tree to display the volume where you will be managing directories and files.

Creating Directories

To create a directory, select (highlight) the location where you want the directory to be created, then complete the following steps:

1. Choose **C**reate from the **O**bject pull-down menu (or press Insert).

2. In the Create Directory dialog box, type a name for the Directory Object.

3. Mark Define Additional Properties if you want to define properties specific to this directory.

4. Choose Create.

5. When the Identification page for this directory opens, choose the Facts, Trustees of this Directory, or Attributes page button to further define properties for this directory.

Viewing and Modifying Directory Information

To view or modify information related to a specific directory, select the directory from the Directory tree, then complete the following steps:

1. Choose **D**etails from the **O**bject pull-down menu.

2. Choose the Facts, Trustees of this Directory, or Attributes page button to open subsequent pages where you can view or modify directory properties.

3. If applicable, when you have made all necessary modifications, choose OK.

Renaming Directories

To rename an existing directory, select the directory from the Directory tree, then complete the following steps:

1. Choose **R**ename from the **O**bject pull-down menu.

2. In the Rename dialog box, type a new directory name (see fig.20.1).

3. Choose OK.

Figure 20.1
The Rename dialog box.

Deleting Directories and Their Contents

To delete a directory and its contents, expand the directory so that its files and subdirectories are displayed, then complete the following steps:

1. Mark the directory and any files and subdirectories to be deleted by pressing the Shift key while you move and click the mouse.

2. Choose **D**elete from the **O**bject pull-down menu (or press Delete).

3. Choose **Y**es at the Do you really want to delete the objects? prompt.

Copying and Moving Directory Structures

To copy or move a complete directory structure, complete the following steps:

1. Mark the directory to be copied or moved, by pressing the Shift key while you move and click the mouse.

2. Choose **C**opy from the **O**bject pull-down menu.

3. Type a Destination for the directory and its structure, or choose the Browse button next to the Destination field and browse the tree.

4. Choose OK.

Copying and Moving Files

To copy one or more files, expand the directory where the files are located so that you can see the file names, then complete the following steps:

1. Mark files to be copied, using the Shift key and mouse button.

2. Choose **C**opy from the **O**bject pull-down menu.

 Note You can also use the mouse to drag and drop the file from one directory to another.

3. In the Move/Copy dialog box, type a Destination for the files (see fig. 20.2), or choose the Browse button next to the Destination field and browse the tree.

4. Choose OK.

Figure 20.2
The Move/Copy dialog box.

 Note You use this same process to move files from one directory to another. The difference is that you mark Move instead of Copy at the top of the Move/Copy dialog box.

Viewing and Modifying File Information

To view or modify information related to a specific file, select the file, then complete the following steps:

1. Choose **D**etails from the **O**bject pull-down menu.

2. Choose the Facts, Trustees of this Directory, or Attributes page button to open subsequent pages where you can view or modify file properties.

3. If you made modifications to a file's properties, choose OK to save those changes.

Deleting, Purging, and Salvaging Files

You delete a file the same way you delete a directory, except that you select the file to be deleted (instead of the directory). You can automatically *purge* (make unrecoverable) a file—either when you delete it or later—or you can choose to not purge the file and make it possible to *salvage* (recover) the file at a later time.

To automatically purge a file when you delete it, set the Purge Immediate attribute for the file (see fig. 20.3).

To purge files that have been deleted but are not yet purged, complete the following steps:

1. Choose Salvage from the **T**ools pull-down menu.

2. Choose where you want the salvageable files to be listed from (Current Directory or Deleted Directory), as well as how you want the files sorted (by Deletion date, File name, and so on).

3. Choose List to see a list of salvageable files (see fig. 20.4).

4. Choose Purge.

5. Answer Yes when prompted with either Purge all files from deleted directories? or with Purge all files from this directory?

6. Choose Close.

To salvage files, complete the following steps:

1. Choose Salvage from the **T**ools pull-down menu.

2. Choose where you want the salvageable files to be listed from (Current Directory or Deleted Directory), as well as how you want the files sorted (by Deletion date, File name, and so on).

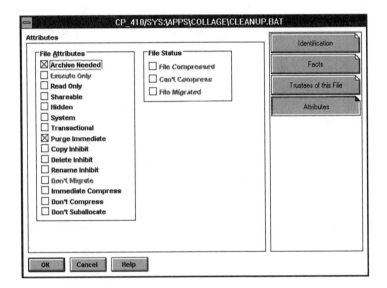

Figure 20.3

The CLEANUP.BAT File Attribute page, with Purge Immediate marked.

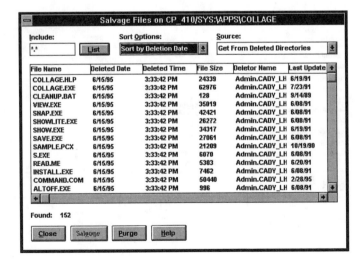

Figure 20.4

The Salvage Files window.

Note If the Salvageable files will be restored to the DELETED.SAV directory at the root of the *volume_name* volume message is displayed, choose OK.

3. Choose List to see a list of salvageable files.

4. Mark files to be salvaged, then choose Salvage.

5. Choose Close.

Managing Volume Space

Volume space usage information is a property of the Volume object. To view information about volume space usage, restrict volume space usage, and change file and directory ownership, use the NetWare Administrator utility, (or the NETADMIN utility), and the NDIR utility.

To view information about volume space usage, complete the following steps:

1. Select the Volume from the NetWare Administrator.

2. Choose **D**etails from the **O**bject pull-down menu.

3. Open the Statistics page to view volume information (see fig. 20.5).

The Volume Statistics page contains the following areas of information:

- ■ **Disk Space.** Shows both the total available disk space and the amount of disk space currently being used

- ■ **Directory Entries.** Shows both the total number of directory entries available and the number currently being used

- ■ **Deleted Files.** Shows the number of deleted files and those not yet purged

Figure 20.5
The Volume Statistics page.

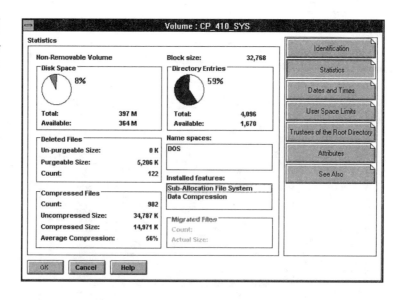

■ **Name Spaces.** Shows which name space NLMs are loaded on the volume

■ **Installed Features.** Shows what features (such as suballocation and data compression) are active on the volume

■ **Compressed Files.** Shows how many files on the volume are stored as compressed files, what the total size of those files is, and the average percentage of file compression

 Note File compression reduces the storage space required for a file, saving as much as 63 percent of storage space. File compression attributes can be set (by using NetWare Administrator, NETADMIN, or FLAG) to indicate whether a file should be compressed as soon as it is closed (Immediately Compress), or not compressed at all (Not Compress). Then, using INSTALL.NLM, you can turn compression on, and all files with the IC attribute will be compressed.

■ **Migrated Files.** Shows how many files have been migrated, and the size of those migrated files

 Note Data migration is used to free up active storage space by transferring inactive files from hard disk to optical storage devices. If HCSS is installed, NDIR, FILER, NETADMIN, or NetWare Administrator can be used to view data migration statistics. Migration is an attribute of directories and files. If data migration is active, you can prevent inactive files and directories from being migrated by applying the Don't Migrate (DM) attribute.

To restrict volume space usage for a user, complete the following steps:

1. Select the volume from the tree, using the NetWare Administrator.

2. Choose **D**etails from the **O**bject pull-down menu.

3. Open the User Space Limit page to view volume information, and browse through the tree until a list of network users is displayed.

4. Select the user whose volume space usage you want to restrict.

5. Choose Modify.

6. In the Volume Space Restriction dialog box, mark the Limited Volume Space box, and type (in the Volume Space Limit (Kb): area) the amount of volume space to be allotted to this user (see fig. 20.6).

Figure 20.6
The Volume Space Restriction dialog box.

 Note You can also limit the amount of space available to a directory by selecting the directory, choosing **D**etails from the **O**bject pull-down menu, opening the Facts page, and typing (in the Limit field) the number of kilobytes to be allowed.

When space usage becomes a problem, one way around that problem is to change the owner of one or more of the directories or files. Changing ownership is particularly helpful also when one user copies files or directories to another user; because these copies now have a new owner, the properties should reflect that fact.

To change file and directory ownership, choose the directory or file, then choose **D**etails from the **O**bject pull-down menu. Next, open the Facts page, and change the Owner field.

Naming Directory Tree Objects

If the Directory tree has only one container, accessing objects in that container is relatively simple. When there is more than one container in the tree, however, accessing objects in containers that are not the user's parent container becomes more difficult. When a user is accessing an object in a different container, NetWare often needs to be told exactly where to look for that object. When looking in the DOS directory structure for a file that is not in the current directory, you provide the exact path. When looking in NDS for an object that is not in the user's current context, you provide an exact object name—either a distinguished name or a relative distinguished name.

 A *common name* (CN) is the name of a leaf object. *Context* is an object's location in the Directory tree. *Current context* is the user's current location (area to which the user is currently pointing, much like the current path in DOS) in the Directory tree.

A *distinguished name* is the object's common name and its context. A distinguished name is identified

with a beginning (leading) period, and all objects in a distinguished name are separated with a period. No two objects can have the same distinguished name.

A *relative distinguished name* lists the path to an object, does not contain a leading period, can contain an ending period, separates objects with a period, and uses the user's current context as a starting point.

To illustrate, using a Directory tree structure for a small business (see fig. 20.7), you would enter a distinguished name for user MICHELLE as follows:

```
.CN=MICHELLE.OU=NOBUS.O=LHC_PARENT
```

If user MICHELLE's current context is .O=LHC_PARENT, you would enter the relative distinguished name for user MICHELLE as follows:

```
CN=MICHELLE.OU=NOBUS
```

NDS has other object names that can be applied to describe an object in the NDS tree. The first— *CONTEXT*—refers to an object's location in the NDS Directory tree. It is written from the [Root] of the tree to the actual location or container of the object within the tree. User MICHELLE's context is stated as follows:

```
O=LHC_PARENT.OU=NOBUS
```

A user can be defined by specifying its context.

In addition, users can be defined by their common name. All leaf objects in the Directory tree have a common name (CN) associated with them. The common name, which is given to the object when it is created, is the name you see next to the icon for the leaf object when you display the Directory tree

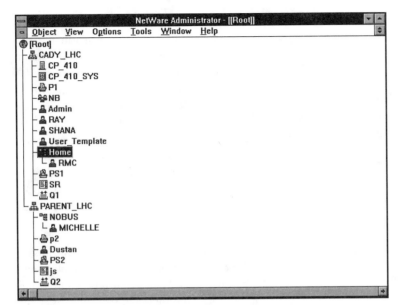

Figure 20.7

The Directory tree structure.

A user's name is also its common name. For example, user MICHELLE's common name is MICHELLE. It is written as CN=MICHELLE.

 You can reference an object by its common name only, if your current context is the same as that of the leaf object. If, for example, your current context is O=LHC_PARENT.OU=NOBUS, you can access the print queue named Q1 by referring to its common name of Q1.

Accessing Objects in the Directory Tree

The NetWare Directory tree is structured to be functional as well as organizational. This structure lets you design and organize your network's Directory tree so that it follows the use of resources on your network. You can base your Directory tree design on a logical use of resources rather than on just a physical organization. You can also organize your Directory tree by your company's organizational structure, its geographical distribution, by job responsibility, or by any combination of these.

How you design your Directory tree affects how objects in the Directory tree are accessed. For example, if the Directory tree is designed around geographical distribution, but users in different locations with similar job responsibilities must share data, access for some users may be different than for other users. Some users may need to access only resources in their parent container. Others may need to access resources in additional containers.

Before users access resources, however, they need to understand not only how the design of the Directory tree affects their access to network resources, but also where their *current context* (the object's current location in the directory structure) is set, and how to change that context.

To change context, you can specify the context by using either typeful naming or typeless naming. In *typeful naming,* you use the abbreviations associated with containers in the tree. To specify an Organization, for example, you use O. When changing context, you specify a typeful name by using the abbreviation, followed by the equal sign (=) and then the name of the object. In addition, typeful names require that you use a period (.) between each object included in the name. User MICHELLE's typeful name would be shown as:

`.CN=MICHELLE.OU=NOBUS.O=LHC_PARENT`

In *typeless naming,* you do not use container name abbreviations or the equal sign. User MICHELLE would be shown as:

`MICHELLE.NOBUS.LHC_PARENT`

To change your current context as well as to view objects in the Directory tree, you can use the NetWare CX command. To view your current context, type **CX** and press Enter. To view the Directory tree structure from below your current context, type **CX /T**. To see see all objects in your current context, type **CX /ALL /T**. To change to [Root], type **CX /R**, or change your context up one level by typing CX followed by a period (**CX.**). You can also type any distinguished name after the CX command, such as CX .OU=NOBUS.O= LHC_PARENT, and change your context to that context.

Although moving about the Directory tree by using the CX command is possible, it can be cumbersome for network users. To make the process of moving through the Directory tree structure easier for users, you can set up in the tree objects designed specifically to enable users to access objects in contexts other than their current context. Objects you can create in the tree for this purpose are Alias, Directory map, and Group objects, which are explained in table 20.1.

Table 20.1
Objects That Enable Easy Access to Different Contexts

Object	*Description*	*Purpose*
Alias	Object that points to another object in the Directory tree	Provides access to an object located in another context and which must be shared
Directory Map	Object that points to a directory on a volume	Makes access to an executable program easier for the user
Group	Object that enables multiple users to have the same rights on the network	Regulates access to network resources for more than one user

Automating User Access to the Directory Tree

You can simplify access to the Directory tree for network users by following two guidelines. First, set the users' current context for them when they log in to the network. Second, when you set up mappings in login scripts for users, be certain to use correct naming.

To set the user's current context, place the following command in the NET.CFG file on the user's workstation:

```
NAME CONTEXT="distinguished name"
```

Replace *distinguished name* with the distinguished name that points to the user's parent container. For example, for user MICHELLE, replace *distinguished name* with OU=NOBUS.O=LHC_PARENT.

 Note Users who log in to the network from a workstation other than their own will not have the correct context set for them. The NAME CONTEXT command is workstation-specific, because it is part of the NET.CFG file of each workstation.

To set up mappings in login scripts for users, use the MAP command. When specifying the path, provide the complete path, using a distinguished name instead of a relative distinguished name.

For example, to map a search drive to the NOBUS container, place the following command in the user's login script:

```
.CP_410_SYS.CADY_LHC
```

The CX command, a variety of utilities (FLAG, NDIR, NetWare Administrator), and so on, are all provided by NetWare to help you successfully manage the Directory tree and file system.

Questions

1. Of the following, which task *cannot* be performed by using the NetWare Administrator utility?

   ○ A. Manage volume space

   ○ B. Move files

   ○ C. Create directories

   ○ D. Create volumes

2. Salvage files by choosing _____ from the _____ pull-down menu.

   ☐ A. Delete

   ☐ B. Tools

   ☐ C. Salvage

   ☐ D. Object

3. Which area of the volume statistics window contains information about NetWare Loadable Modules that make it possible for Macintosh or OS/2 files to be saved on the network?

   ○ A. Directory Entries

   ○ B. Name Spaces

   ○ C. Installed Features

   ○ D. Compressed Files

4. Which THREE utilities can you use to set file compression attributes?

   ☐ A. NetWare Administrator

   ☐ B. NETADMIN

   ☐ C. FILER

   ☐ D. FLAG

5. One way to get around a space usage problem is to _____.

   ○ A. turn compression on and flag all files as NC

   ○ B. create groups and assign all users to a group

   ○ C. change the owner of some files or directories

   ○ D. apply the DM flag to files and directories

6. All leaf objects have a _____ name.

   ○ A. common

   ○ B. disguised

   ○ C. unique

   ○ D. relative

7. Based on figure 20.7, which of the following is a correctly written distinguished name for user DUSTAN?

   ○ A. .CN=DUSTAN.OU=NOBUS.O =PARENT_LHC

   ○ B. .CN=DUSTAN.O=PARENT_LHC

   ○ C. CN=DUSTAN.OU=PARENT_ LHC.O=[Root]

   ○ D. CN=DUSTAN.O=PARENT_LHC

8. The term _____ refers to an object's location in the NDS Directory tree.

   ○ A. context

   ○ B. common name

   ○ C. organization

   ○ D. distinguished name

9. A _____ is the object's common name plus its context.

   ○ A. context

   ○ B. common name

   ○ C. organization

   ○ D. distinguished name

10. If you want to make it easy for a user to access a directory on a volume that contains an executable program, create a _____ object.

   ○ A. Group

   ○ B. Profile Script

   ○ C. Directory Map

   ○ D. Alias

Answers

1. D

2. C, B

3. B

4. A, B, D

5. C

6. A

7. B

8. A

9. D

10. C

Accessing and Using
Network Resources

Most of a network administrator's work involves providing authorized users access to network resources, and preventing unauthorized users from gaining access to the network. After everything is set up and organized on the network, the user must connect to and log in to the network, and use the available resources.

This chapter provides information about how users perform the following tasks:

- ■ *Connect to the network*

- ■ *Log in to the network*

- ■ *Access network data*

- ■ *Access and use applications*

- ■ *Print on the network*

Connecting to the Network

To connect to the network, a user must first have a PC. This PC, with the proper hardware and software, becomes a workstation on the network. For a stand-alone computer to become a workstation, it must have a network board installed and connected to the network cable (see fig. 21.1).

After the physical connection is made, a software connection to the network must also be made. A software connection requires several software files. Each of these files must be loaded into the workstation's memory in the required order. The software files needed to establish network communication are:

- Link Support Layer (LSL.COM)

- Network board driver (such as NE2000.COM)

- Communications protocol (IPXODI.COM)

- NetWare DOS Requester (VLM.EXE and associated VLM files)

Link Support Layer

The LSL.COM file, which loads the Link Support Layer, implements the ODI specification (see the "Communications Protocol" section, a little later in the chapter). Its function is to route network information from various protocols to the network board driver as well as to the related communications software. Because of its function, the Link Support Layer is often called the *switchboard.*

After you load the workstation's operating system (DOS), load the LSL.COM file to provide protocol routing.

Network Board Driver

The *network board driver* is the software that is compatible with the network board installed in your workstation. Its function is to activate the network board and then control its actions. It is the go-between (connection software) for the workstation's software and the physical components that constitute the network hardware.

Figure 21.1

Hardware necessary for network communication.

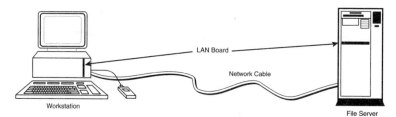

Workstation · LAN Board · Network Cable · File Server

NetWare 4 requires that network board drivers be of a specific type, known as MLID (*Multiple Link Interface Driver*), which support ODI specifications. The communications protocol software used by DOS workstations (see the following "Communications Protocol" section) supports multiple protocols on the same cabling system. MLID network board drivers also support multiple protocols by making it possible for the network board to accept data from various protocols.

Load the board driver by loading the file associated with the network board installed in your workstation. For example, if your workstation has an NE2000 network board installed, load the NE2000.COM file, or the network board file that came with your network board. Load the network board driver file after loading the LSL.COM file.

Communications Protocol

The communications protocol used by DOS workstations is a version of the NetWare IPX communications protocol. The file that loads the communications protocol is called IPXODI.COM because it provides communication based on the ODI (Open Data-Link Interface) specification. By following the ODI specification, users can take advantage of multiple protocols on the same cabling system, even using the same network board.

Load the communications protocol file for DOS workstations by loading the IPXODI.COM file. Load IPXODI.COM after you load the network board file.

NetWare DOS Requester

The NetWare DOS Requester is a series of files, the manager of which is the VLM.EXE file. This file and its associated files are the connection point between the workstation's DOS-based files (the DOS operating system and DOS applications) and the network.

The NetWare DOS Requester enables the DOS operating system and DOS application programs to communicate across the network and to make requests for network services. It also stores information related to the workstation's network connection, information that is deleted when the user logs out of the network and breaks the logical network connection.

To load the NetWare DOS Requester into workstation memory, type **VLM** at the DOS prompt, and press Enter. By default, this loads the NetWare DOS Requester into extended memory. If extended memory is unavailable, or if you prefer to load the NetWare DOS Requester into a location other than extended memory, you can issue this command followed by the /M switch, and your choice of memory locations.

To load the NetWare DOS Requester into conventional memory, for example, follow the /M with a C. That is, type **VLM /MC** and press Enter. Use **X** instead of **C** to load the files into extended memory, or **E** instead of **C** to load the files into expanded memory.

Load the NetWare DOS Requester last, after you load the IPXODI.COM file. The NetWare DOS Requester is the last connection software to be loaded. After all connection software files have been loaded into workstation memory, you can log in to the network.

Note All workstation connection software can be unloaded from workstation memory if you follow two rules.

First, the order in which you must unload the software is opposite the order in which you loaded it. In other words, you must unload the NetWare DOS Requester before you unload the IPXODI.COM file; the IPXODI.COM file must be unloaded before you unload the network board driver file (such as NE2000.COM); and the network board driver file must be unloaded before you unload the Link Support Layer software (LSL.COM).

Second, unload each file by issuing the same command you used to load the file, but following that command with a space, a slash, and the letter U. For example, unload the LSL.COM file by typing **LSL /U** and pressing Enter.

Logging In to the Network

After the physical connection has been made (network board installed in the workstation and connected to the network cable) and all connection software has been loaded into the workstation, you can log in to the network. Before logging in, however, change to the first network drive. (In most cases this is drive F, but the actual drive letter depends on what you specified as the first network drive under the NetWare DOS Requester heading in the NET.CFG file on the workstation.)

After you change to the first available network drive, type **LOGIN** and press Enter. When prompted, provide your login name and password.

 Note If your Name Context was set properly in the workstation's NET.CFG file, you do not have to specify your distinguished name when you log in—you simply specify your login name. Otherwise, specify your distinguished name as your login name when prompted, or as part of the first login command, as shown in the following example:

```
LOGIN .CN=MICHELLE.OU=NOBUS.O=LHC_PARENT
```

Typing **LOGIN** runs the LOGIN.EXE file found in the LOGIN directory on a NetWare 4.1 file server. After you run the LOGIN.EXE file and are successfully logged in to the network, no additional login information is necessary for access to network services.

You can automate the connection and login process by putting the necessary files in your workstation's AUTOEXEC.BAT file, or in a separate file (such as STARTNET.BAT) to be called from the AUTOEXEC.BAT file. The following listing shows a sample STARTNET.BAT file for a network workstation:

```
C:\COLLAGE>TYPE C:\NWCLIENT/STARTNET.BAT
@ECHO OFF
CD C:\NWCLIENT
C:\QEMM\LOADHI /R:2 /LO NWCACHE 1024 1024 /
➥LEND=ON /DELAY=OFF
SET NWLANGUAGE=ENGLISH
LH C:\NWCLIENT\LSL.COM
C:\QEMM\LOADHI /R:2 C:\NWCLIENT\NE2000.COM
C:\QEMM\LOADHI /R:2 C:\NWCLIENT\IPXODI.COM
rem c:\QEMM\LOADHI /R:2 SERVER
rem c:\QEMM\LOADHI /R:0 /LO VLM /ME
rem VLM /ME
rem End of remarked-out section.
CD \
rem C:\NWCLIENT\NET LOGIN
C:\NWCLIENT\VLM.EXE
C:\NWCLIENT\TSASMS.COM

C:\COLLAGE>\
```

Accessing Network Data

After you are granted access to the network file system, you can take advantage of the variety of services it provides—storage space for your data files, application software, shared network printing services, and so on. Before you can store and retrieve data on the network, however, you need a basic understanding of the network file system and how to access and manage it.

The network file system is designed to function in much the same way the DOS file system functions. In DOS, the drive itself is the root of the file system. In NetWare, the volume is the root of the file system. A NetWare *volume* is a logical division (an amount of physical storage space) of the file server's storage area, most commonly the hard disk. A NetWare 4 file server can have as many as 64 volumes, but must have at least one (called SYS). The following are additional facts about NetWare volumes:

■ Maximum storage space is 32 terabytes (TB)

■ Maximum volume space is 32 TB

■ Maximum segments per volume is 32

■ Minimum size for the SYS volume is 2.5 megabytes (MB)

In NetWare 4, volumes have both a physical name and a volume object name. The *physical name* is the name assigned to the volume when you create it. The *volume object name*, which is assigned by NetWare 4 when the volume object is created, consists of the name of the file server and the volume name, with the two being separated by the underscore (_) character. The network administrator can change the volume object name.

Below the NetWare root (volume), directories and files can be added in much the same way that directories and files are added to the DOS root. For example, you can use the DOS MakeDir (MD) command to create directories. You can also use the NetWare Administrator utility to create directories.

Regardless of how you create network directories, after the directories have been created, users can store program and data files in those directories. Users must be able to access the network directories, however. Users can use a variety of NetWare utilities and DOS utilities to access network data.

To access data on the network, the most important NetWare utility users need is the MAP utility. This utility is similar to DOS commands, in that it is entered at the command line, with or without various options. The purpose of the MAP utility is to provide access to data on the network by establishing paths that point to areas in the network file structure where the data can be found. Just as DOS uses drive letters (A, B, C, and so on) to point to the physical resource, NetWare uses letters to point to the logical resource. These letters, and the location of the NetWare directory structure to which they point, are called *drive mappings*. The two types of drive mappings are *network* and *search*. You map network drives to access data on the network, and you map search drives to access executable programs on the network (see the "Accessing and Using Applications" section of this chapter).

Any drive letters not being used by physical DOS devices can be used to map network drives or search drives. Most commonly, the letters F through K are used to map network drives; the letters Z through

L are used to map search drives. Table 21.1 shows the MAP command and the options used to MAP network drive letters.

 Note   A *Directory Map object* is an object on a NetWare 4 network, which acts as a pointer to a specific directory on the network. It is created primarily to provide users with quick access to the exact directory that contains an application program.

Table 21.1
Using MAP to Create Network Drives

Command	Description, Example, and Result
MAP	Displays current mappings (see fig. 8.2) Example: MAP Result: *a list of your current mappings*
MAP N *path*	Maps next available network drive letter to specified path Example: MAP N CP_410\SYS:APPS Result: H: = CP_410\SYS:APPS *(assuming that the last mapped drive was drive G)*
MAP G:=*path*	Maps specified drive letter to specified path Example: MAP G:=CP_410\SYS:APPS\WP Result: G: = CP_410\SYS:APPS\WP
MAP ROOT I:=*path*	Maps specified drive letter to specified path, making drive appear as though it is mapped to the root Example: MAP ROOT I:=CP_410\SYS:APPS Result: I:=CP_410\SYS:APPS \ *(If you type I: at the prompt, it displays as* I:\>)
MAP P K:=*volume:*	Maps specified drive letter to a physical volume Example: MAP P K:=SYS: Result: K:=CP_410\SYS: *(assuming that the file server name is CP_410)*
MAP L:=*name*	Maps specified drive letter to a Directory Map object Example: MAP L:=WORD Result: L:\CP_410\SYS:APPS\WP

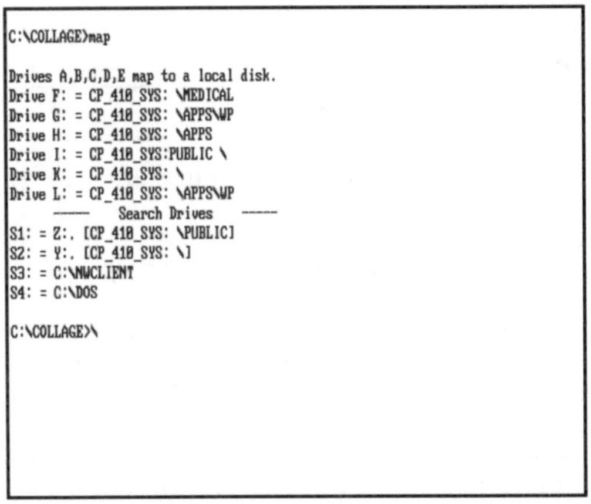

C:\COLLAGE>map
Drives A,B,C,D,E map to a local disk.
Drive F: = CP_410_SYS: \MEDICAL
Drive G: = CP_410_SYS: \APPS\WP
Drive H: = CP_410_SYS: \APPS
Drive I: = CP_410_SYS:PUBLIC \
Drive K: = CP_410_SYS: \
Drive L: = CP_410_SYS: \APPS\WP
---- Search Drives ----
S1: = Z:. [CP_410_SYS: \PUBLIC]
S2: = Y:. [CP_410_SYS: \]
S3: = C:\NWCLIENT
S4: = C:\DOS
C:\COLLAGE>\

Figure 21.2
MAP display.

You can also use the NetWare User Tools utility to map network drives. With the NetWare User Tools utility open, press Alt+D to choose the Drive Connections screen. Choose the exact path to be mapped from the Resources side of the NetWare Drive Connections window, and drag it to the drive letter to which you want to map to that path (see fig. 21.3).

In addition to the MAP command, you can use several other NetWare commands to view and manage the network file system. Table 21.2 lists and describes those commands.

NetWare Drive Connections
Path:
\\CP_410_SYS\APPS\PAINT
Drives:
A:
B:
C:
D:
E:
F: \\CN=CP_410_SYS \PUBLIC
G:
H:
I:
J:
K:
L:
M:
N:
O:
Resources:
CP_410_SYS
APPS
COLLAGE
MEDICAL
PAINT
SIMANT
SPELL
WP
ETC
LOGIN
MAIL
MEDICAL
PUBLIC
QUEUES
SYSTEM
Drive Connections [Alt+D]
Drive Info...
Permanent
Map Delete
Map

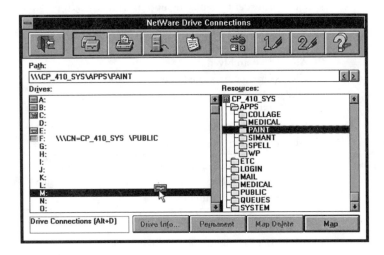

Figure 21.3
Mapping a drive, using the NetWare User Tools utility.

Table 21.2
NetWare File-Management Commands

Command	Description
NDIR	Displays file name, size, last update, and attributes of network files in current context
NDIR /DO	Displays a list of directories in the current context only, as well as the date and time they were created
NDIR /DO /SUB	Displays a list of directories (and their subdirectories) in the current context, as well as the date and time they were created
NDIR /FO	Displays a list of files only (in the current context), with their last update, size, and attributes
NDIR /FO /SO option	Displays a list of files in the current context, with date of their last update, size, and attributes; list is displayed in specific sort order by replacing option with any of the following sort options:
	AC Last accessed date
	AR Last archived date
	CR Created or copied date
	OW Owner
	SI File size
	UP Last updated date
	UN Not (Un-) sorted
NDIR /FO /REV SORT *option*	Displays list of files in current context in reverse sort order, replacing *option* with any of the sort options shown with the preceding command
NDIR /?	Displays help information for the NDIR command
NLIST VOLUME	Lists information about volumes in current context
NLIST VOLUME /N	Lists only names of volumes in current context
NLIST VOLUME /D	Lists detailed information about all volumes in current context
NLIST /?	Displays help information for the NLIST command

Accessing and Using Applications

You map network drives to access *data* on the network. You map search drives to access *applications* on the network. After a search drive is mapped to the directory containing an application, you can run the application by typing the name of its executable file. Because you have a search drive mapped, the executable file is located and run. NetWare uses search drive mappings in much the same way that DOS uses the PATH statement.

When DOS uses the PATH to find an executable file, it searches specified directories in the order in which they appear in the PATH statement. When NetWare uses search drives to find an executable file, it searches in numeric order, beginning with search drive 1 (which is drive letter Z, by default), unless reordered (using the MAP INS command) by the user.

To create a search drive, use the MAP command. Table 21.3 shows different search drive commands and provides information about their use.

Table 21.3
Search Drive Mappings

Command	Description, Example, and Result
MAP S16:=*path*	Maps next available search drive to specified directory for running an executable file Example: MAP S16:=CP_410/SYS:APPS/WP Result: X: CP_410/SYS:APPS/WP (*assuming that next available search drive letter was drive X*)
MAP INS S1:=*path*	Maps next available search drive letter into first search position, moving all other search drive mappings down one level Example: MAP INS S1:=CP_410/SYS:PUBLIC Result: W: CP_410/SYS:PUBLIC (*assuming that next available search drive letter was drive W, because three other letters —Z, Y, and X—have already been used*)
MAP S2:=*path*	Maps next available search drive letter as search drive 2, replacing any mapping that may currently exist for search drive 2 Example: MAP S2:=SYS:SYSTEM Result: X: CP_410\SYS:SYSTEM (*assuming that current context is set to the CP_410 file server, and drive letter X was next available search drive letter*)

Note As was explained earlier, you can also map a network drive to a Directory Map object in order to access an application on the network.

After network search drives have been set up, you can access and run applications on the network. One of the applications that you can run is FirstMail, the electronic mail application provided by NetWare. With Basic MHS installed (refer to Chapter 16, "Setting Up Network Printing and Mail Services"), you can run the FirstMail utility to send and receive e-mail. FirstMail is installed in SYS:PUBLIC, to which a search drive should be mapped from the SYSTEM login script.

Printing on the Network

You can also take advantage of print services provided by print queues, print servers, and printers on a network.

Print queues hold (store) the print jobs you send, until a print server can take the job and route it to the appropriate printer. Print queues—directories in the QUEUES directory on a NetWare volume—can be created on any physical volume. For a print queue to be accessible, however, a corresponding NetWare 4 Print Queue object must exist. The Print Queue object is used to locate the actual print queue directory, and then regulate who can access the printer (by controlling who is allowed to send print jobs to the print queue).

Print servers monitor print queues and printers (up to 256 printers per print server), and pass print jobs from print queues to printers. As with print queues, a corresponding Print Server object must exist on the network.

Printers are the devices that print documents. As with print queues and print servers, a corresponding Printer object must exist on the network. Printers can be physically connected to the following hardware:

- NetWare file servers with the print server software loaded (combination file server and print server)

- Regular NetWare file servers

- Workstations

- Network cable system

Print jobs can be sent to print queues or, if the application from which the print job is being sent is network-aware, directly to a printer on the network. Print jobs that would otherwise be sent directly to the workstation's printer port (such as LPT1 or LPT2) can instead be redirected to a network printer.

To redirect a non-network-aware print job, use the CAPTURE command or the NetWare User Tools for Windows or DOS (also called NETUSER) utilities. Then, from within the application, set up printing by choosing a print driver and then printing jobs to the chosen printer or to a file. From the DOS prompt, use NPRINT or PCONSOLE to send the print job to a printer.

To redirect a print job to a printer by using CAPTURE, place the CAPTURE command in a login script or inside a menu. Use any of the commands associated with the CAPTURE command, the most commonly used of which are shown in table 21.4.

Table 21.4
Commonly Used CAPTURE Commands

Command	Abbreviation	Purpose
Autoendcap	AU	Automatically sends print job when application is closed
Local	L	Specifies local port number
Notify	NOTI	Informs user when print job is finished
Printer	P	Specifies which printer is to receive the print job
Server	S	Specifies NetWare server to which print job should be directed (if server is not the default server)
Show	SH	Displays current status of CAPTURE command
Timeout	TI	Specifies number of seconds that must elapse between receipt of material for printing and indication that the print job is complete

Note You can also issue the CAPTURE command without any parameters, if a default print job configuration exists (was created using the PCONSOLE utility).

To redirect a print job by using the NetWare User Tools utility, choose Printer Connections, then drag-and-drop a print queue or printer from the Resources list to a port in the Port list.

To send a job to a network printer from the DOS prompt (instead of from an application), use the NPRINT utility. To use NPRINT, type **NPRINT** *filename options* and press Enter. Replace *filename* with the name of the file to be printed. Replace *options* with any of the options you can use with the NetWare command. (Refer to table 21.4 for a list of the more common options.)

To use PCONSOLE to send a print job to a printer, start the PCONSOLE utility, then choose Print Queues from the Available Options menu. Next, choose a print queue from the list of Print Queues, and choose Print Job. Press Insert, choose the path where the file is located, choose the file, then choose a print job configuration (if prompted). Press F10 to place the print job in the print queue.

Questions

1. The proper load order for network communication software is _____.

   ○ A. LSL, LAN driver, IPXODI, VLM

   ○ B. IPXODI, LSL, LAN driver, VLM

   ○ C. VLM, IPXODI, LAN driver, LSL

   ○ D. LSL, LAN driver, VLM, IPXODI

2. The _____ file routes information from various protocols to the network board driver.

   ○ A. LSL

   ○ B. IPXODI

   ○ C. LAN driver

   ○ D. VLM

3. The file used to activate the network board is called _____.

   ○ A. LSL

   ○ B. IPXODI

   ○ C. LAN driver

   ○ D. VLM

4. Which of the following files is responsible for managing the related NetWare DOS Requester files?

   ○ A. LSL

   ○ B. IPXODI

   ○ C. LAN driver

   ○ D. VLM

5. The maximum NetWare 4 volume space is _____.

   ○ A. 64 KB

   ○ B. 2.5 MB

   ○ C. 32 KB

   ○ D. 32 TB

6. To map the next available network drive to a given path, use the _____ command.

   ○ A. MAP N:=*path*

   ○ B. MAP N *path*

   ○ C. MAP INS N:=*path*

   ○ D. MAP ROOT N *path*

7. Of the following, which TWO can be used to automate the connection and login process?

   ☐ A. CONFIG.BAT

   ☐ B. AUTOEXEC.BAT

   ☐ C. STARTNET.BAT

   ☐ D. NET.BAT

8. A _____ command can be used to trick an application program into believing that it is being installed and run from root.

   ○ A. MAP ROOT

   ○ B. MAP INS ROOT

   ○ C. ROOT MAP

   ○ D. ROOT INS MAP

9. To see a list of directories only within the current context, type _____ and press Enter.

   ○ A. NDIR

   ○ B. NDIR /SO

   ○ C. NDIR /DO

   ○ D. NDIR /FO

10. To see what the current status of your CAPTURE statement is, use the _____ command.

    ○ A. CAPTURE SH

    ○ B. CAPTURE NOTI

    ○ C. CAPTURE P

    ○ D. CAPTURE TI

Answers

1. A

2. A

3. C

4. D

5. D

6. B

7. B, C

8. A

9. C

10. A

Networking Technologies

Computer Network Concepts

Computer networks enable computers to communicate directly in order to exchange information and services. Because computers are all different, are used in different ways, and might be located at different distances from each other, the task of enabling them to communicate can get quite involved, drawing on a wide variety of technologies.

As you study for the Networking Technologies test, you will be delving into some fundamental networking concepts. This chapter will ensure that you have a basic understanding of those concepts before you plunge into the details. Here you will learn a working definition of a computer network, along with definitions of the types of networks and their components.

Upon completing this chapter, you will be able to do the following:

- Define computer networking

- Describe the following models of network computing: centralized, distributed, and collaborative

- Describe the characteristics of local, metropolitan, and wide area networks.

- Describe the essential elements of a computer network

- Describe servers, clients, and peers as they relate to computer networking

These skills will prepare you to understand the technologies that are examined in greater detail later in this section.

Models of Network Computing

Novell defines *networking* as the sharing of information and services. By this definition, people are networking when they are exchanging information. This course, however, is specifically concerned with computer networking, which has evolved under several different models to respond to different needs. These models are centralized, distributed, and collaborative.

Centralized Computing

The earliest computers were large, difficult to manage, and expensive. Originally, these large mainframe computers were not networked in the sense you are familiar with today. Jobs were entered into the system by reading commands from card decks.

The computer would execute one job at a time and generate a printout when the job was complete. Terminals, which enabled users to interact with the centralized computer, were a much later development.

In the computing environment of the mainframe world, all the processing and data storage are centralized in the mainframe computer. *Terminals* are simple devices that display characters on screens and accept typed input. Because terminals are simply input/output devices and do not process or store data, by Novell's definition of networking, no sharing of information is involved and no networking is taking place in a terminal-host environment. Networks developed when it became necessary for mainframe computers to share information and services.

In summary, the *centralized computing* model involves the following:

- All processing in the central, mainframe computer

- Terminals are connected to the central computer as input/output devices

- Networks may be employed to interconnect two or more mainframe computers

Distributed Computing

As personal computers were introduced to organizations, a new model of distributed computing emerged. Instead of concentrating computing in a central device, PCs made it possible to give each worker an individual computer. Each PC can process and store data independently.

Under the distributed computing model, networking has evolved to enable the many distributed computers to exchange data and share resources and services.

In summary, *distributed computing* involves the following:

- Multiple computers capable of operating independently

- Tasks that are split up among the various computers

- Networks that enable the computers to exchange data and services

Collaborative Computing

Also called cooperative computing, collaborative computing enables computers in a distributed computing environment to share processing power in addition to data, resources, and services. In a collaborative computing environment, computers might "borrow" processing power by running programs on other computers on the network, or processes might be designed so they will run on two or more computers. Obviously, collaborative computing cannot take place without a network to enable the various computers to communicate.

In summary, *collaborative computing* involves the following:

- Multiple computers

- Networks that enable the computers to exchange data and services

- Multiple computers that may cooperate to perform a task

Local, Metropolitan, and Wide Area Networks

Computer networks may be classified according to their size characteristics. The most commonly used categories are the following:

- *Local area networks* (LANs), which are confined to a relatively small area, typically limited to a few tens of kilometers in size. LANs typically employ a single transmission medium and are generally defined within a particular building or campus of buildings.

- *Metropolitan area networks* (MANs) may grow in size to that of a metropolitan area, up to about 100 kilometers in scope. To be able to transmit data longer distances, MANs typically require different transmission media and network hardware.

- *Wide area networks* (WANs) can cross the boundaries of states, countries, or even continents, and can be truly worldwide in scope.

An organization with computer operations at several widely separated sites may employ an *enterprise WAN* to interconnect the sites. An enterprise WAN can use a combination of private and commercial network services, but is dedicated to the needs of a particular organization.

Some WANs can be considered *global* in scope because they cross continental boundaries. An example is the Internet, which interconnects thousands of computers on all continents.

Of the three categories of network sizes, LANs and WANs are those most frequently encountered.

Components of Computer Networks

Until now, the definition of a computer network has been simply "something" that enables computers to exchange information. The time has come for a more thorough definition. Novell's definition of a network includes three components, as follows:

- Two entities that have information to share. On a computer network, computers share *network services.*

- A pathway by which the entities can contact each other. The pathway through which computers contact each other is called the *transmission media.*

- Rules that establish orderly procedures for communication. The rules that govern computer communication are called *protocols.*

Each of these three components is discussed later in further detail.

 Merely having a transmission pathway does not produce communication. When two entities communicate, they do not merely exchange data, but they understand the data they receive from each other. The goal of computer networking is not merely to exchange data, but to be able to understand and use data received from other entities on the network.

Network Services

Networks enable computers to share their resources by offering *services* to other computers. Novell uses the term *service providers* to describe computers (or other entities) that share their capabilities with others. A service provider consists of the hardware and software that provides a specific network service.

Service providers share their capabilities with other entities on the network. A waiter in a restaurant is an example of a human service provider. Examples of network services include the following:

- File services

- Print services

- Communication services

- Electronic mail

Service requesters are entities that utilize network services. A customer ordering lunch in a restaurant is a human example of a service requester.

Service providers will advertise the services they can make available. Service requesters examine the lists of services and request the services they require.

Note Service providers offer services to service requesters.

In this course, remember that the definition of networking is extremely generic. Any entities (human or machine) that are exchanging information are networking. Any entity (human or machine) on a network can become a service provider or a service requester.

Computer networks consist of three types of service providers and service requesters, as follows:

- *Servers* function only as service providers.

- *Clients* function only as service requesters and do not provide services for other computers.

- *Peers* may concurrently provide and request services. In a peer network, a given computer might be requesting file services from one computer, while at the same time providing print services to another.

Whether a computer functions as a server, client, or peer depends on the software the computer is running. Examples from the NetWare world include the following:

- NetWare 3.12, which turns a PC into a file and print server

- NetWare client software (the NetWare Shell or Requester), which turns a PC into a client

- Personal NetWare, which enables a computer to function as a peer, both requesting and providing services

Networks that enable any computer to both provide and request network services (any entity can function as a peer) are frequently called *peer-to-peer* networks.

Many networks are configured so a given computer will function as either a service provider or a service requester, but not both. With this approach, a server is at the logical center of the network and provides all network services. Therefore, this is frequently called a *server-centric approach.* NetWare 3.12 and 4.1 are the most popular software for configuring server-centric networks.

You will learn more about network services in Chapter 23, "Network Services."

Transmission Media

Entities on networks communicate through some media. Human entities may communicate through telephone wires or sound waves in the air. Computers can communicate through cables, light, and radio waves.

Transmission media enable computers to send and receive messages, but do not guarantee that the messages will be understood.

You will learn more about transmission media in Chapter 25, "Transmission Media" and in Chapter 26, "Transmission Media Connections."

Protocols

Rules are necessary to ensure that messages are understood. The rules of English enable two English-speaking people to understand each others' messages.

The rules that govern computer communication are called protocols. A *protocol* is one or more standards that enable two devices to communicate.

Protocols of many types are utilized on networks. Chapter 25 will introduce you to the model that you can use to organize your understanding of protocols. The majority of this section, starting in Chapter 27, "OSI Physical Layer Concepts," will be devoted to expanding your knowledge of network protocols.

Questions

1. Which model of network computing does not take advantage of the processing capability of a user's desktop computer?

   ○ A. Centralize

   ○ B. Distributed

   ○ C. Collaborative

   ○ D. All of the above utilize the processing capabilities of personal PCs

2. In which model do user's personal computers process information independently from each other?

   ○ A. Centralized

   ○ B. Distributed

   ○ C. Collaborative

   ○ D. None of the above

3. In which model of network computing do computers share each others' processing capabilities?

   ○ A. Centralized

   ○ B. Distributed

   ○ C. Collaborative

   ○ D. Departmental

4. Which type of network is most likely confined to a building or a campus?

   ○ A. Local-area

   ○ B. Metropolitan

   ○ C. Wide-area

   ○ D. Departmental

5. What are the size limits of a wide area network?

   ○ A. 100 kilometers

   ○ B. 1,000 kilometers

   ○ C. 10,000 kilometers

   ○ D. Worldwide

6. Which TWO entities can share services on a network?

   □ A. Servers

   □ B. Clients

   □ C. Peers

   □ D. Requesters

7. Which TWO entities can utilize services on a network?

   □ A. Servers

   □ B. Clients

   □ C. Peers

   □ D. Communicators

Answers

1. A

2. B

3. C

4. A

5. D

6. A, D

7. B, C

Network Services

*N*etwork services are the first components of the
network model. Network services are the resources that
servers share with clients, enabling clients to leverage the
computing power of other computers on the network.

An operating system *(OS) is the computer program
that directly manages the resources in a computer,
including memory, disk drives, printing, and input/
output functions. This course regards DOS, OS/2, and
Unix as* local *or* desktop *operating systems—operating
systems that are confined to a single computer. A
network operating system (NOS) such as NetWare
can be distributed on several computers on a network.*

It is possible to build network services as add-ons to local operating systems. Although DOS PCs can be made to network with some add-on programs, the result seldom has the robust, high-level of performance of an operating system that is made for networking. Network operating systems generally include built-in support for file, printing, and other services. Building networking into the NOS improves both performance and reliability, and has the added benefit of being easier to manage than a lot of add-ons.

Services such as file and printer sharing were the earliest incentives for networking computers, but many new network services are now becoming commonplace. In this chapter, you will learn about many network services and how they are managed on NetWare LANs.

When you complete this chapter, you will be able to do the following:

- Describe a variety of network services

- Identify appropriate network services to match organizational needs

- Determine how network services are implemented in centralized and distributed computing environments

In addition, you will examine how the following services function on a network:

- File services

- Print services

- Message services

- Application services

- Database services

File Services

File services enable networked computers to share each others' files. This capability was perhaps the primary reason it became so desirable to network personal computers. Users needed to exchange files, a problem that could be solved, if inconveniently, simply by trading files on disks. More importantly, users needed to share data in common database files, something that can only be done with a network.

The working definition for this course is that file services consist of all network applications that store, retrieve, or move data files. A feature of file services is access control. File services enable users to read, write, and manage files and data, but they should also restrict users to authorized file operations so that files are not accidentally overwritten or deleted.

This section examines the following file services:

- File transfer

- File storage

- File archiving

- Data migration

- File update synchronization

File Transfer

Without a network, the options for transferring files between computers are limited. You can, of course, exchange files on floppy disks, a process that came to be called "sneaker-net" because it consisted of networking by actually running around. Or you could use communication software to dial another computer and transfer files via a modem or a direct serial connection.

Note Although Novell course materials mention this file service first, NetWare 3.*x* and 4.*x* do not excel at file transfer between workstations. It is possible to copy files directly from one server to another, but not directly from one client to another. File transfer with NetWare 3.*x* and 4.*x* is most easily achieved by storing files to be shared on the NetWare server.

It is possible to add file transfer capability to clients using products, such as Novell's Personal NetWare, which enable clients to transfer files directly using peer-to-peer networking techniques.

NetWare 3.*x* and 4.*x* do support file transfer between servers and between clients and servers, but not directly from client to client.

When users are transferring files, the need for security arises. It might be necessary to limit file transfers to authorized users using password-controlled security systems, to assign file attributes that restrict the operations that may be performed with a file, or to encrypt files so they may be read only by authorized users.

File Storage

Most networks have at least some centralized file storage. All NetWare file servers are capable of storing vast amounts of data, sharing it with users, and controlling access to a high degree of precision.

For many years, most storage consisted of *online* storage—storage on hard disks that was always accessible immediately on demand. The files that could be accessed on a server were limited to the amount of hard drive space that was available. Hard drives are fast, but the cost to store a megabyte of data is fairly high. Hard drives have another

disadvantage: Generally speaking, they cannot be removed for off-site storage, exchange, or simply to build a library of files that is seldom required, but must be fairly readily available.

Almost all companies have large amounts of data that is used infrequently. There is no need to keep all of the financial reports available from the previous year, for example, but they had better be available in case of an audit.

One approach is *offline* storage, which consists of removable media that are managed manually. The most popular media used are data tapes or optical disks. Once data is written to a tape or optical disk, the disk can be removed from the server and shelved. Users who require offline data might need to know which tape or optical disk to request. Some systems provide indexes or other aids that make requesting the proper offline storage element automatic. A system operator still has to retrieve the tape or disk and mount it on the server, however.

When the slow response of offline storage is unacceptable, a near-line storage approach may be selected. *Near-line* storage employs a machine, often called a *jukebox*, to manage large numbers of tapes or optical disks automatically. The proper tape or disk is retrieved and mounted by the jukebox without the need for human intervention. With near-line storage, huge amounts of data can be available with only slight delays, but at a much lower cost than would be required to store the data on hard drives.

Data migration is a technology that automatically moves less-used data from online storage to near-line or offline storage. The criteria for moving files can depend on when the files were last used, the owner of the files, file size, or a variety of other criteria. An efficient data migration facility makes it easy for users to locate migrated files. Figure 23.1 illustrates one approach to data migration.

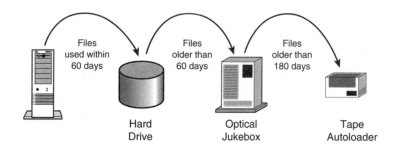

Figure 23.1
Data migration.

Files used within 60 days

Files older than 60 days

Files older than 180 days

Hard Drive

Optical Jukebox

Tape Autoloader

Novell supports the following standards for file storage and migration:

■ *Real-Time Data Migration* (RTDM)

■ *High Capacity Storage System* (HCSS) provides support for optical jukeboxes

■ *Mass Storage Services* (MSS) schedules and maintains distributed hierarchical storage

File Archiving

File archiving (or backup) is basically offline storage that is primarily geared to creating duplicate copies of online files. These backup copies serve as insurance against minor or major system failures.

Networks enable file archiving to be centralized. It is possible, for example, for a single site to back up all the servers on a network. Many current backup systems also have the capability of backing up various client workstations, making it feasible to archive all files on the network to a central facility, whether the files are located on network servers or clients

File-Update Synchronization

In its simplest form, *file-update synchronization* is a means of ensuring that all users have the latest copy of a file. File-update synchronization services can manage files by monitoring the date and time

stamps on files to determine which were saved most recently. By tracking the users who access the file, along with the data and time stamps, the service can update all the copies of the file with the most recent version.

File-update synchronization, however, can be considerably more involved. In a modern computing environment, it is not always feasible for all users to access all files in real time. A salesman, for example, might be carrying a notebook computer on which to enter orders. It would be impractical to dial the central LAN every time an order was to be entered, so the salesman would enter orders offline (while disconnected from the network) and store them in the laptop. That evening, he would call the central LAN, log in, and transmit all of the day's orders at one time.

During this process, files on the LAN must be updated to reflect new data in the salesman's portable computer. In addition, the salesman's PC might need some updating, with order confirmations or new pricing information, for example. The process of bringing the local and remote files into agreement is known as file-update synchronization.

File-update synchronization becomes considerably more challenging when additional users are sharing the data files simultaneously. Complex mechanisms must be in place to ensure that users do not accidentally overwrite each others' data. In some cases, the system simply flags files that have multiple, conflicting updates and requires a human to reconcile the differences.

Print Services

Network printing was the second big incentive to install LANs. Among the advantages of printing on a network are the following:

■ Many users can share the same printers, which is especially useful with expensive devices, such as color printers and plotters.

■ Printers can be located anywhere, not just next to a user's PC.

■ Queue-based network printing is more efficient than direct printing because the workstation can get back to work as soon as a job is queued to the network.

■ Modern printing services are available that enable users to send facsimile (fax) transmissions through the network to a fax server.

In this course, *print services* are defined as network applications that control and manage access to printers, network fax, and other similar devices. The print service functions discussed in this course are as follows:

■ Providing multiple access

■ Servicing simultaneous print requests

■ Operating without distance limitations

■ Managing specialized equipment types

■ Providing facsimile (fax) service

Providing Multiple Access

A typical printer has a limited number of available connecting points, such as parallel or serial interface ports. In fact, many printers can have only a single active port, which means that a limited number of users' PCs can be connected to ports on a given printer. Without a network, this might mean that a printer is required for each PC.

Networks break the relationship of one PC to a port. Any user on the network can print to any network printer simply by printing through the network print service. In most organizations, this means that the number of printers can be reduced, even to a single printer for a department.

Servicing Simultaneous Print Requests

When each printer is servicing several users, print services must have an organized means of achieving two goals, as follows:

■ Enabling any user to print at any time

■ Printing all of the users' jobs in an orderly fashion

Print services manage these complex tasks by employing a technique known as *queuing*. A queue is a line where things wait to be serviced—theater patrons wait in a queue until a ticket clerk can service their ticket requests, for example.

Network print queuing works as shown in figure 23.2. In the figure, you can see how print jobs from several users are collected in the queue. While printing to a queue, the users' PCs are fooled into thinking that they are printing to a directly attached printer. Network printing services reroute printed data to the queue instead of to the PC's printer port.

Figure 23.2

*How print services use
print queues.*

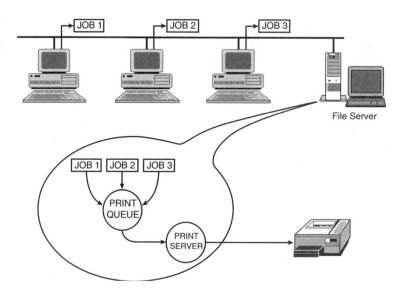

Once the jobs are in queues, the print jobs are sent one-by-one to a printer. Even though a printer can print only one thing at a time, the appearance to the users is that they can print freely, even when the printer is busy.

Interestingly, print queuing usually services print requests more rapidly than printers that are connected directly to users' PCs. A network queue can collect print data at network speeds, which are generally much faster than printers can actually put the data on paper. After the print data is safely stored in a queue, the user can go on about his or her work knowing that the job will be printed as soon as the printer becomes available.

Operating without Distance Limitations

When a printer is connected directly to a PC, it can never be very far from the PC itself. Fifteen to fifty feet is the extreme limit of most printer cables.

Printers on a network, however, can be located anywhere. Any user can use any printer, whether the printer is nearby, in the next building, or across the country. This enables organizations to place printers where they are needed, not just where a user's PC is found.

Managing Specialized Equipment Types

Although many printer types have decreased in cost considerably, some types of printers remain so expensive that they must be shared if owning them is to make sense. Some examples are the following:

- **High-speed printers.** Do you really want to print that 1,000 page report to your personal four-page-per-minute laser?

- **Quality color.** The best color printers, such as thermal transfer, cost many thousands of dollars.

- **Large format printers and plotters.** When 8 1/2×11 is not large enough, it might be nice to have an 11×17 printer or a plotter available.

Providing Facsimile (Fax) Service

A standard fax machine uses a scanner to read the image on a printed form, render that image in electronic signals, and transmit the signals to another fax machine where the original paper image is reconstructed. Fax machines have become so popular that long lines are often encountered by users and much paper is wasted.

A new class of print service directs printed images to a device that can transmit the images as facsimiles. A network fax service enables any user to send a fax directly from a network application, such as a word processor, without needing to print the document and hand-carry it to the public fax machine. The fax service uses queuing so that many users can generate faxes simultaneously. Then the fax service takes care of transmitting the images in an orderly manner.

Moreover, a network fax server can receive faxes and route them electronically to users without generating a printout. Users can view faxes on their PCs, print them if desired, or store them as data files for future use.

Message Services

File services can pass data between users when the data comes in file form. Today, however, many new types of data are available, including audio, video, and graphics. Text data can be simple text, or it can come in exotic forms such as hypertext, which contains electronic links to other text, documents, images, sounds, or other types of data.

Message services consist of a wide variety of services that go beyond simple file sharing to store, transfer, and access text, binary, graphic, video, and audio data.

This course examines four types of message services, as follows:

- Electronic mail
- Integrated electronic mail and voice mail
- Object-oriented applications
- Workgroup applications

Electronic Mail

E-mail is the new reason to install a LAN. In fact, a LAN is an excellent platform for electronic mail because it provides reliable, high-speed service and is low in cost. E-mail is a technology for electronically transferring messages between networked computers.

E-mail systems can service anything from a local workgroup, to a corporation, to the world. By installing e-mail routing devices, mail can be transferred smoothly and efficiently among several LANs. Perhaps the most gargantuan e-mail system is found on the Internet, which enables users in dozens of countries throughout the world to exchange electronic messages more easily than mailing a paper letter.

Early text-based e-mail has given way to elaborate systems that supported embedded sound, graphics, and even video data. Modern e-mail systems also enable traveling clients to "call in" to send and receive mail.

Integrated Electronic Mail and Voice Mail

New messaging technologies are leading to closer interoperation of e-mail and voice mail systems. Voice mail can be more than a simple telephone answering system. Because voice-mail systems are themselves based on computers, they can be connected to networks, and voice data can be managed by messaging services. Eventually, this will enable various voice and e-mail systems to interoperate and freely exchange data.

A traveling user might direct that her e-mail messages should be forwarded to her voice mail. She then could call in and have the messages read electronically by a text-recognition system. Alternatively, speech recognition devices might be used to read a user's voice mail and convert it to a text-based e-mail message.

 Novell's Groupware division has produced a product called GroupWise that has some of these features.

Object-Oriented Applications

Objects are building blocks (consisting of abstract data types and program code) that can be combined to construct large, more complex, object-oriented applications.

Messaging services can be used as intermediaries that enable objects on the network to communicate. Messaging service applications achieve this by acting as agents for the objects. The object simply delivers data to an agent, which is then responsible for delivering the data to the destination object. This eliminates the need for objects to have the capability of communicating with all other objects on the network.

Workgroup Applications

Workgroup applications use network services to improve communication in workgroups. Two types

of workgroup applications are discussed in this course: workflow management and linked-object documents.

Workflow Management Applications

Workflow management applications route electronic forms and documents among workgroup users. When reliable electronic signatures are added to the process, it becomes possible to replace numerous processes that are traditionally paperbound. An electronic purchase order system might function like this:

1. The requester fills in an electronic form.

2. The form is routed to the requesters supervisor for an approval signature which is added electronically.

3. The signed form is routed to a budget manager who ensures that funds are available. Funding verification might even take place automatically before the form is brought to the budget manager's attention.

4. The approved purchase request is used to generate a paper purchase order that can be faxed to the vendor.

You can see how users along the way can add information to the form. The pioneering example of a workflow management application is Lotus Notes. Novell provides an automated forms management package called InForms.

Linked-Object Documents

Documents need no longer be regarded simply as files containing text. Modern documents can consist of many different types of objects, including text, graphics, sound, voice, spreadsheet data, and video. Various types of objects can be assembled to build documents.

Objects are more than just data. An object also has a degree of "intelligence" that enables it to pass messages to documents where they are integrated. Some sense of this operation can be had by experimenting with OLE in Microsoft Windows.

Directory Services

Until recently, most services on a network were operated fairly independently. Suppose that a network consisted of two file servers and an e-mail server. The network administrator would need to manage user accounts on all three servers independently. The larger the network, the more difficult network administration becomes.

Directory services can greatly simplify other network tasks as well. A *directory service* integrates all the information about objects on the network into an overall directory structure. Objects on the network can consult the directory to identify other objects and to enable objects to exchange messages. The objects themselves do not need to know the address, location, or messaging formats required to communicate—all of this information is provided by the directory service.

The directory structure hides the physical structure of the network from applications and from users. A print server is simply a part of the network—it is not a service being offered by a particular computer.

The actual directory, however, is stored in files that physically reside on one or more server. When information in the directory is duplicated on several servers, a *directory synchronization* process is needed to keep all copies of the directory up-to-date.

NetWare Directory Services is a directory service that has been integrated into NetWare 4.*x*.

Application Services

Application services enable applications to leverage the computing power and specialized capabilities of other computers on the network.

For example, business applications often must perform complex statistical calculations that are beyond the scope of most desktop PCs. Statistical software with the required capabilities might need to run on a mainframe computer or on a Unix minicomputer. The statistical package, however, can make its capabilities available to applications on users' PCs by providing an application service.

The client PC would send the request for a calculation to the statistics application server. After the results become available, they would be returned to the client. In this way, only one computer in an organization requires the expensive software license and processing power required to produce the statistics, but all client PCs can benefit.

Application services enable organizations to install servers that are specialized for specific functions. The most common application servers currently are database servers, discussed in the next section. Other application services, however, are beginning to emerge.

Application servers are an effective strategy for making a network more scaleable. New application servers can be added as new types of application needs emerge. If more power is needed for the application, only the application server needs to be upgraded. A database server, for example, might grow from a PC to a multiprocessor RISC system running Unix without requiring many or even any changes to the client PCs.

Each application service does not necessarily need to be hosted on a separate computer. Along with file and print services, NetWare servers can provide e-mail, database, and communication services.

If demand for services loads the server down and hurts performance, it is easy to move an application service to its own computer. This scaleability is one of the advantages of a LAN architecture.

Database Services

Database services are the most common examples of application servers. Because database servers enable applications to be designed in separate client and server components, they are frequently called *client-server databases.*

With a client-server database, the client and server applications are designed to take advantage of specialized capabilities of the client and database systems, as follows:

- The client application manages data input from the user, generation of screen displays, some of the reporting, and generating data retrieval requests that are sent to the database server.

- The database server manages the database files; adds, deletes, and modifies records in the database; queries the database and generates the result required by the client; and transmits results back to the client. The database server can service requests for multiple clients more or less at the same time.

Database services relieve clients of most responsibilities for managing data. A modern database server is a sophisticated piece of software that can do the following:

- Provide database security

- Optimize the performance of database operations

- Determine optimal locations for storing data without requiring clients to know where the data is located

- Service large numbers of clients by reducing the time any one client is accessing the database

- Distribute data across multiple database servers

Distributed databases are becoming increasingly popular. They enable portions of databases to be stored on separate server computers, which may be in different geographic locations. This technique, known as *distributed data*, looks like a single logical database to users, but places the data users need in the most accessible location. East Coast sales data, for example, might be located on a database server in Boston, while West Coast sales data is on a server in San Diego. Special database mechanisms must be in place to keep the data in the copies of the database synchronized.

More simply, databases can simply be replicated; complete copies of the database can be stored in various locations. This provides a redundancy factor because disaster is unlikely to strike all copies at once. Additionally, database replication improves application response time because users can access the database locally rather than through a relatively slow wide area network.

As shown in figure 23.3, the most popular strategies for replication databases are the following:

■ Master server updates, where a single master server receives all updates and, in turn, updates all replicas

■ Locally driven updates, where any local server can receive an update and is responsible for distributing the change to other replicas

Implementing Services in Centralized and Distributed Environments

Just as networks may be organized according to centralized or distributed models, the services offered on networks can be centralized or distributed.

A *centralized* service may be located entirely on a mainframe computer or on a LAN server that uses a server-centric NOS. On networks that employ a peer-to-peer NOS, services may be centralized or may be *distributed* on two or more computers.

 Note A server-centric NOS does not imply a client-server relationship between workstations and the server. When a workstation is configured to function only by requesting services from the network server, network services then are centralized, but do not adhere to a client-server model.

A client-server model implies that the client is an intelligent device that cooperates with the server to manage data.

The remainder of this section discusses issues related to implementing network services.

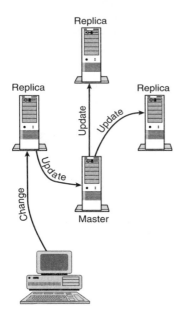
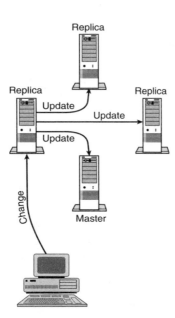

Figure 23.3
Master-driven and locally driven database replication.

Control of Resources

The centralized approach follows the adage "Put all your eggs in one basket and watch that basket very carefully." When hardware and software are concentrated, they can be maintained by experts and closely monitored with management tools. This does not necessarily mean that all devices are physically located in the same area, only that they are grouped for efficient and effective management.

The centralized approach is also logically simpler, and fewer disruptive events are likely to jeopardize data. When resources are distributed through a network, it can be difficult to isolate the causes of problems.

The most important resources that are being controlled on any network are *files* which contain the organization's critical data. In most cases, organizations will choose to store the most critical files on a centralized file server from which all users will access and share the files. This approach is called *server-centric*, *client-server*, or *dedicated server file service*. It is important to understand the advantages and disadvantages of the centralized and distributed approaches.

Centralized File Services

Dedicated file servers have the following benefits:

- Files are in a specific place where they can be reliably archived.

- Central file servers can be managed more efficiently.

- Central file servers can contain expensive, high-performance hardware that expedites file services and makes the file servers more reliable.

- The cost of specialized file server technology is shared by a large number of users.

A few issues, however, should be considered with regard to central file services, as follows:

- When all data is stored on a single server, a single point of failure exists. If the server fails, all data becomes unavailable. This makes proper design and management of the server essential.

- Because all clients are contending for file services from a single source, average file access times might be slower with a centralized file server than when files are stored on individual, local hard drives.

Centralized file services are generally chosen for organizations that want to achieve the highest levels of protection for their data files.

Distributed File Services

In a peer-to-peer environment, any computer can share its files and applications with any other computer. The sharing of services must be established for each individual computer, and each user must have the skills required to manage the networking services on his or her PC. Because services are provided by many different computers, users must become aware of which computers are providing which services. Clearly, the skills and responsibility required of users is higher than for centralized file services.

Some advantages of distributed file storage include the following:

- No single point of failure. When a computer fails, only the files stored on that computer become unavailable.

- Individuals typically experience faster access for files located on local hard drives than for files on centralized file servers.

- No specialized server hardware is required. File services can be provided with standard PCs.

Some issues related to distributed file storage include the following:

- It is more difficult to manage the file service and to protect the integrity of files. File backup is more difficult when files are distributed across many PCs.

- Individual PCs generally do not have high-reliability hardware, including uninterruptible power supplies, disk mirroring, and so forth.

- However, file services provided by peers are typically not as fast as file services provided by a central file server that is specifically designed for the purpose.

- When higher performance is required, rather than upgrading one central file server, each computer must be upgraded.

Organizations tend to choose peer-to-peer networking for two primary reasons. One is a desire to network with their current stock of PCs without the expense of a centralized server. Another is that peer-to-peer is an informal networking approach that fits the working style of many organizations.

Server Specialization

Humans often specialize so that they become very good at one type of task. This approach has benefits for network servers as well. By dedicating each server computer to providing a specific set of services, it becomes possible to carefully tailor the computer to the requirements for that service. This results in optimal performance, simpler troubleshooting, and enhanced scaleability. Server specialization implies that the network is being organized using a centralized approach.

Selecting Network Operating Systems (NOS)

When vendors develop network operating systems, designers will choose whether to use a centralized or a distributed model. Some network operating systems are clearly designed to implement LANs based on centralized models, including the following:

- Novell NetWare

- Banyan VINES

- OpenVMS

- IBM OS/2 LAN Server

- Microsoft Windows NT Server

On the other hand, many products are designed to implement peer-to-peer networking models, including the following:

- Novell Personal NetWare

- Microsoft Windows for Workgroups and Windows NT

- AppleTalk (the networking system for Apple Macintosh computers)

- Artisoft LANtastic

Many peer-to-peer products can be added to networks that are primarily managed by centralized servers. You can, for example, install Personal NetWare on networked PCs, enabling them to interact with each either using a peer-to-peer approach. The PCs, however, retain the capability of accessing the main NetWare servers to utilize centralized services.

Questions

1. Which of the following is a network operating systems?

   ○ A. OS/2

   ○ B. NetWare

   ○ C. Unix

   ○ D. MS-DOS

2. Which TWO of the following are offline file storage media?

   ☐ A. Tape data cartridges

   ☐ B. Removable disks

   ☐ C. Hard disk drives

   ☐ D. Optical jukebox

3. Which of the following is a near-line file storage media?

   ○ A. Optical jukebox

   ○ B. Hard disk drive

   ○ C. Floppy disks

   ○ D. Removable hard drives

4. Which file service is responsible for creating duplicate copies of files to protect against file damage?

   ○ A. File transfer

   ○ B. File-update synchronization

   ○ C. File archiving

   ○ D. Remote file access

5. Which TWO of the following are file services?

   ☐ A. Archiving

   ☐ B. Remote file access

   ☐ C. Update synchronization

   ☐ D. Data integrity

6. What is the most important feature that enables networks to support printing from many users?

   ○ A. Networkable printers

   ○ B. Printer priorities

   ○ C. Queuing

   ○ D. Print servers

7. Which THREE types of information can be processed by a message service?

   ☐ A. Text

   ☐ B. Audio

   ☐ C. Interactive

   ☐ D. Video

8. Which THREE statements are true regarding directory services?

   ☐ A. Directory services enable users to determine physical locations of services.

   ☐ B. Directory services manage resources on multiple servers from a central point.

   ☐ C. Directory services enable users to access network services on multiple servers.

   ☐ D. The directory may be stored on more than one server.

9. Which THREE statements are true regarding application services?

   ☐ A. Clients request services.

   ☐ B. Application services lack scaleability.

   ☐ C. Application servers can be optimized to specialize in a service.

   ☐ D. Multiple services can be offered by the same server PC.

10. Which THREE statements are true regarding database services?

   ☐ A. A database server improves data security.

   ☐ B. All data must be located on the main database server.

   ☐ C. Database performance may be optimized.

   ☐ D. Database services enable multiple clients to share a database.

11. Which THREE are advantages of a centralized approach to providing file services?

   ☐ A. Centralized files may be readily archived.

   ☐ B. It provides the best possible performance.

   ☐ C. Management is efficient.

   ☐ D. The cost of high-performance, high-reliability servers can be spread across many users.

12. Which TWO are advantages of a distributed approach to providing file services?

   ☐ A. There is no central point of failure.

   ☐ B. It is less difficult to manage than a complex, centralized server.

   ☐ C. It is easily scaled to improve performance for all users.

   ☐ D. Specialized equipment is not required.

Answers

1. B

2. A, B

3. A

4. C

5. A, C

6. C

7. A, B, D

8. B, C, D

9. A, C, D

10. A, C, D

11. A, C, D

12. A, D

The OSI Layered Protocol Model

If servers are to provide services to clients, the two parties must be able to communicate. Besides the cables that you see, numerous processes run behind the scenes to keep things running smoothly. These processes are called protocols. As Chapter 22 explains, protocols, along with services and transmission media, make up the three components of a network according to the course model.

After reading this chapter, you will be able to perform the following tasks:

- *Explain the place of rules in the communication process*

- *Describe the seven-layer OSI Reference Model*

- *Discuss how network protocols form protocol stacks*

- *Explain how protocols at given layers interact with peer layers in the protocol stacks of other devices*

Rules and the Communication Process

Networks rely on a great many rules to manage information interchange. Some of the problems that must be solved include the following:

- The procedures used to initiate and end an interaction

- The signals used to represent data on the media

- How to direct a message to the intended destination

- Procedures used to control the rate of data flow

- Methods that enable different computer types to communicate

- How to ensure that messages are received correctly

The process of enabling computers to communicate is an extremely complex one, often too complex to solve all at once with just one set of rules. Instead, the industry has chosen to solve parts of the problem so that the solutions can be put together like pieces of a puzzle. This puzzle comes together a different way each time to build a complete communication approach for any given situation.

The OSI Reference Model

To best understand how the pieces fit together, it is useful to have a model in mind. The most commonly used model is the *Open Systems Interconnection* (OSI) Reference Model, defined by the *International Organization for Standardization* (ISO).

The OSI model organizes communication protocols into seven layers. Each layer addresses a narrow portion of the communication process. The layers of the OSI model are shown in figure 24.1.

Each of these layers are examined in detail, starting with Chapter 27, "OSI Physical Layer Concepts." This chapter, however, introduces only the general characteristics of the model.

Layer 1, the physical layer, consists of protocols that control communication on the network media. Layer 7, the application layer, interfaces the network services with the applications in use on the computer. Between are five other layers that perform intermediate communication tasks.

 You need to know the names and order of the seven layers. Two phrases follow that will help you remember the first letters of the layers:

All **P**eople **S**eem **T**o **N**eed **D**ata **P**rocessing

Please **D**o **N**ot **T**hrow **S**ausage **P**izza **A**way

Choose one, depending on whether you are most comfortable working from the top of the model down or from the bottom up.

 The network media itself is not part of the model, which only deals with protocols. Protocols represent software constructions, whereas cabling is hardware. Networking cannot exist, however, without communication media. Sometimes, you will hear the medium referred to informally as "Layer Zero" of the OSI model.

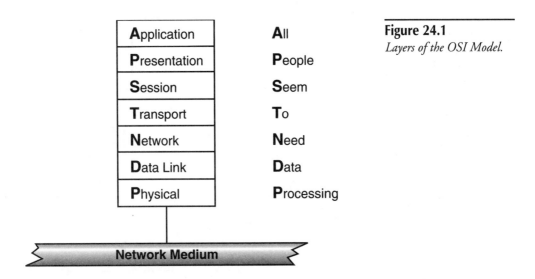

Figure 24.1
Layers of the OSI Model.

Figure 24.1 illustrates the origin of the term "protocol stack." The OSI model breaks the communication process into layers. At each layer, different protocols are selected to solve the needs of a particular communication environment. These protocols are "stacked" one on top of the other until the communication capability is complete. A protocol stack, then, is a set of compatible, layered protocols that have been implemented on a particular computer. Two common examples of protocol stacks are IPX/SPX, the standard NetWare protocols, and TCP/IP, the most widely implemented protocol stack in the computer industry.

A *protocol stack* is a hierarchical set of protocols that coordinate to perform a complete communication process. Each layer makes use of the services provided by the layer below it; and each layer provides services to the layer above it. Formally, layer *N* services layer *N*+1, and layer *N* is serviced by layer *N*-1.

Two computers must be running the same protocol stacks if they are to communicate; each layer in one computer's protocol stack must interact with a corresponding layer in the other computer's protocol stack (see fig. 24.2). The figure originates the path of a message starting in the transport layer. The message travels down the protocol stack, through the network medium, and up the protocol stack of the receiving computer. If the transport layer in the receiving computer understands the protocols used in the transport layer that originated the message, the message can be delivered.

Provided the protocol stacks on two computers are compatible, it is possible for different computer types to communicate. TCP/IP, for example, is available for almost any computer and operation system currently being made. If a Macintosh and a Unix workstation are both running TCP/IP, it is possible for the Mac to access files on the Unix workstation.

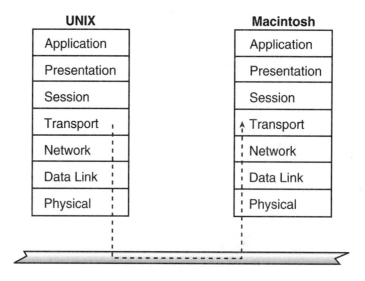

Figure 24.2

Peer communication between protocol stacks.

How Peer Layers Communicate

To communicate with its peer layer in another computer, each protocol layer adds its personal information to the message being sent. This information takes the form of a header added to the beginning of the message (see fig. 24.3).

Headers are added as the message is prepared for transmission, and headers are removed (*stripped*) by the receiver after the information in the header has been utilized.

Notice that the data for each layer consists of the header and data of the next higher layer. Because the data format is different at each layer, different

Figure 24.3

Adding headers to messages.

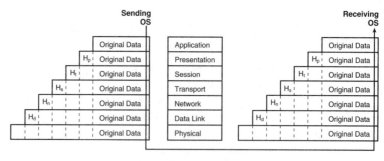

terms are commonly used to name the data package at each level. Table 24.1 summarizes these terms by layer.

> **Note** The physical layer does not append a header because it is concerned with sending and receiving information on the individual bit level. The bits are assembled into longer message units in the data link layer.

Table 24.1
Data Package Names and the OSI Reference Model

Layer	Data Package Names
Application	Message (and packet)
Presentation	Packet
Session	Packet
Transport	Datagram, segment (and packet)
Network	Datagram (and packet)
Data Link	Frame (and packet)
Physical	Bit (and packet)

As you can see in the table, *packet* is a generic term applicable to all layers. It is the term, therefore, to be used for non-layer-specific discussion in later chapters.

Questions

1. The layers of the OSI model (in order) are included in which of the following choices?

   ○ A. Physical, data link, network, transport, system, presentation, application

   ○ B. Physical, data link, network, transport, session, presentation, application

   ○ C. Physical, data link, network, transform, session, presentation, application

   ○ D. Presentation, data link, network, transport, session, physical, application

2. In the OSI model, what is the relationship of a layer (*N*) to the layer above it (layer *N*+1)?

   ○ A. Layer *N* provides services for layer *N*+1.

   ○ B. Layer *N*+1 adds a header to information received from layer *N*.

   ○ C. Layer *N* utilizes services provided by layer *N*+1.

   ○ D. Layer *N* has no effect on layer *N*+1.

3. Which THREE of the following statements regarding protocol stacks are true?

   ☐ A. A given protocol stack can run on only one computer type.

   ☐ B. Layers add headers to packets received from higher layers in the protocol stack.

   ☐ C. A protocol stack is a hierarchical set of protocols.

   ☐ D. Each layer provides services for the next highest layer.

4. Which TWO of the following terms are used to describe data units at the network layer?

   ☐ A. Datagram

   ☐ B. Message

   ☐ C. Frame

   ☐ D. Packet

5. Which TWO of the following terms are used to describe data units at the data link layer?

   ☐ A. Datagram

   ☐ B. Message

   ☐ C. Frame

   ☐ D. Packet

Answers

1. D

2. A

3. B, C, D

4. A, D

5. C, D

Transmission Media

*N*etwork clients must have a channel through which they can communicate with network servers. The channel that carries messages between clients and servers is called the transmission media.

The media for local area networks usually consist of one of the following:

- *Cable (coaxial, twisted-pair, or fiber-optic)*

- *Wireless (radio, infrared, microwave)*

With wide area networks, you don't deal with media so much as you deal with services. You buy wide area network services from a commercial provider or connect to an existing network such as the Internet. In its course through a wide area network, a packet may pass through many types of media, but you as a network administrator need not be concerned with the media being employed. Two networks that provide wide area network support are examined in this chapter:

■ The public telephone network

■ The Internet

In this chapter, you will learn about the following:

■ What transmission media are

■ Common transmission media and their characteristics

■ Public network services that provide wide-area networking support

Network Transmission Media

Transmission media make it possible for the electronic signals in one computer to be transmitted to another computer. These electronic signals express data values in the form of binary (on-off) impulses. The signals are transmitted through the network using a combination of electronic devices (network boards, hubs, and so on) and transmission media (cables, radio, and so on) until they reach the desired destination computer where they again are converted into data signals inside the receiving computer.

All signals transmitted between computers consist of some form of *electromagnetic* (EM) waveform, ranging from radio frequencies, up through microwave, and infrared light. Depending on the frequency of the EM waveform being used, different media are used to transmit the signals. Figure 25.1 illustrates the range of electromagnetic waveforms, known as the *electromagnetic spectrum*, along with their associated frequencies.

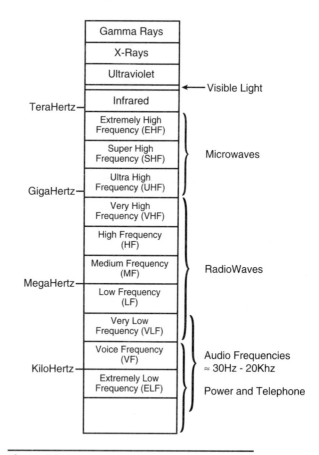

Figure 25.1

The electromagnetic spectrum.

Radio frequency waves are often used for LAN signaling. Radio frequencies can be transmitted using electrical cables (twisted-pair or coaxial) or using radio broadcast transmission.

Microwave transmissions can be used for tightly focused transmissions between two points. Microwaves are used to communicate between Earth stations and satellites. They also are used for line-of-sight transmissions on the Earth's surface. Microwaves also can be used in low-power forms to broadcast signals from a transmitter to many receivers. Cellular phone networks are examples of systems that use low-power microwave signals to broadcast signals.

Infrared light is ideal for many types of network communications. Infrared light can be transmitted relatively short distances and can either be beamed between two points or broadcast from one point to many receivers. Infrared and higher frequencies of light also can be transmitted through fiber-optic cables.

The next sections examine examples of network transmission media, and describe the advantages and disadvantages of each media type.

Characteristics of Transmission Media

Each media type has special characteristics that suit it to a specific type of service. You should be familiar with these characteristics:

■ Cost

■ Installation requirements

■ Bandwidth

■ Attenuation

■ Immunity from electromagnetic interference

The last three characteristics require some explanation.

Bandwidth

Bandwidth is the measure of the capacity of a medium to transmit data. A medium that has a high capacity has a high bandwidth. A medium that has limited capacity has a low bandwidth. The term bandwidth comes about because it is a measure of the range of frequencies that the medium can carry.

Bandwidth can be understood through an analogy to water hoses. A half-inch garden hose that can carry waterflow from a trickle up to 2 gallons per minute might be said to have a bandwidth of 2 gallons per minute. A 4-inch firehose, however, might have a bandwidth of over 100 gallons per minute.

Transmission media have a lower frequency limit and an upper frequency limit. Frequencies are measured in *Hertz* (Hz), or cycles per second. The bandwidth of a voice telephone line is 400–4,000 Hz, meaning that the line can transmit signals with frequencies ranging from 400–4,000 cycles per second.

Data transmission rates frequently are stated in terms of the bits that can be transmitted per second. An Ethernet LAN theoretically can transmit 10 million bits per second and has a bandwidth of 10 megabits per second (Mbps).

The bandwidth that a cable can accommodate is determined in part by the cable's length. A short cable can generally accommodate greater bandwidth than a longer cable. This is one reason all cable designs specify maximum lengths for cable runs. Beyond those limits, the highest frequency signals can deteriorate and errors might be introduced into data signals.

Attenuation

Attenuation is a measure of how much a signal weakens as it travels through a medium. This course does not discuss attenuation in formal terms, but with regard to the impact of attenuation on performance.

Attenuation is a second reason cable designs must specify limits in the lengths of cable runs. When signal strength falls below certain limits, it might be difficult for the electronic equipment that receives the signal to isolate the original signal from the noise that is present in all electronic transmissions. The effect is exactly like trying to tune in distant radio signals. Even if you are able to lock into the signal on your radio, the sound produced generally contains more noise than the sound produced for a local radio station.

Electromagnetic Interference

Electromagnetic interference (EMI) consists of outside electromagnetic noise that distorts the signal in a medium. When you listen to an AM radio, you often hear noise caused by nearby motors or lightning. This is an example of EMI. Some network media are more susceptible to EMI than others.

Cable Media

Three types of cable media are discussed in this section:

- Coaxial
- Twisted-pair
- Fiber-optic

Coaxial Cable

Coaxial cables were the first cable types used in LANs. Shown in figure 25.2, coaxial cable gets its name because two conductors share a common axis; the cable is most frequently referred to as *coax*. The components of a coaxial cable are as follows:

- A center conductor, which is usually solid copper wire (although stranded wire can be used)

- An outer conductor that forms a tube surrounding the center conductor. This conductor can consist of braided wires, metallic foil, or both. Because this conductor also protects the inner conductor from EMI, it is most frequently called the *shield*.

- An insulation layer that also keeps the outer conductor spaced evenly from the inner conductor

- A plastic encasement (jacket) that protects the cable from damage

Types of Coaxial Cable

All coax cables have a characteristic measurement called *impedance*, which is given in ohms. It is important to use a cable with the proper impedance in any given situation. Here are some types of coaxial cable frequently used on LANs:

- RG-8 and RG-ll, 50-ohm cables used with thick Ethernet

- RG-58, a 50-ohm cable used with thin Ethernet

- RG-59, a 75-ohm cable used for cable TV

- RG-62, a 93-ohm cable used with ARCnet

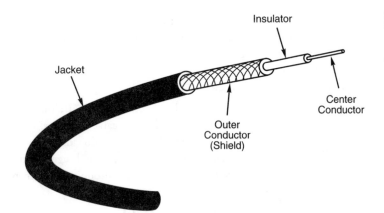

Figure 25.2
The structure of coaxial cable.

Characteristics

You will want to be familiar with the following characteristics of coaxial cable.

Installation

Coaxial cable typically is installed in two configurations: daisy-chained from device to device (Ethernet) and stars (ARCnet). Both are shown in figure 25.3.

You will learn the details of Ethernet cabling in Chapter 26, "Transmission Media Connections."

The Ethernet cabling shown in the figure is an example of thin Ethernet, which uses RG-58 type cable. Devices connect to the cable by means of T-connectors. Cables are used to provide connections between T-connectors. One characteristic of this type of cabling is that the ends of the cable run

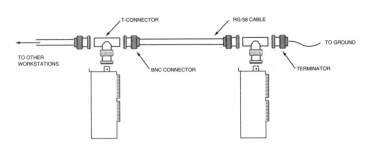

Figure 25.3
Coaxial cable wiring configurations.

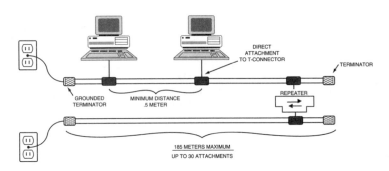

must be terminated by a special connector called a terminator. The *terminator* contains a resistor that is matched to the characteristics of the cable. The resistor prevents signals that reach the end of the cable from bouncing back and causing interference.

Coaxial cable is reasonably easy to install. The cable is robust and difficult to damage, and connectors can be installed with inexpensive tools and a bit of practice. The device-to-device cabling approach can be difficult to reconfigure, however, when new devices cannot be installed near an existing cabling path.

Cost

The coaxial cable used for thin Ethernet falls at the low end of the cost spectrum, whereas thick Ethernet is among the more costly options. Detailed cost comparisons are made after the remaining cable types have been introduced.

Bandwidth

LANs that employ coaxial cable typically have a bandwidth ranging from 2.5 Mbps (ARCnet) to 10 Mbps (Ethernet). Thicker coaxial cables have higher bandwidth, and the potential bandwidth of coax is much higher than 10 Mbps. This potential, however, is not taken advantage of by current LAN technologies.

Attenuation

All media suffer from attenuation, but coax has better attenuation characteristics than other copper cables such as twisted-pair. LANs employing co-axial cable are limited to a few thousand meters in length.

EMI Characteristics

All copper media are sensitive to EMI, although the shield in coax makes the cable fairly resistant to EMI. Coaxial cables, however, do radiate a portion of their signal, and this radiated signal can be detected by electronic eavesdropping equipment.

Twisted-Pair Cables

Twisted-pair cable has become the dominant cable type for all new network designs that employ copper cable. Several reasons account for the popularity of twisted-pair cable, with the most significant being low cost. Twisted-pair cable is inexpensive to install and has the lowest cost-per-foot of any cable type.

Figure 25.4 shows a basic twisted-pair cable, which consists of two strands of copper wire twisted together. The twists are an important part of the characteristics of twisted-pair cable. Twisting reduces the sensitivity of the cable to EMI and also reduces the tendency of the cable to radiate radio frequency noise that interferes with nearby cables and electronic components. The radiated signals from the twisted wires tend to cancel each other out. (Antennas, which are purposely designed to radiate radio-frequency signals, consist of parallel, not twisted, wires.)

Figure 25.4
A twisted-pair cable.

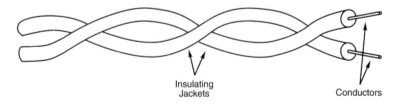

Insulating
Jackets

Conductors

Twisting also controls the tendency of the wires in the pair to cause EMI in each other. Whenever two wires are in close proximity, there is a tendency for the signals in each wire to produce noise in the other. Noise caused in this way is called *crosstalk*. Twisting the wires in the pair reduces crosstalk in much the same way that twisting reduces the tendency of the wires to radiate EMI.

Two types of twisted-pair cable are used in LANs: shielded and unshielded.

Shielded Twisted-Pair (STP) Cable

The first twisted-pair cables used in LANs were shielded twisted-pair, similar to the cable shown in figure 25.5, which shows IBM Type 1 cable, the first cable type used with IBM Token Ring. Early LAN designers employed shielded twisted-pair cable because the shield further reduces the tendency of the cable to radiate EMI and reduces the cable's sensitivity to outside interference.

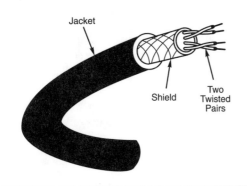

Figure 25.5
A shielded twisted-pair cable.

Coaxial and STP cables use shields for the same purpose. The *shield* is connected to the ground portion of the electronic device to which the cable is connected. A *ground* is a portion of the device, serves

as an electrical reference point, and usually is literally connected to a metal stake that is driven into the ground. A properly grounded shield tends to prevent signals from getting into or out of the cable.

The IBM Type 1 cable shown in figure 25.5 includes two twisted-pairs of wire within a single shield. Various types of STP cable exist, with some shielding each pair individually and others shielding several pairs. The exact configuration used is chosen by the engineers who design the cabling system. IBM designates several twisted-pair cable types for use with their Token-Ring network design, and each cable type is appropriate for a given kind of installation. A completely different type of STP is the standard cable for Apple's AppleTalk network.

Because so many different types of STP cable exist, it is difficult to state precise characteristics. Here, however, are some general guidelines.

Cost

STP cable costs more than thin coaxial or unshielded twisted-pair cables. STP is less costly, however, than thick coax or fiber-optic cable.

Installation

Different network types have different installation requirements. One major difference is the connector used. Apple LocalTalk connectors generally must be soldered during installation, requiring some practice and skill on the part of the installer. IBM Token Ring uses a so-called *unisex* data connector (the connectors are both male and female), which can be installed with common tools such as a knife, wire stripper, and a large pliers.

In many cases, installation can be greatly simplified by using pre-wired cables. You need to learn to install the required connectors, however, whenever your installation requires use of bulk cable.

Most connectors require two connector types to complete a connection. The traditional designation for connector types is male and female. The male connector is the connector with pins, and the female connector has receptacles into which the pins insert. In a standard AC wall outlet, the outlet itself is female and the plug on the line cord is male.

These designations originated when electrical installation was a male province, and the terms male and female gradually are being replaced. A commonly used alternative is "pins and sockets."

The IBM data connector is called a unisex connector because the connector has both pins and sockets. Any IBM data connector can connect to any other IBM data connector.

STP cable tends to be rather bulky. IBM Type 1 cable is approximately $1^{1}/_{2}$ inches in diameter. Therefore, it can take little time to fill up cable paths with STP cables.

Capacity

STP cable has a theoretical capacity of 500 Mbps, although few implementations exceed 155 Mbps with 100-meter cable runs. The most common data rate for STP cable is 16 Mbps, the top data rate for token-ring networks.

Attenuation

All varieties of twisted-pair cable have attenuation characteristics that limit the length of cable runs to a few hundred meters, although a 100-meter limit is most common.

EMI Characteristics

The shield in STP cable results in good EMI characteristics for copper cable, comparable to the EMI characteristics of coaxial cable. This is one reason STP might be preferred to unshielded

twisted-pair cable in some situations. Like all copper cables, STP is sensitive to interference and is vulnerable to electronic eavesdropping.

Unshielded Twisted-Pair Cable

Unshielded twisted-pair (UTP) cable does not incorporate a braided shield. The characteristics of UTP are similar in many ways to STP, differing primarily in attenuation and EMI characteristics. As shown in figure 25.6, several twisted pairs can be bundled together in a single cable. These pairs are typically color coded to distinguish the pairs.

Figure 25.6
A multi-pair UTP cable.

UTP cable is a latecomer to high-performance LANs because engineers only recently solved the problems of managing radiated noise and susceptibility to EMI. Now, however, a clear trend toward UTP is in operation, and all new copper-based cabling schemes are based on use of UTP.

UTP cable is available in the following five grades or categories:

■ Categories 1 and 2 are voice-grade cables, suitable only for voice and for low data rates (below 4 Mbps). At one time, Category 1 was the standard voice-grade cable for telephone systems. The growing need for data-ready cabling systems, however, has caused Category 1 and 2 cable to be supplanted by Category 3 for new installations.

- Category 3 is the lowest data grade cable and is generally suited for data rates up to 16 Mbps. Some innovative schemes, however, make it possible to support data rates up to 100 Mbps with Category 3 cable. Category 3 is now the standard cable used for most telephone installations.

- Category 4 is a data-grade cable suitable for data rates up to 20 Mbps.

- Category 5 is a data-grade cable suitable for data rates up to 100 Mbps. Most new cabling systems for 100 Mbps data rates are designed around Category 5 cable.

 Note In a UTP cabling system, the cable is only one component. All connecting devices also are graded, and the overall cabling system only supports the data rates permitted by the lowest grade of component in the system. In other words, if you require a Category 5 cabling system, it is essential to ensure that all connectors and connecting devices are designed for Category 5 operation.

Category 5 cable also requires more stringent installation procedures than the lower cable categories. Installers of Category 5 cable require special training and skills to understand these more rigorous requirements.

UTP cable offers an excellent balance of cost and performance characteristics.

Cost

UTP cable has the lowest cost of any cable type, although properly installed Category 5 tends to be fairly high in cost. In some cases, existing cable in buildings can be used for LANs, although it is important to verify the category of the cable and

also to know the length of the cable in the walls. Distance limits for voice cabling are much less stringent than for data-grade cabling.

Installation

UTP cable is easy to install. Some specialized equipment might be required, but the equipment is low in cost and can be mastered with a bit of practice. Properly designed UTP cabling systems easily can be reconfigured to meet changing requirements.

As noted earlier, however, Category 5 cable has stricter installation requirements than lower categories of UTP. Special training is recommended.

Capacity

The data rates possible with UTP have pushed upward from 1 Mbps, past 4 and 16 Mbps, and to the point where 100 Mbps data rates are now common. In fact, all new copper-based standards provide at least the option of using UTP cable.

Attenuation

UTP cable shares similar attenuation characteristics with other copper cables. UTP cable runs are limited to a few hundred meters, with 100 meters the most frequent limit.

EMI Characteristics

Lacking a shield, UTP cable is more sensitive to EMI than coaxial or STP cables. The latest technologies make it possible to use UTP in the vast majority of situations, provided reasonable care is taken to avoid electrically noisy devices such as motors and fluorescent lights. Nevertheless, UTP might not be suitable for noisy environments such as factories. Crosstalk between nearby unshielded pairs limits the maximum length of cable runs.

Fiber-Optic Cable

In almost every way, fiber-optic cable is the ideal cable for data transmission. Bandwidths are extremely high, there are no problems with EMI, cables are durable, and cable runs can be several kilometers long. The two disadvantages of fiber optic are cost and more difficult installation.

Figure 25.7 shows two types of fiber-optic cable. In each case, the center conductor is a fiber consisting of highly refined glass or plastic designed to transmit light signals with little loss. The fiber is coated with a cladding that reflects signals back into the fiber to reduce signal loss. A plastic sheath protects the fiber.

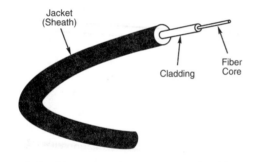

Figure 25.7
A fiber-optic cable.

Loose and tight cable configurations are available. Loose configurations incorporate a space between the fiber sheath and the outer plastic encasement; this space is filled with a gel or other material. Tight configurations include strength wires between the conductor and the outer plastic encasement. In both cases, it is the job of the plastic encasement to supply the strength of the cable. The gel layer or strength wires protect the delicate fiber from mechanical damage.

Although the figure shows cables with single fibers, it is common to bundle multiple fibers into cables. A small-diameter cable can incorporate an astonishing number of optical fibers, making fiber-optic cable ideal for cabling when cable paths are clogged.

Optical fiber cables do not transmit electrical signals. Instead, the data signals must be converted to light signals. Light sources include lasers and *light-emitting diodes* (LEDs). LEDs are inexpensive, but produce a fairly poor quality of light that is suitable for less-stringent applications.

A laser is a light source that produces an especially pure light that is monochromatic (one color) and coherent (all waves are parallel). The most commonly used source of laser light in LAN devices is called an *injection laser diode* (ILD). The purity of laser light makes lasers ideally suited to data transmissions because long distances and high bandwidths are possible. Lasers, however, are expensive light sources and are used only when their special characteristics are required.

The end of the cable that receives the light signal must convert the signal back to an electrical form. Several types of solid-state components can perform this service. The most common are types of photodiodes.

Optical fibers have several characteristics:

- **Mode.** Single-mode cables support a single light path and are commonly used with lasers. Multi-mode cables support multiple light paths and are best suited to lower-quality light sources such as LEDs. At a much higher cost, single-mode cables with laser light sources support the longest cable runs and the greatest bandwidth. Figure 25.8 illustrates the difference between single- and multi-mode cables.

■ **Core diameter.** The cores of fiber-optic cables are small enough to be measured in microns (millionths of a meter). The symbol for micron is μ.

■ **Cladding diameter**. This dimension also is given in microns.

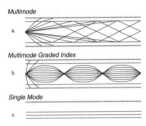

Figure 25.8
Modes of fiber-optic cables.

The following are common types of fiber-optic cables:

■ 8.3 micron core/125 micron cladding/single-mode

■ 62.5 micron core/125 micron cladding/multimode

■ 50 micron core/125 micron cladding/ multimode

■ 100 micron core/140 micron cladding/ multimode

Note the small core diameters of these cables. One of the significant difficulties of installing fiber-optic cable arises when two cables must be joined. The small cores of the two cables must be lined up with extreme precision to prevent excessive signal loss.

Fiber-Optic Characteristics

Like all cable types, fiber-optic cables constitute a blend of advantages and disadvantages.

Cost

The cost of the cable and connectors has fallen significantly in recent years. The electronic devices required are significantly more expensive than comparable devices for copper cable. An Ethernet network board for UTP cable now can cost less than $100. Network boards for use with fiber-optic cables, however, frequently cost in excess of $1,000 each. Fiber-optic cable is also the most expensive cable type to install.

Installation

Greater skill is required to install fiber-optic cable than is needed for most copper cables. Improved tools and techniques, however, have reduced the training required. Still, greater care is required because fiber-optic cables must be treated fairly gently during installation. Every cable has a minimum bend radius, for example, and fibers are damaged if the cables are bent too sharply. It also is important not to stretch the cable during installation.

Capacity

Bandwidths for fiber-optic cables can range as high as 2 Gbps (billion bps). Fiber-optic cable can support high data rates even with long cable runs. UTP cable runs are limited to less than 100 meters with 100 Mbps data rates. Fiber-optic cables can transmit 100 Mbps signals for several kilometers.

Attenuation

Attenuation in fiber-optic cables is much lower than in copper cables. Fiber-optic cables are capable of carrying signals for several kilometers.

EMI Characteristics

Because fiber-optic cables do not use electrical signals to transmit data, they are totally immune to electromagnetic interference. They also are immune to a variety of electrical effects that must be taken into account when designing copper cabling systems.

When electrical cables are connected between two buildings, a common problem to be dealt with is differences between the ground potentials (voltages) between the two buildings. When a difference exists (as it frequently does), current flows through the grounding conductor of the cable, even though the ground is supposed to be electrically neutral and no current should flow. When current flows through the ground conductor of a cable, the condition is called a *ground loop*. The results of ground loops are electrical instability and various types of anomalies.

Because fiber-optic cable is immune to electrical effects, the best way to connect networks in different buildings is by putting in a fiber-optic link segment.

Because they are not electrical in nature, the signals in fiber-optic cables cannot be detected by electronic eavesdropping equipment that detect electromagnetic radiation. Fiber-optic cable is, therefore, the perfect choice for high-security networks.

Summary of Cable Characteristics

Table 25.1 summarizes the characteristics of the four cable types discussed in this chapter.

Table 25.1
Comparison of Cable Media

Cable Type	Cost	Installation	Capacity	Attenuation	EMI
Coaxial	Medium < Cat 5 UTP > Cat 3 UTP Thin<STP Thick>STP <Fiber	Inexpensive/ Easy. May be difficult to reconfigure	10 Mbps typical	Less than STP or UTP. Limited to range of few kilometers	Less sensitive than UTP, but still subject to EMI and eavesdropping
Shielded Twisted-Pair	Medium >UTP =Thin coax <Thick coax <Fiber	Moderate cost/ Fairly easy. More difficult than UTP and coax	16 Mbps typical. Up to 500 Mbps	Limits range to several hundred meters	Less sensitive than UTP, but still subject to EMI and eavesdropping
Unshielded Twisted-Pair	Lowest	Inexpensive/ Easy	1-100 Mbps with 100-meter runs	Limits range to several hundred meters	Most sensitive to EMI and eavesdropping
Fiber-Optic	Highest	Expensive/ Difficult	10 Mbps to 2 Gbps. 100 Mbps typical	Lowest. Range of 10s of kilometers	Insensitive to EMI and eavesdropping

When comparing cabling types, it's important to remember that the characteristics you observe are highly dependent on the implementations. At one time, it was argued that UTP cable would never reliably support data rates above 4 Mbps, but 100 Mbps data rates are now commonplace with UTP.

Some comparisons are fairly involved. Although fiber-optic cable is costly on a per-foot basis, it is possible to construct a fiber-optic cable that is many kilometers in length. To build a copper cable that length, you would need to install repeaters at several points along the cable to amplify the signal. These repeaters could easily exceed the cost of a fiber-optic cable run.

Wireless Media

Cable lends itself to fixed installations and moderate distances. When end points are widely separated or when they are moving, it might be desirable to investigate wireless media. Several wireless media are available, of which the following will be considered:

- Radio
- Microwave
- Infrared

Radio

The radio portion of the electromagnetic spectrum extends from 10 KHz to 1 GHz. Within this range are numerous bands, or ranges of frequencies that are designated for specific purposes. The following are frequency bands with which you are probably familiar:

- Shortwave
- VHF (Very High Frequency): television and FM radio

- UHF (Ultra High Frequency): television

Within the United States, the use of radio frequencies is controlled by the Federal Communications Commission (FCC). The majority of frequency allocations are licensed; an organization is granted an exclusive license to use a particular range of frequencies within a certain limited geographic area. Thus, there only can be one television Channel 5 within an area. Channel 5 allocations are spread out so that they do not interfere with each other. A licensed frequency allocation guarantees the license owner a clear, low-interference communication channel.

A few frequency ranges are unlicensed, meaning that they can be used freely for the purpose specified for those frequencies. The FCC has designated three unlicensed frequency bands: 902–928 MHz, 2.4 GHz, and 5.72–5.85 GHz. The 902 MHz range has been available the longest and has been used for everything from cordless telephones to model airplane remote control. Because the 902 MHz range is quite crowded, many vendors are pushing development of devices for the less crowded 2.4 GHz band. Equipment for the 5.72 GHz remains expensive and is used infrequently.

Use of an unlicensed frequency is done at the user's risk, and a clear communication channel is not guaranteed. Equipment used in these frequency bands, however, must operate at a regulated power level to limit range and reduce the potential for interference.

Radio transmissions can be omnidirectional or directional. A radio station typically transmits an omnidirectional (all-directional) signal that can be received by all radios within the broadcast area. In some circumstances, a directional transmission might be used to direct all of the transmission power toward a specific reception point.

Various types of antennas are used depending on the desired transmission and reception characteristics. Several antenna types are shown in figure 25.9.

- Broadcast towers generally are omnidirectional, although the specific radiation pattern can be adjusted to match the FCC restrictions for a particular licensee.

- Dipole antennas receive a fairly broad range of frequencies and are moderately directional.

- A random-length wire can be used for transmission or reception. Random-length means that the antenna length is not specifically chosen for the frequency being transmitted or received. The antenna on a typical AM/FM radio is a random-length wire.

- A beam antenna uses multiple elements to tune the antenna for a specific frequency range and directiveness. A common antenna design is called the Yagi. A beam antenna is used to produce a fairly focused beam that can be aimed at a specific reception point (although the effect is not completely directional, and some signal leaks in all directions).

Characteristics of Radio Transmission

The characteristics of radio transmissions change dramatically with frequency. Low-frequency radio supports limited data rates, but has a significant advantage in that it can frequently communicate past the horizon. Shortwave operators are familiar with this phenomenon, and it is common for them to be able to monitor transmissions from the other side of the Earth.

As frequency increases, transmissions become increasingly line-of-sight. AM radio broadcast frequencies range from the KHz to the low MHz range. You might have had the experience of picking up an AM radio station that is several states away, particularly late at night. This can occur because AM radio transmissions can bounce off some phenomena in the atmosphere. Some transmissions can bounce a considerable distance.

FM transmissions, however, seldom can be received past the horizon. You will seldom clearly receive an FM broadcast beyond a range of 100 miles. This is partly a function of power, but the primary cause of the range limitation is the inability of FM frequencies to go beyond the horizon.

Figure 25.9

Representative antenna types.

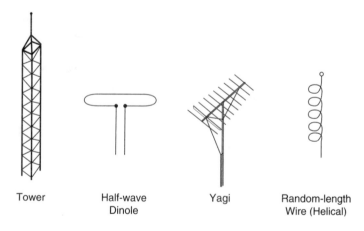

Tower   Half-wave Dinole   Yagi   Random-length Wire (Helical)

On a line-of-sight basis, however, high-frequency transmissions attenuate less rapidly than low-frequency transmissions.

Lower-frequency radio waves can penetrate solid materials to a greater degree than higher frequencies. Very low radio frequencies can be used to communicate with submerged submarines, although the data rates are extremely slow. Penetration capability is also a function of power. Higher-power transmissions penetrate building walls more effectively than lower-power transmissions.

As you can see, designing a radio system to have the ideal characteristics for an application requires a lot of design tradeoffs.

Three classes of radio frequency transmission are discussed in this chapter:

■ Low-power, single frequency

■ High-power, single frequency

■ Spread spectrum

Low-Power, Single-Frequency Radio

Low-power systems are chosen to limit the interference between nearby radio systems. Transmission ranges might be as short as 20 to 30 meters. This approach resembles cellular telephone technology, which divides geographic areas into isolated, low-power cells, enabling frequencies to be reused in nearby cells.

Although low-frequency radio can penetrate building walls, the low power used with this radio class typically requires transmitters and receivers to have a line-of-sight path. The data rates possible with low-frequency radio do not support the data rates required for LANs.

It is theoretically possible to implement mobile stations with this radio class, although walls and low power limit the mobility that is possible.

Frequency Range

Any radio frequency can be used, but higher frequencies, typically in the GHz, generally are chosen to support higher data rates.

Cost

Cost depends on design, but can be low compared to other wireless media. As with most media, higher data rates come at a higher cost.

Ease of Installation

This characteristic is also dependent on design. Some single-frequency systems use licensed frequencies, and a license application must be filed with the FCC. In at least one case, however, a prominent vendor has obtained licenses in many major markets and handles the FCC paperwork for the customer.

Some single-frequency systems use unlicensed frequencies. Some troubleshooting might be needed to prevent interference from other nearby devices that use the same frequencies.

Capacity

Although the theoretical bandwidth of radio LANs is high, currently available products range from 1 to 10 Mbps.

Attenuation

Attenuation is high due to the low power levels used, but proper design turns this into an advantage by creating large numbers of independent areas that do not interfere with each other.

EMI Characteristics

EMI resistance is low, particularly in the 902 MHz band that is shared with other unlicensed devices. All radio LANs are vulnerable to electronic eavesdropping, although the low powers used typically reduce the range at which eavesdropping can occur to the confines of the building in which the LAN is housed.

High-Power Single-Frequency Radio

High-power radio has data capacity similar to low-power radio, but it can cover much larger areas. Transmissions can be line-of-sight or can be extended by bouncing signals off the atmosphere. Because power can be higher, this approach can result in practical mobile networking and can service stations on motor or marine vehicles.

Frequency Range

As with low-power radio, any part of the radio spectrum can be used. Frequencies in the GHz range are generally chosen to achieve high data rates.

Cost

High-power transmission equipment is considerably more expensive. Signal repeaters might be needed to extend the coverage area. Costs for high-power radio can be moderate to high.

Ease of Installation

High-power radio equipment must be operated under an FCC license by licensed personnel. Equipment must be maintained in proper order to remain within the terms of the license. Improperly installed and maintained equipment might function poorly and interfere with nearby radio services.

Bandwidth

Capacity can be high but typically falls between 1 and 10 Mbps.

Attenuation

Attenuation rates for high-power radio are fairly low. Signal repeaters can be employed to extend transmission range.

EMI Characteristics

Immunity to EMI is low, and the potential for eavesdropping is high. Signals might be easily intercepted anywhere within the broadcast area.

Spread Spectrum Radio

Spread spectrum is a technique originally developed by the military to solve several communication problems. Spread spectrum improves reliability, reduces sensitivity to interference and jamming, and is less vulnerable to eavesdropping than single-frequency radio.

Spread spectrum transmission uses multiple frequencies to transmit messages. Two techniques employed are direct sequence modulation and frequency hopping.

Direct sequence modulation breaks original messages into parts called *chips* (see fig. 25.10), which are transmitted on separate frequencies. To confuse eavesdroppers, decoy data also can be transmitted on other frequencies. The intended receiver knows which frequencies are valid, and can isolate the chips and reassemble the message. Eavesdropping is difficult because the correct frequencies are not known, and the eavesdropper cannot isolate the frequencies carrying true data. This technique can operate in environments with other transmission activity since different sets of frequencies can be selected. Direct sequence modulation systems operating at 900 MHz support bandwidths of 2–6 Mbps.

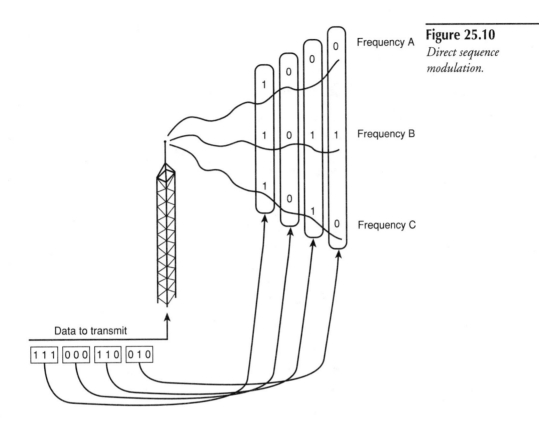

Figure 25.10
Direct sequence modulation.

Frequency hopping switches transmissions among several available frequencies. (See fig. 25.11.) Transmitter and receiver must remain synchronized for this technique to work. Some systems transmit on multiple frequencies simultaneously to increase bandwidth.

Frequency Range

Spread spectrum systems typically operate in unlicensed frequency ranges. 900 MHz devices are common, but 2.4 GHz devices are becoming available.

Costs

Costs are moderate compared to other wireless media.

Ease of Installation

This depends on the system design and the frequencies used. Installation complexity ranges from simple to somewhat complex.

Capacity

All 900 MHz systems support bandwidth capacities of 2–6 MHz. Newer systems operating in GHz frequencies can be expected to offer higher data rates.

Attenuation

This is determined by the frequency and power of the transmitted signals. Spread spectrum LANs typically operate at low power and exhibit high attenuation characteristics.

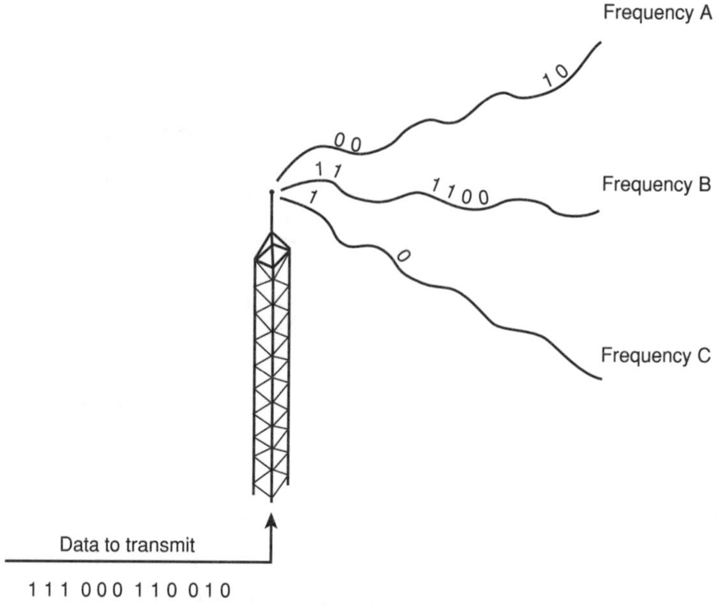

Figure 25.11
Frequency hopping.

Frequency A

Frequency B

Frequency C

Data to transmit

111 000 110 010

EMI Characteristics

Although individual frequencies are susceptible to EMI, the system can seek out clear frequencies on which to transmit. Overall resistance to EMI is, therefore, fairly high. Resistance to eavesdropping is high for the reasons cited earlier.

Microwave

As shown in figure 25.12, microwave communication can take two forms: terrestrial (ground links) and satellite links. The frequencies and technologies employed by these two forms are similar, but distinct differences exist between them.

Terrestrial Microwave

Terrestrial microwave communication employs Earth-based transmitters and receivers. The frequencies used are in the low-gigahertz range, limiting all communications to line-of-sight. You have

probably seen terrestrial microwave equipment in the form of telephone relay towers, which are placed every few miles to relay telephone signals cross country.

Microwave transmissions are typically made using a parabolic antenna that produces a narrow, highly directional signal. A similar antenna at the receiving site is sensitive to signals only within a narrow focus. Since both the transmitter and receiver are highly focused, they must be carefully adjusted so that the transmitted signal is aligned with the receiver.

Microwave is frequently used as a means of transmitting signals where it would be impractical to run cables. If you need to connect two networks that are separated by a public road, you might find that you are not permitted to run cables above or below the road. In such a case, a microwave link is an ideal solution.

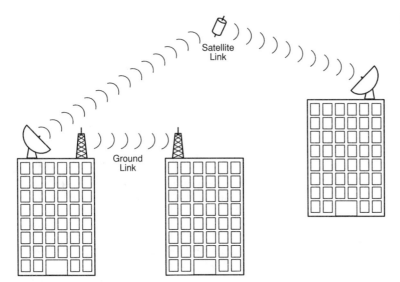

Figure 25.12
Terrestrial and satellite microwave links.

Some LANs operate at microwave frequencies, operate at low power, and use non-directional transmitters and receivers. Network hubs can be placed strategically throughout an organization, and workstations can be mobile or fixed. This approach is one way of enabling workstations to be mobile in an office setting.

In many cases, terrestrial microwave uses licensed frequencies. A license must be obtained from the FCC, and equipment must be installed and maintained by licensed technicians.

Frequency Range

Terrestrial microwave systems operate in the low-gigahertz range, typically at 4–6 GHz and 21–23 GHz.

Cost

Costs are highly variable depending on requirements.

Long-distance microwave systems can be quite expensive, but might be less costly than alternatives. A leased telephone circuit represents a costly monthly expense. When line-of-sight transmission is possible, a microwave link is a one-time expense that can offer greater bandwidth than a leased circuit.

Costs are decreasing for low-power microwave systems for the office. Although these systems do not compete directly in cost with cabled networks, when equipment must be frequently moved, microwave can be a cost-effective technology.

Installation

Licensing usually is required. Many equipment providers take care of licensing along with installation. Installation is a skilled operation generally requiring licensed technicians. Setup of transmitter and receiver sites can be difficult because antennas must be precisely aligned.

The requirement for a line-of-sight communication path might require purchase of access to suitable transmitter sites.

Bandwidth

Capacity can be extremely high, but most data communication systems operate at data rates between 1 and 10 Mbps.

Attenuation

Attenuation characteristics are determined by transmitter power, frequency, and antenna size. Properly designed systems are not affected by attenuation under normal operational conditions. Rain and fog, however, can cause attenuation of higher frequencies.

EMI Characteristics

Microwave systems are highly susceptible to atmospheric interference. They also might be vulnerable to electronic eavesdropping, and signals transmitted through microwave are frequently encrypted.

Satellite Microwave

Satellite microwave systems relay transmissions through communication satellites that operate in geosynchronous orbits 22,300 miles above the Earth. Satellites orbiting at this distance remain located above a fixed point on the Earth.

Earth stations use parabolic antennas (satellite dishes) to communicate with the satellites. Satellites can retransmit signals in broad or in narrow beams depending on which locations are to receive the signals. When the destination is on the opposite side of the Earth, the first satellite cannot transmit directly to the receiver and must relay the signal through another satellite.

Because no cables are required, satellite microwave communication is possible with most remote sites and with mobile devices, including ships at sea and motor vehicles.

The distances involved in satellite communication result in an interesting phenomenon: Because all signals must travel 22,300 miles to the satellite and 22,300 miles when returning to a receiver, the time required to transmit a signal is independent of distance. It takes as long to transmit a signal to a receiver in the same state as it does to a receiver a third of the way around the world. The time required for a signal to arrive at its destination is called *propagation delay*. The delays encountered with satellite transmissions range from 0.5 to 5 seconds.

Unfortunately, satellite communication is extremely expensive. Building and launching a satellite easily can cost in excess of a billion dollars. In most cases, organizations share these costs, or they purchase services from a commercial provider. AT&T, Hughes Network Services, and Scientific-Atlanta are among the firms that sell satellite-based communication services.

Frequency Range

Satellite links operate in the low-gigahertz range, typically at 11–14 MHz.

Cost

Costs are extremely high and are usually amortized across many users by selling communication services.

Ease of Installation

Earth stations can be installed by numerous commercial providers. Transmitters operate on licensed frequencies and require an FCC license

Bandwidth

Bandwidth is related to cost, and firms can purchase almost any required bandwidth. Typical data rates are 1–10 Mbps.

Attenuation

Attenuation characteristics depend on frequency, power, and atmospheric conditions. Properly designed systems take attenuation into account. Rain and atmospheric conditions might attenuate higher frequencies.

EMI Characteristics

Microwave signals are sensitive to EMI and electronic eavesdropping. Signals transmitted through microwave frequently are encrypted.

Infrared Systems

You use an infrared communication system every time you control your television with a remote control. The remote control transmits pulses of infrared light that carry coded instructions to a receiver on the TV. This technology can be adapted to network communication.

Two methods of infrared networking are in use: point-to-point and broadcast.

Point-to-Point Infrared

Point-to-point networks operate by relaying infrared signals from one device to the next. An example of an infrared LAN is shown in figure 25.13. Transmissions are focused in a narrow beam, and the transmitter and receiver must be aligned carefully. Because the devices must be carefully placed and set up, point-to-point infrared is not suitable for use with devices that move frequently.

High-powered laser transmitters can be used to transmit data for several thousand yards when line-of-sight communication is possible. Lasers can be used in many of the same situations as microwave links, without the requirement of an FCC license. Consider infrared lasers for connections between buildings, particularly when they are separated by public rights of way.

Frequency Range

Infrared light falls in a range below visible light and has a frequency range of approximately 100 GHz to 1,000 THz.

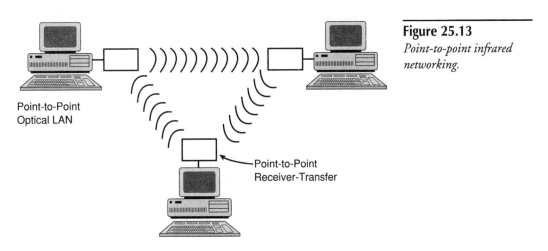

Figure 25.13
Point-to-point infrared networking.

Point-to-Point
Optical LAN

Point-to-Point
Receiver-Transfer

Cost

The cost of point-to-point infrared equipment is higher than the cost for a comparable cabled network. Most systems use transmitters based on LED technology, and the hardware cost is moderate. Long-distance systems use high-powered laser transmitters, which can be quite costly.

Ease of Installation

Installation requires careful alignment of the transmitters and receivers. Lasers used in high-powered transmitters can be hazardous and can burn or damage eyes.

Bandwidth

Bandwidth ranges from about 100 Kbps to 16 Mbps.

Attenuation

Attenuation characteristics are determined by the quality of the transmission, by presence of obstructions, and by atmospheric conditions.

EMI Characteristics

Infrared devices are insensitive to radio-frequency interference but reception can be degraded by bright light. Because transmissions are tightly focused, they are fairly immune to electronic eavesdropping.

Broadcast Infrared

Instead of focusing transmissions in tight beams, broadcast infrared disperses transmissions so that they are visible to several receivers. At least two approaches are possible, as shown in figure 25.14. One approach is to locate an active transmitter at a high point so that it can transmit to all devices.

Another is to place a reflective material on the ceiling; devices transmit toward the ceiling where the light signals are dispersed to other devices in the room.

Frequency Range

Infrared light falls in a range below visible light and has a frequency range of approximately 100 GHz to 1000 THz.

Cost

The cost of point-to-point infrared equipment is higher than the cost for a comparable cabled network. Because lasers produce a tightly focused beam, they are not very suitable to broadcast-type networks.

Ease of Installation

Installation is fairly simple because device alignment is not critical. It is essential that each device has clear transmission and reception pathways. Because these devices are sensitive to light interference, the control of ambient light is a significant installation concern.

Capacity

Typical bandwidths are less than 1 Mbps, although higher bandwidths are theoretically possible.

Attenuation

Attenuation characteristics are determined by the quality of the transmission, by presence of obstructions, and by atmospheric conditions. Typical ranges are limited to tens of meters.

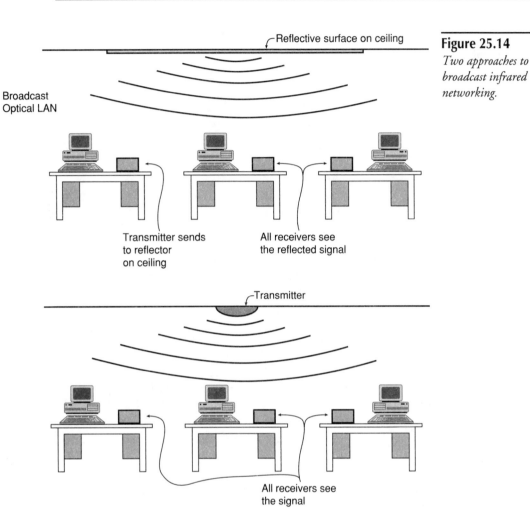

Broadcast
Optical LAN

Reflective surface on ceiling

Transmitter sends
to reflector
on ceiling

All receivers see
the reflected signal

Transmitter

All receivers see
the signal

Figure 25.14
Two approaches to broadcast infrared networking.

EMI Characteristics

Infrared devices are insensitive to radio-frequency interference, but reception can be degraded by bright light. Because transmissions are tightly focused, they are fairly immune to electronic eavesdropping.

Summary of Wireless Media

Table 25.2 summarizes the characteristics of the wireless media discussed in this section.

Table 25.2
Comparison of Wireless Media

Media Type	Frequency Range	Cost
Low-power single frequency	All radio frequencies. Frequencies in the low GHz range are most common.	Moderate for wireless but higher than cabled devices
High-power single frequency	All radio frequencies. Frequencies in the low GHz range are most common.	More expensive than low-power
Spread spectrum	All radio frequencies. 902-928 MHz common in the US. 2.4 GHz most common worldwide.	Moderate
Terrestrial microwave	Usually low GHz, with 6 or 21–23 GHz most common.	Moderate to high but cost effective in many situations
Satellite microwave	Low GHz. 11–14 GHz most common.	High
Point-to-point infrared	100 GHz to 1000 THz	Low to moderate
Broadcast infrared	100 GHz to 1000 THz	Low for wireless, higher than cables systems

Public and Private Network Services

Communication must take place between distant points, but few organizations can justify the costs required to construct a private wide area network. Fortunately, a variety of commercial options are available that enable organizations to pay only for the level of service that they require. One option is the public telephone network. Another is to utilize a public network service, of which the Internet is an example.

The Public Telephone Network

Public telephone networks offer two general types of service:

- Switched services, which the customer pays for on a per-use basis

- Leased dedicated services, to which the customer is granted exclusive access

Switched services operate on the *Public Switched Telephone Network* (PSTN), which we know as the telephone system. Voice grade services have evolved

Installation	Capacity	Attenuation	EMI Sensitivity
Low difficulty	Below 1 Mbps to 10 Mbps	High	High EMI sensitivity. Vulnerable to eavesdropping.
High difficulty	Below 1 Mbps to 10 Mbps	Low	High EMI sensitivity. Vulnerable to eavesdropping.
Moderately difficult	2 to 6 Mbps	High	Some EMI sensitivity. Low eavesdropping vulnerability.
Difficult	Below 1 Mbps to 10 Mbps with higher rates possible	Depends on strength and atmospheric conditions	Low EMI sensitivity. Some eavesdropping vulnerability.
Very difficult	Below 1 Mbps to 10 Mbps with higher rates possible	Depends on frequency, signal strength, and atmospheric conditions	Low EMI sensitivity. Moderate eavesdropping vulnerability.
Moderately difficult	Below 1 Mbps to 16 Mbps	Depends on light purity and intensity as well as environmental conditions	Sensitive to intense light. Low eavesdropping vulnerability.
Low difficulty	Up to 1 Mbps	High	Sensitive to intense light. Low eavesdropping vulnerability.

to high levels of sophistication and can be adapted to providing many data services by using devices such as modems. Newer switched options are providing higher levels of service while retaining the advantages of switched access.

On a switched network, subscribers do not have exclusive access to a particular data path. The PSTN maintains large numbers of paths, but not nearly enough to service all customers simultaneously. When a customer requests service, a path is switched in to service the customer's needs. When the customer hangs up, the path is reused for other customers. In situations when the customer does not need full-time network access, switched service is extremely cost-effective.

In the United States, the following terms are used to describe components of the PSTN (see fig. 25.15):

- The *demarcation point*, or *demarc*, is the point at which outside wiring enters the customer's premises. The demarc is a specific point in the building at which customer wiring connects to the wiring of the local loop.

■ *Subscriber wiring and equipment* consists of all wiring and equipment on the customer side of the demarc. These items are owned by the customer, and the customer is responsible for operation and maintenance.

■ *Local loops* connect the demarc to a central office. The local loop can consist of unshielded twisted-pair wiring, fiber-optic cable, or a combination of the two.

■ The *central office* (CO) switches connections between customer sites. It also supplies reliable, filtered power for the local loop.

Central offices are interconnected by high capacity trunk lines.

Central offices rely on long-distance carriers to communicate with COs that are outside of the local service area. Long-distance carriers use various combinations of fiber-optic, copper, and microwave media to provide high-capacity long-distance service.

When customers require full-time access to a communication path, one option is a dedicated, leased line. Several levels of service are available. Common options are T-1 (1.544 Mbps) and T-3 (44.736 Mbps). Leased lines enable a customer to lease a specified bandwidth between two specified points.

Many organizations need to communicate among several points. Leasing a line between each pair of

Figure 25.15
Elements of the Public Switched Telephone Service.

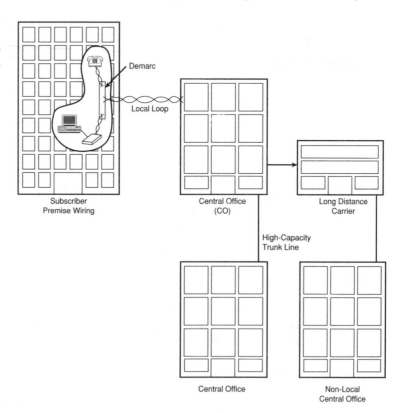

points can prove too costly. Many services now are available that route packets between different sites. Among the services available are X.25, Frame Relay, SONET (Synchronous Optical Network), and ATM. Each of these services has characteristics that suit it to particular uses, and all are available on a leased basis from service providers. An organization that needs to communicate among many sites simply pays to connect each site to the service, and the service takes on the responsibility of routing packets. The expense of operating the network is shared among all of the network subscribers. Because the exact switching process is concealed from the subscriber, these networks are frequently depicted as a communication cloud, as shown in figure 25.16.

Table 25.3 lists common network services and their associated bandwidths.

Table 25.3
Bandwidths of Network Services

Service	Bandwidth
Dedicated 56 KB (DDS)	56 Kbps
Switched 56	56 Kbps
X.25	56 Kbps
T1	1.544 Mbps
Switched T1	1.544 Mbps
Frame Relay	1.544 Mbps
SMDS	1.544 Mbps
ISDN	1.544 Mbps
E1 (Europe)	2.048 Mbps
T3	44.736 Mbps
ATM	44.736 Mbps

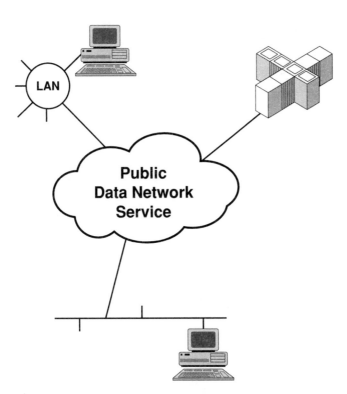

Figure 25.16
An example of a public network service.

These data rates can be compared to common LAN services such as Ethernet (10 Mbps) and token ring (4–16 Mbps).

The Internet

The Internet is a cooperative venture in which huge numbers of government agencies, educational institutions, and businesses have agreed to provide shared network services. Each organization on the Internet provides some amount of communication and computing capability that is freely shared with other network users. As a result of this cooperation, the Internet has grown to encompass computers in over 100 countries on all continents.

The United States has begun to encourage development of a national information infrastructure, popularly called the Information Superhighway. Research is underway to develop practical methods of establishing high-capacity media (>3 Gbps) with the capability of interconnecting large numbers of public and private networks.

Questions

1. Which of the following cable types supports the greatest cable lengths?

   ○ A. Unshielded twisted-pair

   ○ B. Shielded twisted-pair

   ○ C. Large coaxial cable

   ○ D. Small coaxial cable

2. Which TWO are advantages of UTP cable?

   ☐ A. Low cost

   ☐ B. Easy installation

   ☐ C. High resistance to EMI due to twists in cable

   ☐ D. Cables up to 500 meters

3. Which THREE are advantages of coaxial cable?

   ☐ A. Low cost

   ☐ B. Easy installation

   ☐ C. Good resistance to EMI

   ☐ D. Easy to reconfigure

4. Which TWO are disadvantages of fiber-optic cable?

   ☐ A. Sensitive to EMI

   ☐ B. Expensive hardware

   ☐ C. High installation cost

   ☐ D. Low bandwidth

5. Which of the following THREE cable types should be regarded as mature, well-proven technologies?

   ☐ A. Level 3 UTP

   ☐ B. STP

   ☐ C. Fiber-optic

   ☐ D. Level 5 UTP

6. Which of the following is a true statement?

   ○ A. Telephone wiring can be reliably used for most UTP networks.

   ○ B. Thin coaxial networks are easy to install and reconfigure.

   ○ C. Fiber-optic cable supports cable runs of tens of kilometers.

   ○ D. STP cable is insensitive to EMI.

7. Which cable type should be used to connect between two buildings?

   ○ A. UTP

   ○ B. STP

   ○ C. Coax

   ○ D. Fiber-optic

8. Which of the following cable types has the greatest data capacity?

   ○ A. Category 5 UTP

   ○ B. Thick coax

   ○ C. Single-mode fiber-optic

   ○ D. Multi-mode fiber-optic

9. Which statement is true of unlicensed radio frequencies?

   ○ A. Anyone may use them.

   ○ B. 902 MHz and 2.4 GHz are unlicensed frequency bands.

   ○ C. The FCC prevents users from interfering.

   ○ D. They are relatively uncrowded.

10. Which THREE of the following are antenna types?

    ☐ A. Beam

    ☐ B. Duplex

    ☐ C. Dipole

    ☐ D. Random-length wire

11. Which of the following radio transmissions is typically line-of-sight?

    ○ A. AM

    ○ B. FM

    ○ C. Microwave

    ○ D. None of the above

12. Which THREE of the following statements are true:

    ☐ A. Attenuation of radio waves is less with high-power signals.

    ☐ B. High-frequency radio LANs can penetrate office walls.

    ☐ C. Radio-frequency LANs have high bandwidth.

    ☐ D. Spread-spectrum technology reduces sensitivity to EMI.

13. Which TWO wireless technologies would be good choices for connecting two buildings on opposite sides of a highway?

    ☐ A. Satellite microwave

    ☐ B. High-power single-frequency

    ☐ C. Terrestrial microwave

    ☐ D. Broadcast infrared

14. Which TWO wireless technologies are sensitive to radio-frequency interference:

    ☐ A. Microwave

    ☐ B. Spread-spectrum

    ☐ C. Infrared

    ☐ D. High-power, single frequency

15. Which TWO statements are true of the public telephone network?

    ☐ A. Switched services enable customers to pay on a per-use basis.

    ☐ B. The demarc is the place at the Central Office where a user's connection attaches to the network.

    ☐ C. Local loops connect subscriber wiring to the demarc.

    ☐ D. Central offices switch calls between customer sites.

Answers

1. C	9. B
2. A, B	10. A, C, D
3. A, B, C	11. A
4. B, C	12. A, C, D
5. A, B, C	13. B, C
6. C	14. B, D
7. D	15. A, D
8. C	

Transmission Media Connections

This chapter covers a wide variety of devices that are used to connect networks. The devices discussed range from the lowly connector to exotic units, such as routers and CSU/DSUs. Novell divides these devices into two categories, describing them either as network or internetwork devices.

This course defines a network as "a single, independent network." What does this mean? By this definition, a network consists of a single, local cabling system. Any device on the network can directly communicate with any other device on the same network. A network by this definition does not have any connections to other, remote networks.

According to the course definition, an *internetwork* consists of multiple independent networks that are connected together and can share remote resources. It is said that internetworks consist of "logically separate but physically connected networks" that can be dissimilar in type. The device that connects the independent networks together must have a degree of "intelligence" because it must determine when packets will stay on the local network or when they will be forwarded to another remote network.

Connectivity devices perform the following functions:

- Attaching devices to media
- Connecting media segments together
- Utilizing media capacity effectively
- Connecting remote (logically separate) networks

Listed below are the devices to be examined:

- Network connectivity devices:

  Connectors

  Network interface boards

  Hubs

  Repeaters

  Bridges

  Multiplexors

  Modems

- Internetwork connectivity devices:

  Routers

  Brouters

  CSU/DSUs

When you complete this chapter, you will be able to do the following:

- Identify connecting hardware used in computer networking
- Identify connecting hardware used to connect internetworks
- Select connectivity devices to meet specific requirements

Connecting Hardware

Each connection type will specify connectors to be used. Several are discussed in this section.

Connectors for Multi-Wire Cable

A variety of physical layer standards require cables with large numbers of wires. The RS-232 serial interface commonly used for modems can utilize as many as 25 wires (although seldom are all wires actually implemented).

Several types of connectors are used for these types of connections, three of which are shown in figure 26.1. A wide variety of D-type connectors are available, of which the DB-25 and the DB-9 are shown. The number reflects the number of pins or sockets that the connector can accommodate. You will encounter DB-9 connectors in several places. Token-ring network cards are frequently equipped with DB-9 connectors.

The DIX connector is similar to a DB-15 connector, and is used to connect devices with thick-wire Ethernet. The DIX connector differs from a standard DB-15 because the DIX is secured to the mating connector with a sliding clip instead of screws. The sliding clip is installed on the connector that has sockets, which is not shown in the figure. The connector shown in figure 26.1 is equipped with pins and with studs that mate with the sliding clip.

The fourth connector shown in figure 26.1 is a DIN connector. DIN connectors are available in various configurations, with different pin counts and pin arrangements. In networking, you are most likely to encounter DIN connectors when cabling Macintoshes into AppleTalk networks.

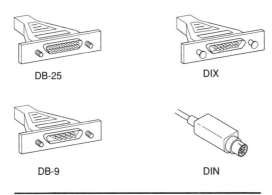

Figure 26.1
Connectors used with multi-wire cables.

Connectors for Twisted-Pair Cables

The most common connector used with UTP cables is the RJ-45 connector, shown in figure 26.2. These connectors are easy to install on cables and are extremely easy to connect and disconnect. The RJ-45 connector has eight pins. You also will occasionally encounter the RJ-11 connector, which resembles the RJ-45, but has only four pins.

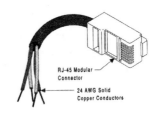

Figure 26.2
A RJ-45 connector.

Although AppleTalk and token-ring networks can both be cabled with UTP cable and RJ-45 connectors, both originated as STP cabling systems. For STP cable, AppleTalk employs a DIN-type connector, shown in figure 26.3. IBM uses the IBM Data Connector, also shown in the figure.

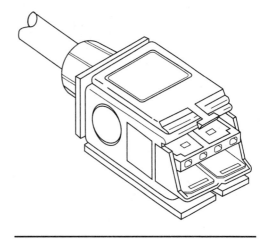

Figure 26.3
Connectors used with STP cable.

The IBM Data Connector is unusual because it does not come in two gender configurations. Any IBM Data Connector may be snapped to any other IBM Data Connector.

Most networking connections for STP token ring are made using IBM Data Connectors. The connection to the workstation, however, is made with a DB-15 connector. Figure 26.4 shows a PC that is set up to connect to a token-ring network.

Connectors for Coaxial Cable

Two types of connectors are commonly used with coaxial cable. The most common connector is the *Bayonette Connector* (BNC) connector, shown in figure 26.5. This figure shows several characteristics of thin Ethernet cabling, as follows:

■ A T-connector is used to connect the network board in the PC to the network. The T- connector attaches directly to the network board, and a cable is never used at this point.

■ BNC connectors attach cable segments to the T-connectors.

■ Both ends of the cable must be terminated. A *terminator* is a special connector that includes a resistor that is carefully matched to the characteristics of the cable system.

■ One of the terminators must be grounded. A wire from the connector is attached to a grounded point, such as the center screw of a grounded electrical outlet.

Thick Ethernet uses N-connectors, which screw on instead of using a twist-lock (bayonette) fitting (see fig. 26.6). As with thin Ethernet, both ends of the cable must be terminated and one end must be grounded.

Figure 26.4

PC ready to connect to a token-ring network.

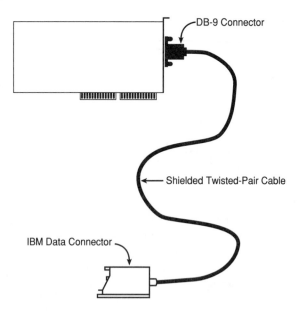

DB-9 Connector

Shielded Twisted-Pair Cable

IBM Data Connector

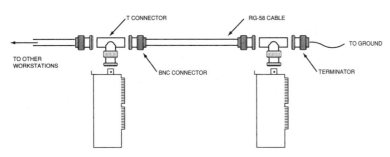

Figure 26.5

Connectors and cabling for thin Ethernet.

Workstations do not connect directly to the cable with thick Ethernet. The cable attachment is made with a *transceiver* (also called a *medium attachment unit* or MAU), which connects to the workstation with a cable called an *AUI cable*. Transceivers can connect to cables in the following two ways:

■ They can connect by cutting the cable and using N-connectors and a T-connector on the transceiver. This, the original method, is now used infrequently.

■ The more common approach is to use a clamp-on transceiver, which has pins that penetrate the cable without the need for cutting it. Because clamp-on transceivers force sharp teeth into the cable, they are frequently referred to as *vampire taps.*

Connectors for Fiber-Optic Cable

A variety of connectors are used with fiber-optic cable. The most common is the ST-connector, shown in figure 26.7. If two devices are to engage in two-way data exchange, two fibers are required, and you will frequently encounter fiber-optic cables with connectors in pairs.

When fiber-optic cable bundles must be interfaced to individual cables, a connection center will be used. Within the splice center, the individual fibers in the cable bundle can be connected to individual connectors that are used to connect to devices. Figure 26.8 illustrates a cabling system based on a splice center.

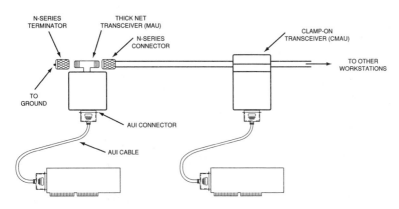

Figure 26.6

Connectors and cabling for thick Ethernet

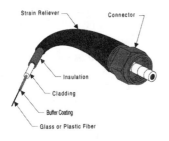

Figure 26.7
An ST connector used for fiber optic cable.

Network Connectivity Devices

This section defines a variety of devices as "network connectivity devices." This definition focuses on the roles of these devices in local networks as opposed to internetworks.

Network Interface Boards

Each workstation must be equipped with hardware that enables the workstation to connect to the network. This course calls all such devices *network interface boards*, although they might not be boards at all:

■ A *network interface card* (NIC) may be installed in one of the computer's expansion slots.

■ The network interface circuitry may be built into the computer's main board. In this case, the connector is built into the computer's case.

■ A transmission media adapter may be used.

Several types of transmission media adapters are in common use, including the following:

■ Ethernet LANs use transceivers to connect DIX connectors on devices to network media. Transceivers are always used with thick coaxial cable and may be used with thin coax or

Figure 26.8
Fiber-optic cable.

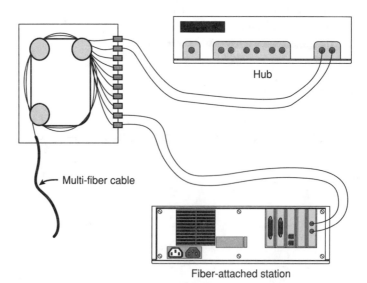

UTP. NICs for thin and UTP Ethernet usually have the transceivers built in so that an external transceiver is not required.

■ When UTP cable is used with token-ring networks, a media filter might be required when operating at 16 Mbps. The media filter prevents noise from getting out onto the LAN. Many token-ring NICs designed for 16 Mbps operation incorporate the media filter on the card.

Transceivers

Regardless of the form of the device, it will include a transceiver of some kind. A transceiver functions as both a *trans*mitter and a re*ceiver.*

The transmitter component translates the computer's internal signals to the signals required for the network. If the network uses UTP cable, the transceiver will supply the proper electrical signals to the proper type of connector. If the network uses fiber-optic cable, the transceiver will translate the computer's electrical signals into the light signals required for the network.

The receiver component performs the opposite service when signals are received from the network, translating them back to a form that matches the computer's internal requirements.

Network Interface Cards (NIC)

Also called an NIC, a *network interface card* is a network board that can be installed in a computer's expansion slot. NICs are the devices most commonly used to connect computers to networks.

NICs incorporate a transceiver, which can service several types of connectors. With the exception of thick Ethernet, NICs are available to connect directly to all types of networks.

Ethernet NICs are equipped with one, two, or possibly all three of the following:

■ RJ-45 connector for UTP Ethernet

■ BNC connector for thin Ethernet

■ AUI connector for thick Ethernet

Token-ring NICs are equipped with one or both of the following:

■ DB-15 connector for STP

■ RJ-45 connector for UTP

Transmission Media Adapters

Novell uses the term *transmission media adapter* to describe a device that adapts one type of connector on the computer to a different type of connector that is required for the network. Several types of devices can be classified as transmission media adapters, including the following:

■ **Transceivers (or MAUs).** Used to connect computers to thick coax Ethernets

■ **Media filters.** Adapt a DB-15 token-ring connector to connect to a UTP network with an RJ-45 connector

■ **Parallel port adapters.** Enable laptop computers to network by communicating through their parallel ports

■ **SCSI port adapters.** Enable computers to connect to networks through a SCSI interface

Hubs

Coaxial cable Ethernet is the only LAN standard that does not use hubs to bring wiring together in a central location, as shown in figure 26.9. Hubs are also called *wiring concentrators.* You will encounter three types of hubs, as follows:

- Passive
- Active
- Intelligent

Passive Hubs

This type of hub is called passive because it does not contain any electronic components and does not process the data signal in any way. The only purpose of a passive hub is to combine the signals from several network cable segments. All devices attached to a passive hub see all the packets that pass through the hub.

Because the hub does not clean up or amplify the signals (in fact, the hub absorbs a small part of the signal), the distance between a computer and the hub can be no more than half of the maximum permissible distance between two computers on the network. If the network design limits the distance between two computers to 200 meters, the maximum distance between a computer and the hub is 100 meters.

ARCnet networks commonly use passive hubs.

Token-ring networks also can use passive hubs, although the industry trend is to utilize active hubs to obtain the advantages cited in the following.

Active Hubs

Active hubs incorporate electronic components that can amplify and clean up the electronic signals that flow between devices on the network. The process of cleaning up the signals is called *signal regeneration.* There are two benefits of signal regeneration: the network is more robust and less sensitive to errors, and distances between devices can be increased. These advantages generally outweigh the fact that active hubs cost considerably more than passive hubs.

Later in the chapter, you will learn about *repeaters,* which are also devices that amplify and regenerate network signals. Because active hubs function in part as repeaters, they are occasionally called *multiport repeaters.*

Intelligent Hubs

Intelligent hubs are active hubs that include something more. Several functions can add intelligence to a hub, as follows:

Figure 26.9
Network wiring with a hub.

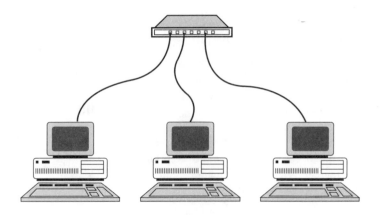

■ **Hub management.** Many hubs now support network management protocols that enable the hub to send packets to a central network console. They also enable the console to control the hub, ordering, for example, a hub to shut down a connection that is generating network errors.

■ **Switching hubs.** The latest development in hubs is the *switching hub*, which includes circuitry that very quickly routes signals between ports on the hub. Instead of repeating a packet to all ports on the hub, a switching hub repeats it only to the port that connects to the destination computer for the packet. Many switching hubs have the capability of switching packets to the fastest of several alternative paths. Switching hubs are replacing bridges and routers on many networks.

Repeaters

As you learned in Chapter 24, "The OSI Layered Protocol Model," all media attenuate the signals that they carry. Each media type, therefore, has a maximum range that it can reliably carry data. Figure 26.10 shows the use of a repeater to connect two Ethernet cable segments. The result of adding the repeater is that the potential length of the overall network is doubled.

Some repeaters simply amplify signals. Although this increases the strength of the data signal, it amplifies any noise on the network as well. Also, if the original signal has been distorted in any way, an amplifying repeater cannot clean up the distortion.

More advanced repeaters can extend the range of network media by both amplifying and regenerating the signals. Signal regenerating repeaters, for example, identify the data in the signal they receive and use the data to regenerate the original signal. This amplifies the strength of the desired signal while reducing noise, and clears up any distortion that might be present. The output of a regenerating repeater duplicates the original data signal.

It would be nice if repeaters could be used to extend networks indefinitely, but all network designs limit the size of the network. The most important reason for this limit is signal propagation. Networks need to work with reasonable expectations about the maximum time a signal might be in transit. This is known as *propagation delay*—the time it takes for a signal to reach the furthest point on the network. If this maximum propagation delay interval expires and no signals are encountered, a network error condition is assumed. Given the maximum allowed propagation delay, it is possible to calculate the maximum permissible cable length for the

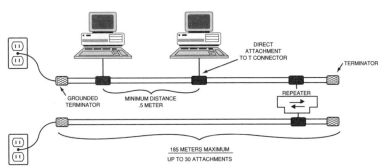

Figure 26.10

Using a repeater to extend an Ethernet LAN.

DIRECT
ATTACHMENT
TO T CONNECTOR

TERMINATOR

GROUNDED
TERMINATOR

MINIMUM DISTANCE
.5 METER

REPEATER

185 METERS MAXIMUM
UP TO 30 ATTACHMENTS

network. Even though repeaters enable signals to travel farther, the maximum propagation delay still sets a limit to the maximum size of the network.

Bridges

Bridges, on the other hand, are capable of extending the maximum size of a network. Although the bridged network in figure 26.11 looks much like the earlier example of a network with a repeater, the bridge is a much more flexible device.

A repeater passes on all signals that it receives. A bridge, on the other hand, is more selective and only passes on the signals that are targeted for a computer that is on the other side. A bridge can make this determination because a device on the network is identified by a unique address, and each packet that is transmitted bears the address of the device to which it should be delivered. The process works like this:

1. The bridge receives every packet on LAN A and LAN B.

2. The bridge learns from the packets which device addresses are located on LAN A and which are on LAN B. A table is built with this information.

3. Packets on LAN A that are addressed to devices on LAN A are discarded. So are packets on LAN B that are addressed to devices on LAN B. These packets can be delivered without the help of the bridge.

4. Packets on LAN A that are addressed to devices on LAN B are retransmitted to LAN B for delivery. Similarly, the appropriate packets on LAN B are retransmitted to LAN A.

Figure 26.11

Extending a network with a bridge.

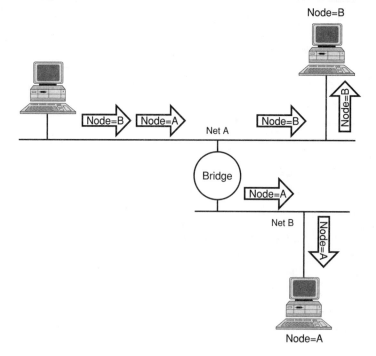

The address tables on older bridges needed to be manually configured by the network administrator. Newer bridges are called learning bridges—they function as described in step 2. *Learning bridges* automatically update their address tables as devices are added to or removed from the network.

Bridges accomplish several things. First, they divide busy networks into smaller segments. If the network is designed so that most packets can be delivered without crossing a bridge, traffic on the individual network segments can be reduced. If the Accounting and Sales departments are overloading the LAN, you might choose to divide the network so that Accounting is on one segment and Sales is on another. Only when Accounting and Sales need to exchange packets will a packet need to cross the bridge between the segments.

Bridges can also extend the physical size of a network. Although the individual segments are still restricted by the maximum size imposed by the network design limits, bridges enable network designers to stretch the distances between segments and extend the overall size of the network.

Bridges, however, cannot join dissimilar types of LANs. Bridges are dependent on the physical addresses of devices. Physical device addresses are functions of the data link layer, and different data link layer protocols are used for each type of network. A bridge, therefore, cannot be used to join an Ethernet segment to a token ring segment.

 Device addresses are functions of the OSI data link layer, which is discussed in greater detail in Chapter 28, "OSI Data Link Layer Concepts." Therefore, bridges are said to function at the data link layer.

Multiplexors

Multiplexors solve a different type of connectivity problem. What if you have several signals to transmit, but only one path that the signals must share? A *multiplexor* is a device that combines several signals so that they can be transmitted together, and then enables the original signals to be extracted at the other end of the transmission. (The process of recovering the original signals is called *demultiplexing*.) Figure 26.12 shows how the process works.

Modems

Standard telephone lines can transmit only analog signals. Computers, however, store and transmit data digitally. *Modems* are capable of transmitting digital computer signals over telephone lines by converting them to analog form.

The process of converting one signal form to another (digital to analog in this case) is called *modulation*. The reverse process of recovering the original signal is called *demodulation*. The term modem is derived from this *mo*dulation/*dem*odulation process.

Modems can be used to connect computer devices or entire networks that are at distant locations. (Before digital telephone lines became available, modems were about the only way of linking distant devices.) Some modems operate constantly over dedicated phone lines. Others use standard *public switched-telephone network* (PSTN) dial-up lines and make a connection only when one is required.

Common uses for modems on LANs include the following:

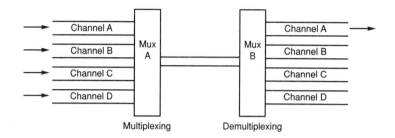

Figure 26.12
Multiplexing and demultiplexing a signal.

Multiplexing   Demultiplexing

- Enabling users to call in and access the LAN

- Exchanging electronic mail between mail-servers

- Transmitting and receiving faxes with a fax server

- Enabling LANs to exchange data on demand

Modems enable networks to exchange e-mail and to perform limited data transfers, but the connectivity made possible is extremely limited. By themselves, modems do not enable remote networks to connect to each other and directly exchange data. In other words, a modem is not an internetwork device. Nevertheless, modems may be used in conjunction with an internetwork device, such as a router, to connect remote networks through the PSTN, or an analog service, such as a 56 KB line.

The point is that a modem cannot enable remote networks to internetwork freely without the assistance of routers or brouters to manage the connection between the networks.

 Modems do not necessarily need to connect through the PSTN. *Short-haul modems* are even frequently used to connect devices in the same building. A standard serial connection is limited to 50 feet, but short-haul modems can be used to extend the range of a serial connection to any required distance.

Many devices are designed to assume that modems will be used. When you want to connect such devices without using modems, you can use a *null modem cable,* which connects the transmitter of one device to the receiver of the other device.

 A modem translates digital signals for transmission on analog phone lines. A codec (*coder/dec*oder) provides a similar service when analog signals are to be transmitted over digital phone lines, translating analog signals into digital form.

Internetwork Connectivity Devices

An *internetwork* consists of two or more independent networks that are physically connected, enabling them to communicate. The networks that make up an internetwork may be of quite different types. An internetwork might include Ethernet and token-ring networks, for example.

Earlier, you saw how bridges can be used to interconnect similar networks. When things get more complex, however, more advanced technologies might be required. This section discusses three such technologies: routers, brouters, and CSU/DSUs.

Routers

Recall that bridges subdivide networks by building tables that list which device addresses can be reached from a particular port on the router. This is a suitable strategy in relatively simple networks, but has shortcomings when networks become more complex.

Consider the network shown in figure 26.13. Let's examine why bridges are unsuitable for interconnecting the network segments in this manner.

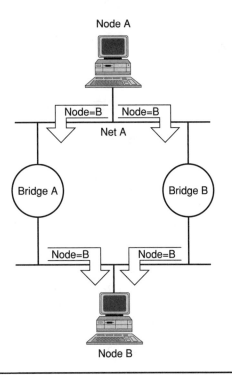

Figure 26.13

A complex network with bridges.

Both bridges are aware of the existence of Node B, and both will pick up the packet from Net A and forward it. At the very least, this means that the same packet will arrive twice at Node B.

A worse case, however, is that these relatively unintelligent bridges will start passing packets around in loops. This results in an ever-increasing number of packets that are circulating on the network and are never reaching their destinations. Ultimately, this activity will saturate the network.

So one restriction of bridges is that the network cannot include redundant paths. However, redundant paths are desirable because they enable the network to continue functioning when one path goes down.

> **Note** An algorithm called the *spanning tree algorithm* enables complex Ethernets to use bridges while redundant routes exist. The algorithm enables the bridges to communicate and to construct a logical network that does not contain redundant paths. The logical network is reconfigured if one of the paths fails.

Another problem is that the bridges cannot analyze the network and determine the fastest route over which to forward a packet. When multiple routes exist, this is a desirable capability, particularly in *wide area networks* (WANs) where some routes can be considerably slower than others.

Routers organize the large network in terms of logical network segments. Each network segment is assigned an address so that every packet has both a destination network address and a destination device address. Figure 26.14 shows a complex network based on routers.

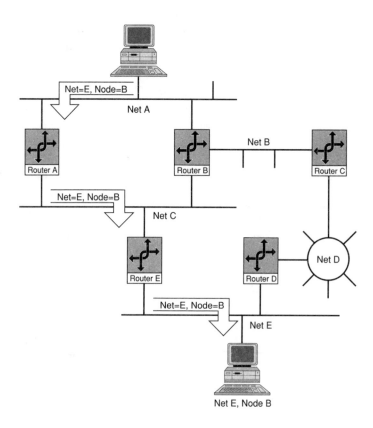

Note Recall the section definition of an internetwork is that which consists of two or more logically separate, but physically connected, networks. By this definition, any network that is segment with routers is an internetwork.

Routers are more "intelligent" than bridges. Not only do they build tables of where networks are located, but they also use algorithms to determine the most efficient path for sending a packet to any given network. Even though a particular network segment might not be directly attached to the router, the router will know the best way to send a packet to a device on that network. Therefore, Router A knows that the most efficient step is to send the packet to Router C, not Router B.

Notice that Router B presents a redundant path to the path provided by Router A. Routers can cope with this situation Because they exchange routing information that ensures that packet loops will not occur. In figure 26.14, if Router A fails, Router B provides a backup message path, making this network more robust.

Routers can be used to divide large, busy LANs into smaller segments, much as bridges can be used. But that is not the only reason for selecting a router.

Routers are also capable of connecting different network types. Notice that the network in figure 26.14 includes a token-ring segment with the Ethernet segments. On such networks, a router is the device of choice.

Because they can determine route efficiencies, routers are usually employed to connect a LAN to a wide area network. WANs are frequently designed with multiple paths, and routers can ensure that the various paths are used most efficiently.

 Device addresses are functions of the OSI network layer, which will be discussed in greater detail in Chapter 29, "OSI Network Layer Concepts." Routers, therefore, are said to function at the network layer.

The network layer functions independently of the physical cabling system and the cabling system protocols—independently, that is, of the physical and data link layers. This is the reason that routers can easily translate packets between different cabling systems. Bridges cannot because they function at the data link layer, which is closely tied to a given set of physical layer specifications.

Brouters

A *brouter* is a router that can also bridge. A brouter attempts to deliver packets based on network protocol information. If a particular network layer protocol is not supported, the brouter bridges the packet using device addresses.

CSU/DSUs

When LANs are connected into wide area networks, the connection is frequently by means of the public telephone network. Connecting to some telephone media requires the use of a *channel service network/digital service unit* (CSU/DSU).

Network service providers design their media for a particular type of signal, and may require use of a CSU/DSU to translate the LAN signals to the signal format required. A CSU/DSU also isolates the local network from the public network to protect each network from noise and voltage fluctuations of the other.

Important Terms from This Chapter

A *network*, according to Novell study materials, is a "single independent network." On such a network, any device can communicate with any other device directly, without the need for a connection to a remote network. Under this definition, network connectivity devices are involved only in local network connectivity.

An *internetwork*, according to Novell study materials, consists of multiple independent networks that are connected together and can share remote resources. Internetwork connectivity devices facilitate connectivity between remote networks.

It is important to realize that "remote" does not necessarily mean "distant." An internetwork can be located entirely within a single building. The important distinction is whether the networks are logically separate, and actually has to do with protocol levels, which you will examine in greater detail in later sections. The crucial level is the network layer, which assigns an address to each network that makes up an internetwork. The following are ways to determine how a message was delivered:

- If a message can arrive at its destination using information that is available at the data link layer of the OSI model, then the message is being delivered by a network.

■ If delivery requires use of the network address information that is available at the network layer, the message is being delivered through an internetwork.

Network connectivity devices, therefore, do not use network address information. Internetwork connectivity devices are capable of using network address information to assist in the efficient delivery of messages. The process of using network address information to deliver messages is called *routing*. The common feature that unites internetwork connectivity devices (routers and brouters) is that they can perform routing.

This distinction will become clearer to you as you progress through the rest of this section. Because each network in an internetwork is assigned an address, each network can be considered to be *logically separate*—that is, each network functions independently of other networks on the internetwork.

 For the purposes of this section, CSU/ DSUs are considered internetwork devices, but this is not strictly correct. The primary purpose of a CSU/DSU is to interface the network to a public data network. A given device may perform routing or it may depend on a separate router, depending on the vendor's hardware design.

Questions

1. Which TWO of the following are characteristic features of internetworks?

   ☐ A. Multiple networks can be interconnected with bridges to form an internetwork.

   ☐ B. Devices can communicate with devices on the local network.

   ☐ C. Devices can communicate with devices on remote networks.

   ☐ D. An internetwork can consist of segments that utilize different network protocols.

2. Which TWO of the following are characteristics of networks?

   ☐ A. Devices can communicate with devices on the local network.

   ☐ B. Devices can communicate with devices on remote networks.

   ☐ C. Routers extend the range of a network.

   ☐ D. A network can include network segments that utilize different protocols.

3. Which TWO of the following are functions of network connectivity devices?

   ☐ A. Enabling devices to interface with media

   ☐ B. Converting protocols between network segments

   ☐ C. Connecting media segments together

   ☐ D. Fully utilizing media capacity

4. Which TWO of the following are functions of internetwork connectivity devices?

   ☐ A. Connecting remote networks

   ☐ B. Enabling networks with different protocols to communicate

   ☐ C. Attaching devices to media

   ☐ D. Extending the range of network segments

5. The DB-15 connector is commonly used with _____.

   ○ A. fiber-optic cable

   ○ B. token-ring connections to NICs

   ○ C. coaxial cable

   ○ D. RS-232 serial interfaces

6. Which TWO connectors are frequently used with STP cable?

   ☐ A. T-connectors

   ☐ B. RJ-45 connectors

   ☐ C. IBM unisex connectors

   ☐ D. AppleTalk DIN connectors

7. Which TWO connectors are commonly used with coaxial cable?

   ☐ A. DB-25 connectors

   ☐ B. N-connectors

   ☐ C. ST-connectors

   ☐ D. BNC connectors

8. Which THREE are some advantages of active hubs?

   ☐ A. They can regenerate network signals.

   ☐ B. LANs ranges can be extended.

   ☐ C. They are inexpensive.

   ☐ D. They function as repeaters.

9. Which TWO networks can use passive hubs?

   ☐ A. Ethernet

   ☐ B. ARCnet

   ☐ C. Token ring

   ☐ D. All of the above

10. Which TWO statements are true of re-peaters?

   ☐ A. Repeaters amplify signals.

   ☐ B. Repeaters extend network distances.

   ☐ C. Repeaters regenerate signals.

   ☐ D. Repeaters can be used to extend the range of a network indefinitely.

11. Which THREE statements are true of bridges?

   ☐ A. Bridges amplify and regenerate signals.

   ☐ B. Bridges can connect logically separate networks.

   ☐ C. Bridges use device address tables to route messages.

   ☐ D. Bridges divide networks into smaller segments.

12. Modems can be used for which THREE of the following purposes?

   ☐ A. To connect remote networks

   ☐ B. To enable users to call in and access a LAN

   ☐ C. To transmit and receive faxes

   ☐ D. To extend the range of a serial interface

13. Which THREE features of routers are not features of bridges?

   ☐ A. Regenerating signals

   ☐ B. Connecting logically separate networks

   ☐ C. Connecting networks using different protocols

   ☐ D. Maintaining tables of network addresses

14. Which TWO of the following are functions of CSU/DSUs?

   ☐ A. Connecting networks with different protocols

   ☐ B. Connecting a network to some types of public telephone networks

   ☐ C. Routing signals between logical networks

   ☐ D. Isolating the local network from the public network

Answers

1. B, C

2. A, B

3. A, C

4. A, B

5. B

6. C, D

7. B, D

8. A, B, D

9. B, C

10. A, B

11. A, C, D

12. B, C, D

13. B, C, D

14. B, D

27

OSI Physical Layer Concepts

Although the OSI physical layer does not define the media used, the physical layer is concerned with all aspects of transmitting and receiving data on the network media. Specifically, the physical layer is concerned with transmitting and receiving bits. This layer defines several key characteristics of the physical network, including the following:

■ *Physical structure of the network*

■ *Mechanical and electrical specifications for using the medium (not the medium itself!)*

■ *Bit transmission encoding and timing*

Although the physical layer does not define the medium, it defines clear requirements that the medium must meet, and physical layer specifications will differ depending on the physical medium to be used. Ethernet for UTP will have different physical layer specifications than Ethernet for coax, for example.

When you complete this chapter, you will understand the following:

■ The purpose of the OSI physical layer

■ Types of network connections

■ Physical topologies

■ Analog and digital signaling

■ Bit synchronization

■ Bandwidth use

■ Multiplexing

Connection Types

All network connections consist of two types of building blocks:

■ Multipoint connections

■ Point-to-point connections

A *multipoint connection* enables one device to communicate with two or more devices. An example is shown in figure 27.1. All the devices attached using a multipoint connection share the same network transmission medium.

A *point-to-point connection* enables one device to communicate with one other device (see fig. 27.2). When two devices are connected through a point-to-point link, they have exclusive use of the data capacity of the link.

Larger networks can be constructed by adding point-to-point links. In this case, devices rely on other devices to relay their messages. Point-to-point links can even come full circle to form a ring, enabling messages to be passed from any device to any other device on the ring.

Physical Topologies

The physical topology of a network describes the layout of the network media. Different physical topologies have different characteristics in terms of performance, ease of installation, troubleshooting, and reconfiguration.

Physical Topologies Based on Multipoint Connections

In fact, only one topology is based on multipoint connections—the bus, shown in figure 27.3. Notice that all devices are connected to a common transmission media. In some cases, the common media is referred to as a *backbone network*.

Figure 27.1

Examples of multipoint connections.

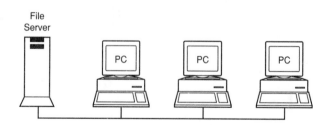

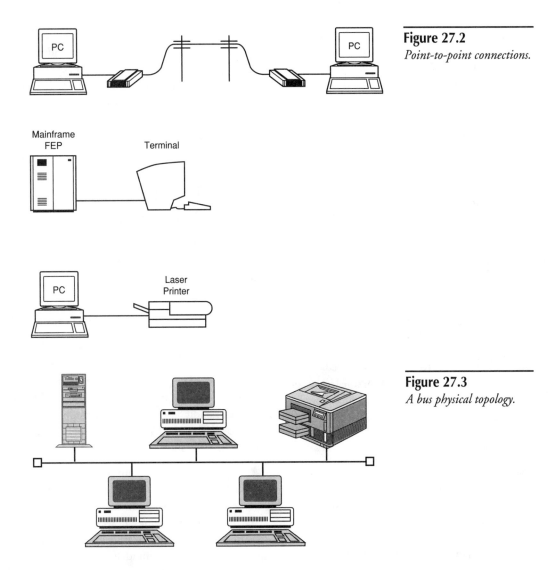

Figure 27.2
Point-to-point connections.

Figure 27.3
A bus physical topology.

Bus Characteristics

Chapters 25 and 26 discussed the cabling and connectors used for bus topologies. Recall that the ends of the cable must be terminated and that devices may be connected along the length of the cable. Connections are performed with T-connectors or with taps (transceivers) that attach directly to the cable and use a drop cable to connect to the workstation.

Typically, signals on a bus network are broadcast in both directions on the backbone cable, enabling all devices to directly receive the signal. With some unidirectional buses, however, signals travel in one direction only and can reach only downstream devices. In this case, the cable must be terminated in such a way that signals are reflected back on the cable and can reach other devices.

Installation

Bus installation is relatively simple and requires only basic tools and skill. Cable runs are generally fairly short because it is not necessary to run a separate cable to a central hub for each device on the network.

Bus networks such as Ethernet have carefully defined rules that must be adhered to for best network performance. Stations on a thick Ethernet cable, for example, should be attached at intervals that are multiples of 2 1/2 meters. All network media have attenuation characteristics that limit the lengths of cables and the number of devices that can be attached.

Reconfiguration

Bus networks can be difficult to reconfigure. If the main cable does not run close to the new device, it might need to be rerouted. Adding new devices often involves cutting the main cable to add a T-connector, which requires the network to be shut down. In the process, it is important to adhere to rules regarding maximum number of devices and distances at which taps are to be spaced.

Troubleshooting

Bus networks can be difficult to troubleshoot because a single fault can render the entire bus inoperative. A broken cable, for example, is the same as having two unterminated cables. Without termination, signals can reflect back into both cable segments interfering with transmissions and making the system inoperable. (In addition, of course, devices cannot communicate with devices that are on the opposite side of the break.) Because all devices are affected by a cable break, it can be difficult to isolate a break to the cable that falls between two devices.

Physical Topologies Based on Point-to-Point Connections

As shown in figure 27.4, several different topologies can be based on point-to-point connections, as follows:

- *Star topologies* utilize a point-to-point link (a "drop cable") to connect each device to a central hub.

- *Mesh networks* establish a point-to-point link between each pair of computers on the network. Because the number of required links rises rapidly as the number of computers increases, large mesh networks are not frequently used.

- *Hybrid mesh networks* are commonly used in wide-area networks. No attempt is made to provide a link between each possible pair of computers. Extra links, however, are installed to provide more direct paths, extra bandwidth, and some redundancy in case links fail.

- *Ring networks* utilize point-to-point links to connect devices together in a ring. Messages are forwarded around the ring and can reach any station in this way.

- *Cellular topologies* divide geographic areas into overlapping cells that are serviced by transmitter/receivers. Point-to-point radio links are established between a cellular data device and the transmitter in a cell. These point-to-point links are constantly reconfigured as the data device moves through the cellular network. (Multipoint links may also be established under appropriate circumstances.)

Each of these topologies is examined in greater detail in the next sections.

The Ring Topology

The ring topology is circular, and signals typically travel around the ring in one direction only. Each device incorporates a receiver and a transmitter and serves as a repeater that passes the signal on to the next device in the ring. Because the signal is regenerated at each device, signal degeneration is low.

Installation

Installation is fairly simple, but the amount of cable required can go higher than with a bus. As with all networks, it is essential to stay within network design restrictions regarding cable lengths between devices, total ring length, and number of devices.

Reconfiguration

Rings can be difficult to reconfigure, particularly when devices are located at large distances.

Troubleshooting

The repeating function makes it fairly easy to isolate cabling faults. When a break is present in the cable, devices will still be able to transmit to downstream devices on the near side of the break. Fault isolation becomes a matter of determining which device is not receiving signals from its immediate upstream neighbor.

Some rings incorporate redundant paths that can be switched in when a cable break occurs. The redundant path takes the form of a second ring that transmits signals in opposite directions from the main ring. When a break occurs in the main ring, the counter-rotating ring can be used to route signals around the break.

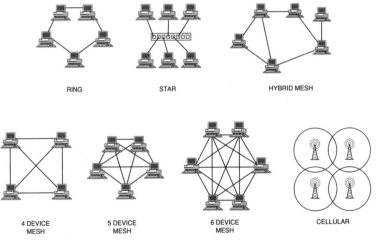

Figure 27.4
Physical topologies based on point-to-point connections.

RING   STAR   HYBRID MESH

4 DEVICE   5 DEVICE   6 DEVICE   CELLULAR
MESH   MESH   MESH

The Star Topology

A star topology networks each device with a cable that connects it to a central hub. The hub receives signals from network devices and routes the signals to the proper destination. Star hubs can be interconnected to form tree or hierarchical network topologies.

Installation

The major installation difficulty is that a separate cable must be run to connect each device to a hub. Cabling requirements are generally considerably higher than for bus or ring physical topologies.

A significant concern with star topologies is that cable lengths between hubs and devices are limited, typically to 100 meters. Therefore, it is necessary to ensure that a hub is located within 100 meters of every potential device location

Reconfiguration

The payoff for cabling to a central hub is that networks are easy to reconfigure. Most adds and moves can be accomplished by simply moving a plug to a new hub port.

Troubleshooting

It is easier to troubleshoot stars than buses and, generally speaking, than rings. It is easy to build troubleshooting features into hubs, which can be monitored centrally.

When the cable to a device fails, it generally affects that device only. In cases where a device cable causes problems for the entire network, it is simple to disconnect the cable from the hub. Many managed hubs will automatically disconnect devices that are producing network errors.

Star topologies are subject to a single point of failure. If the hub fails, all devices are affected.

Mesh Topologies

Mesh networks consist of a point-to-point link between each pair of devices on the network. In most cases, the number of connections required limits the use of true mesh networks to a few stations. A five-device mesh network requires 24 ($4\times3\times2$) connections, but a six-device mesh requires 120 ($5\times4\times3\times2$)!

Two advantages can be stated for a mesh topology. The first is that every device has a guaranteed communication channel capacity with every other device. The other is a high level of fault tolerance. Even multiple media failures will probably leave the network capable of delivering messages to all devices.

More common is the hybrid network, which contains some redundant links, particularly to the most important devices or where the greatest capacity is needed. When it is essential that the network never go down, redundant links are a good form of insurance.

Installation

Mesh networks are difficult to install, with the difficulty increasing rapidly as the number of devices increases.

Hybrid mesh networks are most commonly in wide area networks, where the links consist primarily of leased communication services. Installation is primarily a matter of setting up routers, CSU/DSUs, and so on. WAN connections of this sort can get involved to install and manage.

Reconfiguration

Mesh networks can be extremely difficult to reconfigure.

Troubleshooting

Mesh networks are easy to troubleshoot because each device keeps track of every other device.

Hybrid mesh networks introduce concerns about how signals are routed through the network. This is a skilled task that calls for sophisticated diagnostic and management systems to ensure that the network operates smoothly.

Mesh networks are extremely robust because redundant links abound. They are, therefore, seldom subject to single points of failure. Performance can degrade, however, if failure of one link causes traffic on other links to rise to unacceptable levels.

Cellular Topology

Cellular networks divide the area being serviced into cells, each of which is serviced by a central station. Devices use radio signals to communicate with the central station, and the central station routes messages to other devices. Cellular data networks can be implemented on an office level or in large geographic areas.

Installation

Installation of office-based cellular LANs is quite different from installation of cable-based LANs. Much depends on the degree to which the office building supports the requirements of the cellular system that has been chosen. Transmitters are of limited power and cannot penetrate walls, so some building types are unsuitable. If hubs can be located so they can communicate clearly with devices, installation is relatively simple.

Reconfiguration

Within the area serviced by a hub, devices can be located and relocated easily. Hubs are often connected to other hubs using cable, however, and relocation of hubs can be more involved.

Troubleshooting

Troubleshooting depends on the network design. If hubs maintain a point-to-point link with devices, troubleshooting is simplified.

When a hub fails, all devices serviced by the hub lose service. Because devices are mobile, they can be relocated to a working area to restore service.

Digital and Analog Signaling

Signaling is the process of communicating information. The information being communicated can take one of two forms: analog or digital. Frequently, information in one form must be converted to the other. This frequently involves the use of some encoding scheme that enables the original information to be recovered from a signal after the signal has been received.

When an analog or digital signal is altered so that it contains information to be communicated, the process is called *modulation* or *encoding*. AM radio transmits information by modulating the radio signal, increasing or decreasing the amplitude (signal strength) depending on the information content. Many similar schemes are used to communicate information through different types of signals.

■ *Analog information* is information that changes continuously and can take on many different values. The hands on an analog clock move constantly, displaying time on a continuous scale.

■ *Digital information* is characterized by discrete states. A lightbulb is on or off, for example. A digital clock represents the time in one minute intervals and doesn't change its numbers again until the next minute. A digital clock can represent exact minutes, but nothing in between.

Figure 27.5 illustrates the difference between analog and digital signals. The analog signal is constantly changing and takes on values throughout the range of possible values. The digital signal takes on only two (or a few) specific states.

Digital Signaling Techniques

Computer data is inherently digital, and the majority of networks use digital signaling. This chapter examines two methods of modulating a digital signal to encode digital data, as follows:

■ Current state

■ State transition

Current State Encoding

This encoding technique assigns specific signal states to represent each possible data value. The signal is monitored periodically to determine its current state, from which a data value may be determined. A voltage of +5 might represent a binary 1 and a voltage of -5 might represent a binary 0, for example. Many different signal variations could be used. The important characteristic is that a given state represents one and only one data value. In figure 27.6, a high voltage represents a binary 0, while a low voltage represents a binary 1.

The following encoding schemes make use of current state encoding, although discussion of their specific characteristics is beyond the scope of this chapter:

■ Unipolar

■ Bipolar

■ Return-to-Zero (NRZ)

■ Biphase

State Transition Encoding

This encoding technique uses transitions in the digital signal to represent data. Following are a couple of ways this could be done:

■ A transition from high to low voltage always represents a 1, and a transition from low to high voltage always represents a 0.

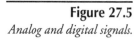

Figure 27.5
Analog and digital signals.

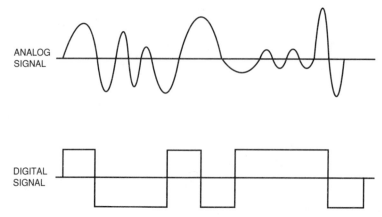

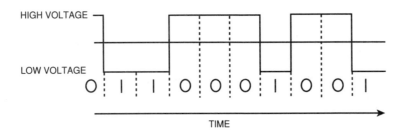

Figure 27.6
Current state encoding.

■ Any transition always represents a 1, and the absence of an expected transition represents a 0. This scheme is depicted in figure 27.7.

The following encoding schemes make use of state transition encoding, although discussion of their specific characteristics is beyond the scope of this chapter:

■ Bipolar-Alternate Mark Inversion (AMI)

■ Non-Return-to-Zero (NRZ)

■ Manchester

■ Differential Manchester

■ Biphase Space (FM-O)

 The terms "current state" and "state transition" were invented by Novell for use in this course and are not standard terms in the industry.

The common industry term for current state is *level triggered* because recognition of a given state is triggered (initiated) by a specific signal level.

The common industry term for state transition is *edge triggered*, since either the leading or trailing edge of a signal transition (the edge of the signal transition) is used to signal that a state change has taken place.

Analog Signaling

Analog signals are constantly varying in one or more values. These changes in values can be used to represent data.

Analog wave forms frequently take the form of sine waves. The sine wave in figure 27.8 illustrates two characteristics that define an analog wave form, as follows:

■ **Frequency.** Indicates the rate at which the waveform is changing. Frequency is associated with the wavelength of the waveform, which is a measure of the distance between two similar peaks on adjacent waves. Frequency is generally measured in Hertz (Hz), which indicates the frequency in cycles per second. Frequency is illustrated in figure 27.8.

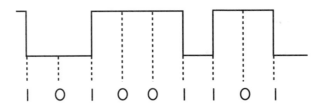

Figure 27.7
State transition encoding.

Figure 27.8

Two analog waveforms differing in frequency.

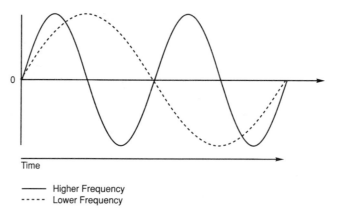

— Higher Frequency
---- Lower Frequency

■ **Amplitude.** The measure of the strength of the waveform. Amplitude is illustrated in figure 27.9.

A third characteristic, *phase*, can also be defined. Figure 27.10 illustrates waveforms that differ in phase. These waveforms have identical frequency and amplitude, but they do not begin their transitions at the same time.

■ In figure 27.10, WAVE B begins to rise from the reference line at the same time that Wave A is peaking. Therefore, Wave B is ¹/₄ of a wave behind Wave A. If a complete wave is represented as having 360 degrees, Wave B lags behind Wave A by 90 degrees.

■ In figure 27.11, notice that Wave B is a mirror image of Wave A. Because Wave B is ¹/₂ of a wave behind Wave A, Wave B lags behind Wave A by 180 degrees. Wave C is ¹/₃ of a wave behind A and lags behind Wave A by 120 degrees.

Each of these characteristics, frequency, amplitude, and phase can be used to encode data.

Figure 27.9

Two analog waveforms differing in amplitude.

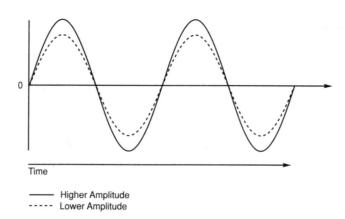

— Higher Amplitude
---- Lower Amplitude

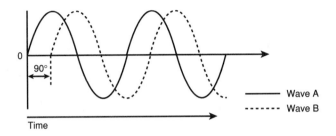

Figure 27.10
Two analog waveforms differing in phase.

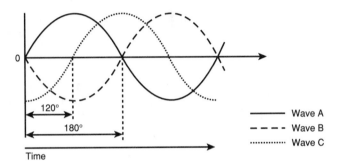

Figure 27.11
Three analog waveforms differing in phase by different amounts.

Amplitude Shift Keying

This is a current state method of modulation in that specific signal amplitudes are assigned specific data values. A high-amplitude signal, for example, might be assigned a value of 1, while a low-amplitude signal is assigned a value of 0. The first example in figure 27.12 illustrates amplitude shift keying.

Frequency Shift Keying

Frequency shift keying is also a current state modulation method. Specific frequency values are assigned specific data values. A high frequency, for example, might represent 0, while a lower frequency might represent 1. The second example in Figure 27.12 illustrates frequency shift keying.

Phase Shift Keying

Phase shift keying is a transition state modulation method. For example, a reference phase might represent 0, while a 180-degree phase shift would represent a 1 value. The process is illustrated in the third example of figure 27.12.

Bit Synchronization

With both current state and transition state modulation methods, the receiving device monitors the signal, looking for an expected characteristic. Timing is important because the receiver needs to know when it should check the incoming signal. If the check is made at the wrong time, erroneous data might be extracted.

Figure 27.12

Keying methods for amplitude waveforms.

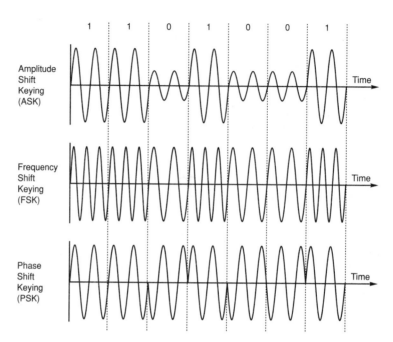

Two methods of coordinating signal timing follow:

- Asynchronous communication

- Synchronous communication

The methods differ primarily in the way they adjust the clocks of the sending and receiving devices.

Asynchronous Communication

Although the sender and receiver have internal clocks, these clocks are not directly synchronized. Each message begins with a start bit that enables the receiver to synchronize its internal clock with the timing of the message. Messages are kept short so the receiver's clock will not drift out of synchronization for the duration of the message. A *stop bit* signals that the message is complete. Asynchronous techniques are primarily used to transmit character data, and the message part of the transmission is limited to 7 or 8 bits.

To make the system work, the sender and receiver must reach a general agreement on the speed at which data is to be transmitted. You are probably familiar with the process of setting the data rate for modems. Even though the sending and receiving clocks are not directly synchronized, if they agree to transmit at, say 9,600 bits per second, their clocks can remain sufficiently synchronized to enable a single short transmission to be completed.

One characteristic to note is that the signals are intermittent and the transmission media is idle except when a transmission is actually taking place. No clock signals are transmitted to keep the receiver's clock synchronized with the sender's clock.

Synchronous Communication

Synchronous communication employs a clocking mechanism to ensure that the sending and receiving devices remain synchronized. Three techniques will be discussed, as follows:

- Guaranteed State Change
- Separate Clock Signals
- Oversampling

Guaranteed State Change

Some encoding techniques are designed to ensure that state changes occur at regular intervals. The receiving device adjusts its internal clock to match the frequencies of the state changes.

Signals of this type are called *self-clocking* because the clocking information is embedded in the signal itself and no other clocking mechanism is required.

Separate Clock Signals

The separate clock signal approach utilizes a separate communication channel to carry clocking information. The common RS-232 serial interface uses this approach. One of the wires in the cable carries clocking signals that enable the sending device to tell the receiver when it should monitor the incoming data.

This approach is useful over short distances, but becomes problematic with longer cables. Signals can travel through different wires in the cable at different rates, and at some point the clocking signal will no longer be synchronized with the signals on the data wires. RS-232 connections, for example, are typically limited to a maximum length of 50 feet for this reason.

Oversampling

With this technique, the receiver samples incoming data at a higher rate than the rate at which the data is being transmitted. If the receiver monitors at ten times the rate at which signal transitions are occurring, it is easy to determine when transitions have taken place. The extra samples also enable the receiver to determine when its clock is drifting and needs to be resynchronized.

Baseband and Broadband Transmissions

There are two ways to allocate the capacity of transmission media, as follows:

- **Baseband.** Devotes the entire capacity of the medium to one communication channel
- **Broadband.** Enables two or more communication channels to share the bandwidth of the communications medium

Baseband is the most common mode of operation. Most LANs function in baseband mode, for example. Baseband signaling can be accomplished with both analog and digital signals.

You have a great deal of experience with broadband transmissions, however, whether you know it or not. The TV cable coming into your house from an antenna or a cable provider is a broadband medium. Many television signals can share the bandwidth of the cable because each signal is modulated using a separately assigned frequency. You can choose the channel you want to watch by selecting its frequency with the television tuner. This technique of dividing bandwidth into frequency bands is called *frequency-division multiplexing* (FDM) and works only with analog signals. Another technique called *time-division multiplexing* (TDM) supports digital signals and will be described in the next section.

Figure 27.13 contrasts the difference between baseband and broadband modes of operation.

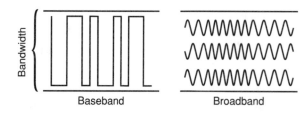

Figure 27.13
Baseband and broadband transmission modes.

Baseband   Broadband

Multiplexing

Multiplexing is the technique that enables broadband media to support multiple data channels. There are several times when multiplexing makes sense, as follows:

- **When media bandwidth is costly.** A high-speed leased line, such as a T-1 or T-3, is expensive to lease. Providing the leased line has sufficient bandwidth, multiplexing can enable the same line to carry mainframe, LAN, voice, video conferencing, and various other data types.

- **When bandwidth is idle.** Many organizations have installed fiber-optic cable that is being used only to partial capacity. With the proper equipment, a single fiber can support hundreds of megabits or even a gigabit or more of data capacity.

- **When large amounts of data need to be transmitted through low-capacity channels.** Multiplexing techniques can divide the original data stream into several lower-bandwidth channels, each of which can be transmitted through a lower capacity medium. The signals can be recombined at the receiving end.

Multiplexing is the process of combining multiple data channels for transmission on a common medium. *Demultiplexing* is the process of recovering the original separate channels from a multiplexed signal.

Multiplexing and demultiplexing are performed by a *multiplexor*, which usually has both capabilities. A multiplexor is sometimes called a *mux*.

The following two techniques are used to multiplex signals:

- Frequency-division multiplexing

- Time-division multiplexing

Frequency-Division Multiplexing

Figure 27.14 illustrates *frequency-division multiplexing*. The technique works by converting all data channels to analog form. Each of these analog signals can be modulated by a separate frequency (called a *carrier frequency*) that makes it possible to recover that signal during the demultiplexing process. At the receiving end, the demultiplexor can select the desired carrier signal and use it to extract the data signal for that channel.

FDM can be used in broadband LANs (a standard for Ethernet exists). One advantage of FDM is that it supports bi-directional signaling on the same cable.

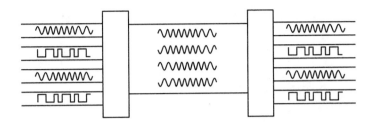

Figure 27.14

Frequency-division multiplexing.

Time-Division Multiplexing

Time-division multiplexing (TDM) divides a channel into time slots that are allocated to the data streams to be transmitted. Figure 27.15 illustrates the process. Provided that the sender and receiver agree on the time slot assignments, the receiver can easily recover and reconstruct the original data streams.

TDM transmits the multiplexed signal in baseband mode. Interestingly, this makes it possible to multiplex a TDM multiplexed signal as one of the data channels on an FDM system.

Conventional TDM equipment utilizes fixed time divisions and allocates time to a channel regardless of how busy that channel is. If a channel is not busy, its time slot is not being fully utilized. Because the time divisions are programmed into the configurations of the multiplexors, this technique often is referred to as *synchronous TDM*.

If it is important to use the capacity of the data medium more efficiently, a more sophisticated technique called *statistical time-division multiplexing* (StatTDM) may be used. A stat-mux uses the time-slot technique, but allocates time slots based on the traffic demand on the individual channels. Figure 27.16 illustrates the process. Notice that Channel B is allocated more time slots than Channel A, while Channel C is allocated the fewest time slots. Channel D is idle and no slots are allocated to it. To make this procedure work, the data transmitted for each time slot includes a control field that identifies to which channel the data in the time slot should be assigned.

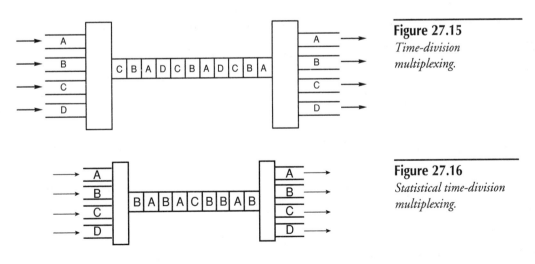

Figure 27.15

Time-division multiplexing.

Figure 27.16

Statistical time-division multiplexing.

Questions

1. Which THREE of the following are functions of the OSI physical layer?

   ☐ A. Mechanical and electrical specifications for using the medium

   ☐ B. Generating electrical signals on the medium

   ☐ C. Network topology

   ☐ D. Bit transmission encoding and timing

2. Which THREE of these network topologies consist of point-to-point links?

   ☐ A. Bus

   ☐ B. Ring

   ☐ C. Star

   ☐ D. Mesh

3. Which network topologies are subject to a single point of failure (that is, one failure can stop all network communication)?

   ○ A. Mesh

   ○ B. Bus

   ○ C. Star

   ○ D. Ring

4. Which THREE are advantages of star topologies?

   ☐ A. Reconfiguration is simplified

   ☐ B. Cable costs are minimized

   ☐ C. Active hubs can regenerate signals

   ☐ D. They are easy to troubleshoot

5. Which TWO are advantages of bus topologies?

   ☐ A. Long cable runs are possible without signal regeneration.

   ☐ B. They often require least amounts of cable.

   ☐ C. They are well-proven technology.

   ☐ D. They are easy to troubleshoot.

6. Which TWO are examples of analog data?

   ☐ A. Light from a switched electric light

   ☐ B. Sound from a radio

   ☐ C. Morse code

   ☐ D. A sine wave

7. Which TWO of the following are analog modulation techniques?

   ☐ A. Phase shift keying

   ☐ B. Binary modulation

   ☐ C. State transition encoding

   ☐ D. ASK

8. Which TWO of the following characteristics of an analog waveform are directly related?

   ☐ A. Amplitude

   ☐ B. Wavelength

   ☐ C. Frequency

   ☐ D. Phase

9. Which bit synchronization techniques can operate without a single-channel medium, such as a single pair of wires?

   ☐ A. Guaranteed state change

   ☐ B. Asynchronous

   ☐ C. Oversampling

   ☐ D. Separate clock signals

10. Which TWO techniques encode data in digital form for transmission on the media?

   ☐ A. Time-division multiplexing

   ☐ B. Frequency-division multiplexing

   ☐ C. Phase shift keying

   ☐ D. Current state encoding

Answers

1. A, C, D

2. B, C, D

3. C

4. A, C, D

5. B, C

6. B, D

7. A, D

8. B, C

9. A, B, C

10. A, D

28

OSI Data Link Layer Concepts

Recall from the previous chapter that the OSI physical layer is concerned only with transmitting and receiving bits. Network communication, however, is considerably more involved than moving bits from one device to another. In fact, dozens of steps must be performed to complete the task of transporting a message from one device to another. This chapter examines the tasks performed by the data link layer.

Real messages consist not of single bits but of meaningful groups of bits. The data link layer receives messages called frames from upper layers (recall the description of OSI layer-to-layer communication in Chapter 24, "The OSI Layered Protocol Model"). A primary function of the data link layer is to disassemble these frames into bits for transmission and then to reconstruct frames from bits that are received.

The data link layer has other functions as well (although all functions may not be performed by a given network protocol stack). This layer performs the following tasks:

- Identifies devices on the network

- Controls (and possibly corrects) errors

- Controls access to the network medium

- Defines the logical topology of the network

- Controls data flow

 Note   The data link layer is conventionally divided into two sublayers:

- *Media access control* (MAC). This sublayer controls the means by which multiple devices share the same media channel.

- *Logical link control* (LLC). This sublayer establishes and maintains links between communicating devices.

This chapter covers the following data link layer topics:

- Logical topologies

- Media access control

- Addressing

- Transmission synchronization

- Connection services

Logical Topologies

Chapter 27, "OSI Physical Layer Concepts," introduces physical topologies, which describe how the media are physically arranged to build a network.

Besides having a physical topology, a network has a logical topology that describes the path that a signal follows on a network. The logical and physical topologies of a network may be the same or different.

Token ring is the most dramatic example of a network having different physical and logical topologies. Figure 28.1 illustrates how computers are connected on a token ring. Each computer transmits signals to the receiver on the next computer. In this way, signals travel through each station on the cabling system, eventually completing a trip back to the station that originated them. Recall that a logical topology describes the manner in which signals travel on the network. It is easy to see why token ring networks have a *ring* logical topology.

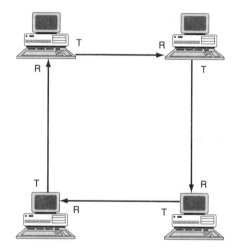

T = TRANSMIT
R = RECEIVE

Figure 28.1
Logical topology of a token-ring network.

Token-ring networks, however, are never physically wired in rings. Hubs are used instead, and each computer is cabled to the hub by a drop cable. Figure 28.2 shows how the computers and cables are arranged. Notice the way the cables are connected within the hub so that the transmitter side of one computer connects to the receiver of the next computer. This is exactly the same logical relationship we saw in Figure 28.1, and the logical topology is still a ring.

Due to the manner in which each computer is cabled individually to a hub, however, the physical topology of a token ring is a star.

Coax Ethernet is an example of a bus network where every station is connected to every other station in a multi-point physical topology. Also, every Ethernet station broadcasts signals to every other station, resulting in a bus logical topology as well. Ethernet, therefore, has a physical bus topology and a logical bus topology (see fig. 28.3).

A 10BASE-T Ethernet uses UTP cable and hub-based wiring, but it remains a logical bus because devices continue to communicate using multi-point communication. A 10BASE-T Ethernet, therefore, is a physical star but a logical bus.

 Note The following are some rules of thumb for distinguishing between physical and logical:

■ If you can see it or touch it, it is physical.

■ If you can't see it or touch it, it is logical.

The following are rules of thumb for distinguishing between bus and ring networks:

■ If signals from each computer are received by every other computer, the network is a bus.

■ If each computer receives signals from only one other computer, the network is a ring.

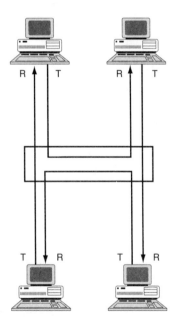

T = TRANSMIT
R = RECEIVE

Figure 28.2
A logical ring is configured as a physical star.

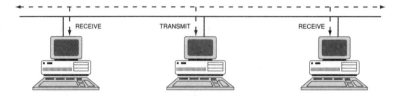

Figure 28.3
Ethernet is both a physical and a logical bus.

Media Access Control

Any given media channel can support only one signal at a time. If two computers transmit on the channel at the same time, their signals will interfere with each other, much as voices interfere when two people speak at the same time. Media access control is the process of controlling access to the media so that interference cannot take place.

This section discusses three forms of media access control:

■ Contention

■ Token passing

■ Polling

Contention

With contention-based access control, any computer can transmit at any time. This system breaks down when two computers attempt to transmit at the same time, in which case a collision occurs (see fig. 28.4). Eventually, when a network gets busy enough, most attempts to transmit result in collisions and little effective communication can take place.

Mechanisms, therefore, are usually put into place to minimize the effects of collisions. One mechanism is *carrier sensing*, in which each computer listens to the network before attempting to

transmit. If the network is busy, the computer refrains from transmitting until the network is quiet. This simple "listen before talking" strategy can significantly reduce collisions.

Another mechanism is *carrier detection*. With this strategy, computers continue to listen to the network as they are transmitting. If a computer detects another signal that interferes with the signal it is sending, it will stop transmitting. Both computers then wait a random amount of time and attempt to retransmit. Unless the network is extremely busy, carrier detection along with carrier sensing can manage a large volume of transmissions.

Both of these mechanisms used together form the protocol used in all types of Ethernet, which is called *Carrier Sense Multiple Access with Collision Detection* (CSMA/CD).

Apple's LocalTalk networks uses the protocol *Carrier Sense Multiple Access with Collision Avoidance* (CSMA/CA). *Collision Avoidance* uses additional techniques to further reduce the likelihood of collisions.

Note According to the course definitions, contention is an access-control *method*. CSMA/CD and CSMA/CA are *protocols* that incorporate contention-access methods.

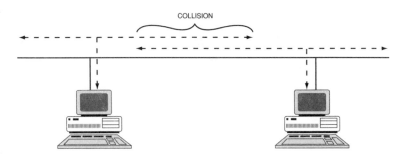

Figure 28.4

A collision on a contention-based network.

The following summarizes the characteristics of contention-access controls:

- Pure contention systems permit all stations to transmit whenever they want (although mechanisms are virtually always in place to limit transmission).

- Collisions always occur at some level on contention-based networks, with the number increasing geometrically as transmissions increase.

- CSMA/CD and CSMA/CA are two protocols that reduce the damage caused by collisions.

Although it sounds as if contention methods are unworkable due to the damage caused by collisions, contention (in particular CSMA/CD) is the most popular media access control method on LANs in the form of Ethernet. (In fact, no currently employed LAN standards utilize pure contention access control without adding some mechanism to reduce the incidence of collisions.)

Contention is a simple protocol that can be managed with simple software and hardware. Unless traffic levels exceed about 30 percent of bandwidth, contention works quite well. Contention-based networks offer excellent performance at low cost.

Because collisions occur at unpredictable intervals, however, no computer is guaranteed the capability

to transmit at any given time. Contention-based networks are called "probabalistic" because a computer's chance of being permitted to transmit cannot be predicted.

Collisions increase in frequency as more computers use the network. When the number of computers on the network climbs to an unmanageable amount, collisions dominate network traffic and few frames are transmitted without error.

All computers on a contention-based network are equal. Consequently, it is not possible to assign certain computers higher priorities and therefore greater access to the network.

 This course recommends contention access control for networks that experience bursty traffic—that is, large intermittent file transfers—and have relatively few computers.

Token Passing

Token passing utilizes a frame called a *token*, which circulates around the network. A computer that needs to transmit must wait until it receives the token frame, at which time it is permitted to transmit. When the computer is finished transmitting, it passes the token frame to the next station on the network. Figure 28.5 shows how token passing is implemented on a token-ring network.

Figure 28.5
Token passing.

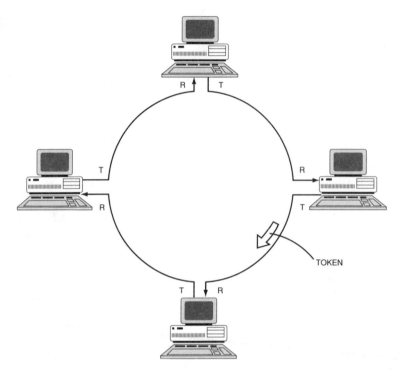

Several network standards employ token passing access control:

■ The most common is token ring, defined by IEEE standard 802.5.

■ IEEE standard 802.4 defines a bus network that also employs token passing. This standard is implemented only infrequently.

■ FDDI is a 100 Mbps fiber-optic network standard that uses token passing and rings in much the same manner as 802.5 Token Ring.

Token passing methods can use station priorities and other methods to prevent any one station from monopolizing the network. Because each computer has a chance to transmit each time the token travels around the network, each station is guaranteed a chance to transmit at some minimum time interval.

 Note   Token passing is more appropriate than contention under the following conditions:

■ When the network is carrying time-critical data. Because token passing results in more predictable delivery, token passing is called deterministic.

■ When the network experiences heavy utilization. Performance typically falls off more gracefully with a token passing network than with a contention-based network. Token passing networks cannot become gridlocked due to excessive numbers of collisions.

■ When some stations should have higher priority than others. Some token passing schemes support priority assignments.

Comparing Contention and Token Passing

As an access control mechanism, token passing appears to be clearly superior to contention. You will find, however, that Ethernet, by far the dominant LAN standard, has achieved its prominence while firmly wedded to contention access control.

Token passing requires a variety of complex control mechanisms to make it work well. The hardware required is considerably more expensive than the hardware required to implement the much simpler contention mechanisms. The higher cost of token passing networks is difficult to justify unless the special features are required.

Because token passing networks are designed for high reliability, it is common to build network diagnostic and troubleshooting capabilities into the network hardware. This further increases the costs of token passing networks. Organizations must decide whether this additional reliability is worth the extra cost.

Conversely, though token passing networks perform better than contention-based networks when traffic levels are high, contention networks have superior performance under lighter loading conditions. The process of passing the token around (and other maintenance operations) eats into the available bandwidth. As a result, a 10 Mbps Ethernet and a 16 Mbps token ring perform comparably under light loading conditions, but the Ethernet costs considerably less. Figure 28.6 illustrates the performance characteristics you can expect from each access control method. (This figure reproduces the graph used for the course, and implies that token passing throughput will eventually reach a zero level, which cannot, in fact, happen, regardless of the loading conditions. Although a station's access to the network may be limited, access is guaranteed with each circuit of the token.)

 Note The course materials emphasize that the comparisons being stated consider only pure contention-based networks, not networks that employ collision reduction schemes such as Ethernet. As noted, however, no current LAN standards employ contention as a media access control method without adding collision reduction techniques.

Polling

Polling is an access control method that employs a central device to regulate all access to the network. Polling is the most common access control method employed with mainframe computer networks.

The central device, called a *primary*, requests data from devices on the network, called *secondaries*. After it is *polled*, a secondary can transmit an amount of data that is determined by the protocols employed on the network. A secondary device cannot transmit unless it is polled by the primary.

Polling guarantees each device fair access to the network, and is suitable for use with time-critical data. In fact, polling has many of the advantages of token passing:

- Access times are predictable. Access is, therefore, deterministic.

- Priorities can be assigned.

- Collisions are eliminated.

A significant difference between polling and token passing is that polling centralizes control. This centralization can be an advantage from a management standpoint, but introduces a single point of failure. If the central control mechanism fails, the network stops functioning. Token passing uses more distributed control functions that are less subject to single points of failure.

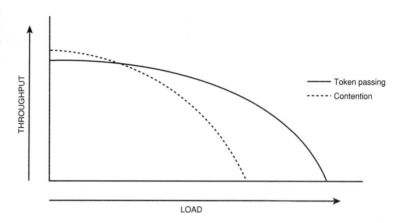

Figure 28.6
Comparison of contention and token passing.

Because polling centralizes control, secondary devices cannot communicate directly with other secondary devices. Rather, they must use the primary as an intermediary.

Furthermore, because the primary must poll each secondary—whether or not the secondary has data to transmit—polling wastes large amounts of network bandwidth. This can result in excessive delays as some secondaries wait while others are polled.

Summary of Access Control Methods

Access Control Method	Advantages	Considerations
Contention	Simple software.	Access is probalistic (not guaranteed).
	Once access is gained, device has complete control of the medium.	No priority mechanism.
		Collisions increase geometrically with demand.
Token passing	Each device is guaranteed media access (deterministic).	More complex software and hardware.
	Priorities might be assigned.	Might require a central control device.
	Collisions are eliminated.	
	High throughput under heavy load.	

Access Control Method	Advantages	Considerations
Polling	Each device is guaranteed media access (deterministic).	Polling uses significant portion of network bandwidth.
	Priorities might be assigned.	Polling requires bandwidth overhead, even for devices that have nothing to transmit.
	Collisions are eliminated.	

Addressing

The data link layer maintains device addresses that enable messages to be sent to a particular device. The addresses used are called *physical device addresses*, which are unique addresses associated with the networking hardware in the computer. In most cases (for example, Ethernet and token ring) the physical device address is burned into the network interface card at the time the card is manufactured.

The standards that apply to a particular network determine the format of the address. Because the address format is associated with the media access control method being used, physical device addresses are frequently referred to as *MAC addresses.*

The device address is not actually used to route a message to a specific device. Frames on LANs are typically transmitted so that they are available to all devices on the network. Each device reads each frame far enough to determine the device address to which the frame is addressed. If the frame's destination address matches the device's own physical address, the rest of the frame will be received. If the addresses do not match, the remainder of the frame is ignored.

As Chapter 26, "Transmission Media Connections," explains, bridges can be used to divide large networks into several smaller ones. Bridges use physical device addresses to determine which frames should remain on the current network segment and which should be forwarded to devices on other network segments. Some bridges must be programmed with the device addresses for each attached network segment, but transparent or learning bridges can learn addresses by analyzing network traffic.

Because bridges utilize physical device addresses to manage frame routing, they function at the level of the data link layer and are data link layer connectivity devices.

Transmission Synchronization

Chapter 27 introduces the need to synchronize bit transmissions between sending and receiving devices. The data link layer, however, operates on data after the bits have been assembled to form characters, frames, or other data groups. At the data link layer, it is also necessary to synchronize frame transmissions. This section discusses three mechanisms:

- Asynchronous

- Synchronous

- Isochronous

Asynchronous Transmission

Asynchronous transmission does not use a clocking mechanism to keep the sending and receiving devices synchronized. Instead, bit synchronization is used to synchronize the devices for each frame that is transmitted.

Each frame begins with a start bit that enables the receiving device to adjust to the timing of the transmitted signal. Messages are kept short so that the sending and receiving devices do not drift out of synchronization for the duration of the message. Asynchronous transmission is most frequently used to transmit character data and is ideally suited to environments where characters are transmitted at irregular intervals, such as when users are typing in character data.

Figure 28.7 illustrates the structure of a typical frame used to transmit character data. This frame has four components:

- **A start bit.** Signals that a frame is starting and enables the receiving device to synchronize itself with the message.

- **Data bits.** Consist of 7 or 8 bits when character data is being transmitted.

- **A parity bit.** Optionally used as a crude method of detecting transmission errors.

- **A stop bit or bits.** Signal the end of the data frame.

Error detection in asynchronous transmission makes use of the parity bit. Several schemes are available for using the parity bit. The most common include the following:

- **Even parity.** The parity bit is set to ensure that an even number of 1 bits are sent. If the data field has three 1's, the parity bit will be set to 1 to produce a total of four 1 bits.

- **Odd parity.** The parity bit is set to ensure that an odd number of 1 bits are sent. If the data field has three 1's, the parity bit will be set to 0 to produce a total of three 0 bits.

Parity techniques can detect errors that affect one bit. They might, however, be unable to detect errors that affect two or more bits.

Asynchronous transmission is a simple, inexpensive technology ideally suited for transmitting small frames at irregular intervals.

Because start, stop, and parity bits must be added to each character to be transmitted, however, overhead for asynchronous transmission is high, in the neighborhood of 20 to 30 percent. This wastes bandwidth and makes asynchronous transmission undesirable for transmitting large amounts of data.

Asynchronous transmission is frequently used for PC-to-PC and terminal-to-host communication. Data in these environments is often of the bursty, character-oriented nature that is ideal for asynchronous communication. In both cases, it is also generally desirable to reduce costs of communication hardware, which is best achieved with asynchronous transmission.

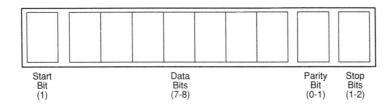

Figure 28.7
Structure of an asynchronous frame.

Synchronous Transmission

Communication can be made more efficient if the clocks on the transmitting and receiving devices are synchronized. This synchronization is accomplished in two ways:

- By transmitting synchronization signals with data. Some data encoding techniques, by guaranteeing a signal transition with each bit transmitted, are inherently self-clocking.

- By using a separate communication channel to carry clock signals, a technique that can function with any signal encoding technique.

Figure 28.8 illustrates two possible structures of messages associated with synchronous transmission.

Both transmissions begin with a series of *synch signals*, which notify the receiver of the beginning of a frame. Synch signals generally utilize a bit pattern that cannot appear elsewhere in messages, ensuring that they will always be distinct and easy for the receiver to recognize.

A wide variety of data types can be transmitted. Figure 28.8 illustrates both character-oriented and bit-oriented data. Notice that multiple characters or long series of bits can be transmitted in a single data frame. Because the transmitter and receiver remain in synchronization for the duration of the transmission, frames may be of great length.

When frames are longer, parity is no longer a suitable method of detecting error. If errors are occurring, it is more likely that multiple bits will be affected and that parity techniques will not report an error properly. The technique used with synchronous transmission is the *cyclic redundancy check* (CRC). The transmitter uses an algorithm to calculate a CRC value that summarizes the entire value of the data bits. This CRC value is appended to the data frame. The receiver uses the same algorithm, recalculates the CRC, and compares the CRC in the frame to the value it has calculated. If the values match, it is virtually certain that the frame was transmitted without error.

An *end bit pattern* unambiguously indicates the end of a frame. As with the synch bits, the end bit pattern is frequently a pattern that cannot appear in the body of the data frame, eliminating confusion on the part of the receiver.

Figure 28.8
Structures of synchronous transmissions.

When synchronous transmission links are idle, it is common to transmit *fill bits* that keep the devices synchronized, eliminating the need to resynchronize devices when a new frame is transmitted.

Synchronous transmission has many advantages over asynchronous transmission. Overhead bits (synch, CRC, and end) are a smaller proportion of the overall data frame, making synchronous transmission far more efficient in its use of bandwidth. Synchronization enables the systems to utilize higher speeds and to improve error detection.

The disadvantage of synchronous transmission is primarily higher cost due to the more complex circuitry required. Consequently, synchronous transmission is employed primarily when high volumes of data must be transmitted.

Synchronous transmission is frequently used in mainframe-to-mainframe communication, and is also used to achieve high efficiency levels on LANs. Both Ethernet and token ring, for example, utilize self-clocking signals.

Isochronous Transmission

Isochronous transmission employs a common device that supplies a clocking signal shared by all devices on the network. The clocking device creates time slots. Devices with data to transmit monitor the network and insert data into open time slots as they become available. A given time slot can be filled to capacity with multiple frames.

Isochronous transmission guarantees transmission rates, is deterministic, and has low overhead. The technique, however, introduces a single point of failure; it is necessary to ensure that the clocking device is fault-tolerant.

Connection Services

Network connection services provide a variety of functions:

- Flow control determines the amount of data that can be transmitted in a given time period. Flow control prevents the transmitting device from overwhelming the receiver. Flow control can take place at several protocol levels, including the LLC sublayer.

- Error control detects errors in received frames and requests retransmission of frames. Error control is a function of the LLC sublayer.

- Sequence control enables receivers to reassemble data frames into their original order. Frame size is limited, and packet fragmentation and reassembly is necessary to transmit large messages. Sequence control is a function of the network layer.

Three types of connection services provide different combinations of the above services:

- **Unacknowledged connectionless services.** Provide no flow, error, or sequence control. When required, these services must be provided by higher protocol layers. Unacknowledge connectionless service provides high performance when network communication can be safely assumed to be reliable (as on most LANs).

- **Connection-oriented services.** Provide flow, error, and sequence control through use of acknowledgments. Connection-oriented services have higher overhead, reducing performance but improving reliability when network reliability is in question (as on most WANs).

■ **Acknowledged connectionless services.** Use acknowledgments to provide flow and error control on point-to-point connections.

Flow Control at the LLC Sublayer

Flow control prevents receiving devices from being overwhelmed by faster transmitting devices. Two common techniques of flow control are guaranteed rate flow control and window flow control.

Guaranteed Rate Flow Control

With *guaranteed rate flow control*, the sending and receiving devices negotiate a mutually acceptable transmission rate. Typically, this transmission rate holds constant for the duration of a communication session.

To ensure that frames are received without error, some protocols require the receiver to acknowledge each frame as it is processed. If no error is detected, an acknowledgment frame is returned to the transmitter, instructing it to send the next frame. If errors are detected, the receiver does one of two things: it sends a retransmission request, or it simply waits until the transmitter times out and retransmits the frame.

Essentially, guaranteed rate flow control assumes that the receiver processes one message unit (bit or frame) for each unit transmitted. This rather inflexible approach often fails to make the most efficient use of transmitter, receiver, and media channel capacities.

Window Flow Control

Buffering is a technique that enables transmitters and receivers to operate with more flexibility. Buffers consist of memory that can receive data from the network and hold it until the receiver can process the data and acknowledge that it has been received.

Windowing is a technique that enables the transmitter to send several data frames prior to receiving acknowledgment from the receiver. Several frames may be buffered in the receiver as they are processed. The number of frames a transmitter can send without receiving an acknowledgment is known as a *window*.

Static window flow control limits the window size to a specific number of frames, usually defined by the number of frames that can fit in the receiver's input buffer. If the window size is 7, the transmitter can have as many as seven outstanding frames. An eighth frame cannot be transmitted, however, until one of the outstanding frames is acknowledged (see fig. 28.9).

Dynamic window flow control improves efficiency by enabling the communicating devices to adjust the window size. Other terms for this technique are *floating* or *sliding* windows. One dynamic window technique enables the receiver to send out a *choke frame* when its input buffer is nearing capacity. This choke frame signals the transmitter to slow down. After the transmitter adjusts its transmission rate downward, it will slowly increase its transmission rate until it receives another choke frame. In this way, bandwidth utilization is optimized.

Error Control

Two LLC error conditions can exist:

■ When CRC errors are detected

■ When expected acknowledgments are not received

Recall from earlier in this chapter that synchronous data frames incorporate a *cyclic redundancy check* (CRC) field that can be used to detect transmission errors. When a receiving device detects a CRC error, it can transmit a *negative acknowledgment* (NAK) that requests retransmission of the frame.

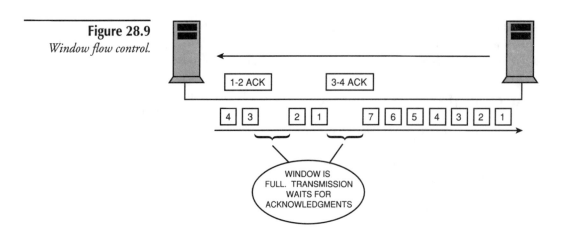

Figure 28.9
Window flow control.

When acknowledged services are employed, the transmitter expects *acknowledgment* (ACK) frames from the receiver for each frame (or a group of frames in a windowed protocol). When a specified interval of time expires without an acknowledgment, the transmitter assumes that the frame was lost and retransmits it.

Questions

1. Which of the following statements is true?

   ○ A. Logical topologies are determined by the cabling system.

   ○ B. A physical bus network may be a logical ring.

   ○ C. A physical star network can be a logical ring.

   ○ D. Contention can be used as an access control medium on a physical ring.

2. Which protocol layer enables multiple devices to share the transmission medium?

   ○ A. Physical

   ○ B. MAC

   ○ C. LLC

   ○ D. Network

3. Which of the following is an error control mechanism?

   ○ A. Contention

   ○ B. Synchronous transmission

   ○ C. CRC

   ○ D. LLC

4. Which of the following layers establishes and maintains a link between communicating devices?

   ○ A. Physical

   ○ B. MAC

   ○ C. LLC

   ○ D. Network

5. Which of the following techniques uses network bandwidth most efficiently?

   ○ A. Static window flow control

   ○ B. Guaranteed rate flow control

   ○ C. Dynamic rate flow control

   ○ D. Dynamic window flow control

6. Which of the following access methods is centrally managed?

   ○ A. Contention

   ○ B. Token passing

   ○ C. Polling

   ○ D. Collision detection

7. Which TWO of the following services provides flow control?

   ☐ A. Acknowledged connectionless

   ☐ B. Unacknowledged connectionless

   ☐ C. Unacknowledged connection-oriented

   ☐ D. Connection-oriented

8. Which of the following access control methods is probabalistic?

   ○ A. Polling

   ○ B. Contention

   ○ C. Token passing

   ○ D. Sliding window

9. Which of the following methods relies on the internal clocks of transmitting and receiving devices?

   ○ A. Synchronous

   ○ B. Isochronous

   ○ C. Asynchronous

   ○ D. Nonsynchronous

10. Which of the following connectivity devices functions at the data link layer?

   ○ A. Repeater

   ○ B. Router

   ○ C. Hub

   ○ D. Bridge

Answers

1. C	6. C
2. B	7. A, D
3. C	8. B
4. C	9. C
5. D	10. D

OSI Network Layer Concepts

The data link layer deals with communication between devices on the same network. Physical device addresses are used to identify data frames, and it is the responsibility of each device to monitor the network and receive frames that are addressed to that device.

The network layer involves communication with devices on logically separate networks that are connected to form internetworks. Because internetworks can be large and can be built of different types of networks, the network layer utilizes routing algorithms that can be used to guide packets from their source to their destination networks.

A key element of the network layer is that each network in the internetwork is assigned a network address that can be used to route packets. The nature of those addresses and how they are used to route packets defines the majority of topics in this chapter, which include the following:

- Addressing
- Switching
- Routing algorithms
- Connection services
- Gateway services

Addressing

You have already encountered the use of physical device addresses, which uniquely identify each device on a network. The network layer makes use of two additional address types, as follows:

- *Logical network addresses,* which are used to route packets to specific networks on the internetwork
- *Services addresses,* which route packets to specific processes running on the destination device

Logical Network Addresses

Logical network addresses are assigned when the networks are configured. If you have installed NetWare servers, you are familiar with the process of assigning a logical network address to each LAN that is attached to the server. One of the tasks a network installer must accomplish is to make sure that each network address is unique on a given

internetwork. Network addresses enable routers to forward frames through the internetwork to the appropriate networks.

Service Addresses

The operating systems on most computers are capable of running several processes at once. When a packet arrives, it is necessary to determine which process on the computer should receive the data in the packet. This is achieved by assigning service addresses, which identify upper-layer processes and protocols. These service addresses are included with the physical and logical network addresses in the data frame. (Some protocols refer to service addresses as *sockets* or *ports.*)

Some service addresses, called *well-known addresses,* are universally defined for a given type of network. Other service addresses are defined by the vendors of network products.

Addressing Summary

A possible format of the address information for a packet is shown in figure 29.1. Three address components appear, as follows:

- *Physical (MAC) network addresses* identify a particular device as the source or destination of a frame.
- *Logical network addresses* identify a particular network on the internetwork as the source or destination of a packet.
- *Service addresses* identify a process or protocol on the computer that is the source or destination of a packet.

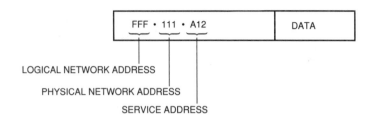

Figure 29.1
Address information showing physical and logical network addresses with a service address.

Switching

Many internetworks include redundant data paths that may be used to route messages. The following switching techniques may be used to route messages:

■ Circuit switching

■ Message switching

■ Packet switching

Circuit Switching

As shown in figure 29.2, *circuit switching* establishes a path that remains fixed for the duration of a connection. Much as telephone switching equipment establishes a route between your telephone on the East Coast and a telephone you dial on the West Coast, circuit switching networks establish a path through the internetwork when the devices initiate a conversation.

Circuit switching provides devices with a dedicated path and a well-defined bandwidth.

Circuit switching is not without disadvantages, however. The process of establishing a connection between devices may be time-consuming. Because other traffic cannot share the dedicated media path, bandwidth may be inefficiently utilized. Because circuit switching networks must have a surplus of bandwidth, they tend to be expensive to construct.

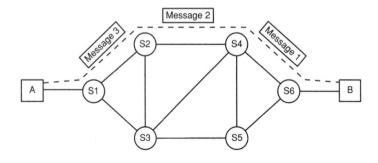

Figure 29.2
Circuit switching.

Message Switching

Message switching treats each message as an independent entity. Each message carries address information that describes the message's destination. This information is used at each switch to transfer the message to the next switch in its route. Message switches are programmed with information concerning other switches in the network that can be used to forward messages to their destinations. They may also be programmed with information about the most efficient routes. Depending on network conditions, different messages may be sent through the network by different routes, as shown in figure 29.3.

Message switching transfers the complete message from one switch to the next switch, where the message is stored before it is forwarded another time. Because each message is stored before it is sent on to the next switch, this type of network is frequently called a *store-and-forward* network. The message switches are often general-purpose computers. They must be equipped with sufficient storage (usually hard drives) to enable them to store messages until it is possible to forward them.

Electronic mail is a common application for message switching. Some delay is permissible when delivering mail, unlike the requirements when two computers are exchanging data in real time. Message switching uses relatively low-cost devices to forward messages and can function well with relatively slow communication channels. Other applications for message switching include group applications such as workflow, calendaring, and groupware.

Message switching has several advantages, as follows:

- Data channels are shared among communicating devices, improving the efficiency of using available bandwidth.

- Message switches can store messages until a channel becomes available, reducing sensitivity to network congestion.

- Message priorities may be used to manage network traffic.

- Broadcast addressing uses network bandwidth more efficiently by delivering messages to multiple destinations.

The chief disadvantage of message switching is that it is unsuitable to real-time applications, including data communication, video, and audio.

Figure 29.3

Message switching.

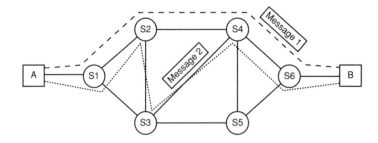

Packet Switching

In *package switching*, messages are divided into smaller packets. Each packet includes source and destination address information so that individual packets can be routed through the internetwork independently. As you can see in figure 29.4, the packets that make up a message may take very different routes through the internetwork.

So far, this looks a lot like message switching. The distinguishing characteristic is that packets are restricted to a size that enables the switching devices to manage the packet data entirely in memory, without the need to store the data temporarily on disk. Packet switching, therefore, routes packets through the network much more rapidly and efficiently than is possible with message switching.

Several methods of packet switching exist. The following two are discussed in this course:

- Datagram
- Virtual circuit

Datagram Packet Switching

Datagram services treat each packet as an independent message. Each packet is routed through the internetwork independently, and each switch node decides which network segment should be used for the next step in the packet's route. This capability enables switches to bypass busy segments and take other steps to speed packets through the internetwork. This is the specific approach that was shown in figure 29.4.

Datagrams are frequently used on LANs. Network layer protocols are responsible for delivering the frame to the appropriate network. Then, because each datagram includes destination address information, devices on the local network can recognize and receive datagrams that they are intended to receive.

> **Note** Packet switching matches the need to transmit large messages with the fairly small frame size that can be accommodated by the physical layer. The network layer is responsible for fragmenting messages from upper layers into smaller datagrams that are appropriate for the physical layer. The network layer is also responsible for reconstructing messages from datagrams as they are received.

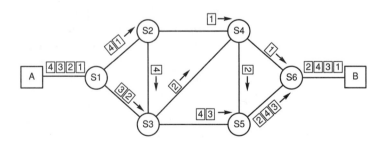

Figure 29.4
Packet switching.

Virtual Circuit Packet Switching

Virtual circuits operate by establishing a formal connection between two devices that are in communication. When devices begin a session, they negotiate communication parameters, such as maximum message size, communication windows, network paths, and so forth. This negotiation establishes a *virtual circuit*, a well-defined path through the internetwork through which the devices communicate. This virtual circuit generally remains in effect until the devices stop communicating.

Virtual circuits are distinguished by the establishment of a logical connection. *Virtual* means that the network behaves as though a dedicated physical circuit has been established between the devices that are communicating. Even though no such physical circuit exists, the network presents the appearance of a physical connection so far as the devices at the ends of the circuit are concerned.

Virtual circuits are frequently employed in conjunction with connection-oriented services, which are discussed later in this chapter.

Advantages of Packet Switching

Packet switching optimizes the use of bandwidth by enabling many devices to route packets through the same network channels. At any given time, a switch may be routing packets to several different destination devices, adjusting the routes as required to achieve the best efficiency possible at the present time.

Because entire messages are not stored at the switches prior to forwarding, transmission delays are significantly less than delays encountered with message switching.

Although the switching devices do not need to be equipped with large amounts of hard drive capacity, they might need a significant amount of real-time memory. Also, they must have sufficient processing power to run the more complex routing protocols that are required for packet switching. Among the new complexities is the need to recognize when packets have been lost so that retransmission can be requested.

Routing Algorithms

Routing is the process of forwarding messages through switching networks. In some cases, routing information is programmed into switching devices. However, preprogrammed switches cannot adjust to changing network conditions. Most routing devices, therefore, have the capability of discovering routes through the internetwork and storing the route information in route tables.

Route tables do not store only path information. They also store estimates of the time taken to send a message through a given route. This time estimate is known as the *cost* of a particular path. There are several methods of estimating routing costs, as follows:

- *Hop count* describes the number of routers that a message would cross before it reaches its destination. If all hops are assumed to take the same amount of time, the optimum path is the path with the smallest hop count.

- *Tic count* is an actual time estimate, where a *tic* is a time unit that is defined by the routing implementation.

- *Relative expense* is any defined measure of the cost (including the monetary cost) to use a given link.

After costs are established, routers can select routes either statically or dynamically, as follows:

- *Static route selection* uses routes that have been programmed in by the network administrator.

- *Dynamic route selection* uses routing cost information to select the most cost-effective route for a given packet. As network conditions change and are reflected in routing tables, the router can select different paths to maintain low costs.

Two methods of route discovery are discussed in this course: distance vector and link-state.

Distance Vector Routing

Distance vector routers advertise their presence to other routers on the network. Periodically, each router on the network will broadcast the information in its routing table. This information can be used by other routers to update their own router tables.

Figure 29.5 illustrates how the process works. In the figure, server S3 learns that server S2 can reach server S1 in three hops. Because Server S3 knows that Server S2 is one hop away, Server S3 knows that its cost to reach Server S1 through Server S2 is two hops.

Distance vector routing is an effective algorithm, but can be fairly inefficient. Because changes must ripple through the network from router to router, it might take a while for a change to become known to all routers on the network. In addition, the frequent broadcasts of routing information produce high levels of network traffic that can hurt performance on larger networks.

 Distance vector routing is the standard routing algorithm for NetWare and is used by the NetWare *Routing Information Protocol* (RIP). You can observe routing information including hop counts by typing **TRACK ON** at a NetWare 3.*x* or 4.*x* server console. Type **TRACK OFF** to cancel the display of routing information.

Figure 29.5

Distance vector routing.

Link-State Routing

Link-state routing reduces the network traffic required to update routing tables. Routers that are newly attached to the network can request routing information from a nearby router.

After routers have exchanged routing information about the network, routers broadcast messages only when something has changed. These messages contain information about the state of each link the router has with other routers on the network. Because routers keep each other updated, complete network routing updates are needed infrequently.

 Note   Link-state routing is employed by Novell's recently introduced *Network Link-State Protocol* (NLSP), which may be substituted for RIP on NetWare 3.*x* and 4.*x* servers.

Connection Services

In Chapter 28, you were introduced to three types of connection services, as follows:

- *Unacknowledged connectionless services*, which provide no flow control, error detection, or packet sequence control

- *Connection-oriented services*, which provide flow control and error detection with acknowledgments

- *Acknowledged connectionless services*, which use acknowledgments to provide flow and error control

The network layer also provides connection-oriented services, including flow control, error detection, and acknowledgments. Network acknowledgments are employed to provide flow control, error detection, and packet sequence control.

Network Layer Flow Control

The data link layer manages flow control based on the capacities of the devices that are in communication.

The network layer manages flow control to avoid congestion on the network. As you learned in the discussion about routing, the network layer determines the number of packets that will be sent through a given route. By routing packets around busy links, available network bandwidth is used more effectively and congestion is reduced. For this reason, network flow control is often referred to as *congestion control.*

Network layer flow control can permit devices to negotiate a guaranteed data rate. Static and dynamic windows may also be employed.

Receiving devices can control congestion by delaying before sending acknowledgments. Under these circumstances, the sender may assume that the packet was lost and retransmit it. To prevent unnecessary retransmission, some protocols define packets that signal congestion and enable receiving devices to explicitly request delays in transmission.

Network Layer Error Control

A variety of error conditions may be detected at the network layer.

Errors in data are typically detected using CRC algorithms. Because packet header information changes at each hop (addresses change), CRC values must be recalculated by each router.

Although the network layer can implement detection of lost and duplicate packets, these functions are typically handled by the transport layer.

Packet Sequence Control

Recall that packet switching networks may route packets by varying routes. As a result, the packets for a message might arrive at their final destination out of order. This can be the case for both datagram and connection-oriented services.

The network layer may be configured to handle packet sequence control, although that function is generally handled at the transport layer.

Gateway Services

Routers can handle interconnection of networks whose protocols function in similar ways. When the rules are sufficiently different on the two networks, however, a more powerful device is required.

A *gateway* is a device that can reconcile the different rules that are used on two different networks. Gateways are commonly required to connect LANs into mainframe networks, which have completely different protocol architectures than LANs. Mainframe networks, such as IBM's SNA, for example, do not use the same device address schemes as LANs employ (they differ in many other ways as well). It is necessary to "fool" the mainframe network into thinking that mainframe devices are on the LAN, and it is also necessary to make the mainframe look like a LAN, so far as devices on the LAN are concerned.

 Gateways may be implemented at the network layer or at higher layers in the OSI model, depending on where the protocol translation is required.

Questions

Because the material is so intertwined, study questions for this chapter can be found at the end of Chapter 33.

OSI Transport Layer Concepts

The transport layer is the next layer of the OSI model. Lower layer protocols are concerned with delivering messages between devices. The transport layer, however, is concerned with delivering messages between processes running on those devices. Whenever a device is using a multi-tasking operating system, and multiple processes might be running on the device, it becomes essential that messages be delivered from one process on the transmitting device to the correct process on the receiving device.

The transport layer can implement procedures to ensure the reliable delivery of those segments to their destination devices. The term "reliable" does not mean that errors cannot occur, only that if errors occur, they will be detected. If errors such as lost data are detected, the transport layer either requests retransmission or notifies upper layer protocols so that they can take corrective action.

The transport layer enables upper layer protocols to interface with the network, but hides the complexities of network operation from them. Among it's functions, the transport layer breaks large messages into segments that are suitable for network delivery.

The following transport layer topics are covered in this chapter:

- Addressing
- Address/name resolution
- Segment development
- Connection services

Addressing

Transport layer addressing is concerned with delivering messages from a specific process on one computer to the correct process running on the destination computer. Messages can be identified in two ways: connection identifiers and transaction identifiers.

Connection Identifiers

A connection identifier (connection ID) might also be called a socket or a port depending on the specific protocol implementation. The *connection identifier* labels each conversation and enables a process to communicate with processes running on other devices. A numeric identifier is assigned to each conversation. A service, running at higher OSI levels, identifies communications with a connection ID number that enables the transport layer to direct lower layer addressing and deliver the messages as required.

Transaction Identifiers

Connection identifiers are used when two devices are engaged in multiple exchanges of data. Transaction identifiers are used when the exchange is a one-time event consisting of a request and a response. Only this simple exchange is tracked, no multiple-message conversations that might be occurring between the devices are tracked.

Address/Name Resolution

Network addresses are always binary numbers, which are often 32 bits in length. These numbers can be expressed in decimal or hexadecimal notation to make them easier for humans to identify. Long decimal and hex numbers, however, are not as recognizable as words. For that reason, some network protocols implement a scheme of logical alphanumeric names that humans use when specifying network devices. These names are translated into numeric network addresses by a service on the network. This translation can be performed by individual network devices or by a central name server.

Service-Requester-Initiated Address/Name Resolution

With this method, a device that requires address information broadcasts a packet requesting the information for a given name, address, or service. The device that corresponds to the name, address, or service responds with the required information.

Service-Provider-Initiated Address/Name Resolution

This method employs a central directory server (also called a name server) that collects information which is broadcast by devices on the network. Devices that require name or address information can request it from the directory server.

Segment Development

When messages from higher-level protocols exceed the size allowed by a protocol stack for a segment, the transport layer divides outbound messages into segments of a suitable size. The transport layer also recombines incoming segments into message formats required by upper layers.

The transport layer also can combine multiple small messages into a single segment to improve network efficiency. As shown in figure 30.1, each message component is identified by a connection identifier (CID). The CID enables the transport layer of the receiving device to deliver each message to the proper process.

Connection Services

Some services can be performed at more than one layer of the OSI model. In addition to the data link and network layers, the transport layer can have some responsibility for connection services.

Segment Sequencing

One connection-oriented service provided by the transport layer is segment sequencing. When large messages are divided into segments for transport, the transport layer must resequence the segments when they are received prior to reassembling the original message.

Error Control

When segments are lost in transmission, or when segments have duplicate segment IDs, the transport layer must initiate error recovery. The following strategies are available:

- Unique segment sequence numbers

- Virtual circuits, permitting only one virtual circuit per session

- Timeouts removed from the network segments that have been misrouted and have remained on the network past a specified time

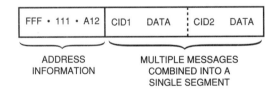

ADDRESS
INFORMATION

MULTIPLE MESSAGES
COMBINED INTO A
SINGLE SEGMENT

Figure 30.1
Identification of messages at transport layer.

The transport layer also detects corrupted segments by managing end-to-end error control using techniques such as checksums.

End-to-End Flow control

The transport layer uses acknowledgments to manage end-to-end flow control between two connected devices.

Besides negative acknowledgments, some transport layer protocols can request the retransmission of the most recent segments. These acknowledgments are called *go back n* or *selective repeat* acknowledgments.

Go back *n* acknowledgments request retransmission of the last *n* packets. Selective repeat acknowledgments can request retransmission of specific packets.

This approach is useful when the receiving device's buffers overflowed before it was able to warn the transmitting device to cease transmission.

Questions

You will find study questions for this chapter at the end of Chapter 33, "OSI Application Layer Concepts."

OSI Session Layer Concepts

The session layer manages dialogs between two computers by establishing, managing, and terminating communications.

The following two session layer topics are discussed in this chapter:

- *Dialog control*
- *Session administration*

Dialog Control

As illustrated in figure 31.1, dialogs can take three forms:

- **Simplex dialogs.** Involve one-way data transfers. An example is a fire alarm, which sends an alarm message to the fire station, but cannot (and does not need to) receive messages from the fire station.

- **Half-duplex dialogs.** Involve two-way data transfers in which the data flows in only one direction at a time. When one device has completed a transmission, it must "turn over" the medium to the other device so that it has a turn to transmit.

  CB radio operators, for example, converse on the same communication channel. When one operator is through transmitting he must release his transmit key so that the other operator may send a response.

- **Full-duplex dialogs.** Permit two-way simultaneous data transfers by providing each device with a separate communication channel. Voice telephones are full-duplex devices, and either party to a conversation may talk at any time. Most computer modems are capable of operating in full-duplex mode.

Costs rise for half- and full-duplex operation because the more complex the dialog technology is, the more expensive it is. Designers of

communications systems, therefore, generally use the simplest dialog mode that satisfies the communication requirements.

Half-duplex communication can result in wasted bandwidth during the intervals when communication is being turned around. On the other hand, full-duplex communication generally requires a greater bandwidth than half-duplex communication.

 Note The Novell course materials associate simplex transmission with broadcast transmission, and therefore imply that simplex transmission is used with multiple receivers. This implication is incorrect, as the above-mentioned example of the fire alarm shows.

Simplex transmission may indeed be implemented as a broadcast technology. Commercial radio is an example of broadcast simplex transmission.

A CB radio is, however, an example of half-duplex communication that also operates in a broadcast mode. Many operators may listen in to CB radio communications. Many operators may also reply to transmissions by waiting for a break in the dialog and pressing the transmit key.

For the purposes of this course, simplex transmissions are defined as providing broad area coverage with the potential for reaching large target audiences.

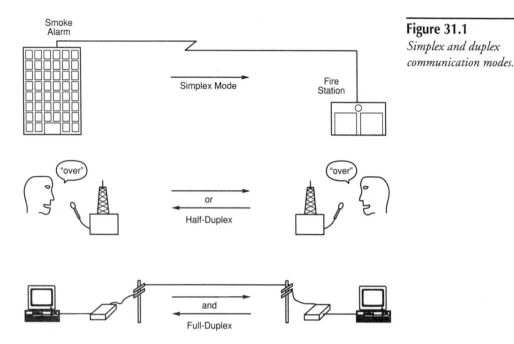

Figure 31.1
Simplex and duplex communication modes.

Session Administration

A *session* is a formal dialog between a service requester and a service provider. Sessions have at least three phases:

- **Connection establishment.** A service requester requests initiation of a service. During the setup process, communication is established and rules are agreed upon.

- **Data transfer.** Because of the rules agreed upon during setup, each party to the dialog knows what to expect. Communication is efficient and errors are easy to detect.

- **Connection release.** When the session is completed, the dialog is terminated in an orderly fashion.

Connection Establishment

Several tasks can be performed at the time a session is initiated:

- Specification of services that are required

- User login authentication and other security procedures

- Negotiation of protocols and protocol parameters

- Notification of connection IDs

- Establishment of dialog control, as well as acknowledgment of numbering, and retransmission procedures

Data Transfer

Once the connection has been established, the devices involved can initiate a dialog. Besides exchanging data, these devices exchange acknowledgments and other control data that manage the dialog.

The session layer can also incorporate protocols to resume dialogs that are interrupted. After a formal dialog has been established, devices recognize a lost connection whenever the connection has not been formally released. A device, therefore, realizes that a connection has been lost when it fails to receive an expected acknowledgment or data transmission.

Within a certain time period, two devices can reenter the session that was interrupted but not released.

Connection Release

This is an orderly process that shuts down communication and releases resources on the service provider.

Session Layer Topics and Methods

Dialog control	Simplex
	Half-duplex
	Full-Duplex
Session administration	Connection establishment
	Data transfer
	Connection release

Questions

Study questions for this chapter can be found at the end of Chapter 33.

OSI Presentation Layer Concepts

*T*he presentation layer deals with the syntax, or grammatical rules, needed when communicating between two computers.

This chapter discusses two major services performed at the presentation layer:

- *Translation of data from one form to another*

- *Encryption/decryption of data*

The name *presentation layer* has caused considerable confusion in the industry because some people mistakenly believe that this layer presents data to the user. However, the name has nothing to do with displaying data, which is performed instead by applications that are running above the application layer.

The presentation layer is so named because it presents a uniform data format to the application layer. As a matter of fact, this layer is not commonly implemented because most presentation layer functions are typically performed by applications.

Data Translation

An important goal to strive for when designing networks is to enable different types of computers to interchange data. Although this goal is seldom met completely, effective use of data translation techniques can make it possible for many types of computers to communicate.

The following discussion covers four forms of data translation: bit order, byte order, character code, and file syntax.

Bit Order

When binary numbers are transmitted through a network, they are sent one bit at a time. Consider the binary number 11110000. The transmitting computer could start at either end of the number:

■ It could start at the *most-significant digit* (the MSD, which is the highest value digit) and send a 1 first.

■ It could start at the *least-significant digit* (the LSD, which is the lowest value digit) and send a 0 first.

Unless the sending and receiving devices agree on bit-order conventions, they will change the values of the binary numbers that are being transmitted.

Byte Order Translation

A similar logic applies to byte orders. Complex values generally must be represented by more than one byte, but different computers use different conventions as to which byte should be transmitted first:

■ Intel microprocessors start with the least-significant byte. Because they start at the small end, they are called *little endian*.

■ Motorola microprocessors start with the most-significant byte and are called *big endian*.

Byte order translation might be needed to reconcile these differences.

Character Code Translation

Most computers use one of the following binary numbering schemes to represent character sets:

■ ASCII, the *American Standard Code for Information Interchange*, used to represent English characters on all microcomputers and most minicomputers (see fig. 32.1)

■ EBCDIC, the *Extended Binary Coded Decimal Interchange Code*, used to represent English characters on IBM mainframes (see fig. 32.2)

■ Shift-JIS, used to represent Japanese characters

7-Bit ASCII Character Set

8	7	6	5		0	0	0	0	0	0	0	0
					0	0	0	0	1	1	1	1
					0	0	1	1	0	0	1	1
					0	1	0	1	0	1	0	1
4	**3**	**2**	**1**									
0	0	0	0	NUL	DLE	SP	0	@	P	`	p
0	0	0	1	SOH	DC1	!	1	A	Q	a	q
0	0	1	0	STX	DC2	"	2	B	R	b	r
0	0	1	1	ETX	DC3	#	3	C	S	c	s
0	1	0	0	EOT	DC4	$	4	D	T	d	t
0	1	0	1	ENQ	NAK	%	5	E	U	e	u
0	1	1	0	ACK	SYN	&	6	F	V	f	v
0	1	1	1	BEL	ETB	'	7	G	W	g	w
1	0	0	0	BS	CAN	(	8	H	X	h	x
1	0	0	1	HT	EM	)	9	I	Y	i	y
1	0	1	0	LF	SUB	*	:	J	Z	j	z
1	0	1	1	VT	ESC	+	;	K	[	k	{
1	1	0	0	FF	FS	,	<	L	\	l	|
1	1	0	1	CR	GS	-	=	M	]	m	}
1	1	1	0	SO	RS	.	>	N	^	n	~
1	1	1	1	SI	US	/	?	O	_	o	DEL

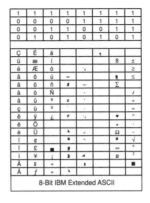

8-Bit IBM Extended ASCII

Figure 32.1
The ASCII character code.

Note Novell and other vendors are beginning to incorporate Unicode in their products. *Unicode*, a 16-bit code that can represent 65,536 characters in English and other languages, is organized into code pages devoted to the characters required for a given language, improving portability of products between different language environments.

File Syntax Translation

When file formats differ between computers, they require translation. Some situations that might require file format translation include:

- Copying files between a Macintosh and a DOS PC. Macintosh files actually consist of two related files called a *data fork* and a *resource fork*. PC files, on the other hand, consist of single file.

- Copying files between DOS PCs and Unix workstations.

Properly done, these translations can be completely transparent. NetWare, for example, enables DOS, Macintosh, and Unix users to share the same files on a NetWare server by using a feature called *name space support*.

Encryption

It is often desirable to ensure that data on a LAN is absolutely secure. Even if an eavesdropper were successful in listening in, sensitive data can be encrypted so that it is unusable.

Encryption techniques employ a form of reversible data scrambling that renders data unreadable without a key. A *key* is a code word or number that allows the encryption/decryption software to scramble and unscramble the data.

Given time, every encryption can be broken. High-speed computers make it feasible to crack many codes by simply trying different key values until the right one is found. A great deal of effort, therefore, has gone into creating powerful encryption algorithms boasting a low probability of failure.

Figure 32.2

The EBCDIC character code.

4321 \ 8765	0000	0001	0010	0011	0100	0101	0110	0111	1000	1001	1010	1011	1100	1101	1110	1111
0000	NUL	DLE	DS		SP	&	-									0
0001	SOH	DC1	SOS				/		a	j	~		A	J		1
0010	STX	DC2	FS	SYN					b	k	s		B	K	S	2
0011	ETX	DC3							c	l	t		C	L	T	3
0100	PF	RES	BYP	PN					d	m	u		D	M	U	4
0101	HT	NL	LF	RS					e	n	v		E	N	V	5
0110	LC	BS	EOB	UC					f	o	w		F	O	W	6
0111	DEL	IL	PRE	EOT					g	p	x		G	P	X	7
1000		CAN							h	q	y		H	Q	Y	8
1001		EM							i	r	z		I	R	Z	9
1010	SMM	CC	SM		¢	!	|	:								
1011	VT				.	$	,	#								
1100	FF	IFS		DC4	<	*	%	@								
1101	CR	IGS	ENQ	NAK	(	)	_	'								
1110	SO	IRS	ACK		+	;	>	=								
1111	SI	IUS	BEL	SUB	|	¬	?	"								

Two common techniques are the following:

- Private keys
- Public keys

Private Keys

Private keys use the same key to encrypt and decrypt the message. This has several disadvantages. The sender and receiver must be sure to inform each other of the key. If the key is intercepted, the message becomes vulnerable. Each time the key is changed, and private keys are changed often in case they are compromised, the new key must be communicated and is vulnerable to discovery.

Public Keys

A *public key* is used to encrypt messages, whereas a *private key* is used for decryption. The public key is created by a user by applying an algorithm to a private key, which is known only to the intended receiver of the message.

The sender of the message uses the public key to encrypt a message and does not know or need to know the private key. In fact, anyone who has a person's public key can encrypt a message for that person.

The receiver decrypts the message by combining the public key with the private key, known only to him- or herself.

The algorithms used for public key encryption are extremely complex and make it unlikely that even a super computer will stumble on the correct key within a reasonable period of time (your lifetime, for example). Nevertheless, the code makers are never far ahead of the code breakers, and more sophisticated encryption techniques are always under development.

Questions

Study questions for this chapter may be found at the end of Chapter 33, "OSI Application Layer Concepts."

OSI Application Layer Concepts

The application layer is concerned with providing services on the network. These services include file services, print services, database services, and the other services discussed in Chapter 23, "Network Services."

A common misunderstanding is that the application layer is responsible for running user applications such as word processors. This is not the case. The application layer, however, does provide an interface whereby applications can communicate with the network.

The application layer performs two functions related to the utilization of services on the network. One function involves the advertisement of available services. Another function involves the use of the services.

Advertising Services

To inform clients of services that are available, the application layer advertises the services to the network. You encountered the use of service addresses when the network layer was discussed in Chapter 29, "OSI Network Layer Concepts." These service addresses provide the mechanism that enables clients to communicate with services.

The application layer can employ *active* and *passive* methods of advertising services.

Active Service Advertisement

When servers actively advertise their services, they broadcast messages announcing the services they offer. Most protocols consider these service advertisements to be valid for a limited time. Unless the information is refreshed within a specified time, clients remove the information from their service tables.

Clients also can transmit messages that request specific services. Servers respond with a list of services they support.

 Note NetWare employs an active service advertisement protocol called the *Service Advertisement Protocol* (SAP).

Passive Service Advertisement

Servers also can list their services and addresses with a central service registry. Clients query the directory to determine which services are available and how to access them—this is called *passive service advertisement.*

Service Use Methods

Clients can access services using three methods:

■ OS call interruption

■ Remote operation

■ Collaboration

OS Call Interruption

Applications on client systems request services by placing service calls to their local operating systems. A *service call* is a formal procedure set up by the designers of an operating system that provides an interface with the programs the operating system supports. Normally, these service calls invoke services on the local client PC.

When a client is configured for network operation, OS call interruption intercepts service requests. Service calls that request local resources are forwarded to the client's OS. Service calls that request network resources are transferred to the network, where they are forwarded to the appropriate server. The process is shown in figure 33.1.

OS call interruption enables a client to utilize network services even when OS has no inherent networking capability.

 Note This is the service access method used by NetWare requesters for DOS and OS/2, as well as for other operating systems supported for NetWare such as Macintosh.

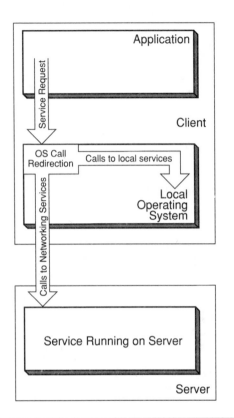

Figure 33.1
OS call interruption.

Remote Operation

When the client OS has network capability built-in, it can access the server by remote operation. The client OS interfaces directly with the network. Requests from the client OS appear to the server to be the same as requests from the server's own systems. In other words, the server is not directly aware of the separate existence of client systems.

Collaborative Computing

Some server and client operating systems are so advanced that the border between them blurs. The operating systems work together to coordinate the use of resources on the two respective computers. Recall from Chapter 22 the discussion of collaborative computing, which consists of far more than computers simply accessing each other's services. Indeed, computers participating in collaborative computing pool all of their resources. One computer can start a process on another, for example, to take advantage of some free processing cycles. This requires the participating operating systems to be capable of a high level of cooperation.

The following table summarizes the topics discussed in this chapter along with the associated methods.

Application Layer Topics and Methods

Topic	Method
Service advertisement	Active
	Passive
Service use	OS call interception
	Remote operation
	Collaborative processing

Questions

Here are some sample questions to help you evaluate your understanding of Chapters 29 through 33.

1. Which TWO address types are associated with individual devices?

   ☐ A. Service

   ☐ B. Network

   ☐ C. Physical

   ☐ D. Virtual

2. Which switching method employs virtual circuits?

   ○ A. Message

   ○ B. Circuit

   ○ C. Packet

   ○ D. All of the above

3. Which network layer is concerned with data encryption?

   ○ A. Network

   ○ B. Transport

   ○ C. Session

   ○ D. Presentation

4. Which network layer is concerned with delivering messages between processes on devices?

   ○ A. Network

   ○ B. Transport

   ○ C. Session

   ○ D. Presentation

5. Which network layer is concerned with address/name resolution?

   ○ A. Network

   ○ B. Transport

   ○ C. Session

   ○ D. Presentation

6. Which switching method makes the most efficient use of network bandwidth?

   ○ A. Message

   ○ B. Circuit

   ○ C. Packet

   ○ D. Methods are about equal

7. Which TWO connection services perform flow-control?

   ☐ A. Unacknowledged connectionless services

   ☐ B. Connection-oriented services

   ☐ C. Acknowledged connectionless services

   ☐ D. Unacknowledged connection-oriented services

8. What is another name for a message switching network?

   ○ A. Connectionless

   ○ B. Datagram

   ○ C. Store-and-forward

   ○ D. Virtual circuit

9. Which is the most common network switching method?

   ○ A. Message

   ○ B. Packet

   ○ C. Circuit

   ○ D. Virtual

10. Which TWO statements about virtual circuits are true?

    ☐ A. They usually are associated with connection oriented services.

    ☐ B. A virtual circuit represents a specific path through the network.

    ☐ C. A virtual circuit appears to the connected devices as a dedicated network path.

    ☐ D. Virtual circuits dedicate a communication channel to a single conversation.

11. Which of the following statements is true?

    ○ A. Hop count is a measure of routing cost.

    ○ B. Distance vector routing methods are technically simple and make efficient use of network bandwidth.

    ○ C. Link-state routing protocols rely on tick counts to make routing determinations.

    ○ D. Link-state routing protocols transmit routing information at regular intervals.

12. Which THREE of the following terms are related?

    ☐ A. Port

    ☐ B. Connection ID

    ☐ C. Socket

    ☐ D. Service address

13. Which switching method fragments messages into small units which are routed through independent paths?

    ○ A. Message

    ○ B. Packet

    ○ C. Circuit

    ○ D. Virtual

14. Which activity involves the use of connection IDs?

    ○ A. Packet switching

    ○ B. Routing

    ○ C. Segment development

    ○ D. End-to-end flow control

15. Which TWO of the following are transport layer error control strategies?

    ☐ A. Using datagram packet switching

    ☐ B. Utilizing unique segment sequencing numbers

    ☐ C. Using time-outs to drop packets that have remained on the network too long

    ☐ D. Using parity checking to detect errors

16. Which TWO of the following statements are true?

    □ A. The data link layer deals with device-to-device traffic.

    □ B. The network layer deals with traffic between upper layer processes.

    □ C. The transport layer deals with traffic between end-nodes.

    □ D. All of the above are true.

17. Which of the following methods of dialog control provides two-way communication?

    □ A. Simple duplex

    □ B. Simplex

    □ C. Half-duplex

    □ D. Full-duplex

18. Dialog control is a function of which layer of the OSI Reference Model?

    ○ A. Network

    ○ B. Transport

    ○ C. Session

    ○ D. Presentation

19. Which THREE of the following are functions of session administration?

    □ A. Connection establishment

    □ B. Checksum error detection

    □ C. Data transfer

    □ D. Connection release

20. Which TWO of the following are functions of connection establishment?

    □ A. Resumption of interrupted communication

    □ B. Login name and password verification

    □ C. Determining required services

    □ D. Acknowledgment of data receipt

21. Which TWO of the following are possible functions of the presentation layer?

    □ A. Data encryption

    □ B. Presentation of data on display devices

    □ C. Data translation

    □ D. Display format conversion

22. Which TWO statements are true about public key data encryption?

    □ A. Encoded data is vulnerable should the public key become known.

    □ B. A public key is generated from a secret key.

    □ C. Public key encryption is less secure than private key encryption.

    □ D. The public key is used to encrypt messages, and a separate key is used to decrypt messages.

23. Which THREE of the following are possible functions of the application layer?

    □ A. Network printing service

    □ B. End-user applications

    □ C. Client access to network services

    □ D. Service advertisement

24. Which of the following methods is used by the NetWare requester to access network services?

    ○ A. Collaborative

    ○ B. OS call interception

    ○ C. Remote operation

    ○ D. Peer-to-peer communication

Answers

1. A C

2. C

3. D

4. B

5. B

6. C

7. B, C

8. C

9. C

10. A, C

11. A

12. A, C, D

13. B

14. C

15. B, C

16. A, C

17. C, D

18. C

19. A, C, D

20. B, C

21. A, C

22. B, D

23. A, C, D

24. B

Protocol Suites

In the preceding chapters, you have seen how the process of designing network protocols is usually done in pieces, with each piece solving a small part of the overall problem. By convention, these protocols are regarded as layers of an overall set of protocols called a protocol suite or a protocol stack.

You have seen one approach to defining the layers of a protocol stack. The OSI Reference Model is useful as a conceptual tool for understanding protocol layering. Although protocols have been designed in strict conformance with the OSI Reference Model, the OSI protocol suite has not become popular. The main influence of the Reference Model is as a conceptual framework in which to understand the process of network communication and in which to compare various types of protocols.

Protocols are real implementations, in program code and hardware, of the conceptual rules defined in the Reference Model. The tasks described in the Reference Model can be performed in various ways, depending on the goals of the network designers, and various protocol suites are in common use. Some protocols and protocol suites existed before the OSI Reference Model was published and can be matched only loosely to the seven-layer model.

In this chapter, you will get down to the task of examining a variety of actual protocols. In the process, you will apply what you have learned about the OSI Reference Model to several of the most popular protocol stacks.

This chapter examines the following protocol stacks:

- NetWare IPX/SPX

- Internet Protocols (TCP/IP)

- AppleTalk

- Digital Network Architecture (DNA)

- Systems Network Architecture (SNA)

Models and Protocols

Three stages take place before a protocol goes to work:

1. A model describes the general function of the protocol.

2. The protocol itself is defined in complete detail.

3. The protocol must be realized by software and hardware designers in real products.

Consider the process of designing a building. The architect first produces sketches that describe the general nature of the building. Then the architect, possibly working with a specialist in particular building trades, develops blueprints that describe every detail of the building. Finally, an actual building is constructed.

Protocols are the blueprints of networking. They are highly-detailed descriptions of all the functions at a given communication layer. Until the protocol is expressed in hardware and software, however, it cannot go to work.

The act of translating a protocol into hardware and software can be a difficult one, and different designers often have difficulty getting their equipment to interact without some tweaking, particularly in the early life stages of a protocol. Eventually, implementation of a protocol becomes fairly routine, but it always is advisable to inquire into the compatibility testing that has been performed on a new piece of equipment.

Because many problems are encountered when attempting to interconnect devices running different protocols, many organizations have pushed for *open systems* (sets of hardware and software standards that could be generally applied throughout the industry to ease communication difficulties).

The OSI Reference Model has been used as one strategy for developing open systems, and some vendors have redesigned existing protocol suites to make them more compliant with the OSI model. Others—a good example is the TCP/IP community—have argued that they already have a highly functional set of protocols that are, in fact, open in the sense that they are freely available to everyone in the industry. As a result, the impact of the OSI model has been limited to the products of some manufacturers.

Figure 34.1 illustrates how the protocol suites discussed in this chapter relate to the layers of the OSI Reference Model.

NetWare IPX/SPX

The protocols utilized with NetWare are summarized in figure 34.2. The NetWare protocols have been designed with a high degree of modularity, making it easy to adapt to different hardware and to incorporate other protocols into the configuration. The discussion of NetWare protocols in this course is fairly brief considering the importance of these protocols to NetWare engineers. For a more detailed description, you might want to consult *NetWare: The Professional Reference, Fourth Edition* from New Riders Publishing.

Each of the protocols in figure 34.2 is discussed later in this chapter. Many of the features of the protocols are summarized in table 34.1.

Multiple Link Interface Driver (MLID)

MLIDs implement the *medium access control* (MAC) sublayer of the OSI data link layer. Practically speaking, MLID is Novell's name for the software that drives a network interface board. The specifications for writing MLIDs are defined by Novell's *Open DataLink Interface* (ODI) specification, which describes Novell's overall architecture for network protocols. An MLID must be written for each board design.

As such, the specific methods incorporated into a specific MLID depend on the underlying physical layer architecture. An MLID written for an Ethernet card uses contention access control, whereas an MLID written for a token-ring card uses token access.

The MLID is implemented in a software driver that usually takes its name from the model number of the network board being supported. An MLID for the Novell/Eagle NE2000 card, for example, is packaged in a file named NE2000.COM.

MLIDs are not dependent on any specific upper layer protocols. One feature of the ODI specification is that multiple protocols can access the same network interface board by linking to the same MLID.

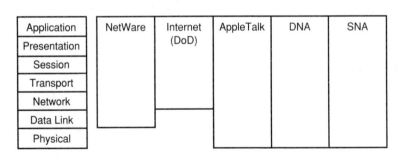

Figure 34.1

A comparison of various protocol suites to the OSI Reference Model.

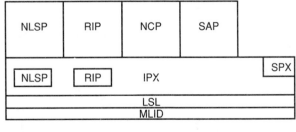

Figure 34.2

The NetWare protocol suite.

Multiple Link Interface Driver (MLID) Topics And Methods

OSI Layer	Topics	Methods
Data link (MAC sublayer)	Medium access	Contention Token passing Polling (Underlying physical layer defines MAC headers)

Link Support Layer (LSL)

The LSL implements the *logical link support* (LLC) sublayer of the OSI data link layer and functions as the interface between the MLID and the upper layer protocols.

When multiple upper layer protocol stacks are being used, the LSL software is responsible for passing packets to the appropriate protocol stack.

On NetWare DOS clients, the LSL sublayer is implemented in a file named LSL.COM.

Link Support Layer (LSL) Topics And Methods

OSI Layer	Topics	Methods
Data link (LLC sublayer)	Protocol specific	Interfaces MLID to upper layer protocols

Internetwork Packet Exchange Protocol (IPX)

IPX is a network layer protocol that provides connectionless (datagram) service. (IPX was developed from the XNS protocol originated by Xerox). As a network layer protocol, IPX is responsible for internetwork routing and for maintaining network logical addresses. Routing uses the RIP protocol (described below) to make route selections.

IPX relies on hardware physical addresses found at lower layers to provide network device addressing. It also makes use of *sockets*, upper-layer service addresses, to deliver packets to their ultimate destinations.

On the client, IPX support is provided as a component of the older DOS shell and the current DOS NetWare requester.

Internetwork Packet Exchange Protocol (IPX) Topics And Methods

OSI Layer	Topics	Methods
Network	Addressing	Logical network service
	Route selection	Dynamic
	Connection services	Connectionless

Router Information Protocol (RIP)

RIP uses the distance-vector route discover method to determine hop counts to other devices. Like IPX,

RIP was developed from a similar protocol in the XNS protocol suite. RIP is implemented as an upper-layer service and is assigned a socket (service address). RIP is based directly on IPX and performs network layer functions.

Router Information Protocol (RIP) Topics and Methods

OSI Layer	Topics	Methods
Network	Route discovery	Distance vector

Network Link Services Protocol (NLSP)

NLSP is a link-state routing protocol derived from an ISO protocol named IS-IS (intermediate system-to-intermediate system). NLSP supports fault-tolerant mesh and hybrid mesh networks with a high level of fault tolerance.

(This protocol is mistakenly named the NetWare Link Services Protocol in the course materials.)

Network Link State Protocol (NLSP) Topics And Methods

OSI Layer	Topics	Methods
Network	Route discovery	Link-state

 Note   Due to the frequency of messages required to advertise routing information, RIP has been a traditional bottleneck in NetWare performance, particularly

with large internetworks that include slower wide-area links. NLSP is a newer protocol that can greatly improve performance of NetWare internetworks. It is shipped with 4.1 and is available as an upgrade for other NetWare implementations such as 3.x and earlier versions of 4.x.

Sequenced Packet Exchange (SPX)

SPX is a transport layer protocol that extends IPX to provide connection-oriented service with reliable delivery. Reliable delivery is ensured by retransmitting packets in the event of error. SPX is derived from a similar SPX protocol in the XNS network protocol suite.

SPX establishes virtual circuits called *connections*. The connection ID for each connection appears in the SPX header. A given upper-layer process can be associated with multiple connection IDs.

On the client, SPX support is provided as a component of the older DOS shell and of the current NetWare requester.

Sequenced Packet Exchange Protocol (SPX) Topics And Methods

OSI Layer	Topics	Methods
Transport	Addressing	Connection ID
	Segment development	Division and combination
	Connection services	Segment sequencing
		Error control
		End-to-end flow control

NetWare Core Protocols (NCP)

NCP provides numerous function calls that support network services such as file service, printing, name management, file locking, and synchronization. NetWare client software interfaces with NCP to access NetWare services.

It is interesting to note that most NetWare services do not rely on a transport layer protocol such as SPX. In almost all cases, NCP provides the upper layer protocol structure that provides services, connection management, and reliable delivery. In most cases, SPX is not required and can even be left out of the client configuration.

NetWare Core Protocols (NCP) Topics And Methods

OSI Layer	Topics	Methods
Transport	Connection services	Segment sequencing
		Error control
		End-to-end flow control
Session	Session administration	Data transfer
Presentation	Translation	Character code
		File syntax
Application	Service use	OS redirector or Collaborative (depending on client)

Service Advertising Protocol (SAP)

SAP is used by NetWare servers to advertise their services to the network. Each server identifies itself once a minute by transmitting a SAP packet. SAP users also can request service information by transmitting a service query packet. SAP implementations obtain service address information from IPX header information.

Service Advertising Protocol (SAP) Topics And Methods

OSI Layer	Topics	Methods
Session	Session administration	File transfer
Application	Service advertisement	Active

Internet Protocols

The Internet protocol suite (also commonly called the TCP/IP protocol suite) was originally developed by the United States Department of Defense (DoD) to provide robust service on large internetworks that incorporate a variety of computer types. In recent years, the Internet protocols have become increasingly popular and constitute the most popular network protocols now in use. If you want more detailed information about the Internet protocols than that provided in this course, you can consult *NetWare TCP/IP and NFS* from New Riders Publishing.

One reason for this popularity is that the Internet protocols are not owned by any one vendor, unlike the NetWare, DNA, SNA, AppleTalk, and various other protocols. The protocol suite evolves in response to input from a wide variety of industry sources. As such, the Internet protocol suite is the most open of the protocol suites and is supported by the widest variety of vendors. Virtually every brand of computing equipment now supports the Internet protocols.

Much of the popularity of the TCP/IP protocols comes from their early availability on Unix. The protocols were built into the Berkeley Standard Distribution (BSD) Unix implementation. Since then, TCP/IP has achieved universal acceptance in the Unix community and is a standard feature on all versions of Unix.

Figure 34.3 illustrates the relationship of the protocols in the Internet suite to the layers of the OSI Reference Model. Notice that the suite does not include protocols for the data link or physical layers. TCP/IP was designed to work over established standards such as Ethernet. Over time, TCP/IP has been interfaced to the majority of data link and physical layer technologies.

It should be noted that the Internet protocols do not map cleanly to the OSI Reference Model. The DoD model was, after all, developed long before the OSI model was defined. The model for the Internet protocol suite has four layers, which are also shown in figure 34.3. From this, you can see the approximate relationships of the layers of the two models. The functions of the layers of the DoD model are as follows:

- The *network access* layer corresponds to the bottom two layers of the OSI model. As previously mentioned, this was deliberately done to enable the DoD protocols to coexist with existing data link and physical layer standards.

- The *internet* layer corresponds roughly to the OSI network layer. Protocols at this layer are concerned with moving data between devices on networks.

- The *host-to-host* layer can be compared to the OSI transport layer. Host-to-host protocols enable peer communication between hosts on the internetwork. (At the time these protocols were designed, personal computers and workstations did not exist and all network computers were host computers. As a result, devices on TCP/IP networks are typically referred to as *hosts*. The concept of a client/server relationship did not exist, and all communicating hosts were assumed to be peers.)

- The *process/application* layer embraces functions of the OSI session, presentation, and application layers. Protocols at this layer provide network services.

A large number of protocols are associated with the Internet protocol suite.

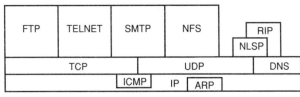

Figure 34.3
The Internet protocol suite.

Internet Protocol (IP)

IP is a connectionless protocol that provides datagram service, and IP packets are most commonly referred to as IP datagrams. IP is a packet-switching protocol that performs addressing and route selection. An IP header is appended to packets, which are transmitted as frames by lower level protocols. IP routes packets through internetworks by utilizing dynamic routing tables that are referenced at each hop. Routing determinations are made by consulting logical and physical network device information, as provided by the *Address Resolution Protocol* (ARP).

IP performs packet disassembly and reassembly as required by packet size limitations defined for the data link and physical layers being implemented. IP also performs error checking on the header data using a checksum, although data from upper layers is not error-checked. The following table shows IP topics and methods.

Internet Protocol (IP) Topics And Methods

OSI Layer	Topics	Methods
Network	Addressing	Logical network
	Switching	Packet
	Route selection	Dynamic
	Connection services	Error control

Internet Control Message Protocol (ICMP)

ICMP enhances the error control provided by IP. Connectionless protocols such as IP cannot detect internetwork errors such as congestion or path failures. ICMP can detect such errors and notify IP and upper layer protocols.

Internet Control Message Protocol (ICMP) Topics And Methods

OSI Layer	Topics	Methods
Network	Connection services	Error control
		Network-layer flow control

Routing Information Protocol (RIP)

RIP in the Internet protocol suite is not the same protocol as RIP in the NetWare suite, although the two serve similar functions. Internet RIP performs route discovery using a distance vector method, calculating the number of hops that must be crossed to route a packet by a particular path. A *hop* is defined as crossing a single router.

While it works well in localized networks, RIP has many weaknesses that limit its utility on wide-area internetworks. These weaknesses are similar to those of NetWare RIP and are causing RIP to be replaced gradually by the OSPF link-state protocol.

Routing Information Protocol (RIP) Topics And Methods

OSI Layer	Topics	Methods
Network	Route discovery	Distance vector

Open Shortest Path First (OSPF)

OSPF is a link-state route discovery protocol that is designed to overcome the limitations of RIP. On large internetworks, OSPF can identify the internetwork topology and improve performance by implementing load balancing and class-of-service routing.

Open Shortest Path First (OSPF) Topics And Methods

OSI Layer	Topics	Methods
Network	Route discovery	Link-state

Transmission Control Protocol (TCP)

TCP is an internetwork protocol that corresponds to the OSI transport layer. TCP provides full-duplex, connection-oriented transport. When the overhead of a connection-oriented transport is not required, the *User Datagram Protocol* (UDP) can be substituted for TCP at the transport (host-to-host) level.

TCP also provides message fragmentation and reassembly, and can accept messages of any length from upper layer protocols. TCP fragments message streams into segments that can be handled by

IP. When used with IP, TCP adds connection-oriented service and performs segment synchronization, adding sequence numbers at the byte level.

In addition to message fragmentation, TCP can maintain multiple conversations with upper layer protocols and can improve use of network bandwidth by combining multiple messages into the same segment. Each virtual-circuit connection is assigned a connection identifier called a *port*, which identifies the datagrams associated with that connection.

Transmission Control Protocol (TCP) Topics And Methods

OSI Layer	Topics	Methods
Network	Addressing	Service
Transport	Addressing	Connection identifier
	Segment development	Division and recombination
	Connection services	Segment sequencing
		Error control
		End-to-end flow control

User Datagram Protocol (UDP)

UDP is a connectionless transport (host-to-host) layer protocol. UDP does not provide message acknowledgments, it simply transports datagrams.

Like TCP, UDP utilizes port addresses to deliver datagrams. These port addresses, however, are not associated with virtual circuits and merely identify local host processes. UDP is preferred over TCP when high performance or low network overhead is more critical than reliable delivery. Because UDP does not need to establish, maintain, and close connections, or control data flow, it generally outperforms TCP.

UDP is the transport layer protocol used with the *Simple Network Management Protocol* (SNMP), which is the standard network management protocol used with TCP/IP networks. UDP enables SNMP to provide network management with a minimum of network overhead.

User Datagram Protocol (UDP) Topics And Methods

OSI Layer	Topics	Methods
Transport	Addressing	Connection identifier
	Segment development	Combination
	Connection services	Connectionless (datagram)

Address Resolution Protocol (ARP)

The following three types of address information are used on TCP/IP internetworks:

- Physical addresses used by the data link and physical layers.

- IP addresses, which provide logical network and host IDs. IP addresses consist of four numbers typically expressed in "dotted-decimal" form. An example of an IP address is 134.135.100.13.

- Logical node names, which identify specific hosts with alphanumeric identifiers. These are easier for humans to recall than the numeric IP addresses. An example of a logical node name is MYHOST.COM.

Given a logical node name, ARP can determine the IP address associated with that name. ARP maintains tables of address resolution data and can broadcast packets to discover addresses on the internetwork. The IP addresses discovered by ARP can be provided to data link layer protocols.

Address Resolution Protocol (ARP) Topics And Methods

OSI Layer	Topics	Methods
Network	Address resolution	Matches logical (IP) and physical device addresses

Domain Name System (DNS)

DNS provides name/address resolution as a service to client applications. DNS servers enable humans to use logical node names to access network resources.

Domain Name System (DNS) Topics And Methods

OSI Layer	Topics	Methods
Transport	Address/name resolution	Service-provider initiated

File Transfer Protocol (FTP)

FTP is a protocol for sharing files between networked hosts. FTP enables users to log onto remote hosts. Logged-on users can inspect directories, manipulate files, execute commands, and perform other commands on the host. FTP also has the capability of transferring files between dissimilar hosts by supporting a file request structure that is independent of specific operating systems.

 Note   NetWare users should note that FTP is more than simply a remote file access protocol. Users are not limited to reading and writing files unlike when they are logged into a NetWare server. FTP is a peer-to-peer protocol that enables users to initiate processes on the remote host.

File Transfer Protocol (FTP) Topics And Methods

OSI Layer	Topics	Methods
Session	Session administration	Connection establishment
		File transfer Connection release
Presentation	Translation	Machine-independent file syntax
Application	Network services	File services
	Service use	Collaborative

Simple Mail Transfer Protocol (SMTP)

SMTP is a protocol for routing mail through internetworks, and it makes use of the TCP and IP protocols. SNMP does not provide a mail interface for the user. Creation, management, and delivery of messages to end users must be performed by an e-mail application. (The most popular e-mail application on the Internet is named Eudora.)

SMTP is implemented by NetWare messaging gateways. SMTP also is provided with UnixWare.

Simple Mail Transfer Protocol (SMTP) Topics And Methods

OSI Layer	Topics	Methods
Application	Network services	Message services

Remote Terminal Emulation (TELNET)

TELNET enables PCs and workstations to function as dumb terminals in session with hosts on internetworks. TELNET implementations are available for most end-user platforms including Unix (of course), DOS, Windows, and Macintosh OS.

TELNET is provided as a part of NetWare XCONSOLE, NetWare NFS, FlexIP, and NetWareIP through UNICON. TELNET also is provided with UnixWare.

Remote Terminal Emulation (TELNET) Topics And Methods

OSI Layer	Topics	Methods
Session	Dialog control	Half-duplex
	Session administration	Connection establishment
		File transfer
		Connection release
Presentation	Translation	Byte order Character code
Application	Service use	Remote operation

Network File System (NFS)

NFS, developed by Sun Microsystems, is a family of file access protocols that are a considerable advancement over FTP and TELNET. Since Sun made the NFS specifications available for public use, NFS has achieved a high level of popularity. NFS consists of the following protocols:

■ eXternal Data Representation (XDR) supports encoding of data in a machine-independent format. C programmers use XDR library routines to describe data structures that are portable between machine environments.

■ Remote Procedure Calls (RPC) function as a service request redirector that determines whether function calls can be satisfied locally or must be redirected to a remote host. Calls to remote hosts are packaged for network delivery and transmitted to RPC servers, which generally have the capability of servicing many remote service requests. RPC servers process the service requests and generate response packets that are returned to the service requester.

Network File System (NFS) Topics And Methods

OSI Layer	Topics	Methods
Application	Network services	File services
	Service use	Remote operation

Remote Procedure Call (RPC) Topics And Methods

OSI Layer	Topics	Methods
Session	Session administration	Connection establishment
		File transfer Connection release

External Data Representation (XDR) Topics And Methods

OSI Layer	Topics	Methods
Presentation	Translation	Byte order
		Character code
		File syntax

AppleTalk

AppleTalk is the computing architecture developed by Apple Computer for the Macintosh family of personal computers. Although AppleTalk originally supported only Apple's proprietary LocalTalk cabling system, the suite has been expanded to incorporate both Ethernet and token ring physical layers.

AppleTalk originally supported networks of limited scope. The AppleTalk Phase 2 specification issued in 1989, however, extended the scope of AppleTalk to enterprise networks. The Phase 2 specification also enabled AppleTalk to coexist on networks with other protocol suites. Table 34.1 summarizes the differences between AppleTalk Phases 1 and 2.

Table 34.1
Comparison of AppleTalk Phases 1 and 2

Characteristic	Phase 1	Phase 2
Maximum zones on a network segment	1	255
Maximum nodes per network	254	About 16 million
Dynamic addressing based on	Node ID	Network+Node ID
supported link access protocols	LocalTalk Ethernet	LocalTalk IEEE 802.2 IEEE 802.5
Split-horizon routing	No	Yes

AppleTalk Phase 1 protocols do not support internetworks because addressing is limited to a unique node ID. This approach is called a *nonextended network* under Phase 2 terminology. Phase 2 also supports extended networks in which addressing is determined by a combination of a network and a node ID, and can make use of the hardware-based device IDs that are coded into Ethernet and token ring cards.

Figure 34.4 presents a layered perspective of the AppleTalk protocols. Each of these protocols is described in this chapter. Each AppleTalk protocol is briefly discussed below.

LocalTalk, EtherTalk, and TokenTalk Link Access Protocols (LLAP, ELAP, and TLAP)

These are link access protocols that integrate AppleTalk upper layer protocols with the LocalTalk, Ethernet, and token ring environments.

LLAP is a protocol developed by Apple for operation with the LocalTalk cabling system, a system based on shielded twisted-pair cabling. LocalTalk is suitable primarily for small, low performance networks. The maximum data rate is 230.4 Kbps (compared to 10 Mbps for Ethernet), and cable segments are limited to 300 meters in length and a maximum of 32 devices.

LLAP uses addresses called AppleTalk addresses that are developed dynamically on the network. LLAP is ideally suited to Apple's "plug and play" Macintosh philosophy because a Macintosh can discover a unique physical address when it connects to the network without the need for any configuration.

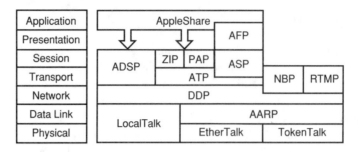

Figure 34.4
*The AppleTalk
protocol suite.*

LocalTalk Topics And Methods

OSI Layer	Topics	Methods
Physical	Connection types	Multipoint
	Physical topology	Bus
	Digital signaling	State transition
	Bit synchronization	Synchronous
	Bandwidth use	Baseband
Data Link (MAC)	Logical topology	Bus
	Media access	Contention
	Addressing	Physical device
Data Link (LLC)	Transmission synchronization	Synchronous
	Connection services	LLC flow control
		Error control

AppleTalk Address Resolution (AARP)

Both Ethernet and token ring make use of physical device addresses that are built into the interfaces when they are manufactured. AARP maps AppleTalk addresses to Ethernet and token ring physical addresses, enabling upper AppleTalk protocols to interface with the Ethernet and token ring physical layers.

AppleTalk Address Resolution Protocol (AARP) Topics And Methods

OSI Layer	Topics	Methods
Network/ Data Link	Address resolution	Matches logical names with physical device addresses

Datagram Delivery Protocol (DDP)

DDP is a network-layer protocol that provides connectionless service between two sockets. A *socket* is the AppleTalk term for a service address. A combination of a device address, network address, and socket uniquely identifies each process.

DDP performs network routing and consults routing tables maintained by RTMP to determine routing. Packet delivery is performed by the data link protocol operating on a given destination network.

Datagram Delivery Protocol (DDP) Topics And Methods

OSI Layer	Topics	Methods
Network	Addressing	Logical network service
	Route selection	Dynamic
	Interoperability	Network layer translation

Routing Table Maintenance Protocol (RTMP)

RTMP provides DDP with routing information based on a distance vector method similar to RIP.

Routing Table Maintenance Protocol (RTMP) Topics And Methods

OSI Layer	Topics	Methods
Network	Route discovery	Distance vector

Zone Information Protocol (ZIP)

ZIP organizes devices into zones, which organize service providers into logically named groups. Zones reduce the complexity of a network by limiting users network views to the devices they need.

ZIP functions with routers to organize service providers into zones and to resolve zone and network names.

Zone Information Protocol (ZIP) Topics And Methods

OSI Layer	Topics	Methods
Session	Protocol-specific	Organization of service providers into zones

Name Binding Protocol (NBP)

AppleTalk enables devices to have logical names in addition to their addresses. These names hide lower-layer addresses from users and from upper-layer processes.

NBP enables an application to match a logical name with it's associated address. Recall that AppleTalk addresses are dynamic and can change from session-to-session. NBP obtains up-to-date information that enables devices to use a logical name to determine address information even though the address varies.

Name Binding Protocol (NBP) Topics And Methods

OSI Layer	Topics	Methods
Transport	Address resolution	Service requestor initiated

AppleTalk Transaction Protocol (ATP)

ATP is a connectionless transport layer protocol. Reliable service is provided through a system of acknowledgments and retransmissions. Retransmissions automatically are initiated if an acknowledgment is not received within a specified time interval.

ATP reliability is based on transactions. A transaction consists of a request followed by a reply.

ATP is responsible for segment development and performs fragmentation and reassembly of packets that exceed the specifications for lower layer protocols. Packets include sequence numbers that enable message reassembly and retransmission of lost packets. Only damaged or lost packets are retransmitted.

AppleTalk Transaction Protocol (ATP) Topics And Methods

OSI Layer	Topics	Methods
Transport	Addressing	Transaction identifier
	Segment development	Division and combination
	Connection services	Error control

AppleTalk Session Protocol (ASP)

ASP is a session layer protocol that establishes, maintains, and releases sessions between service requesters and service providers. The focus of ASP is on providing file services. ASP works with ATP to provide a complete transport service. ATP messages are limited to eight packets, each with a maximum size of 578 bytes. ASP can generate multiple ATP transactions as required to control message overhead on large data transfers.

Multiple sessions can be maintained between service requesters and providers. Sessions can be requested by service requesters, but not by service providers.

AppleTalk Session Protocol (ASP) Topics And Methods

OSI Layer	Topics	Methods
Transport	Connection services	Segment sequencing
		End-to-end flow control
Session	Session administration	Connection establishment
		Data transfer
		Connection release

Printer Access Protocol (PAP)

PAP is a session layer protocol similar to ASP. As the name implies, the protocol provides printing services, but it also supports other types of connections between service requesters and providers.

PAP permits sessions to be initiated by both service requesters and service providers.

Printer Access Protocol (PAP) Topics And Methods

OSI Layer	Topics	Methods
Session	Session administration	Connection establishment
		Data transfer
		Connection release

AppleTalk Data Stream Protocol (ADSP)

Notice in figure 34.4 that ADSP provides a protocol stack that is an alternative to protocols that are layered onto ATP.

ADSP performs services associated with several network layers. It is considered a transport layer protocol in that it establishes, maintains, and releases sessions between sockets. At the session layer, ADSP substitutes for ASP and PAP.

ADSP replaces ATP at the transport layer and incorporates segment sequencing and sliding window flow-control. The service provided is full-duplex.

ADSP is not transaction-based like ATP. Instead ADSP uses a connection identifier and byte streams. ADSP provides better performance on lower-bandwidth channels than does ATP working with ASP or PAP.

AppleTalk Data Stream Protocol (ADSP) Topics And Methods

OSI Layer	Topics	Methods
Transport	Addressing	Connection identifier
	Segment development	Division and combination
	Connection establishment	Error control
		End-to-end flow control
		Segment sequencing

OSI Layer	Topics	Methods
Session	Session administration	Connection establishment
		Data transfer
		Connection release

AppleTalk Filing Protocol (AFP)

AFP provides file services and is responsible for translating local file service requests into formats required for network file services. AFP directly translates command syntax and enables applications to perform file format translations.

AFP is responsible for file system security, and verifies and encrypts login names and passwords during connection setup.

AppleTalk Filing Protocol (AARP) Topics And Methods

OSI Layer	Topics	Methods
Session	Session administration	Data transfer
Presentation	Translation	File syntax
	Encryption	Public key

AppleShare (ASP)

AppleShare provides the following three primary application services:

■ The AppleShare File Server uses AFP to enable users to store and access files on the network.

It logs in users and associates them with network volumes and directories.

- The AppleShare Print Server uses NBP and PAP to support network printing. NBP provides name/address information that enables PAP to connect to printers. The AppleShare Print Server performs print spooling and manages printing on networked printers.

- The AppleShare PC enables PCs running MS-DOS to access AppleShare services by running an AppleShare PC program.

AppleShare Topics And Methods

OSI Layer	Topics	Methods
Application	Network services	File service
		Print service
	Service advertisement	Active
	Service use	Collaborative

Digital Network Architecture

Since it's introduction in 1974, the Digital Network Architecture (DNA) has evolved several times. It's current generation is called Phase V. DECnet is Digital's family of products that implement the DNA architecture.

As DNA has evolved, Digital has placed a strong emphasis on use of standards-based protocols and on achieving close conformance with the OSI Reference Model. A variety of ISO standards are incorporated into the DNA protocol suite.

Prior to DNA Phase V, DNA relied heavily on Digital proprietary protocols above the network layer. This stack—which includes Digital's NSP, Naming Service, Session Control, and other protocols—is still supported for the purpose of backward compatibility. Other pre-Phase V protocols also are supported at the lower network levels.

DNA Phase V introduced an alternative protocol stack based on ISO standards.

Figure 34.5 illustrates the layers of the DNA protocol suite. DNA is based on several physical and data link standards that are discussed in Chapter 35, "Other Protocols and Standards," including IEEE 802.X, FDDI, and X.25/LAPB.

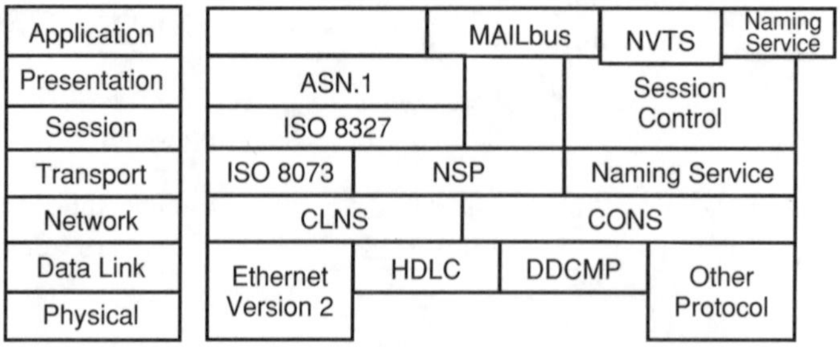

Figure 34.5

Protocols in the Digital Network Architecture.

Application				MAILbus	NVTS	Naming Service
Presentation	ASN.1				Session Control	
Session	ISO 8327					
Transport	ISO 8073		NSP		Naming Service	
Network	CLNS				CONS	
Data Link	Ethernet Version 2	HDLC		DDCMP	Other Protocol	
Physical						

Ethernet Version 2

Digital was joined by Intel and Xerox to develop the first version of Ethernet, physical and data link protocol. Since that time, the standard has been updated, and the current version is Ethernet Version 2.

Ethernet has the following characteristics:

- 10 Mbps signaling over coaxial cable.

- Media access control method is CARRIER-sense multiple access with collision detection (CSMA/CD).

- Signaling uses Manchester encoding.

The IEEE 802.3 standard was developed with slight modifications from Ethernet Version 2. Among those changes was a modification to the frame format, which makes 802.3 frames incompatible with Ethernet Version 2.

 Note   NetWare LANs can interface to DECnet networks using the NetWare for LAT product.

Ethernet Version 2 Topics And Methods

OSI Layer	Topics	Methods
Physical	Connection types	Multipoint
	Physical topology	Bus
	Digital signaling	State transition
	Bit synchronization	Synchronous
	Bandwidth	Baseband

OSI Layer	Topics	Methods
	use	
Data Link (MAC sublayer)	Logical topology	Bus
	Media access	Contention
	Addressing	Physical device

Digital Data Communications Message Protocol (DDCMP)

DDCMP is a data link protocol that dates from the earliest DNA implementations and remains as an optional Phase V protocol. DDCMP has the following capabilities:

- Asynchronous or synchronous service

- Half- or full-duplex modes

- Point-to-point or multipoint operation

- Connection-oriented error control using commands and acknowledgments along with CRC-based error detection

- LLC flow control and message sequencing (Digital uses the term *message* to describe data link level frames.)

 Note   At the time the DNA protocols were being defined, all users interacted with central computers by means of computer terminals. Terminal support was provided by the Local Area Transport protocol (LAT), which enables terminal server devices to support multiple terminals and multiplex their traffic over a single channel. LAT does not conform to the OSI network layer, in that packets

continues

do not incorporate routing information and cannot be routed on wide area networks.

NetWare networks can interface with the DNA environment using the product NetWare for LAT.

Digital Data Communications Message Protocol (DDCMP) Topics And Methods

OSI Layer	Topics	Methods
Physical	Connection types	Point-to-point
		Multipoint
Data Link (LLC Sublayer)	Transmission synchronization	Asynchronous
		Synchronous
	Connection services	LLC-Level flow control
		Error control
		Message sequencing

High-Level Data Link Control (HDLC)

HDLC is a data link protocol that supports transmissions over physical layer modem communication protocols. HDLC has the following features:

- Determines the data frame format and the frame transfer command syntax

- Supports asynchronous and synchronous communication

- Performs LLC flow control

High-Level Data Link Control (HDLC) Topics And Methods

OSI Layer	Topics	Methods
Physical	Connection types	Point-to-point
Data Link (LLC Sublayer)	Transmission synchronization	Asynchronous
		Synchronous
	Connection services	LLC-Level flow control

Connectionless-Mode Network Service (CLNS)

CLNS is a connectionless network layer service that incorporates the following three ISO protocols:

- ISO 8473 is a connectionless-mode network service that manages communication between end systems.

- ISO 9542 is a routing protocol that operates between *end systems* (devices) and *intermediate systems* (routers). This protocol, most frequently referred to as ES-IS, can be relatively simple because it does not need to perform internetwork routing.

- ISO 10589 is a routing protocol that operates between intermediate systems. IS-IS is a more complex protocol than ES-IS because it must be capable of determining routes through complex internetworks. Figure 34.6 illustrates the relationships of the two routing protocols.

These connectionless protocols are used to perform route discovery and selection, addressing, and switching.

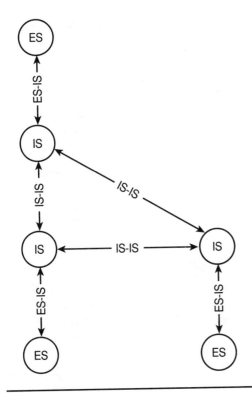

Figure 34.6
ES-IS and IS-IS routing protocols.

Connection-Mode Network Service (CONS)

CONS is a connection-oriented network layer service based on the following protocols:

- ISO 8208 is an ISO version of the X.25 packet-switching protocol, which is discussed in Chapter 29.

- ISO 8878 is an additional protocol that enables X.25 networks to provide connection-oriented services.

CLNS is employed more commonly than CONS to provide network layer services.

Connection-Mode Network Service (CONS) Topics And Methods

OSI Layer	Topics	Methods
Network	Addressing	Logical network
	Route discovery	Link-state
	Route selection	Dynamic
	Connection services	Network layer flow control
		Error control
		Packet
		Sequence control

Connectionless-Mode Network Service (CLNS) Topics And Methods

OSI Layer	Topics	Methods
Network	Addressing	Logical network
	Route discovery	Link-state
	Route selection	Dynamic

Connection-Oriented Transport Protocol Specification (ISO 8073)

ISO 8073 is a transport layer protocol that provides five service classes, tailored to different requirements. Network implementations can select a service level based on required levels of flow, error, and packet sequencing.

Connection-Oriented Transport Protocol Specification Topics And Methods

OSI Layer	Topics	Methods
Transport	Addressing	Connection identifier
	Connection services	Segment sequencing
		Error control
		End-to-end flow control

Network Services Protocol (NSP)

NSP was incorporated in the original DNA protocol suite. NSP is a connection-oriented transport protocol that manages normal or expedited full-duplex subchannels. End-to-end flow control is performed in response to congestion messages from network layer protocols. Either windowing or guaranteed flow rates can be used to control data flow.

Network Services Protocol (NSP) Topics And Methods

OSI Layer	Topics	Methods
Transport	Addressing	Connection identifier
	Connection services	Segment sequencing
		Error control
		End-to-end flow control

Session Control

Session Control is a DNA protocol that performs session and presentation layer functions. Functions performed by Session Control include:

- Address/name resolution.

- Transport connection management.

- Connection identifier management.

- Selection of protocol stacks. When devices initiate a session, Session Control negotiates a protocol stack that is supported on both systems.

Session Control Topics And Methods

OSI Layer	Topics	Methods
Transport	Address/name resolution	Service-requestor initiated
	Addressing	Connection identifier

OSI Layer	Topics	Methods
Session	Session administration	Connection establishment
		Data transfer
		Connection release

Session Protocol Specification (ISO 8327)

ISO 8327 is a session layer protocol that implements the specification ISO 8326, Session Service Definition. OSI 8327 provides the following services:

■ Connection establishment, half-duplex data transfer, and connection release.

■ Support for multiple transport layer connections for each session.

■ Packet synchronization. The method uses tokens that can be used to request retransmission from any point.

ISO 8327 Session Protocol Specification Topics And Methods

OSI Layer	Topics	Methods
Session	Dialog control	half-duplex
	Session administration	Connection establishment
		Data transfer
		Connection release

Abstract Syntax Notation One with Basic Encoding Rules (ASN.1 with BER)

ASN.1 (ISO 8824) is a set of extensible syntax rules that establish data types and structures. The rules themselves are described in the Basic Encoding Rules. These protocols operate at the presentation DNA layer.

These standards are designed to facilitate data exchange between different systems by establishing a common set of data formats. These translations might include conversion between character sets, number representation systems, or other data types. The rules can be extended as required to embrace new data types.

Abstract Syntax Notation (ASN.1 with BER) Topics And Methods

OSI Layer	Topics	Methods
Presentation	Translation	Character code

File Transfer, Access, and Management (FTAM) and Data Access Protocol (DAP)

FTAM (ISO 8571) is an application layer file service protocol. The specification requires a certain set of document types and services, but permits vendors to create customized implementations of the protocol. Standard document types include binary, text, and hierarchical files. Standard services include file transfer and management.

Data Access Protocol (DAP)

DAP performs file services including file creation, deletion, storage, retrieval, and transfer.

File Transfer, Access, and Management (FTAM) and DAP Topics and Methods

OSI Layer	Topics	Methods
Application	Network service	File services

Network Virtual Terminal Service (NVTS)

This service enables multiple terminal types to access computer services. A virtual terminal is a conceptual representation of a computer display. Both the host and the terminal emulating device maintain a copy of this model, which serves as a common intermediate data representation that enables the host and device to exchange terminal data.

Network Virtual Terminal Services (NVTS) Topics And Methods

OSI Layer	Topics	Methods
Presentation	Translation	Character code (commands)
Application	Network service	Terminal service
	Service use	Remote operation

MAILbus and X.400 Message Handling System

These systems provide DNA electronic messaging services. The MAILbus family of products provides proprietary mail services and use the X.400 messaging specification to interface with other X.400-based systems.

MAILbus and X.400 Topics And Methods

OSI Layer	Topics	Methods
Application	Network service	Message service

Naming Service and X.500 Directory

Naming Service is an application-level naming service that provides address/name resolution. A *name service* enables humans to describe network services with logical, alphanumeric identifiers. These identifiers are translated to network addresses by the naming service.

X.500 is a standard for a naming service. Digital has stated that the DNA Naming Service will migrate toward conformance with X.500.

Naming Service and X.500 Topics And Methods

OSI Layer	Topics	Methods
Transport	Address/name resolution	Service-provider initiated
Application	Network service	Directory service

Systems Network Architecture (SNA)

Like DNA, IBM's Systems Network Architecture (SNA) evolved when terminals were the normal devices used to interact with centralized computers. SNA terminal networks are organized hierarchically, and when it was introduced in 1974, SNA supported only hierarchical networks. An example of an SNA network is shown in figure 34.7. The network hierarchy consists of a central control point (the host computer), controllers (communication controllers and cluster controllers), and terminals.

In 1984, SNA was updated to support distributed processing environments with a feature called *Advanced Peer-to-Peer Networking* (APPN). APPN can implement a distributed processing environment that can leverage the processing capabilities of mainframe hosts, minicomputers, and personal computers.

The next refinement of SNA, the Systems Application Architecture (SAA), was announced in 1987 and represents IBM's strategic direction.

SNA and the OSI Reference Model

SNA was not developed from a preconceived, carefully thought-out model from which protocols were developed. IBM literally was pioneering the development of computer networking, and new protocols were added to meet new needs and design criteria. One result of this is that multiple protocols

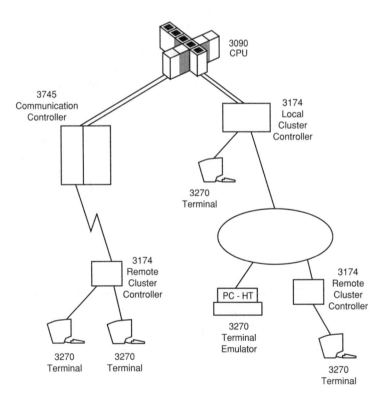

Figure 34.7

An example of an SNA network.

3090 CPU

3745 Communication Controller

3174 Local Cluster Controller

3270 Terminal

3174 Remote Cluster Controller

3270 Terminal

3270 Terminal

PC - HT

3270 Terminal Emulator

3174 Remote Cluster Controller

3270 Terminal

can be present at any given layer. Each protocol serves a somewhat different purpose in the overall scheme of SNA. As such, SNA does not consist of a protocol stack so much as it consists of multiple protocols that work together in different combinations to meet different needs.

SNA was a mature model by the time formulation of the OSI Reference Model was undertaken, and the SNA architecture had a significant influence on the definition of the OSI model. For that reason, this course includes a comparison of the two models.

In addition to showing the organization of the SNA protocols, figure 34.8 compares the layers of the OSI Reference Model to the layers of the SNA model.

The layers of the SNA model and their features are as follows:

- **Physical control** covers the same functions as the OSI physical layer. Both are concerned with the electrical, mechanical, interface, and control characteristics of the physical medium. IBM developed the Token Ring physical layer standard for this layer, but market forces have pushed IBM to extend SNA to embrace other popular physical layer standards such as Ethernet (IEEE 802.3).

- **Data link control** includes many functions of the OSI data link layer. The *Synchronous Data Link Control* (SDLC) protocol is the SNA data link protocol and is responsible for communication between master/primary nodes and slave/secondary nodes.

- **Path control** incorporates functions from two OSI layers. Path control is responsible for flow control, a data link layer function. Path control also is responsible for the routing and packet disassembly/assembly functions of the network layer.

- **Transmission control** is analogous to the OSI transport layer and provides end-to-end connection services. This layer also performs encryption/decryption, services OSI provides at the presentation layer.

- **Data flow control**, like the OSI session layer, controls dialogs.

- **Presentation services** perform data translation services similar to the OSI presentation layer, but also are responsible for sharing resources and synchronizing operations.

- **Transaction services** provide application services, supporting distributed processing and management services. *SNA Distributed Services* (SNADS) is an example of a distributed service.

Figure 34.8						
SNA protocols and the OSI Reference Model.	Transaction Services	Application	DIA	SNADS	DPM	User Applications
	Presentation Services	Presentation	APPC	CICS	IMS	TSO	DB2
		Session				
	Data Flow Control	Transport	APPN	VTAM		
	Transmission Control					
	Path Control	Network	NCP			
	Data Link Control	Data Link	Token Ring	SDLC		X.25
	Physical Control	Physical		V.35	RS-232C	

Network Addressable Units

SNA networks are organized hierarchically and consist of *network addressable units* (NAUs). An NAU is a hardware device or a program (or a combination of hardware and software) that can be addressed on the network. Two types of NAUs can be found: physical units and logical units.

A *physical unit* (PU) is a device consisting of the hardware, firmware, and software required to manage node communication. Communication controllers and cluster controllers are examples of physical units.

 Note By definition under SNA terminology, a node is, by definition, a physical unit (PU). Terminals, printers, and other peripherals are not regarded as nodes.

Logical units (LUs) are the end points of network communication. (The course definition calls LUs "the 'entities' of the network.") Examples of LUs are peripherals such as terminals, printers, and programs that communicate by means of SNA.

SNA defines several types of PUs and LUs, some of which are illustrated in figure 28.9. The types of each are discussed next.

Until the 1980s, virtually all devices on SNA networks operated in a master/slave relationship under which a master device, the control point, controls all network communication. Terminals, printers, and other peripheral devices function as slaves controlled by the master device, which uses polling to manage communication.

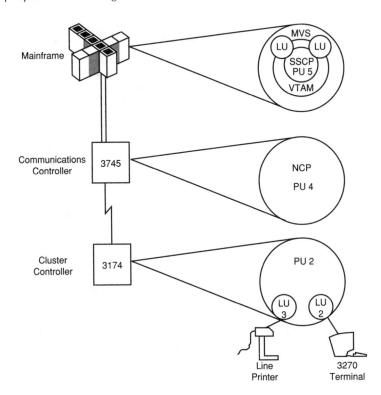

Figure 28.9
PUs and LUs in an SNA network.

During the 1980s, IBM introduced Advanced Program-to-Program Networking (APPN), which enabled LUs to communicate in a peer-to-peer fashion. LU Type 6.2 and PU Type 2.1 were introduced to support APPN.

Physical Units

SNA defines the following three types of physical units:

- **PU type 5** nodes are host nodes. A *host node* is the control point that manages networking in a domain. A *domain* consists of all the PUs, LUs, and other network resources that a given host can control. Domains can be divided into subareas. On SNA networks consisting of multiple hosts, terminals can be configured to access applications on more than one host.

The host node runs a program called *Virtual Terminal Access Method* (VTAM), which provides the *System Services Control Point* (SSCP) service that controls all connection requests and network flow. All SNA network hierarchies are organized around an SSCP.

- **PU type 4** nodes are communication controllers. A *communication controller* is a device that runs a *Network Control Program* (NCP) and serves as a communication front-end for the host node. (For this reason, this device typically is called a front end processor.) A communication controller relieves the host node of the responsibility for directly supervising remote communication resources. The IBM 3745 is a type of communication controller.

- **PU Type 2** nodes are peripheral nodes. Typically, *peripheral nodes* are *cluster controllers*, devices that enable printers, terminals, and other devices to connect to the network. The IBM 3174 is a type of communication controller.

 Note The course materials state that terminals and printers are also examples of PU Type 2 devices. Terminals and printers, however, are more typically defined as logical units, which are discussed in the next section.

Logical units are the network end-points between which communication occurs. Quite often an LU consists of a software process that is running on a type 2 node (a cluster controller). This process in turn services data input and output for a particular terminal, printer, or other peripheral.

The most important thing about PUs and LUs is the *function*, not the hardware in which the function is performed. A terminal, for example, must be serviced by a PU Type 2 function as well as an LU Type 2 function. These two functions typically are performed by the hardware and software operating in a cluster controller.

Some SNA printers might be equipped with hardware that enables them to network as PU Type 2 devices, enabling them to network without a cluster controller. These printers, however, must still include the LU function as well as the PU function.

For purposes of this course, some types of terminals and printers might be considered to be Type 2 PUs.

The course also lists a PU Type 1—a type no longer in use—which is a type of terminal node.

All communication of PU Type 2 nodes is managed by the central control point, the SSCP. Two type 2 devices, therefore, cannot directly communicate.

PU Type 2.1 is a new subclass of PU Type 2 that enables the device to provide a control point. This control point enables type 2.1 PUs to engage in peer-to-peer communication.

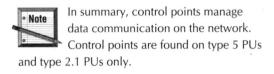

In summary, control points manage data communication on the network. Control points are found on type 5 PUs and type 2.1 PUs only.

Logical Units

Logical units are the endpoints of SNA communication and consist of physical devices (terminals, printers, etc.) and programs. The various LU types are summarized in table 34.2.

Table 34.2
Logical Unit Types

LU	Communication	Description Endpoints
0	Program-to-program	An older LU type supporting program-to-program communication. Replaced by LU type 6.2.
1	Program-to-device	Master/slave. SNA character-stream data on printers, card readers, and hard copy terminals.
2	Program-to-device	Master/slave. Supports terminals using the 3270 protocol.
3	Program-to-device	Master/slave. Supports printers using the 3270 protocol.
4	Program-to-program	Master/slave, peer-to-peer, or program-to-device SNA character stream to printers.
6&6.1	Program-to-program	Peer-to-peer interprogram communication. (Such as CICS-CICS, IMS-IMS, CICS-IMS.)
6.2	Program-to-program	Peer-to-peer Advanced Program-to-Program Communication (APPC).
7	Program-to-device	Communication using 5250 data streams, such as terminals on AS/400, System 36, and System 38.

Key SNA Protocols

The following are brief descriptions of common SNA protocols.

Token Ring

Token Ring is IBM's specification for a token-access LAN based on a ring logical topology. This specification was used as the basis for developing the IEEE 802.5 token ring standard. IBM Token Ring originally operated at 4 Mbps but has been extended to function at 16 Mbps data rates. The Token Ring specification describes various cable types, connectors, hubs, and wiring specifications.

Token Ring Topics And Methods

OSI Layer	Topics	Methods
Physical	Connection types	Point-to-point
	Physical topology	Star
	Digital signaling	State transition
	Bit synchronization	Synchronous
	Bandwidth use	Baseband
Data Link (MAC sublayer)	Logical topology	Ring
	Media access	Token passing
	Addressing	Physical device

Synchronous Data Link Control (SDLC)

SDLC is a high-performance data link protocol developed to support communication between computers and to function with dedicated or dial-up lines. SDLC supports point-to-point and multi-point communication in half- and full-duplex modes. SDLC frame types can be used to communicate data or to perform control functions.

Synchronous Data Link Control (SDLC) Topics And Methods

OSI Layer	Topics	Methods
Data Link (MAC sublayer)	Media access	Polling
	Addressing	Physical device
Data Link (LLC sublayer)	Transmission synchronization	Synchronous Synchronous
	Connection services	Flow control
		Error control

Network Control Program (NCP)

NCP is the protocol that manages network communication on front end processors. NCP functions at the data link and network layers and supports routing and gateway functions.

Network Control Program (NCP) Topics And Methods

OSI Layer	Topics	Methods
Data Link (MAC sublayer)	Media access	Polling
	Addressing	Physical device
Data Link (LLC sublayer)	Connection services	Flow control
Network	Addressing	Logical network
	Route selection	Static
	Gateway services	Network layer translation

Virtual Telecommunications Access Method (VTAM)

VTAM operates on the host control node and provides the *System Services Control Point* (SSCP) function for the network. The SSCP controls the network hierarchy and works in conjunction with NCPs running on front end processors. VTAM can manage single or multiple domains and supports interconnections between networks.

Virtual Telecommunications Access Method (VTAM) Topics And Methods

OSI Layer	Topics	Methods
Transport	Addressing	Connection identifier
	Segment development	Division and combination
	Connection	End-to-end

OSI Layer	Topics	Methods
	services	flow control
Session	Dialog control	Half-duplex
	Session administration	Connection establishment
		Data transfer
		Connection release

Advanced Peer-to-Peer Networking (APPN)

APPN is the SNA architecture for network peer-to-peer communication. Any PU Type 2.1 can communicate with other PU type 2.1 devices directly, without the need for an SSCP control node. Thus APPN supports networking without the requirement for a mainframe computer. APPN provides directory services, route discover, and window-based flow control.

Advanced Peer-to-Peer Networking (APPN) Topics And Methods

OSI Layer	Topics	Methods
Network	Addressing	Logical network
	Route discovery	
Transport	Connection services	Segment sequencing
		End-to-end flow control

Customer Information Control System (CICS)

CICS is a transaction processing environment used to build applications. Transaction processing is intended for critical applications, and CICS provides the security, transaction tracking, error recovery, transaction backout, and restart capabilities that are required in such demanding environments as banking and stocks trading.

Customer Information Control System (CICS) Topics And Methods

OSI Layer	Topics	Methods
Session	Dialog control	Half-duplex
	Session administration	Connection establishment
		Data transfer
		Connection release
Presentation	Translation	File syntax

Information Management System (IMS)

IMS is another application processing environment, and it supports both database and transaction management. The IMS Database Manager is a powerful hierarchical database that can operate under CICS or under the IMS Transaction Manager. IMS databases can be shared among various applications, with IMS scheduling activities and switching messages.

Information Management System (IMS) Topics And Methods

OSI Layer	Topics	Methods
Session	Dialog control	Half-duplex
	Session administration	Connection establishment
		Data transfer
		Connection release
Presentation	Translation	File syntax

Advanced Program-to-Program Communication (APPC)

APPC is the IBM specification that defines LU Type 6.2.

Advanced Program-to-Program Communication (APPC) Topics And Methods

OSI Layer	Topics	Methods
Transport	Addressing	Connection identifier
	Connection services	Segment sequencing
		End-to-end flow control
Session	Dialog control	Half-duplex
	Session	Connection establishment
		Data transfer
		Connection release

Distributed Data Management (DDM)

DDM uses an OS call redirection approach to provide remote file access to SNA applications. DDM receives service requests and executes them locally or directs them to a DDM server elsewhere on the network as appropriate.

Distributed Data Management (DDM) Topics And Methods

OSI Layer	Topics	Methods
Application	Network services	File
	Service use	OS call interception

Document Interchange Architecture (DIA)

DIA defines standards for data interchange between dissimilar computer systems, and coordinates storage, transfer, and retrieval of files.

Document Interchange Architecture (DIA) Topics And Methods

OSI Layer	Topics	Methods
Application	Network services	File

SNA Distributed Services (SNADS)

SNADS provides asynchronous distribution by implementing a store-and-forward distribution service. This service complements the synchronous delivery supported by SNA session capabilities and is useful for distribution of messages and documents. Among its functions, SNADS provides an infrastructure for distribution of e-mail.

SNA Distribution Services (SNADS) Topics And Methods

OSI Layer	Topics	Methods
Application	Network services	File Message

Questions

1. Which TWO protocols are designed to provide reliable delivery?

   ☐ A. IPX

   ☐ B. TCP

   ☐ C. UDP

   ☐ D. SPX

2. Which protocol enables clients to identify available NetWare servers?

   ○ A. IPX

   ○ B. NLSP

   ○ C. SAP

   ○ D. RIP

3. Which THREE protocols translate logical device names into device addresses?

   ☐ A. DNS

   ☐ B. NBP

   ☐ C. SAP

   ☐ D. X.500

4. If your network includes large numbers of NetWare servers, connected via a wide area network, which protocol should you evaluate as a means of reducing network traffic overhead?

   ○ A. SPX

   ○ B. SAP

   ○ C. NLSP

   ○ D. RIP

5. Which of the following protocols are most similar?

   ○ A. NetWare IPX and Internet TCP

   ○ B. NetWare NLSP and AppleTalk RTMP

   ○ C. NetWare NLSP and DNA CLNS

   ○ D. NetWare RIP and Internet OSPF

6. Which Novell protocol usually provides transport-layer functions?

   ○ A. SPX

   ○ B. IPX

   ○ C. NLSP

   ○ D. NCP

7. Which protocol suite provides the standards with the broadest industry support?

   ○ A. AppleTalk

   ○ B. Internet

   ○ C. NetWare

   ○ D. SNA

8. Which types of addresses are used on LocalTalk networks?

   ○ A. Physical node numbers

   ○ B. Static logical IDs

   ○ C. Dynamic logical IDs

   ○ D. Logical device names

9. Which protocol enables Ethernet and token ring networks to interface with AppleTalk protocols?

   ○ A. RTMP

   ○ B. AARP

○ C. LLAP

○ D. ZIP

10. Which protocol is responsible for matching user's logical device names with AppleTalk addresses?

    ○ A. AARP

    ○ B. ZIP

    ○ C. NBP

    ○ D. ATP

11. Which AppleTalk protocols provide session-level services?

    ☐ A. ASP

    ☐ B. PAP

    ☐ C. ADSP

    ☐ D. AFP

12. Which TWO components are required to enable a NetWare LAN to communicate with a Digital computer?

    ☐ A. Ethernet v.2 support

    ☐ B. IEEE 802.3 Ethernet support

    ☐ C. TCP/IP

    ☐ D. NetWare for LAT

13. Which TWO of these DNA protocols are regarded as presentation layer protocols?

    ☐ A. ASN.1

    ☐ B. NVTS

    ☐ C. FTAM

    ☐ D. MAILbus

14. Which THREE of the following statements are true regarding SNA network addressable units?

    ☐ A. A PU type 2 is a communication controller

    ☐ B. An LU 6.2 device is capable of program-to-program communication

    ☐ C. A PU consists of the hardware and software required to manage the resources of nodes.

    ☐ D. Control points are found on Type 5 and Type 2.1 PUs.

15. Which SNA protocols are required to implement peer-to-peer communication?

    ○ A. DDM

    ○ B. SNADS

    ○ C. APPN and APPC

    ○ D. NCP

Answers

1. B, D	9. B
2. C	10. C
3. A, B, D	11. A, B, C, D
4. C	12. A, D
5. C	13. A, B
6. D	14. B, C, D
7. B	15. C
8. C	

35

Other Protocols and Standards

This chapter discusses a variety of network protocols that you are likely to encounter. The following protocols are covered:

- *The IEEE 802 family*
- *Fiber Distributed Data Interface (FDDI)*
- *Serial Line Internet Protocol (SLIP) and Point-to-Point Protocol (PPP)*
- *CCITT/ITU X.25*
- *Frame Relay*
- *Integrated Service Digital Network (ISDN) and Broadband ISDN (B-ISDN)*
- *Asynchronous Transfer Mode (ATM)*
- *Synchronous Optical Network (SONET) and the Synchronous Digital Hierarchy (SDH)*
- *Switched Multimegabit Digital Service (SMDS)*

More information about many of these protocols can be found in NRP's NetWare: The Professional Reference, Fourth Edition.

The IEEE 802 Family

The *Institute of Electrical and Electronic Engineers* (IEEE) is the largest professional organization in the world and is extremely influential with regard to setting standards. The 802 committee of the IEEE has developed a series of standards for LANs, MANs, and WANs. These standards have been recognized and reissued by the *International Organization for Standardization* (ISO) as the ISO 8802 standards.

Twelve subcommittees oversee the 802 standards. (A thirteenth committee has been proposed for the developing 100-BASE-X standard.) Figure 35.1 illustrates the position each standard occupies in the OSI Reference Model. The following table summarizes the topics and methods associated with each standard.

802.2 Topics and Methods

Layer	Topics	Methods
Data link	Protocol specific	Identification of upper-layer protocols
LLC sublayer		

IEEE 802.2

The IEEE 802.2 standard defines an LLC sublayer that is utilized by other lower-layer protocols. Because a single LLC protocol layer is used by lower-layer protocols, network layer protocols can be designed independently of the network's physical layer and MAC sublayer implementations.

The LLC appends a header to packets that identifies which upper-layer protocols are associated with the frame. The header also declares which processes are the source and destination of each packet.

IEEE 802.3

The IEEE 802.3 standard defines a network derived from the Ethernet network originally developed by Digital, Intel, and Xerox. This standard defines characteristics related to the MAC sublayer of the data link layer and to the OSI physical layer. With one minor distinction—frame type—IEEE 802.3 Ethernet functions identically to DIX Ethernet v.2. The two standards can even coexist on the same cabling system, although devices using one standard cannot communicate directly with devices using the other. The following table about 802.3 summarizes the topics and methods associated with each layer.

Figure 35.1

The relationship between the IEEE 802 standards and the OSI Reference Model.

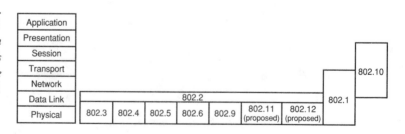

802.3 Topics and Methods

Layer	Topics	Methods
Physical	Physical topology	1BASE5 star
		10BASE5 bus
		10BASE2 bus
		10BROAD36 bus
		10BASE-F star
		10BASE-T star
	Connection types	Multipoint
	Digital signaling	State transition
	Bit synchro-nization	Synchronous
	Bandwidth use	Baseband (except 10BROAD36 broadband)
Data link (MAC sublayer)	Logical topology	Bus
	Media access	Contention
	Addressing	Physical device address

The MAC sublayer uses a variety of contention access called *Carrier Sense Multiple Access with Collision Detection* (CSMA/CD). This technique reduces the incidence of collision by having each device listen to the network to determine if it is quiet ("carrier sensing"); a device only attempts to transmit when the network is quiescent. This reduces but does not eliminate collisions because signals take some time to propagate through the network. As devices transmit, they continue to listen so they can detect a collision should it occur. When a collision occurs, all devices cease transmitting and send a "jamming" signal that notifies all stations of the collision. Then, each device waits a random amount of time before again attempting to transmit. This combination of safeguards significantly reduces collisions on all but the busiest networks.

The physical layer definition describes signaling methods (both baseband and broadband are available), data rates, media, and topologies. Several physical layer variants have been defined. Each is named following a convention that states the signaling rate (1 or 10) in Mbps, baseband (BASE) or broadband (BROAD) mode, and a designation of the media characteristics. The following are the 802.3 variants:

■ **1BASE5** is a 1 Mbps network that utilizes UTP cable with a signal range up to 500 meters (250 meters per segment). A star physical topology is used.

■ **10BASE5** uses a large diameter (10mm) "thick" coaxial cable with a 50-ohm impedance. A data rate of 10 Mbps is supported with a signaling range of 500 meters per cable segment on a physical bus topology. This variant is typically called *Thick Ethernet* or *Thicknet*.

■ **10BASE2** is similar to Thicknet, but uses a thinner coaxial cable that can support cable runs of 185 meters. (In this case, the 2 only approximately indicates the cable range.) The transmission rate remains 10 Mbps and the physical topology is a bus. This variant is typically called *Thin Ethernet* or *Thinnet*.

■ **10BASE-F** uses fiber-optic cables to support 10 Mbps signaling with a range of 4 kilometers. Three subcategories include 10BASE-FL (fiber link), 10BASE-FB (fiber backbone), and 10BASE-FP (fiber passive).

■ **10BROAD36** is a broadband standard that supports channel signal rates of 10 Mbps. 75-ohm coaxial cable supports cable runs of 1,800 meters (up to 3,600 meters in a dual-cable configuration) using a physical bus topology.

■ **10BASE-T** uses UTP cable in a star physical topology. The signaling rate remains at 10 Mbps. Devices might be up to 100 meters from a wiring hub.

■ **100BASE-X** is a proposed standard that is similar to 10BASE-T but supports 100 Mbps data rates.

Note The industry is not in accord regarding the proper use of the name Ethernet. Xerox has placed the name Ethernet in the public domain, therefore no one can claim authority over it. Purists often claim that Ethernet refers only to the original Digital-Intel-Xerox standard. More frequently, however, the term is used to designate any network based on CSMA/CD access control methods.

It is usually necessary to be specific about the standard that applies to a given network configuration. The original standard is called Ethernet version 2 (the older version 1 is still in occasional use) or Ethernet-II. The IEEE standard is distinguished by its committee title as 802.3.

The distinction is important because Ethernet version 2 and 802.3 Ethernet use incompatible frame types. Devices using one frame type cannot communicate with devices using the other frame type. Fortunately, NetWare is conversant with both frame types on both servers and clients.

IEEE 802.4

The 802.4 standard describes a network with a bus physical topology that controls media access with a token mechanism. The standard was designed to meet the needs of industrial automation systems but has gained little popularity. Both baseband and broadband (using 75-ohm coaxial cable) configurations are available.

802.4 Topics and Methods

Layer	Topics	Methods
Physical	Physical topology	Bus
	Connection types	Multipoint
	Digital signaling	State transition
	Bit synchronization	Synchronous
	Bandwidth use	Baseband
Data link (MAC sublayer)	Logical topology	Ring
	Media access	Token passing
	Addressing	Physical device address

IEEE 802.5

The IEEE 802.5 standard was derived from IBM's Token-Ring network, which employs a ring logical topology and token-based media access control. Data rates of 1, 4, and 16 Mbps have been defined. The IEEE 802.5 standard does not describe a cabling system. Most implementations are based on the IBM cabling system, which uses twisted-pair cable wired in a physical star.

802.5 Topics and Methods

Layer	Topics	Methods
Physical	Physical topology	Star/Ring
	Connection types	Point-to-point
	Digital signaling	State transition
	Bit synchro-nization	Synchronous
	Bandwidth use	Baseband
Data link (MAC sublayer)	Logical topology	Ring
	Media access Addressing	Token passing Physical device address

IEEE 802.6

The IEEE 802.6 standard describes a MAN standard called *Distributed Queue Dual Bus* (DQDB). Much more than a data network technology, DQDB is suited to data, voice, and video transmissions. The network is based on fiber-optic cable in a dual-bus topology. Traffic on each bus is unidirectional. When operated in pairs, the two buses provide a fault-tolerant configuration. Bandwidth is allocated using time slots, and both synchronous and asynchronous modes are supported.

802.6 Topics and Methods

Layer	Topics	Methods
Physical	Physical topology	Ring
	Connection types	Point-to-point
	Bandwidth use	Baseband
Data link (MAC sublayer)	Logical topology	Ring

IEEE 802.9

The IEEE 802.9 standard supports a 10 Mbps asynchronous channel along with 96 64-Kbps (6 Mbps total bandwidth) channels that can be dedicated to specific data streams. The total bandwidth is 16 Mbps. This standard is called *Isochronous Ethernet* (IsoEnet) and is designed for settings that have a mix of bursty and time-critical traffic.

IEEE 802.11

IEEE 802.11 is a standard for wireless LANs, currently under development. A CSMA/CD method has been approved, but the final standard is pending.

802.11 (Proposed) Topics and Methods

Layer	Topics	Methods
Data link (MAC sublayer)	Media access	Contention

IEEE 802.12

The IEEE 802.12 standard is based on a 100 Mbps proposal promoted by AT&T, IBM, and Hewlett-Packard. Called 100VG-AnyLAN, the network is based on a star wiring topology and a contention-based access method whereby devices signal the wiring hub of a need to transmit data. Devices can transmit only when granted permission by the hub. This standard is intended to provide a high-speed network that can operate in mixed Ethernet and Token Ring environments by supporting both frame types.

802.12 (Proposed) Topics and Methods

Layer	Topics	Methods
Physical	Physical topology	Star
	Connection types	Multipoint
	Bandwidth use	Baseband
Data link (MAC sublayer)	Logical topology	Bus
	Media access	Contention

Fiber Distributed Data Interface

Fiber Distributed Data Interface (FDDI) is a standard for fiber-based networks that was developed by the X3T9.5 committee of the *American National Standards Institute* (ANSI). The ISO has adopted FDDI as standard 9314. FDDI was developed for WANs but has been used in MANs and LANs as well.

As shown in figure 35.2, FDDI covers the physical layer and the MAC sublayer of the OSI Reference Model. Most frequently, the IEEE 802.2 standard is employed for the LLC sublayer.

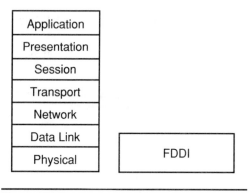

Figure 35.2
The relationship of FDDI to the OSI Reference Model.

FDDI is a 100 Mbps network that functions similarly to 802.5 Token Ring, and is based on token-passing access control and a ring topology. Originally developed for optical fiber cable, the standard has been extended so that it can be supported with copper UTP. Use of optical fiber cable enables FDDI to support physically large networks.

Although FDDI networks can be cabled as physical stars, stars might be impractical with larger networks, and FDDI networks are then typically cabled in physical rings. Stations can be attached in two ways as shown in figures 35.3A and 35.3B. Stations on a single ring configuration are called *single-attached stations*. On a single ring, failure of the medium at any point causes the network to fail.

To provide greater fault tolerance, FDDI is typically cabled with *dual-attached stations* (DASs) using two counter-rotating rings. As figure 35.3B shows, if the cable fails at any one point, the two

rings are automatically reconfigured to maintain a complete ring transmission path. (Note that a failed link between single-attached stations cannot be corrected in this manner.) Under normal operation, both rings can be used for data and traffic can be balanced between rings. It is desirable, however, to design the network to half its dual-ring capacity and to half its size limit. If a ring failure occurs under these conditions, the total length of the two rings will be within specifications and the traffic will be manageable with only a single active ring.

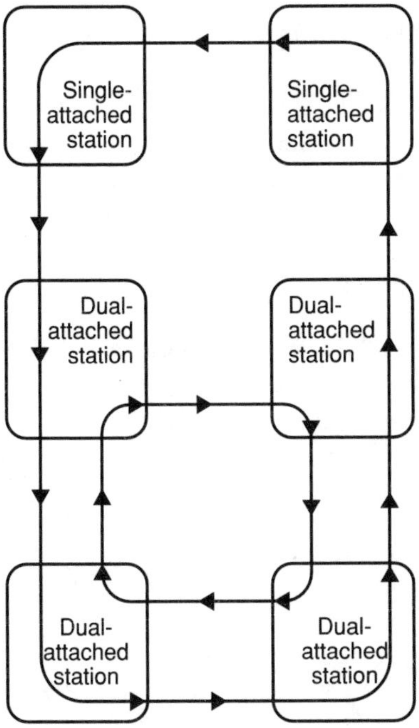

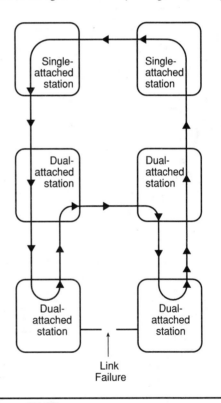

Figure 35.3A

Normal operation of an FDDI network with single- and dual-attached stations.

Figure 35.3B

Dual-attached FDDI stations correcting for a failed link.

FDDI Topics and Methods

Layer	Topics	Methods
Physical	Physical topology	Star or ring
	Connection types	Point-to-point
	Bandwidth use	Baseband
Data link (MAC sublayer)	Logical topology	Ring
	Media access	Token passing

SLIP was developed to provide dial-up IP connections. It is an extremely rudimentary protocol that suffers from a lack of rigid standardization such that different implementations might not interoperate.

SLIP Topics and Methods

Layer	Topics	Methods
Physical	Connection type	Point-to-point

PPP was defined by the *Internet Engineering Task Force* (IETF) to improve on SLIP by providing the following features:

- Security using password login
- Simultaneous support for multiple protocols on the same link
- Dynamic IP addressing
- Error control

Different PPP implementations might offer different levels of service and can negotiate service levels when connections are made.

Serial Line Internet Protocol and Point-to-Point Protocol

The *Serial Line Internet Protocol* (SLIP) and *Point-to-Point Protocol* (PPP) were designed to support dial-up access to networks based on the Internet protocols. SLIP is a simple protocol that functions at the physical layer, whereas PPP is a considerably enhanced protocol that provides physical layer and data link layer functionality. The relationship of both to the OSI model is shown in figure 35.4.

Figure 35.4

The relationship of SLIP and PPP to the OSI Reference Model.

| Application |
| Presentation |
| Session |
| Transport |
| Network |
| Data Link |
| Physical |

PPP Topics and Methods

Layer	Topics	Methods
Physical	Connection type	Point-to-point
Data link (MAC sublayer)	Addressing	Physical device
Data link (LLC sublayer)	Connection services	Error control

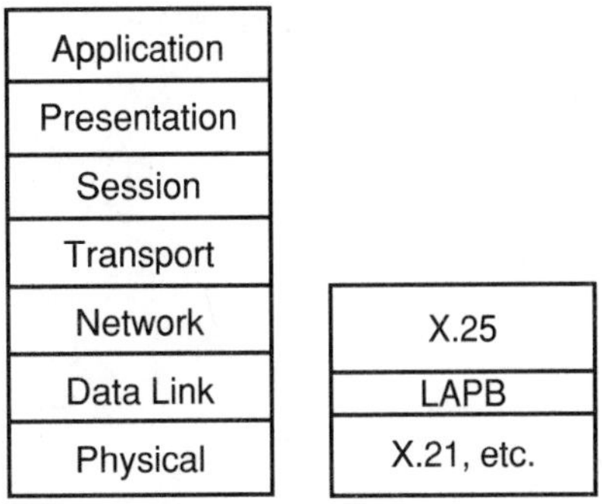

Figure 35.5
The relationship of X.25 to the OSI Reference Model.

CCITT/ITU X.25

X.25 is a packet-switching network standard developed by the *International Telegraph and Telephone Consultative Committee* (CCITT), which has been renamed the *International Telecommunications Union* (ITU). The standard, referred to as Recommendation X.25, was introduced in 1974, and is most commonly implemented in WANs.

As shown in figure 35.5, X.25 is one level of a three-level stack that spans the network, data link, and physical layers.

Physical layer connectivity is provided by a variety of standards including X.21, X.21bis, and V.32.

X.21 Topics and Methods

Layer	Topics	Methods
Physical	Connection type	Point-to-point
	Physical topology	Hybrid mesh
	Bit synchronization	Synchronous

Link Access Procedures-Balanced (LAPB) is a bit-oriented, full-duplex, synchronous data link layer LLC protocol.

LAPB Topics and Methods

Layer	Topics	Methods
Data link control (LLC sublayer)	Connection services	LLC flow
		Error control

X.25 packet-switching networks provide the options of permanent or switched virtual circuits. Although a datagram (unreliable) protocol was supported until 1984, X.25 is now required to provide reliable service and end-to-end flow control. Because each device on a network can operate more than one virtual circuit, X.25 must provide error and flow control for each virtual circuit.

X.25 networks are typically implemented with line speeds up to 64 Kbps. These speeds are suitable for the file transfer and terminal activity that comprised the bulk of network traffic when X.25 was defined. Such speeds, however, are inadequate to provide LAN-speed services, which generally require speeds of 1 Mbps or better. X.25 networks are, therefore, poor choices for providing LAN application services in a WAN environment.

Recommendation X.25 Topics and Methods

Layer	Topics	Methods
Network	Addressing	Channel (logical address maintained for each connection)
	Switching	Packet (virtual circuit)
	Connection services	Network layer flow control
		Error control

Frame Relay

Frame relay was designed to support the *Broadband Integrated Services Digital Network* (B-ISDN), which is discussed in the following section, "ISDN and B-ISDN." The specifications for frame relay address some of the limitations of X.25. Like X.25, frame relay is a packet-switching network service. Frame relay is standardized by ANSI and ITU (CCITT).

Unlike X.25, frame relay assumes a more reliable network. This enables frame relay to eliminate much of the X.25 overhead required to provide reliable service on less reliable networks. Frame relay relies on higher-level protocol layers to provide flow and error control.

Frame relay typically is implemented as a public data network and is, therefore, regarded as a WAN protocol. The relationship of frame relay to the OSI model is shown in figure 35.6. Notice that the scope of frame relay is limited to the physical and data link layers.

Frame relay provides switched and permanent virtual circuits. Frame relay services are typically implemented at line speeds of 56 Kbps up to 1.544 Mbps (T1).

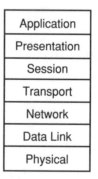

Figure 35.6

The relationship of Frame Relay to the OSI Reference Model.

Customers typically purchase access to a specific amount of bandwidth on a frame relay service. This bandwidth is called the *committed information rate* (CIR), a data rate for which the customer is guaranteed access. Customers may be permitted to access higher data rates on a pay-per-use, temporary basis. This arrangement enables customers to tailor their network access costs based on their bandwidth requirements.

Frame Relay Topics and Methods

Layer	Topics	Methods
Physical	Connection type	Point-to-point
	Physical topology	Hybrid mesh
	Switching	Packet (virtual circuit)
Data link	Connection services	LLC-level flow control (LLC sublayer)
		Error control (detection but not recovery)

ISDN and B-ISDN

Integrated Services Digital Network (ISDN) is a group of ITU (CCITT) standards designed to provide voice, video, and data transmission services on digital telephone networks. ISDN uses multiplexing to support multiple channels on high-bandwidth circuits. The relationship of the ISDN protocols to the OSI Reference Model is shown in figure 35.7.

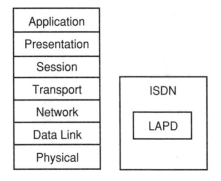

Figure 35.7
The relationship of ISDN protocols to the OSI Reference Model.

A variety of ISDN channel types are defined. These channel types, often called *bit pipes*, provide different types and levels of service. The various channels are described in the following list:

- A channel provides 4 kHz analog telephone service.

- D channels support 64 Kbps digital data.

- C channels support 8 or 16 Kbps digital data, generally for out-of-band signaling.

- D channels support 16 or 64 Kbps digital data, also for out-of-band signaling. D channels support the following subchannels:

  - p subchannels support low-bandwidth packet data.

  - s subchannels are used for signaling (such as call setup).

  - t subchannels support telemetry data (such as utility meters).

- E channels provide 64 Kbps service used for internal ISDN signaling.

- H channels provide 384, 1,536, or 1,920 digital service.

The following three standard channel combinations have been defined:

- *Basic rate* includes two B channels and one D channel.

- *Primary rate* includes one D channel, 23 B channels (in the U.S. and Japan), or 30 B channels (in Europe and Australia).

- *Hybrid* provides one A channel and one C channel.

ISDN functions as a data transmission service only. Acknowledged, connectionless, full-duplex service is provided at the data link layer by the LAPD protocol, which operates on the D channel.

ISDN Topics and Methods

Layer	Topics	Methods
Physical	Multiplexing	Time-division multiplexing
Network	Switching	Packet
		Circuit

LAPD Topics and Methods

Layer	Topics	Methods
Data link (MAC sublayer)	Addressing	Physical device
Data link (LLC sublayer)	Connection services	LLC flow control
		Frame sequencing

Broadband ISDN is a refinement of ISDN that is defined to support higher bandwidth applications such as video, imaging, and multimedia. Physical layer support for B-ISDN is provided by *Asynchronous Transfer Mode* (ATM) and the *Synchronous Optical Network* (SONET). SONET is discussed further in the following section. Typical B-ISDN data rates are 51 Mbps, 155 Mbps, and 622 Mbps over fiber-optic media.

Synchronous Optical Network and the Synchronous Digital Hierarchy

Bell Communications Research developed SONET, which has been accepted as an ANSI standard. SONET is regarded as a WAN standard.

A similar set of standards, published by the ITU (CCITT), is called the *Synchronous Digital Hierarchy* (SDH). Regional variations of SDH, including SDH-Europe, SDH-SONET (North America), and SDH-Japan, have been defined to accommodate local differences. Figure 35.8 illustrates the relationship of the SONET/SDH standards to the OSI Reference Model.

Data rates for SONET are organized in a hierarchy based on the *Optical Carrier* (OC) speed and the corresponding *Synchronous Transport Signals* (STS) employed. The basic OC and STS data rate is 51.84 Mbps. Higher data rates are provided in multiples of the basic rate. Thus OC-48 is 48×51.84 Mbps = 2488.32 Mbps.

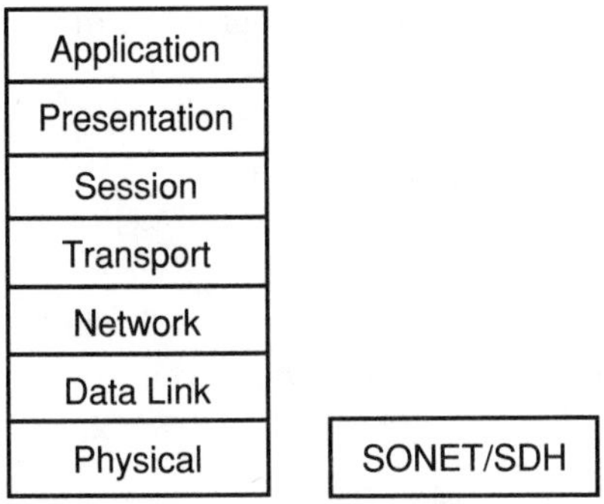

Application
Presentation
Session
Transport
Network
Data Link
Physical

SONET/SDH

Figure 35.8

The relationship of SONET/SD to the OSI Reference Model.

SDH data rates begin at 155.52 Mbps and are calculated in multiples of that rate. Thus an SDH-16 has a data rate of 2488.32 Mbps, equivalent to the SONET STS-48 data rate.

SONET/SDH Topics and Methods

Layer	Topics	Methods
Physical	Connection type	Point-to-point
	Physical topology	Mesh
		Ring
	Multiplexing	Time-division

Asynchronous Transfer Mode (ATM)

ATM is a high-bandwidth switching technology developed by the ITU *Telecommunications Standards Sector* (ITU-TSS). An organization called the *ATM Forum* is responsible for defining ATM implementation characteristics. ATM can be layered on other physical layer technologies such as FDDI and SONET. The relationships of these protocols to the OSI model are shown in figure 35.9.

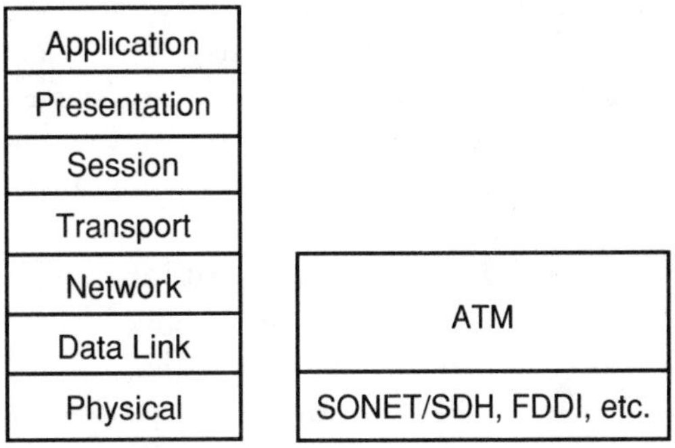

Application
Presentation
Session
Transport
Network
Data Link
Physical

ATM
SONET/SDH, FDDI, etc.

Figure 35.9

The relationship of ATM to the OSI Reference Model.

ATM has several characteristics that distinguish it from other switching technologies discussed in this course. ATM is based on fixed-length, 53-byte cells, whereas other technologies employ frames that vary in length to accommodate different amounts of data. Because ATM cells are uniform in length, switching mechanisms can operate with a high level of efficiency.

The unit of transmission for ATM is called a *cell.* All cells are 53 bytes in length and consist of a 5-byte header and 48 bytes of data. The 48-byte data size was arrived at by the standards committee as a compromise between the needs of audio and data transmission. Audio information must be delivered with little latency (delay) to maintain a smooth flow of sound. Audio engineers preferred a small cell so that cells would be more readily available when needed. For data, however, large cells reduce the overhead required to deliver a byte of information.

Asynchronous delivery is another distinguishing feature of ATM. *Asynchronous* refers to the characteristic of ATM whereby transmission time slots do not occur periodically, but are granted at irregular intervals. ATM uses a technique called *label multiplexing,* which allocates time slots on demand. Traffic that is time critical, such as voice or video, can be given priority over data traffic that can be delayed slightly with no ill effect. Channels are identified by cell labels, not by specific time slots. A high-priority transmission need not be held until its next time slot allocation. It might only be required to wait until the current 53-byte cell has been transmitted.

Other multichannel technologies utilize time-division techniques to allocate bandwidth to channels. A T1 (1.544 Mbps) line, for example, might be time-division multiplexed to provide 24 voice channels. With this technique, each channel is assigned a specific time slot in the transmission schedule. The disadvantage of this technique is that an idle channel does not yield its bandwidth for the creation of other channels.

Devices communicate on ATM networks by establishing a virtual path, which is identified by a *virtual path identifier* (VPI). Within this virtual path, virtual circuits can be established, which are in turn associated with *virtual circuit identifiers* (VCIs). The VPI and VCI together make up a three-byte field that is included in the cell header.

Other networks, such as a routed Ethernet, require a six-byte physical address as well as a network address to uniquely identify each device on an internetwork. ATM can switch cells with three-byte identifiers because VPIs and VCIs apply only to a given device-to-device link. Each ATM switch can assign different VPIs and VCIs for each link. Up to 16 million circuits can be configured for any given device-to-device link.

The following three characteristics define the classes of ATM service:

■ **Time relation between source and destination.** Some data types require a precise time relationship between transmission and reception of cells.

■ **Bit rate.** Constant and variable bit rates are available. Many audio and video signaling techniques require constant bit rates. Newer techniques based on data compression might have the capability to function on variable-rate services.

■ **Connection mode.** Connection-oriented and connectionless services are available.

Using these characteristics, the following service classes have been defined:

■ **Class A.** Timing required, constant bit rate, connection-oriented.

■ **Class B.** Timing required, variable bit rate, connection-oriented. Data for this class must be delivered with a constant delay.

■ **Class C.** No timing, variable bit rate, connection-oriented.

■ **Class D.** No timing, variable bit rate, connectionless.

■ **Class X.** Unrestricted, variable bit rate, connection-oriented or connectionless.

Although ATM was developed primarily as a WAN technology, it has many characteristics of value for high-performance LANs. An interesting advantage is that ATM makes it possible to use the same technology for both LANs and WANs.

ATM Topics and Methods

Layer	Topics	Methods
Data link	Transmission synchronization	Isochronous
	Connection services	Error control
Network	Switching Route selection	Cell switching Static

Switched Multimegabit Digital Service (SMDS)

Switched Multimegabit Digital Service (SMDS) is a technology developed by Bell Communications Research in 1991. SMDS is related to ATM in that it transports data in 53-byte cells. SMDS supports cell switching at data rates of 1.544–45 Mbps.

SMDS is a connectionless data link layer service. IEEE 802.6 (DQDB metropolitan area network) is the primary physical layer standard employed with SMDS, although other physical layer standards are supported as well. Figure 35.10 illustrates the relationships of these protocols in the context of the OSI model.

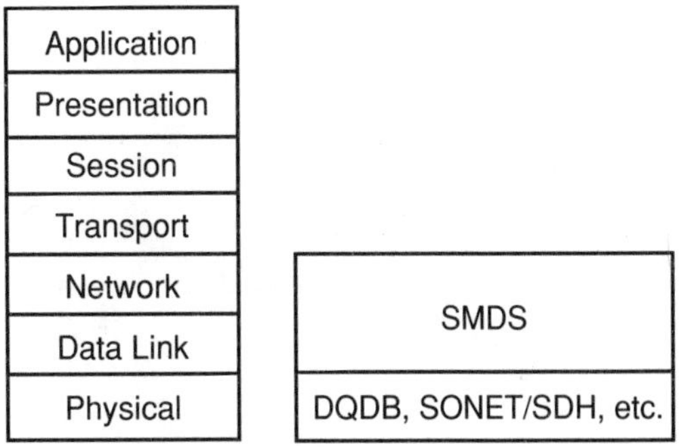

Figure 35.10
The relationship of SMDS to the OSI Reference Model.

SMDS Topics and Methods

Layer	Topics	Methods
Data link (LLC sublayer)	Transmission synchronization	Isochronous
Network	Switching	Cell switching

Questions

1. Which TWO of the following are regarded as WAN protocols?

   ☐ A. Frame relay

   ☐ B. SLIP

   ☐ C. IEEE 802.6

   ☐ D. X.25

2. Which protocols are commonly used with IEEE 802.2?

   ○ A. IEEE 802.3

   ○ B. IEEE 802.5

   ○ C. IEEE 802.6

   ○ D. All of the above

3. What is the primary characteristic that distinguishes a cell from a packet?

   ○ A. Cells are generally smaller than packets.

   ○ B. Cells do not incorporate physical addresses.

   ○ C. All cells have the same fixed length.

   ○ D. Packets cannot be switched.

4. What are the primary differences between Ethernet version 2 and IEEE 802.3 Ethernet?

   ○ A. They require different network hardware.

   ○ B. IEEE 802.3 Ethernet functions at a higher data rate.

   ○ C. They use different frame formats.

   ○ D. Ethernet version 2 does not use CSMA/CD media access control.

5. Which TWO of these protocols are intended primarily for use on fiber-optic cable?

   ☐ A. Frame relay

   ☐ B. FDDI

   ☐ C. SONET

   ☐ D. X.25

6. Which TWO of these standards use token passing for media access control?

   ☐ A. IEEE 802.4

   ☐ B. IEEE 802.6

   ☐ C. Frame relay

   ☐ D. FDDI

7. Which TWO of these standards are designed to support audio data?

   ☐ A. IEEE 802.10

   ☐ B. ISDN

   ☐ C. ATM

   ☐ D. Frame relay

8. Which TWO of these network standards are well suited to delivering time-critical data?

   ☐ A. X.25

   ☐ B. IEEE 802.5

   ☐ C. Frame Relay

   ☐ D. ATM

Answers

1. A, D	5. B, C
2. D	6. A, D
3. C	7. B, C
4. C	8. B, D

Tasks of Network Administrators

The job of network managers involves a wide variety of responsibilities, the basic concepts for some of which this chapter discusses, including the following topics:

- *Configuration management*
- *Fault management*
- *Performance management*
- *Security management*
- *Accounting management*

This book assumes you have had some experience as a network administrator, so discussion is brief and to-the-point, and no review questions follow.

Configuration Management

Configuration management is a process of tracking the components of a network and the configurations of those components. A detailed history of changes to the network is a tremendous aid for troubleshooting. When a problem occurs, the first thing you want to know is, "What's changed?" A configuration management database can tell you.

Following are just a few of the things your configuration management procedures should track:

- All hardware that has vital data, such as firmware (ROM) revisions, when installed (for example, a design change without a new model number), and configuration details, such as interrupts, addresses, and so forth

- Workstation configuration files, such as CONFIG.SYS and AUTOEXEC.BAT, to which many problems trace owing to users making changes

- Network software, such as NetWare shell and Requester versions

- Software licenses, to ensure that your network operates within the bounds of the license terms

- Problems encountered and related solutions; history tends to repeat itself, so the solutions to many problems might already be known and recorded

You can manage proper configuration most easily if you use software designed for that purpose. Novell offers the *NetWare Management System* (NMS). Commercial NetWare configuration management products include Bindview and Cheyenne Monitrix.

Fault Management

Fault management involves using tools and procedures that anticipate network problems and help correct them when they occur.

When failures do occur, having the proper tools can improve the rapidity with which you can isolate and diagnose the fault. Many of these tools have evolved to the point that they report events that are not apparent as problems but that betray a degradation in the network. If a network card generates increasing numbers of damaged packets that must be retransmitted, the right tools report the condition before the NIC fails or generates so many errors that it degrades overall network performance.

Fault management includes some of the following practices:

- **Data archiving and backup.** Properly speaking, archiving and backup are not part of fault management procedure, other than that a good set of backup tapes, properly stored, ensures against catastrophic data loss. Novell's standard for data archiving and backup is the *Storage Management Services* (SMS).

- **Fault-tolerant design.** You can configure many network components in a fault-tolerant configuration such that one hardware failure cannot halt the network. NetWare provides the following three levels of server fault tolerance:

  - **SFT I (hot fix).** Enables servers to recover from minor failure in hard drive media

  - **SFT II (disk mirroring and duplexing).** Enables hard drives to operate in parallel so that a single hard drive failure does not cause data loss or service interruption

■ **SFT III (server duplexing).** Enables pairs of servers to operate in parallel so that even complete failure of a single server does not cause data loss or service interruption

You can achieve network fault-tolerance by designing in redundant data paths, fault-tolerant hubs, uninterruptible power supplies, and other such features.

■ **Network management systems.** Protocols for network management include the *Simple Network Management Protocol* (SNMP—a protocol in the TCP/IP suite that is *the* dominant network management protocol) and *Common Management Information Protocol* (CMIP). Devices that run these protocols (such as routers, hubs, switches, managed NICs, and so on) can generate network management messages that are directed to a network management console that analyzes incoming management information and generates network performance statistics and alerts. The console also can possess the capability to remotely manage network devices. On managed network hubs, for example, the console might automatically shut down a hub port that generates high numbers of errors. Novell's NetWare Management System is an SNMP management console for which you can use "snap-in" accessory products to extend its capabilities.

■ **Protocol analyzers receive all packets on the network and decode them for analysis.** Many network problems betray themselves in the form of abnormal packets. Network managers can capture packets from the network data stream and examine them for abnormalities. The latest versions of protocol analyzers perform much of the analysis automatically and assist with the rest. Some even incorporate expert systems that can intelligently diagnose network problems. Novell offers a software-based protocol analyzer, called LANalyzer for Windows.

■ **Cable testers are available at many levels of sophistication.** The best cable testers isolate faults to a specific area of a cable and even inform you when a cable is operating, but not performing up to specification.

Performance Management

Performance management is the proactive companion to fault management. Monitoring the performance of a network provides "baseline" data that is a snapshot of the network performing well under normal conditions, which proves valuable for identifying deteriorating network performance and as a standard of comparison when network failures occur.

You might monitor the following paramaters:

■ **Response time.**

■ **Throughput.**

■ **Network load.** A measure of network traffic as a percentage of total performance capacity.

■ **Errors.** All networks display some errors, but rising error levels are a clear indication of an impending problem.

Performance management enables you to plan future network enhancements, in addition to helping you anticipate problems. As network demand rises, you can add capacity before users become aware of problems.

Security Management

Anyone who has managed NetWare has dealt with *security management.* One of your tasks is to anticipate security threats and install safeguards. You might consider selecting some of the following security provisions:

- Establishing user and group security

- Restricting internal and external access to data

- Conducting security risk assessments

- Establishing security policies

- Protecting the network from viruses

- Auditing the network to detect security breaches

NetWare 4 provides for auditing the network, by supporting the establishment of network auditors who can function independently of network administrators. NetWare 4 network auditors can monitor all network operations to detect security breaches, including those that supervisors perform.

Accounting Management

Accounting management involves assessing the costs of using network resources. Some organizations use this information to charge departments for network use. These charges can be used to provide incentives for using LAN resources intelligently. User demand for additional LAN storage capacity and performance tends to rise rapidly if not controlled.

Other organizations simply use accounting information to control costs and plan improvements. When network enhancements are anticipated, accounting data can aid in assessing the cost/performance ratio of various options.

Service and Support

Troubleshooting the Network

It is wonderful when everything works as it should, but there is a finite life to everything. This means that no matter how well your network might be operating today, it is only a matter of time before there is a failure in cards, cabling, or any other component from which the network is built.

This chapter explores the following two components of network management:

■ *Preventing problems*

■ *Troubleshooting*

Regardless of how well you do the first, an occasion will come when you will have to do the second. This chapter places primary emphasis on details that can easily become test fodder. Your purpose for reading this chapter is that you want to be able to answer questions on the Novell tests. Aside from that, the material is presented in as practical a manner as possible, and lends itself well to use in the real world.

Problem Prevention

Preventing problems after a network is up and running is one of the primary jobs of an administrator. Because there are so many different types of problems that can occur, one cannot plan for all eventualities. The possibilities, however, can be divided into the following four categories:

- Physical
- Electrical
- Security
- Viruses

The following sections examine each of these.

Physical Problems

Temperature is one of the most critical environmental components affecting a computer's operation—whether a server or a workstation. Ambient temperature figures in, but more importantly is the temperature inside the computer. There can be as much as a 40 degree difference between the inside and outside of a computer due to the heat generated by the components. One reason for leaving computers turned on all the time is to prevent the internal temperature from fluctuating too greatly.

 Note When new equipment arrives, you should allow it to adjust to room temperature before using it. This assures that there will not be undue thermal strain on the components, should they have been bouncing around in a frozen FedEx truck for three days.

It is critical that a server have adequate ventilation to keep from overheating, otherwise "chip creep" can occur wherein integrated circuits lose their seating and contact with the socket. It is equally important that ambient air, which is sucked into the machine, be filtered and be of as high a quality as possible. A consistent temperature in the room should be maintained, and particles such as smoke and dust should be filtered out as much as possible with appropriate filtration devices.

Electrical Problems

Whereas physical problems can deteriorate a server or other computer slowly, electrical problems tend to do it immediately. They can destroy components, trash data, and make you wonder why you didn't keep the job at ChemLawn.

The four types of electrical problems are as follows:

- **Crosstalk.** Crosstalk is when two wires interfere with the magnetic fields of each other. The best solution is to use proper cable shielding and to avoid physical proximity between cables.

- **Static.** It is not the build up that wreaks damage, it is the sudden discharge. What makes it dangerous is that it can build to phenomenal levels before discharging all at once. Also known as *Electro-Static Discharge* (ESD), it must be beyond 3,000 volts for you to even feel it, but charges of 20 and 30 volts can damage equipment. The best solution to avoiding ESD is to use static discharge equipment and ground cords.

You should always ground yourself and any equipment on which you will be working. Never directly touch any electrical leads and always use antistatic bags to store components. You also can control static by keeping ambient humidity low.

 Styrofoam is a common carrier of static buildup. It is highly recommended that Styrofoam cups not be left near servers or workstations.

- **Transients.** Transients are sudden, high voltage bursts of current. Also known as spikes, transients usually occur randomly and last for less than one second. The randomness makes them hard to isolate, and they can often be associated with trouble farther down a power line, such as a blackout or lightning strike. Suppressor diodes are the best line of defense, as well as putting computers on their own circuit with isolated grounds.

- **Line noise.** Low in voltage and low in current, noise usually occurs in an observable pattern. Most of the time, the culprit is another electrical device such as a microwave oven, a motor, or even the ballast of a fluorescent lamp. The best solution is to properly ground equipment and avoid running cable near other sources of interference.

 When discussing noise, there are two acronyms commonly used. *Radio Frequency Interference* (RFI) is caused by microwaves, ovens, and appliances. *Electromagnetic Interference* (EMI) is caused by lights, radar, and industrial tools.

Security

Network security, and the implementation thereof, is the responsibility of the system administrator. *Electronic Data Processing* (EDP) Environmental Security entails thoroughly thinking through all the risks in your installation and creating a plan for dealing with them.

The following are four types of threats:

1. Destruction

2. Corruption

3. Disclosure

4. Interruption

To deal with the possibility of these threats, the administrator should think about each network segment and evaluate what potential risks there are. Next, he should evaluate and implement steps to minimize those risks effectively.

Some examples of security that can be implemented include the following:

- Restricting login times to business hours

- Requiring regular password changes

- Requiring unique passwords

- Turning off modems after working hours

- Building RAID and redundancy into the server

Encryption also can be used to keep an intruder from understanding data that he intercepts. Beginning with NetWare 3.11, encryption is now standard, providing the SET command has ALLOW UNENCRYPTED PASSWORDS set to OFF.

Viruses

In simple terms, *viruses* are programs that interfere with the normal flow of processing. Viruses interfere by changing files and configurations, or by attaching themselves to everything they come in contact with and growing exponentially.

Viruses, by nature, require some action to activate them, and so they attach themselves to executable files. Those files are usually denoted by their extension, which can be BAT, EXE, or COM. Overlays, OVL files, provide other opportunities, however, as do FAT tables and boot sectors.

Very rarely have there been occurrences of viruses shipping with retail software. Most of the time, viruses enter the workplace through pirated software, downloaded shareware, or other suspect software. In a perfect world, the best solution is to prevent anyone other than the system administrator from installing software on the network. In this sense, "network" refers to all things physically attached—not only the server, but all workstations, too.

Given that there is no perfect world, and that you often cannot prevent installation of software on an individual's workstation, you must contend with the possibility of a virus attack. To do so, you should perform the following:

- Regularly back up the server and workstations

- Routinely scan for viruses with third-party software

- Flag EXE and COM files as Read-Only and Execute-Only

- In the PUBLIC and LOGIN directories, grant only Read and File Scan rights

- Check every disk for viruses before you install

- Discourage the downloading of BBS software

- Be prepared for action

Bear in mind that NetWare includes some safeguards against virus attacks. For one thing, the NetWare FAT table is different from that of workstations and cannot be attacked. Therefore, NetWare viruses are not as common as DOS viruses, and most virus attacks occur on workstations, as opposed to the server.

Troubleshooting

After a problem has occurred, prevention is a meaningless word and troubleshooting comes into play. The overall goal of troubleshooting is to restore service in a timely manner. The following are the four steps to the basic troubleshooting model:

1. Gather information.

2. Develop an attack plan.

3. Isolate the problem and execute the plan.

4. Document what was done.

By following these four steps, you can successfully restore a network to its fully operational state in the most efficient time possible. The importance of the fourth step cannot be overstated; it is easy to see where an experienced administrator has an advantage over an inexperienced one.

There are several questions you should ask when someone first reports a problem (and before you ever arrive on site). As rudimentary as these questions might seem, taking the time to ask them will save you an enormous amount of time in the long run.

- **Has it ever worked?** Quite often, when a user calls to complain about something that doesn't work, it might be because she just installed it or has made some other major change that she does not want to mention without prodding.

- **When did it work last?** If the accounting clerk is calling to complain about a printer that is not printing checks, it can be worth knowing that the printer in question has been offline for the last year and a half.

- **What has changed since then?** You should consider, for example, whether you have moved from one building to another, or rearranged your offices? Did you pull your own cable through the ceiling?

The four step troubleshooting model discussed earlier suggests the following steps to solving workstation problems:

1. Rule out any possibility of user error.

2. Check the physical site to verify that all is as it should be. Make certain that an electrical cord or printer cable did not come unplugged.

3. Power everything down and then back up.

4. Back up data if there is a question of storage media (a hard drive or drives).

5. Eliminate as much overhead as you can. If the problem is with a workstation, reduce the CONFIG.SYS and AUTOEXEC.BAT files to the bare minimum and try the process again. Be certain that all terminate-and-stay-resident (TSR) programs that do not need to boot to get on the network are commented out of the AUTOEXEC.BAT file.

Whether solving problems on a workstation or server, you should always think in terms of dollars. During the hypothesis stage, consider what all the possibilities are and try those that cost the least first. Keep in mind that dollars are associated not only with any components that might need replacement, but also with downtime and the time of the administrator.

Documents and Records

As mentioned earlier, the importance of documentation cannot be overstated. The importance of *good* documentation can never be surpassed by any other tool. Even on the smallest of networks, time and money can be saved by documenting problems and keeping good records.

You should maintain three types of records—those relating to the LAN system, the history surrounding it, and the resources available.

For the LAN system, there should be a detailed map identifying the location of users, and all tangible components: printers, routers, bridges, and so forth. You also should keep an inventory of the components and documentation on cabling and the workstations.

The history of the LAN should include user profiles, what the purpose of the LAN is, a log of past problems, and usage information. Not only can this come in handy when an administrator is trying to diagnose a problem, but also when said administrator meets a bus somewhere other than the bus stop. Should a change in administrators take place, there is no better way to keep a business on its feet than to have its network thoroughly documented.

The documentation regarding available resources should include information about the protocols and routing in use, as well as the LAN architecture. The most important resource of all, however, is people. You should have a chart of people and phone numbers readily available for when problems become too difficult for the administrator. VAR numbers, manager numbers, and any other emergency personnel numbers should be kept in an easy to find location.

Diagnostic Software

Third-party, diagnostic software is used to provide information about hardware. That hardware can be virtually anything from the server to a workstation to a cable. A considerable number of packages are available at a variety of prices. The most important consideration should be that they offer information that is useful to you.

Check It PRO is one program that can give quick facts about your hardware and operating system. It can also benchmark the components and show information about the interrupts.

There are a variety of programs with similar features. The following shows an example of output generated at a workstation with System Information—one of the tools available in Norton Utilities:

```
           Computer Name: IBM AT
        Operating System: DOS 6.20
     Built-in BIOS dated: Friday, January 15, 1988
          Main Processor: Intel 80386          Serial Ports: 2
            Co-Processor: Intel 80387        Parallel Ports: 3
   Video Display Adapter: Video Graphics Array (VGA)
      Current Video Mode: Text, 80 x 25 Color
   Available Disk Drives: 13, A: - C:, F: - I:, P:, S:, V:, X: - Z:

DOS reports 639 K-bytes of memory:
   254 K-bytes used by DOS and resident programs
   385 K-bytes available for application programs
A search for active memory finds:
   640 K-bytes main memory     (at hex 0000-A000)
   128 K-bytes display memory  (at hex A000-C000)
   128 K-bytes extra memory    (at hex C000-E000)
 1,024 K-bytes expanded memory
ROM-BIOS Extensions are found at hex paragraphs: C000

  Computing Index (CI), relative to IBM/XT: Testing...                 73.0
      Disk Index (DI), relative to IBM/XT: Not computed. No drive specified.

Performance Index (PI), relative to IBM/XT: Not computed.
```

Much of the same workstation information can be achieved with newer versions of DOS and MSD utility. The following is an excerpt from a report run on the same machine with this utility:

```
Microsoft Diagnostics version 2.01    1/24/95    7:44pm    Page  1
============================================================================


---------------------- Summary Information ------------------------


          Computer: Gateway/Phoenix, 486DX
            Memory: 640K, 15104K Ext, 1024K EMS, 1024K XMS
             Video: VGA, ATI , Ultra
           Network: Novell, Shell 4.10.00
        OS Version: MS-DOS Version 6.20, Windows 3.10
             Mouse: Serial Mouse 7.05
    Other Adapters: Game Adapter
       Disk Drives: A: B: C: F: G: H: I: P:
         LPT Ports: 3
         COM Ports: 2


--------------------------- Computer -----------------------------


      Computer Name: Gateway
  BIOS Manufacturer: Phoenix
       BIOS Version: 680486 ROM BIOS PLUS Version 0.10 G21-2
      BIOS Category: Phoenix PC/AT Compatible BIOS
      BIOS ID Bytes: FC 81 00
          BIOS Date: 01/15/88
          Processor: 486DX
    Math Coprocessor: Internal
           Keyboard: Enhanced
           Bus Type: ISA/AT/Classic Bus
     DMA Controller: Yes
      Cascaded IRQ2: Yes
  BIOS Data Segment: None


--------------------------- Network ------------------------------


           Network Detected: Yes
               Network Name: Novell
     MS-DOS Network Functions: Not Supported
            NetBIOS Present: No
              Shell Version: 4.10.00
                   Shell OS: MS-DOS
           Shell OS Version: V6.20
              Hardware Type: IBM_PC
             Station Number: 3
    Physical Station Number: 0060:8C84:A8DD
              IPX Installed: Yes
              SPX Installed: Yes
          ODI/LSL Installed: Yes
```

Regardless of which utility you use, you should run reports regularly and store them in a place where they are easily accessible. When problems arise, immediately run the utility again and look for any discrepancies that signal problems.

Questions

1. To reduce problems with static electricity, _____.

   ○ A. place a humidifier in the computer room

   ○ B. use proper antistatic protection such as grounded hardware

   ○ C. keep Styrofoam cups away from computers

   ○ D. All of the Above

2. Which of the following is not a type of electrical problem?

   ○ A. Electro-Static Discharge

   ○ B. Crosstalk

   ○ C. Ephemeral

   ○ D. Transients

3. EMI includes all of the following except _____.

   ○ A. appliances

   ○ B. radar

   ○ C. power tools

   ○ D. ignition systems

4. Noise is _____.

   ○ A. low voltage, low current

   ○ B. low voltage, high current

   ○ C. high voltage, low current

   ○ D. high voltage, high current

5. Encrypted passwords _____.

   ○ A. are the default with NetWare 3.1*x*

   ○ B. can be turned on starting with NetWare 3.12

   ○ C. can be implemented with Check It PRO

   ○ D. couldn't keep my big brother out

Answers

1. D
2. C
3. A
4. A
5. A

38

Using Research Tools in Troubleshooting

Anyone who has ever dealt with computers and computer networks knows that increasing the number of computers arithmetically increases the number of problems logarithmically. The number of computer components and peripherals on the market today makes it impossible for network administrators to go without updated research tools at their fingertips. These factors have in no small part influenced Novell's decision to include the knowledge of three basic research tools into their certification curriculum and testing procedures.

This section covers in-depth the tools that Novell has suggested NetWare network administrators use to manage a NetWare network. This chapter reviews Novell's *Network Support Encyclopedia* (NSEPro), Novell's online NetWare assistance database (NetWire), and the Micro House Technical Library, an invaluable hardware reference tool. Each of these products are *query specific* (the data that the program returns depends directly on user input), so the examples that show how the programs work use realistic scenarios.

Any network administrator who uses these three products can shorten the time required to get a system into an operational status. Testing of this portion of the Service and Support CNE examination is three hours, during which you have available a CD-ROM that has NSEPro and the Micro House Technical Library. You need to reference material on these disks much as you would in a real-world situation.

 All NSEPro available is Windows-based. At the same time, when taking the Service & Support test, the machines use a DOS-based version.

NSEPro

Novell's Network Support Encyclopedia is designed to be your front line against outdated software and driver revisions, as well as an answer source for frequently asked NetWare-related questions. Novell distributes it to subscribers monthly on compact disk (and you should install it as soon as you get it).

NSEPro was basically reserved for NetWare and network-related subjects, until February of 1995, when Novell decided to include WordPerfect and QuattroPro in it. Although the move makes sense from Novell's standpoint—and you should peruse

these capabilities for future reference—you should not expect questions on WordPerfect or QuattroPro on the CNE exam.

Installing NSEPro

Installing NSEPro is similar to installing other CD distributed software. If your hard drive is large enough (presently over 170 MB), and you use NSEPro frequently, Novell suggests that you copy all of the data and *Folio* (the database application software) onto your nonremovable media. Should you want to install only NSEPro but not the downloadable files, you only need 100 MB. And if you have next to no available drive space for the NSEPro data, you can select to install only the Windows files necessary to launch NSEPro from your CD. Either of the first two instances not only obviously speeds program access over running applications directly from compact disks, but you then can store your CD in a safe place until a time when your NSEPro data might become corrupted.

If you know how to install software into Windows, you know how to install NSEPro. You can select File, New, Item, Browse, and so on, to install the different modules, or you can use the Windows File Manager application to install the package (the preferred method). To use File Manager to install NSEPro, first open File Manager and select the drive letter that corresponds to your CD-ROM device. Run SETUP.EXE, and you are prompted for which of the three installations you want to use. That's it. One warm or cold system reboot and you can access your NSEPro infobase.

To install NSEPro in a DOS-only environment, simply move over to your CD-ROM device and type **INSTALL** *<drive_letter>* **[DFILES/ NODFILES]**. You want to modify your path environment to include your working NSEPro directory, or move to the NSEPro directory when you want to run the Network Support Encyclopedia.

Using NSEPro

Invoking NSEPro in DOS is as simple as typing **NSEPRO**. If you install NSEPro onto a network, you need a minimum of write rights for the encyclopedia directory. If not, you cannot create a swap file for your graphics and other data. When you initiate NSEPro, you initially are taken to the main menu from which you can select the manual you want.

As with most DOS- and Windows-compatible applications, the MS Windows version is much more user-friendly and less keyboard intensive. After you install NSEPro into your Windows environment, you have an NSEPro program group that consists of your different NSEPro modules. Simply point to the application you want to invoke, double-click the mouse, and navigate the infobase as you please (see fig. 38.1).

Running Queries

Because the NSEPro infobase includes such a vast amount of data, you really do need to familiarize yourself with NSEPro search methods. The most basic form is to search in binary, in which you want to use the "and" and "or" operands. Using generic terminology returns a large number of finds or "hits."

As shown in figure 38.2, if you were to perform a simple search on "ne2000" (a network interface card), the infobase would return 4,996 hits. Nobody really wants to wade through almost five thousand documents, so you might narrow the search by "anding" the ne2000 parameter with the vendor's eagle or smc (which would be 727 and 4,213 hits total in the infobase, respectively), which would drop the number to a slightly (but only marginally) more manageable 3,604. To further

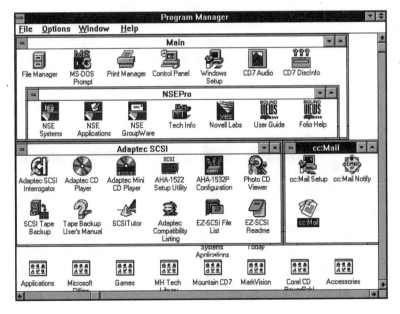

Figure 38.1

The NSEPro Windows program group allows direct access to the different applications.

reduce the number and limit the search, you might "and" the outcome from the previous search concatenation with the term "ethernet," which would bring the outcome to a much more manageable 273. If you were to find 273 acceptable, you would select OK and review the query table of contents.

By focusing the search, the NE2000 NIC example was reduced from almost 5,000 to a much more manageable number. Whether you are in What's New, Service and Support, File Updates, or any of the other NSEPro databases, you have the same basic search and management toolbelt. If you run NSEPro from within MS Windows, you have eight different buttons across your screen. The various buttons enable you to do the following tasks:

- **Query.** Enables you to search the database by selecting combinations of search parameters and keywords

- **Clear Query.** Enables you to clear your previous query criteria so you can easily initiate a new search

- **Next (hit).** When you run a query that returns multiple matches, you can move from one instance to the next by selecting the next button

- **Previous (hit).** Opposite of the next button; you can move back up to the previously matched search criteria instance

- **Backtrack.** Enables you to back through your searches and links so that you can modify your criteria

- **Trail.** Enables you to see the trail you've created with your links and queries and select any part of your trail to move directly to that point

- **Contents.** Enables you to switch from the actual document and the table of contents

- **Print.** Enables you to open your Windows print dialog box and print your search results

You also can run NSEPro from within a DOS environment. The selections in DOS follow the basic MS DOS format; that is, you can select from File, Edit, View, Search, Window, and Help. The display is less graphical than the Windows counterpart, but you basically have a similar representation of the manuals included in the Windows counterpart (see fig. 38.3).

Figure 38.2

The Query dialog box used to search the NSEPro infobase.

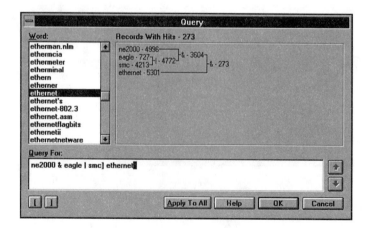

Figure 38.3
*Double-click on the spine
for the manual you want.*

What's New

Anything new or added to NSEPro is covered in this section. Review this section for changes in format for data presentation, as well as any other noteworthy program or driver modifications.

NetWare Support Encyclopedia Modules

As NetWare grows and interfaces with new and different platforms, operating systems, and peripherals, this area will afford you information on various NetWare-related modules.

Service and Support

The Service and Support section is arguably the most used and important section of the CD. It contains the following subsections:

- **Technical Information Documents.** Technical documents and FYI documents written by Novell engineers and technicians

- **Files, Patches, and Fixes.** Names of files available to download from the NetWire BBS, including descriptions of the file names, upload dates, locations, and briefly what the files do

- **Third Party Files.** Items like network interface drivers or "requesters" for various operating systems

- **NetWare Application Notes.** Electronic version of the AppNotes published monthly by Novell, covering new NetWare technologies, implementations, and fine-tuning (for example, NFS and TCP/IP installation and tuning parameters)

- **Novell Professional Developer Bullets.** Another periodical, but more directed toward NetWare-specific application development than addressing the needs of NetWare network administration

- **Novell Lab Bulletins.** Reflect the status of NetWare-compatible third-party products that Novell is testing for compatibility. NetWare compatibility as confirmed by Novell helps network administrators increase the probability of products purchased for certain applications functioning properly

■ **Training-Related Information.** Included in the Service and Support section of NSEPro and includes many typical questions and answers regarding training, classes, and other training-related issues

■ **Service Providers Guide.** Geographical representation of third-party support providers and the number of Novell certified personnel on their staffs

■ **Top Issues.** Most frequently asked questions and answers, particularly useful for newly released products or product versions

■ **Printing Decision Trees.** Enables you to methodically address many NetWare-related problems, beginning from the most logical starting point (as determined by Novell after extensive problem analysis), through a multitude of analytic decisions, drawing conclusions depending on your previous answers; useful for most NetWare problem solving

File Updates

The File Updates section of NSEPro is designed to ensure that critical NetWare and Novell network-related files are up-to-date for a network administrator. Because the number of support are as vast as they are varied, they have been clustered into logical groups for review and download. This issue of NSEPro has fifteen different categories.

Product Manuals

You can find literally dozens of NetWare and Novell product manuals in electronic form in this area. Granted, NetWare literature has shrunk significantly since version 2.*x*, but having manuals available on one thin media is a vast improvement over even the most concise of documentation.

Sales and Marketing

Network administrators frequently underuse the Sales and Marketing tool. Although the terms "sales" and "marketing" basically go 180 degrees against network administration and engineering, the *NetWare Buyer's Guide* is a tool that you simply cannot overuse. Network administrators have no major use for the sales tools themselves, but the buyer's guide provides an invaluable list that has brief descriptions of all Novell-developed products.

Novell Programs

This section contains information about Novell Education Certification Programs such as CNE, NPA, and NUI.

New User Information

New User Information is a great place to start when you first use NSEPro, because it has hints and tips on maximizing time in NSEPro.

NetWire

If you purchased this book, you are more than likely technically literate and familiar with modems and bulletin board systems (BBSes). NetWire is Novell's bulletin board system developed so people who had NetWare network technical questions had an expedient way to get answers to their questions around the clock. The foundation of the NetWire user interface is the CompuServe Information Manager for Windows and DOS (WINCIM), which provides user-friendly access to NetWire via CompuServe.

When you use WINCIM to access NetWire, a user-friendly graphical interface greets you. If you decide to connect to the NetWire system, WINCIM dials the specified CompuServe account and automatically logs you in to the NetWire forum. The main menu for NetWire closely resembles the modules in NSEPro.

Although many people believe BBSes are frivolous and nothing more than an extension of the corporate coffee pot (where people sit and chat), you can use NetWire to do things like ask questions in a variety of forums to perform database searches. Take a look at figure 38.4.

Micro House Technical Library (MHTL)

If you have ever worked with computer hardware, you know that even when you limit the manufacturers and products you use in your network, that versions, as well as form factors, change frequently. And each change basically forces you to relearn how to configure the product, set the jumpers, set the BIOS settings, and on and on. A demo version of MHTL is included with this book.

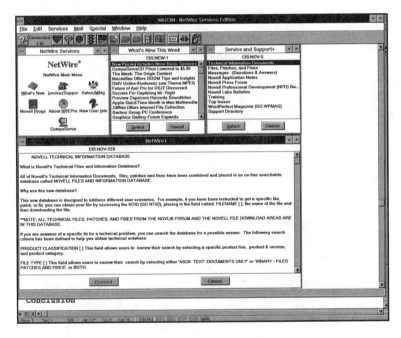

Figure 38.4

By focusing your search criteria, you can travel both up and down your threaded path.

Even the likes of Stephen Hawking could not memorize all the settings and parameters for the products on the market. Micro House Technical Library to the rescue. The MHTL ships on a compact disk and contains information on almost every product that you might encounter while working with computer hardware. Included on the CD are such items as the following:

- BIOS settings for IDE drives

- Jumper settings for popular drives, network interface cards, and other peripheral boards

- A diagnostic program that determines the BIOS settings of your computer

The easiest way to learn how to use the Micro House Technical Library tool would be to follow a couple of examples step-by-step. You can go in one of three basic directions after you boot the MHTL program (see fig. 38.5). The first route you might follow is the Hard Drive Encyclopedia.

Imagine that you have acquired a computer that has lost its CMOS battery and that you must reenter the BIOS information. You can tell by looking that the hard drive is a Seagate ST251-1. You need only click on the Hard Drive Encyclopedia button from the MHTL main menu, click on the Hard Drives button from the Hard Drive submenu, then enter what information you know about the drive into the appropriate fields (see fig. 38.6). After you enter the appropriate information, click on the Search button and the MHTL program searches its database for a search map. If you have entered the information correctly, the odds are that MHTL has the information and you soon see a list of the hard drive settings as suggested by the drive's manufacturer.

Now, assume that your BIOS was actually wiped out due to a surge in your power source, and that your IDE controller was smoked, too. You need to find a controller to replace the one that has passed away and you want MHTL to help.

Buckets and buckets of hard drive controllers are available, so you want to narrow your focus as much as possible. First, open the Hard Drive Encyclopedia module by selecting the Like button from the main menu. Then, select the **C**ontrollers button (refer to fig. 38.6) rather than the Hard

Figure 38.5

The Micro House Technical Library is widely recognized as the resource guide for network hardware configuration.

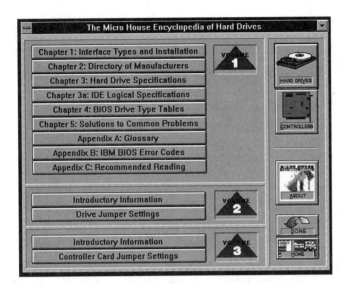

Figure 38.6
The Hard Drive Encyclopedia submenu enables you to access various aspects of hard drive specifications and related data.

Dri<u>ve</u>s button as in the last example. The Hard Drive Controller Card Criteria Search menu appears.

Here, you select the specific parameters you want the product to match; suppose you need a 16-bit ISA IDE-AT half-length card. Further, you want the card to have a 1.2 MB/1.44 MB controller, a serial port, a parallel port, and a game port. After you select the appropriate boxes, you would press the Search button.

Search results show that twenty-two products meet the search criteria (see fig. 38.7). Now you review each product to see whether you like or dislike any additional features before you buy. Suppose you're familiar with Acculogic products and have liked them in the past.

To see the configuration settings for the Acculogics IDE-4/PLUS board, you would simply double-click on the respective Acculogic line on your display. MHTL really shines here in most network administrators' eyes. You are then presented with a series of spreadsheets that display all the possible

switch settings, jumper configurations, and additional specifications (see fig. 38.8). If you want to see what the board physically looks like, use your cursor to select the See Diagram #1 button.

Pressing the See Diagram #1 button brings up a physical representation of the board and any switch, jumper, accessory chip, and connectors locations (see fig. 38.9). The different locations are cross-referenced with the text mentioned in the last paragraph. With this information on CD, most frustration of many network administrators goes the way of the 8-track cassette tape. And if you do not have a photographic memory, you can print the different pages in a variety of sizes and alignments.

Now let's say that not only was the BIOS lost and the IDE controller toasted, but that your motherboard is dysfunctional, and what the heck, as long as the case is open, you want a new network interface card, too. You already have seen basic searching in the hard drive section of the MHTL application. Now, you would select the Main Boards Encyclopedia and Network Interface Technical Guide buttons respectively rather than the Hard Drive Encyclopedia button from the main menu.

Figure 38.7

Our search for a 16-bit ISA IDE controller with additional criteria has resulted in a list of twenty-two products.

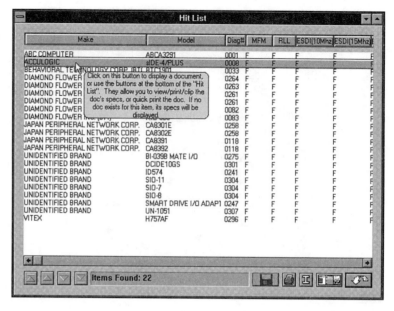

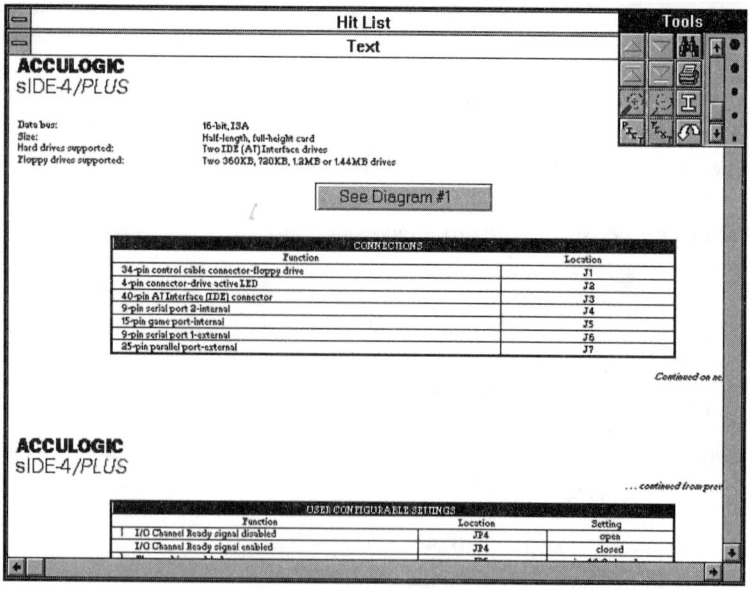

Figure 38.8

The text associated with the various products in the MHTL is as extensive as many expensive hardware encyclopedias.

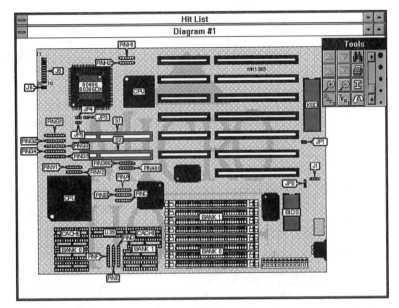

Figure 38.9

Being able to see a representation of the motherboard and match the references to a text chart is invaluable to any network administrator.

The motherboard section of the program enables you to select your criteria much as you did in the hard drive example, but you can select the type of processor, the bus clock speed, the number and type of slots, and other motherboard-related criteria.

You decide you want a 80386/80486/Pentium-compatible board that can handle up to sixty-six MHz. After you narrow your choices, you scrutinize the resulting list and decide you want a TMC Research Corporation PAT34PV board, which can support 32 MB of RAM, a 256 KB cache, and uses AMI BIOS. Good enough, but what is the form factor? As in the drive and controller example, you would double-click on the PAT34PV line, which would bring up the board specifications and chip/connector/jumper location text, and the Diagram button. Click on the Diagram button to bring up a visual layout drawing of the motherboard (refer to fig. 38.9).

In the spirit of avoiding too many redundant details, selecting a network interface card is very much the same. Suffice it to say that having drawings of the different boards, as well as the specifications, is more than just a luxury. Most network environments use few combinations of hardware to ease the support burden. When one comes out, make the new one look the same as the old one, and put the new one in. But what happens when a product you use moves from one vendor to another (which happens frequently)? You know what the board looks like and you usually know a few of the specifications. But do you now know the model number or the manufacturer?

If not, you can enter as much information as you know and then take a look at the board to confirm that you're ordering the right product. For this example, suppose you know that the board is an Ethernet board with 10BASE-T, 10BASE2, and an AUI port. It also has a status LED and is a 10-bit card. You would first enter the proper information into the Network Interface Card Criteria Search menu (see fig. 38.10) and review the listing that results from the MHTL search (see figure 38.11). Fortunately, the second NIC on the list matches the NIC you removed from the computer (except the labels have changed). Figure 38.12 displays the network interface card, which helps an administrator configure the NIC.

After you master searching the MHTL database for one type of product, you should pretty much know how to search for other products. And as for the ways you can use Micro House Technical Library to maximize your computer skill productivity, you can confidently purchase and support virtually any type of desktop computer on the market today.

Figure 38.10

The Network Interface Card Criteria Search menu enables you to select many different hardware/topology/protocol combinations for your search.

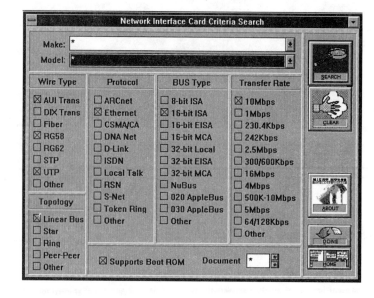

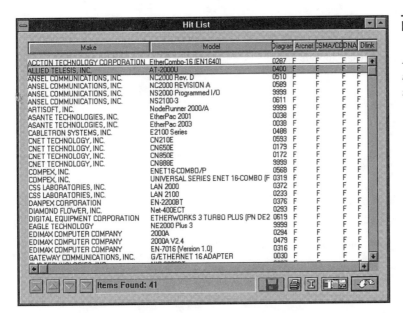

Figure 38.11

The network interface card Hit List affords you enough initial data to drastically narrow your search.

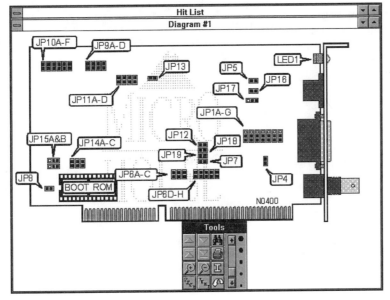

Figure 38.12

The network interface card display helps the network administrator determine how to configure his or her NIC.

Questions

1. Which is not a spine title that appears in NSEPro?

    ○ A. What's New

    ○ B. Sales & Marketing

    ○ C. Patches

    ○ D. Product Manuals

2. The best source of information on network hardware configuration is _____.

    ○ 1. Micro House Technical Library

    ○ 2. NetWire

    ○ 3. NSEPro

    ○ 4. NetWare documentation

3. What is the required hard drive space needed to copy all of NSEPro onto your hard drive?

    ○ 1. 150 MB

    ○ 2. 170 MB

    ○ 3. 190 MB

    ○ 4. 210 MB

Answers

1. C

2. A

3. B

Working with Network Adapter Cards and Cabling

In this chapter, you learn about several of the network interface components used when configuring a NetWare LAN. Proper planning, research, and verification of certified NetWare-compatible components is an integral part of building an efficient network. The items discussed in this chapter include the following:

- *ARCnet board settings, cabling, and troubleshooting*

- *Ethernet board settings, cabling, frame types, and troubleshooting*

- *Token Ring board settings, cabling, and troubleshooting*

- *FDDI cabling, advantages, disadvantages, and troubleshooting*

During the planning phase of a network implementation project, many hardware choices are available. The verification of component compatibility and confirmation of Novell certification of all hardware and software to be integrated is obtained from several sources. Vendor documentation, FAXBACK phone numbers, technical support lines, and peers are good sources for verification. Novell provides a technical support desk that can be reached by dialing 1-800-NETWARE. Access to the technical bulletins in a NetWare Support Encyclopedia can provide some of the information needed.

Without verification that the hardware you want to use has been tested thoroughly using NetWare, you do not know what compatibility problems may occur. If you do not choose hardware that has been verified at the Novell Labs, you will have a much more difficult time troubleshooting problems. You also will not have Novell support to help fix problems. Spending some time at this phase saves you money in the long run. Novell also offers a service called FAXBACK where you can have certain documents sent to your fax. A master document containing all the titles of the documents on FAXBACK helps you choose which item will provide the information you need. In the U.S. or Canada, call 1-800-233-3382 or 1-801-429-5363.

 Note Diagnose and correct incompatibilities between the network adapter card and the CPU data bus.

After you have obtained the equipment to build your network, you must configure the hardware to avoid conflicts. Conflicts among different pieces of hardware occur when their settings match or overlap. Unless the hardware has special features to avoid conflicts, you must be aware of the areas where conflicts are most likely to occur. The

following list contains the most common conflicts that occur when configuring a PC adapter card:

- Interrupt conflicts
- Base I/O and memory address conflicts
- Page memory range conflicts
- DMA channel conflicts
- Node address conflicts

Keep in mind that conflicts are internal to the individual PC. A common misconception is that all network boards on the same network must share the same settings. This is not true and is impractical to enforce unless all your machines are identical in their components. Look at each client individually for configuration information.

Interrupts are dedicated to certain resources. It is possible to use a dedicated interrupt by disabling an unneeded resource. For example, if you do not need a second COM port, you can disable COM2 by using the PC's configuration program, setting switches or jumpers on the system board, or removing the board that supports COM2. This frees up INT 3 for use with a LAN card.

The following is a list of additional items to research as part of the planning process:

- Cabling specifications and requirements
- Hard drive specifications and requirements
- Software drivers to ensure that they are certified with the version of operating system to be used

Now that you have an idea of what needs to be verified, the next section details information about ARCnet, Ethernet, and Token Ring specifications.

Differentiate among media types and physical media protocols.

Exploring ARCnet Specifications

ARCnet is an acronym for Attached Resource Computer NETwork, which was founded by the Datapoint Corporation. Novell uses the term RX-Net to denote its form of this architecture and TRX-Net for the Turbo version. ARCnet uses a token-bus packet passing scheme.

 A Turbo version is an updated RX-Net version that hands packets off to the communications buffers rather than attempting to place the NetWare Core Protocol (NCP) packets in a File Server Process (FSP) buffer.

ARCnet operates at 2.5 Mbps throughput and can be connected using RG-62/U coax cable or unshielded twisted-pair (UTP) wiring. Although ARCnet can support up to 255 node numbers on a single network, systems of this size are not practical.

Figure 39.1 shows the components of a typical ARCnet card. This card is configured for use with twisted-pair wiring. ARCnet cards for use with coax cable have a Bayonet Navy Connector (BNC) twist-on connector. You will find jumpers or DIP (Dual In-line Package) switches for setting the following characteristics:

- Node number
- Base I/O address
- Memory address
- Interrupt
- Network timeout

The node number and network timeout are unique to ARCnet and are described later in this chapter.

Each network interface card (NIC) on an ARCnet network is assigned a node number. This number must be unique on each network and in the range of 1 to 255.

ARCnet manages network access with a token mechanism. The token is passed from the lowest number node to higher number nodes in ascending order. Lower numbered addresses get the token before the higher numbered addresses.

Traffic is controlled by assigning sequential numbers to nodes using the same order in which they are cabled. Choosing random numbers can create a situation in which a node numbered 23 can be a whole building away from the next number, 46, but in the same room as numbers 112 and 142. The token has to travel in a haphazard manner that is less effective than if you numbered the three clients in the same office sequentially, 46, 47, and 48, and the client in the other building 112. With this configuration, the packet stays within the office before venturing on to other stations.

ARCnet was one of the topologies used early on in networking and is rarely used as the topology of choice in current LAN environments. ARCnet, however, still is a functional and cost-effective means of networking.

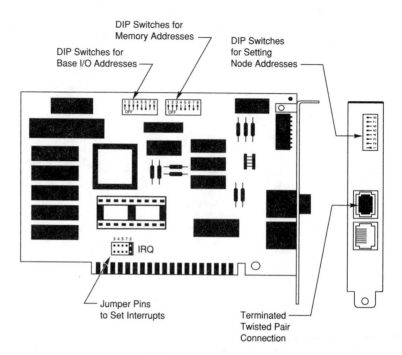

Figure 39.1
Example of an ARCnet NIC.

DIP Switches for Memory Addresses

DIP Switches for Base I/O Addresses

DIP Switches for Setting Node Addresses

IRQ

Jumper Pins to Set Interrupts

Terminated Twisted Pair Connection

ARCnet Board Settings

Depending on the vendor design specifications of your ARCnet card, most base I/O addresses, node addresses, and memory addresses are set by DIP switches. These addresses are set using a binary mode calculation with an on or off setting in the required switch block. Interrupt settings are made by jumper combinations at marked locations on the network interface card. Many types and brands of ARCnet cards are on the market today. Refer to the MicroHouse Technical Library, the documentation for the NIC or, as a last resort, call the technical support group for the specific vendor of the component.

Most ARCnet cards require a shared memory address. Many manufacturers use the area of D000:0 to DFFF:0 as the default. Standard DOS memory is limited to the first 640 KB of a PC's memory.

However, extended or expanded memory managers can be used to make memory above 640 KB available for use by DOS programs. If memory above the 640 KB line (above hex address A000:0) is used for network boards, however, the memory becomes unavailable for use by a memory manager. This makes it difficult to optimize a PC's upper memory area. If a network card requires a memory area such as D000:0-DFFF:0, the memory available for use by DOS memory managers is reduced by 64 KB.

ARCnet Cabling

The ARCnet topology uses coax, twisted-pair, or fiber-optic cabling to connect network devices. An ARCnet network is used primarily with either coax or twisted-pair cable. Coax is an RG-62/U type cable and is terminated with 93-ohm terminators.

Twisted pair uses stranded 24- or 26-gauge wire or solid core 22-, 24-, or 26-gauge type cable and is terminated with 100-ohm terminators. Many ARCnet networks use a mix of both coax and UTP cabling. UTP cable is simple to install and provides a reliable connection to the clients, whereas coax provides a means to span longer distances.

ARCnet can run off a linear bus topology using coax or twisted-pair as long as the cards support BUS. The most popular installations of ARCnet run off two types of hubs:

- *Active hubs* have active electronic signals that amplify signals and split them to multiple ports. The number of ports on an active hub varies with the manufacturer, but eight is typical. A port on an active hub can be connected to a port on another active device (such as another active hub or an NIC) or to a passive hub.

- *Passive hubs* cannot amplify signals. Each hub has four connectors. Because of the characteristics of passive hubs, unused ports must be equipped with a *terminator*, a connector containing a resistor that matches the ARCnet cabling characteristics. A port on a passive hub can connect only to an active device (an active hub or an NIC). Passive hubs can never be connected to passive hubs.

One of the greatest flexibilities of ARCnet is that you can integrate connections from active hubs to a linear bus connection as long as you terminate at the last connection point.

A maximum time limit of 31 microseconds is allotted for an ARCnet signal. This is also called a time-out setting. Signals on an ARCnet can travel up to 20,000 feet during the 31-microsecond default time-out period. You can sometimes extend the range of an ARCnet by increasing the time-out value. However, 20,000 feet is the distance at which ARCnet signals begin to seriously degrade. Extending the network beyond that distance can result in unreliable or failed communication. Therefore, the time-out parameter and cabling distance recommendations should be increased only with great caution.

The maximum cable distances between individual components in an ARCnet network are dependent on how the components are connected (see table 39.1).

In cabling ARCnet networks with coax cable, you must follow several rules:

- Never connect a passive hub to another passive hub directly

- Passive hubs should never be used to connect two active hubs

- Passive hubs are only used to connect an active hub and a node

- Unused connectors on active hubs do not need to be terminated

- Unused connectors on passive hubs must be terminated using a 93-ohm terminator

Figure 39.2 shows an ARCnet configuration using active and passive hubs. Active hubs are required to extend the network for long distances and to configure networks that have more than four nodes. Passive hubs are used as an economical means of splitting a port on an active hub to support three devices.

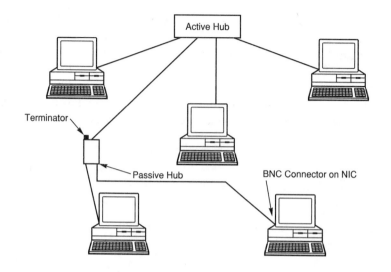

Figure 39.2
Example of an ARCnet topology using active and passive hubs and coax cable.

Table 39.1
Maximum ARCnet Cable Distances

Maximum Distance	From	To
2,000 feet	Network node	Active hub
2,000 feet	Active hub	Active hub
100 feet	Active hub	Passive hub
Not supported	Passive hub	Passive hub
100 feet	Network node	Passive hub
2,000 feet	Network node	Network node
20,000 feet	Farthest node	Farthest node

ARCnet Troubleshooting

Troubleshoot common problems with cards, cables, and related hardware for the three most common networking topologies.

Common sources of problems on ARCnet networks are as follows:

■ No more than one node can have a given node address on the same network. If two or more nodes share an address, one of the two clients will either lose its network connection or will not be able to find a network.

■ Missing terminators might not present visible problems on a small network. Missing terminators cause data retransmits on smaller systems, eventually appearing as transmit time-out errors or network errors.

■ Using a terminator with an incorrect ohm rating. Coax uses 93 ohm; twisted-pair uses 100 ohm. A terminator's value in ohms depends on the impedance of the cable. The cable's impedance and the terminator's value should always match.

■ The ARCnet bus using NICs that do not use the same impedance level. Signals will become attenuated and/or reflected, causing interference with other signals on the wire.

■ Failed NICs.

■ Failed active hubs (or a port on that hub).

■ Cable lengths that exceed specifications (refer to table 39.1). Twisted-pair, cabled in a bus rather than a star, cannot have more than ten NICs per segment. This number varies with different manufacturers. ARCnet UTP installed in a bus configuration is generally used only in very small networks of six nodes or less. This configuration has the major drawback of halting the network if a single cable is disconnected. In an ARCnet bus configuration, the network must be brought down to make any changes or service to the ARCnet cards.

■ Coax connectors not built or crimped correctly. Twist-on connectors are responsible for more intermittent errors on a network than most other failures because of their design.

Twist-on coax connectors became popular in the IBM 3XXX systems. These systems used RG-62 coax cable and operated at 1.5 Mbps throughput.

The twist-on connectors are not recommended for use on any modern LAN cable system because of the higher data rates employed.

The primary characteristics of ARCnet are as follows:

■ The maximum time it takes for the ARCnet signal to travel the length of the network is 31 microseconds.

■ The maximum distance an ARCnet signal can travel between the two nodes farthest away from each other is 20,000 feet.

■ The absolute maximum number of ARCnet nodes that can occupy a given network segment is 255. An ARCnet segment consists of all cabling and nodes that share a given network address.

Understanding Ethernet Specifications

Ethernet was originally developed by the Xerox Corporation, Digital Corporation, and the Intel Corporation in the early 1970s. Ethernet is also known as a *spanning tree topology* because the networks expand by branching in tree structures that do not allow redundant paths between nodes. Ethernet uses the Carrier Sense Multiple Access/Collision Detection (CSMA/CD) media contention access method and supports a maximum throughput of 10 Mbps. The Ethernet and 802.3 protocols are described in the Ethernet Frame Types section of this chapter, as well as in Part IV of the book.

Note The origins of Ethernet are commemorated in the initials DIX, which is a 15-pin connector used to interface Ethernet components. The acronym DIX is derived from the combination of leading letters of the founding Ethernet vendors: Digital, Intel, and Xerox.

The term Ethernet commonly refers to original Ethernet (which has been updated to Ethernet II) as well as the IEEE 802.3 standards. However, Ethernet and the 802.3 standards differ in ways significant enough to make standards incompatible in terms of packet formats. At the physical layer, Ethernet and 802.3 are generally compatible in terms of cables, connectors, and electronic devices.

Today, NetWare 3.11 uses the IEEE 802.3 frame format as a default on its networks. However, a variety of other Ethernet frame formats are supported. NetWare 3.12 and 4.x use the IEEE 802.2 frame format as the Ethernet frame type default. To change this default, change the frame type in the NET.CFG file. Add this frame type if you need to communicate with networks using older Ethernet frame types.

Ethernet is generally used on light-to-medium traffic networks, and performs best when a network's data traffic is sent in short bursts. Ethernet is the most popular network standard. It has become especially popular in many university and government installations.

Ethernet Board Settings

Most older versions of Ethernet NICs are configured using jumpers to set addresses and interrupts.

Current models of NICs can be configured using a diagnostic program that enables changing of interrupt and memory address settings stored in a special memory chip on the NIC.

An example of an Ethernet NIC is shown in figure 39.3. Some of the features of these cards are as follows:

- Shared memory selection; most Ethernet cards do not require the use of shared memory

- I/O address

- Interrupt

- Connectors

- Active connector selection jumpers

- Socket for a remote boot PROM

Ethernet cards can have one, two, or possibly all three of the following connectors:

- BNC connectors support coax cabling

- RJ-45 connectors support 10BASE-T (UTP) cabling

- DIX connectors are used to connect to external transceivers

With some cards, DIP switches or blocks of jumpers are used to select the active connector. In many cases, however, the active connector can be selected with configuration software.

A limitation of 1,024 nodes (physical addresses) per network address exists on an Ethernet network. Addresses are assigned by IEEE to the vendor for the first three bytes of a six-byte address. The vendor is responsible for assigning the rest of the address and ensuring unique IDs.

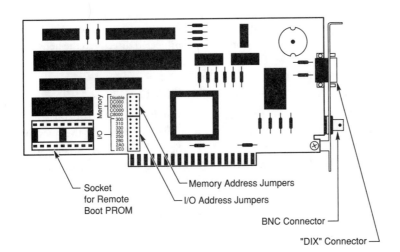

Figure 39.3
Features of an Ethernet NIC.

Socket for Remote Boot PROM

Memory Address Jumpers

I/O Address Jumpers

BNC Connector

"DIX" Connector

As with the Token Ring cards, the card's manufacturer "burns" a unique node address into ROM on each NIC. Unless you override the burned-in address, address conflicts cannot occur on an Ethernet. Vendors sometimes label their cards with the node address. If the address is not visible, use the diagnostic disk supplied by the vendor.

Ethernet Cabling

A variety of cables can be used to implement Ethernet networks. Traditionally, Ethernet networks have been cabled with coaxial cables of several different types. Fiber-optic cables are now frequently employed to extend the geographic range of Ethernet networks.

The contemporary interest in using twisted-pair wiring has resulted in a scheme for cabling using unshielded twisted-pair. The 10BASE-T cabling standard, which uses UTP in a star topology, is described later.

Ethernet remains closely associated with coaxial cable, however. Two types of coaxial cable still used in small and large environments are thin net (also

known as cheapernet) and thick net. The Ethernet networks have different limitations based on thin net and thick net cable specifications. The best way to remember the requirements is to use the 5-4-3 rule of thumb for each cable type.

The 5-4-3 Rule

The 5-4-3 rule states that the following can appear between any two nodes in the Ethernet network:

- Up to five segments in a series

- Up to four concentrators or repeaters

- Three segments of (coax only) cable that contain nodes

10BASE2

The 10BASE2 cabling topology, also referred to as thin net, generally uses the on-board transceiver of the network interface card to translate the signals to and from the rest of the network. Thin net cabling can use RG-58A/U or RG-58C/U coaxial type cable, 50 ohm terminators, and T-connectors that directly attach to the BNC connector on the NIC.

A grounded terminator must be used on one end of the network segment.

 A *transceiver* is a device that takes the digital signal from the node and translates it to communicate on a baseband cabling system. NICs that support thin net or 10BASE-T cable generally have built-in transceivers. External transceivers are used for thick Ethernet although they may be used for thin net and UTP as well.

Use RG-58A/U cable for Ethernet topology, not RG-58U, which is for use with cable TV setups.

Advantages of 10BASE2

The main advantage of using 10BASE2 in your network is cost. When any given cable segment on the network does not have to be run further than 185 meters, 10BASE2 is often the cheapest network cabling option.

10BASE2 is also relatively simple to connect. Each network node is connected directly to the network cable using a T-connector attached to the NIC.

Troubleshooting 10BASE2

The first step in troubleshooting a 10BASE2 network is to ensure that you have met the rules for using 10BASE2. Several additional rules must be adhered to in 10BASE2 Ethernet environments, including the following:

- The minimum cable distance between clients must be 1.5 feet, or 0.5 meters.

- Pig tails, also known as drop cables, from T-connectors should not be used to connect to the BNC connector on the NIC. The T-connector must be connected directly to the NIC.

- You may not go beyond the maximum network segment limitation of 607 feet, or 185 meters.

Figure 39.4

Two segments using 10BASE2 cabling.

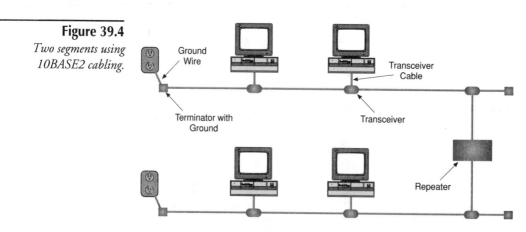

■ The entire network cabling scheme cannot exceed 3,035 feet, or 925 meters.

■ The maximum number of nodes per network segment is 30 (this includes clients and repeaters).

■ A 50-ohm terminator must be used on each end of the bus with only one of the terminators having either a grounding strap or a grounding wire that attaches it to the screw holding an electrical outlet cover in place.

■ You may not have more than five segments on a network. These segments may be connected with a maximum of four repeaters, and only three of the five segments may have network nodes.

Additional troubleshooting tips are found in the Ethernet Troubleshooting section of this chapter.

As mentioned previously, the IEEE 802.3 standard for Thinnet is 10BASE2. This standard describes a 10 Mbps baseband network with a maximum segment length of approximately 200 meters (the actual limit, as stated previously, is 185 meters). Figure 39.4 shows two segments using 10BASE2 cabling.

10BASE5

The 10BASE5 cabling topology, also referred to as thick net, uses an external transceiver to attach to the network interface card (see fig. 39.5). The NIC attaches to the external transceiver by an *Attachment Universal Interface* (AUI) cable to the DIX connector on the back of the card. The external transceiver clamps to the thick net cable. As with thin net, each network segment must be terminated at both ends, with one end using a grounded terminator. The components of a thick net network are shown in figure 39.6.

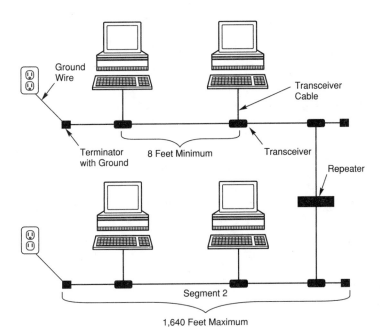

Figure 39.5

Two segments using 10BASE5 cabling.

Figure 39.6

Components of a thick Ethernet.

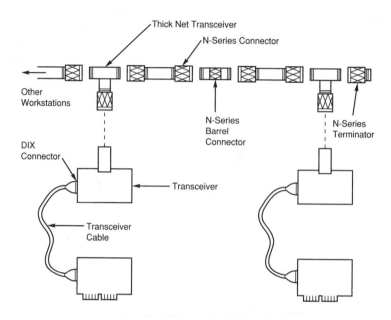

 Note   RG-11 is a 75-ohm cable. 10BASE5 requires 50 ohms.

Advantages of 10BASE5

The primary advantage of 10BASE5 is its ability to exceed the cable lengths to which 10BASE2 is restricted. However, it does have restrictions of its own that should be considered when installing or troubleshooting a 10BASE5 network.

Troubleshooting a 10BASE5 Network

As with 10BASE2 networks, the first consideration when troubleshooting a 10BASE5 network should be the cabling rules and guidelines that have been established. Several additional guidelines, along with the 5-4-3 rule, must be followed in thick Ethernet networks:

■ The minimum cable distance between transceivers is 8 feet, or 2.5 meters.

■ You may not go beyond the maximum network segment length of 1,640 feet, or 500 meters.

■ The entire network cabling scheme cannot exceed 8,200 feet, or 2,500 meters.

■ One end of the terminated network segment must be grounded.

■ Drop cables can be as short as required, but cannot be longer than 50 meters from transceiver to NIC.

■ Cable segments that are cut and connected using a "Vampire Tap" should come from the same cable spool to ensure that each connected piece carries the identical electrical cabling to the other.

■ The maximum number of nodes per network segment is 100. (This includes all repeaters.)

Additional troubleshooting tips are found in the Ethernet Troubleshooting section of this chapter.

The IEEE 802.3 standard that describes thick net is 10BASE5. This standard describes a 10 Mbps baseband network that can have segments up to 500 meters long. Figure 39.7 shows two segments using thick net and the appropriate hardware.

Thin net and thick net cable can be combined to extend the distance of an Ethernet network topology. The following formula can be used to define the maximum amount of thin net cable that can be used in one network segment combination:

Maximum length of = 1,640 feet
thin net that can   (Length of new
be used   network segment to
                           be added)

 A linear bus topology is more economical than wire because it is not necessary to have a separate cable run for each client. However, some local problems on a linear bus have the capability of bringing the entire network down.

If a break is in the cable or a streaming NIC is in the channel, the entire network can go down. Streaming is more frequently referred to as a broadcast storm. This occurs when a network card fails, and the transmitter floods the cable with traffic, just like a faucet that is stuck open. At this point, the network becomes unusable.

10BASE-T

The trend in wiring Ethernet networks is to use unshielded twisted-pair (UTP) cable. UTP or 10BASE-T cable is one of the three most popular implementations for Ethernet. It is based on the IEEE 802.3 standard.

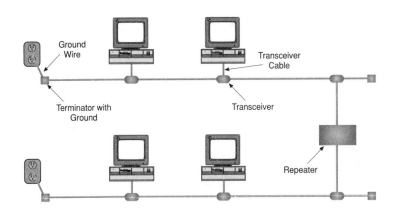

Figure 39.7

Example of thick net Ethernet cabling.

10BASE-T cabling is wired in a star topology. However, it functions logically like a linear bus. The cable uses RJ-45 connectors, and the network interface card can have RJ-45 jacks built into the back of the cards. External transceivers attached to a DIX connector found in combination with RJ-45 or BNC connectors on the NIC can be used to connect standard Ethernet cards into a twisted-pair topology. Figure 39.8 shows Ethernet cabling using twisted-pair cabling and a hub, also called a concentrator.

Advantages of 10BASE-T

The star wiring of 10BASE-T provides several advantages, particularly in larger networks. First, the network is more reliable and easier to manage because 10BASE-T networks use a concentrator (a centralized wiring hub). These hubs are "intelligent" in that they can route network traffic around a bad cable segment, and they can detect defective cable segments. This makes it easier for you to locate and repair bad cable segments.

10BASE-T enables you to design and build your LAN one segment at a time, growing as your network needs grow. This makes 10BASE-T more flexible than other LAN cabling options.

10BASE-T is also relatively inexpensive to use compared to other cabling options. In some cases where a data-grade phone system has already been used in an existing building, this cabling can be used for the LAN.

 Note Networks with star wiring topologies can be significantly easier to trouble-shoot and repair than bus wired networks. With a star network, a problem node can be isolated from the rest of the network by simply disconnecting the cable and directly connecting it to the cable hub. If the hub is considered "intelligent," management software developed for that hub type, as well as the hub itself, can disconnect the suspect port.

Figure 39.8

Example of twisted-pair Ethernet cabling.

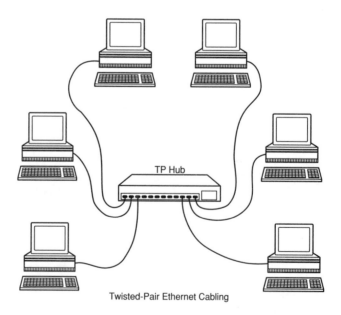

Twisted-Pair Ethernet Cabling

Troubleshooting 10BASE-T

The first step in troubleshooting a 10BASE-T network is to ensure that your network meets the rules for using 10BASE-T. The rules for a 10BASE-T network are as follows:

■ The maximum number of network segments is 1,024.

■ The cabling used should be 22, 24, or 26 American Wire Gauge (AWG), and be rated for an impedance of 85 to 115 ohms at 10 MHz.

 Unshielded twisted-pair uses a terminator resistance level of 100-200 ohms; shielded twisted-pair uses 150 ohms.

■ The maximum number of nodes is 512, and they may be connected on any three segments, with five being the maximum number of available line segments.

■ The maximum unshielded cable segment length is 328 feet, or 100 meters.

 You should be able to translate cable segment lengths from feet to meters, or from meters to feet. A meter is equivalent to 39.37 inches.

Additional troubleshooting tips are found in the Ethernet Troubleshooting section of this chapter.

 10BASE-T requires that the UTP cable system be compliant with the Level IV standard. Level IV is cable-certified to operate at 10 Mbps throughput.

Ethernet Frame Types

In order for information to be transmitted successfully across an Ethernet network, the sending and receiving network nodes must agree in advance on the structure of the information being transmitted. The sending node must organize the information in an orderly and predictable manner so that the receiving node can find and interpret the transmitted information. This orderly arrangement of information traveling across an Ethernet network is known as an *Ethernet frame*. Different Ethernet frame types describe different standards that specify the protocol structure (configuration of the media).

There are four possible Ethernet frame types. The same Ethernet frame type must be loaded at both the server and accessing clients in order for proper communication to take place. The four available frame types are ETHERNET 802.3 (also known as raw ETHERNET), ETHERNET 802.2, ETHERNET SNAP, and ETHERNET II.

Raw ETHERNET (802.3) was developed before the IEEE 802.3 standard was completed and released. Therefore, ETHERNET 802.3 is not in complete compliance with the IEEE standard. ETHERNET 802.3 is used only on IPX/SPX Novell networks. ETHERNET 802.3 does not contain a field to specify which protocols may be contained within the packet. The lack of this field is one feature of ETHERNET 802.3 that makes it almost exclusively unique to Novell's NetWare 2.2 and NetWare 3.*x* Operating Systems.

Common features of the ETHERNET 802.3 standard include the following:

■ A frame size between 64 and 1,518 bytes

- A preamble in the first line of the header (it contains alternating ones and zeroes to synchronize the communicating stations)

- A one-byte Start Frame Delimiter (SFD) field that follows the preamble and designates the beginning of the frame

- A six-byte field that specifies the address of the station to which the packet is being sent

- An originating address indicating the client, server, or router from where the packet was last sent

- A two-byte field that specifies the length of the data portion of the packet, and which must not have a length greater than 1,500 bytes to be considered valid

- A data field which must be no shorter than 46 bytes and no longer than 1,500 bytes

- A four-byte Cyclical Redundancy Check (CRC) or Frame Check Sequence that helps to ensure that the transmitted data is valid

ETHERNET 802.2 is fully compliant with the IEEE 802.3 standard. ETHERNET 802.2 is the default frame type used in NetWare 3.12 and NetWare 4.x networks. Common features of the ETHERNET 802.2 standard include the following:

- All of the same fields as the 802.3 specification

- Three additional Logical Link Control (LLC) fields, one byte long, that act much like an 802.3 header

- A frame size between 64 and 1,518 bytes

ETHERNET SNAP (SubNetwork Address Protocol) is fully compliant with ETHERNET 802.2 and is actually considered an enhancement to the 802.2 specification. Common features of the ETHERNET SNAP standard include the following:

- Two of the LLC fields, which contain fixed data indicating that this is a SNAP packet

- A type field as the third of the LLC fields, which enables the packet to carry other high-level protocols within the frame structure, thus ensuring compatibility and making it possible for network operating systems to carry protocols over other types of media, such as Token Ring

ETHERNET II frame types support TCP/IP for NetWare 3.11. Common features of the ETHERNET II frame type include the following:

- A packet type field located immediately after the source address field, which is the location of the packet length field in other ETHERNET frame types

- A combined preamble and Start Frame Delimiter field that are referred to jointly as the preamble

Although four ETHERNET frame types are available, load only the frame type that you need to use on your network server. If it is necessary in order to support multiple upper-layer protocols, you can load more than one frame type on a server.

Each LAN NIC in the server must have at least one protocol bound to it. To bind a protocol to a NIC, first LOAD the NIC drivers, then bind the protocol to the NIC as in the following:

```
LOAD NE2000 port=320 int=5
frame=ETHERNET_802.3     NAME=ENE5
BIND IPX TO ENE5 NET=BAC1234
```

Ethernet Troubleshooting

Trend measurement and analysis can be applied to all network types. The use of a sophisticated protocol analyzer, such as LANalyzer for WINDOWS and simpler tools, along with your own experience and knowledge, are two other effective troubleshooting techniques for Ethernet networks. This section covers the latter option.

When troubleshooting an Ethernet network, begin with the more obvious physical problems. For example, check to make certain that all connectors are tight and properly connected. Make certain that ground wires and terminators are used when required. Also, be certain that manufacturer's specifications are met, and that cable lengths, maximum number of nodes, and so on, are correct.

Consider the following when troubleshooting Ethernet networks:

- With 10BASE-T, make sure that the cable used has the correct number of twists to meet the data grade specifications.

- Check for electrical interference. Electrical interference can be caused by tying the network cable together with monitor and power cords. Outside interference also can be caused by fluorescent lights, electric motors, and other electrical devices.

- Make sure that connectors are pinned properly and crimped tightly.

- Check the cable lengths to make sure that distance specifications are not exceeded.

- If excess shielding on coax cable is exposed, make sure it is not grounding out the connector.

- Make sure that coax cables are not coiled tightly together.

- Check the grade of the cable being used. For 10BASE2, RG-58/U is required. All 10BASE5 cable must meet Ethernet specifications.

- If using a linear bus setup, make sure that the topology rules are followed.

- Check for missing terminator or terminators with improper impedance ratings.

- Check for malfunctioning hardware, such as a bad NIC, transceiver, concentrator, T-connector, or terminator. Check to make certain that connectors have not been mixed up, such as ARCnet connectors being used on an Ethernet network.

- Test the continuity of the cable, using various physical testing devices, such as an Optical Time Domain Reflectometer, or software, such as Novell's COMCHECK utility.

- If the Fileserver not found error message appears, check for a mismatch in the Ethernet frame type between the server and the client.

- Verify that the LAN card is working properly. Clean the connector fingers (do not use an eraser because it leaves grit on the card); pull the card and replace it with one that you know is in working order; or run the NIC's diagnostics software.

- If NIC resource conflicts seem to be a potential cause of network problems, remove all cards except the file server NICs, then replace them one at a time until the conflicting card is found. Then correct the NIC settings and continue checking NICs one at a time. If you are installing new NICs, avoid using the common COM port interrupts of 3 and 4 to prevent potential Ethernet card conflicts.

- Make sure that all the component cables in a segment are connected together. A user who moves his client and removes the T-connector incorrectly can cause a broken segment.

Understanding Token Ring Specifications

Token Ring uses a token-passing architecture that adheres to the IEEE 802.5 standard. The topology is physically a star, but logically uses a ring to pass the token from station to station. Each node must be attached to a concentrator called a *multistation access unit* (MSAU or MAU).

Token Ring network interface cards can run at 4 Mbps or 16 Mbps. 4 Mbps cards can run only at that data rate. However, 16 Mbps cards can be configured to run at 4 or 16 Mbps. All cards on a given network ring must be running at the same rate.

As shown in figure 39.9, each node acts as a repeater that receives token and data frames from its *nearest active upstream neighbor* (NAUN). After a frame is processed by the node, the frame is passed downstream to the next attached node. Each token makes at least one trip around the entire ring. It

then returns to the originating node. Workstations that indicate problems send a "beacon" to identify an address of the potential failure. You will learn more about this topic later in this chapter.

 To find out if any beacon messages have been sent on your Token Ring network, review your System Error Log, found in SYSCON through Supervisor Options.

Token Ring Board Settings

As with the Ethernet cards, the node address on each NIC is burned in at the manufacturer and is unique to each card. The node address in some cases can be overridden by vendor-specified software instructions. (Check with the vendor of the component.) A maximum of two Token Ring cards can be installed in any node, with each card being defined as the primary or alternate Token Ring card in the machine. A typical Token Ring card is shown in figure 39.10.

Figure 39.9

Operation of a Token Ring.

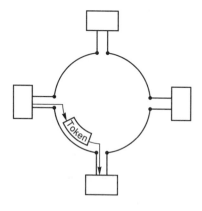

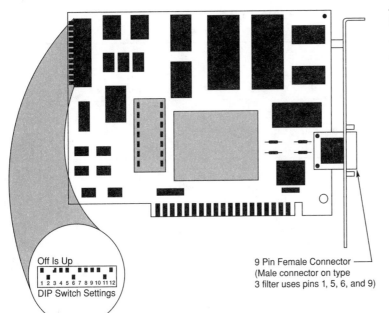

Figure 39.10

Features of a Token Ring NIC.

Off Is Up

DIP Switch Settings

9 Pin Female Connector
(Male connector on type
3 filter uses pins 1, 5, 6, and 9)

The following are features of a Token Ring NIC:

- DIP switches (see table 33.2)
- 9-pin female connector
- Remote boot PROM socket

 Note When loading two Token Ring NICs in a NetWare file server, make sure that you configure the primary card at port address of A20. The alternate card must be set at A24. For v3.1*x* or v4.*x*, in the AUTOEXEC.NCF file or at the file server console, use the following example commands:

```
LOAD TOKEN PORT=A20 INT=2 MEM=CC000
NAME=CARD1

LOAD TOKEN PORT=A24 INT=3 MEM=DC000
NAME=CARD2
```

The interrupt and base memory address on each Token Ring NIC must be set to avoid conflicts with all other components. Table 39.2 defines the proper DIP switch settings for an IBM 16/4 Token Ring card.

Each Token Ring card comes with a diagnostic disk that provides testing for the adapter. Refer to the appropriate documentation for your card for more detailed instructions.

Token Ring Cabling

Traditional Token-Ring networks used shielded twisted-pair cable. The following are standard IBM cable types for Token Ring:

- **Type 1.** A braided shield surrounds two twisted pairs of solid copper wire. Type 1 is used to connect terminals and distribution panels, or to connect between different wiring closets that are located in the same building. Type 1 uses two STPs of solid-core 22 AWG wire for long, high data grade transmissions within the building's walls.

Table 39.2
IBM 16/4 Token-Ring Switch Settings

Switch Blk (Off is Up, On is Down)	1	2	3	4	5	6	7	8	9	10	11	12
ADDRESS												
CC000	Off	On	On	Off	Off	On						
DC000	Off	On	Off	Off	Off	On						
INTERRUPT												
2							Off	Off				
3							On	Off				
6							Off	On				
7							Off	Off				
PRIMARY									Off			
ALTERNATE									On			
SHARED RAM												
8 KB										On	On	
16 KB										Off	On	
32 KB										On	Off	
64 KB										Off	Off	
DATA RATE												
16 Mbps												Off
4 Mbps												On

■ **Type 2.** Type 2 uses a total of six twisted pairs; two are STPs (for networking), four are UTPs (for telephone systems). Additionally, this cable type incorporates two unshielded twisted pairs that can be used for voice circuits. This cable is used for the same purposes as Type 1, but enables both voice and data cables to be included in a single cable run.

■ **Type 3.** Type 3 has unshielded twisted-pair copper with a minimum of two twists per inch, used as an alternative to Type 1 and Type 2 cable because of its reduced cost. It has four UTPs of 24 AWG solid-core wire for networks or telephone systems. Type 3 cannot be used for 16 Mbps Token-Ring networks. It is used primarily for long, low data-grade transmissions within walls. Signals will not travel as fast as with Type 1 cable because Type 3 does not have the shielding used by Type 1.

■ **Type 5.** With Type 5, fiber-optic cable is used only on the main ring. Type 5 can use two 100-um or 140-um optical fibers in one fiber jacket.

■ **Type 6.** A braided shield surrounds two twisted pairs of stranded copper wire. It is made up of two 26 AWG stranded-core STPs.

This cable supports shorter cable runs than Type 1, but is more flexible due to the stranded conductors. Type 6 is the IBM standard for patch cables and extension cables, used also in wiring closets.

- **Type 8.** Type 8 uses a single 26 AWG stranded-core STP and is especially designed for use under carpet.

- **Type 9.** Type 9 is the same as Type 6 cable except that it is designed to be fire-resistant for use in plenum installations. It uses two STPs of solid-core 26 AWG wire and is used for long runs within the walls of a building.

Token ring cabling is used to connect clients to the MSAU, or to connect one MSAU to another. Cables that connect between MSAUs are called patch cables. Patch cables may also be made of IBM Type 6 cable.

 Note Novell defines Token-Ring cabling in terms of two types of systems:

- Small movable

- Large non-movable

The small movable system supports up to 96 clients and file servers and 12 MSAUs. It uses Type 6 cable to attach clients and servers to IBM Model 8228 MSAUs. Type 6 cable is a shielded twisted-pair cable with stranded conductors. This cable is flexible, but has limited distance capabilities. The characteristics of this cable make it suitable for small networks and for patch cords.

The large non-movable system supports up to 260 clients and file servers, with up to 33 MSAUs. This network configuration uses IBM Type 1 or Type 2 cable. These are shielded twisted-pair cables with solid-wire conductors

suitable for carrying signals greater distances than are possible with Type 6. The large nonmovable system also involves other wiring needs such as punch panels or distribution panels, equipment racks for MSAUs, and wiring closets to contain the previously listed components.

The MSAU is the central cabling component for IBM Token-Ring networks. The 8228 MSAU was the original wiring hub developed by IBM for Token-Ring networks. Figure 39.11 shows 8228 MSAUs. Each 8228 has ten connectors, eight of which accept cables to clients or servers. The other connectors are labeled RI (ring in) and RO (ring out). The RI and RO connectors are used to connect multiple 8228s to form larger networks.

8228s are mechanical devices that consist of relays and connectors. Their purpose is to switch clients in and out of the network. Each port is controlled by a relay powered by a voltage sent to the MSAU from the client. When an 8228 is first set up, each of these relays must be initialized with a setup tool shipped with the unit. The setup tool is inserted into each port and held there until a light indicates that the port is properly initialized.

IBM Token Ring networks use two types of connectors. NICs are equipped with a nine-pin D-connector. MSAUs, repeaters, and most other equipment use a special IBM data connector. Two types of cables are employed:

- *Patch cables* have IBM data connectors at both ends. These cables interconnect MSAUs, repeaters, and most other Token-Ring components.

- *Token Ring adapter cables* have an IBM data connector at one end and a nine-pin connector at the other. Adapter cables connect client and server NICs to other network components that use IBM data connectors.

Figure 39.11 shows an example of a network cabling several clients and MSAUs. The distances noted in the figure are based on the rules for the small movable cabling system.

When you are connecting a Token-Ring network, make sure that you do the following:

1. Initialize each port in the 8228 MSAU by using the setup tool shipped with the MSAU (wait for the click) before connecting a cable.

2. If using more than one MSAU, connect the RO port of each MSAU with the RI port of the next MSAU in the loop. This must physically complete a circle or ring.

A variety of rules must be observed when configuring Token Rings. The following rules apply to small, movable Token-Ring networks:

■ The minimum patch cable distance between two MSAUs is eight feet.

■ The maximum patch cable distance between two MSAUs is 150 feet. Patch cables come in standard lengths of 8, 30, 75, and 150 feet for Type 6.

■ The maximum patch cable distance connecting all MSAUs is 400 feet.

■ The maximum adapter cable distance between an MSAU and a node is 150 feet.

A small movable IBM cable system consists of the following:

■ Maximum 96 nodes

■ Maximum 12 MSAUs

■ Uses Type 6 cable

A large non-movable IBM cable system consists of the following:

■ Maximum 260 nodes

■ Maximum 33 MSAUs

■ Uses Type 1 or Type 2 cable

 Token-Ring networks also can be cabled using UTP cabling, which IBM calls Type 3 cable. The IEEE 802.5 standard describes 4 Mbps Token Ring using UTP cable. However, level 5 UTP is currently used for 16 Mbps Token Ring.

When using UTP wiring, a media filter must be installed between the NIC and the UTP cable. Some newer Token Ring NICs have built-in media filters and RJ-45 jacks ready to interface with UTP wiring.

Token Ring Troubleshooting

When troubleshooting a Token-Ring network, as with troubleshooting other types of networks, begin with the more obvious physical problems, checking such things as connectors to see if they are tight and properly connected. You also should check to see that manufacturer's specifications are met, and that cable lengths, maximum number of nodes, and so on, are correct.

When troubleshooting Token-Ring networks, you also should look for the following:

■ Any base I/O, DMA shared memory, or interrupt conflicts with other boards.

■ The version of the client or server software driver, to make sure that its revision level is compatible with your NIC (drivers are different for file servers and clients).

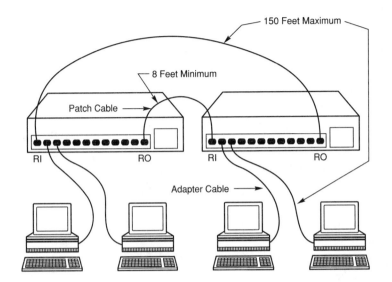

Figure 39.11
An example of Token-Ring cabling using MSAUs.

Token-Ring Cabling

▦ Proper connections of MSAUs, with ring out ports connecting to ring in ports throughout the ring. In troubleshooting problems that you have first isolated to a particular area of the network, if you suspect the MSAU, isolate it by changing the ring in and ring out cables to bypass the MSAU. If the ring is now functional again, consider replacing the MSAU. You may also find that if your network has MSAUs from more than one manufacturer, they are not wholly compatible. Impedance and other electrical characteristics may show slight differences between manufacturers, causing intermittent network problems.

▦ Other MSAU problems. Some MSAUs other than the 8228 are active and require a power supply. These MSAUs fail if they have a blown fuse or a bad power source.

▦ Correct attachments of patch cables and the adapter cable. Remember, patch cables connect MSAUs together, and the adapter cable connects the NIC to the MSAU. Patch cables, adapter cables, and MSAUs are common sources of problems. Isolating the problem is easier to do if you have a current log of your network's physical design. Once you have narrowed down the problem, you can isolate potential problem areas on the network from the rest of the network, and then use a cable tester to find the actual problem.

▦ A failed NIC. Try substituting another one known to work properly. NICs that have failure rates that exceed a preset tolerance level may actually remove themselves from the network.

▦ A bad MSAU or MSAU port. Ports may need to be reinitialized with the setup tool. Removing drop cables and reinitializing each MSAU port is a "quick fix" that is useful on relatively small Token-Ring networks.

▦ Incorrect card speeds; for example, a 16 Mbps card is inserted into a 4 Mbps ring or vice versa. Neither situation is correct. The speed of the NIC is displayed when the Token-Ring driver is loaded at the client.

■ The wrong type of cable for the speed of the network.

■ Bent or broken pins on the adapter cable.

■ Duplicate node addresses. If you are overriding the burned-in network addresses, it is possible that duplicate node addresses may be set.

■ The Type 3 media filter, if connecting to a 4 Mbps twisted-pair network.

One of the advantages of a Token-Ring network is its built-in ability to monitor itself. This process provides electronic troubleshooting and, when possible, repair processes. When it is not possible for the Token-Ring network to make its own repairs, a process called *beaconing* is helpful. Beaconing narrows down the portion of the ring where the problem is most likely to exist. This potential problem area is referred to as the *fault domain*.

The Beaconing Process

The design of the Token Ring network itself contributes greatly to the ability of the beaconing process to troubleshoot its own network. The design includes two types of network stations known as Active Monitors and Standby Monitors. Only one Active Monitor can exist on a network at a time. All other stations are Standby Monitors.

Generally, the first station that is powered-up and becomes part of the network is automatically the Active Monitor station. The responsibility of the Active Monitor station is to announce itself to the next active downstream station as the Active Monitor station, and request that station to announce itself to its next active downstream station. The Active Monitor station sends out this beacon announcement every seven seconds.

Once each station has announced itself to its next active downstream neighbor, the announcing station becomes the nearest active upstream neighbor (NAUN) to the downstream station. Each station on a Token-Ring network has an upstream neighbor as well as a downstream neighbor.

Once each station is aware of its NAUN, the beaconing process continues every seven seconds. If for some reason a station does not receive one of its expected seven-second beaconed announcements from its upstream neighbor, it attempts to notify the network of its lack of contact from the upstream neighbor. It sends a message out onto the network ring, which includes the following:

■ The sending station's network address

■ The receiving NAUN's network address

■ The beacon type

From this information, the ring can determine which station may be having a problem and attempt to fix the problem without disrupting the entire network. This problem fix is known as *autoreconfiguration*. If the autoreconfiguration is unsuccessful, manual correction is required. Figure 39.12 shows a Token-Ring network utilizing the beaconing process.

The preceding section detailed common characteristics of ARCnet, Ethernet, and Token Ring. Other components also must be examined for conflicts and proper configuration. The next section describes these items.

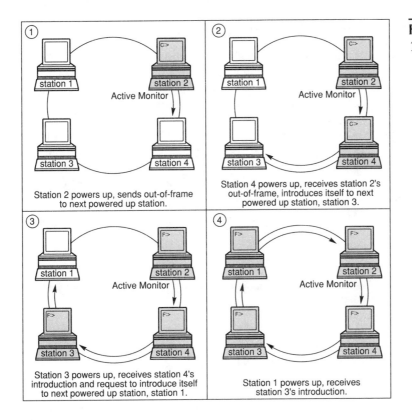

Figure 39.12
Token Ring beaconing.

Understanding FDDI

Fiber Distributed Data Interface is a LAN standard that, like Token Ring, follows the IEEE 802.5 standard for accessing the network. FDDI carries both LED and laser-generated LAN communications through fiber-optic cables.

| Note | Decide when it is appropriate to consider the installation of FDDI. |

Fiber optic cable is primarily made of pure glass that is pulled into very thin wires or fibers. Many of these fibers are bundled together to form a core. This core is surrounded by another layer of glass called *cladding*. The LED sends the signals through the core of this cable, and the cladding contains these signals to the core. The signal on each fiber can go in only one direction at a time. The bundle of fibers enables the LED to send multiples of signals at a time.

Unlike Token Ring and its related network interface cards that transfer data across the network at speeds of 4 or 16 Mbps, FDDI transfers information at a rate of 100 Mbps. In addition, FDDI is structured to take advantage of two rings, rather than one. This Dual Counter Rotating Rings structure enables FDDI to transfer data across one ring while it performs backup and other services on the second ring.

In addition, FDDI uses multiple tokens and has the ability to bypass network stations designated as low priority, so it can provide faster service to high-priority network stations.

Like a Token-Ring LAN, FDDI uses a token to transfer data frames around the network. After the data frame is processed by the correct network station, the token is passed on to the next attached network node.

The second ring in the FDDI network rotates in the opposite direction of the first ring. This counter-rotation enables the network to compensate for a break in the fiber. If one ring in the network becomes broken due to a problem at one of the network stations, those stations located on either side of the break can isolate the break in the fiber by forming a single ring (wrapping) from their own ports, as shown in figure 39.13.

Each network station can be attached to either one ring or to both rings, depending on the class of the connected station. There are two types of station classes: Class A and Class B.

Class A stations, also called *Single Attached Stations* (SAS), can be attached to only one ring at a time. Only Class B stations, or Dual attached Stations (DAS), can be connected to both rings simultaneously. This designation of station classes helps to keep unstable network devices from breaking both network rings.

Another method of isolating faulty nodes in the network is through the use of wiring concentrators. Wiring concentrators function in theory much like the Token-Ring MSAU. They act as centralized cabling connection devices for network stations. Unlike MSAUs, however, wiring concentrators are capable of communicating with stations and verifying the integrity of the station-to-concentrator connection.

Advantages of Using FDDI

The ability to isolate a break in the cable and continue network communication makes FDDI an extremely reliable cabling option. FDDI has several other advantages.

FDDI overcomes some of the performance problems experienced by traditional Token-Ring networks. It accomplishes this by implementing a standard that provides fair and timely access to the network.

Increased reliability is another advantage of using FDDI. That reliability comes in several forms, including the following:

- **Information security.** Fiber-optic cable is difficult to wiretap.

- **Physical security.** Fiber-optic cable is more resistant to cable breakage than are other types of cabling.

- **Electrical security.** Fiber-optic cable is not susceptible to electrical interference and does not conduct electricity.

FDDI also can transmit network packets over its cable for distances that are significantly longer than other types of cabling. For example, on a fiber-optic cable with no cable bends or breaks that would otherwise reduce the integrity of the transmission, information theoretically can travel hundreds of miles.

FDDI also has built-in management of three aspects of the network, including the following:

- **Ring Management (RMT)** is responsible for finding and resolving faults in the network ring.

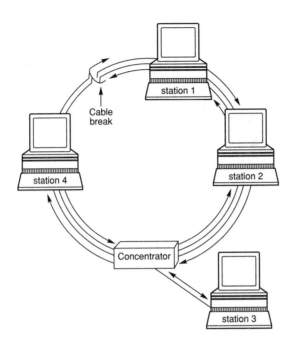

Figure 39.13
Isolated cable break in an FDDI network.

■ **Connection Management (CMT)** is responsible for controlling stations that are inserting themselves into the network, or removing themselves from the network.

■ **Station Management (SMT)** makes it possible for special high-level programs to monitor the ring.

As noted earlier, FDDI networks are substantially faster than Token-Ring networks, capable of communicating at a rate of 100 Mbps. They accomplish this speed not only as a result of the type of cable (fiber optic) that they use, but also as a result of their use of multiple tokens and their ability to service only the high-priority network stations, bypassing the low-priority stations whenever necessary.

A fiber-optic cable is also significantly lighter in weight than is, for example, twisted-pair cabling with an equivalent bandwidth.

 Note   Don't look directly at fiber-optic cable without eye protection. To check to see whether a fiber-optic port is transmitting, darken the room and place a piece of paper in front of the port. If it is transmitting, a light will be reflected onto the paper.

Disadvantages of Using FDDI

There are two primary disadvantages of using FDDI in your network. First, because of the complexity and newness of FDDI technology, you need a great deal of expertise to install and subsequently maintain an FDDI network.

Second, although the cost of the cable itself is comparable to that of unshielded twisted-pair (UTP) cabling, the concentrators and LAN adapters are relatively expensive. For example, a typical FDDI concentrator runs between $1,000 and $1,500 per network node. Therefore, the overall cost of an FDDI network for a LAN of any size can quickly become quite costly.

FDDI Cabling

Various types and wavelengths of fiber-optic cables are available. A typical fiber-optic cable consists of a core made from silica, surrounded by a primary and secondary buffer, and then enclosed in a jacket. Kevlar may be added to provide strength.

The important thing to remember about choosing a fiber-optic cable is to select one based on its intended use, and to match the cable to its appropriate connectors. Figure 39.14 shows a typical duplex fiber-optic cable.

FDDI Troubleshooting

As with troubleshooting all types of networks, begin by looking for the obvious problems, such as loose connectors, damaged cables, and so on. After ruling out these types of problems, consider other possible causes. Look first at those problems considered typical of FDDI networks:

- Incorrect cable type for actual distance between nodes. On an FDDI network where network information must travel thousands of feet, Multimode Fiber should be used. When distances between nodes begin to reach tens of thousands of feet, or exceed distances of two kilometers, Single-Mode Fiber is necessary.

- Problems with communicating between network nodes. Even small breaks in a fiber-optic cable can result in network communication problems. There are several ways to detect cable problems, except for one that requires special equipment. If a break in a segment of

the cable is a complete break, you can detect the break using a flashlight. Otherwise, you can use an optical power meter and a source of light energy to test the cable. If either of these methods is insufficient, you can use the most expensive method, an Optical Time Domain Reflectometer (OTDR).

- Dirt on connectors is another cause of communication problems between network nodes. Data is transmitted through fiber-optic cables using light. Therefore, it is important that you keep connectors free from dust and dirt. You can clean connectors using any type of lint-free cloth dampened with alcohol. Do not use water or any type of cleaning fluids other than alcohol.

- Communication problems also can be caused by bad connectors or by a segment of the cable that is open (incorrectly terminated). A loss of optical power that exceeds 13.0 decibels is an indication that cable problems of this nature may exist. To correct these problems, replace faulty connectors and properly close any open cable segment.

- A delay of up to four milliseconds in communication is not unusual for fiber-optic cable. If communication delays are a problem, consider using NetWare's Packet Burst Protocol to send multiple rather than single frames across the network, thus reducing transmission delay.

- When the network does not efficiently handle transmissions across cable that exceeds 50 meters, or which requires 10 Mbps or more throughput, this problem may be directly related to the type of fiber-optic cable. If you are using plastic fiber-optic cable in your network, consider replacing all or at least some of

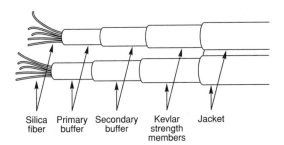

Figure 39.14
*Fiber-optic duplex cable
assembly.*

Silica   Primary   Secondary   Kevlar   Jacket
fiber   buffer   buffer   strength
                               members

this cable with glass cable. Speed can be affected by the type of fiber-optic cable used.

■ The path that network information must travel should be the most efficient. If you are using bridges instead of routers in your network, consider switching to network routers. NetWare network routers, or routers such as CI500 and Wellfleet that are certified by Novell, can choose the best path for any given packet. They are somewhat slower than bridges, however, because of the increased processing that they perform. The design of FDDI translation bridges makes routers the preferred choice for FDDI networks running NetWare.

Which Topology Should I Use?

As a network administrator or support engineer, you have to make some tough decisions on the best type of topology to incorporate into your network environment. It is similar to choosing what type of vehicle and size of engine you need to drive your loads on local streets, freeways, or highways. You need to consider using Token Ring (4 Mbps or 16 Mbps) or Ethernet (10 Mbps). You also need to consider which type of cabling system you need for your network.

The factors that are involved in your choice include the following:

■ Type of applications and their percentage of overall use

■ Flexibility of setup

■ Cost

■ Knowledge level of your support or vendor source

■ Availabilty of replacement or add-on components

No one topology is better than another. Your choice is dependent on how the factors affect your network environment.

Choose the Ethernet topology for those types of networks with a light-to-medium workload. If you are using standard applications, such as word processing, spreadsheets, gateway host sessions, electronic mail, and calendaring packages, Ethernet will work efficiently.

Ethernet has a maximum throughput of 10 Mbps. (Standard loads usually are working around 8-9.1 Mbps.) The cost is nominal, and interchangeable components are readily available. Clients can attempt to transmit more quickly rather than waiting their turn, as is done with the Token Ring topology.

The disadvantage of Ethernet is that the size of the data frames in the packets may require more traffic to pass along the data files on the media. Also, the collision-oriented system can be degraded with the heavy use of database, imaging, multimedia, or CAD/CAM applications.

Token Ring topology is a choice for networks that tend toward heavy workloads. The size of the data frame in the packet is larger than in Ethernet. Token Ring can handle large file transfers, such as database, CAD/CAM, and multiple accesses to imaging files, more easily. Token Ring runs at 4 Mbps or 16 Mbps on many types of media. Some applications of 16 Mbps Token Ring speed are not always as efficient as using the 4 Mbps or the Ethernet 10 Mbps.

Token Ring is more reliable because no collisions occur with the token passing scheme. The disadvantages of Token Ring are cost, station transmission capabilities, and the overhead for management of the token scheme. Also, the more clients you add to a ring, the more that performance can be degraded. Consider splitting the ring into smaller rings with fewer clients attached.

Use your best judgment on your network setup. Where your applications reside, the location of your workloads, and the availability of your network components will determine whether you should use one topology or perhaps mix them.

Questions

1. Which is the least important when configuring a client?

   ○ A. Avoiding conflicts

   ○ B. How other clients are configured

   ○ C. Checking that cables meet specifications for their intended topology

   ○ D. Matching drivers to operating system revisions

2. Which statement about ARCnet is false?

   ○ A. ARCnet can be cabled in star or bus.

   ○ B. ARCnet uses RG-62/U for coax.

   ○ C. ARCnet has the unique feature time-out setting of 31 microseconds.

   ○ D. ARCnet can span a distance of 25,000 feet.

3. Which combination is not supported?

   ○ A. Passive hub to passive hub

   ○ B. Active hub to passive hub to active hub

   ○ C. Active hub to passive hub

   ○ D. Network node to passive hub

4. Which is not a feature of an Ethernet board?

   ○ A. Ethernet boards usually have DIX connectors.

   ○ B. Ethernet boards can have thick (DIX), thin (BNC), or twisted-pair (RJ-45) connectors.

   ○ C. Ethernet boards have internal transceivers for thin net.

   ○ D. Ethernet boards have a time-out setting.

5. Which level cable is correct for 10BASE-T?

   ○ A. Level I

   ○ B. Level II

   ○ C. Level IV

   ○ D. Level VI

6. Which statement about Token Ring cabling is true?

   ○ A. Small, movable systems support up to 96 clients and 12 MSAUs. Token Ring networks cannot use UTP cabling.

   ○ B. The maximum patch cable distance between two MSAUs is 75 feet.

   ○ C. The minimum patch cable distance is 2.5 feet.

   ○ D. Token-Ring uses Type 2, Type 4, and Type 6 cabling.

7. Which TWO of the following statements regarding FDDI are true?

   ☐ A. It follows the IEEE 802.5 standard.

   ☐ B. Like Token Ring, it uses only a single token.

   ☐ C. FDDI can transfer data at speeds of 100 Mbps.

   ☐ D. Stations must attach to the cable by a concentrator.

8. FDDI stands for _____.

   ○ A. Fiber-based Data Distribution Interface

   ○ B. Fiber Distributed Data Interface

   ○ C. Fiber Optic Data Distributed Interface

   ○ D. Fiber Data Distribution Interface

9. Plastic and glass fiber-optic cables can be used equally well in all situations except _____.

   ○ A. when the cable distance is less than 50 meters

   ○ B. when the cable has an open condition

   ○ C. when stations are attached using a concentrator

   ○ D. when throughput of 10 Mbps or greater is required

10. Which of the following is one advantage that FDDI has over Token Ring?

   ○ A. Fiber optic cable is difficult to wiretap.

   ○ B. FDDI is capable of isolating cable breaks.

   ○ C. FDDI provides fair and timely access to the network.

   ○ D. FDDI has built-in ring management.

11. What is the main advantage of using 10BASE2 when network segments do not have to exceed 185 meters?

   ○ A. It is relatively simple to connect.

   ○ B. Drop cables can be used, making it easier to troubleshoot.

   ○ C. Each node connects directly to the cable.

   ○ D. It is the least expensive of the cabling options.

12. Which TWO of the Ethernet cabling options requires that each end of the bus be terminated?

   ☐ A. 10BASE2

   ☐ B. 10BASE5

   ☐ C. 10BASE-T

   ☐ D. Thin net

13. Which of the cabling options is considered the trend for wiring Ethernet networks?

   ○ A. 10BASE2

   ○ B. 10BASE5

   ○ C. 10BASE-T

   ○ D. Thick net

14. Which of the following is not an advantage in using 10BASE-T for cabling a network?

   ○ A. It is easier and more reliable to manage.

   ○ B. Centralized hubs make it easier to detect bad cable segments.

   ○ C. Beaconing helps to isolate cable breaks.

   ○ D. It is relatively inexpensive to use.

15. Which of the following Ethernet frame types
    is designated as raw Ethernet?

    ○ A. ETHERNET_802.2

    ○ B. ETHERNET_802.3

    ○ C. ETHERNET_SNAP

    ○ D. ETHERNET_II

Answers

1. B

2. D

3. A

4. D

5. C

6. C

7. A, C

8. B

9. B

10. A

11. D

12. A, B, D

13. C

14. C

15. B

Troubleshooting Network Storage Devices

In this chapter, you will learn about the advantages and disadvantages of different types of storage devices that can be used on the network. There are many storage devices that have evolved throughout the history of the computer industry. Understanding how these devices operate and what their limitations are is an important function of a network administrator's job. The following are the types of storage devices that will be discussed in this chapter:

- *Hard drives*

- *CD-ROM players*

- *Magneto-optical drives*

Hard Drives

The hard drive is perhaps the most important storage device on your network. Great care and attention must be given to the hard drive because it is the core of the file server. The operating system that gives a network its functionality must reside on that core drive. If that core drive fails, the entire network will go down. A network administrator is responsible for developing a design for fault tolerance in protecting the core of the network. You also must be able to diagnose potential failure points and be proactive in preventative maintenance. An experienced network administrator must be able to do capacity planning and know how to react in a contingency management mode.

The terminology in the computer industry uses the term *fixed disk* to mean *hard disk*. The fixed disk or the *platters* are contained in the hard drive casing, as opposed to inserting a removable disk in the floppy drive (see fig. 40.1). The technology of a hard drive enables it to provide speed, reliability, and a lot of storage in a small space in one location.

The device that enables the communication between the hard drive and the CPU is called the *disk controller card.* The disk controller card can be built into the motherboard, as part of the drive or as a separate component. The controller interprets the commands from the CPU and sends the interpreted signals to either seek, read, or write data to the hard drive.

 The drive casing is sealed by the manufacturer in a dust- and moisture-free environment. Do not open this drive casing for any reason—dust particles can scratch your platters. They can become inoperable and you could lose valuable data.

The hard drive is made up of many components that work in unison and can be described as an electronic wonder. The drive contains a spindle motor that rotates the platters inside the drive casing. The voice coil actuator moves the read/write heads to the needed position on the disk platter. The time it takes for the read/write heads to find the correct track is called *seek time.*

After the track has been located, the amount of time it takes for the needed piece of data to rotate under the read/write head is called *drive latency.* The combination of seek time and drive latency (the total amount of time it takes to get to the data on the platter) is called *access time.* To "settle" a drive is the time it takes for the head to stabilize above the track after the process or the motion for seeking data has stopped.

The *data transfer rate* is the speed at which data is moved from the disk to the electronic "brains" of the CPU. The amount of data moved is measured in megabytes per second. All these timing features in a hard drive are important to how quickly data can be accessed on the network.

 A cluster is the minimum unit of space for the storage of a file allocated by DOS. A block is the minimum unit of space (usually 4 KB) for the storage of file information by NetWare.

Types of Hard Drive Interfaces

There are several types of hard drive interfaces and encoding schemes used with these interfaces in the networking environment. As a network administrator or support engineer, you should become familiar with each type because of the varied install base that still exists. An early example of a type of

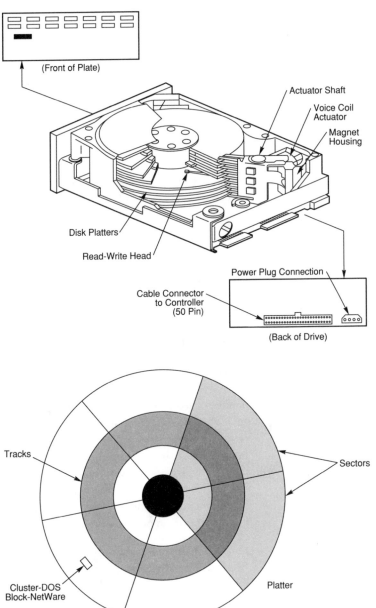

Figure 40.1

Internal components of a hard drive.

(Front of Plate)

Actuator Shaft

Voice Coil Actuator

Magnet Housing

Disk Platters

Read-Write Head

Power Plug Connection

Cable Connector to Controller (50 Pin)

(Back of Drive)

Tracks

Sectors

Cluster-DOS Block-NetWare

Platter

a hard drive is an ST-506 model manufactured by Seagate. The ST-506 originally was built for 5MB size drives. The *Run Length Limited* (RLL) or the *Modified Frequency Modulation* (MFM) encoding scheme is used for the larger ST-506 drives.

 MFM is referred to as double-density recording and is used as a coding system to pack more information on hard disks. MFM is still used today on floppy disks and small hard drives.

RLL has increased data density capabilities over MFM by the way it manipulates electronic flux transitions. Fluxes are defined as the way the magnetic field handles the 0s and 1s of digital information. The RLL handles a higher data throughput over the MFM encoding scheme.

Integrated Drive Electronics (IDE) Drives

The Integrated Drive Electronics drive uses the mechanics of having the controller interface integrated with the electronic controls of the hard drive. The IDE terminology often is identified as an AT-type interface with the cable connector for the controller built into the CPU's motherboard. The IDE drive is a cost-effective solution that uses the RLL encoding scheme. Even though the IDE solution has widely replaced the ST-506 drives, there are some limitations on using IDE drives with NetWare:

- Unless a special nonstandard BIOS is used, there is a maximum drive capacity of 528MB.

- IDE does not support drive command overlapping, nor can it multitask I/O. If you are mixing IDE drives in a file server with other types of drives, the network operating system must wait for the IDE to complete any

commands issued before the network operating system can issue any commands to any other drives.

- IDE does not support any optical or tape drives (the SCSI interface does).

- IDE does not support bus-mastering.

 It is recommended that you never do a low-level format on an IDE drive. If you do this repair task, you could erase the manufacturer's bad block information that is written in a special format on the IDE drive.

Enhanced Small Device Interface (ESDI) Drives

The Enhanced Small Device Interface uses one cable for floppy control, one for hard drive control, and one for data. The ST-506 drive uses the same cabling system, but it is not interchangeable with the ESDI drive. The ESDI drive became more popular than the ST-506 because of its capability of having a higher performance level and using a larger storage capacity. The ESDI also can store information about bad tracks onto the disk, and the interface is designed to work with tape systems. The popularity of ESDI was fairly short-lived, however, and SCSI drive systems have replaced ESDI as the drives of choice on network servers.

Older ESDI drives are supported by the computer's BIOS. Newer drives that have 1,024 or more cylinders do not work well in older ESDI machines. Drives that have more than 1,023 cylinders and 33 sectors per track are not likely to be supported by DOS versions before v3.3. The controllers of XTs, ATs, and Western Digital WD1002 controllers cannot recognize the cylinder count above 1,023 in larger drives.

Note If you are using PS/2 CPUs as file servers (older ones came with ESDI drives) and early versions of NetWare, be careful in updating disk information with the reference disk after NetWare has been loaded. The older operating systems wrote the Cold Boot Loader to part of the track 0 on the ESDI drive.

When the reference disk updates drive information, it writes to track 0 and it will write on top of the cold boot loader. You will have to use your backup copy of the NET$OS.EXE file and boot from a floppy drive to get the server back up. If you want to boot from the hard drive again, you have to rebuild the file server from scratch.

Small Computer Systems Interface (SCSI) Drives

The Small Computer Systems Interface provides an expansion bus architecture that allows up to seven SCSI-type devices (hard drives, CD-ROM, tape units). These can all be the same tape device, be used in combination, or be only one device on one bus slot (see fig. 40.2). These devices are attached to the cable chain that is attached to the SCSI controller card installed in a server or a client.

The devices that are installed internally in the CPU use ribbon cables designed for SCSI. External devices attach by cables that are built with the appropriate connectors for each of the devices attached to the SCSI chain.

The SCSI arbitration scheme allows a faster data transfer rate among the devices attached to each bus slot chain. The advantage in using SCSI is that the CPU does not have to intervene with the processing on the chain in order for the SCSI devices to complete their operations. The SCSI controller has its own BIOS that will run in the upper memory area of the CPU. It also uses hardware port addresses, memory addresses, and DMA channels to ensure compatibility with other components in the CPU.

Each SCSI address can support a controller that provides access to one or two hard drives. An *advanced SCSI programming interface* (ASPI) device driver is provided by the manufacturer and is needed to coordinate communications between

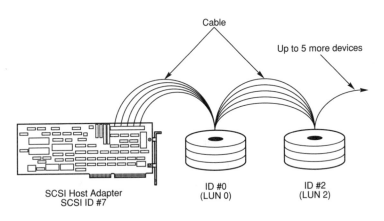

Figure 40.2

SCSI drive device addressing.

SCSI Drive Device Addressing

different types of devices. There are SCSI controllers that are available with connector ports for use with floppy disk drives. If you want to use the floppy controller already built into your CPU, you can disable the floppy controller on the SCSI board.

The SCSI bus must be terminated at both ends (see fig. 40.3). A SCSI device driver cannot interpret the difference between the original signals or returned signals as an Ethernet bus does. To prevent confusion caused by reflected signals, terminators are used to absorb or prevent signals from becoming unstable. Each SCSI device connected to this terminated bus must have a unique address. This unique address is called a *Logical Unit Number* (LUN).

The American National Standards Institute (ANSI) X3T9.2 committee sets the standards for the SCSI interface. The newest SCSI standard, SCSI-2, defines the protocols, hardware, and command set to run devices other than hard disks. The older SCSI standard could not reliably control the devices beyond the hard drive setup. It is not recommended that you mix SCSI-1 and SCSI-2 standards in the same host, unless the SCSI adapter provides a method of handling both standards. The ISA bus has a transfer data rate maximum of 2 MB per second, whereas the SCSI-2 can transfer data at 4 MB, and, during the FAST operation, can transfer data up to 10 MB per second. You should use the EISA, MCA, or PCI bus with the appropriate SCSI interface cards for the FAST SCSI-2 operation to work efficiently.

There is an implementation of SCSI called WIDE SCSI-2 that is not used as much as the FAST SCSI-2 standard, as WIDE SCSI-2 is fairly new. WIDE SCSI-2 uses a second data path that offers the capability of 20 MB per second data transfer

rate. The WIDE SCSI-2 controller integrates the 68-pin SCSI cable and the differential signaling process. Standard SCSI devices use a 50-pin cable and the single-ended signaling process. There are SCSI host adapters that have a combination of connection slots for a SCSI internal bus with both 68-pin and 50-pin cables. These combination type adapters use either the differential or single-ended signaling process, but not both.

You cannot mix the differential and single-ended devices on the same SCSI bus—they are electronically incompatible. If you have both types of SCSI devices, use one adapter for WIDE SCSI using differential signaling, and another adapter that uses the single-ended devices. Future implementations for the WIDE SCSI devices will develop enhancements for using single-ended signaling.

Tips for Working with SCSI Devices

The use of SCSI devices is rapidly becoming an industry standard. These devices are flexible, affordable, and are relatively easy to install. As a network administrator or support engineer, you should use the following tips in setting up a SCSI environment:

- When selecting your hardware and software, make sure the revision levels are current and that each can work within the same bus with the other devices.

- Use all SCSI-2 devices when designing a network. Older SCSI-1 hard disks will mix with SCSI-2 equipment if you have to use available resources.

- Use SCSI host adapters that use a software setup for jumper and termination settings. Then you do not have to remove the card from the CPU each time you need to change the settings.

Internal SCSI Setup

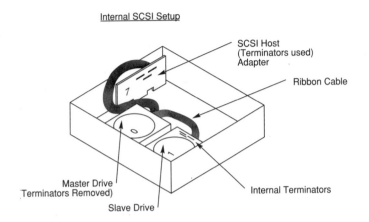

SCSI Host
(Terminators used)
Adapter

Ribbon Cable

Master Drive
(Terminators Removed)

Slave Drive

Internal Terminators

Figure 40.3

Termination of SCSI internal/external setups.

Internal/External SCSI Setup

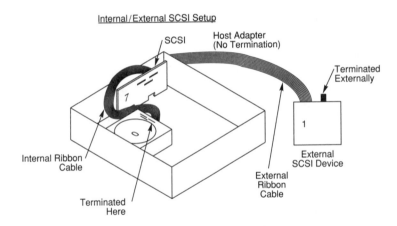

SCSI

Host Adapter
(No Termination)

Terminated
Externally

Internal Ribbon
Cable

Terminated
Here

External
Ribbon
Cable

External
SCSI Device

External SCSI Setup

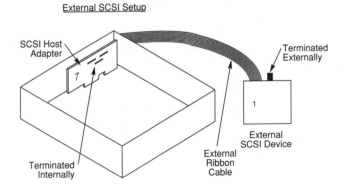

SCSI Host
Adapter

Terminated
Externally

Terminated
Internally

External
Ribbon
Cable

External
SCSI Device

■ Make sure that you use the proper pin number and connector size for the SCSI host adapter and the devices attached to complete the bus. Watch for cables with FAST SCSI-2 adapter connections attaching to the standard Centronics connector on the external SCSI devices. Unfortunately, the proper SCSI connector cables are not always shipped to meet the needs in your environment.

■ Always confirm that each SCSI bus is properly terminated and that the cables are fitting snugly into the connector slots. The maximum length for a SCSI bus is 19 feet, 10 inches. Make sure that the external disk subsystems are using cables that match the proper impedance level.

■ The SCSI bus requires a stable current for the signals to operate properly. Verify that your host adapter and other SCSI devices are supplying the necessary terminating power.

■ Make sure your SCSI host adapter's BIOS, port address, IRQ, and DMA channel addresses do not conflict with other components in the CPU.

■ Make sure that each SCSI device has a unique identifier number (LUN). Each SCSI adapter has a default address of 7 set by the manufacturer. The first bootable hard disk must have a SCSI LUN of 0. Other standard SCSI devices on the bus should be numbered 1-6 in the sequential order that the devices are located in the SCSI chain. Some Hewlett-Packard and IBM PS/2 CPUs use a SCSI adapter with an ID of 7 and the devices on the bus start at LUN 6; then each device is numbered sequentially downward to 0.

■ It is best not to mix models of SCSI adapters if they are being used in the same computer. The ASPI software manager that is used by the adapter is written uniquely for that card. Mixing ASPI managers—even by the same manufacturer but different models—can cause operating conflicts.

■ SCSI host adapters can coexist with other types of hard disks and their controllers. Still, it is best to keep device models consistent in the computer.

Note There are many third-party software utilities that can be used to determine what drive interface is used in a client or file server. Tools such as CHECKIT PRO, as shown in figure 40.4, can assist a network administrator in determining the needed details.

Figure 40.4
CHECKIT PRO Hard Drive information screen example.

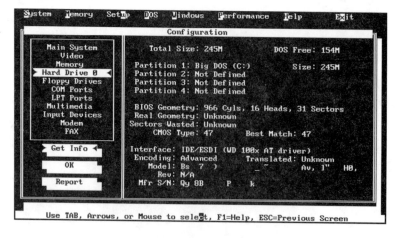

Disk Coprocessor Boards (DCBs)

Disk Coprocessor Boards are controller cards that offload the I/O from the CPU onto the DCB's own coprocessor chip. This frees up the CPU's processor to assist in improving network performance. DCBs also are referred to as *Host Bus Adapters* (HBAs) in Novell literature.

A file server can handle up to four DCB channels. A *disk channel* is a DCB and its disk subsystems. Each DCB can handle a maximum of eight SCSI controllers, with each controller supporting up to two disk drives. SCSI external disk subsystems can be daisy-chained off the DCB port on the end of the card (see fig. 40.5). DCBs are developed for the ISA (AT bus), EISA, and Micro-channel architecture. Development of DCBs today is done by third-party vendors.

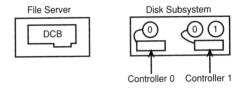

Figure 40.5

Disk Coprocessor Board configuration.

The original DCBs were developed by Novell and had an 80188 on-board processor. The DCB also served as a UPS monitor that could gracefully down a server in the event of a UPS "battery low" condition. DCBs also were used as a keycard for serialization of early versions of NetWare 2.*x*. The DISKSET utility is required for using Novell's DCBs to send disk and drive configuration information to the EEPROM on the DCB. Any physical adds or deletions to the controller or disk drive setup required the use of DISKSET. Current DCBs by third parties use the utilities provided by the

vendor. Most extended channel disk subsystems or internal multiple drives today use internal SCSI cards in the file server instead of DCBs.

Although the DCB was at one time the preferred method for constructing high-performance disk storage systems, many current SCSI controllers offer much higher performance.

■ A file server can handle up to 4 DCB channels.

■ A disk channel consists of a DCB and the disk subsystems that attach to it.

■ Each DCB can handle a maximum of eight SCSI controllers.

Proper integration of hardware components in a network is integral for efficient LAN performance. Verification from vendors and Novell Technical Support can help in your network planning. You must pay attention to potential conflicts for interrupts, memory addresses, and node addresses. Cabling limitations, hard drive requirements, addressing and termination, and certified software drivers also must be considered. If you do the proper homework and planning, you will reduce the chances of cost overruns and unplanned down time.

Setting Up Hard Drives

The hard disk is the most important device in a file server for storing both data and the applications that provide the glue for the network to function. The speed, the capacity, and the reliability of the hard disk can make or break your everyday operations (and maybe your sanity!). Understanding the hard disk, using the proper setup features, and performing proactive maintenance is an important function of a network administrator.

Working with Jumpers on the Hard Drive

When the hard drive arrives from the manufacturer and is unpacked from the box, all the jumpers on the drive are set at default options. These settings may or may not work in your computer. As a network administrator or support engineer, you must confirm that the settings on the drive will work for the interface type and encoding scheme required for that computer. Depending on your drive type, the following jumpers might need to be set directly on the drive:

- **ACT.** Set primarily on IDE and SCSI drives, and lights an external LED to indicate that the drive is active.

- **Drive Select.** Used primarily by ESDI, MFM, and RLL drives, depending on the number of drives and if you are using a flat or twisted cable.

- **C/D or DS.** Used by IDE to determine if the drive is to be a C or a D drive.

- **SCSI Address.** A unique address set by three jumpers that define a binary number. The manufacturer sets this address at 0. Check your drive documentation for all SCSI drives—this setting can vary with different vendors.

- **DSP.** Used by IDE to designate when a cable is being shared or which one of the drives is the master drive.

The controller card (if used by the drive) might need to have the following jumpers set:

- **Controller Interrupt.** You also might need to establish this setting in the STARTUP.NCF file on your file server when the DSK file is loading. Usually, this setting is made by the

manufacturer and should be left at this default setting.

- **Base I/O.** This should not conflict with any other device in the computer. This is set as a default from the manufacturer and rarely is changed unless there is a conflict.

- **DMA Channel.** NetWare does not recommend sharing a DMA channel between two devices. There are some ESDI and SCSI controllers that may need to have this setting verified.

- **Base BIOS Address.** Some controller cards use ROM BIOS and may need to have this set. Addresses over E000h may not be supported by some motherboards. Conflicts may arise with this setting and network interface cards or VGA cards.

Types of Cables Used with Hard Drives

The cable setup is important; it should be installed so that the pins in the connectors on the cable can receive and transmit the proper signals for data transfer. As a network administrator or support engineer, you must be aware of different cable types and proper installation of these cables. Improper installation can cause the loss of data and the potential destruction of drive components. Use the following recommendations when working with drive cables:

- Make sure that the colored stripe (usually red) is attached to Pin 1 on the controller card and to the hard drive (see figure 40.6).

- In an AT standard computer, the floppy and hard drive cables have different twists and cannot be interchanged.

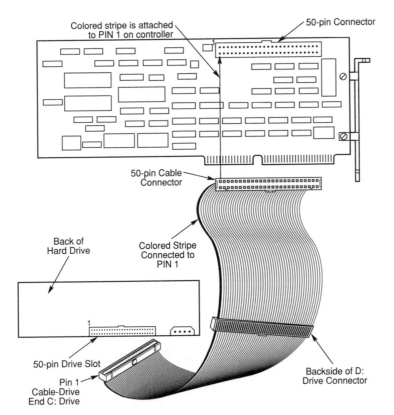

Figure 40.6

Proper connection of Pin 1 between a hard drive and a disk controller card.

 Practical TIP MFM and RLL hard drive cables have five twisted lines, and a floppy cable has seven twisted lines.

Floppy cables have the twists in the lower pin numbers.

■ Small-numbered wires: twisted, smaller drive (that is, floppy disk drive).

■ High-numbered wires: twisted, larger drive that is, hard drive).

■ A SCSI cable may have 25 or 50 pins on the connector, and the bus it is attached to must have exactly two terminated ends. Terminators may be found near the connector slot on the SCSI device in packs of three resistors.

■ An IDE cable must not be longer than 18 inches, and it uses a 40-pin cable.

■ You need three cables to connect two RLL or MFM drives to one controller: two data cables and one control cable. The control cable regulates the way the disk functions. If you are using two drives, remove the terminator that is on the drive in the middle of the chain (see fig. 40.7).

Figure 40.7

Types of drive cables.

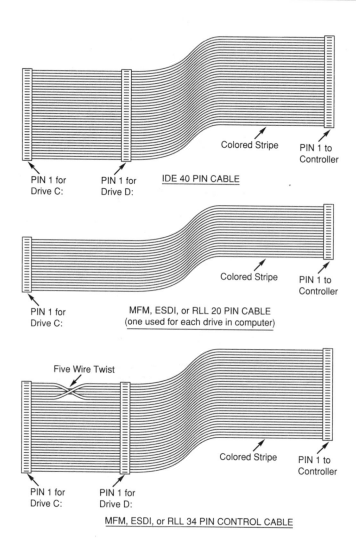

Colored Stripe   PIN 1 to Controller

PIN 1 for Drive C: PIN 1 for Drive D: IDE 40 PIN CABLE

Colored Stripe   PIN 1 to Controller

PIN 1 for Drive C: MFM, ESDI, or RLL 20 PIN CABLE
(one used for each drive in computer)

Five Wire Twist

Colored Stripe   PIN 1 to Controller

PIN 1 for Drive C: PIN 1 for Drive D:

MFM, ESDI, or RLL 34 PIN CONTROL CABLE

Formatting the Hard Drive

Physical installation of a hard drive into a computer, setting the jumpers, and connecting the cables are the initial necessary tasks in preparing the drive for network use. When you receive a new hard drive or are reusing an existing drive, you must prepare these drives in the required format so that data can be stored on them.

There are four important steps in preparing a hard drive to operate as it is designed:

1. Low-level formatting

2. Entering CMOS setup information

3. Establishing partitions

4. Performing a high-level DOS format

Low-Level Formatting

Low-level formatting usually is done by the manufacturer of the drive at the factory. It is a destructive process and should only be done as the last resort in attempting to repair a drive. A low-level format is the process of defining sectors and the bad spots on the hard drive. Sectors provide the marking points (or indexes such as in a phone book) where information can be read, retrieved, or written.

There are third-party programs such as CKLLFMT in the CheckIt PRO software package. Some versions of DOS or the advanced drive diagnostics disk for the drive include low-level format utilities. You should check with the manufacturer of your drive for the proper procedure and program to do a low-level format.

A low-level format not only establishes sector IDs, it marks off bad sectors, tests the disks by performing a surface analysis, temporarily fills each sector, and sets the interleave ratio entered. Besides using a low-level format to give a new hard drive the directions on getting started, a low-level format can be done to remark the sectors of a drive that have been previously used, make an attempt at repairing a drive that is exhibiting a large number of errors, or change the interleave ratio.

 If for some reason you have to low-level format a drive, make sure you format the drive in the same temperature and in the same position it will be used— flat or sideways. The temperature and gravity environment are very important to disk drives.

Setting the Interleave Ratio

Establishing the interleave ratio helps the drive to manage the flow of information between the computer and the disk better. Setting the interleave factor is not as necessary a concern for newer drives. Older drives used to be faster than what the CPU's microprocessor could handle; therefore, the interleave factor was developed to slow the drive down but still make it functional. The interleave ratio can help prevent bottlenecks if it is set properly.

 Technology has enabled newer drives to set sector sparring, which is similar to NetWare's hot fix. This new feature will reserve one sector on every track for the remapping of bad sectors. This reduces the capacity of your new drive and should only be used if there are a lot of problems with the drive.

The physical sector arrangement and the logical arrangement of how the sectors are numbered in a track determines the interleave ratio (see fig. 40.8). An interleave factor is chosen by setting a ratio for the computer to use in determining how it is to read disk information. A ratio is defined as the length of a sector and the distance between two logical sectors. One sector is used as the starting point for measuring the length of an interleave. Setting an interleave factor too low or high can impede performance.

 IDE drives use cache and really have no need for an interleave setting. Some SCSI drives and all MFM encoded drives can manage interleave ratios. The following interleave ratios are recommended:

continues

Figure 40.8

Sector reading by a hard drive set at a 2:1 interleave ratio.

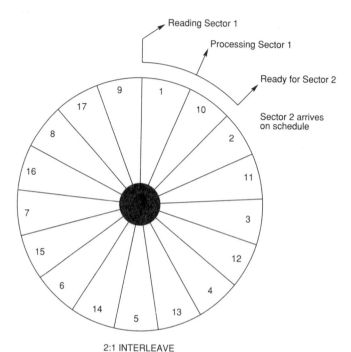

Reading Sector 1

Processing Sector 1

Ready for Sector 2

Sector 2 arrives on schedule

2:1 INTERLEAVE

- 1:1 for machines running NetWare that are 10 Mhz or faster, using 286 or 386 system boards. DOS machines at 20 Mhz or faster using 286 or 386 motherboards use this interleave. All 486 machines use 1:1.

- 2:1 for machines running DOS that are 10–16 Mhz and are using 286 or 386 motherboards.

- 3:1 for 6–8 Mhz AT class computers and for XT type machines running DOS applications.

  - 4:1 for all 4.77 Mhz XT class machines.

Establishing Partitions

The hard drive must be partitioned after a low-level format has been completed. Modern drives that are new out of the box are already low-level formatted and ready to be partitioned. The operating system must be compatible with the format of the logical structure of the hard disk. The logical structure is set up with a DOS program called FDISK (see fig. 40.9). FDISK sets the partitions needed on a hard drive.

 Note For NetWare 3.*x* and above file servers, a DOS partition of only 10 MB is recommended. DOS must be installed in a Primary DOS partition, which must be configured as the drive's Active partition. This can be done with an FDISK program.

```
   Current fixed disk drive: 1

   Choose one of the following:

   1. Create DOS partition or Logical DOS Drive
   2. Set active partition
   3. Delete partition or Logical DOS Drive
   4. Display partition information

   Enter choice: [1]

Press Esc to exit FDISK
```

Figure 40.9

Opening screen using an FDISK program to partition hard drives.

The DOS operating system recognizes the rest of the NetWare-ready hard drive as a non-DOS partition. After the NetWare operating system is loaded, NetWare identifies the DOS partition as *Physical partition #0* and the NetWare partition as *Physical partition #1.*

 The low-level format utility that is shipped with a SCSI drive is the best program to use if you need to perform the low-level format process. Generic-type low-level format utilities usually will not work with the SCSI drives.

Entering CMOS Setup Information

The *Complementary Metal-Oxide Semiconductor* (CMOS) is a battery-operated chip that is found on the motherboard of the computer. The CMOS chip is an important microprocessor found primarily in the newer generation of personal computers. This chip is important to the operation of the computer because it is responsible for telling the electronics of the PC what is contained in the CPU and the location of these components in the scheme of being able to operate together. The CMOS chip provides the electronic current management for

the positive and negative electrons that provide the flow of electrical signals to the components.

 If your computer shows unexplained erratic behavior or is losing the date or time, replace the battery with a new one that meets the same voltage requirements. This voltage number is printed or stamped on the battery.

The CMOS must be told what type of components the computer has and where they are located. The information about the hard drive is an important setup requirement in CMOS. You can get to CMOS with most computers during the power-up process by pressing Ctrl+Alt+Esc. You also can view CMOS information through third-party utilities such as CheckIt PRO, as shown in figure 40.10. The CMOS setup characteristics require the TYPE number of the drive, which is found marked on the drive or in the manufacturer's documentation. The type information includes the number of cylinders, heads, sectors, and the size of the hard drive. If the drive requires write precompensation information, the CMOS asks for this detail also.

Figure 40.10

CMOS Setup Information found by CHECKIT PRO.

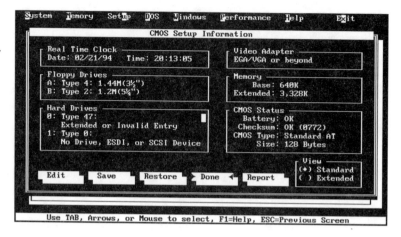

The drive you install does not have to match one of the CMOS drive types perfectly. IBM's CMOS Type 1 is used for most ESDI drives. The Type 1 represents a 10 MB drive, and at power-up the BIOS from the ESDI controller card overwrites this information to what is needed for ESDI operations. SCSI drives use the Type 0 or Not Installed parameter. The MicroHouse Technical Library has an extensive listing of drive types from which to find a type that closely represents your drive. Choose a type that has the cylinder count that is equal to or less than the number of cylinders available on your drive. Do not use a type that exceeds the megabyte size or the number of heads on your physical drive.

 Note Write precompensation is used primarily by older drives. This process manages the timing of retrieval of information from the platters as the sectors get closer together toward the center of the drive. The magnetic field that is passed to the read/write heads on a hard drive is made stronger to handle the changes in the geometric division of the drive as the read/write heads move to the center of the disk. As a default, write precompensation is determined by taking the maximum number of cylinders on that individual drive and dividing that number by two.

High-Level DOS Format

The fourth part in setting up a hard drive is performing a high-level format. The DOS program FORMAT accomplishes this task on a new or used drive. The high-level format can be used to erase all the files in an entire DOS partition.

For a file server to have a bootable partition, you must format the primary DOS partition with the following command:

FORMAT /S

The /S parameter places the hidden DOS system information files and the COMMAND.COM in the DOS partition. The format process also accomplishes the following tasks:

- Creates a blank root directory (except when using the /S parameter)

- Creates a DOS boot sector and a DOS *file allocation table* (FAT)

- Scans the disk and notes the bad sectors

It is a benefit to have a DOS bootable partition on a NetWare 3.x and above file server. The server boots up faster from the hard disk. You can set the necessary statements to remotely reboot a server. You also can load a communication package on the DOS partition, down the server, then have an on-site person set the server as a host. Then you could dial in to copy updated files, such as DSK or NLM drivers, or maybe run CheckIt PRO to investigate server details.

Before you format a used drive that already contains data, make sure you back up all the files you need to protect. Low-level formats never allow the data to be recovered by an unformatted utility. There are some third-party utilities that can recover high-level formats, provided the hard drive has not been written to since the format was performed. Professional data recovery services such as On-Track can assist in recovering data from a destroyed drive. As a network administrator or support engineer, you should be aware that most disks have bad sectors—don't panic if you see a few. A manufacturer considers a hard drive to be acceptable to be shipped if the bad sectors are less than 1 percent of the total size of the drive.

NetWare Drive Information

NetWare calculates a unique device code for each device on the bus or for each hard drive. System error messages use this code to display failure messages. As an example, the device code 20010 refers to the first drive (0) on the second controller (1) on the first host bus adapter (0) on the first instance the ISADISK.DSK driver (20) is found. NetWare uses the ISADISK device driver for ST-506 drives using RLL or MFM encoding schemes. These types of drives have the disk controller and the host bus adapter on the same physical drive. The controller digit found in the device code always is zero. The IDE type drives can use the

ISADISK.DSK file or preferably the IDE.DSK device drivers. The SCSI drivers are provided by the manufacturer of the host adapter card. The device code for SCSI is always set to 0.

 The device drivers that come in the core package of a new 3.11 operating system box are slightly outdated. Although they are operational, enhanced ISADISK and IDE drivers are available on NetWire or on NSEPRO.

When a 3.x server is setting up the operating system, it establishes the hot fix redirection area first. NetWare considers the location from the beginning of the NetWare data area to the end of the NetWare data area as a *logical partition*. A NetWare logical partition holds the NetWare operating system files and the data that is loaded to be accessed by the network users. Each logical partition has its own identifying number. A NetWare logical partition can be made up of more than one physical partition, contiguous with a physical partition, or be made as part of a physical partition. NetWare uses physical partition numbers for housekeeping tasks performed by the operating system. Logical partition numbers are used for mirrored drive designation.

After you set up NetWare partitions through the INSTALL.NLM, you also must establish volume information. NetWare 3.x (20) enables volumes to be spanned across multiple hard drives. Volume segments are made up of the same volume information on different hard disks. There can be up to 8 segments on a hard drive and 32 segments per volume. Performance can be improved by spanning volumes. The disadvantage to spanning is that the loss of one drive and its partial volume segment can cause the loss of access to the entire volume. RAID, mirroring, or duplexing can help prevent the loss of an entire volume from happening.

Working with RAID Drives

The network environment of today has evolved from having only a file server, a printer, and a few client stations, to having large enterprise designs requiring unlimited availability. The critical nature of data accessibility requires that network administrators or support engineers provide the best storage and recovery solutions as cost effectively as possible. The reliability of the network is not required for just the file server, but for the client also. The early history of the computer environment lacked the flexibility of the PC world, and the critical data needed was kept on a mainframe machine. Data manipulation on a mainframe requires many lines of code and cooperation from several differently skilled computer technicians. With the flexibility of the PC environment, extra precautions must be made in protecting against human or mechanical error.

The *Redundant Array of Inexpensive Drives* (RAID) can work with NetWare's System Fault Tolerance (SFT) features to protect data in a network environment. The use of RAID enables you to set up the best disk array design to protect your system. RAID is defined in detail as the architecture of combining two or more disks to create a large virtual disk structure to develop a source for redundancy of data. In a disk array, the drives are coordinated into different levels of RAID to which the controller card distributes the data as it is designed to do.

RAID uses a format of splitting data among drives at the bit, byte, or block level. The term *data striping* refers to the capability of arranging data in different sequences across drives. An example demonstration of this data splitting is shown in figure 40.11.

Your input in designing the most reliable drive setup for your network is an important responsibility. You must choose the best RAID implementation level that will meet your users' requirements in data integrity and cost. There are seven levels of RAID available on the market today. The numbers that represent RAID levels are 0, 1, 2, 3, 4, 5, and 10. A higher number does not necessarily mean that it is a better choice than the lower number. You must select the best for your environment. The following paragraphs present a brief discussion of each of the seven available levels.

RAID 0

Level 0 uses data striping and block interleaving. This level distributes the data block-by-block across the disk array in the same location across each drive. Data can be read or written to these same sectors from either drive, improving performance. The failure of a single drive can bring down the system. Redundancy of data is not provided.

RAID 1

Drives are paired or mirrored with each byte of information being written to each identical drive. You can duplex these devices by adding a separate host adapter for each drive. Mirroring provides a better performance benefit than that of RAID 0. If one drive in the pair fails, the other drive can continue to operate. This level can get expensive with the cost of drives to meet your needs for capacity. You will need to make sure your power source has enough wattage to handle the additional devices.

RAID 2

This level uses data striping with bit interleave. This means that data is written across each drive in succession, one bit at a time. Faulty bits are isolated

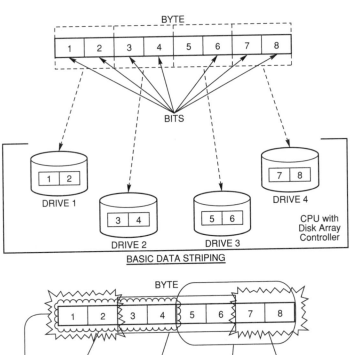

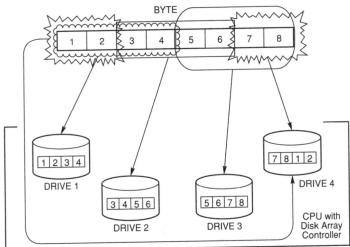

Figure 40.11

Examples of data striping.

by using checksum-capable drives. This level does not require total data redundancy. RAID 2 drives are transmitting in a parallel mode, enabling a faster data transfer rate. The write mode can be slower because each drive is working on every write attempt. The data used for checksum information is redundant. This level is not effective or cost-efficient for use in personal computers.

RAID 3

This level uses bit interleave data striping with parity checking capabilities. Data striping is done across the drives, one byte at a time. There usually are four or five drives at this level, with one drive dedicated for parity information to ensure the integrity of the data. RAID 3 has a very high data transfer rate and can handle long data transfers. This level is more reliable than RAID 2. Parity maintenance can be an overhead problem and cause the write performance to slow because the parity drive must be accessed for every write. There also could be major system problems if any two drives fail. The failure of a single drive will not affect the availability of data; the array controller will use the parity drive to reconstruct the contents of the failed disk. RAID 3 is not ideal for NetWare 3.x. As a default, NetWare accesses data in 4 KB blocks, which is not considered a long transfer rate.

RAID 4

This level uses block interleave data striping with parity checking. This means that this level uses a single parity drive, as does RAID 3, and uses block data striping, as does RAID 0. The drives in this RAID level function individually, with an individual drive reading a block of data. The combination of multiple drives has the ability to do multiple simultaneous reads. The block-level striping process is more efficient than RAID 3 byte-level striping. The downfalls of this level are the same as RAID 3, with the addition of the parity drive not being used to store data. If the array controller fails, the entire array cannot function.

RAID 5

This level uses block interleaved data striping with distributed check-data on all drives in the array. RAID 5 is efficient in handling small blocks and has quicker transfer rates because reads and writes can happen in parallel mode. The capability of virtual redundancy at an inexpensive cost is a benefit of RAID 5. This level is not as fast as RAID 0 or RAID 1 because it distributes parity information across all drives. Large file transfers are done in blocks and can be slower than RAID 3, which uses parallel

bytes. RAID 5 efficiency goes up as the number of disks in the array increases. You can use hot spares mounted in the array cabinet. These extra drives can be picked up by the array automatically, replacing the failed drive. The data will be rebuilt to the added drive to function in sequence with the rest of the array as if nothing happened. This failed drive can then be replaced on the fly.

RAID 10

This level is defined as data that is duplicated across two identical RAID 0 arrays or hard disk drives. All data that is contained on a physical drive in one array is mirrored on a drive in the second array. RAID 10 uses the similar concept that NetWare's SFT III mirrored file servers use.

When you are choosing RAID for the customer, consider the following factors to make the best selection:

- The importance of the applications and data to the cost of downtime and lost business

- The number of users and the amount of drive capacity needed

- The size of the data blocks and whether they require direct or sequential access on the drives

- The proportion of reads to writes to the I/O activity, and the maximum transfer rate needed

There are many vendors that offer RAID solutions. Some examples of these vendors include AST, Compaq, Dell, IBM, and Storage Dimensions. Dell Computer offers a reliable high-end file server that uses RAID 10, PCI bus architecture, a Pentium processor, and FAST SCSI-2 host adapters. This combination can be used for the mission-critical environment using NetWare.

Understanding Disk Mirroring and Disk Duplexing

Disk mirroring and disk duplexing are two important system fault tolerance features added in SFT II to protect information in the event of hardware failure.

Disk Mirroring

Disk mirroring is defined as two hard drives—one primary and one secondary—using the same disk channel (controller cards and cable). The process is illustrated in figure 40.12. Disk mirroring is most commonly configured using disk drives contained in the server. You soon see that duplexing enables you to configure a more robust hardware environment.

All changes to the primary disk are duplicated on the secondary so that the secondary is a mirror image of the primary. In the event that the primary drive fails, users can access data on the secondary drive as if nothing happened. Disk mirroring can be done internally in a file server if enough drive and card slots are available. A DCB can be used to provide access to an external disk subsystem. Disk drives must be the same logical size, terminated properly, and addressed correctly.

Disk Duplexing

In the event of a disk channel failure (controller card or cable), access to all data on the channel is stopped. A message is displayed on the file server console screen (if your users do not let you know about it first). Even though drives can be mirrored, if they are connected to the same disk controller, all disk activity on the mirrored pair ceases.

Disk duplexing performs the function of simultaneously writing data to disks located on different channels. As figure 40.13 illustrates, each hard disk in a duplexed pair is connected to a separate hard disk controller. This figure shows a configuration in which the drives are housed in separate disk subsystems. Each subsystem has a separate power supply. This is a more reliable setup than is possible with mirroring, because a failure of one disk drive power supply does not disable the server, which continues to work with the system that remains under power.

A duplex configuration has two disk channels. In this example, each channel has two disks. NetWare identifies the drives by their channel and drive numbers, as shown in figure 40.13.

Duplexing enables NetWare to perform split seeks, in which NetWare seeks with both drives of a duplexed pair and retrieves data from the first drive on which the data is found. Split seeks are a distinct advantage of duplexing when compared to mirroring and can significantly improve a server's file access time.

Working on the same channel is analogous to going to a baseball game when only one gate is open to the stadium. You can enter or exit through only one gate (channel) at the stadium (file server), and the crowd (data) can get backed up on both sides. If more than one gate (another channel) is open, the crowd (data) does not get backed up on both sides of the fence (file server or workstation).

 Note   Duplexing protects information at the hardware level with duplicate channels (controller cards and cables) and duplicate hard drives (refer to fig. 40.12).

continues

Figure 40.12

How disk duplexing works.

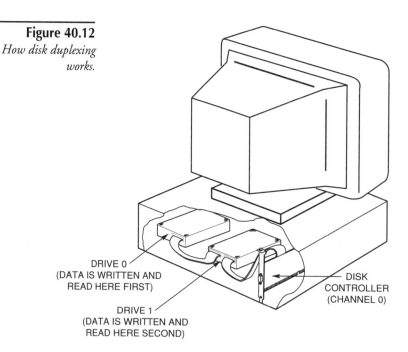

DRIVE 0
(DATA IS WRITTEN AND
READ HERE FIRST)

DRIVE 1
(DATA IS WRITTEN AND
READ HERE SECOND)

DISK
CONTROLLER
(CHANNEL 0)

Mirroring uses one controller card and two hard drives (refer to fig. 40.13). The point of failure for this setup is primarily the controller card or the cable connecting the drives to the controller card. Disk duplexing uses two controller cards and a minimum of one drive per controller card. The point of contention for failure is reduced with duplicate hardware.

Disk Mirroring or Duplexing in Version 3.*x*

Use the INSTALL.NLM to mirror or duplex in 3.*x*. The following example is done on a network

drive after the original operating system installation was completed. The following steps must be completed to install a disk pair as mirrored or duplexed:

1. Install the hardware components with the correct termination and hardware addresses. Document the model of the controller card and drives.

2. Bring the server up and at the file server console (or through RCONSOLE) load the

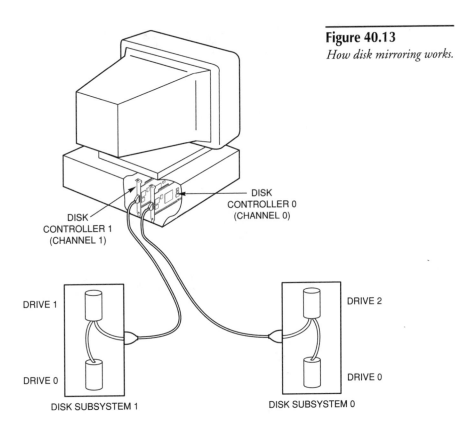

Figure 40.13

How disk mirroring works.

INSTALL.NLM. From the Installation Options menu, select Disk Options. The screen shown in figure 40.14 displays the Available Disk Options menu.

3. Select Mirroring and press Enter. The Partition Mirroring Status screen appears as shown in figure 40.15. This screen contains the status of all the drives in the 3.*x* file server

to be edited. Select the drive designated as Logical Partition #1 to be the primary drive and press Enter.

4. The screen displays the Mirrored NetWare Partitions menu as shown in figure 40.16. Press Insert to add another partition to the Mirrored NetWare Partitions screen. The menu screen shown in figure 40.17 then displays the Available Partitions from which to choose.

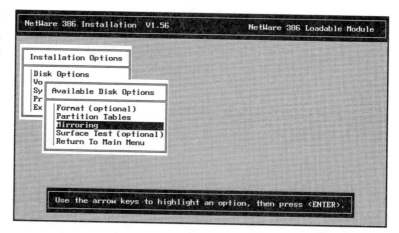

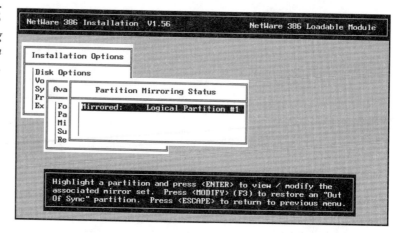

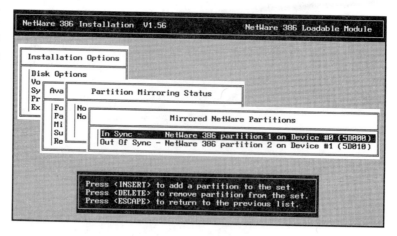

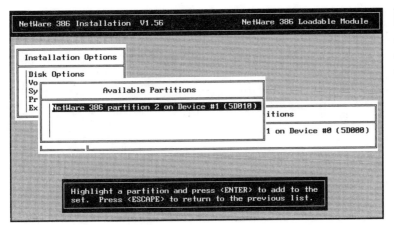

Figure 40.17

Display of partitions available for assignment as mirrors.

Highlight an available partition and press Enter. The Device numbers come from the addressing and termination of the SCSI drive installation.

5. The Mirrored NetWare Partitions screen menu (see fig. 40.18) displays the In Sync status of the primary mirrored partition. In Sync means that the designated partition is unmirrored and has no data problems. The Partition 2 shows an Out Of Sync status. Within ten seconds, the Partition 2 drive begins synchronizing with Partition 1.

To check the status of the remirroring process, press Alt+Esc to get to the colon prompt. The message Remirroring partition # appears, indicating that the process has begun.

The synchronization process takes several minutes, depending on the size of the drive being mirrored.

6. The Partition Mirroring Status menu screen (see fig. 40.19) then shows confirmation of the logical partition as being mirrored when the synchronization process from step 5 is completed. The partitions are now mirrored and in operation.

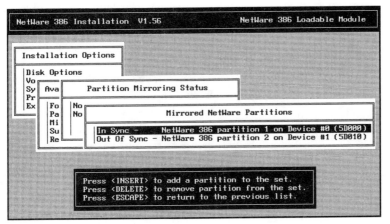

Figure 40.18

The Mirrored NetWare Partitions box displaying information about an out-of-sync mirrored pair.

Figure 40.19

Mirrored drives in process of synchronization.

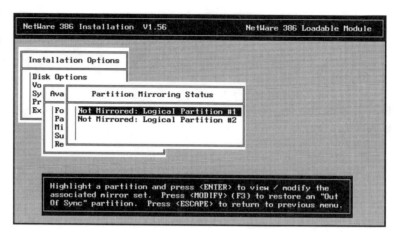

Press Esc until you exit from the INSTALL.NLM. You now can continue to do normal processing.

 Note The mirroring process should be performed during nonproduction hours, and all user logins should be disabled.

Tips for Working with Mirrored/ Duplexed Drives

As a network administrator or support engineer, you must plan appropriately the use of mirrored/ duplexed drives in your file server. Improper setup or lack of monitoring these types of hard drive setups can cause loss of data and destruction of hardware. As part of your maintenance process, use the following recommendations in your planning design:

■ Mirroring and duplexing should not take the place of backups—keep doing them on a regular basis.

■ Always load the disk drivers in the same order—the internal controllers should be loaded first, in the order they are to be addressed.

■ NetWare does not differentiate between mirroring or duplexing in its system messages.

■ Periodically check the status of your mirrored or duplexed drives to see if they are still "in synch." Check the physical and the logical window using the INSTALL.NLM on the file server.

■ As part of your network documentation, keep a record of the device codes of your hard drives. This could help you troubleshoot the load order of your disk drivers using system messages.

■ IDE drives should not be used as duplexed drives because of how the built-in controllers piggyback each other in a master/slave relationship. If the primary drive goes down, the second drive will also. Exceptions to this rule are the use of a motherboard that has dual IDE ports or the use of paddle boards.

Working with CD-ROM Drives

CD-ROM players can enhance your network environment by adding flexibility to your resources for multitudes of information. You can have a CD-ROM player attached as a device on your SCSI bus that is connected to your file server. A CD-ROM drive can be found that has multiple drive bays, with each bay recognized as a volume on the server. For 3.1x, software packages such as SCSI-Express and Corel SCSI can do this volume setup. NetWare 3.12 has a CDROM.NLM that enables the CD-ROM to be seen as a built-in volume. The client can use a locally attached CD-ROM player with the proper MSCDEX driver extensions and parameters loaded in the CONFIG.SYS and AUTOEXEC.BAT files. The CD-ROM unit in the NetWare environment must be ISO-9660-compliant.

The following are the advantages of a CD-ROM player in a networked environment:

■ The file formats are standardized and can be accessed easily.

■ There is access to more volumes of information. Keyword searches on some applications increase data resources in one setting.

■ Media is lightweight, can be stored easily, and costs for duplication are low.

The following are the disadvantages of a CD-ROM player:

■ CD-ROM players can get expensive, but continually are coming down in price.

■ CD-ROM players are slower than hard disks. Modern hard drives are 20 times faster than the 200–300-millisecond seek rate of the CD-ROM. Newer CD-ROM players coming to the market that are available for networks will have 3X and 4X speed capabilities.

Tips for Working with CD-ROM Players

CD-ROM players can be an enhancement to any network. A network administrator or support engineer must be knowledgeable in this hardware arena. As with any other device included in your network environment, improper planning can cause expensive data recovery and troubleshooting delays. Use the following tips when using CD-ROM players in your network:

■ Check for incompatibilities by having the CD-ROM player and the hard drive on the same SCSI controller. Review the manufacturer's documentation and check the software vendor's requirements.

■ Some CD-ROM players require a "caddie" box for the CD-ROM platter to be placed in before it can be inserted into the player. Make sure your users know about this—failure to properly use a caddie box can result in severe damage to your CD. (*Please* read your documentation before using the player!)

■ Do not install a CD-ROM player in a drive bay in the CPU that is located directly above a hard drive in the CPU casing. The magnetic fields created by the CD-ROM unit can erase data from the hard drive.

■ The error message Invalid drive specification means that the MSCDEX file is loaded too low in your AUTOEXEC.BAT file. The error message Disc not High Sierra Format means you need to upgrade the version of your currently installed MSCDEX extension drivers to work with the newer ISO-9660 CD-ROM format.

Working with Magneto-Optical Drives

Magneto-optical Drives (M-O) are used to capture text, audio, video, and other types of integrated media in a combined format on the optical platter. M-O drives are used as a compromise between *digital access tape* (DAT) drives, which are an inexpensive, slower medium, and hard drives, which are expensive, yet faster in speed. M-O drives are faster than tape and more expensive than hard drives.

The use of optical drives can replace the standard tape and hard drives for backup, archiving (which is the best use for M-O), and storage of data-intensive applications such as CAD/CAM type programs. The setup of M-O drives is similar to tape backup units; they can be jukeboxes, external, or internal devices. M-O should not be confused with *Write Once Read Many* (WORM) systems because WORM drives cannot have the data changed on the optical-type disk after it has been written.

A magneto-optical drive operates with the use of laser beams and magnetism. An M-O disk is coated with layers on which spiral grooves have been molded. To write data, a polarized laser beam is reflected onto the surface of the M-O platter. The reflection is measured for its rotation on the plane of the disk that has been polarized magnetically.

The data is then interpreted from how the rotation is magnetically oriented. Reverting the magnetic orientation to the way it was directed prior to the M-O disk being written to will erase data.

The following are the advantages of magneto-optical disks:

- **Removable Media.** Disks can be removed and are capable of being changed with another M-O disk.

- **Capacity.** M-O can handle capacities from 650 MB to 1,000 GB and can be loaded into jukeboxes for increased capacity of data accessibility.

- **Random Access.** M-O supports many read/write operations, unlike streaming tape cartridges.

- **Durability.** Head crashes are impossible because of the use of laser beams.

- **Backup.** It can be used for large unattended backups and archiving of data.

The following are the disadvantages of magneto-optical disks:

- **Cost.** Very expensive currently. Drive prices range from $3,500 to $5,000, and the optical disk platter ranges in price from $180 to $300.

- **Speed.** Magneto-optical drives are not as fast as SCSI drives. M-O drives need a double pass to the platter to write any data.

- **Size.** These drives are too big to fit inside laptops. This may interfere with the requirements for the mobile network of today.

Questions

1. The most important storage device on the network is _____.

    ○ A. fixed disk

    ○ B. CD-ROM

    ○ C. magneto-optical disk

    ○ D. floppy disk

2. Communication between the hard drive and the CPU is handled by which device?

    ○ A. NIC

    ○ B. Fixed disk cable

    ○ C. Disk controller card

    ○ D. Floppy drive cable

3. The time it takes for the read/write heads to find the correct track on a fixed disk is known as _____.

    ○ A. access time

    ○ B. transfer rate

    ○ C. megabytes per second

    ○ D. seek time

4. Which of the following is NOT one of the components of a hard drive?

    ○ A. Spindle motor

    ○ B. Voice coil actuator

    ○ C. Platter

    ○ D. Cluster block

5. Which of the following is NOT a limitation of an Integrated Drive Electronics (IDE) drive?

    ○ A. It cannot multitask I/O.

    ○ B. It has a maximum drive capacity of 528M even when a special non-standard BIOS is used.

    ○ C. It does not support any optical or tape drives, as does the SCSI interface.

    ○ D. It does not support bus-mastering.

6. The main reason that you should never do a low-level format on an IDE drive is that _____.

    ○ A. you might erase the manufacturer's bad block information

    ○ B. you might be unable to access the IDE drive again to reestablish it

    ○ C. it removes the drive's ability to support overlapping and multitasking of I/O

    ○ D. electronic flux transitions of the drive might be reversed

7. Which TWO of the following are cited as reasons why ESDI drives have become more popular than ST-506 drives that use the same cabling system?

    ☐ A. ESDI drives are interchangeable with ST-506 drives.

    ☐ B. ESDI drives are capable of performing at higher levels.

    ☐ C. ESDI drives allow the Cold Boot Loader to be written to track 0, freeing disk space for data storage.

    ☐ D. ESDI drives have a larger storage capacity.

8. Which drive type provides an expansion bus that allows up to seven types of devices to be connected?

   ○ A. IDE

   ○ B. ESDI

   ○ C. SCSI

   ○ D. ASPI

9. Which of the following is NOT true of the WIDE SCSI-2 implementation of SCSI?

   ○ A. It uses a 50-pin cable and the single-ended signaling process.

   ○ B. It uses a second data path offering up to 20 MB per second data transfer rate.

   ○ C. It implements a 68-pin SCSI cable with the differential signaling process.

   ○ D. It is not used as much as the FAST SCSI-2 standard.

10. Which drive device is rapidly becoming the industry standard?

   ○ A. ASPI

   ○ B. ESDI

   ○ C. SCSI

   ○ D. IDE

11. If you do not want to remove the SCSI host adapter each time you need to change its settings, you should do which of the following?

   ○ A. Make sure that the same cabling is used for all SCSI devices on the network.

   ○ B. Make sure that you use a SCSI host adapter that uses software for setup of jumpers and termination settings.

   ○ C. Make sure that each SCSI device has a unique identifier number.

   ○ D. Make sure that all SCSI devices are the same, using either all SCSI-1 or all SCSI-2 devices.

12. The SCSI LUN required for the first bootable hard disk on all except for some HP and PS/2 machines is _____.

   ○ A. 0

   ○ B. 1

   ○ C. 6

   ○ D. 7

13. One primary use of the third-party tool called CHECKIT PRO is _____.

   ○ A. to set up hard drives for storage

   ○ B. to modify jumpers on the drive

   ○ C. to enable you to mix SCSI devices

   ○ D. to determine a workstation's drive interface

14. Which of the following is not a jumper that might have to be set on the hard disk?

   ○ A. ACT

   ○ B. IDE

   ○ C. DS

   ○ D. DSP

15. Although usually set for the controller card by the manufacturer, you might need to put which setting into the STARTUP.NCF file of a network server?

    ○ A. Controller interrupt

    ○ B. Base I/O

    ○ C. DMA channel

    ○ D. Base BIOS address

Answers

1. A		9. A	
2. C		10. C	
3. D		11. B	
4. D		12. A	
5. B		13. D	
6. A		14. B	
7. B, D		15. A	
8. C			

Troubleshooting the DOS Workstation

Several versions of DOS are installed in the workplace today. Many businesses, either for economic reasons or because they have never seen a need to upgrade, are still running version 3.3. If upgrade decisions are made on a departmental basis, then it is possible that one LAN administrator could be supporting PCs running versions 3.3, 4.x, 5.0, and 6.x.

Not only do all of these Microsoft versions exist, but there are also DOS versions from IBM and Novell. Novell's DOS was acquired in a purchase of Digital Research. DR DOS 5.0 gave way to DR DOS 6.0, which in turn gave way to Novell DOS 7. All of these combine together to make a fine stew for the administrator to stay on top of.

The majority of problems arise when one resource is accessed by more than one entity, for example, memory. This chapter examines these problems as well as the following topics:

- Working with IPX/NETX

- Working with ODI

- Working with the DOS Requester

- Working with Remote Boot

- Troubleshooting with TRACK

- Diagnosing conflicts

- Conflict resolution

- PC memory

- DR DOS

Working with IPX/NETX

Figure 41.1 depicts the Internetwork Packet Exchange (IPX) architecture and shows how the components work together. NCP is the NetWare Core Protocol going to the server, while the NetWare shell is going to the workstation. The LAN driver could be Ethernet, ARCnet, Token Ring, or any other.

With NetWare, as with any client/server system, one station interacts with another as the client makes requests of the server. The IPX.COM and the NetWare shell carry out this interaction between the two components.

 Note The command IPX I shows information about the version of IPX running on your workstation.

The purpose of IPX is to function as a go-between for the NIC card and communication link. This is described in the Administration sections of this book, and it is strongly encouraged that you review the specific coverage there. Here, suffice it to say that IPX is responsible for communication functions and management of the sockets used in the workstation. It also is responsible for ascertaining the address of the network segment to which the workstation is connected, the network number, and the node address.

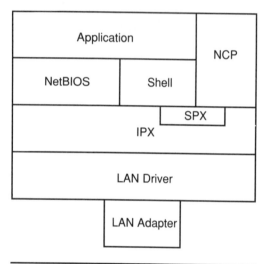

Figure 41.1
The IPX architecture for a DOS workstation.

The NetWare Core Protocol regulates how connection control information is passed. Every server packet must have the connection number and a sequence number assigned to it. The only purpose for the sequence number is to ascertain when a packet is lost.

What To Do If You Cannot Connect to the Server

The following steps should be followed if a workstation cannot connect to the server:

1. Verify proper seating of the NIC and connection of the cables.

2. Verify that the NIC is set to the same configuration as the IPX.COM.

3. Look for conflicts in interrupts, memory, and hardware addresses.

4. Verify that the server LAN driver is bound to IPX.

The Watchdog

When users leave a workstation, they should log out from the server to clear their connection and free resources. The Watchdog process, running at the server, routinely sends a poll to workstations to verify if they are active or not. If they are not active for a specified period of time, they automatically are cleared.

Working with ODI

ODI is nothing more than a specification of how the data link layer works in the OSI model. Developed by Novell and Apple in 1989, it provides support for multiple protocols on the same network with one driver. Up to four network cards can be active in the same machine, and drivers can be unloaded as easily as they were loaded. This means that IPX and TCP/IP can live in network harmony, and ODI drivers have replaced IPX.COM in the workplace.

The components of ODI, as discussed in the Administration sections, include:

■ LSL.COM

■ The LAN driver

■ IPXODI.COM (which includes SPX)

The *Multiple Link Interface Driver* (MLID) is a part of the LAN driver specification, which controls communication between the board and the LSL. Figure 41.2 illustrates the interaction between the components.

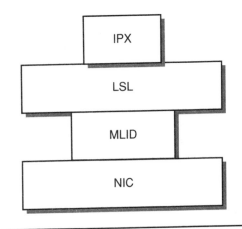

Figure 41.2
The ODI architecture.

Protocol stacks figure into the equation as they receive packets from the LSL. They operate independently of the board type and remove the header information that is pertinent only to them. Protocol stacks include TCP/IP, AppleTalk, OSI, and IPX/SPX.

Troubleshooting ODI

The first step when trying to diagnose ODI workstations is to check the board and cabling to make certain there are no obvious physical problems. Next, check that you have an ODI LAN driver for the board. Following that, boot with a bare-bones AUTOEXEC.BAT and CONFIG.SYS—loading no drivers of any kind. When booted, load LSL, the LAN driver, IPXODI, and the NETX.

Note Any of the four networking components can be unloaded in the opposite
order they were loaded by following
their command with a *U*:

NETX U

IPXODI U

{LAN driver} U

LSL U

If problems persist, turn your attention to the
NET.CFG file. Within that file, main headings
must be left-justified, with other entries indented
by a tab or space. Headings must precede each
section and end with a carriage return, but case
sensitivity does not apply. The following is an
example of a NET.CFG file:

```
Link Driver NE2000
        INT 5
        PORT 340
        MEM D0000
        FRAME ETHERNET 802.2
NETWARE DOS REQUESTER
        FIRST NETWORK DRIVE=F
```

INT must match the IRQ set on the board, while
PORT gives the I/O address. MEM shows the
memory range used by the board, and FRAME is
used with boards that support multiple types. Other
entries that can be present, or needed, include the
following:

- **DMA.** Allows the DMA channels to be
  configured

- **NODE ADDRESS.** Used to override hard
  coded board addresses

- **SLOT.** Makes the driver see a specific board
  first

- **PROTOCOL.** Signifies that existing LAN
  drivers can handle new protocols

Working with DOS Requester

The DOS Requester replaces NETX and all the
variants that Novell traditionally shipped with
successive versions of NetWare. Providing complete backward compatibility, it uses a modular
approach to anticipate future enhancements.

Within DOS, the COMMAND.COM file serves
as the shell. It accepts commands and determines
whether the request can be handled internally, or if
a search of the PATH statement directories
is necessary to find an executable file to carry out
the command. When NetWare is installed,
the DOS Requester encompasses the DOS shell
and intercepts commands before they get there. It
then decides whether the command typed in is a
NetWare command—in which case it directs it
appropriately—or a DOS command—in which
case it passes it through to the DOS shell for regular
processing. Figure 41.3 symbolizes the relationship
between these two shells.

The Requester actually is more than one entity; it
is composed of a number of VLM files. Each VLM
(Virtual Loadable Module) is a TSR program that
can be loaded and unloaded by VLM.EXE as
needed. These are stored, by default, in the
NWCLIENT subdirectory on the workstation,
and are loaded and unloaded by the manager
(VLM.EXE). If the VLMs are in another directory,
there must be a VLM= line in NET.CFG to point
to the appropriate path.

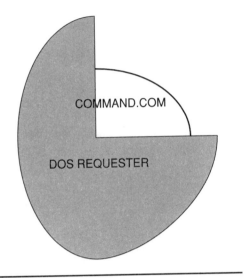

Figure 41.3

The relationship between the DOS Requester and the DOS shell.

Installing the DOS Requester

The steps to installing on a client machine are as follows:

1. Run INSTALL.EXE. This creates the NWCLIENT directories and copies in the VLMs.

2. Give the Windows path when prompted, if you are using Windows.

3. Give the configuration information when prompted—this is used to build the NET.CFG file.

The files you should see are shown in the following table.

VLM File	Function
AUTO.VLM	Automatic reconnect
BIND.VLM	Protocol bindery service
CONN.VLM	Connection table manager
FIO.VLM	File input\output
GENERAL.VLM	Miscellaneous NETX functions
IPXNCP.VLM	Transport protocol using IPX
NETX.VLM	Shell compatibility
NWP.VLM	Protocol multiplexer
PRINT.VLM	Print redirector
REDIR.VLM	DOS redirector
RSA.VLM	Encryption
TRAN.VLM	Transport protocol multiplexer

Working with Remote Boot

With diskless workstations, there is a read-only memory chip on the NIC. The code within that chip is executed on boot-up and is responsible for contacting the server and getting the necessary information to establish a communication link. Typically, the ROM size is 8 KB.

DOSGEN is the utility used to create the remote image the workstation communicates with on the server. Reasons for using diskless workstations include the following:

- Cost

- Convenience

- Security

- Speed

The created image appears to the workstation as a virtual drive, and the workstation functions as if there were a drive installed within it. To the workstation, the image is seen as a floppy from which it is booting, thus it needs files such as the following:

- CONFIG.SYS

- AUTOEXEC.BAT

- IPX

- NETX

It also needs the necessary command to get to the LOGIN routine (this can be within the AUTOEXEC.BAT file).

The file NET$DOS.SYS is created and placed in the working directory; it must be flagged as sharable to properly function.

 Note   Remote booting DOS 5 requires RPLFIX run against the existing NET$DOS.SYS. The sole purpose of this utility is to change parameters since COMMAND.COM is larger in 5.0 than other DOS versions.

Troubleshooting with TRACK

TRACK is a console command used to diagnose router and server problems. It shows the network, server, and connection request information on a Router Tracking Screen. Information is depicted as it comes in and goes out. TRACK ON turns the monitor screen on, while TRACK OFF removes it.

The two requests to keep in mind are *Router Information Protocols* (RIP) and *Service Advertising Protocols* (SAP). RIPs are transmitted from routers to servers to advertise their presence, and SAPs are sent by print servers, gateways, and all servers to denote their presence.

A file server is seen by a workstation when it is "SAPing." Thus, the workstation knows it is there and attempts to connect to it—preferably the one within the nearest proximity. If a file server is not SAPing, there can be a problem with IPX not being bound to the card, or volumes not being mounted.

When a workstation shell loads, TRACK should report the following three things on the console if all is working as it should:

1. Get Nearest Server

2. Give Nearest Server *server_name*

3. Route Request

SLIST can be detrimental in isolating problems if a message of Unknown file server appears when the user tries to log in at the workstation.

Diagnosing Conflicts

Interrupt Request Channels (IRQ) conflicts can take a long time to diagnose. This is because the connection might work properly for a considerable amount of time, then die off at unexpected moments. IRQ conflicts do not happen until two devices attempt to access the same IRQ at the same time.

IRQs are directly tied to hardware components such as modems and printers. When a call is made to their device, the CPU puts other jobs on a wait status and processes the request made of that interrupt—in essence, they are interrupting other processing. A number of utilities can be used to diagnose IRQ problems, and Check It PRO is one worth noting. On DOS machines running version 6.*x*, MSD can offer similar information. The following listing depicts an example of an MSD report.

Normally, COM1 and COM3 use IRQ4, while COM2 and COM4 use IRQ3. It also is worth noting that early machines (XTs) have only eight interrupts, and newer ones have sixteen (numbered 0-15).

The I/O address gives the memory range reserved by the CPU. These are areas set aside specifically for each interrupt. If more than one device is using the same address, conflicts occur. The range of CA000 to DFFFF is safe for network adapter configurations.

Conflict Resolution

System configuration, once the domain of dip switches, now resides in CMOS memory. Usually, you can access CMOS during bootup by pressing a key sequence, which can be anything from the Esc key to Ctrl+Alt+Ins. The necessary key sequence is determined by the hardware manufacturer, and there is no standard throughout the industry.

The EISA Configuration Utility is a menu-driven approach to configuring EISA boards and solving conflicts. It reads the CFG file that comes with the board, and Verification Mode can be used to automatically check to see if conflicts can occur with other devices.

```
Microsoft Diagnostics version 2.01   1/24/95   7:44pm   Page  6
=========================================================================


.......................... IRQ Status ...........................

    IRQ  Address   Description        Detected           Handled By
    ..   ........  ...............    ...............    ...............
     0   2AB6:0000 Timer Click        Yes                win386.exe
     1   0A79:1923 Keyboard           Yes                Block Device
     2   08B4:0057 Second 8259A       Yes                Default Handlers
     3   08B4:006F COM2: COM4:        COM2:              Default Handlers
     4   0364:02C2 COM1: COM3:        COM1: Serial Mouse MS$MOUSE
     5   08B4:009F LPT2:              Yes                Default Handlers
     6   08B4:00B7 Floppy Disk        Yes                Default Handlers
     7   0070:06F4 LPT1:              Yes                System Area
     8   08B4:0052 Real-Time Clock    Yes                Default Handlers
     9   F000:9C54 Redirected IRQ2    Yes                BIOS
    10   166A:01D4 (Reserved)                            3C509
    11   08B4:00E7 (Reserved)                            Default Handlers
    12   08B4:00FF (Reserved)                            Default Handlers
    13   F000:9C45 Math Coprocessor   Yes                BIOS
    14   08B4:0117 Fixed Disk         Yes                Default Handlers
    15   F000:FF53 (Reserved)                            BIOS
```

Working with PC Memory

The following list shows the memory detail displayed with DOS 6's MSD utility.

When the 8088 CPU was first designed, it divided the 1 MB address space into several areas, including 640 KB for application usage. To maintain compatibility, subsequent CPUs have kept the same scheme. Memory optimizers, such as MEMMAKER (MS DOS) and OPTIMIZE (QEMM), enable you to avoid manual memory tuning and automatically configure your system for optimal memory performance.

Real Mode is the term used to indicate the backward compatibility between subsequent models of CPU boards and the 8088. All x86 machines, when running in real mode, act as if they were running an 8086 chip.

Protected mode is the native mode for all CPUs from 80286 on up. Protected mode refers to the fact that memory is not used without first requesting it from the operating system.

```
-------------------------- Memory --------------------------------

      Legend:  Available "  "  RAM "##"  ROM "RR"  Possibly Available ".."
      EMS Page Frame "PP"  Used UMBs "UU"  Free UMBs "FF"
     1024K FC00 RRRRRRRRRRRRRRRR FFFF  Conventional Memory
           F800 RRRRRRRRRRRRRRRR FBFF              Total: 640K
           F400 RRRRRRRRRRRRRRRR F7FF          Available: 442K
      960K F000 RRRRRRRRRRRRRRRR F3FF                    452976 bytes
           EC00                  EFFF
           E800                  EBFF  Extended Memory
           E400                  E7FF              Total: 15104K
      896K E000                  E3FF
           DC00 PPPPPPPPPPPPPPPP DFFF  MS-DOS Upper Memory Blocks
           D800 PPPPPPPPPPPPPPPP DBFF          Total UMBs: 28K
           D400 PPPPPPPPPPPPPPPP D7FF       Total Free UMBs: 0K
      832K D000 PPPPPPPPPPPPPPPP D3FF    Largest Free Block: 0K
           CC00 UUUUUUUUUUUUUUUU CFFF
           C800 ...UUUUUUUUUUUUU CBFF  Expanded Memory (EMS)
           C400 RRRRRRRRRRRRRRRR C7FF         LIM Version: 4.00
      768K C000 RRRRRRRRRRRRRRRR C3FF  Page Frame Address: D000H
           BC00 ................ BFFF              Total: 1024K
           B800 ................ BBFF          Available: 1024K
           B400 ................ B7FF
      704K B000 ................ B3FF  XMS Information
           AC00 ................ AFFF         XMS Version: 2.00
           A800 ................ ABFF      Driver Version: 2.05
           A400 ................ A7FF    A20 Address Line: Enabled
      640K A000 ................ A3FF    High Memory Area: In use
                                             Available: 1024K
                                    Largest Free Block: 1024K
```

Memory Types

Conventional memory, also known as base memory, is everything within the first 640 KB that is available to DOS applications. The following 384 KB is known as upper memory and is used by adapter cards, video, and serial ports. This completes the first 1 MB, or 1,024 KB of memory. Expanded memory is nothing more than pages of memory that can be swapped in and out of the upper memory space.

Extended memory comes next, and it is everything above the 1 MB space. High memory is a subset of extended memory and comprises the first 64 KB of extended memory. Within the range of 1,024 KB to 1,088 KB, it is available to DOS applications with an XMS memory manager.

Figure 41.4 illustrates this concept.

Loading LAN drivers into high memory can free up more of the lower 640 KB for applications. This is accomplished by placing lines in CONFIG.SYS similar to the following:

```
DEVICE=C:\DOS\HIMEM.SYS
DEVICE=C:\DOS\EMM386.SYS NOEMS
DOS=HIGH,UMB
```

This is followed up in the AUTOEXEC.BAT file with this:

```
LH LSL
LH 3C509 (or your card type)
LH IPXODI
LH NETX
```

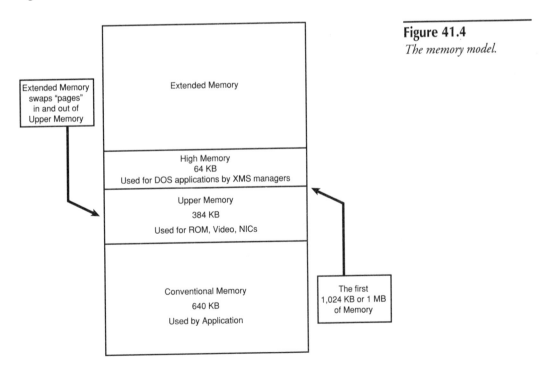

Figure 41.4
The memory model.

DR DOS

DR (Digital Research) DOS, from Novell, is a workstation operating system fully compatible with Microsoft's DOS. It features data compression, disk defragmentation utilities, a read/write cache, task switching, and enhanced memory management.

Enhancements have been made to the following external DOS commands:

- CHKDSK
- DISKCOPY
- HELP
- MEM
- REPLACE
- TREE
- UNDELETE
- XCOPY

Typing any command and following it with /H or /? displays all the options available. The following are additional features DR DOS offers over other products:

- DISKMAX is the set of compression utilities.

- DOSBOOK offers online documentation of the available commands.

- HIDOS.SYS is a driver for configuring memory on 80286 and earlier machines.

- HIDOS=ON, HIBUFFERS=xx are used in conjunction to move the operating system out of base memory.

- LOCK is used to lock the keyboard and keep anyone from using it without entering the password. This provides additional security at the workstation level.

- SETUP is a full screen menu used to configure any of the DOS features, including TASKMAX, MEMMAX, and DISKMAX.

- TASKMAX is the task switcher, enabling you to move between DOS programs in much the same manner as Windows does.

Questions

1. Which of the following is a connectionless protocol?

   ○ A. SPX

   ○ B. IPX

   ○ C. NCP

   ○ D. NetBios

2. The utility used to generate workstation files on the local drive is _____.

   ○ A. WSUPDATE

   ○ B. DOSGEN

   ○ C. IPXODI

   ○ D. WSGEN

3. Which THREE of the following are network communication protocols:

   ☐ A. TCP

   ☐ B. SPX

   ☐ C. NFS

   ☐ D. IPX

4. Unloading drivers is accomplished by _____ and _____.

   ☐ A. using the U option

   ☐ B. running the command a second time

   ☐ C. specifying the drivers in reverse order of their load

   ☐ D. using a memory management utility to remove the TSRs

5. Features of the DOS Requester do not include _____.

   ○ A. backward compatibility

   ○ B. modular design

   ○ C. architecture independent protocol support

   ○ D. the use of current technology

6. The Protocol Mulitplexer is loaded with which VLM?

   ○ A. NWP.VLM

   ○ B. MULTI.VLM

   ○ C. NDS.VLM

   ○ D. RSA.VLM

7. How many interrupts do XT machines have?

   ○ A. 2

   ○ B. 4

   ○ C. 8

   ○ D. 16

8. How many interrupts do current machines have?

   ○ A. 2

   ○ B. 4

   ○ C. 8

   ○ D. 16

Answers

1. B
2. D
3. A, B, D
4. A, C
5. C
6. A
7. C
8. D

Troubleshooting Network Printing

Network printing is one of the most difficult processes to install and maintain. Because the process is so mechanical in nature, a series of problems can occur. When they do occur, the cause is not always visible. This chapter explores the issue from two sides:

■ *Preventing problems*

■ *Troubleshooting*

Before you consider taking the certification test, you should review the administrative topics pertinent to printing that are covered in the book's two administration course sections. The following topics are of particular interest:

- PCONSOLE
- PRINTCON
- PRINTDEF
- PSERVER
- RPRINTER

You should know how to create a print server and print queue; assign print servers to file servers; configure ports and printers; and manage queue and spool assignments.

Preventing Problems

Most of the steps used to prevent printer problems can be thought of as common sense precautions. They include cleaning paper and ribbon paths on a regular basis and vacuuming paper particles from inside the unit.

Temperature ranges and humidity should be kept as constant as possible, and there should be adequate space for ambient air to circulate around the printers. Laser printers should never be pointed directly at anyone, for the thermal radiation they give off can be harmful.

Troubleshooting

Printer problems can be broken into the following subcategories:

- Physical problems
- Print queues

- Print servers
- Remote printers
- Printer configuration
- Printer utilities
- PostScript printers

When diagnosing a problem, check the obvious components first. Make certain the electrical cord and printer cord are firmly attached and connected to the appropriate place. If there are any lights on the printer that indicate the power is on, check that they are lit. Also check to be sure that any switch boxes, electrical or A/B type, are working properly.

After you are convinced that the connections are functioning as they should be, turn the printer off and on again, and try sending your print job once more. If this attempt is unsuccessful, run a self-test on the printer and verify that it is working properly as a stand-alone. If it is, try printing to it again with a different application, such as a print screen, to see if the application is the culprit.

Physical Problems

Physical problems are the easiest problems to verify, and the first for which you should check. You should begin by checking the cables, as mentioned already. Next, make sure that the paper is not jammed, and that there is a ribbon or toner cartridge in working condition in the unit. If the ribbon is damaged or the toner cartridge is empty, replace the faulty component and try again.

 Parallel printing is four to six times faster than serial printing, and the faster the machine's CPU, the more obvious this becomes. Novell recommends that parallel printers be used as often as possible. The maximum standard cable length for parallel printers is 10 feet (150 by some manufacturers) compared to the standard of 50 for serial printers (500 by some manufacturers).

Parallel printers are, moreover, universally compatible, although serial printers are not. Only limited error checking is available on parallel printers; serial printers have parity checking, which slows printing speed by 10 percent.

Print Queues

The print queue's physical representation is the directory on the file server where the print jobs wait until they are printed by the print server. Problems can occur if you run out of hard drive space, or if the queue has become corrupted. You can monitor job entries with PCONSOLE to show their status.

 If problems occur when using NPRINT, check for older versions of IPX and update them.

One of the first things you should do when a user complains that a job won't print is use PCONSOLE to verify that the job is still in the queue. If it is not in the queue, the application might not be network-aware. Check to see that CAPTURE is active on the workstation before going further.

Print Servers

If the job is still in the queue, and all the physical checks appear correct, re-enable the server's capability to service queues. Verify that the latest version of PSERVER.NLM is running; then, using PCONSOLE, take the print server down and bring it back up again.

 PSERVER needs 512 KB of memory. An additional 10 KB is needed for every extra printer added to the server.

When using PSERVER.EXE (as opposed to PSERVER.NLM), make sure that your SPX CONNECTIONS are set to at least 60.

 NETERR.ZIP is a file of utilities useful for problem solving with print servers and a variety of other hardware devices. It is highly recommended that this file be downloaded from NOVLIB on NetWire or taken from NSEPro and extracted for use.

Remote Printers

Remote serial printers demand constant attention. If the error message Not Connected appears, RPRINTER has not yet been run to activate the defined printer.

If RPRINTER has been run, and there are still problems, the problems might be attributed to a lack of memory, older versions of the software, or an incompatible PC clone.

Many times, conflicts can occur between RPRINTER and the NIC card installed in the machine. If such is the case, change the interrupt setting on the card to solve the problem.

Routers between RPRINTER workstations and print servers can cause problems and cause the remote printer to periodically hang. If such is the case, increase the NET.CFG parameters for the following two fields:

- SPX ABORT TIMEOUT
- IPX RETRY COUNT

Printer Configuration

PRINTDEF and PRINTCON are utilities used to create printer and job definitions. It is imperative that the printer definitions be correct in order for the print jobs to function as efficiently and error-free as possible. Often, a slight problem in the configuration means that short jobs will print without any errors, but large graphics jobs will fail.

Printer Utilities

You can solve many printing problems by upgrading older printer utilities, such as PSERVER.EXE and others, to the newest ones available. The latest utilities can be found on NSEPro or on the NOVLIB forum of NetWire.

Incorrect buffer sizes can cause characters to get lost on a printout. If such is the case, use PCONSOLE to increase the buffer size.

You can use PRINTCON when files are printing with improper page breaks. Redefine the configuration and change the Timeout Count.

PostScript Printers

PostScript is a printer language created by Adobe that provides a method of interfacing with a printer to create high-end, high-quality graphics. A great many PostScript problems can be solved by updating application drivers to the latest available.

It is important to verify that any cartridges used on the printer to generate PostScript are properly inserted and seated. It is also highly recommended

that when printing in PostScript, you use the following settings:

- **/NB.** No banner
- **/NT.** No tabs
- **/NFF.** No form feed

Questions

1. The standard maximum length of a serial cable is _____.

   ○ A. 10 feet

   ○ B. 30 feet

   ○ C. 50 feet

   ○ D. 500 feet

2. The Print Server does which of the following THREE tasks?

   ☐ A. Stores print jobs in the queue

   ☐ B. Sends data to a remote printer

   ☐ C. Accepts data from the queue

   ☐ D. Polls the queue for print jobs

3. Parity checking is used with print jobs sent _____.

   ○ A. to a remote printer

   ○ B. to a serial printer

   ○ C. to a parallel printer

   ○ D. to any printer

4. When unloading PSERVER.NLM because of a problem, you should _____.

   ○ A. reboot the print server

   ○ B. unload the NLMs in an orderly manner

   ○ C. use PRINTCON to stop incoming jobs

   ○ D. laugh like a pirate

5. RPRINTER is _____.

   ○ A. used to define remote print jobs

   ○ B. the main utility for establishing network printing

   ○ C. a loadable server module for remote printing

   ○ D. a utility used at a workstation to activate remote printing

Answers

1. C

2. B, C, D

3. B

4. B

5. D

Network Optimization and Disaster Recovery

Let's think about the two most basic needs of network administrators—how to best utilize the software and hardware resources on hand, and how to best ensure that your precious data will be there when you need it. This section of the Service and Support test is arguably by far the most important aspect of administering any network.

The SET Parameter

NetWare is generally quite good at optimizing the SET parameters. You can degrade system performance drastically by altering memory SET parameters incorrectly. If the alterations are performed correctly, however, your system and peripherals will function optimally.

On the other hand, as with any popular network operating system, you must know how to change these parameters. With NetWare you can alter communications, memory, file caching, directory caching, file system, locks, transaction tracking, disk, and miscellaneous parameters by adding the necessary SET commands into the appropriate STARTUP.NCF or SYS:SYSTEM\AUTOEXEC.NCF files.

 Unless you have a full understanding of the ramifications involved in changing the various SET commands, do not change them. Although the system should remain intact after you make the changes, the potential exists for devastating results.

Communications Parameters

The following paragraphs give explanations for the parameters and their defaults and options.

Console Display Watchdog Logouts: OFF [ON, OFF]

If this parameter is set to ON, a message is displayed at the console when a connection is cleared.

New Packet Receive Buffer Wait Time: 0.1 Seconds [0.1 to 20]

This parameter determines how long the system will wait after receiving a request for another packet. If you have an EISA NIC in your server, you should not have to worry about your system granting too many receive buffers during high usage periods.

Maximum Physical Receive Packet Size: 1130 [618 to 4202]

As indicated by the name, this parameter establishes the maximum size of the packets that a system can receive. The parameter is configured in the STARTUP.NCF. The default is 1 KB (with packet header). If you have a NIC that can transmit packets larger than 512 bytes, you should increase this number to equal the largest packet size supported by your NIC.

Maximum Packet Receive Buffers: 100 [50 to 2000]

Use MONITOR to establish the number of service processes and packet receive buffers that your system is currently using. Increase the number in increments of 10 until you have 5 buffers per EISA or microchannel board, or until each workstation has 10.

Number of Watchdog Packets: 10 [5 to 100]

This value represents the number of watchdog packets that your server will send without receiving a reply before it disconnects the workstation.

Delay between Watchdog Packets: 59.3 Seconds [1 to 626.2]

Simply put, this is the amount of time that exists between sending the watchdog packets if the system receives no reply.

Delay before First Watchdog Packet: 240 Seconds [15.7 to 172.3]

This is the amount of time that a system will wait without receiving a request from a workstation before the system sends a watchdog packet to that workstation.

Memory Parameters

The following paragraphs give explanations for the parameters and their defaults and options.

Cache Buffer Size: 4096 Bytes [4096, 8192, or 16384]

If your block allocation size is smaller than 4096, increasing this value will diminish your system performance. If, however, your block allocation sizes are larger than 4096, system performance will increase if you increase this value.

Maximum Alloc Short-Term Memory: 2097152 [50000 to 16777216]

This critical memory pool stores drive mappings, loadable module tables, queued broadcast messages, open and locked files, service request buffers, and user connection information. The default 2 MB should be sufficient for 250 users with 26 drive mappings apiece.

Auto Register Memory above 16 Megabytes: ON [ON, OFF]

Care should be taken when altering this variable. If you install a NIC or disk controller that uses 24-bit address lines, only 16 MB of memory can be accessed properly. If your server can address more than 16 MB and you have installed one of the aforementioned EISA boards, only low memory will be addressed (in lieu of high), and the low memory that is being used by the NOS may become corrupted.

File Caching Parameters

The following paragraphs give explanations for the parameters and their defaults and options.

Maximum Concurrent Disk Cache Writes: 50 [10 to 100]

Increasing this variable increases the efficiency of write requests. Decreasing, on the other hand, increases read efficiency. If your dirty cache buffers rises above 70 percent of the total cache buffers, you should increase this number.

Dirty Disk Cache Delay Time: 3.3 Seconds [0.1 to 10]

This parameter sets the duration that your NOS will hold a write request before writing the data to the disk. This parameter is best left at the default.

Minimum File Cache Report Threshold: 20 [0 to 1000]

Your server will warn you when it has allocated some number greater than the minimum. Although changeable, this variable should be left at default in the vast majority of installations.

Minimum File Cache Buffers: 20 [20 to 1000]

As named, this variable sets the minimum number of file cache buffers that can be allocated at any given point in time. Increasing this number too high decreases resources available for other server processes.

Directory Caching Parameters

The following paragraphs give explanations for the parameters and their defaults and options.

Dirty Directory Cache Delay Time: 0.5 Seconds [0 to 10]

This parameter determines the amount of time that the system will wait until a directory table write request is written to disk. Increasing this parameter increases both system performance and the possibility of directory table corruption.

Maximum Concurrent Directory Cache Writes: 10 [5 to 50]

In a manner similar to the previous Maximum Concurrent Disk Cache Writes, when you increase this variable, you increase write efficiency at the cost of cache reads. The converse is also correct.

Directory Cache Allocation Wait Time: 2.2 Seconds [0.5 to 120]

How long will the operating system wait between allocating allocation buffers? Here is where this value is determined. If you notice that when you run DIR or NDIR the response time is lagging, try reducing this parameter.

Directory Cache Buffer Nonreferenced Delay: 5.5 Seconds [1 to 120]

Logically, some time must pass before your NOS can overwrite a nonreferenced directory entry with another. Increasing this value will increase allocated directory cache buffers and increase performance.

Maximum Directory Cache Buffers: 500 [20 to 4000]

This value is permanent until a server is rebooted and determines how large the directory cache is. Increase this number if directory searches are sluggish.

Minimum Directory Cache Buffers: 20 [10 to 2000]

This parameter is inverse parameter to the previous Maximum Directory Cache Buffers. For obvious reasons, don't set the Minimum Directory Cache Buffers greater than the Maximum Directory Cache Buffers.

File System Parameters

The following paragraphs give explanations for the parameters and their defaults and options.

Maximum Extended Attributes per File or Path: 32 [4 to 512]

This variable establishes the number of extended attributes that a file or path can have. This applies to all volumes on the server.

Immediate Purge of Deleted Files: OFF [ON, OFF]

If this self-explained variable is set to ON, no SALVAGE features will be able to recover deleted files. If set to OFF, deleted files are salvageable.

Maximum Subdirectory Tree Depth: 25 [10 to 100]

This variable determines how deep your deepest directory tree can be. Increasing this variable requires more system memory.

Volume Low Warn All Users: ON [ON, OFF]

If you value the data on your system and are not one to check your system variables regularly, you will want to leave this option ON so you are alerted if your drives approach full. If you change this option to OFF, you should run VOLINFO or CHKVOL daily.

Volume Low Warning Reset Threshold: 256 [0 to 100,000]

After you receive an initial warning that your volume is getting low (as set in Volume Low Warning Threshold), space is freed up by deleting files. Volume Low Warning Reset Threshold determines the amount of threshold space that must be exceeded for a second volume low warning.

Volume Low Warning Threshold: 256 [0 to 1,000,000]

Because this value is in blocks rather than bytes, you will first need to establish your system's block size (determined when you set up your volume during installation). If you want your system to warn you when your volume has only 5 MB left, you need to divide your desired volume-free size by your block size to establish the number of blocks that will trigger the warning. If your volume block size is 4 KB, then you would select 1280 blocks to be warned at 5 MB.

Turbo FAT Re-Use Wait Time: 329.6 Seconds [0.3 to 1 Hour 5 Minutes 54.6 Seconds]

If a program randomly accesses a file containing greater than 64 FAT entries, a turbo FAT index is automatically built. These builds take time, so a re-build wait time is implemented so your NOS doesn't immediately rebuild the index every time a file is closed.

Minimum File Delete Wait Time: 65.9 Seconds [0 to 7 days]

This is an extremely valuable variable in environments where people delete files by accident. Since this situation could happen in just about every network in existence, increase this value if you have the resources. Realize, however, that this value is absolute, and that deleted files will not be purged until this time limit has been met (even if the volume is full and users are not able to create new files).

File Delete Wait Time: 329.6 Seconds [0 to 7 days]

Similar to the Minimum File Delete Wait Time, this value lets the system know when a deleted file may be marked as purgeable. Because NetWare tries to keep a minimum of $1/32$ of the total volume for new files, if your free space drops below $1/32$ and files are marked as purgeable, they will automatically be purged. At this point the file is history and can not be salvaged.

NCP File Commit: ON [ON, OFF]

Files can typically flush all pending file writes to disk.

Don't mess with this parameter unless you know what you are doing or a Novell representative instructs you to do so.

Maximum Percent of Volume Used by Directory: 13 [5 to 50]

How much of a volume may be used as directory space? This parameter provides the answer.

Maximum Percent of Volume Space Allowed for Extended Attributes: 10 [5 to 50]

This value is typically fine at the default setting, and is addressed only when the volume is being mounted.

Lock Parameters

The following paragraphs give explanations for the parameters and their defaults and options.

Maximum Record Locks per Connection: 500 [10 to 10,000]

A setting of 500 is usually more than sufficient in non-SQL environments (and even when you are in one). This parameter enables you to determine how many records each connection can establish. You might need to increase the value if you have a system-to-system *pipeline* in which multiple users will use one connection.

Maximum File Locks per Connection: 250 [10 to 1000]

If you have one connection that needs more than 250 files locked at one time, you have a unique environment! Suffice it to say that the default value should be fine.

Maximum Record Locks: 20,000 [100 to 200,000]

See the aforementioned Maximum Record Locks Per Connection, and take it to the server level. Changing this parameter is pretty straightforward.

Maximum File Locks: 10,000 [100 to 100,000]

This parameter enables you to set the number of files you can lock per connection.

Transaction Tracking Parameters

The following paragraphs give explanations for the parameters and their defaults and options.

Auto TTS Backout Flag: OFF [ON, OFF]

Although the default is OFF, if it is more important for your system to automatically boot after crashing, you might want to consider changing this value to ON. This enables your system to automatically back out of any incomplete transactions without asking you if it may do so.

TTS Abort Dump Flag: OFF [ON, OFF]

If you change the Auto TTS Backout Flag to ON, you will probably want to change this value to ON as well. If you do so, the system will create a log file that reflects what data has been backed out of the TTS.

Maximum Transactions: 10,000 [100 to 10,000]

Simply put, this parameter controls the number of transactions that can be performed at any given time on the system.

TTS Unwritten Cache Wait Time: 65.9 Seconds [11 to 659.1]

Certain transactional blocks are more courteous than others and for other blocks to be written to disk before they go. This value is the maximum time that any TTS block may wait in memory before being written to disk.

TTS Backout File Truncation Wait Time: 59 Minutes 19.2 Seconds [65.9 Seconds to 1 Day 2 Hours 21 Minutes 51.3 Seconds]

This parameter controls how long allocated blocks are available to the TTS backout file.

Miscellaneous Parameters

The following paragraphs give explanations for the parameters and their defaults and options.

Enable Disk Read After Write Verify: ON [ON, OFF]

If your media is "raided" or mirrored, then you may want to consider turning off this variable to increase performance. If not, or if you want to have a backup failsafe procedure in place, let your system verify that what it has just written to disk is the same as what was just in memory (default setting).

Maximum Outstanding NCP Searches: 51 [10 to 1000]

Normally your network will have only one NetWare Core Protocol directory search going on at any time. Ten searches are probably more than you will ever need, but if your network environment involves software that makes multiple NCP calls concurrently, you might need to increase this value. If your software needs this, it will let you know up front. Make any changes accordingly.

Allow Unencrypted Passwords: OFF [ON, OFF]

If you are running NetWare 3.0 or later, leave this OFF. Setting the variable to ON allows your passwords to be sent across your wire unencrypted.

New Service Process Wait Time: 2.2 Seconds [0.3 to 20]

This variable assigns how long the NOS waits after receiving a request for a new service before it actually allocates the new process.

Pseudo Preemption Time: 2000 [1000 to 10,000]

Certain types of software (NLMs) are CPU time-sensitive. Change this parameter only if your software suggests.

Display Spurious Interrupt Alerts: ON [ON, OFF]

This value should not be altered, because it reflects whether you have a hardware interrupt conflict in your file server. If this alarm is displayed at the system console, remove all unnecessary add-on boards and begin troubleshooting.

Display Lost Interrupt Alerts: ON [ON, OFF]

Again, this value should not be altered from the default value. An alarm will appear on the system console if a hardware interrupt call is made, but lost before the CPU can respond.

Display Disk Device Alerts: OFF [ON, OFF]

This is not a bad variable to change in any environment. Novell suggests turning this ON if you are experiencing hard drive problems.

Display Relinquish Control Alerts: OFF [ON, OFF]

This is a CPU watchdog control. If an NLM holds the CPU for more than 0.4 seconds, an alarm is displayed on the system console if this variable is turned ON.

Display Old API Names: OFF [ON, OFF]

This variable can be changed periodically to verify that new APIs are being used. Old APIs should still function, but they do so more slowly and should be updated.

Maximum Service Processes: 20 [5 to 40]

Increase this number only if you have sufficient resources (memory), and MONITOR reflects that you are using the number that is currently allocated.

Performance Modifications and Considerations

If your system requires that data be stored on the NetWare server in various file system formats, it is best that you do not mix file systems and name spaces on one volume. If you do require multiple name services on one volume, increase the Minimum Directory Cache Buffers setting, and the volume will mount more rapidly.

If you are going to implement more than one name space on a volume, install all name spaces on the volume when it is initially installed. If you are not able to do so and are adding a name space after your server has been running for some period of time, consider backing your system, re-installing the drive, adding all of the required name spaces, and then restoring the data. This will make efficient use of the Disk Directory Entry Table Blocks.

Monitoring with MONITOR

Whoever was on the development team of MONITOR.NLM is a friend to every network administrator. With MONITOR you have the ability to monitor various aspects of your network in real time, including various system utilizations, cache memory, network connections, drives, volumes, network drivers, modules, open file status, and memory usage.

When you invoke MONITOR.NLM, your initial screen will display information about the basic health of your system (see fig. 43.1). Some information, such as file server up time, is nifty, but it is usually nothing more than a basis of bragging rights between network administrators. The remainder of the information is very pertinent indeed. The Utilization number reflects what percentage of your overall resources are being used. If this number is consistently over seventy, add memory and

tune how these resources are being used. The Cache buffers numbers are also critical. If your Dirty Cache Buffers are close to or match your Total Cache Buffers, you have a bottleneck somewhere, and unless you find the source (that is, faulty cabling), your system will hang and need to be rebooted. Lastly, Current Disk Requests are transactions that are waiting for the disk to become available. Again, if your transactions get too stacked, your system will hang and need to be rebooted.

Connection Information

This section provides various information you need concerning connections.

List Active Connections

Displays connection time, network address, requests, kilobytes read, kilobytes written, semaphores, logical record locks, and open files for the user that is highlighted.

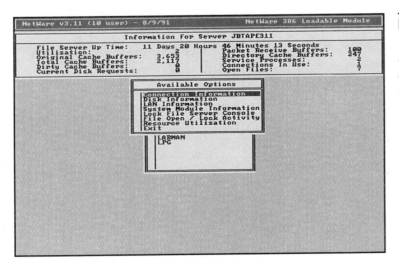

Figure 43.1
The MONITOR.NLM is an invaluable tool for anyone needing to tune a NetWare network.

List Physical Record Locks for a User

Show the beginning and ending offsets for locked files, how the record is locked, and the status of the file.

Clear a Connection

You can clear a connection using this section of the MONITOR program. Simply select the connection you want cleared, press Delete, and answer Yes when prompted to clear the connection. If you want to clear multiple connections, press F5 to select multiple connections before pressing the Delete key.

List Open Files

Lists the open files for the user that is highlighted. See figure 43.2.

Disk Information

This section discusses things you'll need to know about disks and other memory devices.

List System Hard Disks

This option enables you to view information about all system volumes. Select the desired drive from the drive list, and you will see a variety of information about the drive. Included is the driver for the disk, the disk size, partitions, mirror status, hot fix status, partition blocks, data blocks, redirection blocks, redirected blocks, and reserved blocks.

List Volume Segments per Hard Disk

This option displays basic information about a hard drive's volume segments.

Change the "Read After Write Verify" Status of the Hard Disk

Can change the read after write status between software level verify, hardware level verify, and disable verify events.

Flash the Hard Disk Light

Flashes the drive light.

Figure 43.2

The Connection Information screen.

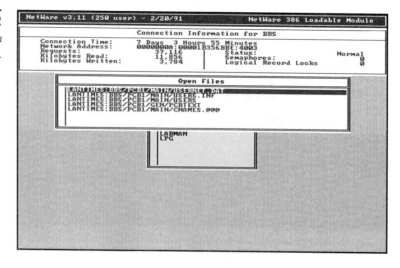

Activate/Deactivate a Hard Disk

Can switch a system drive between active and inactive.

Mount/Dismount a Removable Media Device

Makes it possible to mount and dismount devices such as magnetic optical or compact disk devices before they are removed. You can also view the status of the various removable devices from this utility (see fig. 43.3).

Lock/Unlock a Removable Media Device

It is good practice to lock a removable device prior to mounting it as a NetWare volume. This renders most eject buttons on removable media devices useless. Figure 43.3 shows the Drive Status screen.

LAN Information

This section covers information concerning details about local area networks.

LAN Drivers and Statistics

Displays information about the various network interface devices and connect points (see fig. 43.4). Included in the information is the driver name, version, node address, protocols, network address, total packets sent, total packets received, no ECB available count, send packet too big count, send packet too small count, receive packet overflow count, receive packet too big count, receive packet too small count, send packet miscellaneous errors, receive packet miscellaneous errors, send packet retry count, checksum errors, and hardware receive mismatch count.

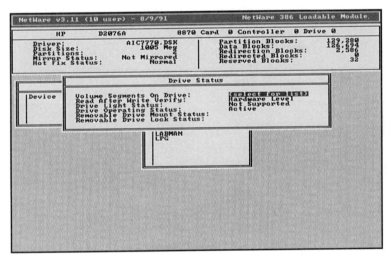

Figure 43.3

The Drive Status screen shows you pertinent information about your various hard drive media.

System Module Information

◼ List system modules (see fig. 43.5)

◼ List resources used by system modules

Lock File Server Console

◼ Lock the file server console

◼ Unlock the file server console

File Open/Lock Activity

◼ Check the status of a file

◼ View mounted volumes

Figure 43.6 shows the File Open/Lock Activity screen.

Figure 43.4

The LAN Information screen is your first reference point when using the MONITOR.NLM program.

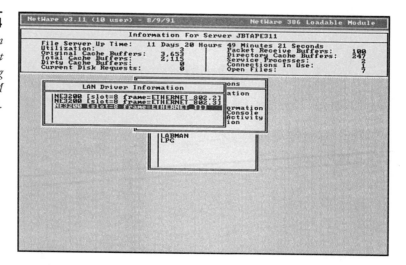

Figure 43.5

The System Modules screen affords you detailed information about your server status.

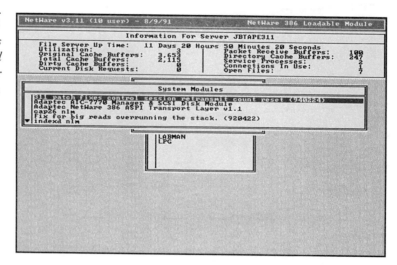

Resource Utilization

- View memory statistics

- View tracked resources

Figure 43.7 shows the Resource Utilization screen.

PATCHMAN

PATCHMAN is a utility available on NetWire and NSEPro that enables administrators to ensure that network modules are current and up to date. This is performed by means of the PATCHMAN.NLM that tracks and manages all official patches for

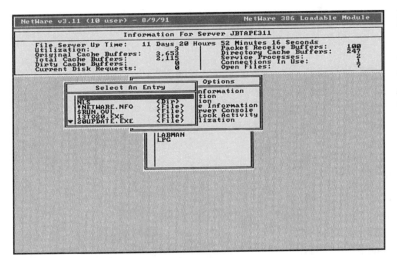

Figure 43.6

The File Open/Lock Activity screen lets you see at a glance what files a person presently has held open.

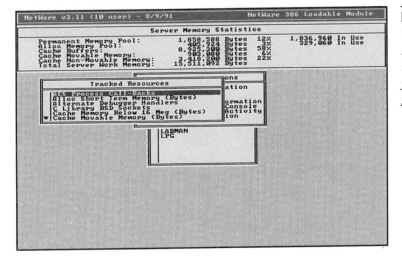

Figure 43.7

The Resource Utilization screen can give you detailed information about how your network resources are presently being used.

NetWare 3.11. The following list presents three basic types of patches for NetWare:

- **Dynamic.** Patches that can be loaded and unloaded at will. They are called *dynamic* because the server need not be powered down to have the changes take effect.

- **Semi-Static.** These semi-static patches can be loaded while the server is running (similar to dynamic patches), but cannot be unloaded unless you power down the server.

- **Static.** A *static* patch literally alters the SERVER.EXE file. It is good practice to back up your original SERVER.EXE prior to implementing any static patches.

Following is the PATCHMAN, dynamic, and semi-static patch installation procedure:

1. PATCHMAN is installed by first running the self-extracting file UPD311.EXE. This uncrunches the PATCHMAN.NLM that needs to be placed into the SYS:\SYSTEM directory.

2. Rename any patches that are currently on the system so that any new patches that have the same name as the current will not overwrite the old (in case you want to return the system to the pre-patch state).

3. Copy the new patches into the SYS:\SYSTEM directory.

4. Put LOAD PATCHMAN into the same script that holds your other system boot loadable modules.

To modify your SERVER.EXE file using a static patch, do the following steps:

1. Back your existing SERVER.EXE some-where safe.

2. Copy the static patches into the directory that holds your existing SERVER.EXE file.

3. Patch your SERVER.EXE by typing the patch name followed by SERVER.EXE.

In the same way that you type MODULES to display the modules that are currently running on your server, you can type PATCHES to display what patches are currently in place in your server's memory. The patches will be grouped with regard to whether they are dynamic, semi-dynamic, or static.

Bridges, Routers, and Hubs

If your channel utilization exceeds 60 to 70 percent, split the channel with the bridge or router. The answer to the question of how much data should flow locally versus over bridges and routers, 80 percent should be local with a maximum of 20 percent over the bridge or router.

Bridges and routers do not always play well together. Routers cannot properly route packages when bridges are involved, and there is a possibility of data getting "trapped" in a segment of the topology.

Remember that no more than four repeaters can be included in any local topology. This includes many hubs that amplify the incoming signal prior to shipping it back out.

Speed should always be an issue. Realize that since routers need to make decisions as to how to route the packet, they typically take substantially longer to receive the packet and then send it along its merry way.

Protocol Analyzers

There is nothing quite like having a good protocol analyzer on your side when troubleshooting a network wire problem. If you have ever spent hours trying to find out where the intermittent break or short in a 10BASE2 cable is, even on a relatively small network, you can appreciate why so many administrators have sent buckets of money in the direction of the Hair Club for Men.

Spend just one evening, weekend, or holiday searching for cable gremlins, and you know that you can put almost no dollar value on a device that not only tells you how far and in what direction a problem exists, but what the problem actually is!

Realize that many protocol analyzers perform such intricate tasks such as capturing the packets and disseminating the information for you to review, but for the CNE exam you only need to know how to start an analyzer, stop the capture, and what data will help you analyze your problem.

Novell usesLANalyzer for Windows as its example for the CNE exam. This product is commercially available and is simple to use. It is not the most extensive network-monitoring package on the market today, but with it you can monitor real-time activity, identify trends, create reports, and troubleshoot your system.

When you use LANalyzer for Windows, you can monitor real-time activity either graphically or in text form. The main graphical dashboard display shows you in real time the packets per second, utilization percentage, errors per second, and the size of your capture buffer for your network, server, or router. These easy-to-read dials move accordingly with the respective network/server/router activity.

Identifying trends is an important aspect of troubleshooting any network. If you have a network card that is going bad and is "chattering" on your network, you will notice a network speed degradation that could possibly bring that segment to a halt. LANalyzer for Windows has a variety of charts that enable you to track trends. For the chattering NIC, the station monitor display would probably be most useful. If you were monitoring the station monitor screen while a NIC was merrily sending garbage away, you would probably notice an inordinate amount of data being generated from one station. Couple this discovery with minimal to no activity on the other stations and an increase in the error count, and your first action might be to swap out the NIC in the suspect machine to see if this rectifies your problem. Realize that just because one workstation is much more active than the others does not necessarily mean that the NIC is faulty. You might just have one workstation that is more communication-intensive than the others.

If you decide to frequent your LANalyzer for Windows program, you will undoubtedly want to set some thresholds for alarms within the program. "Settable" parameters include packets per second, utilization percentage, broadcasts per second, fragments per second, CRC errors per second, and server overload per minute. These parameters are self-explanatory, but unless you intend to scrutinize every aspect of your LANalyzer program every time you turn it on, take a moment to set your defaults so that you are alerted to any potential network problems.

Third-Party Disaster Recovery Products

Nowadays, when everybody seems to be coming out with backup and restoral products, it is important to take a look at a product's certified compliance. In the NetWare realm of backup products, the most popular certified compliance is *Storage Management System* (SMS) compliance. This standard began years ago with Novell's SBACKUP, but Novell has since released the standard to a standards committee in hopes that SMS will become the industry standard.

Without a standard, the backup and restore industry was becoming segmented. Segmentation is not necessarily a bad thing in the free-enterprise system; in this case, however, the end-user was frequently the loser. Frequently network administrators purchased "whiz-bang" backup utilities only to realize the utilities' shortcomings after a year or two. Upon attempting to contact the vendor to inquire about an upgrade path, network administrators frequently discovered that, in the cut-throat tape backup industry, their vendors had either gone away or merged with other companies. Often the vendors changed their formats (which were frequently not readable by other backup products anyway), which meant that if an administrator decided to purchase and use a new version (or merged product), past backups were history.

It cannot be stressed enough how important system backups are. Here are a few guidelines to follow when handling your backup procedures:

1. If a backup product does not allow for you to verify-after-write, don't buy it. You should always have this feature turned on.

2. Test the data that you back up. Ideally, you should have a mirror server identical to your online server. You can test that your backed-up data is valid by restoring it to your mirrored server. Realistically, you will only have a small area into which you can restore a small portion of your backup to ensure that the backup was valid.

3. Take an electronic look at your backup to verify that the data that you want to be backed up actually is. With many products, there is a log file that displays the names of all of the files that are backed to tape.

4. Obvious but necessary—do not ever overwrite your most recent tape.

Novell suggests that you verify that your data is indeed corrupted prior to restoring your server from tape. There are a couple of tools that can assist you in performing these tasks. The first is INSTALL.NLM. If you are having problems with drives or data, INSTALL displays useful information about the status of your drive and volume.

VREPAIR.NLM can be an invaluable tool when dealing with a suspect drive or volume. As invaluable as it is, however, if your hardware is damaged, there is nothing that you can do about it with software.

Burst Mode Advantages and Drawbacks

Normally, when a workstation makes a request to a server, the server responds with an acknowledgement that it has received a request. On smaller networks this is of little concern, but as your network grows, every little bit of optimization helps to keep the users from complaining about how slow their system is running. By enabling packet burst mode, you can increase performance on a larger LAN or WAN by expanding the size of the packet to over 512 bytes, as well as by allowing more than one packet to be included to the server before an acknowledgement is sent.

Although it might sound like enabling packet burst mode is a feature that should be implemented from the get go, by doing so you increase the possibility of damaging packets because of the congestion that will result in having to resend. This is where the argument for virtual loadable modules rather than NETX comes into play. NETX (or NET4, NET5, NET6, and so forth) is quite literal and will take packet sizes and order as law. VLMs, on the other hand, are more intelligent than NETX, and can dynamically adjust the packet window on the fly for both performance and speed. Although NETX's packet burst increases performance by an average of 38 percent, the VLM version displays an efficiency increase of 82 percent. Learn your VLMs and you will be happy that you did.

Questions

1. SET parameters can be changed _____.

   ○ A. in AUTOEXEC.NCF

   ○ B. in STARTUP.NCF

   ○ C. All of the Above

   ○ D. None of the Above

2. SET can be used to alter parameters for all except _____.

   ○ A. file caching

   ○ B. communications

   ○ C. palette colors

   ○ D. memory

3. Dirty Directory Cache Delay Time is used to determine the amount of time _____.

   ○ A. the system will wait until a directory table write request is written to disk

   ○ B. directory contents are stored in read-ahead buffers

   ○ C. the system will hold corrupted (dirty) data before discarding it

   ○ D. a user must wait before a response is given to their DIR request

4. By default, NetWare 3.0 and later use encrypted passwords.

   ○ A. True

   ○ B. False

Answers

1. C

2. C

3. A

4. A

NetWare 3.1x Installation and Configuration

Preparing for a NetWare Installation

This section of the book is designed to provide you with the knowledge and skills necessary to complete the NetWare 3.1x Installation and Configuration Workshop portion of Novell's CNE program. It is intended for experienced network administrators who have a basic understanding of general NetWare principles and procedures. In this section, you learn how to plan a NetWare 3.1x installation, as well as perform all necessary installation steps.

This section does NOT discuss the administrative commands and utilities such as SYSCON. As a CNE candidate, you do need to have a thorough knowledge of these utilities and commands; this chapter focuses on the installation of NetWare. The administrative commands are thoroughly documented in the administrative sections of this book.

This section should help you accomplish the following objectives:

- Understand the terms used for NetWare 3.1*x* operating system installation

- Demonstrate the ability to find third-party software drivers required for NetWare 3.1*x* operating systems installation

- Identify the software needed to install NetWare 3.1*x* operating systems

- Describe the hardware needed to install NetWare 3.1*x* operating systems

- Describe the various methods available for installing NetWare 3.1*x*

Terms and Files

Novell's operating systems for NetWare 3.1*x* and above have the distinguishing factor of being able to be dynamically configured. In earlier NetWare versions and with other network operating systems, object modules selected during installation have to be "bound" together to form the operating system. This procedure is known as *static linking*, or *generating*. Through static linking, the operating system is configured to operate with a particular hardware configuration. In NetWare 3.1*x*, however, the ability to dynamically link operating system modules enables the module to be added to the operating system as it is loaded into memory—on-the-fly.

The reverse is also true—that is, modules can be unloaded and thus dynamically removed from the operating system. These software modules are referred to as *NetWare Loadable Modules* (NLMs)—a group of cooperating software tasks or engines that enable NetWare to be dynamically configured to operate with almost any hardware configuration.

 NetWare's dynamic linking is similar to the *Dynamic Link Libraries* (DLLs) found in Windows and OS/2. The difference between NetWare's NLMs and other forms of Dynamic linking is NetWare NLMs are linked at load time, rather than at execution.

NLMs are activated from the server's console with NetWare's LOAD command, as in the following line:

```
LOAD MONITOR
```

NLMs are deactivated by simply unloading the NLM. You can unload an NLM by using NetWare's UNLOAD command, as follows:

```
UNLOAD MONITOR
```

NLMs can be loaded or unloaded whenever the network administrator desires.

The flexibility of NLMs enables third-party hardware and software providers to take advantage of being a part of the operating system. Certain NLMs, such as network card drivers and disk controller drivers, can be added to the operating system at any time. These specialty NLMs can also be designed to accept command-line parameters, which enable the driver behavior to be modified, as in the following line:

```
LOAD NE2000 port=300 int=3
➡frame=Ethernet_802.2 Net=38823
```

In this situation, the command-line parameters enable the NetWare administrator to load the driver at the correct port, interrupt, frame type, and network segment.

 Note NLMs written specifically for a network card will have a file extension of LAN. NLMs written for a disk driver will have a file extension of DSK.

NetWare has the capability to be dynamically configured because it is based on a software bus-like architecture. This *bus* allows services to be loaded or attached to the operating system so that it can communicate with the device that is providing the service. The server cannot communicate with the hard disk without first loading the disk driver (*.DSK), for example, nor can it communicate with the network board without first loading the appropriate LAN driver (*.LAN). Likewise, other services can be loaded into the software bus, as shown in figure 44.1.

Because of NetWare's dynamic configuration properties, there are a lot of installation parameters that are not automatically set during installation. For this reason, you must be aware of the correct configuration information, especially for the network card and disk driver. If these settings are not correct, NetWare will not properly function.

Finding Third-Party Drivers and NLMs

Knowing you have the correct drivers for your particular hardware is crucial to a successful NetWare installation. Thus, you will need to know where you can find the drivers for the LAN card, as well as the driver for the disk controller.

NetWare ships with several different LAN and DSK drivers. The third-party drivers that ship with NetWare can be found in the System directory of the System-2 and System-3 floppy disks. After NetWare is installed, all of the third-party NLMs are located in the System directory on the SYS volume.

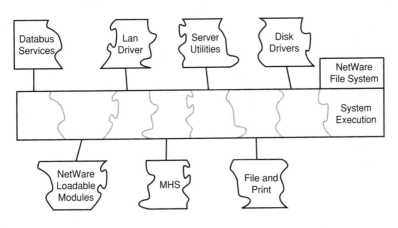

Figure 44.1
NetWares Dynamically configurable bus-like architecure.

If you are installing NetWare 3.12 from CD-ROM, the disk and network card drivers can be found in either of the following directories:

```
Disk drivers <CD-ROM drive letter>
➥\NetWare.312_____\diskdrv

LAN drivers <CD-ROM drive letter>
➥\NetWare.312_____\landrv
```

Most vendors ship NetWare drivers with their cards. Never assume that the drivers with the card or the drivers that come with NetWare are the latest version, however. The only way to be absolutely sure which driver is the latest is to contact your hardware manufacturer.

Contacting the manufacturer does not necessarily mean via phone. Most manufacturers have bulletin boards, forums on a public network such as CompuServe, or even fax-back services. Most of these services will inform you of the latest driver release dates.

Required Software

Besides having all of the necessary hardware drivers (disk driver and LAN driver), you will also need a copy of NetWare and a copy of DOS version 3.3 or later.

DOS is required because NetWare first needs to boot to DOS. After booting to DOS, you will be able to store the NetWare boot files, such as SERVER.EXE, on the DOS device. SERVER.EXE is the primary NetWare operating system file and makes the machine a NetWare 3.1x file server.

 Note During the initial server installation, you need to copy the SERVER.EXE file to the hard drive. Doing this enables you to load the file from the hard drive, instead of from a floppy.

With NetWare 3.12, the SERVER.EXE file, along with all the other necessary boot files, is copied to the SERVER.312 directory on the DOS partition of the hard drive. With 3.11, however, it is left up to you to copy the SERVER.EXE and other boot files to the hard drive.

After SERVER.EXE is executed, it loads the NetWare file system and takes over the operation of the computer. Because NetWare does not use the services of any other operating system (including DOS), it is important to verify that no memory managers or other device drivers are loaded prior to executing NetWare.

Required Hardware

As client software becomes increasingly resource intensive, the lines between client and server hardware continue to gray; it is the function of the machine that determines if it is a client or a server, not the hardware configuration. However, it is common for the file server to have more memory, disk space, and other enhancements than a workstation. Again, the differentiation comes when NetWare is loaded because once it is loaded it will provide services to all the network users, manage the file system, provide security, and control communication services for clients and other devices.

Even though a server uses many of the same hardware components as a PC or a client workstation, there are some minimal server hardware requirements that must be met before you can install NetWare 3.12. They are as follows:

- 386 or better Intel-based processor

- Minimum of 6 MB of memory

- Network card with LAN driver

■ A hard disk with at least 10 MB of free space

■ Disk controller with disk driver

■ Floppy drive

■ (Optimal) CD-ROM drive

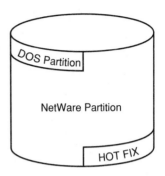

NetWare is a multitasking operating system, and therefore requires at least a 386-based processor. Each server must also contain at least 6 MB of memory, although 8 MB or more is recommended. Actually, the amount of RAM your server needs for its optimal operation depends on the overall hardware configuration—the more disk space you have, the more memory you need.

Figure 44.2

NetWare supports internal as well as external drives.

A NetWare 3.1*x* server must have a bare minimum of 10 MB of free disk space. Again, this is the bare minimum, which will only enable you to load the NetWare files.

When preparing for your NetWare installation, you will need to know your disk channel configuration as well as your disk space requirements. This knowledge will help you in planning for future disk expansion, and in determining the appropriate initial server configuration.

For example, if you do not plan to grow, you might be able to get along with a single, internal drive. If growth is probable, you might want to consider using an internal drive for your boot partition, and use external drives as your main storage area. This concept can be seen in figure 44.2.

As you plan your disk configuration you will also want to keep in mind NetWare's hot fix area. This is an area of the drive that is reserved for storing data in the event a drive encounters any bad blocks (areas of the drive not stable enough to accept data). To prevent data loss, NetWare automatically redirects data to the reserved section or hot fix area of the drive. By default, approximately two percent of the drive is reserved for the hot fix area.

Questions

1. What group of software components is required before installing NetWare?

   ○ A. Third-party drivers (LAN and disk channel), NetWare, and DOS

   ○ B. DOS, OS/II, and Windows NT

   ○ C. NetWare loadable moudles, disk drivers, and LAN drivers

   ○ D. DOS, STARTUP.NCF file, and NetWare

2. An NLM is loaded from which of the following?

   ○ A. Workstation

   ○ B. Windows System Directory

   ○ C. DOS prompt

   ○ D. NetWare Console

3. What extension is found on a NetWare NLM that provides the interface between a disk controller card and the NetWare operating system?

   ○ A. NCF

   ○ B. DSK

   ○ C. NLM

   ○ D. LAN

4. What extension is found on a NetWare NLM that provides the interface between a network card and the NetWare operating system?

   ○ A. NCF

   ○ B. DSK

   ○ C. NLM

   ○ D. LAN

5. What is the minimal amount of memory required to load NetWare 3.12?

   ○ A. 10 MB

   ○ B. 6 MB

   ○ C. 4 MB

   ○ D. 12 MB

Answers

1. A

2. D

3. B

4. D

5. B

Installation and Configuration

This chapter offers two methods of installation. First, it provides a quick guide, or list of steps, that must be performed during the installation process. It then provides a more detailed version, discussing in depth— and illustrating—several of the NetWare 3.12 installation steps.

After reading this chapter, you should be able to list, in order, all the steps required for installing NetWare. You should also understand why each step is necessary.

The following lists the steps required to install a NetWare 3.1x file server. Each step is necessary and must be completed in the proper order.

1. Partition the hard disk for DOS.

2. Format the hard disk with DOS.

3. Load and boot to DOS.

4. Load INSTALL.BAT.

5. Enter a server name.

6. Assign a unique internal IPX number.

7. Enter the source and destination paths.

8. Select the locale configuration settings.

9. Select the file format.

10. Specify any special startup set commands.

11. Elect to have the AUTOEXEC.BAT file load SERVER.EXE.

After you have completed the steps listed above, you will also need to complete the following:

1. Load the HBA driver.

2. Load INSTALL.NLM.

3. Create a NetWare partition.

4. Create a NetWare volume.

5. Mount volume SYS.

6. Copy public and system files to the file server.

7. Load the LAN driver.

8. Create AUTOEXEC.NCF and STARTUP.NCF files.

 Note   Performing each step in order is not absolutely necessary, but following this sequence ensures that nothing is forgotten.

If you are not familiar with all of the above steps, read on. The following section discusses each of the individual installation steps.

Performing a NetWare 3.12 Installation

This section discusses all the steps required to install a NetWare file server successfully.

Partitioning the Hard Disk for DOS

When a NetWare server boots, it must first load DOS, which means a server has to boot either from a floppy drive or from a small DOS partition located on the active, primary partition of the hard drive.

There are several advantages to creating a DOS partition over booting from a floppy drive. The most obvious advantage is simply speed. Other advantages include: a place to store necessary startup files, convenience, security, and so forth.

Older *Host Bus Adapters* (HBAs) known as *Disk Controller Boards* (DCBs) do not support the use of a DOS partition.

Formatting the Hard Disk with DOS

The NetWare installation utility requires a DOS partition on your hard disk in order to install the NetWare operating system. NetWare's installation utility creates a DOS partition using Novell DOS. If you do not want NetWare's installation to create this partition for you, exit and manually create the partition using DOS's FDISK and FORMAT commands.

By default, most setup routines use the entire drive for DOS, leaving no room for NetWare. When the DOS installation routine asks if you want to use the entire drive for DOS, answer No. A 10 or 20 MB DOS partition should suffice.

 NetWare's installation routine requires a DOS partition; however, the NetWare operating system does not. If you do not want a DOS partition on your server's hard drive, you will have to install NetWare manually.

Creating the DOS partition to store NetWare files is no different for a server than it is for a typical PC.

Most versions of DOS provide an automatic installation routine or setup program. These installation aids automatically partition the drive, assign the first partition on the drive as the active partition, format the drive, and install DOS on the active partition.

 To boot from the partition, the partition must be a primary DOS partition and be designated as the active partition. Most DOS setup routines automatically create a partition and set it active. If you are using a SCSI controller, however, you often have to set the partition active manually.

You can also let NetWare's installation routine guide you through the creation of the DOS partition. This process uses Novell DOS's FDISK command to create the primary boot partition. After creating the partition, you will have to reboot the server and reload the INSTALL.BAT file.

After restarting the INSTALL.BAT file, the installation routine recognizes that a partition now exists, but that the partition has not yet been formatted. It prompts for your permission to format the new partition.

 Creating a partition and formatting the drive deletes all the information on the drive.

After formatting the partition, the server must once again be rebooted. Your server should now have a DOS partition and be freshly booted. Start the INSTALL.BAT file again. After starting the installation routine, the Disk Partition Options screen reflecting the newly created and formatted DOS partition will appear.

NetWare's installation routine, as mentioned previously, formats the server so it can be booted. This formatting requires that the DOS system files be transferred to the computers boot sector. It also means that the COMMAND.COM file needs to be located on the hard drive. It does not, however, mean that a complete copy of DOS will be installed on the server boot partition.

NetWare does not require any of the DOS files; however, some of the DOS files, especially utility type files that are used for maintenance, such as EDIT, XCOPY, DELTREE, and so on, are very handy to have on the partition. If you do not mind using the disk space, you might want to go ahead and install a complete copy of DOS onto the boot partition. You need to be sure, though, that none of the DOS memory managers are loaded.

 If you are installing 3.11, you will want to manually copy supporting startup files—such as VREPAIR.NLM, a volume repair utility necessary if the NetWare partition is inaccessible—to the DOS partition of the hard drive. You also should keep your LAN drives on the DOS partition.

Entering a Server Name

After loading INSTALL.BAT, you are prompted to enter a server name which can be 2 to 47 characters long. It should be used to bring meaning to the server, yet be as short as possible. Give the server a name that indicates its primary function or who is using it. This scheme is easier for users to remember, and the shorter the server name, the easier it is to type. Also, the name must be unique from any other servers on the network.

 The server name can be any length of characters from 2 to 47 long. It can contain any alphanumeric character (letters A–Z, numbers 0–9). It can even contain some special characters such as a hyphen or an underscore; it cannot, however, contain spaces or periods.

Assigning a Unique Internal IPX Number

After entering a server name, you assign an internal IPX number, which is an internal two to eight-digit hexadecimal number (using numbers 0 through 9 and letters A through F). The Internal IPX number is a "logical" network number used by NetWare to identify each server on the network. Because it is used as a unique identifier, you must ensure that no two servers have duplicate IPX numbers. The uniqueness of the internal IPX number is very important—so important that large sites will devise a scheme of assigning internal IPX numbers in an attempt to guard against accidental duplications.

The NetWare 3.12 installation routine creates a NETWARE.312 directory on the DOS partition of the hard drive. After you assign a unique name and Internal IPX number to the server, the routine transfers all the necessary startup files from the source (CD-ROM, floppy disks, or another server) to the target directory on the server's boot drive.

The transferred files include SERVER.EXE, VREPAIR.EXE, disk drivers, LAN drivers, and other necessary startup files.

A bar graph shows the progress of the file copy. If you are installing from floppy disks, you are prompted to change disks during the copy procedure.

Entering Local Support Codes

NetWare supports several different languages (French, English, German, Spanish, and so on). To ensure that the correct message files are displayed, the installation routine prompts you to enter the correct Country Code, Code Page, and keyboard mapping.

Selecting the File Name Format

NetWare shells prior to NetWare 3.12's Requester technology supported file names that included extended characters and lowercase letters. To continue this support, you must use the shells (NETX.EXE) rather than the requesters (VLM.EXE). To avoid confusion and problems, you should simply select the DOS file format, which maps lowercase characters to uppercase file names.

After choosing your local settings, the installation prompts you for any special commands that you would like to have stored in the STARTUP.NCF or AUTOEXEC.NCF files, which are much like batch files in DOS; that is, they store a list or *batch* of commands that are automatically execute when the file is launched. Furthermore, these files are much like the CONFIG.SYS and AUTOEXEC.BAT files in that they are automatically executed when the server is started.

Note Additions to these files can be made at anytime using INSTALL.NLM.

Like with DOS batch files, you can also create a file with an NCF extension and have the file process the commands when the file is processed. If, for example, you want to load MONITOR, INSTALL, RCONSOLE, and so forth, you could store the load commands in an NCF file called START.NCF. Typing **START** at the file server's console would then launch the batch of commands.

After you have entered any special startup commands, the install utility automatically loads SERVER.EXE. Once SERVER.EXE is loaded, DOS commands will no longer function. NetWare is now loaded, and the install utility returns you to a colon prompt, which is known as the *NetWare console* prompt.

Loading the Disk Driver

The disk drivers provide the communication interface between the controller, the drive, and NetWare. In addition to loading the driver, you need to provide the disk controller settings. These settings usually include the appropriate interrupt (INT) and I/O address.

Note If you are using an EISA machine, enter the slot where the controller is located.

If you are using an ISA-based machine, enter the correct interrupt and I/O address.

Although NetWare ships with several SCSI disk controller drivers, it is good practice to use the very latest driver. This driver will usually whip the SCSI controller; however, you should check with the controller's manufacturer to verify that you have the most current driver.

If you are using an MFM controller and hard disk combination, use the drivers (ISADISK.DSK) that ship with NetWare.

If you are using an IDE disk controller, use the IDE.DSK file that ships with NetWare, or, if the manufacturer of the IDE controller ships a NetWare drive, use it.

After the disk drivers are loaded, NetWare can access the hard drives, which enables you to define NetWare disk partitions.

Loading INSTALL.NLM

INSTALL.NLM is the Install utility that creates NetWare disk partitions and volumes. INSTALL.NLM is loaded at the server console by typing:

LOAD INSTALL

The INSTALL utility is used for the initial installation of NetWare, plus much more. It manages disk drives, performing such tasks as formatting, partitioning, mirroring, and surface testing. INSTALL provides information concerning your NetWare volumes, such as volume name, block size, and disk size. It indicates whether or not a particular volume is mounted. Moreover, it is the easiest place in NetWare to create, edit, and save crucial startup files, such as the AUTOEXEC.NCF and STARTUP.NCF files.

Creating a NetWare Partition

With the Install utility, you can divide the drive into logical sections called partitions. A NetWare *partition* consists of a data area, which should be the largest portion of the drive, and a hot fix redirect area, which should be about two percent of the drive.

To partition a server's drive, select Create NetWare Partition from the partition table menu. After indicating a partition size for NetWare, press Enter. A partition verification screen appears, where you can complete the following tasks:

■ Change hot fix

■ Create a NetWare partition

■ Delete any partition

After selecting the Partition Tables option, a partition options menu appears. If your drive does not contain any partitions, the Partition Type area of the box indicates that the drive has free space, or contains no partitions. If your drive is partitioned, the Partition Type indicator specifies the type of partitions installed on the drive, as seen in figure 45.1.

Creating a partition in NetWare is similar to performing a low level format and running FDISK on a DOS drive. You can only have one NetWare partition on a drive. Likewise, every drive in the server, if it is to be accessed by NetWare, has to have a NetWare partition.

Creating a NetWare Volume

After creating a partition, you must create a NetWare volume. Creating a NetWare volume is like formatting a DOS drive, in that it allows NetWare to store files on the drive's surface. With NetWare you can have more than one volume on a single drive. You can also have a single volume span multiple drives.

To create a NetWare volume, select Volume Options from INSTALL's main menu. These options enable you to create, delete, rename, or expand a volume. If your server currently has volumes created, selecting this menu item initiates a list of those volumes. To view the configuration or to modify a volume, highlight the volume and press Enter.

To create the very first NetWare volume on your server, press Insert, and the screen in figure 45.2 appears.

The first volume on your NetWare server must be named SYS. Consequently, when you create the first volume, the Volume Name box is automatically filled in with "SYS." You can, however, change the first volume's (SYS) block size and volume size.

Figure 45.1

NetWare's partition creation screen.

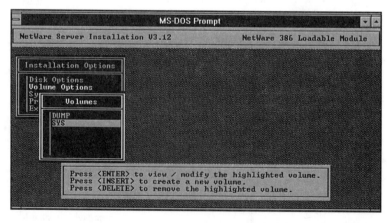

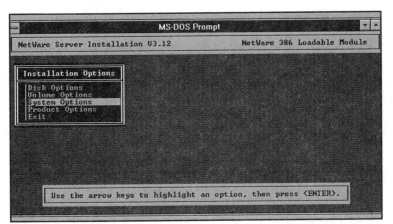

Figure 45.2
NetWare 3.12's create volume screen.

If the volume you want to create is not the first on the server, enter its name and press Enter. Press Esc and type **Y** at the Create Volume prompt, then specify the block size and volume size.

In the volume information screen, you have the option of changing the block size of the volume. The smaller the block size, the more memory your server needs. The larger the block size, the more sequential the storage and the better the data retrieval time; the drive, however, holds less data (that is, if the volume block size is set to 64 KB, then a 2 KB file consumes an entire 64 KB block).

Mount Volume SYS

After creating the volumes, you are ready to mount them. Mounting a volume enables you to copy the necessary NetWare files onto the drive.

You can mount a volume using INSTALL.NLM's Volume Options, or you can press Alt+Esc, switching from the INSTALL utility back to the server's console prompt. At the console, type the following:

MOUNT SYS

After pressing Enter, a message appears indicating that the volume is in the process of mounting.

Copying Public and System Files

Before continuing you should have first completed the following tasks: loaded SERVER.EXE, assigned a name and IPX number to the server, loaded INSTALL, defined a NetWare partition, created a volume SYS, and mounted volume SYS. After performing these initial installation steps, you are ready to install the NetWare files to the file server.

From Install's main menu, select System Options, as seen in figure 45.3.

Remember the SYS volume must be mounted before the operations in this menu selection can be used.

 If the volume is not mounted and one of these items is selected, a dialog box appears asking if you would like to mount volume SYS. To mount the volume, simply select the YES option.

Selecting System options provides access to the operations.

Figure 45.3

The System Files option of Install's main menu.

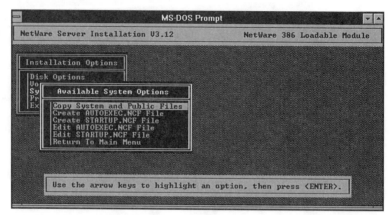

To install NetWare's operating system files and utility files, select Copy System and Public Files. You are then given the option either to insert the NetWare disks in the A drive, or to press F6 to change the location of the source drive.

> **Note** In NetWare 3.11 you have to load INSTALL with a /J parameter to be able to change the location of the source drive.

With either version, the source drive does not necessarily have to be a floppy drive; it can be a CD-ROM, a NetWare mapped drive, or even a DOS partition on the same drive.

Loading the LAN Driver

Much like disk drivers, LAN card drivers are an integral part of the network installation. They enable the server to communicate with other network stations (workstations and servers). NetWare 4 ships with several LAN drivers; but they, like disk drivers, are the responsibility of the card manufacturer. Again, contact the manufacturer to obtain the most current drivers.

Before installing a network card driver, you need to perform the following tasks:

- Select the correct interrupt

- Verify the I/O port and memory addresses

- Choose your network's frame type

- Bind the LAN driver to a network address

An IRQ is an Interrupt Request Line that enables the computer to interrupt whatever the processor is doing so some other "important" job can be completed, such as receiving a packet coming across the Ethernet card.

Unfortunately, confusion explodes when more than one device is using the same interrupt (IRQ); even more unfortunate is the difficulty of determining what devices are using what interrupts. The scarcity of interrupts and the confusion caused by not understanding which device uses which interrupt, makes resolving interrupt conflicts one of the most difficult network workstation problems.

If, for example, the addition of a sound card or modem to a network workstation—a workstation that has been functioning properly—causes problems, most likely you have placed a new device at the same interrupt as an existing device.

Each card in the computer's bus must use a different IRQ setting, including the Ethernet, Token Ring, or ARCNET card that hooks your computer to the network cable.

If two cards, or devices, are using the same IRQ setting, a conflict occurs: either the machine hangs up or one of the cards is completely ignored. The best way to determine the current setting is to use a software diagnostic utility or consult your PC documentation.

An Ethernet or other network board driver could load when the wrong interrupt is specified, causing a tremendous amount of confusion. The entire installation might appear to have gone smoothly, yet no stations are able to connect to the server.

After the actual loading of the LAN driver, you need to specify the frame type(s) your network is currently running. You also need to bind the driver to a specific network address.

You should have already loaded the LAN card, selected an interrupt, selected an I/O port, and chosen a memory address. After completing these steps, continue loading the network card driver by performing the following steps:

- At the server's console, type **BIND *IPX* to *NE2000*.** *IPX* is the protocol you are using, and *NE2000* is the name of the driver you previously loaded.

- Enter the appropriate network address.

The BIND command is one of the final steps in the LAN driver loading process. It's the step that links the LAN driver to a communication protocol and to a specific network board in the NetWare server. Unless you link a communication protocol to the board, the board cannot process packets.

NetWare 3.1*x* allows protocols other than IPX to function on the network. The following steps use IPX as an example protocol to bind each LAN driver to the file server.

To bind IPX to each LAN driver, type the following:

```
BIND IPX to LAN_driver
```

 It is only necessary to use the BIND command the first time you load a LAN driver, or if you have not previously saved the BIND command in the AUTOEXEC.NCF file. If you let the INSTALL utility create an AUTOEXEC.NCF file for you, the BIND command and the correct parameters are added to the AUTOEXEC.NCF file, and thus, loaded each time the server is brought up.

This binds only to IPX. For other protocols, you must edit the AUTOEXEC.NCF file, or manually enter additional bind commands.

It is also important to note that you can link more than one frame type to the same network board. If you want an Ethernet card to run both 802.2 and 802.3 frame types, for example, simply load the network card driver again. You are then given the following message:

```
Do you want to add another frame type for a
previously loaded board?
```

If you do, press **Y**.

NetWare displays a message (see fig. 45.5) indicating all available frame types for that particular network board (ones that are not currently loaded) (see fig. 45.4).

To load an additional frame type, enter the number to the left of the listed frame type.

Each LAN driver must be assigned the correct network address; that is, it must be assigned the network address that correctly identifies the cabling system on which it resides. In other words, the same network address must be assigned to all the network cars needed to communicate with similar LAN drivers on the network.

If this is the first server on the network, any random network address will work.

If this is not the first server on the network, you need to know the correct network address of the LAN segment to which the server is attached, as executed in the following command:

```
BIND IPX to LAN_driver NET=A
```

The network address is not the same as the internal IPX network number that you assigned to the file server.

If you are using multiple frame types on a single LAN, you must assign a different network address for each of the loaded and bound frame types on any given segment or card.

The network address is an eight-digit hexadecimal number that uniquely identifies a server's network boards and cable segments. A network address identifies a network cabling scheme, much like a node number identifies a network station along the cable. Each packet on a network is stamped with a source and destination address, which consists of a network address and a node number.

A network, therefore, is a single cabling scheme identified by a unique address to which one or more stations are attached, each of which are identified by numbers unique along the network.

There is no set convention for assigning network numbers—they are arbitrary (unless your company has a set policy for network numbering/naming conventions).

Figure 45.5 shows a multiserver network, along with the network numbers and node addresses.

Multiple servers on one network have the capability to route packets back and forth. This connection means the clients hooked to this segment (wire) will be able to see all the servers on the same network segment. It also means that all the servers on this segment must be using the same network number (if they are using the same frame type).

Further, with NetWare, a server can internally route between different network segments. If server A, for example, is using a different protocol (perhaps ARCNET) than server D (using Ethernet), you can use server B to route packets between the two different protocols (see fig. 45.6).

By having one of the network servers internally route between different protocols, the users on each segment are able to access both of the servers. In other words, users on the ARCNET segment are able to access the server using Ethernet, even though their workstations do not have Ethernet cards.

Figure 45.4
Available frame type screen.

```
                              MS-DOS Prompt
COMPAQ:LOAD NE2000
Loading module NE2000.LAN
Do you want to add another frame type for a previously loaded board? y
Supported frame types for NE2000 using I/O Port 340h to 35Fh, Interrupt 4h are:
     1. ETHERNET_II
     2. ETHERNET_SNAP
Select new frame type:
     Attempt to reinitialize re-entrant module FAILED
COMPAQ:
```

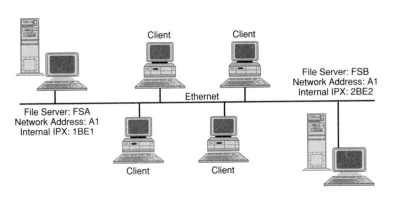

Figure 45.5

A multiserver network.

The first time you load a network card, the driver automatically loads a frame type. The default frame type for NetWare 3.12 is 802.2; the default frame type for NetWare 3.11 is 802.3. Consequently, if you want the two servers to communicate, you need to change the frame types to be the same or load both frame types on all the servers.

Loading both frame types on all the servers increases the amount of packets each server has to look at. Thus, performance is affected—the slower the server, the more it is affected.

Creating AUTOEXEC.NCF and STARTUP.NCF Files

After SERVER.EXE is loaded, the STARTUP.NCF and AUTOEXEC.NCF files are automatically loaded. These files contain the necessary information to bring up the server. The files are usually created with the INSTALL utility during the installation procedure.

The STARTUP.NCF file is loaded first. It contains those settings that must be present before NetWare actually loads (it can be compared to DOS's CONFIG.SYS file). It holds the disk controllers

NetWare driver commands, for example, which must be loaded before you can access any NetWare drives.

The AUTOEXEC.NCF file stores the server name and internal network number, loads the LAN drivers and setting for the network boards, and binds the protocols to the installed network drivers. Just as with DOS's AUTOEXEC.BAT file, you can also launch other programs or utilities, such as MONITOR, or INSTALL.

 An NCF file can be used just as a DOS batch file. If you have a list of commands that you load on a regular basis but do not want to include them in your AUTOEXEC.NCF file, you can simply create an NCF file using any text editor. The only requirement is that you use the NCF extension, just as you have to use the BAT extension when naming a DOS batch file.

The AUTOEXEC.NCF is located on the SYS volume in the system directory. Remember, the AUTOEXEC.NCF is used to load modules and to set the NetWare operation system's configuration. It stores items such as the server's name, internal IPX number, and other configuration options.

Figure 45.6
Internal routing.

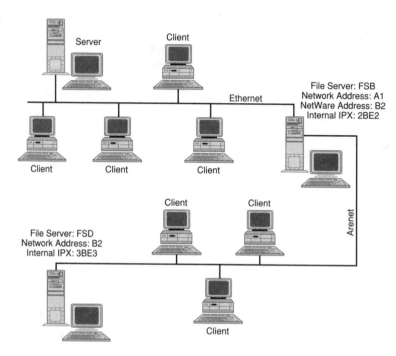

To create an AUTOEXEC.NCF or START UP.NCF file, select System Options from Install's main menu. The Available System Options screen appears. From this menu you can select one of the following options:

- Copy Public and System Files
- Create AUTOEXEC.NCF File
- Create STARTUP.NCF File
- Edit AUTOEXEC.NCF File
- Edit STARTUP.NCF File
- Return to Main Menu

After making one of the above NCF file selections, an editing screen appears. If you do not currently have an AUTOEXEC.NCF file, the screen displays the files that have been manually loaded at the server's console since the server was last loaded. If you do have an AUTOEXEC.NCF file, select the EDIT option; the editing screen then displays the

commands currently in the AUTOEXEC.NCF file. Add or delete the commands you want. Press Esc to save the changes.

Remember, commands loaded by the STARTUP.NCF are the first files loaded by the NetWare operating system; so the STARTUP.NCF file contains such commands as disk drivers, name-space option, and various SET parameters. Because these options have to be loaded before a volume is mounted, the STARTUP.NCF file is located on your boot device.

After choosing the Create STARTUP.NCF File option, an editing screen appears. This screen displays the commands loaded when you first brought up the server. If the commands listed are sufficient, simply press Esc and type **Y** to save the changes. If the commands need editing, make the necessary changes and then press Esc.

Changes made to the STARTUP.NCF do not take effect until the server is downed and brought back up. The STARTUP.NCF file needs to be located on the boot device (DOS partition).

Differences between a NetWare 3.11 and NetWare 3.12 Installation

One the biggest differences between NetWare 3.11 and 3.12 is that 3.12 can be installed from a CD-ROM drive.

The steps are the same when installing from disk, but some of the default settings have changed. The default frame type for NetWare 3.11 is 802.3, for example, and the default frame type for NetWare 3.12 is 802.2.

CD-ROM Installation Issues

Because NetWare 3.12 can be installed from a CD-ROM drive, you should become familiar with CD-ROM drive installation issues; they are covered in this next section.

The steps you need to complete to gain access to your CD-ROM device depend on the type of CD-ROM you are using. CD-ROM devices are available in several different interfaces. These different interface styles are usually determined by the type of controller providing a link between the CD-ROM drive and the computer. The Five most popular CD-ROM interface types are CD-ROMs that use a proprietary interface controller; CD-ROM drives that hook to a Sound Blaster controller interface; CD-ROM drives that hook to a computer's parallel port; CD-ROMS that use the IDE channel; and CD-ROM drives that use the SCSI interface. Each of these is capable of installing NetWare, but if you want to have NetWare access the CD-ROM device after the operating system is installed, you want a SCSI type CD-ROM device. SCSI CD-ROM drives also usually provide the best throughput and access times (that is, they are faster).

A SCSI CD-ROM hooks to a SCSI controller, which provides the CD-ROM device access to the computer's bus. After having gained access to the computer's bus, you need to make sure that the drive and controller "hook into" the operating system. This connection between the operating systems and the CD-ROM is usually accomplished by loading operating specific drivers. You need a driver for DOS and a driver for NetWare. The driver for DOS enables you to access the CD-ROM device as a DOS drive.

Gaining access to a SCSI CD-ROM device from DOS usually consists of several steps. First, you need SCSI software for DOS, obtainable from the manufacturer of the SCSI controller or from a third-party software developer. You also need a DOS device driver, which usually ships with your version of DOS. MS DOS 6.O, for example, ships with a Microsoft CD-ROM extension driver called MSCDEX.EXE. This file needs to be loaded and is usually found in your AUTOEXEC.BAT file. The Microsoft CD-ROM extension file often ships with your CD-ROM configuration. You must be certain, however, that the MSCDEX.EXE file matches the version of DOS you are using.

If your CD-ROM extension does not match your DOS version, an error message appears, informing you that an incorrect version of DOS is being used. If this happens, either find the correct version of the MSCDEX.EXE file, or add this file and the correct DOS version to DOS's SETVER.EXE file listing. Also, add the SETVER.EXE command to your CONFIG.SYS file. (See your DOS manual for further instructions on how to add a file to the SETVER.EXE listing as well as how to load device drivers from your CONFIG.SYS file).

After gaining access from DOS to the CD-ROM device, most of the battle is over.

NetWare 3.12's INSTALL.BAT File

NetWare 3.12 has an install batch file utility. When this utility is launched, it starts an automatic installation routine, which simplifies the installation process by automatically loading SERVER.EXE. It then provides the following prompts:

- Create and format a DOS partition

- Create DOS partition (optional)

- Prompt for a server name

- Assign an IPX internal number

- Copy the NetWare 3.12 server boot files to the server 3.12 directory on the DOS partition

- Set code page information

- Select DOS filename format

- Create an AUTOEXEC.BAT file

- Load SERVER.EXE

NetWare 3.12 ships with the necessary portions of DOS to create and format a DOS partition. If you have a DOS partition already created and you start the INSTALL.BAT file, you are asked if you want to retain or create new DOS partition information.

If you select to create new DOS partition information, all current information on the DOS partition is lost.

In NetWare 3.12, you are prompted for each of these steps. After completing them, you must complete the following tasks (just as in NetWare 3.11).

1. Load INSTALL.NLM.

2. Create a NetWare partition.

3. Create a NetWare volume.

4. Mount volume SYS.

5. Copy public and system files to the file server.

6. Load the LAN driver.

7. Edit AUTOEXEC.NCF and STARTUP.NCF files.

For information regarding any of the individual steps, see the "Installing NetWare 3.11" section of this chapter.

The Automatically Installed File System

During the previous steps, you will have copied the public and system file to your new NetWare file server. Most of the files are copied into one of two directories: the Public directory or the System directory.

The files that need to be accessed by the majority of—or by all—the NetWare users are located in the Public directory (that is, the SYS:PUBLIC directory). This general-access directory is created automatically and is also flagged as being read-only. Files located in the directory cannot be erased without changing the file's attributes.

NetWare utilities, help files, and some message and data files (such as the system log in script file and the NET$LOG.DAT) are public files to which all NetWare users have Read, Open, and Search rights.

The files accessed primarily by the network system's supervisor, or by the system itself, are copied into the SYS:SYSTEM directory.

Questions

1. Which of the following information is NOT needed when you are installing NetWare 3.12?

   ○ A. Server Name

   ○ B. Serial number

   ○ C. Disk Type

   ○ D. LAN Driver Type

2. Which of the following LAN card information is needed during a NetWare 3.12 installation?

   ☐ A. Frame Type(for Ethernet)

   ☐ B. LAN Driver Type

   ☐ C. I/O address

   ☐ D. Interrupt (for ISA bus)

3. Which of the following sequences best describes a NetWare 3.12 installation?

   ○ A. Load Disk driver, load DOS, load LAN driver, load NetWare

   ○ B. Load NetWare, load LAN driver, load disk driver, configure DOS

   ○ C. Load DOS, invoke SERVER.EXE, load disk driver, configure NetWare, copy NetWare files

   ○ D. Copy NetWare files, invoke DOS, load LAN driver, load disk driver, start SERVER.EXE

4. After loading the LAN driver, you must also complete which of the following steps?

   ○ A. Reentrantly load any other frame types

   ○ B. Bind communications by attaching the communication protocol to the correct LAN driver

   ○ C. Enter the correct network number for the cable that will be attached to the network adapter

   ○ D. All of the above

5. Which of the following file sequences is the most correct?

   ○ A. AUTOEXEC.NCF, STARTUP.NCF, SERVER.EXE, AUTOEXEC.BAT

   ○ B. AUTOEXEC.BAT, SERVER.EXE, STARTUP.NCF, AUTOEXEC.NCF

   ○ C. STARTUP.NCF, SERVER.EXE, AUTOEXEC.NCF, AUTOEXEC.BAT

   ○ D. SERVER.EXE, STARTUP.NCF, AUTOEXEC.BAT, AUTOEXEC.NCF

6. Which of the following names must be assigned to the first volume on a NetWare server.

   ○ A. VOL1

   ○ B. SYS

   ○ C. SERVER

   ○ D. PUBLIC

7. Which of the following directories is NOT created for you automatically?

   ○ A. Applications

   ○ B. Public

○ C. System

○ D. Mail

8. A file server name is automatically generated for you.

○ A. T

○ B. F

9. Each server on any given cable segment should have an identical internal IPX number.

○ A. T

○ B. F

10. During the protocol binding process, you must enter a network number for the server that is the same as all other servers on that particular wire segment.

○ A. T

○ B. F

11. Under normal operations, you will have to assign a network number for every LAN card in the server.

○ A. T

○ B. F

12. During installation, an internal IPX number is randomly generated for you. This number can be changed as long as it is unique from any other server on the network.

○ A. T

○ B. F

Answers

1. B

2. A, B, C, D

3. C

4. D

5. B

6. B

7. A

8. F

9. F

10. T

11. T

12. T

46

Migrating a 3.11 Server to a 3.12 Server

*P*art of a NetWare administrator's job is to keep the system up to date. This often requires that you upgrade NetWare itself. Currently, there are several methods to upgrade NetWare. The method you use will depend on your current situation, as well as the hardware you will have available. This section covers all the available migration tools, as well as their options.

In this chapter, you'll learn about the utilities used for a NetWare 3.11 to 3.12 migration, suggested preparations to perform prior to an upgrade, the procedures and results of the NetWare 3.11 to 3.12 upgrade, and how to upgrade a 3.11 server to a 3.12 server.

Overview

Before upgrading you should take the opportunity to "clean up" or perform some housekeeping tasks on your file server before actually starting the migration processes. The following list contains examples of "housecleaning tasks" that should be done before you begin a server migration:

1. Delete any outdated users or groups.

2. Verify all your user default settings (as you want them on the new server).

3. Eliminate unnecessary security equivalencies and workgroup or user account manager designations.

4. Verify the security of the system with the SECURITY.EXE file.

5. Run BINDFIX.

6. Remove unnecessary files from user directories and public areas.

7. Restrict the directory tree depth to 25 subdirectories.

8. Perform two complete system backups.

9. Verify that you have at least 6 MB of RAM on the server.

10. Verify that you have at least 25 MB of free space on your server's SYS volume.

11. Log out all user and print servers from the server.

12. Guard against users logging in during the upgrade (type DISABLE LOGIN at the console).

13. Verify that the frame types and other communication parameters are the same for both servers.

14. Bring down the server that is to be upgraded.

Besides performing some of the housekeeping tasks in the preceding list, you should make sure you are using the best possible migration utility. Table 46.1 lists the advantages and disadvantages of each migration option.

Table 46.1
NetWare Upgrade Advantages and Disadvantages

Upgrade from–to	Options	Advantages	Disadvantages
Upgrade 2.*x* to 3.12	Across-the-wire to an installed 3.1 server	No risk of data loss	Need a 3.12 server installed
		Can migrate many servers to one server	
		Can choose what data you want to migrate	
		Can direct data to specific volumes or directories	

Upgrade from–to	Options	Advantages	Disadvantages
	Same-server migration	Can choose what data you want to migrate	Some risk of data loss Need a workstation (or tape backup) with enough disk space for data files
	In-place upgrade from 2.1*x* or 2.2 to 3.12	Need only one 2.1*x* server	Cannot upgrade from 2.0a Need 80386 or higher processor If upgrade fails, you may have to restore your 2.1*x* data from backup
NetWare 3.*x* to 3.12	Across-the-wire to an installed 3.12 server	No risk of data loss Can migrate many servers to one server Can choose what data you want to migrate Can direct data to specific volumes or directories	Need a 3.12 server installed
	Same-server migration	Can choose what data you want to migrate	Some risk of data loss Need a workstation or tape device capable of handling all your current data
	In-place upgrade from 3.*x* to 3.12	Just need one 3.*x* server—no additional hardware is needed	Cannot upgrade from 3.0 If upgrade fails, you will have to use a backup to restore the server to its original state

Note Regardless of the migration method used, you want to have a solid, reliable, proven backup. It is good practice and recommended that you have at least two verified backups of your data and bindery information before starting any major work on the server, including a migration.

The following sections discuss each migration method in more detail.

Across-the-Wire Migration

Across-the-wire migration is a method of migrating your existing data and bindery files from a NetWare 3.1x file server to a 3.12 server (see fig. 46.1). Across-the-wire migration is a workstation-based utility that transfers your network information (files, users, print queues, and so on) to a working directory on the workstation's hard drive (the workstation from which you start the migration utility). The bindery and files are then translated into 3.12 format so that they can be transferred to the new server. After translation, the objects are placed in the 3.12 file server's bindery.

The across-the-wire method provides you the option of migrating your data from your old server to a new server that is attached to the same physical network. With across-the-wire migration utility you also can temporarily copy information from the old server to a workstation and then transfer it back to your original server, in the new format. This same-server approach is more risky, but does not require a second server. Migrating across-the-wire to a new server leaves the existing server and all of its information intact, and is much safer (you can always go back to the old server).

The following list contains information that should be migrated during a system upgrade.

- ■ User information:

   Login scripts

   Account restrictions

   Station restrictions

   Time restrictions

   Security equivalencies

Figure 46.1

Across-the-wire migration.

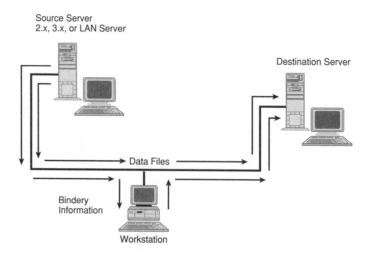

- Printing information:

  Print queues

  Print queue users and operators

  Print servers

  Print server users and operators

  Print server control files

- Information about groups:

  Group rights

  Group members

- Default account restrictions

- Accounting information

The following information should not be migrated:

- Data files

- Passwords

- Volume restrictions

The following list explains some key points on data and server migration when the across-the-wire method is used:

- NetWare 3.1*x* file server system files are not migrated.

- A file on the source server will not be copied if the file name already exists on the destination server (an error will be listed in the error log).

- The system login script is not migrated.

- User login scripts are migrated.

- If the destination server contains a directory with the same name as a directory on the source server, then the files in both directories will be merged.

- During a server consolidation, if users with the same user name exist on more than one file server, the user accounts will be merged.

The Same-Server Method

The same-server migration takes the bindery information on an existing 3.11 server, copies it to a working directory on a workstation, upgrades (translates) the bindery information into a 3.12 format, then migrates it from the workstation back to the server.

The MIGRATE.EXE utility is located on the NetWare 3.12 CD-ROM in the following directory:

    D:\CLIENT_____\MIGRATE\ENGLISH

There are two options with the MIGRATE.EXE utility: Custom migration and Standard migration. The Custom option, as its name implies, enables you to select from a list the information that you want migrated. This selection process enables you to create a custom destination server.

Although the Standard migration option is less flexible and therefore easier to use, it migrates all information from the source server, across the network, to the destination server. You cannot select specific information to migrate; all data files and LAN information are automatically migrated.

The same-server upgrade uses a DOS client station to manage the migration process and uses the same computer as both the source and the destination device (see fig. 46.1). This method does not migrate data, so you must back up your data files and restore them to the server after NetWare 3.12 is completely installed.

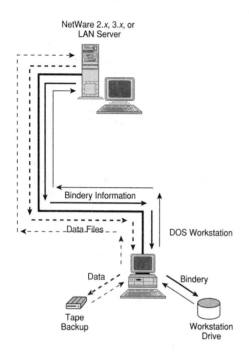

NetWare 2.*x*, 3.*x*, or
LAN Server

Bindery Information

Data Files

DOS Workstation

Data

Bindery

Tape
Backup

Workstation
Drive

Figure 46.2

Same-server migration.

After creating a backup, you use the
MIGRATE.EXE utility to migrate the bindery
information to the working directory of the client.
Now the server is ready to have NetWare 3.12
installed as a new installation. Restore the data
from the tape backup and then execute the migration utility to migrate the bindery information to
the new NetWare 3.12 server.

 Passwords are not migrated to the
NetWare 3.12 server. The utility assigns
either random passwords or no passwords. If you choose to have random passwords
assigned, a file (NEW.PWD) is created in the SYS:
SYSTEM directory. This file contains a list of all the
users' passwords.

The in-place upgrade method involves the following four phases:

- Analysis of the file system
- Analysis of the disk drives
- Modification of the disk drives
- Creation of a NetWare 3.12 bindery

Phase one, the analysis of the file system, takes
inventory of the disk drives and attempts to determine how much memory is required to complete
the upgrade process.

Phase two, the disk analysis, locates the Hot Fix
area, File Allocation Tables, and Directory Entry
Tables. It then re-creates such areas on the new
NetWare 3.12 server. The Directory Entry Tables
and File Allocation Tables are translated, and directory file attributes are upgraded.

 Macintosh files also are migrated. Be
sure to load the Macintosh Name
Space on any volumes that contain
Macintosh files, however.

Phase two also verifies that you have enough memory to complete the upgrade process. If you do not
have enough memory, the procedure will halt. You
can restart it again after more memory is added.

Phase three is the phase in which modification of
data on the disk actually occurs—the partition
table is upgraded and the system files are written to
the system area (track zero).

If the upgrade process fails or is stopped during
phase three of the upgrade, you have to restore the
old NetWare 2.*x* file server to its original state and
start the migration process again.

Phase four, creation of a NetWare 3.12 bindery, upgrades the 2.1x bindery to a 3.1x bindery. As with the MIGRATE.EXE, you have the option to have the system generate random passwords, or you can perform the migration without passwords (passwords are not migrated).

Performing the 3.11 to 3.12 Upgrade Steps

This section provides you with the steps necessary to perform an upgrade from a NetWare 3.11 to a 3.12 file server:

1. Start the INSTALL.BAT file from the 3.12 server CD-ROM by changing to the *<CD-ROM Drive>*:\NETWARE\ENGLISH directory and typing **INSTALL.BAT**.

2. Access the upgrade portion of the NetWare 3.12 installation utility (see fig. 46.3).

3. Copy files to the DOS partition.

At this point you are given some information about drivers that were not copied to the new server. It is important that you verify that none of these drivers need to be used.

4. Assign locale information—country code, code page, and keyboard mappings—and file format. The DOS file format is almost always recommended.

5. Decide whether to invoke the existing STARTUP.NCF file.

Usually you will not invoke the STARTUP.NCF file unless all the disk controller drivers and other startup paramaters are identical. If these files are not identical and the STARTUP.NCF is used, errors occur and the boot process is halted. Thus, it is better to skip the STARTUP.NCF file and load the drivers manually (unless you have settings that have to be loaded from the STARTUP.NCF file—for example, memory settings).

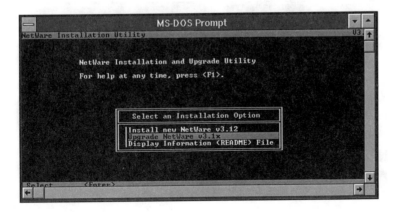

Figure 46.3

Selecting to upgrade an existing NetWare 3.1x server.

Perform the following steps if you did not invoke the STARTUP.NCF file:

1. Assign a server name.

2. Start SERVER.EXE.

3. Assign an IPX internal network number.

4. Load the disk driver.

5. Mount all volumes (load name spaces).

6. Load the INSTALL.NLM from the DOS partition.

7. Install system and public files to the SYS volume (see fig. 46.4).

8. Load and bind the LAN driver.

9. Verify that the AUTOEXEC.NCF and STARTUP.NCF files contain the appropriate changes.

10. Reboot the server using the newly created AUTOEXEC and STARTUP files.

11. Log in to the NetWare 3.12 server as a user that existed on the old server, to verify the migration.

Post-Migration Procedures

After you finish the migration process, perform the following tasks before you count the migration as complete:

1. Update user login scripts.

2. Check system login scripts.

3. Check user restrictions and accounting change rates.

4. Check printing services.

5. Test your applications.

6. Check data integrity.

After all these procedures are complete you should make a backup of the new server.

Figure 46.4

Copying the public and system files.

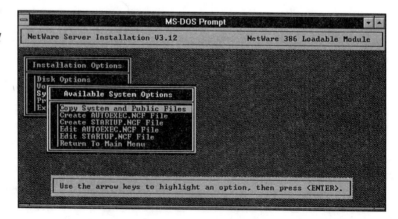

Questions

1. What information is needed prior to upgrading 3.11 to 3.12?

   ○ A. Country code information

   ○ B. Code page information

   ○ C. Keyboard mapping type

   ○ D. All of the above

2. What is the default frame type for NetWare 3.12?

   ○ A. Ethernet 802.3

   ○ B. Ethernet 802.2

   ○ C. Ethernet_SNAP

   ○ D. TCP/IP

3. Which TWO of the following are valid file name formats for a NetWare server?

   ☐ A. DOS

   ☐ B. HPFS

   ☐ C. NT Advanced server

   ☐ D. NetWare

4. Which TWO of the following are valid migration methods?

   ☐ A. Across-the-wire

   ☐ B. Same server

   ☐ C. Backup and restore

   ☐ D. Restore

5. During a migration, you have the opportunity not to use the STARTUP.NCF file. Which of the following is a reason not to invoke the STARTUP.NCF file?

   ○ A. Country code information has changed.

   ○ B. The default frametype has changed.

   ○ C. The LAN card is different.

   ○ D. The Disk controller drive is different.

6. When performing a 3.11 to 3.12 migration, which of the following are true?

   ☐ A. NetWare system files are not migrated.

   ☐ B. Code page information must be entered.

   ☐ C. AUTOEXEC.NCF files must be changed to reflect the default frametype changes.

   ☐ D. Passwords will not be migrated.

7. Starting the NetWare 3.12 INSTALL.BAT file will give you access to which TWO of the following migration utilities?

   ☐ A. Custom migration

   ☐ B. Standard migration

   ☐ C. 2XUPDATE.NLM

   ☐ D. All of the above

Answers

1. D	5. D
2. B	6. A, B, C, D
3. A, D	7. A, B
4. A, B	

Installing Client Software

This chapter provides you with much more than the basic steps for installing a NetWare client. It also provides you with an understanding of the basic differences between the shell style client and the new requester technology, and, in addition, covers the enhancements to the client in the NetWare 3.12 software.

After you finish this section, you should be able to identify the different types of client technology and explain how to use and configure them. You also should be able to install a NetWare requester client and name the installation steps.

Client Support in NetWare 3.12

NetWare supports all the popular client platforms. This section informs you of the types of clients NetWare supports, as well as some of the software required for each particular client technology. NetWare 3.1*x* supports the following types of clients:

- Macintosh
- OS/2, 2.1 and above
- Unix
- DOS (Windows)

Macintosh

NetWare 3.12 now includes a five-user version of NetWare for Macintosh version 3.12. It also is backward compatible with 3.11, and incorporates software fixes and the management utilities necessary for some of the system administrator functions to be completed from a Macintosh client.

If you need to support more than five Macintosh clients, you can buy a separate 200-user license.

OS/2

NetWare 3.1*x* supports OS/2 2.1 and above.

OS/2 remote printing support uses NPRINTER.EXE rather than RPRINTER.EXE. NPRINTER.EXE is the same remote printing file used in NetWare 4.*x*.

Unix

For Unix support, NetWare includes routing services for TCP/IP connections. The necessary files are placed in the SYS:ETC and SYS:SYSTEM directories of the automatically installed file system.

To support a Unix client on a NetWare 3.12 server, use version 1.2b of NetWare for NFS.

DOS

NetWare also obviously supports DOS-based machines (with or without Windows).

The DOS support includes the following software components:

- Open Data LINK interface (ODI)
- NetWare DOS Requester
- NetWare DOS *Virtual Loadable Module* (VLM)

All your clients should run the latest version of the DOS requester. If you run the latest version of the requester, you provide your DOS clients with the most stable and feature-rich network client support.

Open Data-Link Interface (ODI) provides flexibility by supporting multiple transport protocols for a single network board. Before ODI, multiple-protocol support required that you install multiple network boards in each of the client stations, not to mention reset the workstation whenever the board or transport method was needed. The ODI client drivers include the following files:

- LSL.COM (Link Support Layer)

- LAN driver file (Multiple Link interface driver or MLID)

- IPXODI.COM (Communication protocol)

These three files replace the older, dedicated IPX.COM file that was generated using WSGEN.EXE or SHELLGEN.EXE. The older IPX.COM driver was incapable of simultaneously supporting multiple protocols.

Furthermore, DOS technologies have been updated from shell to requester. The DOS Requester is required to use NetWare 4.x as well as to get all of the functionality from 3.12. The new requester technology, for instance, provides a NetWare DOS client the following functionality:

- Memory swapping technology and DOS redirection capabilities

- Faster client speeds and response times with Packet Burst

- Enhanced MS windows client support

- Backward compatibility with NETX.EXE

Furthermore, the new client design incorporates modularity, which ensures that the Requester is equipped for future functionality.

Differences between the Shell and Requester

In the NetWare 3.x shell, NETX.EXE acts as a front end for DOS, intercepting user and application requests before they reach NetWare. Any commands heading for the workstation operating system are intercepted, interpreted, and then passed to the appropriate location—DOS or NetWare. So, if the request is not for the network, the shell passes the instructions on to DOS. If the request is for the network, the instructions are passed to NetWare.

The DOS requester has the following two components:

- The Manager (VLM.EXE)

- Virtual Loadable Modules (VLMs)

The manager component, or VLM.EXE, loads and subsequently manages the VLMs. Its major responsibilities include the following:

- Handling requests from applications and routing them to the proper VLM

- Managing communication between modules

- Controlling memory services, allocation, and management

The Virtual Loadable Modules are composed of small pieces of code, which are files that have a VLM extension.

Each VLM provides a specific function. For instance, the PRINT.VLM controls printing functions. VLMs can be one of two types:

- Child VLMs

- Multiplexer (Parent VLMs)

The VLM manager transparently loads a *child VLM* into the workstation's memory. You also can specify which VLMs the VLM manager loads by placing or removing them from the NET.CFG (network configuration) file. If you choose to specify the load files, know that you must load child VLMs before their associated multiplexers.

In the past, Novell has used the Shell, however, they are moving to a requester style client for several technical reasons.

The files that compose the VLM technology can be arranged into the three following layers, as seen in figure 47.1:

- **DOS Redirection Layer.** Provides all the DOS file services through the DOS redirecter (REDIR.VLM).

- **Service Protocol Layer.** Contains several parallel services, such as NWP.VLM, RSA.VLM, FIO.VLM, and PRINT.VLM, each of which contains several other "child" VLMs.

  - NWP.VLM

  - RSA.VLM

  - FIO.VLM

  - PRINT.VLM

- **Transport Protocol Layer.** Mechanism responsible for maintaining the connections, providing packet transmissions between connections and performing other transport-specific functions.

The requester performs the same functions as a shell—passes information from the client to the network operating system—but does so differently. The NetWare shell had to retain its own set of internal resource tables for network file and print services. In contrast, the more tightly integrated DOS Requester can actually share resource tables with DOS, thereby eliminating the need to maintain redundant tables and decreasing memory requirements for the DOS Requester.

If DOS receives a request it cannot service, it uses the interrupt to call a redirected service (REDIR.VLM). When an application makes a request to DOS, for example, DOS first attempts to qualify the request to determine ownership of the requested resource, such as a drive letter, a file handle, or a print device. If DOS determines that it does not own the resource, DOS polls the redirecters to allow them to determine ownership. If a redirecter claims ownership, DOS then makes the appropriate calls to that redirecter so that it can complete the request.

As part of the Requester technology, Novell has made it possible for workstations running applications that use the old DOS shell calls to be compatible with the new Requester technology.

Figure 47.1

Novell's client arcitecture.

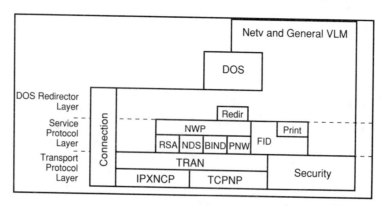

Owing to the different methods they use to manage resources, the NetWare shell (NETX.EXE) and the DOS Requester (VLM.EXE) cannot coexist, meaning that you cannot load them together. After you install the VLM client kit for Windows, in fact, you have to use the VLMs.

The architecture of the Requester technology is much more modular than its Shell counterpart, enabling you to set up the VLMs in a variety of memory configurations. You can load them into extended memory, expanded memory, or conventional memory. You even can make the VLMs use the upper memory blocks, if any exist. When you load VLM.EXE, it relocates its startup code at the top of conventional memory, which enables it to load and unload modules as needed, so memory is not unnecessarily waited. In a sense, the VLM.EXE file is its own memory manager; when you load the VLM.EXE, it temporarily loads each of the VLM modules specified by the NET.CFG file for loading. After it loads each module, it reports its ID, memory requirements, and global transient information.

 This temporary loading procedure causes a series of dots to appear on-screen. During this initialization stage, each VLM module executes its initialization code, including initializing internal variables, hooking interrupts, notifying other VLMs of its presence, and detecting the presence of other dependent VLMs.

Because VLM.EXE now knows the amount of memory each module can use, it can calculate the total memory requirement for the overall configuration. It then sets aside enough memory for the transient portions and the global portions for each requester module.

The global portion contains the global segments of each VLM's code. After initialization, the global segment is stored in conventional memory or, if available, the upper memory blocks. This code often must remain in conventional memory for compatibility or backward compatibility issues.

VLM.EXE automatically detects and selects the type of memory that is available. After it determines the available memory, it allocates its use. It tries to use the best possible configuration by using extended memory first, expanded memory second, and conventional memory last. If you do not have a memory manager loaded, VLM.EXE must reserve space in conventional memory for both the global and transient portions of VLM module code, which can quickly consume memory.

To determine where the VLMs transient portions are loaded, use the following command-line commands: /mx, /me, and, /mc (extended, expanded, and conventional).

The transient portion is often called the Swap block. It consists of the sections of requester code that do not always have to be loaded into memory, and thus are swapped in and out of memory. The transient swap block is roughly the size of the largest VLM module at initialization, but afterward is reduced to match the largest transient segment of the largest VLM module.

VLM Functions fall into one of the following three service categories:

- DOS Redirection
- Service Protocol
- Transport Protocol

You use REDIR.VLM to manage DOS redirection services. The Service protocols portion of the VLM technology handles requests for very specific services, such as connection establishment, broadcast messages, file reads and writes, and print redirection, whereas the Transport protocol portion of the VLMs handles maintaining server connections and providing packet transmissions and other transport-related services.

NET.CFG File

The VLM-Requester technology is modular and uses the NET.CFG file or its configuration. The following section provides you with some examples of different configurations optimized for different situations. You use entries in the NET.CFG file to change the workstations network environment or configuration. For example, you might want to change the configuration for the following reasons:

- You changed the default hardware setting on your network board.

- You use Novell's LAN Workplace.

- You use multiple protocols on the same network board.

- You want to optimize your workstation's configuration.

As a rule of thumb, NET.CFG file should be located in the same directory as the rest of the VLM files.

Several different types of configuration options are set in the NET.CFG file, including the network interface card settings, protocol settings, and so on. The NET.CFG file is created during installation of the client software and can be edited with any text editor.

The NET.CFG file is similar to the old SHELL.CFG file, as well as the NET.CFG file used with the ODI drivers.

You must follow certain rules when you work with a NET.CFG file, such as the following:

- You must begin each option section at the very left of the file (flush left).

- You can list only one option per line.

    An *option section* is a line that performs a function, such as the following:

    LINK DRIVER NE2000

- Each option section can have several parameters, such as the following:

    - INT 4

    - PORT 340

    - Frame Ethernet_802.2

- You must indent each parameter line (at least one space) and locate the line beneath its respective option section (only one parameter per line).

- You must place a hard return at the end of each parameter setting in each line (including the last line of the file).

- You can remark out a text or comment line by placing REM or a semicolon in front of the line.

The NET.CFG file is not case-sensitive.

Because the VLMS is so easy to configure, you can optimize a client for several different purposes; you can configure the client for the best possible performance, memory optimization, or even for specific configuration that combines performance and memory optimization.

This section includes three sample NET.CFG files. The first grants higher performance but sacrifices memory. The second conserves memory at the expense of performance. The third and final example attempts to find a common ground at which you do not sacrifice performance for memory, nor memory for performance. In each of these example NET.CFG files, the boldface entries are by default set for a specific purpose (performance or memory). For simplicity, the options that have no relevance are omitted.

Performance

When you optimize VLMs for performance, you use about 100 KB of conventional memory.

```
CACHE WRITES = ON
CHECKSUM = 0 (only use with 802.2)
LARGE INTERNET PACKETS = ON
LOAD LOW CONN = ON
LOAD LOW IPXNCP = ON
MINIMUM TIME TO NET = ON
NETWARE PROTOCOL = NDS, BIND, PNW (only use
necessary options e.g. NDS, BIND - BIND -
PNW)
PB BUFFERS = 0
PRINT BUFFER SIZE = 256
SIGNATURE LEVEL = 0
TRUE COMMIT = OFF
```

If you are optimizing for memory, you will want to make some of the following changes in your NET.CFG file.

```
AUTO LARGE TABLE = OFF
AUTO RECONNECT = OFF
CACHE BUFFERS = 0 (PERFORMANCE HIT
AVERAGE NAME LENGTH = CALCULATED VALUE, (48-
DEFAULT)
CONNECTIONS = CALCULATED VALUE, (8 DEFAULT)
LOAD LOW CONN = OFF
LOAD LOW IPXNCP = OFF
EXCLUDE VLM = <VLM>
NETWORK PRINTERS = 0
PB BUFFERS = 0 (0 SETS PACKET BURST OFF)
PRINT HEADER = 0
PRINT TAIL = 0
SIGNATURE LEVEL = 0
```

When you optimize for memory, be sure not to load the VLMs that you don't need. The following is a list of the optional VLMs:

- AUTO.VLM_
- PRINT.VLM_
- SECURITY.VLM_
- NDS.VLM_
- BIND.VLM_
- PNW.VLM_
- NETX.VLM_
- RSA.VLM_
- WSSNMP.VLM_
- WSREG.VLM_
- WSTRAP.VLM_
- MIB2IF.VLM_
- MIN2PROT.VLM_
- NMR.VLM_

 Disabling VLMs means also disabling its respective functions. For example, disabling the last seven VLMs in the preceding list effects SNMP services. Disabling PRINT.VLM, for example, means you can't print. Disabling NDS.VLM means you can't access NetWare 4 Directory Services. Disabling BIND.VLM means you can't connect to a NetWare 3.x server.

You can disable, or not load, specific VLMs in three ways:

- Delete the VLM
- Rename the VLM file to a different name, using an extension other than VLM

■ Include the line **Exclude VLM = <VLM name>** under the NetWare DOS requester section of the NET.CFG file

VLMs come with default configurations for optimizing both memory and performance. The default values are as follows:

```
AUTO LARGE TABLE = OFF
AUTO RECONNECT = ON
AVERAGE NAME LENGTH = 48
CACHE BUFFERS = 5
CACHE BUFFER SIZE = <MAX MEDIA SIZE>
CACHE WRITES = ON
CHECKSUM = 1
CONNECTIONS = 8
LARGE INTERNET PACKET = ON
LOAD LOW CONN = ON
LOAD LOW IPXNCP = ON
MINIMUM TIME TO NET = 0
NETWARE PROTOCOL = NDS BIND PNW
NETWARE PRINTERS = 3
PB BUFFERS = 3
PRINT BUFFER SIZE = 64
PRINT HEADER = 64
PRINT TAIL = 16
SIGNATURE LEVEL = 1
TRUE COMMIT = OFF
```

The NetWare DOS requester is the preferred workstation, or client software. Some applications, however, might use specific Application Program Interfaces (API) that employ calls that can't be redirected, in which case you might need to use NETX.EXE (shells). Novell includes all the files necessary to use the older shell workstation software.

These files, NETX.EXE (and the extended and expanded memory versions), are automatically copied into the SYS:LOGIN directory during a NetWare file server installation. These files can also be retrieved from the installation disks, specifically the SYSTEM_3 disk from the LOGIN subdirectory.

The DOS requester architecture offers the following advantages:

■ Provides a modular architecture that has advantages for current and future applications

■ Takes advantage of memory-swapping technology and DOS redirection capabilities

■ Includes Packet Burst and Large Internet Packet (LIP) support

■ Provides backward compatibility with NETX.EXE

Performing Workstation Installation Steps

During the workstation software installation, you must know some specific information regarding your network boards and client configuration. The following list can help prepare you for the questions you have to answer during the installation process.

■ Interrupt your network board uses

■ Base I/O address your network board uses

■ Frame type your network uses

■ Other settings your card might use

You can usually get this information from the network boards documentation.

After you obtain the preceding information for your configuration, you need to make sure that you have the following disks:

WSDOS_1

WSWIN_1

WSDRV_1

WSDRV_2

If you install an OS/2 client, you also need the following disks:

WSOS2_1

WSOS_2

WSDRV_1

Besides these NetWare client disks, you also need to be sure to have a recent third-party driver for your network board. Because both the network cards, as well as NetWare itself, might have been sitting on a vendor's shelf, you want to verify that you are installing the latest drivers; never assume the drivers that came with the card or drivers that came with NetWare are the latest.

Installation Methods

Installing workstation software varies, depending on the type of network card you use, as well as the version of NetWare drivers you try to load. This section assumes that you use an Ethernet card and the drivers that come with NetWare (opposed to the ones that ship with your network card).

Currently three methods are available for installing the NetWare client software: from disk, from the CD-ROM, or off the server.

Installing the client software directly from the NetWare Operating System CD-ROM is simple and quick. You must, however, have a CD-ROM drive in every workstation.

When you install the NetWare server, you can create and install the client software. You always should install the client software to the server, even if it is not your preferred choice of client installation, because having the software on the server enables you to update any client software from the server if the clients are currently connected. This method of installing client software assumes that you already have client-to-file server connection, and is the best in situations where you are upgrading.

Creating Client Disks

Creating a set of client disks is absolutely necessary if all your workstations do not have CD-ROMs or if you do not currently have a client-to-server connection (and you should do so even if one or both of the above conditions are met). Creating a set of client disks requires that you have several preformatted disks before you begin duplication.

Before you can create installation disks from a NetWare 3.12 operating system CD, you must have the CD-ROM as a DOS volume or as a Network volume. After you gain access to the CD-ROM, you need to complete the following steps:

1. Use the DOS FORMAT command to format five high-density disks.

2. Change to one of the following subdirectories in the client directory of the CD-ROM:

   ■ DOSWIN

   ■ OS/2

3. Set the NWLANGUAGE environment variable by typing the following at the command line:

   `Set NWLANGUAGE=Language`

4. Type the following command:

   `MAKEDISK drive_letter`

After you enter the MAKEDISK command, you are prompted to insert the blank disk in the selected target drive. If anything at all interrupts the MAKEDISK routine, you must start over from the beginning.

The disk creation procedure simply copies the client files off the CD-ROM to disk. Thus, you really need to use blank disks. If the disks are not blank, the copy procedure returns an error indicating the disk does not have enough room, in which case, you must start all over again, regardless of the progress already made. In other words, if the last disk that you attempt to make is not blank, you must re-create the first four.

After you begin the copy procedure, a message appears indicating that the copy is in progress. After the first disk is completed, the copy routine informs you to label the disk and to insert the next disk. After all of the disks in the set are created, you are returned to the DOS prompt.

Installing from a File Server or Network Directory

To install the client software from network directory you must have all the client installation prerequisites, as well as having the client connected to the server with a previous version of the network workstation software. You must also have a complete copy of the workstation software loaded on the server.

To install the software from a file server, complete the following steps:

1. Log in to the file server.

2. Map a drive to the directory on which the client software resides.

The next section covers the basic tasks that you must do, regardless of client installation method, to successfully install the NetWare client software for a DOS workstation.

Installation Steps

DOS and MS Windows workstation share the same DOS-based installation routine. To start the client install process, type **INSTALL.**

Be sure you are completely out of Windows and not in a DOS box because the install procedure needs to modify some of the Windows files.

After you type **INSTALL**, a screen appears (see fig. 47.2).

During installation, a directory is created in the root of the drive from which you boot DOS (with the default name of \NWCLIENT). All workstation files for DOS and Windows are copied to this newly created directory, including the NetWare user tools for DOS and Windows, VLM program files, VLM manager files, Network board drivers, and Unicode tables with their corresponding code pages, numbers, and country codes.

Also, during the installation a Windows group file is automatically created. This group file contains a User tools icon.

In the first installation screen, you are asked to verify several installation options. Most of these options, such as whether you want to install MS Windows support, or whether to use the default client directory, are pretty straightforward. However, you also must identify the correct hardware and hardware settings for your network card at this installation screen.

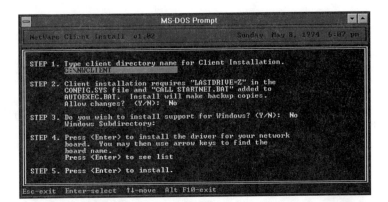

Figure 47.2
Workstation installation screen.

To select a network card, move the cursor to step four and press Enter. The screen shown in figure 47.3 then appears, from which you can select the appropriate network card.

If you currently have an older version of network software loaded, the installation routine recognizes the settings in use and simply uses the same driver and card settings. So, if you are upgrading, loading the client drivers and then installing the new client software is your best option.

If the correct network card driver can't be found, an error message appears, informing you that you have two options:

■ Copy the driver to the current directory and start the install routine over

■ Modify the LINK DRIVER section of your NET.CFG to load the appropriate driver file after the installation is completed

After you select the driver that matches your network card, you must specify the correct settings (if you have changed the card from its default

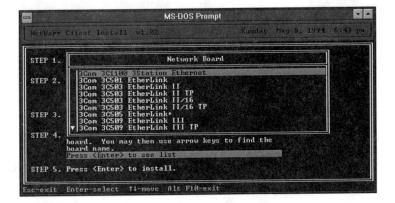

Figure 47.3
Select the appropriate network card.

settings). To specify the correct settings, select option five, and the screen shown in figure 47.4 appears.

To change the settings of your network board, highlight the location you want and press Enter. A dialog screen appears, from which you can make your selection. If you select the Hardware interrupt line, for instance, you receive the options similar to the one shown in figure 47.5.

The options box lists all of the interrupts your card supports. To select an interrupt, move the highlight bar to the correct setting and press Enter.

If you're installing from floppies, you are informed which disks you need to use. If you're installing from one of the other methods, the installation begins to copy the client files to your workstation's boot drive.

Figure 47.4

Selecting the correct network card settings.

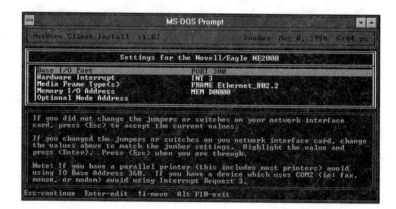

Figure 47.5

The Hardware Interrupt options box.

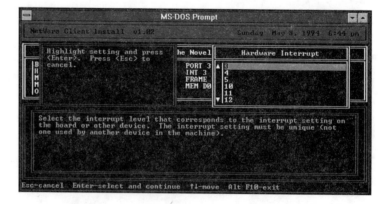

Questions

1. Which THREE of the following methods are valid client installation methods?

   ☐ A. From CD-ROM

   ☐ B. From disk

   ☐ C. From the server

   ☐ D. From the router

2. Which part of the VLM drive acts as a memory manager?

   ○ A. CONN.VLM

   ○ B. NWP.VLM

   ○ C. VLM.EXE

   ○ D. REDIR.VLM

3. Which file is used to determine the configuration of the VLMs?

   ○ A. VLM.EXE

   ○ B. AUTOEXEC.NCF

   ○ C. NET.CFG

   ○ D. AUTOEXEC.BAT

4. When using the VLM client, which of the following changes must be made to the CONFIG.SYS file?

   ○ A. LASTDRIVE=Z

   ○ B. SET NWLANGUAGE=ENGLISH

   ○ C. LASTDRIVE=F

   ○ D. BUFFERS=100

5. Which of the following are main sections of the NET.CFG file?

   ☐ A. Link Driver

   ☐ B. Link Support

   ☐ C. Protocol IPX

   ☐ D. NetWare DOS Requester

Answers

1. A, B, C

2. C

3. C

4. A

5. A, B, C, D

Tuning for Performance

The NetWare 3.1x operating system is a set of dynamically linked collections of components and software subsystems. Each component can directly or indirectly affect the performance of the entire NetWare operating system. This chapter looks at how you can optimize the following NetWare components:

■ *Server memory*

■ *File system and cache*

■ *Communications subsystem*

■ *System processor*

This chapter also teaches you how to use the NetWare set commands to "tweak" NetWare for your particular environment.

Only network administrators who understand how changing one portion of the operating system can affect each operating system component should use these "fine tuning tips." These configuration changes should be tested in a nonproduction environment before being implemented.

NetWare 3.1*x* has a modular design that lends it the capability to automatically allocate and deallocate memory and other resources as needed by the operating system. You can use the tunable SET parameters to manually configure these dynamic allocating features to create a very efficient, customized implementation, but little information is available on how you use them. Therefore, the server usually is simply left with the default parameters.

NetWare is a specialized networking operating system designed and coded to give optimum speed and performance to most configurations. Changing a default setting can actually result in a performance loss.

The most vital factor when you tweak the NetWare operating system is realizing that any tweaking of a NetWare server is not an exact science, and that any performance tuning must be based on the characteristics of the server's actual production workloads.

NetWare 3.11 Server Components

Server hardware tuning is the most critical factor in the optimization of NetWare systems. However, after you tune and balance the server's hardware, you can effectively optimize NetWare.

To optimize NetWare, you need to understand each of the subsystems and the characteristics of those subsystems, including the following:

- **Memory.** Because NetWare uses file caching extensively, it is extremely memory oriented. You need to have a basic understanding of how the server allocates memory because you must consider the memory impact of each tuning parameter.

- **Communications system or server LAN I/O channel.** The communications system can affect performance in a number of ways: packet size, communication buffers, Burst Mode protocol, SAP traffic, and network interface cards. Because each of these components affect the overall network performance, you can tweak them to enhance overall network response times.

- **File system.** The NetWare file system is very cache oriented; any change in available memory for cache directly affects overall performance. A bottleneck in the physical disk channel also directly degrades overall network performance.

- **System processor.** The system processor typically is a subsystem that requires a lot of attention; NetWare is very rarely processor bound. The processor, however, is tied directly to the server's bus, which is the most common bottleneck. Because of the relationship of the processor and the bus, these components are discussed together.

Memory Pools

Memory allocation refers to reserving specific memory locations in RAM for processes, instructions, and data. NetWare 3.12 uses memory pools to manage RAM. These memory pools are designed to be allocated and optimized based on whether they are to have long-term or short-term usage.

Short-term memory is used to perform such activities as mapping drives, providing user-connection information, locking files, and so on. *Long-term memory* is used for the servers's communication buffers, directory cache buffers, and so on.

Figure 48.1 illustrates NetWare 3.12's use of memory. Table 48.1 represents how these memory pools are used.

After memory resources are released from the file cache buffer pool to the permanent memory pool or to the allocated short-term memory pool, they cannot be returned to the main memory pool until after the server is brought down and the primary memory segment is reestablished.

Frequent loading and unloading of NLMs causes fragmentation of your file server's memory, so it might not have enough contiguous RAM to actually service all requests of memory.

You can optimize your file server's memory allocation in one of two ways:

- Minimize loading and unloading of NLMs to prevent RAM fragmentation.

- If the RAM becomes fragmented, bring down the server and start it back up. This eliminates fragmentation and makes contiguous memory available to NLMs.

 The memory model for NetWare 3.12 is based on the use of 32-bit registers, which enables NetWare to provide access to one flat segment of RAM up to 4 GB.

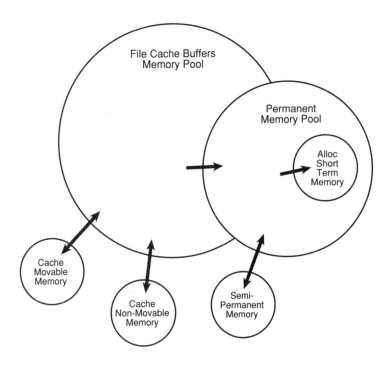

Figure 48.1

NetWare 3.12 memory pools.

Table 48.1
Memory Pool Utilization

Memory Pool or Subpool	Description and Use	Status
File Cache Buffer	Main memory pool; used for caching reads and writes	Primary memory segment
Cache Movable	Subpool used by NetWare; used for internal system tables that change size dynamically: Hash tables File allocation tables (FATs) Directory entry tables (DETs) No fragmentation Expandable	Returnable to file cache buffer in contiguous blocks
Cache Non-Movable	Subpool used by NLMs, including CLIB, when loaded Causes fragmentation Non-expandable	Returnable to file cache buffer in non-contiguous blocks
Permanent Memory	One-way allocation pool for long-term memory needs used for communication buffers and directory cache buffers	Not returnable to file cache buffer
Semi-Permanent	Subpool used by LAN and disk drivers	Returnable to permanent memory, but not to file cache buffer
Allocated Short-term	Pool used for small, short-term memory allocations such as drive mappings, SAP and RIP tables, Queue manager tables, and connection information	Not returnable to permanent memory or to file cache memory Unused allocated memory remains in the pool for other uses

Rather than allocating chunks of memory at the time of installation, most resources (such as memory for communication buffers and drive mappings) are allocated as needed.

Any preassigned values must be specified in the server's STARTUP.NCF and AUTOEXEC.NCF files.

NetWare 3.12 uses the same memory architecture as earlier versions of 3.11. In 3.12, however, Novell made some changes to the core operating systems. These changes require 3.12 to have a greater use of the alloc short term memory pool.

NetWare 3.12 commonly needs more than 2 MB in its ALLOC memory pool. Other demands—such as users not logging out, clients using MS-Windows and OS/2, and some disk drivers—cause the alloc short term memory pool to reach its maximum value quickly.

Therefore, the default value and the range of values available have been increased. The default value for the Alloc Short Term Memory pool has changed from 2 MB in NetWare 3.11 to 8 MB in 3.12. The maximum value of the Alloc Short Term memory pool has also been increased from 16 MB in 3.11 to 32 MB in 3.12.

To change the default value of the Alloc Short Term memory pool, use the following SET command:

`SET MAXIMUM ALLOC SHORT TERM MEMORY = value`

Practical TIP The range of values is 50,000 to 33,554,432 bytes (32 MB).

You can view the Resource Utilization option in the Monitor utility, from the console screen, to verify the amount of memory the alloc short term memory pool is using.

The best policy for adjusting the alloc short term memory pool is to let the server *self-adjust*, that is, to let the server run under normal situations for about three or four days. During this period, the server uses the amount of memory it most likely needs. Then, if you want to manually change the alloc short term memory levels to always reflect your environment, you can enter the SET command manually.

You might want to adjust the alloc short term memory value based on the information found in the MONITOR.NLM. You might want to decrease the value, for instance, if your server does not use the allotted memory. Or, you might want to increase the value if the server issues warnings that an operation cannot be completed because this memory pool has reached its limit.

File System Adjustments

Optimizing the NetWare 3.12 caching mechanism includes adjusting parameters that affect NetWare Core Protocol (NCP) reads and writes, as well as adjusting the disk block size, buffer size, FATs, and directory entry tables.

The following list provides some common rules of thumb for adjusting the components of the NetWare file:

■ Increasing the amount of file cache buffers optimizes the file system. The default is to use all remaining memory for file cache buffers, under which circumstance adjustments made to other subsystems that require more memory can negatively affect performance.

■ The larger the disk block size, the more efficient the read-ahead cache, which equate to better performance (however disk space is sacrificed).

■ Modifying the cache block size adds efficiency to the file server by increasing response time between server and client.

■ Increasing the Turbo FAT reuse wait time ensures that Turbo FAT index structures are not flushed as often; that is, if the file is reused, the location of the file can be obtained from cache memory rather than from the hard drive.

■ Adding any extra name spaces to a volume requires multiple FATs and DETs to be cached, which decreases performance. If multiple name spaces are required, consider using separate volumes for each name space, which divides files that require name spaces, to help optimize NetWare file system performance. However, multiple volumes also chew up valuable RAM.

■ For optimal performance, consider using the SET parameters to turn read-after-write verification to OFF and Immediate Purge of files to ON, as follows:

```
SET ENABLE DISK READ AFTER WRITE VERIFY = OFF

SET IMMEDIATE PURGE OF DELETED FILES = ON
```

■ Using an intelligent controller—or in some RAID systems, an intelligent driver—often provides support for data retrieval and writing techniques, such as scattering, merging, queuing, mingling, and so on. These intelligent components help optimize disk I/O.

 Note For some controllers (such as those used with Compaq disk arrays), the hot fix verification is perceived as redundant and the hardware turns off the read-after-write and hot fix functionality.

Some SCSI controllers implement read-after-write verification, providing a redundant level of error checking.

Several enhancements were made to NetWare 3.12 (over 3.11), including the following:

■ Read-ahead cache

■ Enhanced extended attribute support for OS/2 2.1

■ Ability to mount a CD-ROM as a volume

Cache read-ahead allows the server to read more into the cache buffer when the server is performing a sequential file read, which allows for faster file access. You use the SET parameter to control cache read-ahead, as follows:

```
READ AHEAD ENABLED = ON     (default)
```

Communications Subsystems

You need to consider several factors you made to evaluate the performance of a network's communication channel. Most of these considerations deal with the actual design of the network, the amount of segments being used, the medium (Ethernet, token ring, and so on) being used, the type of hardware connecting the network segments (internal or external routing connections mechanisms), and the list goes on. Although these types of questions provide more insight to the overall tuning effort, this section concentrates on those items that the network administrator uses to tune the internal server communications channel, which includes the following components:

■ Packet size

■ Communication buffers

■ Burst Mode technology

■ SAP traffic filtering

Packet Size

The best advice for optimizing the communication channel is simply to use the largest packet size possible. The packet size is a function of the network card.

 Note The default packet receive buffer size for a NetWare 3.11 server is 1 KB (1,024 bytes).

To enable the server to use a packet size other than the default of 1 KB, you must modify a SET parameter in the server's STARTUP.NCF file, as follows:

`SET MAXIMUM PHYSICAL RECEIVE PACKET SIZE =`

The following table lists the most common packet sizes.

Drivers	Default	Packet Size
Token Ring	4 Mbps	2154 KB
Token Ring	16 Mbps	4202 KB
Ethernet		1130 KB
ARCnet		618 KB

 Note Although using the largest supported packet size is the best way to go, you should be aware that using an overly large packet size is about the worst configuration mistake you can make. If you choose a 4 KB packet size, for instance, you need only a 1 KB packet size, and the communication buffers needs to be 4 KB, too. Because communication buffers are allocated in permanent memory, it requires more memory to be permanently allocated out of file cache buffers, which slows disk access.

Communication Buffers

Communication buffers are allocated dynamically based on an aging algorithm in the OS. A minimum number of buffers can be allocated when the server boots, and a maximum number specified to prevent an out-of-control growth situation. A lack of packet receive buffers results in a No ECB Available Count error message.

NetWare's communication buffers support all protocols that the underlying network card drivers could possibly use. Any change to the size of these buffers reflects across all protocol stacks. Remember this when you set about to modify the buffer size.

You use a SET parameter in the STARTUP.NCF file to modify buffer size, as follows:

`SET MAXIMUM PHYSICAL RECEIVE PACKET SIZE =`

 Note The value for this parameter equals the size of the data portion plus the protocol overhead.

In NetWare 3.11, when a packet passes through an intermediate NetWare router, NetWare reduces the packet size to 512 bytes (to accommodate different topologies it must assume the least common denominator).

 Practical TIP To get around this 512-byte router packet size limitation in NetWare 3.11, you need to use LIPX.NLM.

The network administrator can use SET parameters in the STARTUP.NCF and AUTOEXEC.NCF files to control the increase in the number of communication buffers. Two SET parameters work to reconfigure or reallocate the number of buffers based on usage. The first SET parameter controls the minimum number of buffers that can ever be allocated:

```
SET MINIMUM PACKET RECEIVE BUFFERS =
```

The network administrator can use the MONITOR utility to compare the number of configured buffers versus the number currently in use. If the total number of communication buffers peaks at 100 after several months of continuous server operation, for example, the administrator can take advantage of the SET Minimum Packet Receive Buffers parameter to reallocate more than the default of 10 buffers the next time the server is rebooted.

The second SET parameter controls the maximum number of buffers that can ever be allocated:

```
SET MAXIMUM PACKET RECEIVE BUFFERS =
```

If occasional peaks in server usage cause the number of buffers to grow significantly, you might need to control this growth to control the impact on memory.

The administrator can set the maximum at 200 to prevent these peaks from causing unnecessary allocations into permanent memory.

A third SET parameter controls the amount of time the system waits before spawning a new buffer:

```
SET NEW PACKET RECEIVE BUFFER WAIT TIME =
```

You use this parameter in conjunction with the SET Maximum Packet Receive Buffers parameter, acting as a peak inhibitor.

All three of these SET parameters are very closely related and you should use them in a complementary fashion. However, you should use good judgment; these buffers are allocated out of permanent memory, so the memory they use is never returned to the main memory pool.

Burst Mode

Packet Burst is a protocol built on top of an IPX that expedites the transfer of multiple-packet NCP file reads and writes. In older versions of NetWare, for instance, when a NetWare client made an NCP request, a *one-request/one-response method of communication* was followed; that is, each packet of the request had to be followed by an individual acknowledgment—quite inefficient, especially when the requested data requires more than one packet.

Packet Burst is more efficient because it allows client read requests without acknowledgment. Thus, the server can return the requested data in a "burst."

Packet burst is now built into the NetWare 3.12 operating system code and enabled by default in the new client software.

 When Packet Burst is enabled at a server and is communicating with a client at which Packet Burst is not enabled, the server communicates with this client in the old one-request/one-response mode.

Service Advertising Protocol (SAP) Traffic

The *Service Advertising Protocol* is used by servers, print servers, gateways, and so forth, to advertise their respective services. Normally, SAP broadcast traffic is very efficient, except for in large Internet works, or WANs. In these situations SAP traffic can occasionally clog the lines.

To reduce this possibility of NetWare SAP traffic clogging the lines, use the new NetWare Link Services Protocol (NLSP).

Note NLSP replaces RIP and SAP, offering better performance, reliability, and management of NetWare traffic. Yet it retains compatibility with existing routers, enabling you to upgrade servers and routers on your network one at a time.

Novell's implementation of NLSP is offered as a NetWare Loadable Module (NLM). It will run on versions 3.11 and later on the NetWare operating system.

Large Internet Packet (LIP)

Large Internet Packet is another factor for enhancing the network environment. It works to increase the speed of data transmission of router communication.

LIP allows the client and server to negotiate the packet size used when communication occurs through a router. With LIP, the packets can be set to a maximum of 4,202 bytes. The negotiated packet size depends on the maximum physical packet size of the server.

Network administrators would want to take advantage of the NLSP for three main reasons:

- Reduce SAP traffic

- Prevent users from seeing specific servers

- Lower information coming from remote servers

Note Like Packet Burst, LIP is included in the operating system code of NetWare 3.12 and in the client connection software. LIP is enabled by default at both the server and the client. In some cases, packet size is hard-coded in the router. LIP is not effective in these instances.

Network Interface Card Issues

In NetWare 3.1x, a single network card can support multiple frame types (such as 802.3, Ethernet II, and Ethernet_SNAP) and multiple protocols (such as IPX/SPX, TCP/IP, and AppleTalk). Given this flexibility, configurations are often used where the NIC is simply saturated. Determining whether the network interface card and driver is a bottleneck, however, is not a simple endeavor.

NetWare's MONITOR utility does provide some useful information for determining the status of the network card.

Not every NIC's manufacturer will provide you with all the information you need.

There are basically two sets of NIC statistics: general error information and custom statistics.

The general error statistics, as its name implies, consists of general error entries. All network card manufacturers are urged to write its drivers such that these 15 different statistics are maintained. These include statistics such as total packets sent and received, packets dropped due to no available communication buffers, and so forth.

The optional statistics, which consist of another 15 to 20 additional statistics, provide custom driver information. Thus, and unfortunately, not all Ethernet cards will have the same set of custom statistics.

Some of this information can be extremely helpful. For instance, if the network card displays this level of information, you can use these statistic to determine if the network card is "keeping up."

The Enqueued Send Counts reports the number of packets the NIC had to buffer because the driver or card was too busy to send a packet that the processor had ready.

If this count increments regularly and reaches 1 to 2 percent of the total packets transmitted, it indicates that the NIC driver is having trouble keeping up with the server and is reaching or has reached its saturation point.

System Processor

The system processor is the last frontier for performance optimization. High server CPU utilization does not always mean the server lacks in system processor power. Many resources, including NLMs and NICs, contend for CPU time. Network administrators frequently make the mistake of assuming that 90 percent utilization means the CPU is saturated. Replacing the server with a new 80486 machine may not yield the expected performance gains. Typically, the other server subsystems must be optimized before the system processor emerges as a bottleneck.

Using the NetWare's MONITOR utility, you can evaluate your server's CPU utilization. To do so select the Processor utilization option. It will provide you with a list of processes by interrupt, which identifies inefficient or CPU-intensive resources in the server.

The regularity with which an interrupt is triggered is an indication of which hardware device is being accessed most frequently. For example, if a NIC configured for interrupt 3 is constantly servicing packets and utilizing a large percentage of CPU time, that NIC could be a possible bottleneck.

Managing the server's CPU utilization is often best accomplished by balancing the server's hardware. For example, using 32-bit disk controller technology in an EISA bus machine with a slower ISA bus network card will ultimately be a bottleneck. You should also use technologies such as Bus Mastering cards. This technology allows the server to move data in and out of system memory and on to the card without interrupting the CPU.

Questions

1. Each of the server components can directly or indirectly affect the performance of the entire NetWare operating system.

   ○ T

   ○ F

2. Adding any extra name spaces to a volume requires multiple FATs and DET to be cached, which decrease performance.

   ○ T

   ○ F

3. Which of the following enhancements made to NetWare 3.12 (over 3.11) is most likely to affect performance?

   ○ A. Read-ahead cache

   ○ B. Enhanced extended attribute support for OS/2 2

   ○ C. Ability to mount a CD-ROM as a volume

   ○ D. None of the above

4. Network administrators would want to take advantage of the NLSP for which one of the following reasons?

   ○ A. To reduce SAP traffic

   ○ B. To prevent users from seeing specific servers

   ○ C. To lower information coming from remote servers

   ○ D. All of the above

5. Which of the following server subsystems is not a concern to overall network performance?

   ○ A. Server memory

   ○ B. File system and cache

   ○ C. Communications subsystem

   ○ D. None of the above

Answers

1. T
2. T
3. A
4. D
5. D

NetWare Printing

Understanding Printing and NetWare Printing Services

*O*ne of the earliest—and continuous—benefits of networking your computer environment is the capability to share printers and related print services. A detailed understanding of printers and printing helps you take full advantage of this capability. To that end, this chapter discusses printers and printing in NetWare networks, and provides information about the following related topics:

■ *Understanding printers and printing*

■ *Identifying printing environments and components*

■ *Understanding NetWare 2.x core printing*

Understanding Printers and Printing

As early printing design is based on printing through DOS applications, so too is much of today's network printing. Three methods of printing are commonly used in DOS-based applications. An understanding of these three methods may help you better understand network printing.

The following three printing methods are used by DOS-based applications:

- Interrupt 21 DOS function calls

- Interrupt 17 BIOS function calls

- Hardware direct I/O

The Interrupt 21 DOS function calls method is the simplest. Applications that use this method of printing simply send the print request directly to the printer, waiting until it is ready to accept its print job if it is presently busy with another. The drawback of this method is that it carries with it a great deal of printing overhead. The advantage is that it is readily compatible with most printing software and utilities.

The second method, the Interrupt 17 BIOS (Basic Input Output System) function call, is somewhat more complex than the first method. In this second method, the application accesses the printer by using the services of the ROM BIOS parallel printer port controller. Although somewhat more complex to use, this method provides additional features, including access to printer and controller status information.

The third method, hardware direct I/O (Input/Output), is the most direct of the three methods. This method ignores DOS and BIOS and instead interfaces directly with the printer. The main drawback to this approach is that the application itself must be correctly written to provide all interface with the printer. This method is useful for devices other than printers, if those devices need speed and minimal delay.

The first two options—Interrupt 21 DOS and Interrupt 17 BIOS—are compatible with NetWare printing redirection, using the CAPTURE command. The third method—hardware direct I/O—is not. It is better suited to video, serial devices, and similar devices.

 Note Applications that need to print to a serial device but which use this third printing method can still use the DOS MODE command to redirect the printing request from a parallel port to a serial port. To use the MODE command, type **MODE *parallel_port = serial_port*** and press Enter. Other options are available for use with the DOS MODE command, depending on which version of DOS you are running. Details about these other options can be found in your DOS manual.

Table 49.1 lists other printing-related terms and provides a brief explanation of and comments related to each term.

Table 49.1
Printer-Related Terms to Know

Term	Description	Comments
Redirection	Sending a print job to one location when it was originally intended for another location	The DOS MODE and NetWare CAPTURE commands can be used to redirect print jobs
Print Buffer	Temporary storage area for data being sent to a printer	There are three types of print buffers: external (between printer port and printer interface), internal (inside the printer), and memory-resident (in PC's memory)
Print Queue	A directory for temporarily storing print requests	Found on a NetWare file server
Spooling	Sending a print job to a queue on a NetWare server	CAPTURE, PCONSOLE, NPRINT, and NetWare-aware applications can use spooling
NetWare-aware	Capable of sending print jobs directly to NetWare print queues	Other networking software have network-aware printers
Print server	Responsible for polling print queues for job requests and routing the job to the correct network printer	Can be part of a NetWare server or a separate computer
Polling	Checking for jobs to be printed	Used with core printing services

Following are the three phases in the network printing process:

▪ Spooling

▪ De-spooling

▪ Printing

Spooling is the process of sending the actual print job across the network to a print queue. NetWare-aware applications and DOS applications with print services redirected to the network perform this process.

De-spooling is the process of transferring the print job from the print queue to the designated printer. Specialized NetWare Loadable Modules (NLMs) and Value Added Processes (VAPs) perform this function.

> **Note** On NetWare 3 and 4 network file servers and on NetWare 3 multiprotocol routers, the NLM is PSERVER.NLM. On NetWare 3 and NetWare 2 external routers, the VAP is PSERVER.VAP. On dedicated DOS workstations in NetWare 2 or 3, the executable program is PSERVER.EXE.

Printing is the process of translating the print job into a printed document.

Identifying Printing Environments and Components

The different components associated with printing in a network environment (workstations, the NetWare Operating System, print servers, print queues, NetWare file servers, and printers) all play a role in the effective and efficient use of network printing. So too does the fact that NetWare printing services can support multiple workstation platforms (DOS, MS Windows, IBM OS/2, Apple Macintosh, and Unix BSD and AT&T hosts). In addition, the NetWare OS itself affects printing (core printing services provided in NetWare 2, or NetWare print services provided in NetWare 3 and 4). Each of these components and workstation platforms ultimately affect the quality of printing services on your network. Just how they can affect the quality of printing services on your network is important to developing an understanding of network printing.

The goal of printing services is to make their access and use as simple and as invisible as possible to network users. Supporting a variety of workstations on a NetWare network helps to accomplish that task. The workstations themselves contribute to this process whenever a network workstation is used to provide network printing services.

Workstations can provide printing services in two ways: through local printers and remote printers. A local printer, one attached to a workstation and accessible only to the workstation's user, does little

to contribute to network printing services except for the service it provides to the local workstation. Having a printer attached to a workstation does not prevent the user from accessing files, printers, and print queues on the network, even though the local printer is not accessible by other network users.

On the other hand, remote printers are attached to workstations but can be accessed by other network users. Remote printers are accessible when the appropriate software is loaded at the workstation. In NetWare 2 and NetWare 3 environments, that software is the RPRINTER.EXE file. In NetWare 4 networks, that software is NPRINTER.EXE.

Besides direct attachment to a workstation, printers can be part of a network in the following ways:

- **Network direct.** Printers with a built-in network interface ("smart" printers) may be connected to the network cable at convenient locations.

- **External network direct.** Printers with external network interfaces can also be connected directly to the network cable.

- **Wide area remote.** Printers in LANs can be shared when LANs are connected using various communication methods to form WANs.

- **Print server.** A maximum of seven printers can be directly connected to a NetWare print server.

 Note   The main benefit of print servers is that print jobs can be directed to any printing device located anywhere on the network. In addition, there is no limit to the number of print servers that can be used on a network at one time. There can be only one print server per NetWare server, however.

The use of multiple print servers increases printing performance, and provides flexibility and convenience when placing printers on the network. Strategically placing printers, however, benefits not only the users and network administrators, but the efficiency of network printing as well.

Placing printers close to print servers, for example, generally increases printing performance. So too does placing the print server software on a dedicated PC instead of on a NetWare file server.

■ **NetWare server.** A maximum of five printers can be directly connected to a NetWare server, provided that the print server software also is loaded on the NetWare server.

 Note Not only can printers be directly connected to NetWare servers, but servers can also provide subdirectories (print queues) in which print jobs can be temporarily housed. Print jobs stored in these print queue subdirectories are recognizable by their Q file extension.

Various benefits are associated with using print queues on NetWare servers. First, certain network users can be assigned the responsibility of managing these queues. Those responsibilities may include deleting, ordering, holding, viewing, modifying, and flagging print jobs.

In addition, one or more servers can accept print requests from a single print queue (multiple printers assigned to a single queue), and a single server can service more than one print queue. The first option provides low-delay print

services, and better distribution of print jobs. The second option provides distributed queue management, printing by form type, priority access to printers, cost-effective resource sharing, and job grouping by Print Description Language (PDL).

Finally, print management can be simplified by assigning queues to specific printers, and the priority of print jobs can be determined by the print queue into which the job is placed.

Understanding NetWare 2.x Core Printing

Core printing services are available only on NetWare file servers running versions earlier than NetWare 2.2. Using NetWare core printing services, you can attach a maximum of five printers directly to serial or parallel ports (COM1, COM2, LPT1, LPT2, and LPT3) on the NetWare file server, to be used as network printers. While in a very small network, connecting all printers to the file server may be sufficient, NetWare core printing services have two major drawbacks.

First, connecting all network printers to the file server adds the printing process to the server itself, thus possibly slowing other services normally provided by the NetWare file server. Second, print servers cannot be used, nor can workstation-attached or network-attached printers.

Installing NetWare 2.x core printing by using the Basic installation establishes some defaults. The defaults include: the creation of a print queue named PRINTQ_O on the server; generation of the NET$OS.EXE file with core printing included; the ability of all users (because they are members of group EVERYONE) to access and use these printers; and the establishment of polling at 15-second intervals, a time option that, depending on the network's demand for print services, may be too frequent or not frequent enough.

> **Note**   The following commands can be used with core printing services:

■ **QUEUE.** To create a new print job (QUEUE *queue_name* CREATE), view a list of print queues (QUEUE), change a job's priority in the print queue (*queue_name* CHANGE JOB *n* TO PRIORITY *x*), remove a print queue (*queue_name* DESTROY), remove a job from the print queue (*queue_name* DELETE JOB n/*), and see a list of print jobs in the queue (*queue_name* JOBS).

■ **PRINTER.** To alter or view a printer's configuration (PRINTER *n* CONFIG), assign a queue to a printer (PRINTER *n* ADD *queue_name*), or view available options for this command (PRINTER Help or PRINTER ?).

■ **PSTAT.** To view the status of a printer from a workstation (PSTAT S=*server_name printer_name or printer_number*).

You can automate the process of loading the NetWare core printing services by placing the appropriate commands in the file server's AUTOEXEC.SYS file. To edit this file, start the SYSCON utility, choose Supervisor Options from the Available Topics menu, then choose Edit System AUTOEXEC File from the Supervisor Options menu (see fig. 49.1).

Figure 49.1
The SYSCON utility.

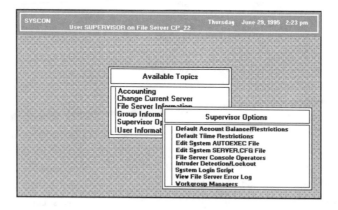

Questions

1. The printing method that enables the application to access the printer by using the ROM BIOS parallel printer port controller services is called _____.

   ○ A. Interrupt 21 DOS function calls

   ○ B. Interrupt 21 BIOS function calls

   ○ C. Interrupt 17 BIOS function calls

   ○ D. Hardware direct Input/Output

2. Which THREE printing methods are used by DOS-based applications?

   ☐ A. Interrupt 21 DOS function calls

   ☐ B. Interrupt 21 BIOS function calls

   ☐ C. Interrupt 17 BIOS function calls

   ☐ D. Hardware direct Input/Output

3. The _____ method of printing is NOT compatible with NetWare network printing redirection.

   ○ A. Interrupt 21 DOS function calls

   ○ B. Interrupt 21 BIOS function calls

   ○ C. Interrupt 17 BIOS function calls

   ○ D. Hardware direct Input/Output

4. A _____ is a temporary storage area used for data being sent to a printer.

   ○ A. redirector

   ○ B. print buffer

   ○ C. spooler

   ○ D. print server

5. The software responsible for polling print queues for job requests and then routing the job to the correct network printer is called the _____.

   ○ A. redirector

   ○ B. print buffer

   ○ C. spooler

   ○ D. print server

6. The phase of printing that transfers the print job from the print queue to the designated printer is called _____.

   ○ A. redirecting

   ○ B. spooling

   ○ C. de-spooling

   ○ D. printing

7. Of the following, which THREE perform de-spooling?

   ☐ A. NPRINTER.EXE

   ☐ B. PSERVER.NLM

   ☐ C. PSERVER.VAP

   ☐ D. PSERVER.EXE

8. In NetWare 2 and NetWare 3 environments, the software which must be loaded on a workstation to make that workstation's attached printer a remote printer is _____.

   ○ A. RPRINTER.EXE

   ○ B. NPRINTER.EXE

   ○ C. PSERVER.EXE

   ○ D. RSERVER.EXE

9. A maximum of _____ printers can be directly connected to a NetWare file server.

   ○ A. 3

   ○ B. 5

   ○ C. 7

   ○ D. 9

10. Choosing the Basic installation option when installing core printing on a NetWare 2 network causes the _____ file to be generated by default.

   ○ A. RPRINTER.EXE

   ○ B. NET$OS.EXE

   ○ C. SERVER.EXE

   ○ D. NET$SYS.EXE

Answers

1. C

2. A, C, D

3. D

4. B

5. D

6. C

7. B, C, D

8. A

9. B

10. B

Planning and Installing Basic Printing Services

You've heard the old cliché: Keep it simple. Sometimes simple is the best. Sometimes it is not. For example, using the NetWare 4 Basic Installation option to set up printing for your network certainly is simple, but that does not necessarily make it the best option because the simple setup may not truly meet your network's needs. To ensure that the network's needs are met, a well-planned and appropriately implemented network printing environment is necessary. This chapter deals with network planning and basic installation, and provides information about the following related topics:

■ *Planning the printing environment*

■ *Setting up and managing print queues*

■ *Setting up and managing print servers and printers*

Planning the Printing Environment

There are two primary phases to planning a printing environment. The first is to understand what factors should be considered when you identify network printing requirements. The second is to understand the hardware, software, and other resources necessary for a well-designed network printing environment. This section discusses these two important phases of planning a printing environment.

Network Printing Requirements

The first step to determining network printing requirements is to conduct a needs analysis. A *needs analysis* is a study of current and future needs. Obtaining answers to the following types of questions should provide the basic information required to determine the printing needs of most network environments:

- How many current users need to print documents, and how many new users requiring access to print services are anticipated, in both the short and long term?

- How much printing does the average user do, based on the number of pages printed by each user in a single day?

- Do all users print to the same types of forms, or do forms vary (different size and shape of paper, preprinted documents, and so on)?

- How long can most users afford to wait for their printed documents, and will delays be detrimental to productivity?

- Is the layout of the building suitable to placing shared printers for ready access, or must additional printers be located so as to handle users who need easier access?

- Does the location of printers present any security issues, such as whether confidential data will have to be printed on a readily accessible printer?

- Have environmental factors such as excess noise, heating and cooling, fumes and odors, and so on been considered?

With the answers to these questions in hand, you can begin to decide such important issues as how many printers you will need, where the printers should be located, whether you will need only one or several print servers, and so on.

Network Printing Resources

Having analyzed your network's printing needs, you can then consider your available resources, as well as any additional resources you may need to provide. The following three types of resources should be considered:

- Physical (hardware)

- Applications and operating systems (software)

- Print services administrators (print server and print queue operators) and other human resources

Following are the physical resources to consider:

- The number and type (CPU) of workstations, and whether they can handle printers

- The number and type (not only CPU, but also version of NetWare OS) of file servers on the network, and their availability for printer attachment

- The number of print queues and print servers needed

- The number and types of printers available, including the amount of RAM available, types of interfaces they use, and fonts they provide

- Supplies needed to service the printers

Software resources to consider are the operating systems running at workstations (DOS, MS Windows, Unix, and so on), the NetWare OS versions running on network file servers, whether core printing services are to be used, and which applications are available to network users.

Print services administrators can include print queue operators as well as print server operators, in addition to the network Supervisor (or administrator, in NetWare 4) or users with Supervisor-equivalent rights.

Also to be considered are the rights end users will have to network printing services; the cost of providing printing services and service and support, both initially and as an ongoing benefit; and the training necessary not only for network users, but also for administrators, supervisors, and operators.

Setting Up and Managing Print Queues

Print queues (subdirectories located either in the SYS:SYSTEM directory on NetWare 2 and 3 servers, or on any volume in NetWare 4 servers) are an important part of network printing in all versions of NetWare—2, 3, and 4. In NetWare 2 and 3, print queues are bindery objects. In NetWare 4, print queues are NetWare Directory Services (NDS)

objects. Print queues are used to maintain information about print jobs and print servers. Queue operator flags enable Supervisors, administrators, and print queue operators to control print queue access and use.

The PCONSOLE utility can be used to create and manage print queues in all versions of NetWare.

 The NetWare Administrator tool provided in NetWare 4 also can be used to create and manage print queues.

Using PCONSOLE, you can create print queues, rename or delete a print queue, view the Print Queue object ID, add or delete print queue operators and users, and modify operator flags. To use this utility, type **PCONSOLE** and press Enter. Next, choose Print Queue Information from the Available Options menu (see fig. 50.1). Now you can perform any of the listed tasks, some of which require that you have Supervisor rights.

To create a print queue, press the Insert key with the Print Queues screen open. At the New Print Queue Name prompt, type a name for the print queue, and then press Enter.

To rename a print queue, select a print queue from the list of print queues, press F3, delete the existing name, then type a new name and press Enter.

To delete a print queue, select a print queue from the list of print queues, press Delete, and answer Yes when prompted.

To view a print queue's object ID number, choose a print queue. From the Print Queue Information menu, choose Print Queue ID.

Figure 50.1
*The PCONSOLE
Available Options menu.*

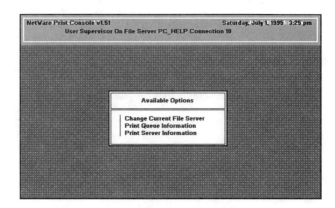

To add or delete a print queue operator, select a print queue from the list of print queues, then choose Queue Operators. Press Insert to see a list of queue operator candidates from which to choose. Select one and press Enter, or mark several by pressing F5, and then press Enter. To delete queue operators, select one or mark several with the F5 key, then press Delete. Answer Yes at the Delete Queue Operator prompt.

To add or delete a print queue user, select a print queue from the list of print queues, then choose Queue Users. Press Insert to see a list of queue users from which to choose. Select one and press Enter, or mark several by using the F5 key, and then press Enter. To delete queue users, select one or mark several with the F5 key, then press Delete. Answer Yes at the Delete User prompt.

Access to print queues by users and print servers can be managed and controlled by using NetWare's print queue operator flags. The following three operator flags can be modified:

■ **Users can place entries in queue.** When set to No, users cannot add print jobs to the print queue.

■ **Servers can service entries in queue.** When set to No, print servers cannot access the queue to service print jobs.

■ **New servers can attach to queue.** When set to No, new print servers cannot attach to the print queue for the purpose of servicing print jobs.

To modify any of these operator flags, select the flag and press Y to toggle the flag on, or press N to toggle the flag off.

You also use print queues to view information about print jobs. Figure 50.2 shows a typical print queue entry.

Table 50.1 describes the function of each field in the Print Queue Entry Information screen, and provides additional information about some of the fields.

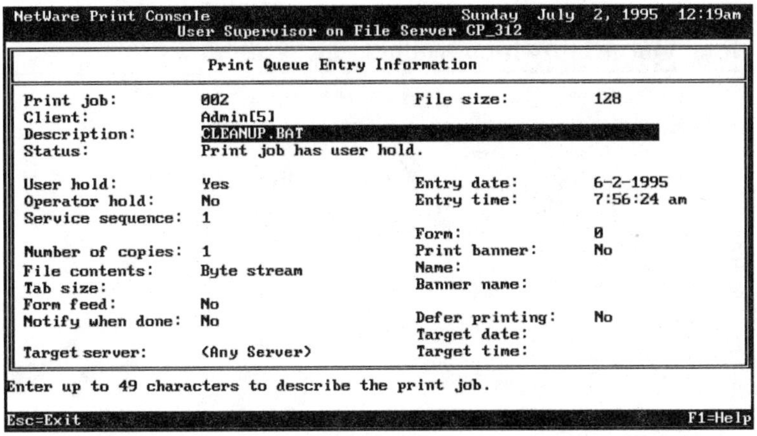

Figure 50.2

The Print Queue Entry Information screen.

Table 50.1
Print Queue Entry Information Fields

Field Name	Description	Additional Information
Print job	Number assigned to this print job request	Cannot be changed
Client	User's name and connection number	Cannot be changed
Description	Name of file being printed	
Status	Condition of print job	Shows whether job is on hold or ready to print
User hold	User can prevent job from printing by setting to Yes	
Operator hold	Queue operator can put any print job on hold	
Service sequence	Order in which job is to be printed	Queue operator can change job order to be printed

continues

Table 50.1, Continued
Print Queue Entry Information Fields

Field Name	Description	Additional Information
Number of copies	Quantity of copies to be printed, as requested by user	From 1 to 250, inclusive
File contents	If set to text, tabs replaced by spaces; if set to byte stream, data sent directly to printer	Choose Text or Byte stream
Tab size	Sets number of spaces to use when replacing a tab	Use 1 to 18, inclusive
Form feed	Prevents form feed from being sent to printer	
Notify when done	Notifies sender when print job is done	Set to Yes to notify, No to not notify
Target server	Print server to service this print job	"Any Server" indicates no server was specified
File size	Size of this file (in bytes)	Cannot be changed
Entry Date	Date job sent to queue	Cannot be changed
Entry Time	Time job sent to queue	Cannot be changed
Form	Name of form to be used for this job	Specified by form number
Print banner	Specifies whether to print a banner page	Set to Yes or No
Name	Text for upper part of banner page	Maximum of 12 alphanumeric characters

Field Name	Description	Additional Information
Banner name	Text for lower part of banner page	Maximum of 12 alphanumeric characters
Defer printing	Set to Yes to print at a later date and time	
Target date	Date when job is to be printed if Defer printing field is set to Yes	Use any standard format
Target time	Time when job is to be printed	Examples: 3 pm, 03:00:00, or 3:00 pm

Setting Up and Managing Print Servers and Printers

Print servers poll print queues looking for jobs to be printed. They then take ready-to-print jobs from print queues and send them to the appropriate print server.

The following three types of print servers differ in location and the type of file used to run them:

■ **NetWare Loadable Module.** The NLM print server is created by loading the PSERVER.NLM file on a NetWare 3 or NetWare 4 file server. This type of print server can control a maximum of 16 printers on a NetWare 3 network, and a maximum of 255 printers on a NetWare 4 network.

■ **Value Added Process.** The VAP print server is created by loading the PSERVER.VAP file

on an external router (bridge) or a NetWare 2 (2.15c or higher) file server. This type of print server can control a maximum of 16 printers.

■ **Executable.** The DOS executable print server is created by running the PSERVER.EXE file on a dedicated DOS-based NetWare workstation.

To create, configure, delete, or change a print server, use the PCONSOLE utility. To create a print server, start PCONSOLE and complete the following steps:

1. Choose Print Server Information from the Available Options menu.

2. Press Insert.

3. Provide a name for the print server (47 characters maximum) and press Enter.

Note Upon creation of a print server, a subdirectory is created in the SYS:SYSTEM directory, and a bindery object is created. When the print server is brought up the first time, a file called FILESERV is created. When additional print servers are brought up, information about those servers is added to this file, increasing its size by 48 bytes for each NetWare server added to the service list.

The following other configuration actions occur as print servers are configured:

■ Each time a printer is defined for a print server, a file called PRINT.*nnn* (with *nnn* representing the printer's number) is created. This file contains such information as the name of the printer, its IRQ number, buffer size, baud rate, and so on.

■ Each time a print queue is assigned to a printer, a file called QUEUE.*nnn* (with *nnn* representing the printer's number) is created. This file contains such information as the queue's name and its printing priority.

■ Each time a notification list is added for a printer, a file called NOTIFY.*nnn* (with *nnn* representing the printer's number) is created. This file contains such information as the name and type of the object to be notified, and how much time should elapse before notification is first sent (as well as between notifications).

After you choose a print server from the list of print servers, you can delete the print server (see fig. 50.3) or modify various aspects of information related to the print server.

To modify print server information (that can be modified), you first choose the appropriate option from the Print Server Information menu, then complete the steps related to that option.

The following options are available for NetWare 2 and 3 print servers:

■ **Change Password.** Provide a new password and press Enter, retyping the password at the prompt.

Figure 50.3
NetWare 4's prompt to delete a print server.

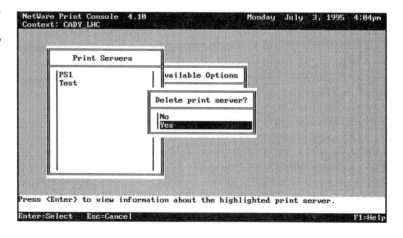

- **Full Name.** Type a descriptive name of no more than 62 alphanumeric characters, and press Enter.

- **Print Server Configuration.** Choose File servers to be Serviced, then choose one or more (mark with F5) NetWare servers, to authorize each server to service a print queue. (To discontinue service, press Delete after you choose the file servers.) To add a print server, press Insert, then provide a name and additional information (see the following Note).

 With this option, you can also configure printers to be serviced by this print server. You can use this option also to assign a permanent service mode (choose Queue service mode), create or edit a list of users to be notified when the printer needs attention (Notify List for Printer), or permanently assign a print queue to a printer (Queues Serviced by printer).

To configure printers being serviced by this print server, after choosing Printer Configuration from the Print Server Information menu, choose an existing printer number, provide the following information, then press Escape and, when finished, answer Yes at the Save changes prompt:

- **Type of printer.** If the printer is directly connected to the print server's I/O port, choose a serial port such as COM1, or a parallel port such as LPT1. If the printer is connected to a DOS workstation running NPRINTER or RPRINTER, choose one of the Remote (parallel or serial) options.

- **Method of port handling.** Choose either interrupt-driven or polling. At the Use Interrupts prompt, answer Yes (for

quickest printing), then provide the correct interrupt number. If other devices use the same interrupt number as the port, choose No.

- **Buffer size.** Enter the number of kilobytes for the print buffer. A maximum of 20 and a minimum of 3 are allowed.

- **Starting form.** Provide the number of the form to be used when the print server is loaded.

- **Queue service mode.** Enables you to choose to change forms as necessary, minimize form changes across queues, minimize form changes within queues, and service only currently mounted forms.

- **Communication parameters.** Define information such as baud rate, data bits, stop bits, parity, and whether to use X-On/X-Off for serial printers.

- **Print Server ID.** View object ID shown for this print server, as well as the name of the NetWare server on which this print server was defined.

- **Print Server Operators.** Add or remove print server operators by using the Insert or Delete keys.

- **Print Server Users.** Add or remove users by using the Insert or Delete keys.

- **Print Server Status/Control.** Attach or detach a print server to/from a NetWare printer by choosing the File Servers Being Serviced menu option and adding (press Insert and choose from the list) or removing (select one or more servers and press Delete) attached servers.

The following options are available for NetWare 4 print servers (see fig. 50.4):

- **Printers.** View, add (press Insert), or delete (press Delete) printers assigned to this print queue.

- **Information and Status.** View type, version, print server's advertising name, and status of this print server, as well as the number of printers being serviced (if the print server is up), or the print server's status (Down) if it is not presently up and running.

- **Users.** View, add (press Insert), or delete (press Delete) users who can use this print server.

- **Operators.** View, add (press Insert), or delete (press Delete) operators responsible for this print server.

- **Description.** Add, view, or change (press F3) the description associated with this print server.

- **Password.** Add or change this print server's password.

- **Audit.** Enable and configure auditing of this print server, and view or delete the print server audit log.

Figure 50.4

The Print Server Information menu.

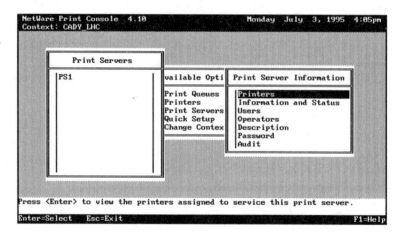

Questions

1. The version of NetWare running on the file server is a _____ printing resource to be considered.

   ○ A. hardware

   ○ B. software

   ○ C. administration

   ○ D. human

2. The TWO phases of planning a printing environment are _____ and _____.

   ☐ A. understanding network printing requirements

   ☐ B. creating print queues and servers

   ☐ C. understanding resources necessary for a well-designed network

   ☐ D. conducting a needs analysis

3. The _____ is NOT a physical resource issue to be considered when designing network printing.

   ○ A. workstation's CPU

   ○ B. number of print servers

   ○ C. OS running at the workstation

   ○ D. supplies required for printers

4. In addition to PCONSOLE, the _____ utility can be used to create and manage print queues.

   ○ A. NetWare User Tool

   ○ B. PRINTCON

   ○ C. PSERVER

   ○ D. NetWare Administrator

5. Which of the following is NOT a print queue operator flag?

   ○ A. Users can place entries in queue

   ○ B. Operators can hold print jobs

   ○ C. Servers can service entries in queue

   ○ D. New servers can attach to queue

6. To view information about print jobs, use the _____ option in PCONSOLE.

   ○ A. Print Job Description

   ○ B. Current Queue Status

   ○ C. Print Servers

   ○ D. Print Queues

7. Of the following, which THREE are items of information provided on the Print Queue Entry Information screen?

   ☐ A. Buffer Size

   ☐ B. Print Job

   ☐ C. Service Sequence

   ☐ D. Operator Hold

8. Which of the following is NOT a type of print server?

   ○ A. PSERVER.NLM

   ○ B. PSERVER.VAP

   ○ C. PSERVER.EXE

   ○ D. PSERVER.VLM

9. When a print server is brought up the first time, a file called _____ is created.

   ○ A. FILESERV

   ○ B. PRINTSER

   ○ C. PRINTQ

   ○ D. PSERVER

10. If you want to assign a permanent service mode to a print server, you must _____.

   ○ A. choose Type of Printer and specify a port in PCONSOLE

   ○ B. choose Queue service mode from the Print Server Configuration option in PCONSOLE

   ○ C. load PSERVER.EXE on the file server and choose the appropriate print server

   ○ D. load PSERVER.VAP on a NetWare 3 file server

Answers

1. B
2. A, C
3. C
4. D
5. B
6. D
7. B, C, D
8. D
9. A
10. B

Customizing Printing for DOS and Windows

*M*any applications are capable of interfacing directly with the network to provide printing services. Some applications are not. In addition, most MS Windows applications can access network printing, but there are some differences between local printing and network printing under MS Windows 3.1. Various NetWare programs can be used to accommodate not only those applications incapable of directly accessing network printing services, but also the variations expected while printing from within applications compatible with MS Windows 3.1.

This chapter, which provides information about printing on the NetWare network, is divided into the following two sections:

- Printing from DOS Applications
- Printing from MS Windows 3.1 Applications

Printing from DOS Applications

The following NetWare utilities provide printer control to DOS applications:

- PRINTDEF
- PRINTCON
- CAPTURE
- SMODE
- NPRINT
- RPRINTER
- NPRINTER
- NetUser (NetWare 3.12 and 4)
- NetWare Administrator (NetWare 4)

This section discusses these utilities and how to use them to customize printing and enable access to printer capabilities that may not otherwise be supported by the DOS application.

PRINTDEF

The PRINTDEF utility enables you to create custom definitions for network printers and forms. It stores these custom definitions in a server-wide database file called SYS:PUBLIC\NET$PRN.DAT. Network users can access this file, but it must be created by the network administrator. After printer definitions have been created, copies of definitions can be made (exported). Other existing printer definitions can also be copied (imported) by using the PRINTDEF utility.

To use this utility, type **PRINTDEF** and press Enter. The PrintDef Options menu opens (see fig. 51.1).

Choose the Print Devices option to create, change (edit), or delete network *printer definitions* (files containing strings of printer commands that control and specify the printer's actions). The names of these files end in the PDF extension. Choose the Forms option to create, change, or delete network

Figure 51.1
The PrintDef Options menu.

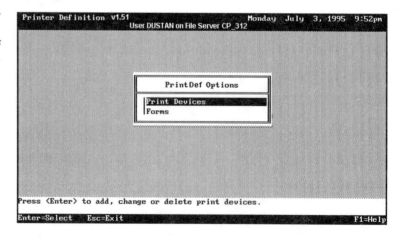

form types (definitions of paper or preprinted forms to be used in the printer). After the PRINTDEF database is created, it is used by PRINTCON, CAPTURE, and other printing-related utilities to accomplish various printing tasks.

 Note The PRINTDEF utility in NetWare 4 is slightly different from its counterpart in NetWare 2 and 3. If you compare figure 51.2 to figure 51.1, you can see that the wording for menu names (Available Options versus PrintDef Options) and options (Printer Forms instead of Forms) is slightly different. Note also that the NetWare 4 version has a third option (Change Current Context), with which you can change your context in the NDS tree before creating, deleting, or modifying a print device or form.

To create, delete, or edit a printer definition, choose Print Devices from the Available Options (or PrintDef Options) menu. The Print Device Options menu (see fig. 51.3) is the same for all three versions of NetWare. Then complete the following steps:

1. Choose Edit Print Devices.

2. Choose a printer from the list of defined printers.

3a. Add a print device by pressing Insert, typing a name, and pressing Enter.

3b. Or, delete a print device by selecting the device, pressing Delete, and choosing Yes at the prompt.

3c. Or, edit a print device by choosing the device to be edited, then making changes to print modes and print functions.

 Note To edit print device functions or modes, first choose either Device Functions or Device Modes from the Edit Print Devices menu. Next, choose either an existing function or an existing mode. (Alternatively, instead of choosing an existing function or mode, at this point you can add a new function or mode by pressing Insert and then providing a name for the function or mode.) Finally, edit the contents of the function or mode, then exit the PRINTDEF utility and save the changes.

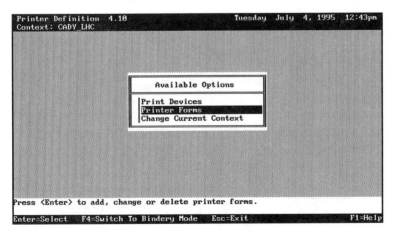

Figure 51.2

The Available Options menu in NetWare 4 version of PRINTDEF utility.

Figure 51.3

The Print Device Options menu.

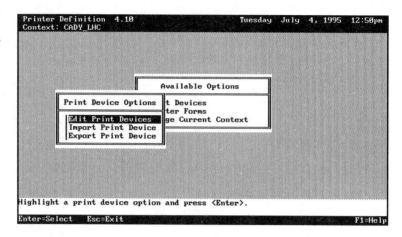

To copy an existing printer definition into your PRINTDEF database (import), or from your PRINTDEF database to another one on another file server (export), choose Print Devices from the PrintDef Options menu, then complete the following steps:

1a. Choose Import Print Device.

1b. Or, choose Export Print Device.

2a. Type **SYS:PUBLIC** in the Source Directory field, and press Enter if you are importing a print device.

2b. Or, choose a print device (.PDF) file to export.

3a. Choose a file to import from the Available .PDFs list.

3b. Or, type the path to the location to which the print device file is to be copied (Destination Directory), as well as a name (without the PDF extension) for the print device file, and press Enter.

To create, delete, or edit a form type, choose Forms from the PrintDef Options menu, then complete the following steps:

1. Choose a form from the Forms list.

2. Add a form by pressing Insert, typing a name (12 characters maximum), pressing Enter, and giving the form a number (0 to 255, inclusive).

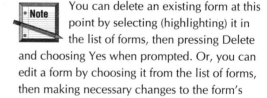 You can delete an existing form at this point by selecting (highlighting) it in the list of forms, then pressing Delete and choosing Yes when prompted. Or, you can edit a form by choosing it from the list of forms, then making necessary changes to the form's definition (length and width).

3. Provide the length of the form, based on the number of lines that can be printed on the page. You can enter any number from 1 to 255, inclusive.

   For example, if your printer can print 6 lines of text per inch of paper length, and your paper is 11 inches long, enter 66 (6 times 11).

4. Provide the width of the form, based on the number of characters that can be printed across the page in a single line. You can enter any number from 1 to 999.

For example, if your font size is 10 characters per inch and your page is 8 1/2 inches wide, enter 85 (10 times 8.5).

5. Save the form and exit the PRINTDEF utility.

PRINTCON

The PRINTCON utility enables both users and network administrators to set up print job configurations that help to customize the working environment. The CAPTURE, NPRINT, and PCONSOLE utilities can then use the custom print job configurations.

To use this utility, type **PRINTCON** and press Enter. From the Available Options menu (see fig. 51.4), you can then choose to accomplish any of the following tasks:

■ **Edit Print Job Configurations.** Enables you to choose an existing print job configuration and modify various parameters set for this template, delete an existing print job configuration (select the configuration, press Delete, and answer Yes to the prompt to confirm), or rename a print job configuration (press F3, type a new name, and press Enter).

■ **Select Default Print Job Configuration.** Enables you to choose which print job

configuration to use as the default when you send a print request.

■ **Copy Print Job Configurations.** Provides the capability to copy any individual user's PRINTCON.DAT database file to another user. Groups cannot have configurations set; therefore, a print job configuration must be created or copied for each user.

 In NetWare 4, significant changes have been made to the format of the PRINTCON database. In addition, a public database—instead of several private printing configuration databases—can be created (stored in SYS:PUBLIC). If your network does not include applications or utilities that use the PRINTCON.DAT databases created for individual users in the NetWare 2 or 3 environments, then delete these older DAT files from each user's SYS:MAIL*UserID* directory.

In addition, administrators can use the NetWare 4 NetWare Administrator utility to manage print job configurations.

Note also that in NetWare 4, the Copy Print Job Configurations option has been replaced by the Change Current Object option (see fig. 51.5). This option enables you to change your current user to that of another user, or to change your current container object.

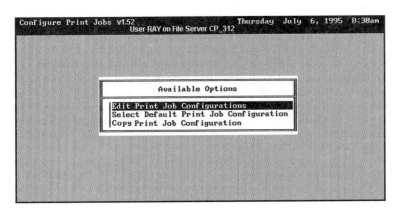

Figure 51.4

NetWare 2/3 PRINTCON Available Options menu.

Figure 51.5

NetWare 4 PRINTCON
Available Options menu.

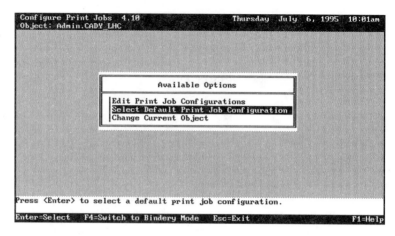

When you create or edit a print job configuration, the parameters you work with are the same as those used with the CAPTURE and NPRINT utilities.

CAPTURE

The CAPTURE utility enables network users to customize their printing environment and accomplish a variety of printing-related tasks. For example, using the J (JOB) CAPTURE command option, the user can choose to apply a print job created by using the PRINTCON utility. You can use the J and other options when you issue the CAPTURE command, as well as when you create print job configurations. Several of the most commonly used CAPTURE options are shown in table 51.1.

Figure 51.6 shows the screen used to set options for print job configuration, using the NetWare 4 version of the PRINTCON utility. Note similarities between the field names in this figure and several of the CAPTURE options in table 51.1. The Notify and No Notify CAPTURE options, for example, are set by using a toggle (Yes/No) in the Notify when done field of this screen.

Table 51.1
Commonly Used CAPTURE Commands

Command	Use	NetWare Version	Purpose
All	ALL	4	Used with EC (ALL EC), ends capture of all LPT ports. Used with /?, provides online help
Autoendcap	AU	2, 3, 4	Automatically sends print job when application is closed

Command	Use	NetWare Version	Purpose
Banner	B	4	Specifies text to be placed in lower half of banner page. No more than 12 characters can be used
Local	L	2, 3	Specifies local port number
Notify	NOTI	2, 3, 4	Informs user when print job is finished
No Notify	NNOTI	3, 4	Does not inform user when print job is done
Printer	P	4	Specifies which printer is to receive print job
Server	S	4	Specifies NetWare server to which the print job should be directed if server is not the default server
Show	SH	2, 3, 4	Shows current status of CAPTURE command
Timeout	TI		Specifies how many seconds to wait after printing text has been received before the print job is deemed complete

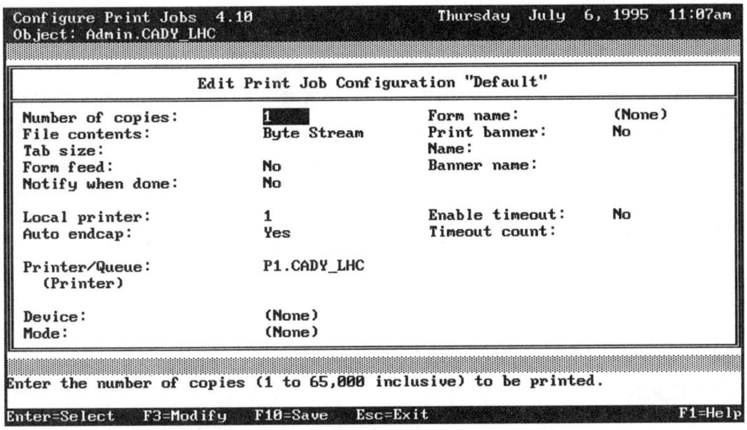

```
Configure Print Jobs  4.10                    Thursday  July  6, 1995  11:07am
Object: Admin.CADY_LHC


┌─────────────────────────────────────────────────────────────────┐
│              Edit Print Job Configuration "Default"               │
│                                                                   │
│ Number of copies:      1            Form name:        (None)      │
│ File contents:     Byte Stream      Print banner:     No          │
│ Tab size:                           Name:                         │
│ Form feed:             No           Banner name:                  │
│ Notify when done:      No                                         │
│                                                                   │
│ Local printer:         1            Enable timeout:   No          │
│ Auto endcap:           Yes          Timeout count:                │
│                                                                   │
│ Printer/Queue:     P1.CADY_LHC                                    │
│   (Printer)                                                       │
│                                                                   │
│ Device:                (None)                                     │
│ Mode:                  (None)                                     │
└─────────────────────────────────────────────────────────────────┘

Enter the number of copies (1 to 65,000 inclusive) to be printed.

Enter=Select   F3=Modify   F10=Save   Esc=Exit                      F1=Help
```

Figure 51.6

The Edit Print Job Configuration screen.

SMODE

The NetWare 2 and 3 SMODE command-line utility is used to modify how PCONSOLE, CAPTURE, and NPRINT function, so as to enable all currently logged-in users to use one PRINTCON database on a single file server. (In NetWare 4, the equivalent to using SMODE is to create and use a Public PRINTCON database stored in the SYS:PUBLIC directory on a NetWare 4 file server.)

Search mode (SMODE) is set to 0 by default. This setting causes all NetWare executable files to search the individual user's mail directory for a PRINTCON.DAT file. By changing the search mode setting to 5, NetWare executable files can use search drive mappings to find the PRINTCON.DAT file stored in SYS:PUBLIC, effectively using a global print job configuration instead of a private one.

To change the SMODE default of 0 to 5 for the PCONSOLE, CAPTURE, and NPRINT utilities to use, type the following nine lines of commands, pressing Enter after each command:

FLAG SYS:PUBLIC\PCONSOLE.EXE N

FLAG SYS:PUBLIC\CAPTURE.EXE N

FLAG SYS:PUBLIC\NPRINT.EXE N

SMODE SYS:PUBLIC\PCONSOLE.EXE /
➡**Mode=5**

SMODE SYS:PUBLIC\CAPTURE.EXE /
➡**Mode=5**

SMODE SYS:PUBLIC\NPRINT.EXE /
➡**Mode=5**

FLAG SYS:PUBLIC\PCONSOLE.EXE SRO

FLAG SYS:PUBLIC\CAPTURE.EXE SRO

FLAG SYS:PUBLIC\NPRINT.EXE SRO

The first three commands set the flags on the PCONSOLE, CAPTURE, and NPRINT utilities to normal, so that their SMODE level can be changed. The next three commands change the SMODE level from the default of 0 to 5, for each of these three utilities. The last three commands change the flags on the three related utilities back to their original settings (-Shareable, Read-Only).

 Remember to remove the individual user's PRINTCON.DAT file from each users SYS:MAIL\ *UserID* directory.

NPRINT

As a workstation utility, NPRINT enables you to print DOS text files, or files preformatted by a DOS application program, to a network printer. You can use a variety of options with this command, most of which are the same as those used with the CAPTURE utility. The SHow, Autoendcap, NoAutoendcap, TImeout, Local, CReate, and Keep CAPTURE options do not apply to the NPRINT command.

RPRINTER

The RPRINTER utility enables you to connect or disconnect a *remote* printer (connected to a workstation) on a NetWare 3 network. NetWare 4 networks also can use remote printers, but they use NPRINTER instead of RPRINTER.

NPRINTER

As with RPRINTER on a NetWare 3 network, NPRINTER enables you to connect printers to workstations, which can then be accessed by other network users. NPRINTER.NLM is loaded on the NetWare 4 file server to provide remote printing services.

NetUser

This utility, available in NetWare 3.12 and NetWare 4 networks, is designed to enable users to add, modify, or delete their own print jobs. Figure 51.7 shows the NetUser utility Available Options menu running on a NetWare 4 file server.

NetWare Administrator

The NetWare Administrator utility can be used to create and administer printing services in the NetWare 4 environment. It is a GUI (Graphical User Interface) utility, which is run from inside MS Windows. Logged in to the network as the Administrator, you can accomplish the following tasks by using the NetWare Administrator utility:

■ Create, control, monitor, and manage print queues

■ Create, control, monitor, and manage print servers

■ Delete, change, monitor, and reorder print jobs

■ Assign print queue objects to printers, and printer objects to print servers

Printing from MS Windows 3.1 Applications

As with DOS-based network printing, a printer must be directly attached to the workstation, or the workstation must be connected to a network in order to print through MS Windows. In addition, a driver file for the printer must be available and properly configured to support the printer being accessed. MS Windows printer drivers can be used to access printing while still supporting the MS Windows environment and applications.

 A print driver file is a DLL (dynamic link library) file with the DRV extension instead of a DLL extension. Print driver files are capable of communicating with a specific printer in order to translate application print requests into information the printer can use. MS Windows driver files enable users to access particular attributes of different printers. For example, a print driver makes it possible to specify such things as the margins to be used when printing a document, which typeface to use, which paper tray to choose from, and so on.

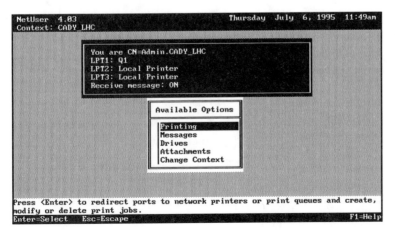

Figure 51.7
NetUser Available Options menu.

MS Windows applications access printing by using the GDI (Graphics Device Interface). GDI formats the output sent to the printer, as well as that sent to the monitor. Applications running under MS Windows use the GDI to call the active MS Windows Print Manager. From there, print jobs are formatted and printed one page at a time. When there is more to be printed than can be immediately sent to the printer, the additional print pages are stored in either the MS Windows TEMP directory, or the root directory of the default drive's hard disk. From either of these locations, jobs then can be sent directly to a NetWare print queue, to a local queue, or to a local printer port.

When the MS Windows Print Manager is not active or is not installed, GDI sends the data directly to a DOS device rather than to a print queue on the hard disk.

When the MS Windows Print Manager is installed and local printing is enabled, the formatted pages are sent by GDI to a queue file on the local hard disk, which the Print Manager controls.

When the Print Manager is enabled and network printing is available, the formatted pages are sent by GDI to a network queue file, bypassing the Print Manager's local queue file.

 Note The NetWare CAPTURE command can be used with MS Windows to redirect printing to a NetWare queue. By using the CAPTURE command, the user can specify which queue to use for print jobs. The command also enables users to monitor and manipulate jobs in the print queue before they are printed, and to otherwise exercise a greater degree of control over print jobs (after they have been sent to a print queue) than might be possible with local printing only.

You can use MS Windows 3.1 to set up printing for each application that needs print support, as well as for each type of printer being used. The setup for a specific printer is called the printer's *device context*. Most applications check the printer's device context before attempting to print. When a print request is made, MS Windows checks to see whether the application itself has established any specific print settings. If it has, MS Windows follows those settings. If it has not, MS Windows checks memory for the most recent print settings and uses those. If no print settings are stored in memory, MS Windows checks for print settings established in the WIN.INI file and uses those. If the WIN.INI file does not contain the necessary printer and port settings, MS Windows uses the defaults in its own setup to complete the print request (see fig. 51.8).

To take full advantage of MS Windows printing, you may need to set up printing by using the Printers dialog box in the MS Windows Control Panel (see fig. 51.9).

To install, configure, set up, or remove a printer, complete the following steps:

1. Open the MS Windows Control Panel.

2. Choose Printers.

3. Choose a printer, then choose one of the following:

   ▪ **Setup.** To adjust settings such as DPI resolution (the number of dots per inch), paper tray to use, and so on

   ▪ **Remove.** To remove or delete a printer from the list

   ▪ **Set as default printer.** To choose the selected (highlighted) printer as the default print driver

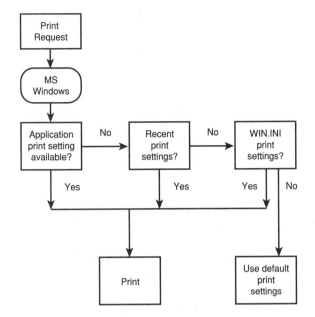

Figure 51.8
The steps taken by MS Windows when WIN.INI contains no printer settings.

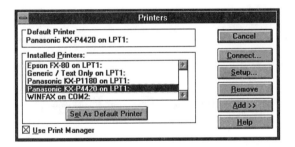

Figure 51.9
The MS Windows Printers window.

■ **Connect.** To connect the printer to a local port (LPT or COM) or to a network drive

When you choose Connect and then choose Network to connect the printer to a NetWare network drive, the NetWare User Tools utility opens (see fig. 51.10). From this utility you choose to connect or disconnect a printer. In addition, you can make any printer connection a permanent one by marking the Permanent box.

Making a printer connection Permanent overrides CAPTURE redirection for the specified printer port.

You use the MS Windows Print Manager to set the following printing options:

■ Priority (Low, Medium, or High)

■ Alert Always

■ Flash (or Ignore) if Inactive

- Network Settings

- Network Connections

- Printer Setup

Using the Print Manager, you can also view a NetWare print queue, temporarily pause any print job, resume a paused print job, or delete print jobs (see fig. 51.11).

The MS Windows WIN.INI file contains commands that help establish default printing settings.

The following main commands are included in the WIN.INI file:

- **Device=** Defines the default printer that MS Windows uses

- **DeviceNotSelectedTimeout=** Specifies how long MS Windows waits for a printer to be turned on before it sends a print request to a printer that currently is turned off (default is 15 seconds)

Figure 51.10

The NetWare User Tools Printer Connections window.

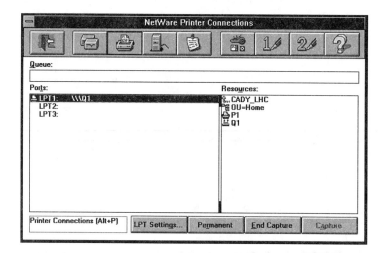

Figure 51.11

The Print Manager window.

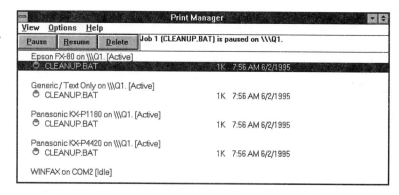

- **DosPrint=** Uses Interrupt 21 for printing if set to Yes, or Interrupt 17 if set to No

- **Spooler=** Enables Print Manager, if set to Yes (the default); if set to No, disables Print Manager and does not display it in the Main window

- **TransmissionRetryTimeout=** Sets the number of seconds (default is 90) the printer will wait before sending out an error message when the printer is not accepting characters

- **LPT1:=** Specifies where the I/O port is redirected, if it has been redirected (such as the redirection that occurs when you use the NetWare User Tools to set a connection and specify it as Permanent)

- **LPT1-Options=** Lists all options associated with printing to this printer port, such as No Form Feed, number of copies to be printed, and so on (uses several of the same options used by the CAPTURE utility)

Questions

1. The PRINTDEF utility is used to _____.

   ○ A. create custom printer and form definitions

   ○ B. set up print job configurations

   ○ C. customize user's printing environment

   ○ D. connect or disconnect a remote printer

2. The file in which printer definitions are stored for server-wide use is called _____.

   ○ A. NET$PRN.DBS

   ○ B. NET$PRN.DAT

   ○ C. NET$DAT.PRN

   ○ D. NET$DBS.DAT

3. The _____ utility/command is used to set up job configurations to customize the user's environment.

   ○ A. PRINTDEF

   ○ B. PRINTCON

   ○ C. SMODE

   ○ D. CAPTURE

4. When creating or editing a print job configuration, many of the parameters that can be used are the same as those used in the _____ and _____ utilities.

   ○ A. PRINTCON, PRINTDEF

   ○ B. PRINTDEF, NPRINT

   ○ C. NPRINT, CAPTURE

   ○ D. CAPTURE, SMODE

5. The default setting for search mode (SMODE) is _____.

   ○ A. 0

   ○ B. 3

   ○ C. 5

   ○ D. 9

6. Which utility is used to connect or disconnect a remote printer?

   ○ A. PRINTDEF

   ○ B. PRINTCON

   ○ C. SMODE

   ○ D. RPRINTER

7. Of the following, which THREE are NetWare 2, 3, and 4 CAPTURE command options?

   ☐ A. AUtoendcap

   ☐ B. NoNOTIfy

   ☐ C. NOTIfy

   ☐ D. SHow

8. The _____ utility is designed to let users add, modify, or delete their own print jobs.

   ○ A. NPRINTER

   ○ B. RPRINTER

   ○ C. NetUser

   ○ D. NetWare Administrator

9. When the MS Windows Print Manager is not active, _____.

   ○ A. GDI sends the formatted pages to a print queue on the local hard disk

   ○ B. GDI sends the data directly to a DOS device

   ○ C. GDI sends the formatted pages directly to a NetWare print queue

   ○ D. GDI holds the print job until the Print Manager is activated

10. If you want to direct print jobs to a network printer by using the Printers option in the MS Windows Control Panel, you must choose _____.

   ○ A. Capture

   ○ B. Setup

   ○ C. Set as default

   ○ D. Connect

Answers

1. A

2. B

3. B

4. C

5. A

6. D

7. A, C, D

8. C

9. B

10. D

Understanding Printing in NetWare 4

There are some basic differences between printing in the NetWare 4 (NDS) environment and printing in the NetWare 2 and 3 (bindery) environment. Other chapters in this section discuss NetWare 4 printing in contrast to NetWare 2 and 3. In this chapter, the following topics provide more detailed information about printing in the NetWare 4 environment:

■ *NetWare 4 printing basics*

■ *NetWare 4 printing configuration and administration*

NetWare 4 Printing Basics

Because NetWare 4 is based on NetWare Directory Services (NDS), print services must function in that environment as well. To some extent, print service configuration and administration in NetWare 4 is easier than in NetWare 2 or NetWare 3. Standard printing elements—print servers, print queues, and printers—are NDS objects in NetWare 4. As such, their administration is similar to that of other NetWare 4 objects.

Printing utilities such as PCONSOLE, PRINTCON, and PRINTDEF have been enhanced for NetWare 4 printing, functioning through bindery-emulation. In addition, the NetWare User Tools and NetWare Administrator utilities are available in NetWare 4, enabling you to administer and use NetWare print services.

NetWare 4 Printing Configuration and Administration

To administer NetWare 4 printing, you can use the NetWare Administrator utility as well as PCONSOLE. With the NetWare Administrator utility, you can accomplish the following tasks:

- Create, modify, and delete print queues and print servers

- Monitor, modify, reorder, and delete print jobs

- Control and monitor printers and print servers

Figure 52.1 shows the first screen of the NetWare Administrator utility.

Figure 52.1

The main screen for the NetWare Administrator utility.

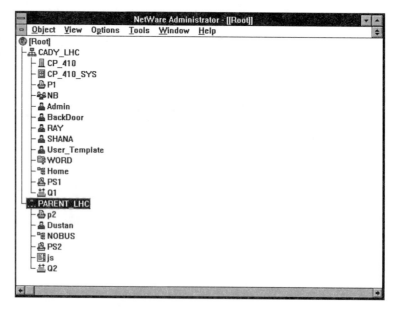

With the NDS tree expanded in the NetWare Administrator utility, you can create Print Server, Print Queue, and Printer objects by selecting (highlighting) the container in the NDS tree where you want to place the object, then choosing **C**reate from the **O**bject pull-down menu (see fig.52.2).

Next, choose the type of object you want to create (Print Server, Print Queue, or Printer) from the New Object window (see fig. 52.3).

When the related Create *object_name* dialog box opens, provide the necessary information. For example, if you choose to create a Print Queue object, the Create Print Queue dialog box opens. You must provide a Print Queue **N**ame and a Print Queue **V**olume. You can also choose to either **D**efine Additional Properties for the Print Queue object, or to Create **A**nother Print Queue. In addition, you can choose to make this a NetWare Directory **S**ervice Print Queue, or to **R**eference a Bindery Queue (see fig. 52.4).

You can also move, rename, or delete Print Server, Print Queue, and Printer objects by selecting the object and choosing the related action from the **O**bject pull-down menu.

To rename a Print Queue object, for example, choose Re**n**ame from the **O**bject pull-down menu, and enter the new name in the Rename dialog box. If you want to, you can save the old name as well by marking the **S**ave Old Name box (see fig. 52.5).

You can also use NetWare Administrator to monitor, modify, reorder, and delete print jobs. To accomplish these tasks, you must choose either a Print Queue object or a Printer object. If you choose a Print Queue object and then open the Jobs List page for this Print Queue object (see fig. 52.6), you can perform various tasks (view details about the job, hold the job, delete the job, and so on) by choosing the corresponding button.

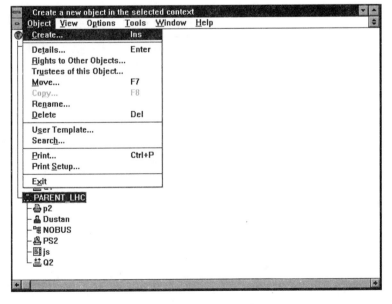

Figure 52.2

The Object pull-down menu.

Figure 52.3

The New Object window.

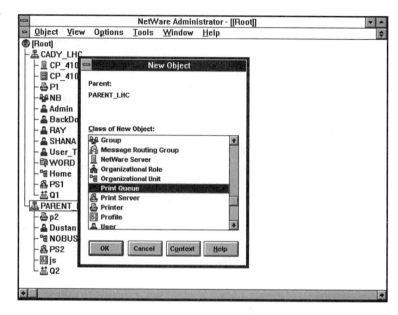

Figure 52.4

The Create Print Queue dialog box.

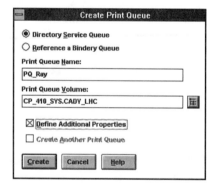

Figure 52.5

The Rename dialog box.

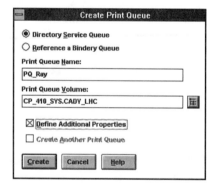

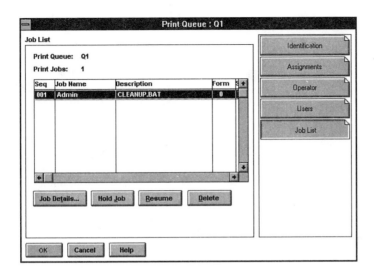

Figure 52.6

The Print Queue Jobs List page for Print Queue Q1.

You can also use the NetWare Administrator utility to control and monitor Printer objects and Print Server objects. To monitor a Printer object, for example, select the Printer object, choose De**t**ails from the **O**bject pull-down menu, then choose Configuration to open the Configuration page for this Printer object. Figure 52.7 shows a Configuration page.

From this page you can monitor information about the Printer object's configuration, such as the type of printer (Parallel or Serial), the type of banner, the service interval, buffer size, and so on. In addition, you can open the Printer Status page for this Printer object and monitor information such as the printer's status, which form is mounted, and so on.

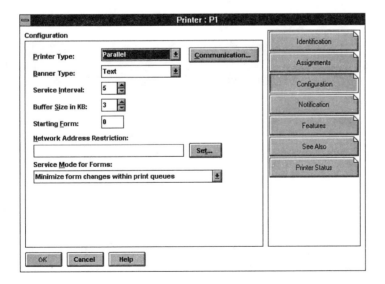

Figure 52.7

The Configuration page.

In addition to the NetWare Administration utility, the NetWare Tools and NetUser utilities are included in NetWare 4 to provide greater access to printing services. The NetWare Tools utility enables you to use the MS Windows drag-and-drop feature to capture printer ports to network print drives. Figure 41.8 shows the NetWare Tools utility with the NetWare Printer Connections window open.

The NetUser utility is used from DOS workstations to control printing. Its menu interface makes it possible for users to enable or disable printing redirection, set redirection parameters, and make printer redirection settings permanent. Figure 41.9 shows the Available Options menu for the NetUser utility.

Another significant change between NetWare 4 and earlier versions of NetWare is the addition of the Quick Setup option in the NetWare 4 version of the PCONSOLE utility (see fig. 52.10). With this option, the task of setting up the printing environment for a single Print Server, Printer, and Print Queue object is very quick and very easy.

NetWare 4 also provides a workstation and an NLM version of a utility called NPRINTER. NPRINTER enables users on the network to share printers attached to workstations and servers. (For DOS and OS/2 workstations, DOS and OS/2 versions of NPRINTER exist.) With the NPRINTER.NLM loaded at a NetWare 4 file server, up to seven printers can be attached to the server and shared by network users.

Printing in a NetWare 4 NDS environment and printing in a NetWare bindery environment differ in a few other ways.

First, in bindery-based versions of NetWare, print queues were always located on the SYS:SYSTEM volume. In NetWare 4, print queues can be located on any volume in the QUEUES directory.

Second, in NetWare 4, the ENDCAP command is not available as a separate command as it is in NetWare 3.1*x.*

Third, although NetWare 3.1*x* has three types of print servers—PSERVER.NLM, PSERVER.EXE, and PSERVER.VAP—NetWare 4 supports only one print server type: PSERVER.NLM.

Figure 52.8

The NetWare Tools NetWare Printer Connections window.

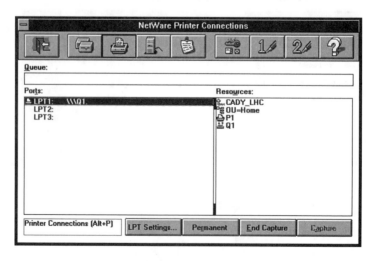

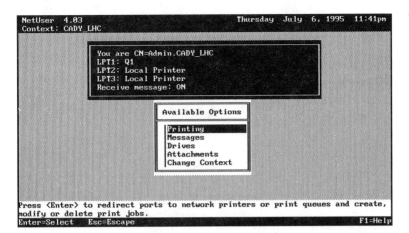

Figure 52.9
*The NetUser Available
Options menu.*

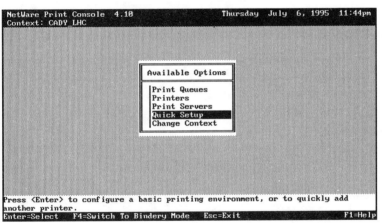

Figure 52.10
*The PCONSOLE
Available Options menu.*

Fourth, print servers in the NetWare 3.1*x* environment can control a maximum of only 16 printers. In the NetWare 4 environment, however, Print Server objects can control up to 255 printers.

Finally, shared printers on a NetWare 4 network can only be connected to servers, DOS or OS/2 workstations, or directly to the network cable. In NetWare 3.1*x*, printers can be connected to NetWare servers, dedicated DOS print servers, external routers, DOS workstations, or directly to the network cable.

Questions

1. Which of the following utilities has *not* been enhanced for NetWare 4 printing services?

   ○ A. NPRINT

   ○ B. PRINTDEF

   ○ C. PCONSOLE

   ○ D. PRINTCON

2. Which TWO of the following are true?

   ☐ A. NetWare Administrator provides many of the same capabilities as PCONSOLE.

   ☐ B. PCONSOLE, PRINTCON, and PRINTDEF have all been enhanced for NetWare 4.

   ☐ C. CAPTURE cannot be used with NetWare 4.

   ☐ D. You must use the PCONSOLE utility to perform a quick printing setup.

3. The _____ utility CANNOT be used to set up or manage both NetWare 3 and NetWare 4 printing environments.

   ○ A. PCONSOLE

   ○ B. PRINTCON

   ○ C. NetWare Administrator

   ○ D. PRINTDEF

4. The _____ utility also can be used to administer printing in NetWare 4.

   ○ A. PCONSOLE

   ○ B. CAPTURE

   ○ C. SMODE

   ○ D. RPRINTER

5. To create a Print Queue object, you must provide at least _____ and _____ information in the Create Print Queue dialog box.

   ○ A. Print Queue Name, Print Queue Volume

   ○ B. Print Queue Name, Print Queue Server

   ○ C. Print Queue Volume, Printer Name

   ○ D. Print Queue Server, Printer Name

6. You can create, rename, or move a Print Queue object by first selecting the object, then choosing the related option from the _____ pull-down menu.

   ○ A. View

   ○ B. Window

   ○ C. Options

   ○ D. Object

7. Of the following, which TWO are provided with NetWare 4 and not with NetWare 3.1*x*?

   ☐ A. Quick Setup option in PCONSOLE

   ☐ B. PRINTCON and PRINTDEF

   ☐ C. NetWare Administrator utility

   ☐ D. NetWare User Administration utility

8. Open the _____ page to monitor information about a Printer object's configuration.

   ○ A. Assignments

   ○ B. Notification

   ○ C. Configuration

   ○ D. Features

9. The _____ utility makes it possible for users to enable or disable printing redirection, set redirection parameters, and make printing redirection permanent.

   ○ A. NETUSER

   ○ B. NETADMIN

   ○ C. NWUSER

   ○ D. NWADMIN

10. Which of the following is NOT a difference between printing in NetWare 3.1x and NetWare 4?

   ○ A. PSERVER.NLM is the only type of print server in NetWare 4.

   ○ B. NetWare 3.1x print servers can service up to 16 print servers only, whereas NetWare 4 print servers can service up to 255 printers.

   ○ C. Printers cannot be connected to external routers in a NetWare 4 environment.

   ○ D. None of the above

Answers

1. A

2. A, B

3. C

4. A

5. A

6. D

7. A, C

8. C

9. A

10. D

Improving Network Printing Performance

*N*etwork printing performance depends on several factors,
the most important of which are included in this
chapter's discussions of the following topics:

- ■ *Avoiding and correcting printing bottlenecks*

- ■ *Troubleshooting network printing problems*

Avoiding and Correcting Printing Bottlenecks

Chapter 49, "Understanding Printing and NetWare Printing Services," discussed the following three phases of printing:

- **Spooling.** Sending the print job across the network to a print queue

- **De-spooling.** Transferring the print job from the print queue to the designated printer

- **Printing.** Translating the print job into a printed document

At any point in these three phases of printing, a *bottleneck* (a significant reduction in processing speed) can occur. Several factors can affect printing performance. An understanding of these factors can help you to find and correct performance problems with your network.

The following primary factors affect printing performance:

- How quickly the print job can travel between the printer port on the host computer and the printer (network interface speed)

- How effectively the application program and print drivers communicate (printer interface speed)

- How long and complex the document is that is being printed (spooling)

- How well the printing-related hardware handles the printing process (de-spooling)

When you consider the network interface speed, consider the design of the network itself, how

traffic moves around the network (pattern), and the types of print information traveling across the LAN. For example, Token Ring networks can transfer data across the network at speeds ranging from 230.4 Kbps to 16 Mbps.

When you consider the printer interface speed, consider how the type of cable and connection affect how data is transferred to the printer. A parallel interface, for example, commonly transfers data at the rate of 1 Kbps to 40 Kbps.

 Note A printer with its own network interface, such as those that use the HP Jetdirect card, can be directly connected to the network through the printer's parallel port. The speed of printing for devices connected in this manner is determined primarily by the parallel interface the printer uses. These devices function, however, by taking the print job directly from the NetWare print queue and then printing it. These devices do not wait for a print server to poll the print queues and send the jobs to them.

When you consider spooling bottlenecks, consider such performance-affecting factors as the print drivers provided by the application requesting the print service, whether NetWare CAPTURE or NetWare Core Protocol (NCP) printing is being used, the speed and capability of the workstation's CPU and network board, and the topology of the network, as well as the NetWare server's configuration (network board, number of NLMs currently loaded, and so on).

When you consider de-spooling bottlenecks, consider such factors as the length of time between queries of the queue by the print server, where the print server is physically located on the network in relation to the printer, and the maximum performance of which the print server is capable.

You should also consider the printer's capabilities. Factors such as the printer's interface, the formatter, the print engine, language/context switching, multiple port and protocol selection all affect printing performance.

Printer Interface

Printer interfaces include elements such as the speed at which the printer can accept input, the capability of the printer's parallel port, and the size of the printer's print buffer. Printers that cannot accept print jobs from the network as quickly as the network sends them can create a bottleneck. This applies also to the capability of the parallel port. Many parallel ports can transfer and receive data at speeds from 1 to 14 Kbps. The use of a newer bidirectional, high-speed (up to 40 Kbps) printer port can reduce bottlenecks of this type. Larger print buffers also can reduce bottlenecks by allowing complete jobs to be sent to the printer and held until the formatter is ready for them.

Formatter

The printer's formatter converts print data signals into signals the printer engine can recognize. Those printer formatters that operate at speeds below the speed at which the parallel port can transfer and receive data become a bottleneck. When you use the bidirectional high-speed printer ports on a printer with a formatter that functions at a slower speed, you limit the speed of the printer to that of the printer's formatter.

Print Engine

The print engine takes the print data converted by the formatter and transfers the information to paper. The speed of the print engine is measured by using the number of lines per minute, pages per minute, or characters per second that the print engine is capable of managing.

Language/Context Switching

Some printers can accommodate different languages. Some automatically switch to the required language by examining the print data (context switching). Others accommodate a single language, which cannot be changed. Still others can accommodate different languages, but some method to enable the changes must be provided. Although the language change itself may initially be a little time-consuming, bottlenecking seldom occurs after the printer is changed. On the other hand, when automatic context switching is part of a printer's features, some bottlenecking may occur when the language used in different print jobs varies.

Multiple Port and Protocol Selection

Often, resources such as ports, protocols, fonts, macros, and so on must be downloaded to the printer before a print job can be completed. Sometimes, changing languages can necessitate that all this information be downloaded again. Printers that can retain this information, even when the language used changes, are less of a bottleneck than are those that necessitate downloading the information once again.

Troubleshooting Network Printing Problems

To effectively troubleshoot and solve network printing problems, you first need to understand the basics of printing on a NetWare network.

In NetWare versions 3.0 and higher, printing is a process separate from the NetWare Operating System. Printing is provided by separate software, called PSERVER, that can be added as a NetWare Loadable Module (NLM), value-added process (VAP), or as an executable (EXE) file on a workstation. The PSERVER software performs most of the NetWare printing process.

The Effect of Setting Up Printing Services

Using the NetWare Administrator (NetWare 4 only) or PCONSOLE utilities, you create print servers (or Print Server objects) and print queues (or Print Queue objects). When you create a print server, a directory for each print server is also created under the SYS:SYSTEM directory. The same is true for print queues, but the print queue directories are created on the same file server as the print queue. Alphanumeric characters are used to name both print server and print queue directories. Their names correspond to the Object ID number for print servers (found in the Print Server ID options of PCONSOLE's Print Server Information menu), and for print queues (found in PCONSOLE's Print Queue ID field for a chosen print queue).

 Note To see a list of print queues, type **LISTDIR** in the SYS:SYSTEM directory. NetWare 3.1x print queue directories are displayed with a QDR extension.

The print queue directory holds print jobs, SRV files, and a SYS file. Print jobs are placed in the print queue in the order they are sent. Each print job is assigned a number. After a print job is sent to a printer, the job is deleted from the print queue, and the job number becomes available for another print job to use. The print queue directory also contains a hidden SRV file for each print server to which the print queue sends print jobs. Print servers that are not currently available have zero bytes in their related hidden SRV file. The SYS file contains information required by the server to maintain the print queue. Information in this file includes such things as the number of the station that sent the print job, the ID number of the user who sent the print job, print job file names, and so on.

The print server directory contains four types of files, which contain information about the following:

- The file server this print server services (FILESERV)

- The printers being used (PRINT)

- The print queues being serviced by these printers (QUEUE)

- The users on the notify list for each printer (NOTIFY)

Because NetWare 3 can support as many as 16 printers per print server, as many as 16 sets of these files can be found in the print server directory. (Related files have the same extension; for example, all files in a set might have the extension .000 or .001.) When you run the PCONSOLE utility and make changes to print configurations, these files are updated. The updates become effective, however, only when the print server is brought down and then reloaded by typing PSERVER.

The Dynamics of Printing with NetWare

To use NetWare printing services, load and run the print server software—PSERVER.VAP (NetWare 2), PSERVER.NLM (NetWare 3 and 4), or PSERVER.EXE (dedicated workstation). Figure 53.1 shows what happens when you issue the PSERVER command. First, PSERVER checks its ID directory for information about the file servers it is to service. It then connects to each file server listed in the FILESERV file, and creates a table based on the information it finds in the PRINT, QUEUE, and NOTIFY files. Finally, it attaches print queues to their assigned printers.

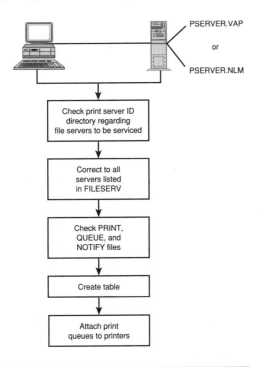

Figure 53.1

The dynamics of printing with NetWare.

After PSERVER is loaded and set up, it polls the assigned print queues and sends the print jobs it finds to the appropriate printer.

You can also provide network printing through a printer attached to a regular network workstation, if that workstation has a RPRINTER.EXE file loaded. When RPRINTER is loaded, the associated print server sends its configuration information to the workstation running RPRINTER. RPRINTER waits for a print job to be sent to it, then prints jobs as they are received. Because limited print buffer space is available, RPRINTER must notify PSERVER when it is ready for additional print job data (if the buffer cannot hold the entire print job when it first receives the job).

Printing Problems and Suggested Solutions

Printing problems are not uncommon, and most of them can be solved. With printing problems, as with medical problems, the first step toward solving the problem is correct diagnosis. Following are some common printing problems, their symptoms, and solutions:

■ **Problem:** *Corrupted print queue or print server definitions.*

   Symptoms: Request for a print server password when none has been set; slow printing; RPRINTER errors that occur when network print data is sent or received.

   Solution: Delete and re-create print queues or print servers, and if necessary, any related subdirectories in the SYS:SYSTEM directory, if no corresponding PCONSOLE Print Server ID exists.

■ **Problem:** *Faulty cabling, concentrators, terminators, network boards, or other printing-related hardware.*

Symptoms: When you reboot the workstation to reestablish a lost connection, message indicates that RPRINTER is still in use

Solution: Add settings to the SHELL.CFG or NET.CFG file to prevent the SPX connection from timing out before it receives a response. Add the following lines: IPX RETRY COUNT=35 and SPX ABORT TIMEOUT=700.

■ **Problem:** *Conflicts between RPRINTER and the network interface board settings, or with other TSRs.*

Symptoms: RPRINTER hangs when it loads.

Solution: Change the settings on the network board, and rerun WSGEN to match the IPX to the new settings. If ODI drivers are used at the workstation, change the NET.CFG file to load the network board with the new settings. Also, before running RPRINTER, try unloading any other TSRs that may be loaded at the workstation.

■ **Problem:** *Conflicts between PSERVER.EXE and the network interface board.*

Symptoms: PSERVER.EXE hangs the workstation.

Solution: Unload, then reload the print server to reset the print server. If this does not correct the problem, check various items of hardware such as the network board and the cabling for problems. Also, if you are using an older version of an IPX driver, update the driver to a newer version.

■ **Problem:** *Third-party VAPS are in conflict with the PSERVER.VAP; the first LAN uses*

ARCNET topology and no workstations are powered on; the print server uses shadow RAM and is experiencing sporadic problems.

Symptoms: The PSERVER.VAP used on NetWare 2 networks hangs or *stops advertising its presence* (SAPs) on the network.

Solution: Check the order in which third-party VAPs are loading, and eliminate those that are causing conflicts. You can also power up a workstation in the ARCNET LAN if none are currently running. Also, remove shadow RAM and run PSERVER without it to see whether that corrects the problem.

■ **Problem:** *PostScript printers delete any print job that does not appear to be properly formatted for a PostScript printer. Banner pages and jobs sent in Text mode are seen as improperly formatted print jobs.*

Symptoms: Print jobs containing graphics files are not printed when sent to PostScript printers.

Solution: Use the /NT (No Tabs), /NB (No Banner), and /NFF (No Form Feed) parameters when you use CAPTURE or NPRINT on graphics jobs sent to PostScript printers. In addition, you can update the driver files for the PostScript printer, and add the following line to the SHELL.CFG or NET.CFG file: PRINT HEADER=n (replacing n with a number between 64 and 255).

■ **Problem:** *Applications that print to plotters use the COM port, while NetWare uses LPT ports for printing.*

Symptoms: Plotter printing jobs sent through a related application program do not print.

Solution: Use the application to save the print job to a file, then use NPRINT or PCONSOLE to print the job.

■ **Problem:** *The implementation method used for handshaking a serial printer to the network is not compatible with one or more printers.*

Symptoms: Communication between serial printers and the network is nonfunctional or sporadic.

Solution: Use Novell's recommended pin-out for serial printer cabling, as shown in table 53.1.

Table 53.1
Serial Cable Pin-Out Recommended by Novell

Pin No. at PC	Cable Type	Function	Pin No. at Printer
(none)	9-pin	Frame Ground	1
1	25-pin	Frame Ground	1
3	9-pin	Transmit Data	2
2	25-pin	Transmit Data	3
2	9-pin	Receive Data	3
3	25-pin	Receive Data	2
7	9-pin	Request to Send	4
4	25-pin	Request to Send	4
8	9-pin	Clear to Send	20
5	25-pin	Clear to Send	20
6	9-pin	*Data Set Ready	6
6	25-pin	*Data Set Ready	6
5	9-pin	Signal Ground	7
7	25-pin	Signal Ground	7
1	9-pin	Data Carrier Detect	8
8	25-pin	Data Carrier Detect	8
7	9-pin	Data Terminal Ready	4
4	25-pin	Data Terminal Ready	4

* NetWare does not use Data Set Ready, but DOS does. Novell recommends tying pins 5 and 6 together to provide DOS printing support.

Questions

1. One of the primary factors that affects printing is _____.

   ○ A. network interface speed

   ○ B. application speed

   ○ C. other network devices on the cable

   ○ D. version of DOS being run

2. The _____ and _____ factors, which affect printing, are also steps in the printing process.

   ☐ A. printing

   ☐ B. spooling

   ☐ C. queuing

   ☐ D. de-spooling

3. Printers with their own network interface can be directly connected to _____.

   ○ A. a print server

   ○ B. a workstation

   ○ C. the printer's parallel port

   ○ D. the printer's print server

4. An element of a printer interface is _____.

   ○ A. de-spooling

   ○ B. the speed at which the printer can accept input

   ○ C. print drivers provided by applications

   ○ D. none of the above

5. The printer's _____ converts print data signals into signals the printer engine can recognize.

   ○ A. language switch

   ○ B. port selection

   ○ C. context switch

   ○ D. formatter

6. Printers that can switch automatically to the necessary language are said to have _____ ability.

   ○ A. language switching

   ○ B. port switching

   ○ C. context switching

   ○ D. formatter switching

7. Of the following, which THREE are elements of the printer's interface, which can be a cause of printing bottlenecks?

   ☐ A. Speed of accepting input

   ☐ B. Capability of the parallel port

   ☐ C. Type of connection to the network

   ☐ D. Size of the print job buffer

8. Which of the following is NOT a method of providing print services in NetWare 3.0 and later versions?

   ○ A. PSERVER.VAP

   ○ B. PSERVER.COM

   ○ C. PSERVER.NLM

   ○ D. PSERVER.EXE

9. The _____ file in the print queue contains information the server needs to maintain the print queue.

   ○ A. SRV

   ○ B. DRV

   ○ C. 000

   ○ D. SYS

10. If you are prompted for a print server password but no password was set, you must _____ to solve the problem.

   ○ A. delete and re-create the print server and print queue

   ○ B. change settings on the network board and rerun WSGEN

   ○ C. unload and then reload the print server to reset it

   ○ D. use the /NT, /NB, and /NFF parameters with the CAPTURE or NPRINT commands

Answers

1. A

2. B, D

3. C

4. B

5. D

6. C

7. A, B, D

8. B

9. D

10. A

Using Alternative Printing Configurations

Printers are commonly attached to devices attached to the network, such as servers and workstations. Printers also can be attached directly to the network cable if those printers have interfaces that enable them to be placed anywhere on the network, including direct cable attachment, and if network software is provided to manage those printers. In NetWare, the QServer and RPRINTER software make possible the direct network connection of printers.

In order for printers to be successful when connected directly to the network cable, they must be capable of dealing with the variety of choices implemented on the network. For example, they must be capable of supporting the following:

■ A variety of technologies, such as Ethernet, Token Ring, and Local Talk

■ A variety of communication frame types, such as 802.2, 802.3, Ethernet II, and Ethernet SNAP

■ A variety of protocols, such as TCP/IP, IPX/SPX, and AppleTalk

This chapter provides more detailed information on direct connection of printers and the associated network software, emphasizing the following topics:

■ Alternate network printer interfaces and administration

■ Remote printer administration and configuration

Alternate Network Printer Interfaces and Administration

Direct-connect printers use either an internal interface card to connect to the network (such as that used by the HP IIISi and HP 4Si), or an external connection device (such as that used by the HP JetDirect). The method of connection is a less important consideration in network printing, however, than the features or capabilities provided by the printers themselves.

Printer capabilities must be considered and may include any of those shown in table 54.1.

Table 54.1
Printer Capabilities

Capability	*Description*	*Function*
Duplexing	Prints one side, then turns the paper over and prints on the other side	Printing on both sides of paper
Multiple Input Ports	Simultaneously accepts multiple print jobs	Servicing print requests simultaneously
Resource Saving	Stores printer-related resource information in the printer's memory	Retaining downloaded fonts, forms, and so on to save time
Media Selection	Enables choice of what to print on—labels, paper, envelopes, and so on	Selecting the print media
Media Management	Enables choice of print trays when issuing a print job	Providing multiple types of print media

Capability	Description	Function
Language Switching	Provides choice of PCL or PostScript job printing language	Providing automatic or controlled switching
Plotters	Enables CAD packages to send print jobs across the network to plotters that can be connected directly to the network	Providing access to plotters for Computer Aided Design
Color Printers	Provides access to color printers	Enabling color print jobs to be used on the network

In addition to the printer's capabilities, consider the software method to be used for implementing direct-connect printers. The options are QServer mode and RPRINTER mode.

With the QServer mode, the printer's interface also functions as a print server. In addition to the network connection duties it performs, it is also responsible for polling print jobs directly from the network queue and then sending them to the printer. Benefits of this method include the fact that no external print server is needed, redundant printer traffic is prevented, and setup is relatively easy compared to setting up a printer that uses the RPRINTER mode.

The main disadvantage of the QServer mode is that it requires a user connection. On a network with limited available user connections, users may be prevented from connecting to the network if too many printers functioning under the QServer mode are connected to the network.

With the RPRINTER mode, the printer's interface emulates the RPRINTER communication method used by workstations connected to the network with a printer attached. The main benefit of using the RPRINTER mode is that a separate user connection is not required. In addition, this method provides reasonably good performance and does not require the use of unencrypted passwords, because the data itself is password protected from the NetWare server to the print server.

The main drawbacks associated with this method are the need for a Novell NetWare print server and the fact that setup requires more steps than setting up a printer running under the QServer mode.

Remote Printer Administration and Configuration

Because the HP JetDirect, HPIII, and HP4 printers are commonly used on NetWare networks when a direct-connect printer is required, an understanding of remote printer setup and administration of these printers is also commonly required. Two utilities are used to set up and administer these HP printers—JetAdmin and JetPrint.

JetAdmin

The JetAdmin program provides remote installation, configuration, management, troubleshooting, and monitoring of any printer using the HP JetDirect interface. For example, once you open the HP JetAdmin main menu and choose a printer, you can view the status of that printer (see fig. 54.1).

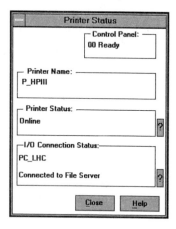

Figure 54.1

The HP JetAdmin Printer Status window.

The Printer Name area displays the name given to the printer when it was installed. The Printer Status area shows the current condition of the printer—Offline, Online, Out of paper, or Printing. Additional status information, such as Door open, Toner low, and so on, may also be displayed. The I/O Connection Status area displays any number of up to 38 different messages, each of which have context-sensitive help (F1) available to describe them.

You can also configure and manage the printer by using the JetAdmin software. Start JetAdmin from the DOS prompt (type **JetAdmin** and press Enter)

or from MS Windows (choose the associated icon). Next, choose the printer to configure and choose Configuration. To configure Queue Server Mode, choose Queue Server Mode under Operating Mode; then assign a printer name, choose Add Queue, and add a New Queue.

To configure the Remote Printer Mode, choose Remote Printer from the Operating Mode option, provide a name for the printer, then choose a printer number and exit JetAdmin.

You can configure various aspects of the remote printer, such as printer drivers, advanced settings, notification, test pages, and user sheets. To use an MS Windows print driver for your JetDirect printer, make the copy available in the SYS:LOGIN\HP_PRINT directory on the NetWare server, if the one you need is not already stored there or needs to be updated. You can also modify printer settings or network interface settings.

The following are printer settings that you can modify:

- **JetDirect Broadcasts.** Sets the frequency at which broadcasts are made to locate the printer's interface on the network.

- **Queue Server job Poll Rate.** Sets the frequency at which print queues are polled for print jobs.

- **NetWare Protocol Restart.** Reinitializes the NetWare protocol.

- **PJL Settings.** Establishes how the HP JetDirect interface uses the Print Job Language.

- **Toner-Low Messages.** Determines which toner-low message is to be displayed (available only when operating in QServer mode).

- **Protocol Stacks.** Turns on or off other protocol stacks.

- **Frame Type Settings.** Chooses the frame type to be used.

JetAdmin printer network interface settings enable you to use the HP JetDirect interface in QServer mode, eliminating the need to assign the printer to a NetWare print server. You can also set the poll rate, adjusting it low to speed up the printing service or high to reduce the amount of network traffic.

You can also choose to Restart Server Connections, which restarts JetDirect interfaces and rereads the configuration files. You also can choose to Force Complete Re-Initialization Immediately, which restarts the NetWare protocol stack. This option stops jobs currently being printed, immediately implementing any changes in frame types, polling rates, and so on.

You can use Notification to specify which users or groups should be notified of printer problems. You can send a self-test page to the printer to verify its functionality by using the Test Page option, and you can send information about the printer to the printer by using the User Sheet option.

JetPrint

JetPrint is an HP utility designed to enable management of a remote printer from an MS Windows network client. You can install drivers, print by using the MS Windows drag-and-drop feature, view network printer and interface status, set up default print queues for use by MS Windows applications, and assign different sounds to different printer functions. The JetPrint main menu provides a list of printers and print queues from which to choose. It also provides information on the default printer, status of the selected printer, and print jobs submitted by users that are currently being serviced.

The JetPrint utility is a graphical utility, available through MS Windows. The main menu provides buttons from which to choose in order to perform various tasks:

- Exit closes the HP JetPrint Network Printing Utility main menu.

- Printer Setup enables you to specify information about the printer.

- Job Options enables you to set print job configuration information, such as whether a banner page should be printed and, if so, the banner name and user name to be used. It also enables you to set whether to enable the NetWare Form Feed option and whether to notify the user when the requested print job is complete.

- File Servers enables you to detach from NetWare servers (if no network drives are mapped or the server is not the NetWare server containing the default queue) or attach to NetWare servers (up to a maximum of eight).

- Search enables you to search for printer types associated with queues, or words or phrases that are part of the description of a queue.

- Preferences enables you to customize the user environment for JetPrint.

- Help enables you to search for and view information about the HP JetPrint utility and its associated fields of information.

When you choose the Preferences button and open the Preferences window (see fig. 54.2), you can set or choose to configure the following:

■ Options

■ ToolBar Buttons

■ Prompt When

■ Advanced Options

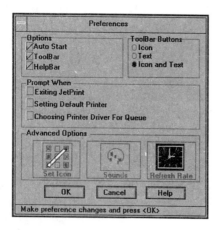

Figure 54.2

The HP JetPrint Preferences window.

The Options field can be toggled to include or not include Auto Start, ToolBar, and HelpBar. Those options toggled to On, as displayed by a check mark next to each option, are active when the JetPrint utility is running.

The ToolBar Buttons field enables you to choose whether to display the icon only, the text only, or both the icon and associated text on buttons within the HP JetPrint utility's button bar.

The Prompt When field enables you to specify when the utility is to prompt you. The options are when Exiting JetPrint, when Setting Default Printer, and when Choosing Printer Driver For Queue.

The Advance Options field enables you to choose from three advanced JetPrint options, which you then can configure. Those three advanced options are Set Icon, Sounds, and Refresh Rate.

If you choose the Set Icon button, you can choose any available MS Windows icon file to associate with a printer. The purpose of this configuration option is to make it easier for users to view graphically and choose the appropriate printer based on its capabilities, language selection, print options, or other features you choose to highlight by selecting a different icon.

If you choose the Sounds button, you can associate a given sound file (such as those you can choose from to play when you perform tasks such as closing MS Windows) with different printer events. The purpose of this configuration option is to inform the user of different printer-related events or conditions (such as when the printer is out of paper or has been taken offline) by using sound rather than just a message displayed on the user's workstation monitor.

If you choose the Refresh Rate button, you can set the frequency at which the JetPrint utility polls the NetWare server or printer to obtain printer and print job status information. This field cannot be set to a frequency of less than 15 seconds.

Questions

1. The _____ printer capability makes it possible to print on both sides of the paper.

   ○ A. duplexing

   ○ B. resource saving

   ○ C. media selection

   ○ D. media management

2. Direct-connect printers use either a/an _____ or a/an _____ interface.

   ☐ A. internal

   ☐ B. central

   ☐ C. distributed

   ☐ D. external

3. The _____ is NOT a printer capability.

   ○ A. resource-saving capability

   ○ B. QServer mode

   ○ C. duplexing capability

   ○ D. media-management feature

4. A _____ is a printing device that enables CAD packages to print on network printers.

   ○ A. duplexor

   ○ B. multiple input port

   ○ C. color printer

   ○ D. plotter

5. The main disadvantage of the QServer mode is _____.

   ○ A. that it emulates the RPRINTER communication method

   ○ B. that its interface also functions as a print server

   ○ C. that it requires a connection

   ○ D. that it does not require the use of unencrypted passwords

6. To view the name of the printer using the JetAdmin utility, look at the _____ area on the main menu.

   ○ A. Printer Name

   ○ B. Printer Status

   ○ C. I/O Connection Status

   ○ D. Control Panel

7. Of the following, which THREE are direct-connect printers?

   ☐ A. HP JetDirect

   ☐ B. HPIII

   ☐ C. HP AppleWriter

   ☐ D. HP4

8. A _____ is NOT a printer setting you can modify by using JetAdmin.

   ○ A. JetDirect Broadcasts

   ○ B. JCL Setting

   ○ C. Queue Server job Poll Rate

   ○ D. Protocol Stacks

9. The _____ button on the JetPrint utility main window enables you locate a print queue by a word in its description.

   ○ A. Printer Setup

   ○ B. Job Options

   ○ C. Search

   ○ D. Preferences

10. If you want to customize the user's environment for JetPrint, you must _____.

   ○ A. use the JetPrint Printer Setup option and set configuration information, such as whether to print a banner page

   ○ B. choose the Job Options button on the JetAdmin main menu

   ○ C. detach from the default file server

   ○ D. use the Preferences option of the JetPrint utility

Answers

1. A
2. A, D
3. B
4. D
5. C
6. A
7. A, B, D
8. B
9. C
10. D

Printing Using Unix and Macintosh Devices

*B*oth Unix and Macintosh workstations can access
printers in a NetWare (DOS-based) network environment. Both the NetWare server and the Unix client
must be configured in order for a Unix client to access
NetWare printing services. Additional products
(NetWare NFS or NetWare Flex/IP) are required in
order for Unix clients to print to NetWare print queues.
This is not true, however, for Macintosh clients.
NetWare print services have been available for
Macintosh clients since the early versions of NetWare 2
were released (NetWare 2.15).

In addition, NetWare clients may send print jobs to printers attached to Unix workstations by using the lpr (*line printer remote*) protocol and the NetWare-to-Unix gateway, providing the Unix host is correctly configured to service those print requests.

This chapter provides printing-related information on the following topics:

- Unix-to-NetWare Printing
- NetWare-to-Unix Printing
- Macintosh-to-NetWare Printing

Unix-to-NetWare Printing

Unix-to-NetWare printing requires that both the NetWare file server and the Unix client be set up for use before Unix systems can access NetWare network printers. Setting up the NetWare server includes such tasks as creating print queues and print servers, and assigning printers. This section explains the NetWare file server setup and the Unix client setup required before Unix users can print to NetWare printers.

NetWare File Server Setup

Setting up the NetWare file server for Unix-to-NetWare printing requires that NetWare print queues are first exported for use by lpd (line printer daemon), one of the two protocols used by Unix systems to send print jobs to other Unix systems. Several NLMs must be loaded in order to implement Unix-to-NetWare printing. Two of those NLMs are particularly important for setup (PLPD.NLM and PLPDCFG.NLM). The following are the NLMs used for Unix-to-NetWare printing:

- PLPD.NLM
- PLPDCFG.NLM
- PLPDMSG.HLP
- FILTER.NLM
- FLTRLIB.NLM
- POSTSCPT.PRO
- ENSCRIPT.PRO

By loading the PLPDCFG.NLM at the NetWare file server (see fig. 55.1), network administrators can then export NetWare print queues, identify those Unix systems that are considered to be *trusted hosts*—clients allowed to access the Unix-to-NetWare print gateway—and map Unix users to NetWare user accounts.

Figure 55.1

The PLPDCFG.NLM Main Menu.

To export NetWare print queues for use by Unix system clients, choose Select Print Queues for use by LPD from the Main Menu. Then choose which NetWare print queues will be accessible to Unix system users from the list of Available Print Queues. Choose a print queue from the list of Print Queues Selected. When the Print filter and Device configuration menu opens, provide information on the Print Filter to use (choose None, Line Printer, or Postscript), the Form Type (anyone previously defined using the NetWare PRINTDEF utility), the Print Device (type of printer such as HP4), and the Printer Mode (the command for the start of the job).

To choose which Unix hosts will be trusted hosts, choose Select Trusted Hosts from the Main Menu, then press the Ins key to see a list of Available Hosts. Choose a host to add to the Trusted Hosts List.

 Note Unix hosts are listed in the HOSTS database in the SYS:ETC directory on the NetWare file server with the PLPDCFG.NLM and associated NLMs loaded. If the Unix host for which you are looking does not appear when the Available Hosts list opens, the database file does not contain an entry for that Unix host.

To map Unix users to NetWare user accounts, choose Select Username Mapping Mode from the Main Menu. Next, choose All Clients use same NetWare Account from the Current Mode menu (see fig. 55.2). This normally sets user GUEST as the default user for all Unix users to use when accessing NetWare print services. If only specific Unix users will be able to access NetWare print services, a table of Unix users and their associated NetWare User Name(s) can be created by using the Setup Table for Username Mapping option in the Current Mode menu. In addition, the Unix client user name can be used as the NetWare user name (choose the Use Client Username as NetWare Username option). Remember, Unix user names are case-sensitive and thus must be entered with case in mind. NetWare user names are not case-sensitive.

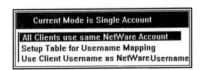

Figure 55.2
The Current Mode window.

Once the Unix-to-NetWare printing configuration is set up, the related print server can be loaded. To load the Unix-to-NetWare print server, type **LOAD PLPD** at the NetWare file server console and press Enter.

Unix Client Setup

One of the aspects of Unix that makes it an interesting operating system is that there are so many versions of it currently in use. NetWare supports several of those versions, two of which are considered to be the most commonly encountered—the BSD (Berkeley Source Distribution) and System V (a version from UniVel) versions.

The UnixWare (a version of the System V Unix OS) system administrator sets up access to NetWare servers running the NFS or Flex/IP products from the UnixWare desktop, using Printer_Setup found in System_Setup. To set up the UnixWare-to-NetWare printer, the system administrator uses the following steps:

1. Choose the Printer button.

2. Select New and Remote Unix System.

3. Provide requested information, including the name of the printer, the type of printer, the name of the NetWare NFS or Flex/IP NetWare server (in the Remote System Name field), and the name of the NetWare queue (in the Remote Printer Name field).

4. Choose BSD at the Remote Operating System is prompt.

5. Add the new printer definition and a new icon in the Printer Setup window.

6. Select the printer's icon, then choose the Actions and the Set Remote Access buttons.

7. Enable BSD by choosing the NetWare NFS or Flex/IP server.

8. Save the changes to finish the setup.

The following are System V-based utilities for administering remote and local printing:

- lpstat to view printer status information

- lpsched/lpshut to control printer operation

- lp to send print jobs to a remote printer

- lpstat to view jobs in the queue

- cancel to delete jobs from a print queue

The Berkeley (BSD) uses a printing database file called Printcap to establish printing capabilities. To set up Unix-to-NetWare printing on a BSD system, use a text editor to add the following lines to this file. Then create the spool directory for the printer on the Unix host (use the Unix mkdir command and create the directory in the default directory (/var/spool). Once these steps are complete, start the printer by using the Unix lpc utility.

Include the following lines in the Printcap database file:

```
Printer Name:\
lp=:\
rm=<NetWare Server Name>:\
rp=<NetWare Queue Name>:\
sd=<Unix Spool Directory>:\
```

The following are BSD-based utilities for administering remote and local printing:

- lpstat to view printer status information

- lpc to control printer operation

- lpr to send print jobs to a remote printer

- lpq to view jobs in the queue

- lprm to delete jobs from a print queue

NetWare-to-Unix Printing

NetWare users can also print to printers attached to Unix systems if the NetWare-to-Unix print gateway is installed on a NetWare 3 or NetWare 4 server and configured, and if the Unix host is configured for NetWare clients to access the printers.

To install and configure the NetWare-to-Unix print gateway, complete the following steps:

1. Type **LOAD NFSADMIN -NWPRINT** (at the console of a NetWare NFS server) or **LOAD FLEXCON -NWPRINT** (at the NetWare Flex/IP server) and press Enter.

2. Add a printer to the list of Configured Unix Printers by pressing Ins, typing a descriptive name for the new printer in the Printer Name field of the UNIX Printer Setup Options window (47 alphanumeric characters maximum), and pressing Enter (see fig. 55.3)

 You can also delete a printer by selecting the printer to delete, pressing Del, then answering Yes when prompted.

3. Choose the UNIX Host Name field and select a UNIX host from the Available UNIX Hosts list.

4. Choose the UNIX Printer Name field, and type the name of the UNIX printer.

5. Choose the NetWare Queues field and press Ins to display a list of Available NetWare Queues from which to choose, or press Ins again and type a name for a new queue in the Create Queue field and press Enter.

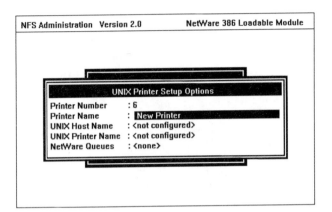

Figure 55.3
The UNIX Printer Setup Options window.

You can now exit the NFSADMIN or FLEXCON NLM utility and start the lpr print gateway by typing the following two commands at the NetWare file server console (press Enter after each command):

```
LOAD LPR_PSRV
LOAD LPR_GWY
```

Once the lpr print gateway is started, the Unix host must be configured. To configure the Unix host, complete the following steps:

1. If not already done, install the TCP/IP package on the Unix host by using the pkgadd program, and re-create the Unix OS kernel.

2. Log in to the Unix host as the root user.

3. Type **pmadm -l -p tcp -s** and press Enter. Then verify that values 0 and lpd exist for SVCTAG.

4. Type the following command (replacing *NetWare_FileServer_name* with the name of the file server) and press Enter:

    lpsystem -t bsd -R 5 -T 10
    ➥ *NetWare_FileServer_name*

5. Define the printer on the UnixWare host (if it does not already exist) by typing the following command (replacing italicized items with the actual names associated with them, such as the type of printer in place of *Printer_Type*) and pressing Enter:

    lpadmin -p *Printer_Name* **-v** *Device* **-T**
    ➥ *Printer_Type*

For a BSD-based Unix system, edit the Printcap database file to include the following lines, replacing the italicized items with the name associated with it (such as the name of the actual printer in place of *Printer Name*):

```
Printer Name ¦ Description:\
lp=Local Printer Port:\
rm=:\
rp=:\
sd=Spool Directory
```

Macintosh-to-NetWare Printing

The NBP and PAP AppleTalk protocols enable communication between Macintosh clients and network printers. The ATPS.NLM is responsible for the front-end receipt of print data, as well as for the back-end distribution of print data to ATPS printers. To function properly, the ATPS.NLM must be configured. The ATPS.CFG file contains the configuration information for the ATPS.NLM. Once properly set up and configured, DOS, MS Windows, and other NetWare workstations can submit properly formatted print jobs to NetWare for Macintosh print queues. In addition, with NetWare for Macintosh v3.10-or-higher installed, Macintosh workstations with compatible print drivers loaded can print to non-AppleTalk printers attached to NetWare file servers.

Regarding printing in the Macintosh environment, keep the following in mind when preparing NetWare-compatible printing by using Macintosh:

- The Macintosh Chooser provides the capability of choosing a printer to which all print jobs then will be sent.

- AppleTalk printers can be attached to Macintosh computers or directly connected to the network.

- AppleTalk print services use the AppleTalk protocol architecture for sending print jobs from Apple workstations to printers or print queues.

- AppleTalk is compatible with LocalTalk, the Apple Computer, Inc., proprietary hardware interface, EtherTalk, TokenTalk, and networks using standard Token Ring or Ethernet media.

- AppleTalk printers use bi-directional communications, establishing a communications dialog before printing occurs; therefore, they require special drivers that support both AppleTalk protocol and bi-directional communications.

> **Note** Because of the amount of network traffic created by bi-directional communication, the AppleTalk protocol is not recommended for wide area networks because of limited bandwidth.

- The Apple ImageWriter and Apple LaserWriter are the most commonly used AppleTalk network printers, and both include a printer interface that provides workstation or print server communication with the printer.

- The AppleTalk environment most commonly uses the PostScript page description language, supporting its own list of fonts—another feature that relies on bi-directional communication.

Several AppleTalk printing protocols are used for the various print devices used in the AppleTalk network:

- **Address Resolution Protocol.** The method whereby network nodes are arbitrarily assigned a node id (name) each time the node is activated on the network.

- **Datagram Delivery Protocol (DDP).** The connectionless delivery method for communication between the ATPS client and the printer. At this layer, two phases can be distinguished—phase I and phase II. Phase I networks are *nonextended* (a unique number must be assigned to each node). Phase II networks are *extended* (able to communicate across routers).

AppleTalk print services can use printer names to track printers (Name Binding protocol) and zone names to provide logical groupings of network nodes (Zone Information protocol).

■ **AppleTalk Transaction Protocol (ATP).** The method of delivery service between ATPS clients and printers, considered to be very reliable because delivery is acknowledged by ATM and retransmission is reinitiated after a specified period of time if the first transmission is not acknowledged.

■ **Printer Access Protocol (PAP).** The method of establishing communication between the workstation and printer. Used for communications related to connection setup and teardown, maintenance, and printer status.

NetWare print services can also be provided to most Macintosh users or other ATPS workstations by using NetWare for Macintosh AppleTalk print services. Unlike NetWare print queues, which receive data and store it in temporary print files, ATPS print queues establish and maintain bidirectional communication during the print request. This service is provided by the NetWare for the Macintosh print spooler. This is considered to be a front-end print service. In this front-end configuration, ATPS advertises NetWare print queues to appear to ATPS clients as if they were standard ATPS printer names. The NetWare PSERVER can service the NetWare print queue in this particular configuration.

Back-end print services are usually provided by the print server, such as NetWare's PSERVER.NLM and PSERVER.EXE files, or the NetWare for Macintosh ATPS print server. When binary data must be transferred to the printer, the ATPS back end requires an ATPS-compatible printer. Back-end print services include taking print jobs from the NetWare print queue, and sending the jobs across an AppleTalk network to an ATPS-compatible printer when the NetWare server is connected to an AppleTalk printer through an AppleTalk network.

 Version 3.01 and later of NetWare for Macintosh enable the ATPS back-end process to be used without the front-end process when no ATPS clients are in use and the AppleTalk printer-to-NetWare network connection occurs across an AppleTalk network. This provides any workstation with access to a print queue with the capability of submitting print jobs to ATPS printers using CAPTURE or NPRINT commands.

Printing from a Macintosh application functions slightly differently (see fig. 55.4).

When a Macintosh application sends a print job, that print job is sent in a generic format called QuickDraw. A connection is made and a dialog is initiated between the Print Manager and the printer. The Print Manager then makes sure the printer is available or finds it on the network by using Name Binding Protocol (NBP). Next, the print driver converts the QuickDraw-formatted print job into printer commands, establishes a connection to the printer, then initiates print driver and printer interaction. The LaserPrep file, which specifies operating system and drive-related information from the computer to the printer, is then downloaded as needed, and any fonts needed for the print job are downloaded. Next, the print job is sent to the printer, the job is printed, the connection is terminated, and the job is complete.

Figure 55.4

The printing process for Macintosh applications.

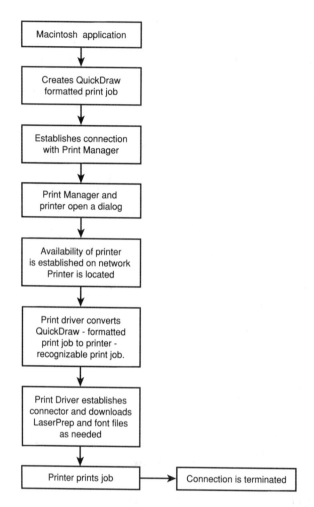

To configure AppleTalk print services, you can include the configuration options at the command line when you load AppleTalk print services, or you can provide the configuration information in a text file that can be referenced when AppleTalk print services are loaded. The configuration file used is called ATPS.CFG.

Use the NetWare Install console utility to create and edit the ATPS.CFG file.

Table 55.1 lists the configuration options that can be used at the command line or included in the ATPS.CFG file when loading AppleTalk print services.

Although some differences exist between printing with DOS or MS Windows applications and Macintosh applications, NetWare makes it relatively easy to print from the network from applications running under any of these operating systems.

Table 55.1
AppleTalk Print Services Configuration Options

Option	Option Name	Description
-o	Object Name	Name of the queue that accepts ATPS print jobs (31 characters maximum)
-p	Printer Name	Name of the AppleTalk printer, from which a default queue name consisting of the prefix of NW and the printer name can be created if the -o option is not included (31 characters maximum)
-wb	Without Back End	Assumes PSERVER or another print server other than an AppleTalk print server is to be used
-wf	Without Front End	Assumes no AppleTalk print spooler, and that PC users but not Macintosh or other ATPS users can use the queue
-z	Zone Name	If provided, gives the name of the zone in which the AppleTalk printer resides; otherwise, the internal network's zone is used as the default

Questions

1. The first step in setting up the NetWare file server for Unix-to-NetWare printing requires _____.

   ○ A. the administrator to load PLPD.NLM on the Unix host

   ○ B. that a trusted host be selected

   ○ C. Unix users to be mapped to NetWare user accounts

   ○ D. NetWare print queues to be exported for use by lpd

2. To choose Unix hosts as trusted hosts, choose the _____ and _____ options from the main menu of the NLM.

   ☐ A. Selected Trusted Hosts

   ☐ B. Username Mapping Mode

   ☐ C. PLPD

   ☐ D. PLPDCFG

3. The Unix lpd acronym refers to _____.

   ○ A. line printer display

   ○ B. live printer deployment

   ○ C. line printer daemon

   ○ D. live printer display

4. A list of trusted Unix hosts is contained in the _____ database file.

   ○ A. SYS:SYSTEM\DATABASE

   ○ B. SYS:PUBLIC\HOSTS

   ○ C. SYS:ETC\HOSTS

   ○ D. SYS:MAIL\HOSTDB

5. Load the Unix-to-NetWare print server by using the _____ NLM.

   ○ A. PLPDCFG

   ○ B. PLPDMSG

   ○ C. FILTER

   ○ D. PLPD

6. The NetWare-to-Unix print gateway is configured by using the _____ or _____ NetWare loadable modules.

   ☐ A. NFSADMIN

   ☐ B. FLEXCON

   ☐ C. LPR_PSRV

   ☐ D. LPR_GWY

7. Of the following, which THREE are utilities used to control printer operation on System-V or BSD Unix systems?

   ☐ A. lpstat

   ☐ B. lpsched

   ☐ C. lpshut

   ☐ D. lpc

8. Edit the _____ database file to configure a BSD-based Unix host.

   ○ A. PrintDB

   ○ B. Printcap

   ○ C. PMADM

   ○ D. ATPS.CFG

9. Which protocol is used to provide connectionless delivery for communications between the ATPS client and the printer?

   ○ A. DDP

   ○ B. ARP

   ○ C. ATP

   ○ D. PAP

10. If the -o option to specify an object name is not included when loading AppleTalk print services, information provided by the _____ option is used to specify a default print queue.

    ○ A. -wf

    ○ B. -z

    ○ C. -p

    ○ D. -wb

Answers

1. D

2. A, D

3. C

4. C

5. D

6. A, B

7. B, C, D

8. B

9. A

10. C

INDEX

Symbols

A

J–L

N

X–Z

GET CONNECTED
to the ultimate source
of computer information

The MCP Forum on CompuServe

Go online with the world's leading computer book publisher!
Macmillan Computer Publishing offers everything
you need for computer success!

Find the books that are right for you!
A complete online catalog, plus sample
chapters and tables of contents give
you an in-depth look at all our books.
The best way to shop or browse!

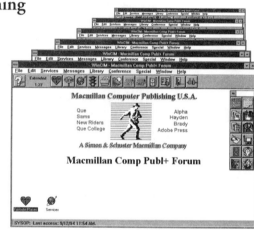

➤ Get fast answers and technical support for
  MCP books and software

➤ Join discussion groups on major computer
  subjects

➤ Interact with our expert authors via e-mail
  and conferences

➤ Download software from our immense
  library:

  ▷ Source code from books
  ▷ Demos of hot software
  ▷ The best shareware and freeware
  ▷ Graphics files

Join now and get a free
CompuServe Starter Kit!

To receive your free CompuServe Intro-
ductory Membership, call **1-800-848-
8199** and ask for representative #597.

The Starter Kit includes:
➤ Personal ID number and password
➤ $15 credit on the system
➤ Subscription to *CompuServe Magazine*

Once on the CompuServe System, type:

GO MACMILLAN

for the most computer information anywhere!

MACMILLAN
COMPUTER
PUBLISHING

PLUG YOURSELF INTO...

THE MACMILLAN INFORMATION SUPERLIBRARY™

Free information and vast computer resources from the world's leading computer book publisher—online!

FIND THE BOOKS THAT ARE RIGHT FOR YOU!

A complete online catalog, plus sample chapters and tables of contents give you an in-depth look at *all* of our books, including hard-to-find titles. It's the best way to find the books you need!

- **STAY INFORMED** with the latest computer industry news through our online newsletter, press releases, and customized Information SuperLibrary Reports.

- **GET FAST ANSWERS** to your questions about MCP books and software.

- **VISIT** our online bookstore for the latest information and editions!

- **COMMUNICATE** with our expert authors through e-mail and conferences.

- **DOWNLOAD SOFTWARE** from the immense MCP library:
  - Source code and files from MCP books
  - The best shareware, freeware, and demos

- **DISCOVER HOT SPOTS** on other parts of the Internet.

- **WIN BOOKS** in ongoing contests and giveaways!

TO PLUG INTO MCP: ➤   WORLD WIDE WEB: **http://www.mcp.com**

GOPHER: gopher.mcp.com

FTP: ftp.mcp.com

WANT MORE INFORMATION?

CHECK OUT THESE RELATED TOPICS OR SEE YOUR LOCAL BOOKSTORE

CAD and 3D Studio

As the number one CAD publisher in the world, and as a Registered Publisher of Autodesk, New Riders Publishing provides unequaled content on this complex topic. Industry-leading products include AutoCAD and 3D Studio.

Networking

As the leading Novell NetWare publisher, New Riders Publishing delivers cutting-edge products for network professionals. We publish books for all levels of users, from those wanting to gain NetWare Certification, to those administering or installing a network. Leading books in this category include *Inside NetWare 3.12*, *CNE Training Guide: Managing NetWare Systems*, *Inside TCP/IP*, and *NetWare: The Professional Reference*.

Graphics

New Riders provides readers with the most comprehensive product tutorials and references available for the graphics market. Best-sellers include *Inside CorelDRAW! 5*, *Inside Photoshop 3*, and *Adobe Photoshop NOW!*

Internet and Communications

As one of the fastest growing publishers in the communications market, New Riders provides unparalleled information and detail on this ever-changing topic area. We publish international best-sellers such as *New Riders' Official Internet Yellow Pages, 2nd Edition*, a directory of over 10,000 listings of Internet sites and resources from around the world, and *Riding the Internet Highway, Deluxe Edition*.

Operating Systems

Expanding off our expertise in technical markets, and driven by the needs of the computing and business professional, New Riders offers comprehensive references for experienced and advanced users of today's most popular operating systems, including *Understanding Windows 95*, *Inside Unix*, *Inside Windows 3.11 Platinum Edition*, *Inside OS/2 Warp Version 3*, and *Inside MS-DOS 6.22*.

Other Markets

Professionals looking to increase productivity and maximize the potential of their software and hardware should spend time discovering our line of products for Word, Excel, and Lotus 1-2-3. These titles include *Inside Word 6 for Windows*, *Inside Excel 5 for Windows*, *Inside 1-2-3 Release 5*, and *Inside WordPerfect for Windows*.

Orders/Customer Service **1-800-653-6156** Source Code **NRP95**

New Riders Publishing 201 West 103rd Street ◆ Indianapolis, Indiana 46290 USA

Fold Here

BUSINESS REPLY MAIL
FIRST-CLASS MAIL PERMIT NO. 9918 INDIANAPOLIS IN

POSTAGE WILL BE PAID BY THE ADDRESSEE

**NEW RIDERS PUBLISHING
201 W 103RD ST
INDIANAPOLIS IN 46290-9058**

Name _____ Title _____

Company _____ Type of business _____

Address _____

City/State/ZIP _____

Have you used these types of books before? ☐ yes ☐ no

If yes, which ones? _____

_____

How many computer books do you purchase each year? ☐ 1–5 ☐ 6 or more

How did you learn about this book? _____

Where did you purchase this book? _____

Which applications do you currently use? _____

_____

Which computer magazines do you subscribe to? _____

_____

What trade shows do you attend? _____

_____

Comments: _____

_____

_____

Would you like to be placed on our preferred mailing list? ☐ yes ☐ no

☐ **I would like to see my name in print!** You may use my name and quote me in future New Riders products and promotions. My daytime phone number is: _____

New Riders Publishing   201 West 103rd Street ◆ Indianapolis, Indiana 46290 USA

Fax to **317-581-4670**   Orders/Customer Service **1-800-653-6156**   Source Code **NRP95**